Introduction to Global Business

UNDERSTANDING THE INTERNATIONAL ENVIRONMENT AND GLOBAL BUSINESS FUNCTIONS

Julian E. Gaspar
Texas A&M University

Antonio Arreola-Risa
Texas A&M University

Leonard Bierman
Texas A&M University

Richard T. Hise
Texas A&M University

James W. Kolari
Texas A&M University

L. Murphy Smith
Murray State University

SOUTH-WESTERN
CENGAGE Learning®

Australia • Brazil • Japan • Korea • Mexico • Singapore • Spain • United Kingdom • United States

Introduction to Global Business: Understanding the International Environment and Global Business Functions

Julian E. Gaspar, Antonio Arreola-Risa, Leonard Bierman, Richard T. Hise, James W. Kolari, and L. Murphy Smith

Senior Vice President, LRS/Acquisitions & Solutions Planning: Jack W. Calhoun

Editorial Director, Business & Economics: Erin Joyner

Sr. Acquisitions Editor: Michele Rhoades

Developmental Editor: Suzanna Bainbridge

Marketing Manager: Jonathan Monahan

Sr. Content Project Manager: Colleen A. Farmer

Media Editor: Rob Ellington

Manufacturing Planner: Ron Montgomery

Production Service: Integra Software Services Pvt. Ltd.

Sr. Art Director: Stacy Shirley

Cover and Internal Designer: cmiller design

Cover Image: © Steven Bourelle/Shutterstock

Rights Acquisitions Specialist (Text and Photo): John Hill

Library of Congress Control Number: 2012947564

Student Edition ISBN 13: 978-0-547-15212-7
Student Edition ISBN 10: 0-547-15212-4

South-Western
5191 Natorp Boulevard
Mason, OH 45040
USA

Cengage Learning products are represented in Canada by Nelson Education, Ltd.

For your course and learning solutions, visit **www.cengage.com**
Purchase any of our products at your local college store or at our preferred online store **www.cengagebrain.com**

Printed in the United States of America
1 2 3 4 5 6 7 16 15 14 13 12

brief contents

© C Miller Design/ Getty Images

contents

preface

Business is global in nature! Opening the door to global business, however, involves many challenges for both instructors and students. The goal of *Introduction to Global Business* is to provide the keys to success that will lead to a rewarding educational experience and set the stage for pursuing a successful domestic or international business career. Any business, big or small, is fraught with risk, and unless students have a clear understanding of the global business environment, they will be taking unnecessary risk, and such risk could lead to failure. The global business environment is rapidly changing. Understanding the foundations of globalization—shift in geopolitical alliances, active role of global policy institutions, and advances in information technology—is also crucial to business success. Gaspar et al. *Introduction to Global Business*, 1e introduces comprehensively the foundational and functional tools to better prepare students for the global business landscape. As part of that functional approach, the text flows smoothly and clearly from concept to application, asking students to implement their learning into real-world personal and professional applications. The purpose of this book is to introduce students to the fundamentals of globalization—and in a way that is interesting, relevant, and engaging, in the hope that they may develop the knowledge for a successful business career.

A Team of Experts Can Make a Difference

The introduction to global business course covers a lot of ground, starting with the foundations of global business, moving on to the global business environment, and ending with global business strategy and management. We recognize that it is a challenge for students to understand how these major issues of global business are interrelated, and it is a challenge for an instructor to cover all these areas with equal amounts of enthusiasm and expertise. Other introduction to global business texts are written by authors who have expertise in one, two, or three functional areas. One thing that makes our book unique is our author team of six functional area experts. Our specialized author team introduces globalization through unparalleled scholarship and world-view presentation of the fundamental pillars of the global landscape—culture, economic development, ethics, and information technology. For more than three years, we have met weekly as a team to share ideas, review manuscript, examine market feedback, and make sure that we created a cohesive, comprehensive, authoritative presentation of global business that is unparalleled in the market. Helping us all the way in this process—making sure that the material is presented consistently, and clearly—has been our lead author. He has taught thousands of introduction to global business students and understands the challenges they and you, the instructor, face.

Goals and Key Themes of the Book

Throughout the planning and writing of *Introduction to Global Business*, we have sought and listened to the advice of instructors across the country that have taught this course for many years. We also sought student feedback to be sure that the content is appealing and relevant to students. As a result, the features of this book have been carefully designed to respond to both student and instructor needs. Anyone who listens to the news and follows current business events knows that contemporary business is global in nature, regardless where it is conducted and is heavily influenced by cultural diversity, economic development, enforcement of ethical standards, and advances in information technology.

Accessible, Relevant Text

Since this is an introductory business text, we have aimed to keep the narrative conversational and concise. Reviewers have commented positively about the readability of the text. We hope this text will be "user-friendly" so that students will read the chapters and come to class prepared. Every aspect of *Introduction to Global Business* aims at getting the reader to think deeply about the subject—the foundations and environment of global business as well as global business entry strategies and management. Our primary goal is to help the reader fully appreciate the fundamentals of global business and pursue a career—either as an entrepreneur or as an employee.

Key Features of the Text

Chapter Openers

Each chapter begins with an *outline* and a list of *learning objectives* to help direct student reading. The learning objectives are repeated in each section of chapters so that students can map their progress through the chapter. The chapter summary is also organized by the learning objectives to help students retain their focus on key concepts and issues.

Chapter Opening Vignettes

Each chapter opens with a short but interesting story—something that students can relate to easily—that corresponds to the chapter's topic. Within the chapter, reference is made to the chapter openers to connect the opening story to chapter content.

Theme Boxed Features

Each chapter also includes two boxes that deal with one of the four themes, *Culture, Economic Developments, Ethics, and Information Technology*, that is relevant to that chapter. Every box concludes with questions that encourage students to think about what they have read and can lead to interesting in-class discussion.

Graphics, Color, and Real Examples

The layout of the book has been designed for clarity, with an uncluttered, sophisticated look. At the same time, this streamlined approach is enhanced with color and graphics meant to heighten interest in the topics and focus the reader's attention on the most important globalization concepts. Real-world examples are used throughout the text to show how the topic at hand has an impact on big and small businesses. The important role that culture, economics, ethics, and information technology play in the future of business should stand out because of these features.

Margin Notes

The introduction to global business course is packed with terms that may be new to students. To make this new vocabulary more accessible, all new terms appear in bold type in the chapters and are defined clearly in the text, margin notes, and the comprehensive glossary at the end of the text.

Reality Check

Each learning objective section ends with a Reality Check, questioning the impact that section's learning objective has had on the students. By bringing global business issues to a personal level, students are more likely to be engaged in the subject.

End-of-Chapter Pedagogy

The end-of-chapter pedagogy carefully reinforces the relevance of chapter content as well as the learning terminology, concepts, business environment, operations, and strategy. A menu of assignments allows instructors to choose which activities are most appropriate for their courses.

- **Chapter Summary** Each chapter summary is organized according to the learning objectives. By the time students finish going through the summary, they will have read the learning objectives at least three times and, hopefully, will know where to find the required information related to them.
- **Chapter Questions** At least one question per learning objective is assigned at the end of each chapter. The objective is to help students recall global business concepts, understand how these concepts are applied, and challenge students to use judgment when developing their answers.
- **Mini-cases** Brief case studies highlight specific companies to help bring the chapter concepts alive.
- **Point-CounterPoint** Honing in on the necessary critical thinking skills to make intelligent and ethical business decisions, the point-counterpoint provides insight into the varying perspectives of a controversial business issue and asks students to make choices and support their decisions.
- **Interpreting Global Business News** Based on typical and/or current global business news items that readers would generally find in periodicals such as *The Wall Street Journal, Financial Times, Bloomberg Businessweek, The Economist*, etc. students must interpret the meaning of the news items using their understanding of the material covered in that chapter.
- **Portfolio Projects** To help students build their own business portfolios, one or both of the *Portfolio Projects* may be assigned as individual or group activities that span the course. The objective of *Exploring Your Own Case in Point* is to encourage and enable each student to conduct a comprehensive analysis of a large multinational company (e.g., a *Fortune 500 or Financial Times Global 500* company). Each student selects a company that is publicly traded and obtain information that is readily available on the Web and from library sources. By answering chapter-specific questions in these sections, the student will have conducted a comprehensive analysis of the company by the end of the course. The questions in *Starting Your Own Business* are intended to provide each student with the opportunity to act as an entrepreneur and put together a comprehensive international business plan—the first steps in the start-up of a new enterprise. The objective here is to enable students to become successful global entrepreneurs by helping them to establish clear business goals, strategies, and methods of international operation.

Teaching and Learning Resources

For Instructors

Instructor's Manual

The Instructor's Manual, available via download from the companion Website or the Instructor's Resource CD (IRCD), contains such elements as chapter and lecture outlines, teaching objectives that mirror the student learning objectives, discussion starters and reality check discussion guides, synopsis and answers to the *Ethical Perspectives* and the *Economic Perspectives* features, and answers and guided responses to all of the end-of-chapter content.

We would like to thank and acknowledge the expertise of Dr. Daria Panina, Texas A&M University, in her contribution of the text development and the authoring of this instructor's manual.

Test Bank in *ExamView*

The test items, available in the IRCD, have been designed to demonstrate student comprehension of the functional elements of global business. By focusing on the learning objectives of each chapter, the test questions have been created to illustrate learning—from conceptual understanding to application. Each question includes a tag reflecting AACSB standards and a Bloom's level of learning.

Many thanks to Dr. Amit Shah, Frostburg University, for his expert contribution to the creation of this test bank.

PowerPoint® presentation

The PowerPoint, available via download from the companion Website or the IRCD, helps bring lectures to life with visual images and lecture points specific to each chapter.

DVD Guide

The DVD guide, available via download from the companion Website or the IRCD, provides fantastic overviews and discussion questions based on the videos available on the accompanying DVD (sent separately from the IRCD).

Instructor's Resource CD (IRCD)

As previously mentioned, the IRCD contains all necessary instructional components to assist you in your class presentation. Specifically, it contains the Instructor's Manual, testing items and software, the PowerPoint presentations, and the DVD guide.

Global Business DVD

This compilation of BBC and CBS video segments feature real-world footage from China, India, South America, United Kingdom, and the United States of America. Your students will discover critical issues effecting the global business environment such as expatriation, outsourcing, international trade, international agriculture, and economic booms and busts. Through these real-world examples, students will start to see the true nature of global business and their places within the world community.

CourseMate, text companion website

This dynamic interactive learning tool includes student and instructor resources. For instructors, you can download electronic versions of the instructor supplements from the password-protected section of the site, including the Instructor's Resource Manual, Test Bank, and PowerPoint® presentations. To access companion resources, visit www.cengagebrain.com. On the CengageBrain.com homepage, use the search box at the top of the page to search for the ISBN of your title (from the back cover of your book). This will take you to the product page where you will find free companion resources.

WebTutor

WebTutor is a web platform containing premium content such as unique web quizzes, audio summary and quiz files, lecture PowerPoint slides, and crossword puzzles for key terms from the text.

CengageNow

This robust online course management system gives you more control in less time and delivers better student outcomes—NOW. CengageNow™ includes teaching and learning resources organized around lecturing, creating assignments, casework, quizzing, and gradework to track student progress and performance. Multiple types of quizzes, including *DVD-specific media quizzing* and quizzes tied to *Interactive Maps*, are assignable and gradable. Flexible assignments, automatic grading, and a gradebook option provide more control while saving you valuable time. A Personalized Study diagnostic tool empowers students to master concepts, prepare for exams, and become more involved in class.

Also available via CengageNow (**GlobalBusiness** CengageNow +LivePlan), **LivePlan**, from Palo Alto Software, a proven web-based business plan software that allows your students to work as teams, receive intuitive advice, and produce professional-grade business plans through software used by real entrepreneurs. GlobalBusiness CengageNow + LivePlan goes beyond the book to deliver what you need!

Student Learning Resources

CourseMate, text companion website

Make the grade with CourseMate! This interactive website helps you make the most of your study time by accessing everything you need to succeed online in one convenient place. CourseMate provides numerous interactive learning tools, such as quizzes, flashcards, PowerPoint to support your lecture comprehension, and videos to help you master today's global business concepts.

CengageNow

This robust online course management system gives you more control in less time and delivers better student outcomes—NOW. CengageNow™ includes learning resources organized around lecturing, assignments, quizzing, and gradework to track your progress and performance. Multiple types of quizzes, including *DVD-specific media quizzing* and quizzes tied to *Interactive Maps*, are assignable and gradable. Flexible assignments, automatic grading, and a gradebook option provide more control while saving you valuable time. A Personalized Study diagnostic tool empowers students to master concepts, prepare for exams, and become more involved in class.

Also available via CengageNow (**GlobalBusiness** CengageNow +LivePlan), **LivePlan**, from Palo Alto Software, a proven web-based business plan software that allows students to work as teams, receive intuitive advice, and produce professional-grade business plans through software used by real entrepreneurs. GlobalBusiness CengageNow + LivePlan goes beyond the book to deliver what you need!

Acknowledgments

This textbook owes a debt of gratitude to Texas A&M University's Center for International Business Education and Research (CIBER), which played an important role in identifying a dedicated author team and motivating them to focus and integrate the role of four critical themes of our book: cultural diversity, economic development, international business ethics, and information technology. We would also like to acknowledge support from Dean Jerry Strawser of Mays Business School and Executive Associate Dean Bala Shetty who provided the collegial and scholarly environment necessary to fulfill such an ambitious project.

In addition, many professors provided us with constructive criticism throughout the writing process. Also, numerous professors acted as reviewers and Advisory Board Members, contributing ideas and comments that have improved the quality of our text:

David Blake
University of California-Irvine

Gary Carini
Baylor University

Kimra Coons
Webster University

Donna Davisson
Cleveland State University

Paul Dowling
University of Utah

Mark Fenton
University of Wisconsin-Stout

P. Roberto Garcia
Indiana University

Debora Gilliard
Metropolitan State College-Denver

Kurt Gleichauf
University of North Carolina-Charlotte

Robert Goldberg
Northeastern University

Andrew Gross
Cleveland State University

Yu-Feng Lee
New Mexico State University

Tomasz Lenartowicz
Florida Atlantic University

Sviatoslav Moskalev
Adelphi University

Daria Panina
Texas A&M University

Joseph Petrick
Wright State University

Christine Probett
San Diego State University

Charlie Shi
Diablo Valley College

Richard Sjolander
University of West Florida

Jon Steele
Mid-State Technical College

Miriam Thangaraj
University of Wisconsin-Madison

Sharon Toler
College of DuPage

Mindy West
Arizona State University

Finally, this book would not have been possible without the splendid support of Suzanna Bainbridge, Development Editor, and the editorial team at Cengage who worked tirelessly to produce this quality textbook. Their attention to organization, content, graphics design, and mundane details is much appreciated by all of the authors. Specifically, we'd like to thank Michele Rhoades, Senior Acquisitions Editor; Colleen Farmer, Senior Content Project Manager; Sreejith Govindan, Project Manager; John Hill, Senior Rights Acquisitions Specialist; Kristine Janssens, Text Permissions Project Manager; Corey Geissler, Senior Permissions Project Manager; Shiela Mary, Associate Project Manager; and Kelly Lydick, copy editor. All helped to ensure a smooth publishing process.

Introduction to Global Business
Gaspar/Arreola-Risa/Bierman/Hise/Kolari/Smith
November, 2012

about the authors

Julian Gaspar

Dr. Julian Gaspar, is the director of Texas A&M University's Center for International Business Education and Research (CIBER) and is responsible for internationalizing Mays Business School's academic programs and faculty research. As the director of one of America's 33 CIBER business schools, Dr. Gaspar's mission is to infuse internationalization in business courses. Dr. Gaspar has been the architect of institutionalizing internationalization in Mays business curriculum at the undergraduate and graduate levels through international business course design and development, and implementation of overseas study programs. Dr. Gaspar teaches international finance with Mays Business School in College Station and in Strasbourg (France) where he conducts an annual five-week summer study abroad program with 30 Mays students. Dr. Gaspar is an International Economist by training with three decades of international expertise in country risk analysis, project economic and financial analysis, and financial and industrial restructuring of developing/transition economies. His corporate experience stems from his years of work with Bank of America in Tokyo and San Francisco, where he conducted country risk analysis and researched and analyzed debt problems of developing countries. During his tenure as an international economist with the World Bank Group in Washington, DC, Dr. Gaspar worked on funding over 45 investment projects in East Asia for the International Finance Corporation (IFC). He also designed financial and industrial restructuring programs for Poland and Cyprus while working with the International Bank for Reconstruction and Development (IBRD). Dr. Gaspar received his Ph.D in international and monetary economics from Georgetown University, an MBA from Indiana University, and BS in Chemical Engineering from the University of Madras, India. Dr. Gaspar has travelled/worked in over 55 countries and consults with the U.S. Department of State on business education reform in Central Asia and Africa. Dr. Gaspar and some of his Mays Business School colleagues have written six Russian business cases and he is the lead author of two textbooks—*Introduction to Business* and *Introduction to Global Business.*

Antonio Arreola-Risa

Dr. Arreola-Risa is an Associate Professor in the Information & Operations Management Department, Mays Business School, Texas A&M University. He received his B.S. in industrial and systems engineering from Monterrey Institute of Technology (ITESM) in Mexico, his M.S. in industrial engineering from Georgia Institute of Technology, and his M.S. and Ph.D. in operations management from Stanford University. Prior to joining Texas A&M University, Dr. Arreola-Risa worked as a production and inventory control analyst at a manufacturing firm, and later he taught at ITESM and at the University of Washington in Seattle. His primary research, teaching, and consulting interests are in production-inventory systems as well as in service operations, with emphasis on enterprise resource planning, supply-chain management, and health care systems management. He currently teaches undergraduate, masters, and doctoral courses. He has also lectured in executive education programs and consulted for numerous companies in the United States and abroad. Dr. Arreola-Risa is a member of the Decision Sciences Institute, the Institute of Industrial Engineers, and the Institute for Operations Research and the Management Sciences. Some of his research can be found in the academic journals *Decision Sciences, European Journal of Operational Research, IIE Transactions, Management Science, Naval Research Logistics,* and *Production and Operations Management.* He is the co-author of the textbooks *Linear Programming: an introduction to quantitative decision making* (Thomson Learning Inc., 2003) and *Introduction to Business* (Houghton Mifflin Company, 2006).

Leonard Bierman

Professor Bierman does research and writing in the areas of strategic management and human resource management, with particular emphasis on topics related to corporate governance and professional service firms. Earlier in his career he held positions in the federal government at the EEOC, the U.S. Department of Labor, and the U.S. International Trade Commission.

Richard T. Hise

Richard T. Hise is Professor Emeritus of Marketing, Texas A&M University. He is the author of seven text books and more than eighty articles in marketing strategy, product planning and development and international marketing. His bio is contained in *Who's Who in America* and *Who's Who in International Business Education and Research.*

James W. Kolari

Professor Kolari has taught financial markets and institutions at Texas A&M University and been active in international education, consulting, and executive education. In 1994 he was awarded the JP Morgan Chase Professorship in Finance in the Mays Business School at Texas A&M University. In 1986 he was a Fulbright Scholar at the University of Helsinki and worked with the Bank of Finland and large banking organizations there. He has served as a Faculty Fellow with the Mortgage Bankers Association of America and a Visiting Scholar at the Federal Reserve Bank of Chicago in 1982, in addition to being a consultant to the U.S. Small Business Administration, American Bankers Association, Independent Bankers Association of America, and numerous banks and other organizations. In recent years he has worked as a Senior Research Fellow at the Swedish School of Business and Economics (Hanken), Vaasa, Finland. Previously, he served as an advisor on the North American Free Trade Agreement for the State of Texas, consultant for the Mexican government in financing technology, and member of the Academy of Sciences for Higher Education in Russia. With more than 100 articles published in refereed journals, numerous other papers and monographs, 11 co-authored books, and more than 100 competitive papers presented at academic conferences, he ranks in the top 1-2 percent of finance scholars in the United States, according to recently published guides of research productivity among finance professors. His papers have appeared in such domestic and international journals as the *Journal of Finance, Review of Financial Studies, Journal of Business, Review of Economics and Statistics, Journal of Money, Credit and Banking, Journal of Financial Research, Journal of Banking and Finance, Real Estate Economics, Journal of Economic Dynamics and Control,* and the *Scandinavian Journal of Economics.* Papers in Russian, Finnish, Dutch, and Italian have appeared outside of the United States. He is a co-author of leading college textbooks in commercial banking.

L. Murphy Smith

Dr. L. Murphy Smith, CPA, is the David and Ashley Dill Distinguished Professor of Accounting at Murray State University. Dr. Smith's academic record includes numerous professional journal articles, research grants, books, and professional meeting presentations in the United States and abroad. His work is cited in various news media, including *Fortune,*

USA Today, and *The Wall Street Journal*. He has received numerous teaching and research awards, including the Outstanding Researcher Award from the American Accounting Association Strategic and Emerging Technologies Section and the Outstanding Educator Award from the Texas Society of CPAs. He ranks in the top one percent of authors on Social Sciences Research Network (SSRN.com) by downloaded articles. During his career, he held a number of leadership positions in academic and professional organizations e.g. President of the American Accounting Association Gender Issues and Work-Life Balance Section. His major research interests are ethics, international accounting, systems, and auditing. Dr. Smith serves on several journal editorial boards and his research has appeared in leading journals such as *Accounting Horizons, Contemporary Accounting Research, Advances in Accounting, International Journal of Economics and Accounting,* and *Research on Professional Responsibility and Ethics in Accounting.*

i

Foundations of Global Business

ndar Todorovic/ erstock.com

Ricardo De Mattos/iStockphoto.com

ArtisticPhoto/Shutterstock.com

Noel Hendrickson/Blend Images/ Jupiter Images

Jorg Hackemann/Shutterstock.com

CH 1

The Rise of Globalization

After studying this chapter, you should be able to:

- **LO-1** Explain the characteristics of globalization and describe how it functions.
- **LO-2** Identify how major international institutions facilitate globalization.
- **LO-3** Evaluate the need for strong and transparent institutions to adapt to global competition.
- **LO-4** Describe the key policy measures that make globalization sustainable.
- **LO-5** Describe the role of information technology in bridging the global digital divide.
- **LO-6** Describe the validity of the anti-globalization argument.
- **LO-7** Explain the case made to temporarily support those people negatively affected by globalization.

Global Credit Crisis Puts Globalization at Risk![1]

The global credit crisis, a sudden freeze in short, medium, and long-term lending by banks to regular customers and other banks that began in September 2008 with the collapse of Lehman Brothers (an American investment bank headquartered in New York), led to a global economic recession. This event had a rippling impact on many economies worldwide triggering a disruption in world trade, capital, and labor flows, and putting globalization in danger. Since the 1980s, increased financial deregulation has made credit markets around the globe more intertwined; national governments and their residents are able to borrow, spend, and invest abroad more freely. Furthermore, imports of commodities (like crude oil and iron ore), goods, and services have grown rapidly. After rising steadily for over a decade, world trade fell in 2009 as the global economy has slowed. Countries face contracting export markets, falling export prices, and vanishing trade finance and migration flows.

A close analysis of the impact of the global credit crisis on four diverse countries in different regions of the world shows how interdependent and integrated the global economy has become (see Exhibit 1.1). Commodity exporters such as Burkina Faso and Ukraine saw export prices and volume drop, while Singapore's electronic component manufacturers and Ireland's information technology service sector witnessed a massive slump in external demand for their goods and services.

Cotton accounts for about 60 percent of exports in Burkina Faso, sub-Saharan Africa's largest cotton producer. The cotton sector directly employs some 700,000 people, or 17 percent of the country's population. Indirectly, many more people gain from the cotton sector by providing services like housing, retailing, and restaurants. The global credit crisis depressed world demand for textiles and apparel, especially in developed countries; this in turn reduced the demand for Burkina Faso's cotton. The net result was loss of jobs and lower living standards in Burkina Faso.

Ukraine, a former Soviet bloc country, did not fare much better. Ukraine's economy, the world's eighth-largest steel producer, depends heavily upon developments in the global steel sector. With the fall in global steel demand, prices fell correspondingly and Ukraine's economy was dragged down as well.

Singapore is a highly open country (i.e., an economy primarily based upon free trade and free markets) and about one-third of its economic output has been directly affected by demand for consumer electronics, information technology products, and services from industrialized countries. With the global recession, Singapore's electronics and information technology exports stalled—and so did its economy.

Beginning in the mid-1990s, Ireland's economy grew rapidly, largely because of its free market and open trade and investment policies, which were

EXHIBIT 1.1

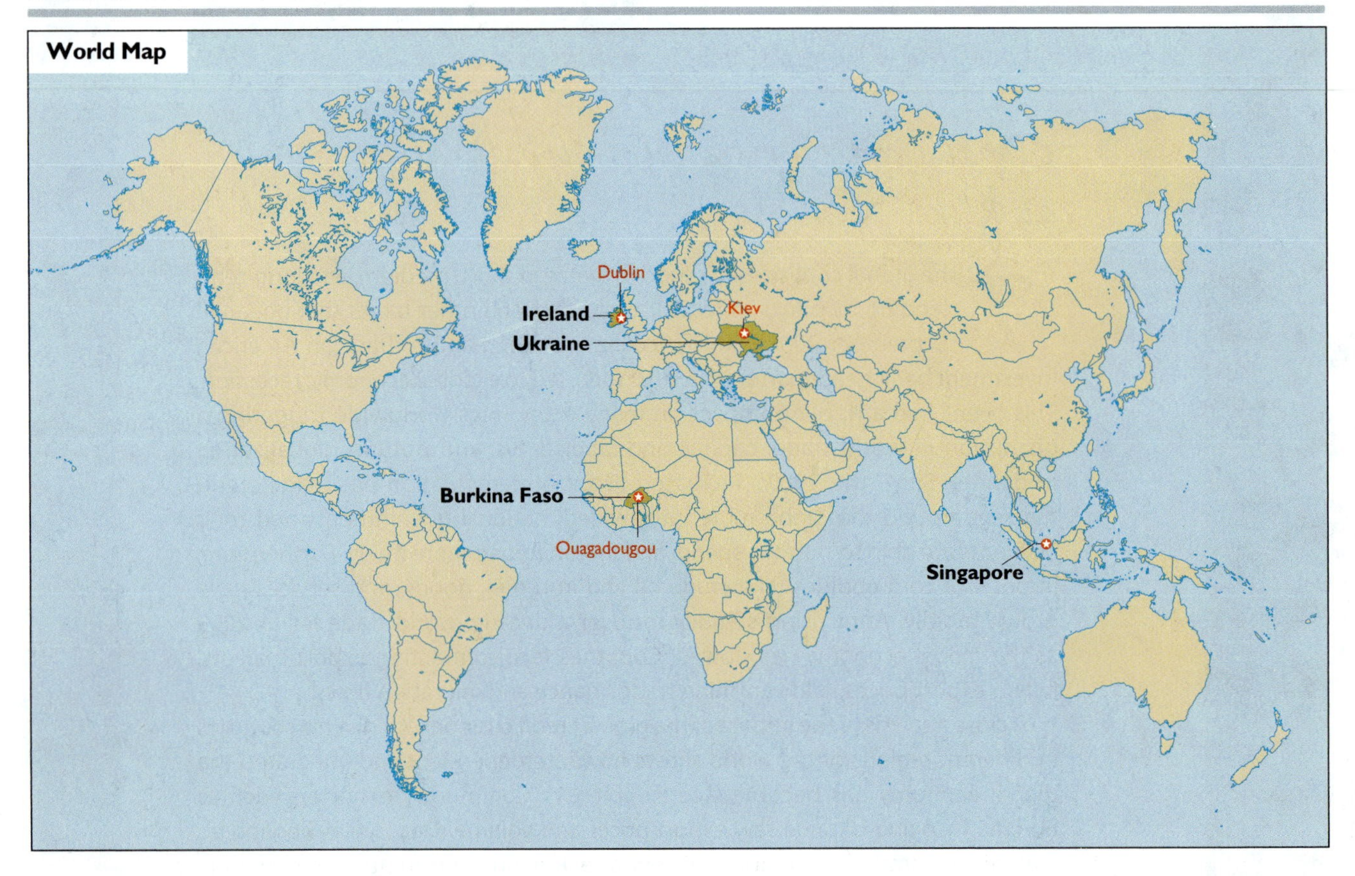

(Source: The International Monetary Fund, "Deep Impact," *Finance & Development*, March 2009, pp. 13–18.)

boosted significantly by low-cost borrowing from abroad. In the resulting economic boom, Ireland became known as the "Celtic Tiger," and was transformed from a land of emigrants to a land that attracted immigrants, especially from Poland. Industries like information technology and housing construction flourished. But the global financial crisis suddenly made it extremely difficult for Ireland to service its foreign loans and continue to grow its economy. Soon emigration increased, immigration slowed, and the economy stalled.

In the wake of financial shock, policymakers may resort to nationalist or protectionist policies that shelter domestic companies by curtailing world trade and investment and bringing the globalization process to a halt. This is a major global concern, especially to international organizations such as the International Monetary Fund, the World Bank, and the World Trade Organization.

Introduction

The opening vignette illustrates that we live in a highly integrated and interdependent world. The credit crisis had an impact not only on residents of the country of its origin—the United States—but also on farmers in Burkina Faso, miners and steel workers in Ukraine, assembly-line workers in Singapore, and white-collar workers at information technology firms in Ireland. Business has become increasingly global in nature, so that the success of businesses—big and small—depends not only on the domestic economic environment but also on developments abroad.

What Is Globalization?

LO-1

Explain the characteristics of globalization and describe how it operates.

globalization
the socio-economic reform process of eliminating trade, investment, cultural, information technology, and political barriers across countries, which in turn can lead to increased economic growth and geo-political integration and interdependence among nations of the world

Globalization encompasses the socio-economic *reform process* of eliminating trade, investment, cultural, information technology, and political barriers across countries, which could lead to increased economic growth and geo-political integration and interdependence among nations of the world. Details will be discussed in the remainder of this chapter.

Consider a real-world situation. Imagine sitting and relaxing on a leather couch in your house or apartment, sipping a cup of hot coffee or tea, and watching a TV show on the Discovery Channel. Chances are high that the leather couch you are seated on was made in Italy, the cup was made by Corning of the United States, the coffee came from Colombia but was processed by Nestlé of Switzerland, or the tea came from India and was processed by Lipton's of the United Kingdom, the Sony TV was manufactured in Japan, and the Discovery Channel program was broadcast live from Masai Mara in Kenya. Perhaps the clothes that you may be wearing are from China.

This cultural lifestyle has been made possible by certain key aspects of globalization: the elimination of barriers to trade, investment, culture, and information technology that separate countries. It also reflects the growing integration and interdependence among people, communities, and economies around the world. Globalization has made it possible for goods, services, capital, technology, and culture to cross national borders.

david pearson/Alamy

News media may give the impression that globalization has only been a relatively recent phenomenon, but that is not the case. The fundamental basis of globalization represents freer international trade and investment, or the free flow of goods and services (including cultural and belief systems) between countries. Thus, globalization and international trade and investment are interlinked. However, globalization reaches further. It includes a process of integrating the nations of the world so that they become more economically efficient and interdependent. That process has been based upon changes in national policies, which aim to promote private enterprise and reduce or eliminate economic, cultural, and social barriers between countries. These policies could include: moving toward strengthening the role of the private sector; supporting free-market pricing; eliminating barriers to free movement of goods, services, capital and information technology; and promoting institutions that enforce transparency, disclosure, and rule of law. Therefore, the actions taken by one country could affect others.

Aleksandar Todorovic/ Shutterstock.com

International organizations facilitate globalization. *Tea leaves harvested for exports from Sri Lanka.*

For example, the dawn of globalization can be traced back to the fifteenth century, when the Portuguese navigator and explorer Vasco da Gama made voyages to Kerala State, on India's West coast, in search of spices to satisfy European palates. At about the same time, Arab and Chinese traders were making similar voyages to trade in spices and silk. Goods, people, and ideas have been traveling around the globe ever since that time. More recently, however, globalization began to *accelerate* after World War II beginning in 1944 with the creation and implementation of open market policies advocated by such international institutions as the World Bank, the International Monetary Fund, and, a few years later, by the General Agreement on Tariffs and Trade (GATT), now called the World Trade Organization. While most ascertain that globalization can be good for society as a whole, much of its value depends upon how the "rules of the game" are implemented: fair trade, flexible exchange rates, open foreign investment policies and harnessing the Internet (including social media outlets such as Facebook), for example, all can influence the results. These changes could bring about "openness, accessibility, accountability, connectivity, democracy, and decentralization"—all the "soft" qualities essential to globalization. Yet, globalization does create "winners" and "losers."

Emerging Market Economies

Prior to 2000, globalization generally implied that business expanded from developed or industrialized countries to developing or emerging economies. When the dot-com bubble burst in 2000, however, the flow of business had moved in both directions, and also increasingly from one developing country to another. For example, according to the World Bank[2], the value of merchandise exports between East Asia and South Asia increased at an average annual rate of 27.2 percent between 1999 and 2009, because of lower tariff and non-tariff barriers while exports to the European Union and the United States grew by 18.9 and 15.2 percent, respectively, over that same period. This increase led to much faster economic growth rates in emerging Asian economies than in their western counterparts, and this growth could continue for a good while. Business today centers around "competing with everyone from everywhere for everything," according to the Boston Consulting Group.

The growing number of companies from **emerging market economies**—countries that have been moving toward more open trade and free-market policies—that appear in the *Financial Times Global 500* latest[3] ranking of the world's biggest firms indicates this is true. The recent (2010) list included 127 companies, primarily from the "BRIC economies" (Brazil, Russia, India, and China, discussed more in Chapter 2), up from 32 in 2002, and forecast by analysts to rise to fully one-third of the *Financial Times Global 500* list by 2020. The past decade has been to a large degree the success story of emerging market economies. In the recent past, there has been a sharp increase in the number of emerging-market companies acquiring established businesses and brands in Europe and the United States (e.g., Tata-Corus, Mittal-Arcelor, Lenovo-IBM), clearly demonstrating that "globalization" will no longer simply be another word for "Westernization" or "Americanization."

The world's center of economic gravity is shifting toward emerging markets. Purchase a mobile phone or laptop computer and you will find it most likely was made in China. Call a customer service helpline for computer service and personnel outside of the United States may answer the call. Emerging economies are no longer sources of inexpensive labor; they are becoming hotbeds of innovation in diverse fields such as telecommunications, automobile manufacturing, biotechnology, and health care. Increasingly, more research and development has recently been conducted in emerging market economies.

Companies in emerging markets are redesigning products without sacrificing quality to reduce costs—not by 10–20 percent—but up to 90 percent such as a no-frills car for $3,000 (the Tata "Nano") and $300 laptop computers from China's Lenovo. This comes as good news for the billions of people who live in emerging economies. But cheaper goods and services will help industrialized countries' consumers as well, especially because these consumers are likely to face years of slow income growth, as shown in Exhibit 1.2. Innovation in emerging economies will encourage rather than hinder innovation in rich countries.

emerging market economies
countries that are implementing more open trade and free-market policies

EXHIBIT 1.2 STRATEGIC COMPETITORS 2020

World's Ten Largest Economies: PPP Basis (US$2009)

	Country	PPP GNI (billions) 2009	Real GNI Growth 2009–2020 p.a. est.	PPP GNI (billions) 2020	Population (millions) 2009	Population Growth rate 2009–2020	Population (millions) 2020	PPP GNI per Capita ($) 2009	PPP GNI per Capita ($) 2020
1	**United States**	14,011	2.20%	17,800	307	0.9%	338.8	45,640	52,540
2	**China**	9,170	8.00%	21,381	1,331	0.6%	1,421.5	6,890	15,041
3	**Japan**	4,265	1.50%	5,024	128	−0.3%	123.8	33,440	40,568
4	**India**	3,786	7.00%	7,969	1,155	1.3%	1,331.3	3,280	5,986
5	**Germany**	3,017	2.00%	3,751	82	−0.3%	79.3	36,850	47,284
6	**Russia**	2,599	5.00%	4,445	142	−0.3%	137.4	18,330	32,356
7	**U.K.**	2,217	2.00%	2,757	62	0.5%	65.5	35,860	42,087
8	**France**	2,191	2.00%	2,724	63	0.3%	65.1	33,950	41,840
9	**Brazil**	1,968	5.00%	3,366	194	0.7%	209.5	10,160	16,069
10	**Italy**	1,919	2.00%	2,386	60	0.1%	60.7	31,870	39,332
	European Union (27)	15,590	2.00%	19,384	497	0.30%	513.6	31,368	37,738
	World TOTAL	71,774	2.70%	96,215	6,775	1.10%	7,641.4	10,594	12,591

Source: The World Bank: *World Development Indicators, 2011*, pp. 10–12 and 36–38.

Decoupling and the Move to a Multi-Polar World Economic Order[4]

In the past, the developing world has generally been perceived as a drag on global economic growth. However, recent evidence shows that the developing world, especially the emerging market economies of Asia, could instigate worldwide growth in the future as developed countries try to recover from the global credit crisis. While many western populations are becoming increasingly wary of globalization, evidence of this in Asia has not been noted. Indeed, most Asian countries welcome globalization as a means to enhance their business and economic growth. Despite fears that they could be among the leading victims of the global financial crisis, emerging giants like Brazil, India, and China grew strongly by an average of more than seven percent a year during 2009–2010 while advanced countries of Europe, the United States and Japan stagnated.

The Paris-based Organization for Economic Cooperation and Development (OECD) believes that while the U.S. economy has generally powered strong rebounds from global downturns, the future could be significantly different. Economic data for robust emerging economies such as Brazil, China, and India stand in sharp contrast to the outlook for Europe, Japan, and the United States, suggesting that the once-popular, then much-derided theory of "decoupling" between emerging economies and the developed world may be valid.

decoupling
a fundamental global shift in which industrialized country-dependent developing economies begin to grow based on their own underlying economic strengths rather than the ups and downs of the world's richest countries

Decoupling refers to a fundamental global shift in which developing economies that were once dependent upon industrialized countries for economic advancement, begin to solidly grow based on their own underlying economic strengths rather than the ups and downs of the world's 30 richest countries, which make up the OECD (and account for roughly 60 percent of the world economic output in nominal terms).

EXHIBIT 1.3 A MULTIPOLAR WORLD ECONOMIC ORDER

ECONOMIC PERSPECTIVES Asia: Reducing Export Dependency and Increasing Domestic Demand

The rapid economic advances witnessed by East Asian economies before the Asian financial crisis of 1997 were fueled largely by those countries' emphasis on "export-led" growth. To an extent, the recent high-level growth of BRIC countries can also be attributed to merchandise exports from China, services exports from India, and raw material (minerals and crude oil) exports from Brazil and Russia. Yet, these countries have also been reforming their large domestic economies by making them more market oriented. As illustrated in the opening vignette, the 2008 global financial crisis showed that countries that had pursued a policy of "export-led" growth could find difficulty sustaining rapid economic expansion during periods of external shock.

A few lessons, especially for developing countries, are becoming clear. First, with the ongoing decoupling of the global economy, it seems imperative that export-oriented nations diversify their market to include major emerging markets like BRICs. Second, countries emphasizing exports should base their strategy on their true competitive advantages and not subsidize the export sector directly or indirectly (such as keeping their currency weak). Governments that maintain a weak currency policy not only unfairly subsidize exports but they also tax imports, thereby contributing to domestic inflation and worsening consumer welfare in the exporting nation. Third, for countries with large populations, the size of the domestic market (especially the size and growth of that country's middle class) remains most important. Large populations act as a built-in stabilizer during periods of external downturns. As recent events have shown, the economies of China, India, and Indonesia performed well despite the global financial crisis. Fourth, overindulgence (living of credit) can lead to disaster. Consumers need to live within their means, corporations should not be over-leveraged, and governments must keep their budget deficits under control. Finally, countries' financial sectors—banking and capital markets, which are the heart of an economy—need to be adequately regulated to prevent the excessive risk taking that can lead to economic crisis.

Globalization has its merits, but it also requires participants to play by the rules of the game and avoid excessive risk taking, as it could send the global economy into a tailspin.[5]

QUESTIONS:

1) How should countries diversify from a purely "export-led" growth strategy?

2) What are some of the major lessons learned by countries to better prepare them for the next global economic crisis?

To see how decoupling works, consider the middle class in any country as the crucial segment of that nation, because it provides consumption of goods and services, savings (hence investment), and government tax revenues. The current fundamental shift in BRIC economies has been the growing size and income levels of the middle class. For example, the size of the middle class in China and India has been estimated at nearly 400 million and 300 million, respectively, and continues to grow. Furthermore, China and India each have a sizable world-class technical labor force and high savings and/or investment rate that help contribute to their rapid and stable economic growth. These countries provide high potential for decoupling, which could lead to more stable global economic growth with less cyclicality.

A sustainable decoupling process would eventually lead to a **multi-polar world**—a world economy in which the engines of growth could comprise the United States, the European Union, China, India, Brazil, Russia, and South Africa rather than the United States alone! Exhibit 1.2 and Exhibit 1.3 illustrate what the multi-polar world may look like based on the author's estimates. The final outcome could be a more stable global economic order.

multi-polar world
a world economy in which the engines of growth could comprise several major industrialized and emerging market economies such as the United States, the European Union, China, India, Brazil, Russia, and South Africa rather than the United States alone

REALITY CHECK LO-1

How have job opportunities for business majors from your school been affected by globalization? Do you see any particular trends or challenges?

LO-2

Identify how major international institutions facilitate globalization.

Key International Institutions that Facilitate Globalization

Globalization has not been a new phenomenon. Yet, it also has broader cultural, political, and environmental dimensions. Globalization has progressed throughout the course of recorded history, although not in a sustained fashion as it has since the early-1950s. Globalization seems to be gaining momentum; at what pace will it continue?

Here we will discuss three important institutions that will continue to guide the future direction of globalization. But the role of another important entity—sovereign governments—should not be overlooked. Governments still have the power to erect significant obstacles to globalization, ranging from protectionist policies to ignoring environmental standards to immigration restrictions to military hostilities. Nearly a century ago, the global economy operated in a relatively open environment, with goods, services, and people able to move across borders with comparatively little difficulty. That openness began to wither away with the onset of World War I in 1914, followed by the Great Depression in late-1920s through the 1930s, and World War II, which ended in 1945. The interwar period was chaotic as countries did not follow free trade rules. A recovery of globalization that was lost during that time still affects society today. Since World War II, governments in the free world have recognized the importance of international cooperation and coordination, which has led to the emergence of three major international organizations and financial institutions, namely, the International Monetary Fund (IMF), the World Bank, and the present World Trade Organization (WTO) that play a crucial role in the globalization process. We will now discuss the origins of these institutions, their functions and their role in globalization.

The International Monetary Fund

During the Great Depression of the 1930s, countries attempted to boost their failing economies by implementing nationalist or protectionist trade policies: sharply raising trade

Danita Delimont / Alamy

A typical IMF Board Meeting includes discussing the right policy reforms for countries.

barriers, weakening their currencies to compete against each other for export markets, and curtailing their citizens' freedom to hold foreign currencies. These attempts proved to be self-defeating. World trade declined sharply, and employment and living standards fell in many countries. This breakdown in international cooperation led the IMF founders to plan an institution charged with overseeing the **international monetary system**—the global system of exchange rates and international payments that enables countries and their citizens to buy goods and services from each other. The new institution's mission was to ensure stable national currencies and encourage its members to eliminate foreign exchange restrictions that hinder trade.

The IMF was conceived in July 1944, shortly after the surrender of the Axis powers in World War II, when representatives of 45 countries met in Bretton Woods, New Hampshire in the United States, and agreed upon a framework for international economic cooperation. They believed that a framework was necessary to avoid a repetition of the disastrous economic policies that had contributed to the Great Depression. The IMF came into formal existence in December 1945, when the first 29 member countries signed its Articles of Agreement. It began operations on March 1, 1947 in Washington, DC. IMF membership began to expand in the late-1950s and the 1960s as many African nations, formerly European colonies, became independent and applied for membership.

The IMF and Globalization As of June 1, 2011, 187 countries were members of the IMF, a part of the United Nations family of 192. This near-global membership means that the IMF has been uniquely placed to help its member governments take advantage of the opportunities—and manage the challenges—posed by globalization. The IMF tracks global economic trends and performance, alerts its member countries when it sees problems on the horizon, provides a forum for economic policy dialog, and disseminates information to governments on how to implement **economic reforms** to meet global challenges. Marked by massive movements of global capital and abrupt shifts in countries' comparative advantage, globalization affects countries' choices in many areas, including labor, trade, environment, and tax policies. Helping countries enjoy globalization's benefits while avoiding its downsides has been an important task for the IMF.[6] In many ways the IMF's main purpose—to provide global financial stability—has remained the same today as it was when the organization was first established. More specifically, the IMF continues to:

- Provide a forum for cooperation on international monetary problems;
- Facilitate the sustainable growth of international trade, thus promoting job creation, economic growth, and poverty reduction;
- Promote exchange rate stability and an open system of international payments; and
- Lend countries foreign exchange when needed, on a temporary basis and under adequate safeguards, to help address balance of payment problems (discussed in greater detail in Chapter 4).

The IMF recognizes the fact that the benefits of globalization are not without risks—such as those arising from the recent global credit crisis. The IMF works with countries to help them manage or reduce these risks, through economic analysis and policy advice and through technical assistance in areas such as macroeconomic policy reforms, financial sector sustainability, and exchange rate management.

The World Bank

Like its sister institution the IMF, the World Bank was conceived at the Bretton Woods Conference in 1944. The World Bank's initial primary role was to aid the reconstruction of Europe after the war; its first loan of $250 million was to France in 1947 for postwar reconstruction. Today, reconstruction and restructuring economies to make them efficient

international monetary system
the system of exchange rates and international payments that enables countries and their citizens to purchase goods and services from one other

economic reforms
economic policy changes that promote private sector development, competitive markets, market-pricing, freer trade, and deregulation

Table 1.1: The World Bank Group's Developmental Institutions

International Bank for Reconstruction and Development (IBRD)	Supports reconstruction and restructuring of member countries using funds raised in international capital markets
International Development Association (IDA)	Provides long-term low-interest social sector and infrastructure loans to the poorest members using foreign aid funds provided by the rich nation members
International Finance Corporation (IFC)	Provides loans and takes equity position in private companies of developing countries and works toward developing **capital markets** in those economies
Multilateral Investment Guarantee Agency (MIGA)	Provides political risk coverage for private investments made in developing countries
International Center for the Settlement of Investment Disputes (ICSID)	Works on issues related to foreign investment disputes

remain a major role of the Bank, along with poverty reduction. Also headquartered in Washington, DC, the Bank has become a bigger, broader, and far more complex organization than it was at its inception with the same membership countries as the IMF. Now called the World Bank Group, it encompasses five closely associated developmental institutions, presented in Table 1.1 by function.

The World Bank and Globalization The World Bank sees globalization as an opportunity to reach global solutions to national challenges.[7] Concern for the natural environment coupled with the need for sustainable economic growth and development in developing countries has been embedded in the Bank's work. As part of the Bank's Strategic Framework, there are five focus areas that accommodate and facilitate the globalization process.

First, trade expansion has been a leading factor in global integration, especially since the early-1970s. Several developing countries have participated in trade liberalization, but the gains from trade have been uneven, with Asian economies moving fast, while Africa in general has been less able to capitalize on world trade growth.

Second, the Bank's analytical and advisory role has been essential; supporting national policies to strengthen free-market institutions and infrastructure has provided the potential for creating large gains from trade.

Third, the financial crises of 1997–1998 and 2008–2009 instigated broad agreements in the Bank that support international standards, especially in financial systems that are a necessary foundation in a global economy. The Bank participates in various forums with the IMF and other financial institutions to strengthen financial sectors (banking and capital markets) of member countries.

Fourth, the Bank considers its role as a knowledge and information technology transfer agent to developing countries as the engine for sustainable development. The Bank's work in bridging the digital divide has been aimed at speeding the globalization process.

Finally, the Bank focuses on eradicating communicable diseases without neglecting the importance of cultural heritage in a shrinking, globalized world.

capital markets
a stock exchange where long-term financial instruments such as stocks and bonds can be bought and sold

The World Trade Organization

The World Trade Organization (WTO) commenced operation on January 1, 1995, but its trading system (which sets trade rules) began in 1948 under the General Agreement on Tariffs and Trade (GATT). Whereas GATT primarily dealt with merchandise trade, the WTO and its agreements now cover trade in agriculture, services, inventions, and intellectual property. GATT **liberalization of the trading system** (lowering and/or removing trade barriers such as tariffs, quotas, and subsidies) was developed through a series of trade negotiations, or "rounds." The first of eight GATT rounds primarily dealt with tariff reductions, but later negotiations included other areas such as anti-dumping and non-tariff measures.

Lowering trade barriers has been one of the most simplistic ways to encourage trade and globalization. The barriers concerned include custom duties (or tariffs) and measures such as import bans or quotas that selectively restrict quantities. From time to time, other issues such as deregulation and exchange rate policies have also been discussed. Because of trade liberalization, there has been an exceptional increase in world trade, and merchandise exports have grown by an average of 6 percent annually since 1950. For example, world trade in 2000 was 22 times as high as it was in 1950. The eighth and last GATT round—the 1986–1994 Uruguay Round—led to the creation of WTO.

The WTO, based in Geneva, Switzerland, has no branch offices anywhere else in the world. Its 153 member nations account for more than 97 percent of world trade in goods and services. Another 30 countries are in the process of negotiating membership to join the organization. Simply put, the WTO addresses the rules of trade between nations at a near-global membership level. But more than that, the WTO has been an organization for liberalizing trade, a forum for governments to negotiate trade agreements, and a place for member governments to settle trade disputes. It operates a global system of trade rules.

The WTO and Globalization The WTO's overriding objective helps global trade to flow smoothly, freely, fairly, and predictably. It does this by:

- Administering trade agreements
- Acting as a forum for trade negotiations
- Settling trade disputes
- Reviewing national trade policies
- Assisting developing countries with trade policy issues, through technical assistance and training programs
- Cooperating with other international organizations like the IMF and World Bank[8]

At the heart of the system—known as the multilateral trading system—are the WTO's agreements, negotiated and signed by a large majority of the world's trading nations, and ratified in their parliaments. These agreements lay the legal ground rules for international commerce. Essentially, they are contracts that guarantee member countries important trade rights. They also bind governments to keep their trade policies within agreed limits to every member's benefit. WTO agreements are lengthy, complex legal texts covering a wide range of activities including agriculture, textiles and clothing, banking, telecommunications, government purchases, industrial standards and product safety, food sanitation regulations, intellectual property, and much more.

A number of simple, fundamental principles run throughout all these documents; the following five principles are the foundation of the multilateral trading system.

- Trade without discrimination: Member countries should not discriminate between their trading partners (giving them equally "most favored nation" or MFN status); and member countries should not discriminate between their foreign products and services.
- Freer trade: Gradually removing trade barriers through negotiations.
- Predictability: Foreign companies, investors, and governments should be confident that trade barriers (including tariff and non-tariff barriers) will not be raised arbitrarily; tariff rates and market-opening commitments are "bound" in the WTO.

liberalization of the trading system
lowering and/or removing trade barriers such as tariffs, quotas, and subsidies

- Promoting fair competition: Discouraging "unfair" practices such as export subsidies and dumping products in the export market at below cost.
- Encouraging economic reforms in developing countries: Giving emerging economies more time to adjust to a free trade environment, greater flexibility, and special privileges to meet WTO requirements[9].

In 2000, new trade talks started on agriculture and services. However, progress has been slow. Emerging economies, especially Brazil, China, and India, have made it clear that further liberalization in the industrial sector will not proceed unless the European Union, Japan, and the United States drastically cut their huge agricultural subsidies. The concept of curtailing agricultural subsidies in developed economies was incorporated into the ninth (most recent) round to trade negotiations called the "Doha Round" or Doha Development Agenda (DDA), which was launched in Qatar in November 2001.

REALITY CHECK LO-2

What is the status of the Doha Round of trade negotiations? Identify the key stumbling block of this trade negotiation and describe its impact on globalization.

LO-3
Evaluate the need for strong and transparent national institutions to adapt to globalization.

Institutional Structure and Its Impact on Globalization[10]

As discussed earlier, most countries cooperate multilaterally on important global economic issues through membership in the IMF, the World Bank and the WTO. These three organizations address a very wide range of international economic concerns, but they were not designed to be all-encompassing.[11] There are several key challenges that require national attention. These include building institutions that support (1) a democratic system of government,

SALVATORE DI NOLFI/EPA/Newscom

The WTO is responsible for interpreting trade laws and resolving dispute brought by member countries.

(2) free markets, (3) an independent judiciary, and (4) a free press. As an institution, an independent judiciary can be paramount for interpreting the rule of law, with courts enforcing the laws, and a free press that can be important for transparency of business practices. The need for such national institutions must be addressed if globalization will be sustained.

What is Institutional Structure?

In business, when we speak of **institutions** we mean the rules, enforcement mechanisms, and organizations that support market transactions. Institutions help transmit information, enforce contracts and property rights, and promote market competition across extremely diverse developed and developing countries. Building effective institutions takes time and results from a cumulative process.[12] Within each country, institution building may stall or reverse over time because of political conflicts or economic, social, and cultural conditions. Merely establishing institutions will not be enough: they must be effective and people must want to use them ethically. Successful institutions play three important roles: they channel information about market conditions, goods, services, and participants; they define property rights and contracts, determining who gets what and when; and they promote competition and innovation in markets.

Transparency of Political Institutions

Many people believe that globalization addresses economics, information technology, and business culture. But, before markets, modems, and manufacturers can work, appropriate political systems must also be in place. The foundations of the globalized business world are political—and so are the biggest threats to the system.[13] Technocrats, especially in the Americas, Asia, and Europe, are struggling to convince their citizens that globalization does not just benefit the rich. If these technocrats are unable to successfully convey the nationwide benefits of globalization in any of the 10 major world economies listed in Exhibit 1.2, then globalization could unravel.

The political change that accelerated the globalization process in the recent past took place during a relatively short period (1978–1991). It started in 1978 with China moving away from Maoism to market reforms, followed by Thatcherism in 1979 in the United Kingdom, Reaganomics in 1980, the creation of the European Union in mid-1980s, and the 1989 collapse of the Berlin wall and the Soviet Union. Finally in 1991, when India faced a balance of payments crisis, through IMF support, it was forced to dismantle bureaucratic regulation and protectionism that had hobbled its economy for decades. Thus, in a span of less than 13 years, the political elites in the world's major power centers came to similar conclusions. They embraced globalization and a move toward free-market economics.

Yet, in all of these countries it appears that the poor have suffered as a result of globalization due to increased global competition and decreased subsidies for basic items such as cooking fuels and food. The World Bank encourages political institutions and leaders to be transparent and convince their constituents that while globalization does create "winners" and "losers," appropriate policies will be in place to retrain and uplift the downtrodden. Otherwise, the Bank believes that social unrest will rise, leading to political instability and ineffective and inconsistent economic policies. This, in turn, will wreak havoc on markets and the benefits of globalization will be stalled. Political stability has been greatest among long-standing democracies.

Adaptive Institutions to Strengthen Public Participation

Adaptive institutions are government organizations that create strong incentives for private investment and operate under a system of checks and balances that function best in a democratic system of government. Here, **accountability** and **transparency** emerge as key

institutions
the rules, enforcement mechanisms, and organizations that support market transactions

adaptive institutions
government organizations that create strong incentives for private investment and operate under a system of checks and balances

accountability
a system of responsibility in which an authority, such as the government, is answerable for its actions

transparency
a system of full disclosure and openness that aims to avoid any semblance of corruption and cronyism

Stephen Ferry/Getty Images news/Getty Images

The collapse of the Berlin Wall was just one political event that helped accelerate globalization.

factors for institutional reform that promotes political stability, sustainable economic growth, and globalization. The potential for social unrest such as violent strikes recedes in these societies because civil liberties, political and human rights, and opportunities for citizens to select and influence a government's policies exist. Democracies strive to nurture such institutions by instilling transparency with the help of various communication channels. Historically, newspapers or print media have been the dominant route for conveying in-depth investigation, analysis, and thoughts. That was followed by the advent of the TV, which is the most dominant form of instantaneously conveying current developments and information, today. The Internet with the help of desktop and laptop computers has made visual and readable information even more readily available. The most recent device that enables greatest ease in portability and accessibility of information are the iPhone and iPad, which use wireless connections and social media that even espouse a strong tradition of individual rights and a free press. Such countries tend to have a vibrant free enterprise system, a competitive market structure, and companies that actively seek to be engaged in globalization.

Independent Judiciary and Free Press

Investors have greater confidence when conducting business in countries with low crime, effective courts, dependable contract enforcement, and free press. In this regard, the judiciary system in a country remains an extremely important institution, which has a primary responsibility of interpreting the laws and resolving disputes. Countries seeking to become established as good places to do business will maintain fair, transparent and functioning legal systems along with a free press that could expose and investigate misdeeds by public officials and corporate leaders.

For example, countries like Nigeria, Iraq and Afghanistan that rank at the bottom of Transparency International's[14] (a Berlin-based, anticorruption organization) list of most corrupt countries in the world to conduct business have dysfunctional legal systems (i.e., legal systems that exist only in name but not in practice). Even emerging economies like the BRIC nations struggle to deliver adequate legal protection. Respect for the rule of law enhances the predictability businesses require to make decisions based upon the sanctity of contracts.

REALITY CHECK LO-3

Identify an adaptive institution in your city or state that promotes globalization. What are some of the measures advocated by that institution?

Effective Policy Measures that Promote Globalization

LO-4

Describe the key policy measures that make globalization sustainable.

Countries cannot thrive on high-quality institutions alone, they also need effective policies as complements to globalization. Countries with sound economic policies will be more successful in the global economy, encouraging further opening and cross-border integration. To attract foreign and domestic private investments, which are crucial engines of sustainable economic growth and globalization, governments need to put in place good governance, competitive markets, and property rights, and assist in the fight against corruption.

ETHICAL PERSPECTIVES

Canadian *Terroir*?

Canadians love wine. Unfortunately, because of its frigid weather conditions, most of Canada is unsuitable for the development of vineyards. The two notable regional exceptions include British Columbia's Okanagan Valley, which is blessed with a Mediterranean climate, and southern Ontario, which rests at the same latitude as France's Languedoc wine region. Wines from these Canadian regions have been awarded international honors and have been able to export some of their output. Yet without Canadian government subsidies, wineries may not be globally competitive.

The small wineries of British Columbia and southern Ontario produce Canadian *terroir* that is relatively more expensive and of better quality than the wines produced by Canada's two biggest wine companies, Vincor Canada and Andrew Peller. *Terroir* (derived from "terre," the French word for "land") is defined as a group of vineyards or vines from the same region, belonging to a specific appellation, and sharing the same type of soil, weather conditions, grapes and wine-making, which contribute to a specific personality of the wine.

The small wineries of British Columbia and southern Ontario believe that the image of Canadian *terroir* is being tarnished by Ontario government's Liquor Control Board, which has approved labeling wine with up to 70 percent imported content (i.e., only 30 percent Canadian content) to be sold as Canadian wine. The "big two" wine companies that primarily sell these blended wines argue that because Canada is incapable of being self-sufficient in wine production, there is no choice but to blend the limited amount of Canadian wine with cheaper imports from Australia and Chile to effectively compete in the Canadian market. However, the fine print on the bottle labels indicates that the imported wines were "cellared in Canada."

In the interest of transparency in government policy, the small Canadian wineries want the labeling to be changed. Wineries would like the Liquor Control Board to "call a spade a spade" and indicate on the bottle labels that the blended wine is "bottled" in Canada but not "cellared" in Canada.

For that matter, why blend the wines? Why not sell the pure Canadian wines as Canadian, and the imports as Australian and Chilean wines bottled in Canada, as it is done in the United States?

QUESTIONS:

1) In the interest of globalization, do you believe that Ontario's Liquor Control Board is ethical in its wine labeling process? Explain your position.
2) With the ongoing globalization process, do you think that as an institution, Ontario's Liquor Control Board is practicing good governance?

Source: "Outsourcing Terroir," *The Economist*, September 12, 2009, pp. 44.

Taken together, these provide a baseline measurement for gauging the relative quality of a country's economic policies and performance. These policies will now be discussed in greater detail.

Good Governance

Countries that have successfully adapted to globalization realize that they cannot succeed without high-quality government management at home. Singapore, a country in which government actions are fully disclosed and discussed before they are implemented, posits an appropriate example. This type of policy transparency makes it very attractive for domestic and foreign investors to funnel resources into the country to fuel economic growth and quickly adapt to globalization. On the other hand, most government policies and transactions in Central Asia are conducted in secrecy, therefore, economic progress and global integration has been slow in this region.

The quality of administration is also important; fine policies alone do not inspire respect and confidence without competent administrators and consistency over time. The quality of government services, the capabilities of civil servants, the political independence of public agencies, and the credibility of the government's commitment to good policies can measure effective governance.

Competitive Markets

Successfully globalized economies strive to attain competitive market structures at home. To achieve this objective, countries must enforce regulations that promote free markets such as **antitrust laws**. Although some might argue that antitrust laws interfere with the natural growth of successful businesses, they are meant to encourage competition and prevent problems like the "too big to fail" phenomenon that occurred in the 2008 American credit crisis.

In competitive market economies, governments minimize the role of state-owned enterprises, which makes them less likely to impose wage and price controls. For example, commissioner, Mr. Joaquin Almunia, of the European Union's Competition Commission in Brussels, Belgium, has had a primary role as watchdog on competition (i.e., to make sure that companies—domestic or foreign—that operate in the European Union do not monopolize any business sector) to ensure that the region's market structure for goods and services remains competitive. The planned merger of GE and Honeywell announced in 2000 was blocked by European Union's Competition Commission on the grounds that the merger would have lead to an uncompetitive market for GE-Honeywell products and services in the European Union, thereby impeding globalization.

Property Rights

Protection of property rights has always been fundamental to market economies, as this protection enables buyers and sellers to conduct transactions with a high degree of trust. Studies by the World Bank have shown that countries that have successfully adapted to globalization guarantee property rights, whereas the least-globalized countries offer less protection. If government actions call into question the ownership and transfer and/or sale of property, conducting business could become risky and economic activity could stall.

In communist and state-controlled economies like those in Central Asia and parts of Africa and the Middle East, property rights either do not exist or are not well defined. This discourages domestic and foreign investors from making long-term commitments in these countries despite any competitive advantage in terms of labor productivity or raw materials those countries may have. As a result, these countries will most likely fall behind nations that guarantee property rights and will not be able to take advantage of globalization.

antitrust laws
national laws aimed at maintaining competition in all sectors of the economy and preventing monopolistic behavior of firms

Anticorruption Policies

Illicit dealings undermine economic performance by raising costs, creating uncertainty, and thwarting competition and transparency. More globalized economies (e.g., New Zealand, the Nordic countries, and Singapore) are less likely to tolerate corruption and they rank at the top in index for absence of corruption by Transparency International (the global civil society organization leading the fight against corruption). Some countries of the former Soviet Union, in contrast, rank near the bottom of the index.

REALITY CHECK LO-4

Search Transparency International's website and identify the ranking of the United States and the top ten countries with least corruption. Were you surprised with the ranking? Why?

Impact of Information Technology on Globalization

LO-5

Describe the role of information technology in bridging the global digital divide.

Innovations in information technology (computers, software, wireless telecommunication, the cell phone, and the Internet) are radically changing the way people all over the world live, communicate, and work.[15] Take a few moments to think about what life was like ten—or even five—years ago. IT has fundamentally changed everything people do in daily life, at home, at school, at play, and at work. We are in a period of profound transformation—adjusting lifestyles to make the Internet and wireless technologies a part of everyday life—called the **digital era**. The economic, social, and political benefits of new information technologies, of which the Internet and wireless telecommunications are by far the most publicly visible form, are changing the relative competitiveness of nations as access to those technologies spreads rapidly around the globe. For example, farmers in Kenya can now directly make payments for their inputs and have deposits made to their accounts for crop sales by using cell phones and not spend hours or days working on their banking transactions. Similarly, fishermen off India's coastal regions are now able to obtain the best price possible for their catch by negotiating and finalizing the sale while at sea! On the political front, the democracy movements in the Middle East were largely fueled by social networking using the cell phone. As **bandwidth** expands and communications costs fall, more people will be linked together via computers, iPads, and cell phones. The economic efficiency of online communication will increase exponentially with the number of these kinds of connections. Increasingly, as communication networks become more established, they will reshape the way people all over the world live, entertain, communicate, and work. The same technological changes that are transforming the business world now will also revolutionize the nature of social networks and the way that governments operate in the future.

digital era
the period of transformation that adjusts lifestyles to make the Internet and wireless technologies a part of everyday life

bandwidth
the amount of data and other information that can be transferred in a second via the Internet

The Digital Generation

Imagine life without the Internet and cell (mobile) phone. Though these technologies are relatively new, already a world without **the web** and wireless network has become as unthinkable for many of us as a world without land-line telephones.[16] But what about the future? Can the benefits of this extraordinary technology be multiplied and globalized? The network's infrastructure has also been fundamentally transformed in the past decade; dial-up Internet access has given way to an "always-on" broadband technology. Furthermore, users are accessing the Internet via many types of wireless devices, from laptops to cell

the web
the world wide web, abbreviated as "www" and commonly known as the web; a system of interlinked documents contained and accessed via the Internet

phones (including iPhones, iPads, tablets, etc.) in order to have mobile access to email and other applications. Communication has become the fastest-growing part of household expenditures since 1993 in many countries. Millions of people all over the world now use the Internet for everything including online banking, investments, research, publishing, Skype, doing homework, buying books, playing or downloading books, data, games, music, movies, and recipes. Levels of user participation and publication on the Internet have also surged, from blogs, podcasts and interactive wikis that anyone can modify, to services for sharing photos and video clips, such as YouTube and Flickr. Social networking sites such as Facebook, LinkedIn, and MySpace, and instant broadcasting sites like Twitter, represent additional rapidly developing global frontiers of communication.

Expanding the Global Use of Information Technology

It may be less apparent that Internet-based applications underlie major advances in science, business organization, environment monitoring, transport management, education, and e-government. Without the Internet, planes would not fly, financial markets would not operate, supermarkets would not restock, taxes would not get paid, and power grids would not balance the supply and demand for electricity. This reflects our increasing global reliance on the Internet for business and social activity, including health and education. In addition, seeking information on health has become one of the most frequent uses of the Internet.

Because broadband prices have been falling, governments in emerging economies such as China, India, and South Africa are facilitating the spread of broadband to rural towns and villages to provide instant access to market information and government programs to remote villagers. This will enable policymakers to maximize the economic potential of remote communities and make globalization sustainable.

Unlike changes instigated by technological revolutions such as electricity and the railroad, which took decades to spread around the globe, the IT revolution has been relatively instantaneous. This reinforces the fact that IT and globalization are closely

Olivier Asselin/Alamy

Advances in information technology and the Internet is enabling school children in Nigerian to become globally competitive.

related. By reducing communications costs, IT has helped to globalize production of goods and services and has encouraged a freer flow of these items, including capital, across national boundaries. In fact, IT acts as a catalyst in the globalization process by lowering operating costs.

Internet-related technologies help reduce corporate and societal hierarchies because of greater access to information for everyone concerned. Therefore, Internet and wireless technologies could make many authoritarian governments uneasy thereby restricting public access to social media. This appears especially true in relatively closed societies where political freedom, especially of speech, press, or other forms of expression are severely curtailed—as in China and several countries in Central Asia and the Middle East. Political authorities in these societies, particularly nondemocratic governments such as China and North Korea, have expressed their belief that uncensored information from countries abroad will corrupt local cultures. As events in Egypt, Tunisia, Libya, Syria, and others (the so-called 2011 "Arab Spring") have shown, there are fears that Internet-related technologies could bring about rapid social and political change, and access to communications technology could shift the balance of power between ordinary people and their governments, making dissent safer. Therefore, it may be unlikely that Internet and related technologies will remain, or completely thrive, free of government interference.

The Digital Divide Myth

Digital divide describes the perceived economic gap between countries or people with easy access to digital and information technology (and its benefits) and those with very limited or no access. However, as described in this section, the rapid and progressive fall in prices of digital IT equipment and services has increased access and accelerated globalization, thereby narrowing the digital gap. The question that should be asked: will globalization make digital divide a myth?

Most people like what modern technology has to offer, and developing countries are now making the same transition that the United States, Europe, and Japan made earlier—only more rapidly and in a less expensive way. In the transition period, this could cause political strain, especially in nondemocratic societies. Failure to adapt will likely negatively impact some countries more than others. As current technologies become even cheaper, they will spread faster the world over. While some governments may hold their countries back, the vast majority will move forward.

The number of mobile phones that can access the Internet has been growing at a phenomenal rate, especially in the developing world. In China, for example, more than 73 million people (or 29 percent) of all Internet users in the country use mobile phones for online access[17]. In 2008, China surpassed the United States as the country with the largest number of Internet users—more than 300 million in 2010—as well as some 600 million cell phone subscribers, more than any other country. The potential for mobile Internet service remains enormous. Mobile web-browsing has been growing the fastest in developing countries, including India, Indonesia, Russia, and South Africa.

Behind these statistics lies a more profound social change, such as web banking and web commerce, which enhances worker productivity and economic efficiency in these countries. A couple of years ago, a favorite example of cell phones' impact on the developing world was that of an Indian fisherman calling different ports from his boat to get a better price for his catch. However, cell phones are now increasingly being used to access more elaborate data services such as M-PESA, a cell phone payment service introduced by Safaricom Kenya. M-PESA allows subscribers to deposit and withdraw money by text message. Similar services have proved popular in the Philippines, South Africa, and even the Maldives Islands in the Indian Ocean.

digital divide
the perceived economic gap between countries or people with easy access to digital and information technology (and its benefits) and those with very limited access, or none at all

How Countries "Leapfrog" into the Internet and Cell Phone Era

As of 2010, only one-fifth of the world's population of 6.7 billion had access to the Internet. These 1.34 billion people have been empowered by the opportunities that the Internet presents for business, social interaction and civic engagement. The question now is: What will be the characteristics of the next several billion Internet users?[18]

Analysts believe that the next billions of Internet users will be vastly different from the first billion. Because of market saturation in developed economies, the majority of users will be from developing countries, and they will connect to the Internet principally via wireless networks. In many developing countries, the number of cell phone subscribers now outnumbers those for fixed-line networks by more than 20:1. For example, the number of new mobile subscribers added each month in India exceeds Sweden's entire population! As cheaper "Internet-capable" mobile phones become the norm and competition and economies of scale lowers access prices, the same can be expected for Internet services. As communication access spreads in developing countries, businesses rather than governments will lead the way by offering lower prices and more choices for services and devices, with economic liberalization as an enabling factor.

Safaricom's parent company, Vodaphone, launched M-PESA's mobile payment service in Tanzania and Afghanistan, and plans to introduce it in India, where unlimited wireless access to the Internet can be purchased for less than $6 a month. Furthermore, since mobile phones are often shared by several members, say of a family, the number of calls made and/or received on a single cell phone in India is two to three times the average seen in most developed economies. It has become apparent that developing countries are skipping the use of land-line technology and moving directly to wireless systems, thereby leapfrogging an entire generation of technology and catching up faster with the developed world.

Non-profit organizations in developing countries believe that text messaging will likely predominate emerging economies' mobile phone usage for three reasons: (1) all cell phones, however inexpensive, can send text messages; (2) users know what it costs to send a text message; and (3) cell-web access requires more sophisticated handsets and may not always supported by cell phone companies. However, as countries continue to develop, more consumers will have full access to cell phones with web capabilities.[19] National regulators are also likely to help by fostering cheap cell access. The developing world missed out on much of the excitement of the initial web revolution, largely because of its lack of an Internet infrastructure and the initial high cost of new technologies. Now that access costs have been decreasing and infrastructure has been expanding, developing countries may be poised to leapfrog the industrialized world in the era of the cell phone-to-web technology.

REALITY CHECK LO-5

Research and determine whether the typical middle-class citizen in Mexico is already in the cell-to-web era.

LO-6

Describe the validity of the anti-globalization argument.

The Globalization Controversy[20]

To its fiercest critics,[21] globalization—the impact of an increasingly free flow of ideas, people, goods, services, and capital that leads to closer integration and interdependence of economies and societies—can be a force for exploitation and injustice. Some socialist-leaning citizens and labor unions believe that capitalism exploits man in the economic sense just as communism exploits man in the political sense. Anti-globalists have drawn support from a broad range of public opinion, and as a result, they are likely to remain politically influential. Arguments against globalization highlight problems such as the costs of disruptive economic change including job losses and stagnant wages, the loss of local control over economic policies and developments, the disappearance of old industries, and related erosion of communities. This section will examine several arguments against globalization and their counter arguments. To address this issue objectively, one must also understand the benefits of globalization; e.g., why closer economic integration is a force for good, and how globalization reduces poverty.

Job Losses and Income Stagnation

In developed economies, support for further trade liberalization that could lead to acceleration of globalization is uncertain; in some European countries, voters are hostile to it, which is part of the reason why the Doha Round of trade liberalization has stalled. Critics argue that globalization harms the poor through loss of jobs and stagnant, if not falling, wages. Critics also argue that open trade and foreign direct investment may take jobs from workers in advanced industrial economies (blue-collar and, increasingly, white-collar workers) and transfer them to less expensive workers in developing countries. This leaves the workers in the richer country, out of work. This increase in local labor supply drives down wages, causing wage stagnation. Meanwhile, the workers in developing countries are drawn into jobs that may exploit them. These workers often get paid much less than their counterparts in richer countries and they are often required to work longer hours in sub-standard environments.

As the world enters a "knowledge-based" global economy, advanced countries should expect greater development (based on Heckscher-Ohlin and factor price equalization trade theory discussed in Chapter 2). Workers in high-income countries will need to use more technology and be more productive in order to maintain or enhance their wage rates. The only way workers in industrialized countries can compete with their counterparts in the developing world will be through increased productivity by using technologically intensive manufacturing techniques.

Ron Yue / Alamy

Globalization creates "winners" and "losers". *Japanese farmers protesting WTO call for cutting rice subsidy.*

What about the workers in the richer countries who are not displaced (laid off), but whose wages may stagnate because of foreign competition? The answer to this question will be hard to conclude, because it will depend on the industry, the worker skills needed, and specific market conditions. For instance, the wages of such workers may fall, or fail to rise as quickly as they would have without globalization. However, all workers would benefit from lower-priced imports. Researchers at University of Chicago's Graduate School of Business have shown that inexpensive imports from China have disproportionately benefited the American poor.[22] Meanwhile, in developing countries, globalization will lead to increased demand for labor and will raise wages even for workers who are not directly employed in the new trade-related jobs, e.g., engineers will generally witness an increase in domestic wages when the demand for IT and software engineers increases because of outsourcing.

Sustainable Development and Environmental Degradation

What does **sustainable development** mean? The term was first used around 1983 by the Brundtland Commission[23], which was set up by the United Nations to address growing concerns "about the accelerating deterioration of the human environment and natural resources." The Brundtland Commission defined sustainable development as development that "meets the needs of the present without compromising the ability of future generations to meet their own needs,"[24] whether environmentally, socially, or economically (including natural resource conservation). While the concept of sustainable development has been discussed since 1987, it only recently gained popularity as a powerful force as awareness about climate change, the production of greenhouse gases, and rapid and uncontrolled deforestation of the world's tropical rain forests has grown. Sustainable development has also become a source of increasing tension between the developing world and developed nations, especially between China, the United States, and the European Union. Globalization and Asia's role in it has become particularly contentious.[25] For example, China's unprecedented economic growth since 1978 has left a legacy of environmental degradation. Pollution has made cancer China's leading cause of death. Likewise, the debate over deforestation, which focuses on countries ranging from Brazil to Indonesia and Malaysia, does not have simple solutions. In order to produce biofuels, some forests have suffered, but the drive in Europe and the United States to find alternatives to fossil fuels has spurred the growth of biofuels. Clearly there are complex issues involving tradeoffs and difficult challenges for governments, the private sector, and non-governmental organizations. Finding solutions depends upon a shared, single vision—meeting the needs of the present without compromising the future—and working toward that vision together.

Some businesses have adopted sustainable development policies. In 2008, for example, British retailer Marks & Spencer introduced the slogan "Plan A. Because there is no Plan B." A five-year, 100-point, ecological plan to tackle some of the biggest challenges facing its business (and the larger market in which it operates) includes working with customers and suppliers to combat climate change, reduce waste, safeguard natural resources, and ethically trade.

A survey by the World Bank indicates that corporate social responsibility (CRS) practices are now a significant factor in determining where multinational corporations conduct business.[26] Of the companies surveyed, 90 percent have board-approved policies on environmental management. Other issues featured in CRS practices include labor rights, corruption, human rights, community health, and land rights. The World Bank survey also found that 48.5 percent of multinationals will make their decisions based on CSR issues with regard to foreign direct investment (FDI)—corporate investment abroad to build new manufacturing or service facilities, or to purchase existing companies abroad. Furthermore, CSR factors such as the unwillingness of some corporations to pay bribes had caused 36.4 percent of respondents to withdraw from a country. The World Bank study also indicates that rather than FDI sparking a "race to the bottom," (i.e., companies rushing to invest abroad in order

sustainable development
economic development that meets the needs of the present generation without compromising the ability of future generations to meet their own needs, whether environmentally, socially, or economically

to take advantage of poor environmental and labor standards), these companies are largely being prudent and looking for long term commitment to countries. CSR issues consistently implemented for the long term, as in the case of PepsiCo, lead to sustainable business and development. Under these circumstances, FDI does improve labor and environmental conditions, particularly in the developing world.

REALITY CHECK LO-6

Determine whether there have been any industrial job losses in your region of the country because of globalization, and ask those workers who have lost their jobs about their experiences.

Making Globalization Work for All

LO-7

Explain the case made to temporarily support those negatively affected by globalization.

Policymakers in many countries have come to the conclusion that the globalization debate should center on how to best manage the globalization process—at both national and international levels—so that the benefits are widely shared and costs are kept to a minimum. Most economists would agree that greater integration into the world economy and more openness to efficiency and modernization offers all citizens of the global village a more hopeful future. The world has experienced successive waves of what is now described as "globalization." These periods have all shared certain characteristics with our own: the expansion of trade, the diffusion of technology, extensive migration, and cross-fertilization of diverse cultures. For China, globalization has, since 1978, brought about more trade, financial flows, and faster economic growth than any corresponding period in history, leading to higher living standards, bigger declines in poverty, and larger increases in life expectancy.

Globalization has the *potential* to increase the quality of life for people; however, there cannot be a guarantee that quality of life for all people will increase, or that all changes caused by globalization will be positive. Globalization does create winners and losers. For example, in the search for profits to maximize shareholder wealth, some multinational corporations may try to pay substandard wages to the workers they employ in developing countries. To prevent this from happening, developing countries could enforce regulations that would require multinational corporations to pay living wages that are fair by local standards. As an additional enforcement, export barriers could be imposed by the WTO on countries that do not comply with regulations.

Globalization's Winners and Losers

According to the World Bank, more than 400 million Chinese citizens have climbed out of poverty since the implementation of economic reforms that started in 1978 in their country. Since India's initiation of economic reforms in 1991, that country has become a rapidly growing economy with a middle class approaching 300 million out of a total population of some 1.16 billion. Brazil has been flourishing as well, and recent economic growth successes in South Africa, Tanzania, and Ghana show that Africa, too, may be poised for brighter economic prospects. A number of factors have affected economic growth, but they likely could not have occurred without globalization. In addition, closer participation with institutions such as the IMF, the World Bank, and the WTO has promoted civil liberties by proliferating information and increasing choices. While rapid growth in emerging market economies could lead to higher commodity prices, such price increases are a reflection that economic growth accelerates at a faster rate than the supply of resources, including crude oil and food. In examples such as this, supply will eventually catch up to demand, and

Lisa F. Young/IStockphoto.com

Globalization's losers need support. *A laid-off auto assembly worker being retrained for jobs in the promising solar energy sector.*

commodity prices will stabilize, perhaps at a higher level, thereby increasing the income levels of commodity exporters.

Globalization's Losers Need Support

Those that suffer most from the effects of globalization are those countries that have not been able to seize the opportunities to participate in this process. Countries that fall under this category of "real" losers especially include those that do not provide economic and political freedoms to their citizens. Most of these countries are governed by authoritarian regimes with minimum rule of law and insignificant transparency. They include Central Asia, much of Africa, and countries such as North Korea.

Because globalization does create winners and losers even in relatively open countries like the U.S., economists have argued that national policies ought to be implemented to help retrain and educate displaced workers. This will enable displaced workers to become more productive and earn a higher income. In the United States, however, globalization does not provide the only source of the problem for American workers. Something more structural has occurred: high school education needs reform especially in math and the sciences; universal access to basic health care must be addressed; worker retraining programs like those in Germany must be emulated; and a need for more ethical corporate managers has not been filled. Reforms in those areas, together with more effective help (lengthening the unemployment benefit period and de-linking healthcare benefits from employment) for people forced to change jobs because of globalization, would address the challenge directly and enhance society's resources and competitiveness. Efforts to hold back globalization or technological progress are bound to fail.

REALITY CHECK LO-7

Would you consider yourself a "winner" or "loser" of globalization? Explain.

SUMMARY

Globalization has become a new word to describe an old process that began in the 15th century. Globalization encompasses the *reform process*, i.e., economic and social policy changes that most countries participate in by eliminating barriers of trade, investment, culture, information, and political divisions that separate countries. This has led to closer integration and interdependence of nations of the world and has resulted in faster economic growth, rising incomes, and better living standards in those countries.

At the end of World War II, foundations were laid for the establishment of three crucial international organizations: the International Monetary Fund, the World Bank, and the World Trade Organization. The primary role of these institutions was to rebuild the broken world financial and trade systems that could help lead to global peace and prosperity.

While multilateral institutions could establish the rules of international monetary and trade systems, they were not designed to be all-encompassing. Therefore, progressive countries developed key national institutions that set domestic rules, enforcement mechanisms, and organizations that supported transparency of political systems, a functioning judiciary, and adaptive market mechanisms. To make globalization sustainable, these institutions must have effective policies in place that promote good governance, competitive markets, property rights, and ethical decision-making.

Information technology has played an important role in globalization by narrowing the income gap between developed and developing countries. The Internet and wireless technologies such as cell phones are enabling developing countries to leapfrog older information technologies like land lines, thereby making it possible to bridge the digital divide more quickly.

While globalization does create "winners" and "losers," funding well-designed retraining and educational programs for the adversely affected will lead to better-paying jobs and increased productivity of displaced workers.

Environmental degradation caused by globalization can be overcome if sustainable business and development policies can be implemented. This will call for cooperation between governments and private sectors through the implementation of sustainable business models, i.e, long-term corporate social responsibility practices. Those negatively affected by globalization are those countries that have not been able to seize the opportunities to participate in this process.

KEY TERMS

globalization, *p. 5*
emerging market economies, *p. 6*
decoupling, *p. 8*
multi-polar world, *p. 9*
international monetary system, *p. 11*
economic reforms, *p. 11*
capital markets, *p. 12*
liberalization of the trading system, *p. 13*
institutions, *p. 15*
adaptive institutions, *p. 15*
accountability, *p. 15*
transparency, *p. 15*
antitrust laws, *p. 18*
digital era, *p. 19*
bandwidth, *p. 19*
the web, *p. 19*
digital divide, *p. 21*
sustainable development, *p. 24*

CHAPTER QUESTIONS

1. What are some underlying factors that are causing decoupling to happen as societies move from a uni-polar to a multi-polar world? In your opinion, in which direction is the balance of global-economic power shifting?

2. What are some of the major economic reform themes that are common to the three international organizations promoting globalization?

3. Globalization can be facilitated only if national governments are willing to participate in that process. What roles can the three major international institutions play to be a part of this facilitation process?

4. While domestic institutions play an important role in the globalization process, what are some of the fundamental policy measures that those countries need to promote in order to benefit from globalization? How might these policies be implemented and promoted?

5. Do you believe that there is a "digital divide" in the global economy? Is globalization narrowing that gap? If so, how?

6. Is sustainable business and economic development the answer to the globalization controversy?

7. Globalization temporarily creates "winners" and "losers." What reform programs would you suggest to help those who are not benefiting from globalization? How might these reforms be implemented?

MINI CASE: BIOFUELS: A CASE FOR SUSTAINABLE DEVELOPMENT AND ENERGY SECURITY?

Concern over politically controlled supply and finite availability of non-renewable energy resources such as crude oil and natural gas has prompted large crude oil-consuming nations to seek alternate renewable energy sources. Furthermore, environmental concerns associated with carbon dioxide and other greenhouse gas emissions have prompted countries with large agricultural tracts of land to seek and develop clean, renewable biofuels that are not only environmentally friendly, but which also contribute to sustainable economic growth and energy security. Developing biofuels does not need to be a panacea, however, real challenges must be overcome to prevent economic costs from exceeding social benefits. For example, countries should take extreme care in implementing national biofuel policies because in the rush to energy independence, more pollution may occur, and resources may be misallocated.

Biofuels can be described as one of two major types. Bioethanol, which has a global production of some 50 billion liters, and which can be blended with gasoline (as is done in China, Europe and the United States) or used as a substitute for gasoline (as is done in Brazil). Note that industrial ethanol is a distillate or byproduct of crude oil and not a non-renewable energy source, and bioethanol is purely from plants (sugarcane, corn, etc.) and is a renewable energy resource. Sugar cane provides the raw material for nearly half of the global bioethanol production, with Brazil being the dominant producer, followed far behind by the Philippines. The other raw materials used for extracting bioethanol are corn (maize) and wheat. U.S. bioethanol production is corn-based, and Europe's bioethanol is wheat based. Bioethanol derived from sugar cane will be much more cost and pollution efficient because its single-cycle processing remains relatively inexpensive, and it consumes less energy than what is produced by burning the resulting bioethanol. In contrast, bioethanol from corn and wheat undergo a more expensive double-stage process. Moreover, critics of corn-based bioethanol argue that the energy used in its production and the corresponding pollution it creates may exceed the energy content of corn-based bioethanol.

Biodiesel has a global production of some 13 billion liters, has often been used as a substitute for diesel, and has mainly been produced in Indonesia, India, Malaysia, Thailand, as well as some European countries. The major raw materials used for biodiesel production include soybeans, rapeseed, sunflower seed, and palm oil; more recently, biodiesel producers in India have

(continued)

MINI CASE: BIOFUELS: A CASE FOR SUSTAINABLE DEVELOPMENT AND ENERGY SECURITY?

also begun using plants such as jatropha and pongamia which are weeds that grow wild along highways and on arid land.

Variations in climatic and soil conditions in Asia explain the wide range of crops (including coconut in the Philippines and jatropha and pongamia in India) used in biodiesel production in the region. Their national goals also differ. Palm oil has been the most energy-efficient crop for biodiesel production to date, and Malaysia exports 90 percent of its output to earn foreign exchange. For India, where imports cover 73 percent of its petroleum needs, developing domestic biodiesel can help to achieve energy security. India's government believes that some 70 million hectares of wasteland could be targeted to grow biodiesel crops. Cultivating these low-maintenance arid land crops could also become a source of income for the rural poor without displacing prime agricultural land. Their benefits are many and significant: easing poverty, reducing air pollution, mitigating global warming, and rehabilitating degraded wasteland. In Indonesia, forests and swamps have been stripped to make way for palm plantations, enabling the country to become the largest producer of palm oil in the world.

As the demand for biofuels (bioethanol and biodiesel) has increased, sugar, corn and palm oil prices have risen sharply, which in turn has helped exporters at the expense of higher sugar, corn and cooking oil prices to domestic consumers. Much of East Asia's push to biofuels is based upon the promise of huge shipments to Europe.

QUESTIONS:

1) What are the advantages and disadvantages of biofuels in terms of addressing the challenge of sustainable development? Explain fully.
2) Should bioethanol production from corn be encouraged, given that corn is used as a basic cereal (and in other food products) in many societies? Should bioethanol production be subsidized in the United States, and also be protected against competition from Brazilian sugar cane-based bioethanol?

Greenfield Projects: Buying Farmland Abroad

In recent years, countries that do not have much agrarian land and cannot grow enough to feed their own populations have been acquiring vast tracts of land in nations with sizable quantities of underutilized fertile agricultural land. Questions have been raised to determine whether this is beneficial foreign direct investment or a form of neocolonialism. For example, through the King Abdullah Initiative for Saudi Agricultural Investment Abroad, a group of Saudi investors spent $100 million in 2009 to grow wheat, barley, and rice on land leased from the government of Sudan. The investors will be income-tax exempt for the first few years and may export the entire crop back home. The Saudi program exemplifies a powerful trend sweeping the developing world. Capital-rich food-deficit countries have been investing in countries that badly need capital and have good agricultural land to spare. Instead of purchasing food commodities in world markets, governments and politically connected companies lease farmland abroad, grow crops, and ship them back to their investment country's location. Similar deals have been successfully concluded in target countries such as Cambodia, Malawi, Mozambique, and Turkey by investors from China, Kuwait, United States, India, United Kingdom, Egypt, Qatar, and Bahrain. So, what's all the fuss about?

(continued)

Greenfield Projects: Buying Farmland Abroad (continued)

POINT Supporters of free trade and investment believe that such investments reflect efficient allocation of resources and bring along with them new seeds, agricultural technology, and cash to countries that have suffered from underinvestment for decades. Investment in foreign farmland has occurred for a long time. The phrase "banana republic" originally referred to the friendly dictators of the West who ran countries (e.g., in Central America) dominated by foreign-owned fruit plantations (for example, the notorious but now defunct United Fruit Company, and others today such as Dole, Chiquita, and Del Monte). After the collapse of the Soviet Union, foreign investors snapped up some state-owned and collective farms. One could argue that by purchasing farmland abroad, food-deficit countries will be putting land resources to efficient use in order to meet growing global food demands.

COUNTERPOINT Opponents argue that investment in farmland elicits nothing but "land grab" on a global scale, which takes advantage of vulnerable capital-deficit countries. They further argue that because of political connections, foreign investors may be able to circumvent the law of the land and push out native subsistence farmers from the land they have farmed for generations. Opponents also ague that these large, controversial projects may not actually result in technology transfer but may instead lead to dependency on expensive imported seeds and chemicals.

What Do You Think?

Use the Internet or other sources to research this issue. Which argument would you support? Provide your own reasoning.

INTERPRETING GLOBAL BUSINESS NEWS

Business newspapers and magazines such as the *Financial Times*, *The Wall Street Journal*, *Bloomberg Businessweek*, and *The Economist*, include various statements made by economic analysts and business gurus. At the end of each chapter you will be given the opportunity to explain a global news item as it relates to that chapter. How can the following examples of financial news related to the concepts in this chapter be interpreted?

1) Economists have argued that globalization is here to stay, and that society needs to adapt to this process or it will be left behind. Historically, four groups have done the most to bring about globalization: traders, preachers, adventurers, and warriors. Though the motives for these groups—to profit, convert, learn or conquer—have usually been selfish, the overall impact of their actions has been to bring about greater integration and interdependence of nations of the world. Put this view of history into the context of today's globalization and explain why you agree or disagree.

2) The Doha Round of trade negotiations that began in 2001 stalled in 2007 when the G-4 nations—Brazil, India, the United States, and the European Union—could not agree on further trade and investment liberalization. The breakdown had less to do with India and Brazil's protectionism than with the U.S. and EU's political inability to respond to long-standing world-wide demands for the reduction of their agricultural subsidies.

The United States and the European Union must reduce agricultural subsidies before they can expect the rest of the world to liberalize trade further. What is the reasoning for this? Make your case.

3) Persistent poverty and increasing environmental degradation in developing countries, changing climate patterns around the globe, and the use of food crops to produce biofuels all pose new and unprecedented risks and opportunities for global agribusiness in the future. Explain what this means.

4) Mexican billionaire Carlos Slim made huge profits over the years and became the world's richest man in 2010, but not by playing nice with rivals. Competitors in Mexico's telecommunications industry accuse him of being a monopolist who has kept phone and Internet charges high by erecting barriers to entry. Investigate the situation and determine the effectiveness of Mexico's antitrust institution.

PORTFOLIO PROJECTS

Throughout the 15 chapters of this text you will be exposed to many examples of real world companies to help illustrate how the concepts that you are learning in each chapter can be applied to real business situations. The Portfolio Projects at the end of every chapter consist of: (1) ***Explore Your Own Case in Point:*** enhancing your understanding of your company of choice; and (2) ***Develop an International Business Strategy for Your Own Small Business.*** Gather your data from sources such as company annual reports; agencies like Standard & Poor's, Moody's, and Value Line; and the following websites:

www.state.gov/r/pa/ei/bgn/

https://www.cia.gov/library/publications/the-world-factbook/

www.xmarks.com/site/

www.stat-usa.gov/tradtest.nsf

www.globaledge.msu.edu/resourceDesk/

Explore Your Own Case in Point: Understanding the Global Environment of Your Company

The objective of this portfolio project is to enable you to conduct an independent analysis of a large company (e.g., a Fortune 500 company). Select a company that you admire, a company that intrigues you, or a company that you've always wanted to know more about. Select a company listed in a major stock exchange like London, New York, Tokyo, Shanghai, Hong Kong, Singapore, Bombay, Frankfurt, or Paris so that various types of information (financial or otherwise) are readily available. Each chapter focuses on a specific topic, and the end-of-chapter questions will encourage you to analyze how that particular topic relates to your company. By the time you have completed Chapter 15, you will have learned a great deal about your chosen company.

After reading this chapter you should be prepared to answer some basic questions about your favorite company.

1) Identify three major countries with which your chosen company operates. Preferably, these three countries are in different continents.

2) Are these three countries members of the IMF, the World Bank, and WTO? Do you believe that these three countries actively follow guidelines of these three major international institutions?

3) Compare the institutional structure of these three countries to determine if they promote globalization, i.e., (a) are their political institutions transparent? and (b) do they have a functioning judiciary system?

4) Do you believe that the three countries under consideration practice policies that promote globalization? For example, what are those countries' policies toward (a) governance, (b) competitive markets, (c) property rights, and (d) corruption?

Develop an International Strategy for Your Own Small Business: Your Target Country's Institutions and Policies

In this portfolio project you will have the opportunity to apply key concepts that you learn in each chapter of the course to a small business of your own, which may be hypothetical or, if you actually run a small business, real. Most multinational corporations (MNCs) started as small firms that initially focused on exporting a single product or service to another country. For your project, your "home base" is your country of citizenship (or residence) and the "target" country is the foreign country with which you plan to start business. During the period of this course, you should focus your effort on conducting business with the target country that you identified; you will deal with the target country's business practices, culture, currency, and so forth. Issues addressed in various chapters of this course will allow you to systematically develop an international business strategy while providing you with a global perspective. Take a closer look and analyze your target country's institutions, policies, and IT environment. Use the research sources identified at the end of the exercise for your activity. The following questions will help deepen your understanding of your target country:

1) Is your target country in the process of implementing certain basic reforms recommended by the IMF, the World Bank, or the WTO? What reforms?

2) Since you plan to conduct business in the target country you should be concerned about transparency of political institutions and judiciary. How good is your target country in enforcing the rule of law of the country? How is your target country ranked by Transparency International?

3) For business to be successful anywhere, we need to have a clear idea of the information technology environment in the target country. How prevalent is Internet and wireless communications technology in your target country? Is there a digital divide within the target country that could hinder your business performance?

Data sources:

The International Monetary Fund: www.imf.org

The World Bank: www.worldbank.org

World Trade Organization: www.wto.org

Transparency International: www.transparency.org

United States Department of State: www.state.gov/r/pa/ei/bgn/

United States Central Intelligence Agency https://www.cia.gov/library/publications/the-world-factbook/

Global Edge: www.globaledge.msu.edu/resourceDesk/

CHAPTER NOTES

[1]The International Monetary Fund, "Deep Impact," *Finance & Development,* March 2009, pp. 13–18.
[2]The World Bank, "World Development Indicators 2011," *Direction and Growth of Merchandise Trade,* pp. 332–334.
[3]D. Oakley, "Emerging Markets Grow Internally, Expand Internationally," *Financial Times*, June 8, 2011. pp. 2–3 (Supplement: Mastering Growth Part 4-Emerging Markets), and *Financial Times Global 500*, June 24, 2011.
[4]K. Mahbubani, *The New Asian Hemisphere: The Irresistible Shift of Global Power to the East* (New York: Public Affairs, 2008).
[5]M. Ayhan Kose, E. Prasad, K. Rogoff, and S. Wei, "Beyond the Blame Game," *Finance & Development,* March 2007.
[6]IMF Staff, *Globalization: A Brief Overview*, Issues Brief, May 2008.
[7]J.D. Wolfensohn, "The Challenge of Globalization: The Role of the World Bank," *Public Discussion Forum,* Berlin, Germany, April 2001.
[8]www.wto.org/english/thewto_e/whatis_e/whatis_e.htm
[9]www.wto.org/english/thewto_e/whatis_e/tif_e/utw_chap1_e.pdf "2. Principles of the Trading System," pp. 10–13.
[10]The World Bank, "Building Institutions for Markets, *World Development Report*, 2002. pp. 3–27.
[11]E. Aninat, "Surmounting the Challenge of Globalization," *Finance & Development*, March 2002.
[12]W. Michael Cox, "Racing to the Top: How Global Competition Disciplines Public Policy, *2005 Annual Report,* Federal Reserve Bank of Dallas.
[13]G. Rachman, "The Political Threats to Globalization," *Financial Times*, April 8, 2008, p. 12.
[14]www.transparency.org
[15]J.E. Gaspar et al., *Introduction to Business* (Boston: Houghton-Mifflin Co., 2006), pp. 35–39.
[16]S. Huttner, "The Internet Economy–Towards a Better Future," *OECD Observer,* No. 268 (July 2008): pp. 5–7.
[17]"The Meek Shall Inherit the Web," *The Economist Technology Quarterly,* September 6, 2008, p. 3.
[18]S. Paltridge, "The Next Several Billion," *OECD Observer* No. 268 (July 2008): pp. 16–18.
[19]"The Meek Shall Inherit the Web," *The Economist Technology Quarterly,* September 6, 2008, pp. 3–4.
[20]"Globalization and its Critics," A Survey of Globalization, *The Economist,* September 29, 2001.
[21]J.E. Stiglitz, *Making Globalization Work,* (New York & London: W.W. Norton & Company, 2006); *Globalization and Its Discontents,* (New York & London: W.W. Norton & Company, 2002).
[22]T. Cowen, "No Need to Apologize for International Trade," *The New York Times,* June 9, 2008.
[23]In December 1983, the Secretary General of the United Nations, Javier Peréz de Cuéllar, appointed Gro Harlem Brundtland, former Prime Minister of Norway to chair the World Commission on Environment and Development (WCED), the Brundtland Commission, to unite countries to pursue sustainable development together because of heavy deterioration of human environment and natural resources caused by economic growth.
[24]Our Common Future, Chapter 2: Towards Sustainable Development in *"Report of the World Commission on Environment and Development: Our Common Future"* Transmitted to the United Nations General Assembly as an Annex to *Document A/42/427,* Development and International Co-operation: Environment, June 1987.
[25]"The Challenge of Sustainable Development in Asia," *International Herald Tribune*, June 16, 2008.
[26]"The Challenge of Sustainable Development in Asia," *International Herald Tribune,* June 16, 2008. p. II.

CH 2

The Evolution of International Business

© C Miller Design/ Getty Images

Nikada/iStockphoto.com

After studying this chapter, you should be able to:

LO-1 Briefly explain why trade and foreign investment are good for society as a whole.

LO-2 Describe the major international trade theories and how they operate.

LO-3 Evaluate trade policy, the main instruments of trade policy, and their impact on business, consumers, and governments.

LO-4 Explain the rationale behind a country's choice of managing trade.

Asia's Century: The Re-emergence of China and India

During the early-19th century, the world's two largest economies in terms of national income were China and India[1]. Because of foreign invaders and rule by various domestic feudal factions and foreign colonial powers, these two countries restricted free enterprise and open trade while increasing government's role in commerce. After its independence from Britain in 1947, India, under the leadership of Prime Minister Jawaharlal Nehru, adopted the practice of democratic socialism.[2] In 1949, China's move to communism with Chairman Mao Zedong at the helm led to a command, or government-directed, economic system. As a result, China's and India's economic systems stifled domestic entrepreneurship as well as business growth and left both countries relatively poor.

In 1978, recognizing the economic failure of the communist system, China under the leadership of Deng Xiaoping decided to jump-start its economy by encouraging private enterprise—capitalism with communist roots—as well as opening the economy to foreign trade and investment. India's socialist economic policies led the country to near bankruptcy in 1991, when Finance Minister Dr. Manmohan Singh (with economic policy advice and financial assistance of the International Monetary Fund in Washington, DC) agreed to change the country's economic strategy through systematic deregulation, privatization, and implementation of freer trade and foreign investment policies.

These changes in economic policies have led both China and India to rapidly grow. For example, during 2000–2009 China's economy grew by an average of 10.9 percent each year while India's economy grew by an average of 7.9 percent a year during the same period. This compares with U.S. annual growth of 2.0 percent and Japan's 1.1 percent for that period. Thus, by 2009, China had become the world's second largest economy after the United States; India became the fourth largest economy after Japan[3] (see Exhibit 2.1).

Interestingly, while both China and India have unleashed their pent-up domestic consumption and competitive advantage in the global marketplace, their paths to economic success have been different.[4] China has followed the traditional route by becoming a global center for relatively low-wage manufacturing and exporting of consumer goods like apparel, toys, and electronics—items that can be found every day in stores such as Walmart and Target in the United States. India, on the other hand, has focused more on using its large English-speaking labor force to provide services such as call centers, medical transcription, data processing, and software development for companies worldwide.

Based on current economic trends, analysts believe that by 2020 China will become the world's largest economy, followed by the United States and India (see Exhibit 1.2). China has recently been expanding its manufacturing capabilities by producing greater value-added goods such as automobiles, aircraft, and semiconductor chips. India has also been expanding the service value chain by

EXHIBIT 2.1 WORLD'S TEN LARGEST ECONOMIES: PURCHASING POWER PARITY (PPP) BASIS* (US$2009)

Source: *World Development Indicators 2011*, The World Bank, pp.10–12.

*PPP conversion factor is the number of units of a country's currency that is required to buy the same amount of goods and services in the domestic market that a U.S. dollar would buy in the United States.

**GNI is the total value of goods and services produced by a country plus net receipts of employee compensation and property income from abroad.

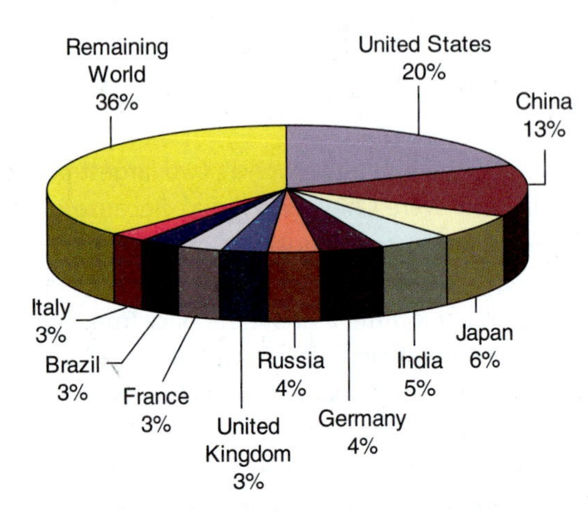

becoming a center for information technology services, research and development, and biomedical sciences. Over time, economists believe that India's approach may work better because the wealth of nations eventually depends more on services than manufacturing.

Introduction

The growth trends in China and India[5] today illustrate the impact that **international business** has on blue-collar and white-collar workers in wealthy countries (such as the United States and in Europe) as relatively low-skill factory jobs as well as high-skill service profession jobs migrate overseas. Business has become increasingly international in nature and has been accelerated by low cost communications technology. What is International Business? And, how did all this development happen?

international business all commercial transactions, both private and public between nations of the world

One could trace international business to a story from fertile Mesopotamia (present-day Iraq).[6] In the 3,000 B.C., Sumerian farmers realized that the grain surplus they produced could be used as barter for things they did not have. Therefore, the Sumerians obtained copper from Sinai Desert traders who were located several hundred miles to the west in order to make weapons and repel nomadic raiders. Thus, international trade yielded to the Sumerian farmers not only a bounty of material goods (copper and armaments for security) but also an understanding of the culture of their neighbors and a mutual desire to sell things to other groups rather than to annihilate them.

LO-1 Explain briefly why trade and foreign investment are good for society as a whole.

Benefits of Trade and Foreign Direct Investment

The earliest and simplest form of international business is **trade**, which can be defined as the sale (exports) and purchase (imports) of goods (textiles, wine, spices, etc.) and services (transportation, education, consulting, etc.) across national borders. International trade benefits consumers in three major ways by providing:

trade the two-way flow of exports and imports of goods (merchandise trade) and services (service trade)

- A greater amount of choice in the availability of goods and services;
- Lower prices for goods and services consumed; and
- Higher living standards.

JOHN ANGELILLO/UPI /Landov

Foreign Inflow of Capital: *The New York Stock Exchange (NYSE) which like other stock exchanges attracts foreign capital.*

Largely for better, but sometimes for worse, trade has affected our world. Trade has influenced culture, shaped history, raised living standards, and expanded knowledge to include new ways of thinking.[7] In fact, one could ask: Where would the history of civilization be without trade? Yet, even today, policymakers in some countries continue to question the benefits of trade by asking whether to open national borders to freer trade and **foreign direct investment (FDI)**, foreign inflow of capital, technology, and skills to enhance domestic investment and economic growth.

Open trade and investment does create winners and losers and, as discussed later, the gains from open trade and investment are always greater than the losses.[8] The right to export and import freely enhances the quality of life and living standards of people in the countries involved in trade. In addition, trade brings with it cultural and technological riches; it can also make the world a more peaceful place because of national interdependence.

Trade generates jobs in both the export and import sectors of an economy. For example, it is estimated that for every billion dollars worth of exports from the United States 20,000 domestic jobs are created. As seen in Exhibit 2.2, U.S. exports in 2010 were about $1.3 trillion, which would imply creating some 26 million jobs in the export sector of the country. In addition, 2010 U.S. imports of approximately $2 trillion also created more U.S. jobs, for example, at imported car dealerships.[9]

Exhibit 2.2 also shows that despite the deep global recession in 2009, trade around the world increased by some 24 percent over the 2006–2010 period, thereby improving the income of all those involved in trade. One could argue that the living standard of people in the developed countries of Europe, Japan and North America has been enhanced because of the low-cost goods and services imported from China and India that were mentioned in the opening vignette. At the same time, trade has given an astonishing boost to China's and India's economies as millions of Chinese and Indian workers move from subsistence farming and clerical work into more comfortable middle-class prosperity. As the income of Chinese and Indian workers increases, they will purchase more foreign goods and services, thereby giving a boost to the global economy.

Open trade increases competition, and like rivalry from new domestic companies, it does have a negative impact on some because of this disruptive change. In the case of the United States, the "losers" include workers in manufacturing as well as service sectors who lose jobs

foreign direct investment inflows of capital from abroad for investing in domestic plant and equipment for the production of goods and/or services as well as for buying domestic companies

EXHIBIT 2.2 WORLD TRADE PATTERNS

Source: International Monetary Fund: *International Financial Statistics*, July 2011, pp. 52–57.

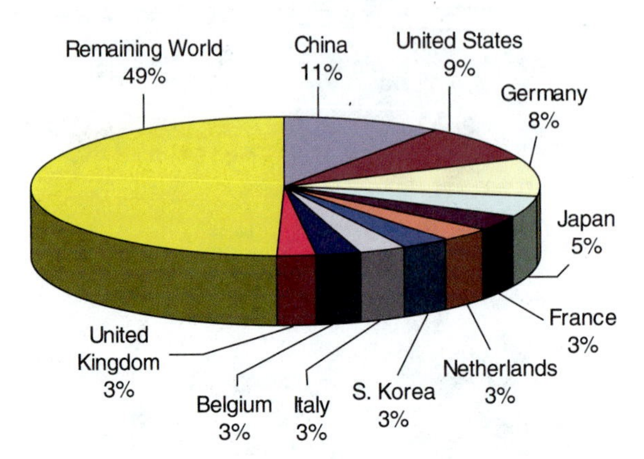

or are forced to accept reduced or stagnant wages and a lower or sluggish standard of living in exchange for working in globally uncompetitive industries. This generally happens when assembly-line jobs in uncompetitive manufacturing sectors (e.g., microwave ovens) migrate to countries like China and Vietnam, or when service sector jobs (e.g., call centers, software development) are **outsourced** abroad to countries like India or the Philippines. In general, countries in the developed world try to soften the disruptive nature of trade by retraining and re-educating those in the negatively affected workforce and enabling those workers to learn new skills in order to become more productive and gainfully employed.

Foreign direct investment (FDI) in a country brings funds and business culture from abroad, creates new well-paying jobs, introduces innovative technologies, and enhances the skills of domestic workers. Because of the largely positive impact that FDI has on countries, governments all over the world try to create a business-friendly environment to attract such investments. In addition, emerging countries like Brazil, Russia, India, and China (BRIC) that have large populations, an expanding middle class, and a combination of relatively low wage-rates and rapidly growing economies (as indicated in Exhibit 2.1) tend to attract sizeable amounts of foreign investment.

Exhibit 2.3 summarizes net (inflow minus outflow) foreign direct investment inflows during 1990–2009 based on national income levels and geographic regions of the world. It is important to note that 69 percent of net inflows of foreign investment in 2009 went to high-income countries in Europe and North America; the U.S. has been almost consistently the largest recipient of FDI in the world followed by the United Kingdom.[10] This reflects that both the U.S. and the U.K. have been practicing, at least until the financial crisis of 2008, a private-sector-driven open economic system with free and flexible markets as well as rule of law.

For these reasons, foreign investors have great faith in the high-income economies listed in Exhibit 2.3. Foreign investment flows are generally based on long-term global or country outlook. For example, the largest increase in world FDI flows in 2000 reflects the euphoria of the dot-com era with approximately $321 billion in net inflows of FDI to the U.S. Soon after the dot-com bubble burst in late-2000, net inflows of FDI to the U.S. fell by almost two-thirds. Among middle-income countries, China, as we discussed earlier, has been consistently attracting the largest amount of FDI because of its well-developed infrastructure and its emerging position as the low-cost manufacturing center of the world. Singapore, a regional center for global companies, continues to attract sizable amounts of foreign investment given its strategic location, world-class infrastructure, and productive workforce. India, as mentioned earlier, is a major player in the service sector, and has recently witnessed a significant increase in FDI inflow. Oil- and gas-rich Colombia, Russia,

outsourcing
the corporate practice of acquiring or producing quality goods or services abroad at a lower cost thereby eliminating domestic production

EXHIBIT 2.3 NET INFLOWS OF FOREIGN DIRECT INVESTMENT BY REGION AND INDUSTRIALIZATION

Foreign Direct Investment by Region and Industrialization (billions of U.S. dollars)*

	1990	1995	2000	2005	2006	2007	2008	2009
World Total	**205**	**328**	**1518**	**1050**	**1352**	**2139**	**1823**	**1164**
High Income	**181**	**230**	**1358**	**773**	**998**	**1613**	**1225**	**805**
Belgium	8	11	215	34	62	72	100	-39
Canada	8	9	66	29	69	112	45	20
France	13	24	42	81	81	160	100	60
Germany	3	12	210	35	43	52	21	39
United Kingdom	34	22	122	196	140	198	94	73
United States	48	58	321	109	181	238	320	135
Low & Middle Income	**24**	**99**	**161**	**276**	**355**	**527**	**598**	**359**
East Asia & Pacific	**11**	**51**	**45**	**104**	**105**	**175**	**188**	**101**
China	3	36	38	79	78	138	148	78
Indonesia	1	4	-5	8	6	7	9	5
Malaysia	2	4	4	4	6	9	7	1
Singapore	6	12	16	15	24	24	23	17
Thailand	2	2	3	8	9	10	10	5
Vietnam	0	2	1	2	2	7	10	7
Europe & Central Asia	**3**	**10**	**20**	**63**	**114**	**156**	**172**	**86**
Kazakhstan		1	1	2	6	10	15	14
Poland	0	4	9	10	10	23	15	14
Russia		2	3	13	31	55	73	37
Turkey	1	1	1	10	20	22	18	8
Latin America & Carib.	**8**	**30**	**80**	**70**	**71**	**107**	**126**	**77**
Argentina	2	6	10	5	5	6	10	4
Brazil	1	5	33	15	19	35	45	26
Chile	1	3	5	7	8	15	17	13
Columbia	0	1	2	10	6	9	11	7
Mexico	3	10	18	20	19	25	23	15
Middle East & N. Africa	**1**	**1**	**5**	**14**	**27**	**29**	**30**	**28**
Yemen	0	0	0	0	1	1	2	0.1
South Asia	**1**	**3**	**4**	**10**	**23**	**30**	**49**	**38**
India	0	2	4	7	17	23	42	5
Sub-Saharan Africa	**1**	**5**	**7**	**15**	**15**	**29**	**34**	**29**
Nigeria	1	1	1	2	5	6	4	6

* Net inflows of investment to acquire or establish an enterprise in another country

Source: World Bank: World Development Indicators database and 2011 World Development Indicators, pp.364–367

Kazakhstan, and Nigeria have been attracting foreign investment primarily in the energy sector. Because of NAFTA, Mexico consistently draws a significant amount of investment from the United States and Canada. Brazil, rich in natural resources, and also a manufacturing powerhouse in the Western Hemisphere, will continue to draw significant amounts of foreign investment.

REALITY CHECK LO-1

Visit the retail store where you purchase everyday necessities and pick out ten items that you regularly use. Now, look at the labels and find out how many of them come from abroad. Can you imagine what your life would be like if we did not have international trade?

LO-2
Describe the major international trade theories and how they operate.

Major Theories of International Trade

No single nation in the world is capable of producing and consuming all the goods and services that its citizens want or need. Neither does any nation have the required resources—minerals, agricultural land, skilled labor, machinery, technology, and the like—to produce the wide range of goods and services that people in our modern economy desire. Therefore, nations of the world need to trade.

An understanding of how major trade theories have evolved is important. First, these theories provide an appreciation for the progress made in understanding how trade (and gains from trade) really works in an open economy. Second, these theories present a rationale why restriction to trade should be minimized even when domestic economic and business conditions seem awful. If policy-makers ignore trade theory, they are likely to repeat past mistakes, which could then lead to trade retaliation and lower global living standards.

Wealth Accumulation as a Basis for Trade Theory: Mercantilism

Mercantilism is a theory of international trade that supports the premise that a nation could only gain from trade if it had a trade surplus, i.e., more exporting than importing. Mercantilism is the oldest form of trade theory; it was practiced during the 1500–1750 period as Europe emerged from the feudal systems of the Middle Ages and moved toward nationalism. During this period, money consisted almost exclusively of gold and silver coins; bank notes were rarely used, largely because of a lack of trust in them. Wealth, at a personal or national level, was largely determined by the amount of precious metal (gold and silver) to which one had access. Land and labor were considered less important, because they were primarily **factors of production** that were needed to generate wealth—gold and silver.

mercantilism
a theory of international trade that supports the premise that a nation could only gain from trade if it had a trade surplus

factors of production
endowments used to produce goods and services: land (quantity, quality, and mineral resources beneath it), labor (quantity and skills), capital (cost), and technology (quality)

trade surplus
when the value of exports exceeds the value of imports; the opposite of a trade deficit

Mercantilists believed that for a nation to become wealthy, that nation must export as much as possible and, in turn, import as little as possible. Their objective was to see that, as a nation, the value of exports must always exceed those of imports so that the country would have a **trade surplus**. Their rationale was simple: exports generate income, causing gold or silver to flow into the country. On the other hand, imports were determined to be a cost, as gold or silver must leave the country to pay for them. Therefore, when countries have a trade surplus, the inflow of gold and silver will exceed the outflow of gold and silver; the result will be a net gain of gold and silver, hence the wealth of the nation will be enhanced. National wealth was seen as the foundation of national power and global influence. Mercantilists also believed that accumulation of gold and silver by way of exportation was the only way that countries without gold and silver mines could become wealthy.

Mercantilists did not want, or care, to see the big picture. If every trading nation decided to increase its exports and decrease its imports, there would be surplus of exported goods in the world market. This would lead to two unpleasant results. First, the surplus of exports in the world market would depress prices and, therefore, earnings for exporting countries (in the form of gold and silver) would drop. This decrease in wealth would result in lower wages in the export sector, meaning that exporters would become poorer, not richer. Second, as the demand for exports drops, competitors in the export market would want to undersell each other by further lowering their prices in order to get rid of their exports. This would further depress wages in those countries.

To keep labor costs low, Mercantilists encouraged their people to produce large families by providing bounties for children and penalties for the unmarried. The inflow of gold and silver to the nation—hence national wealth—was what mattered, not the prosperity of its citizens. Mercantilists championed this short-sighted view of wealth.

Specialization as a Basis for Trade Theory: Absolute and Comparative Advantage

During the mid-18th century, British economist Adam Smith, who came to be known as the father of free market and open trade systems, recognized the absurdity of Mercantilism. He argued and proved that free trade without restrictions would increase the wealth—in terms of rising real income—of all those who participated in free, unrestricted trade. At the heart of Adam Smith's international trade theory was his belief that free trade encourages countries to specialize in the production of those goods and services that they most efficiently produce. There are two basic theories that explain this behavior: the theory of absolute advantage in production and the theory of comparative advantage in production. These theories are best explained with the help of examples.

Theory of Absolute Advantage As a hypothetical example, consider two countries, Brazil and the United States, and try to determine what each of these countries would export if each opened their countries to free trade. Assume that because of soil and climatic conditions, Brazil is more efficient (measured in pounds of coffee beans produced per acre of farmland) in the production of coffee than the United States. Also assume that for the same reasons (soil and climate), the United States is more efficient than Brazil in the

Ron Buskirk / Alamy

Specialization as a Basis for Trade Theory: *The United States has a comparative advantage in corn production.*

production of corn. It would make more sense for Brazil to concentrate on producing coffee rather than corn; part of the coffee produced would be kept for domestic consumption, and the remainder exported to the United States. The United States could do the same by concentrating on corn production, saving some for domestic consumption, and exporting the rest to Brazil.

The gains from trade are quite significant. Citizens from both Brazil and the United States would enjoy the benefits of lower-cost coffee and corn because of trade. If these two countries did not trade, the United States would need to produce its own coffee and Brazil would need to grow its own corn, which in both cases would be inefficient and at a high cost to citizens. Using terminology of international trade, Brazil has an **absolute advantage** in coffee production and the United States has an absolute advantage in corn production. An absolute advantage exists when one country can produce a good—such as coffee or corn—more efficiently than another.

Theory of Comparative Advantage Now suppose that one country has an absolute advantage over another in the production of two (or more) products. Should trade between these two countries occur? The answer is yes. This approach is a refinement of Adam Smith's theory of absolute advantage and can be attributed to another great British economist, David Ricardo.[11] Let's analyze the rationale behind this assertive answer.

Continue with the Brazil-U.S. case that was just explored. *Assume* two small changes: that Brazil can produce both coffee and corn more efficiently than the United States (measured in terms of pounds of coffee or corn per acre of farmland); and that Brazil can produce five times more coffee than the United States but only two times more corn than the United States, using the same quantity of resources (land and labor). Therefore, Brazil has an absolute advantage over the United States in the production of both coffee and corn. In which commodity, coffee or corn, does Brazil have a greater production advantage than the United States? It is in coffee production, because Brazil can produce five times as much, compared with only twice as much corn. What should Brazil do? The answer is that Brazil should produce the commodity in which it has the greatest advantage: coffee.

You will notice that Brazil not only has an absolute advantage in coffee production, it also has a **comparative advantage** in coffee production over corn production. Despite the fact that Brazil has an absolute advantage over the United States in the production of both coffee and corn, free trade will ensure that both countries will have a higher standard of living if Brazil concentrates its efforts on producing coffee and the United States concentrates on producing corn.

It is important to remember that resources (land, labor, and capital) in all countries are scarce, which is why countries must choose the most efficient use of their scarce resources. When all countries follow this approach, resources can be used most efficiently, and the total output and standard of living of the world can be increased.

Factor Endowments as a Basis for Trade Theory: Heckscher-Ohlin and Factor Price Equalization

In the 1930s, two Swedish economists, Eli Heckscher and Bertil Ohlin, refined David Ricardo's theory of comparative advantage and showed that nations primarily export goods and services that intensely use their abundant factors of production. The next two theories described use the concept of factor intensity as the basis of trade.

The **Heckscher-Ohlin (H-O) Theory** attributes the comparative advantage of a nation to its factor endowments: land (quantity, quality, and mineral resources beneath it), labor (quantity and skills), capital (cost), and technology (quality). By implication, a country rich in minerals such as Australia would have global competitive advantage in the production and exports of minerals such as iron and uranium ore, and coal.

absolute advantage
the ability of one country to produce a good or service more efficiently than another

comparative advantage
the ability of one country that has an absolute advantage in the production of two or more goods (or services) to produce one of them relatively more efficiently than the other

Similarly, Saudi Arabia, with the world's largest reserve of easily extractable crude oil, will export crude oil to other nations. The key assumptions for the H-O theory to work are: (1) perfect competition in the marketplace; and (2) perfect immobility of factors of production among countries. As indicated in the opening vignette, China's abundant factor has been relatively low-wage workers, who migrate from villages to large cities for assembly line work. The H-O theory, therefore, helps explain why the export of manufactured goods is China's competitive advantage. On the other hand, India's abundant factor has been relatively well-educated, English-speaking labor that provides a low-cost gateway to global services exports. The two key requirements of H-O are met, because the markets for labor in both China and India are very competitive and severe external restrictions prevent labor from moving abroad.

A related theory, **factor price equalization theory**, states that when factors (labor, for example) are allowed to move freely among trading nations, efficiency increases, which leads to superior allocation of production of goods and services among countries. For example, when Poland entered the European Union—where there is free movement of labor across member countries—some of the abundant Polish plumbers migrated to the United Kingdom to fill the shortage there. The net result was that wages for plumbers in the U.K. stabilized or softened and wage rates for plumbers in Poland increased. As the U.K. consumer of plumbing services benefited from this development, one could argue that the real income of the British consumer was, therefore, enhanced.

The Polish plumber's real income received a boost as well, because earnings in Britain were higher than what would have been earned in Warsaw. In Poland, wages of plumbers will gradually rise because of a decrease in the supply of plumbers (when some plumbers migrated to Britain). The real income of all Polish plumbers will increase over time. As is shown, free mobility of factors will lead to efficient reallocation of resources (factors of production) until price equilibrium is reached. That is, over time the wage rates for plumbers doing similar work in Britain and Poland will be the same. Then, **factor price equalization** would have been attained.

A similar scenario is happening in the United States as well. Software and IT engineers from India are allowed to enter the United States on H-1B visas, which enable Indian engineers to work in the United States for up to five years. Because of factor price equalization, wages for software and IT specialists (with similar educational background and work experience) in the United States have stabilized at a lower level than during the dot-com days of 2000. At the same time, wages for software and IT engineers in India have considerably gone up. Over time, wages for software and IT engineers in India and the U.S. (adjusted for cost of living) will move toward equilibrium.

Porter's "Diamond" Model of National Competitive Advantage[12]

In 1990, American economist and Harvard Business School professor Michael Porter published his seminal work, *The Competitive Advantage of Nations,* which reported the results of his four-year study of ten nations on why some countries excel in certain industries and markets. Porter found that trade theories broadly explained the basis upon which countries exported certain goods, services, or commodities. However, Porter believed that the trade theories did not explain enough. For example, why did some countries export certain products and import similar products? Also, he argued that firms and not countries conduct most trade. Therefore, Porter looked more closely at the theory of firm and industry specifics to identify characteristics that made firms and industries in countries "winners" or "losers" in international trade.

Porter's model of National Competitive Advantage is based upon the trade theories discussed earlier in this chapter. The robustness of Porter's model can be attributed to his integration of the theory and structure of a firm's behavior to trade theory. Porter's hybrid model was designed to operate within an environment of government actions and unforeseen external events—shocks, positive or negative. Porter neatly explains his model in terms of a "diamond" that consists of four groups of company-specific and country-specific characteristics, positioned at the edge of a diamond. Porter's model also explains that the interaction of these four groups of characteristics will determine a country's competitive advantage in the global arena. Hence the success or failure of firms can be attributed to how country- and company-specific characteristics are nurtured. Each group of characteristics is discussed next.

Factor Conditions The theory of comparative advantage in production and Heckscher-Ohlin theory provide factor endowments as a basis for international trade. Porter's model looks more closely at the quality of the factor endowments (i.e., land, labor, capital, and technology). For example, how can the quality of labor in a specific country be described—skilled, unskilled, highly technical? Can the quality of educational systems and research institutions be determined? Are schools and institutions aimed at producing a significant number of quality engineers and scientists, or musicians and artists? Regarding the earlier example of land, Porter's model would focus upon the quantity of land, as well as upon its quality, management, and development. With regard to capital, the availability and ability to raise capital at a low cost will be an important characteristic. Technology becomes crucial in a knowledge-based economy, therefore, the prevalence and quality of technology and telecommunications are crucial factor characteristics.

Porter exemplifies Japan as a powerhouse for consumer electronics because of the quality and quantity of its engineers, and the ability and willingness of Japanese consumers to try out new electronic products that are perfected and later exported. Porter found that Japan has more engineers per capita than any other country in the world. When we analyze current emerging market economies, Porter's model would explain why R&D and IT services are moving to India: the availability of quality English-speaking engineers and scientists at very competitive wage rates. Similarly, the supply of skilled, productive factory workers coupled with modern infrastructure makes China a global manufacturing hub.

Demand Conditions Porter stresses the importance of domestic demand for goods and services when determining a nation's competitive advantage. When domestic demand remains high, the number of suppliers will also be high. With sizable demand, domestic competition among suppliers will intensify and result in lower prices as well as sophisticated,

-/EPA/Newscom

Porter's "Diamond" Model: *India's factor conditions make the $3,000 Tata Nano possible.*

innovative new products. This could lead to product specialization. In the United States, which has a sophisticated marketing and distribution network, the demand for web-enabled cell phones and related items (the iPhone, iPod, iPad, etc.) has been strong and rapidly growing. As a result, the United States has become a global leader for these products, which are also in strong demand in other high-income countries. In the emerging market economies of China and India, which have a fast-growing middle class, the demand for automobiles has been strong; China became the world's largest market for automobiles in 2009. Because of this fact, domestic competition among automobile companies in these countries has increased considerably, spurring the development of such innovative cars as India's $3,000 four-seat Tata "Nano," which will likely enter the global market for low-cost cars by 2015.

Related and Supporting Industries The presence of supporting industries and companies in a country will always be important for its competitive advantage. The quality and competitive nature of supplier industries will determine how successful a country will be. Silicon Valley, California, where there are numerous world-class suppliers that provide semiconductors to the IT hardware industry, posits a good example. The availability of a full range of world-class supporting industries makes Silicon Valley the envy of the world. China's southern province of Guangdong has become the center for textile and apparel production, and the province teems with textile industry supporting industries, including manufacturers of textile machinery, yarn manufacturers, and sources of dyes and related chemicals. Similarly, India's southern coastal city of Chennai houses the country's automotive, truck, and motorcycle industry. The large cluster of supporting supply companies create a highly competitive environment, enabling Chennai to put out quality products at reasonable prices, with automobile exports going to East Asia, Africa, and Europe.

Firm Strategy, Structure, and Rivalry The final set of characteristics in Porter's diamond relate to a firm's strategy, structure and rivalry. Firm strategy deals with the way companies in an industry manage their operations as well as the structure of the organization. Management style—top down, bottom up, or consultative—has a large impact on a firm's performance. Also, the background of top managers holds great importance, as Porter points out in the case of Japanese and German companies versus American companies. Japanese and German firms often employ engineers to run manufacturing companies, hence their emphasis on product and product quality and the reason why German and Japanese companies are generally known for their machinery and engineering goods. American firms are often run by finance and marketing professionals with an emphasis on sales and short-term profits, which may not be too helpful in the long term.

Firm structure and rivalry address the competitive structure of industries in a nation. Monopolistic industrial structures are unlikely to create innovative or dynamic firms willing to compete abroad, or have the capability of competing abroad. However, a competitive industry will foster innovative, cost efficient, aggressive firms that can adjust to changing economic conditions at home and will be well prepared to compete abroad.

According to Porter's "diamond" model, the success or competitive advantage of a nation at the global stage would crucially depend upon the interaction of the four groups of characteristics identified above. Yet, Porter also identified two other crucial variables outside the diamond that play an important role in the competitiveness of nations: chance and government.

Chance refers to an external shock or development that could drastically change or hasten the course of economic development. Innovation in information technology, for example, has, to a considerable extent, made some countries very competitive all of a sudden. Innovation in IT has increased efficiency all over the world, and has increased connectivity among citizens globally. IT has propelled economic growth in some countries; India, for example, has recently become a major supplier of IT services worldwide (see more detailed discussion in Chapter 1).

In contrast, some external shocks could have negative affects on countries. For example, the Icelandic volcano eruption of 2010 disrupted air travel in northern Europe for six days at an estimated cost of $200 million per day to the airlines alone.[13] The massive 2011 earthquake off Sendai in Japan led to an unprecedented tsunami, several hundred billion dollars in damages, and severe global supply chain disruptions in the auto industry. The global nuclear power industry also came under great scrutiny because of the crippling effect on Japan's Fukushima-Daichi nuclear power plant. Human-caused shocks such as terrorist attacks could also result in negative business affects by raising the cost of conducting business because of security-related outlays.

The second and even more important variable outside Porter's "diamond" is: the role of *government*. Government institutions and policies could help or hurt competitiveness of nations (as discussed in Chapter 1), due to the fact that government institutions and policies have the potential to affect all four sets of characteristics associated with Porter's diamond. For example, in the case of factor conditions, if government policy does not support or provide incentives for higher education, the quality and quantity of labor force will be detrimentally impacted with corresponding loss in the nation's global competitiveness. Similarly, inflationary monetary policies would lead to high cost of capital and diminished competitiveness. Also, inadequate investment in physical infrastructure will increase business cost and lower competitiveness.

Government policy could also stifle demand through excessive taxation or perverse incentive programs. Such policies will stifle rational investment and innovation, and hence, national competitiveness. Government policies could also stunt the growth of related and supporting industries through the implementation of programs that divert resources to sectors in which companies do not have core competencies.

Finally, government policies could impact market structure, or the level of competitiveness in an industry. For example, privatization of public enterprises will have a major positive impact on economic growth, economic efficiency, and competitiveness. Furthermore, the institution of antitrust policies, for example, could also lead to increased competition, growth of supporting industries, and overall competitiveness of nations.

From the above analysis, one can conclude that Porter's model of national competitive advantage provides a neat, comprehensive framework with which to analyze global trade patterns in industrial subsectors. The predictability of the model will depend on how well the four clusters of characteristics (i.e., factor conditions; demand conditions; related and supporting industries; and firm strategy, structure and rivalry) interact within the external framework of chance and government. Therefore, a company that exhibits relatively positive characteristics in all four diamonds will be an exporter of certain types of goods or services. And a country that exhibits relatively negative characteristics will be a net importer of goods or services.

REALITY CHECK LO-2

Have you witnessed any changes in international business activity in your hometown over the past five years? Which of the above discussed theories can you attribute to that business development?

LO-3

Evaluate trade policy, the main instruments of trade policy, and their impact on business, consumers, and governments.

The Practice of Trade Policy

Trade theory clearly shows how free trade has had a positive effect on the economic well-being of all trading partners. This can be achieved through improvements in the living standards of people in those countries due to a greater amount of choice in goods and services, and lower prices to the consumer. Equally important, free trade also creates jobs in the exports and imports sectors of economies. Despite these benefits, individuals, firms, and lobby groups continue to pressure government policymakers to impose barriers to imports or subsidize exports of goods and services. Special interest groups primarily attempt to save good-paying jobs and prevent increased competition in their industries at home—at least for the short term—thereby preventing companies from reorganizing their businesses. **Trade policy** refers to all government actions that seek to alter the free flow of merchandise or services from or to a country.[14] A look at daily newspapers will show that governments do not adhere to free trade principles. A country's trade policy will, therefore, have direct impact on the value and volume of their exports and imports. Historically, the main instrument of trade policy has been import tariff; however, more recently, non-tariff barriers and export subsidies have become equally important in international business. Some of the main instruments of trade policy that countries use to interfere with free trade are described next.

trade policy
all government actions that seek to alter the size of merchandise and/or service flows from and to a country

tariffs
taxes on imports; also known as **custom duties** in some countries

Tariffs, Preferential Duties, and Most Favored Nation Status

Tariffs are taxes on imports; they are also known as **custom duties** in some countries. Like domestic taxes, import tariffs generate revenues for governments. In many developing countries, import tariffs are a major source of government revenue. Tariffs come in two forms: specific and ad valorem.

custom duties
taxes on imports that are collected by a designated government agency responsible for regulating imports

A **specific tariff** describes an import tax that assigns a fixed dollar amount per physical unit. Until January 1, 2012[15] the price for ethanol consumers in the United States was higher than world free-market price by $0.54 per gallon because of the $0.54 per gallon tariff imposed by the U.S. government on ethanol imports. This also implied that domestic (U.S.) producers of ethanol could domestically sell ethanol at a price not exceeding the world price by $0.54.

specific tariff
an import tax that assigns a fixed dollar amount per physical unit

An **ad valorem tariff** describes a tax on imports levied as a constant percentage of the monetary value of one unit of the imported good. For example, the ad valorem tariff on passenger cars imported into the United States has been around 2.5 percent.[16] Thus the tariff bill will depend upon the cost the car being imported into the United States. If the car dealer imports a $50,000 BMW from Germany, the tariff that the dealer must pay the U.S. government that will be passed on to the customer, is $1,250.

ad valorem tariff
a tax on imports levied as a constant percentage of the monetary value of one unit of the imported good

Preferential duties refer to low tariff rates applied to specific imports coming from certain countries, especially from the developing world. Under this system, the same good imported from a country outside the preferred group will be subject to a higher tariff. Preferential duties are, therefore, geographically discriminatory as certain countries receive different or preferential treatment. The **Generalized System of Preferences (GSP),** where a large number of developed countries have agreed to permit duty-free imports of a selected list of products that originate from specific countries provides a good example. GSP could be based on colonial relationships or based upon helping developing countries succeed in trade—trade could be better than aid. Countries that are part of a free-trade area allow duty-free entry of imports. (This type of regional trade agreement will be discussed in Chapter 3, "Regional Economic Integration.")

preferential duties
an especially advantageous or low import tariff established by a nation for all or some goods of certain countries and not applied to the same goods of other countries

generalized system of preferences (GSP)
an agreement where a large number of developed countries permit duty-free imports of a selected list of products that originate from specific countries

Finally, in addition to imposing import tariffs, some countries also interfere with the free flow of exports by enforcing **export subsidies,** or **export taxes**. Export subsidies are aimed at protecting certain groups within their economy, such as agriculture. An export subsidy refers to a negative tariff or tax aimed at boosting exports by lowering export prices. On the other hand, export taxes are meant to discourage exports and to keep production at home. For example, when food grain prices shot up dramatically in late-2008, governments in several rice exporting countries such as India and Thailand imposed export tariffs to reduce rice exports and increase domestic supply of rice in order to keep local rice prices under control.

export subsidy
a negative tariff or tax aimed at boosing exports

At the end of World War II, three major international organizations were established to accelerate trade and economic growth among countries of the world. The Bretton Woods conference of 1944 instituted the International Monetary Fund (IMF) and the World Bank, and the General Agreement on Tariffs and Trade (GATT), an offshoot of a conference held at Geneva,

export taxes
taxes meant to raise export cost and divert production for home consumption

ECONOMIC PERSPECTIVES Predatory Trade Practices: A Game of Chicken?

In September 2009, U. S. President Barack Obama imposed a three-year, sliding-scale tariff on tires imported from China starting at 35 percent for the first year and decreasing to 25 percent in the final year. Critics noted that this decision seemed hypocritical considering that the president had accused China of unfair trade practices. China decided to challenge the U.S. decision by deferring the matter to the World Trade Organization's dispute resolution branch. China retaliated by initiating an investigation regarding the United States' possible violation of WTO sanctions by unfairly dumping chicken feet and auto parts into China's market. Global concerns were raised about how a tit-for-tat trade war could lead to rapid contraction of global trade, economic growth, and accelerating unemployment, thereby deepening the global recession.

China has been accused of predatory trade practices on several counts and many believed the Chinese should be held accountable for their actions. First, the value of the Chinese currency, the yuan, has not been market determined, but rather managed and kept artificially low (some economists claim by as much as 15–20 percent), thereby providing an unfair competitive advantage for all Chinese exporters. In addition, cheap credit, subsidized land, low cost energy, and controlled wages add to China's competitiveness to the detriment of nations that practice fair trade worldwide. These actions have led China to accumulate some $3 trillion in foreign exchange reserves in 2011 that are available for investment abroad.

Until the Obama decision, the United States had been unwilling to impose broad trade sanctions on China lest they curtail buying U.S. Treasury securities that finance the United States' large federal deficits. If that were to happen, U.S. interest rates would need to rise, leading to ballooning debt service, increasing the cost of capital to U.S. firms, and slowing economic growth in the United States.

Why impose tariffs on Chinese tires? The U.S. used a trade law against Chinese tire exports because their unfair exchange rate could "cause or threaten to cause market disruption"[17] in the domestic tire manufacturing industry. China's share of the U.S. tire market increased from 3 percent to 11 percent over the 2004–2008 period; during this time four U.S. tire plants were closed, and approximately 5,200 workers were laid off. Further, tire plant closings and additional worker layoffs were a distinct possibility. Meanwhile, China's government announced plans to impose restrictions on imports of U.S. chicken feet (a product for which there was little to no demand in the U.S.). The chicken feet were priced at $0.02 per pound, less than one-tenth of their domestic cost in China.

QUESTIONS:

1) Is China practicing fair trade? Explain in detail what China is trying to achieve, and the implications on the result for the rest of the world.

2) Why did the U.S. impose a "sliding-scale" tariff on China's tires? And why only for a three-year period? What should the U.S. do if China were to impose a 50 percent tariff on American chicken feet?

Source: "The China Conundrum: Using Tires to Send a Message," *Newsweek*, September 28, 2009, p. 24.

was established in 1948. (Details about these three institutions were discussed in Chapter 1). When GATT was established, 22 member countries committed to lower approximately 45,000 tariff rates within rules laid down by that organization. GATT was renamed World Trade Organization (WTO) and formally established on January 1, 1995 to set rules of trade among nations on a near-global basis. The WTO's primary objective was (and still is) to extend tariff reduction to agriculture and services, and also to settle trade disputes among member countries (as in the example on Chinese tire exports). By 2011, 153 nations had become members of the WTO and a further 29 countries were in negotiations to join the organization[18].

most favored nation (MFN)
an agreement among WTO countries in which any tariff concession granted by one member to any other country will automatically be extended to all other countries of WTO

Under the **most favored nation (MFN)** principle, any tariff concession granted by one member to any other country will automatically be extended to all other countries of WTO—nondiscrimination in tariff policy. WTO members are *obligated* to apply the MFN principle only to other WTO members, but they can apply MFN to nonmember countries as well. WTO members periodically assemble to discuss major trade negotiations with the prime objective of lower tariffs and increased trade among member nations.

Nontariff Barriers

Since 1948, GATT (and later, the WTO) has been able to significantly lower tariffs. During that same time period, however, countries have resorted to various forms of non-tariff barriers to restrict imports and, hence, trade. Some of the important forms of non-tariff barriers are described next.

Import quotas, also known as Quantitative Restrictions (QRs), limit the amount or number of units of products that can be imported to a country. Import quotas are generally worse than import tariffs because when a quota is reached, that particular good can no longer be imported or purchased. In the case of an import tariff, the price of imports can only increase by the amount of the tariff. But under an import quota, with high demand, the price of goods will increase to extremely high levels.

import quotas
also known as Quantitative Restrictions (QRs are regulations that limit the amount or number of units of products that can be imported to a country

Voluntary export restraint (VER) occurs when an efficient exporting nation agrees to temporarily limit exports of a product to another country to allow competitors in the importing country to become more efficient. For example, in the early-1980s, soon after the second oil shock of 1979 that quadrupled the price of crude oil, U.S. consumer demand for small cars significantly increased. However, the bulk of small, fuel-effective cars available in the world market were built in Japan. The Detroit "Big Three" faced severe financial strain because they could not compete against the Japanese automakers. The Japanese and U.S. governments negotiated a VER whereby Japan's automobile manufacturers voluntarily agreed to limit their export of cars to the U.S. to approximately 1.6 million units a year for three years. This gave the American automobile firms three years to retool and become relatively efficient and competitive; at the end of this period the VER was removed.

voluntary export restraint (VER)
a non-tariff barrier in which an efficient exporting nation agrees to limit exports of a product to another country for a temporary period

Domestic content provisions are another form of non-tariff barrier. Countries may require that a certain percentage of the value of import be domestically sourced. For example, the U.S. government may require that apparel imported into the United States should use U.S. cotton, or use a certain amount of American labor. Domestic content provisions aims to protect jobs in the home country.

domestic content provisions
regulations requiring that a certain percentage of the value of import be sourced domestically

REALITY CHECK LO-3

Visit your local foreign car dealer and find out what type of tariff or non-tariff barriers they face when importing cars from abroad. If tariffs are imposed on imported cars, find out whether it is ad-valorem or specific, and for how much.

Current Practice of "Managed" Trade

LO-4
Explain the rationale behind a country's choice of managing trade.

This text has, so far, evaluated arguments for free trade and protection, examined multilateral trade negotiations and agreements under GATT (WTO), and analyzed tariff and non-tariff barriers to trade. Remember that global trade today cannot be completely based upon the economics of free trade, but also encompasses a response to geo-political and socio-economic factors. **Managed trade** refers to agreements, sometimes temporary, between countries (or a group of countries) that aim to achieve certain trade outcomes for the countries involved.[19] Managed trade aims to replace global market or economic forces with government actions to determine trade outcomes. Under a managed trade regime, policymakers may use various socio-economic or geo-political rationales to protect specific companies or industries and achieve particular strategic objectives.

managed trade
agreements, sometimes temporary, between countries (or a group of countries) that aim at achieving certain trade outcomes

Socio-Economic Rationale

In general terms, socio-economics addresses the study of the relationship between business or economic activity and the social life of residents in a nation. In the context of international trade, socio-economics explores the relative negative impact of free trade upon society's welfare, as well as government policy measures that are implemented to minimize the negative outcomes to society in a country. Several forms of managed trade are part of the socio-economic category; these include countertrade, export cartels, the infant industry argument, and considerations of ethics and safety.

Countertrade In **countertrade,** an exporter of goods or services to another country commits to import goods or services of corresponding value from that country. The terms of export and import exchange are predetermined through negotiations. However, most countertrade transactions are still paid through the banking system; relatively few are done through outright barter (e.g., Iranian crude oil exports for imports of Chinese goods and infrastructure services). During the Cold War period (and even today in several countries of the former Soviet bloc[20], as well as some developing countries) the Soviet bloc countries practiced countertrade.

As you can imagine, countertrade can be extremely inefficient. Countries participate in countertrade especially when they do not have adequate amounts of foreign currencies (U.S. dollars, euros, etc.) to pay for their imports. Countries may also pursue countertrade because they may not be capable of producing goods of international quality, or because a banking embargo has been imposed on them. For example, during the Soviet days, the government of India imported Soviet fighter jets and other defense hardware in exchange for Indian-made consumer goods such as soaps, detergents, and copy machines.

countertrade
agreement in which an exporter of goods or services to another country commits to import goods or services of corresponding value from that country

export cartel
a group of countries that could effectively control export volume to keep their export prices, revenues, and economic growth stable or high

Export Cartels Rich, developing countries dependent upon certain non-renewable natural resources have generally seen their export earnings and economic growth widely fluctuate. Commodity price changes caused by business cycles, as well as a limited number of countries competing with one other in the same market cause this to happen. In order to maintain stable economic growth, natural-resource-rich countries have tried to join together to form **export cartels**, which could control export volume and prices. The Organization of

Jo Yong-Hak/Reuters/Corbis

Managed Trade: *South Koreans protesting free trade with the United States that would lead to job losses in uncompetitive industries.*

Petroleum Exporting Countries (OPEC), which today has considerable influence over crude oil supply and prices throughout the world, exemplifies an export cartel.

There are certain requirements for export cartels to be successful; all cartel members must agree not to cheat on the agreement, substitutes for the good in question must not exist, and demand for a particular product must be relatively inelastic.

Infant Industry Argument Economists have successfully argued that at times when a country gets a "late start" in a particular industry where it has a potential to become a world class competitor, short-term protection for that industry or firm may be justified. This **infant industry argument** expects that economies of scale and the comparative advantage of an industry can only be exploited by providing temporary protection. During this period, the firm or industry will grow and become globally competitive, thereby enhancing society's gains from trade for the long term. For example, in the past several South Korean firms in the semiconductor and automotive sectors have been provided protection under the infant industry premise.

infant industry argument temporary provision of protection to nascent industries that have good prospects of becoming globally competitive in the medium term

Questionable Labor Practices and Environmental Considerations Developed countries often resort to managed trade for reasons of unethical labor practices and violation of basic human rights. International Labor Organization (ILO) standards does not

ETHICAL PERSPECTIVES

Stabilizing Sierra Leone's Devastated Economy

Sierra Leone, a small country in West Africa, sandwiched between Liberia and Guinea, has a population of six million. The end of Sierra Leone's civil war in 2002 brought much hope to this mineral-rich, but fiscally poor nation. With a gradual return to democracy and rule of law, Sierra Leone's economy has slowly grown and has been diversifying away from the export of "blood diamonds," which illicitly finance civil wars for more commercial production of diamonds, gold, bauxite, and rutile (a mineral used as a whitening agent in the production of paint, paper, etc.). Blood diamonds, mined by poor panhandlers at the mercy of local militias, will not fetch international market price because they have been banned (by the Kimberley Process set up in 2003) in global trade and can only be sold illegally.

As the country's civil war ended, South Africa-based Koidu Holdings, a major global commercial mining operator, replaced local freelance panhandlers in Sierrra Leone's Kano district (in the east of the country), which was known for its diamonds. As part of the deal with Sierra Leone's government, Koidu Holdings negotiated profit-sharing arrangements that would benefit the local population as soon as the mines became profitable. In addition, local small-time miners who were competing with the "mining majors" have been required to pay a 3 percent tax on their diamond sales. Approximately 0.75 percent (a quarter of the sales tax) will be returned to the local government to develop social infrastructure (e.g., education, health, sanitation, and roads). This trickle-down effect aims to economically benefit the local community and also bring peace and stability in the once militia-infested region.

Since the end of 2002, Sierra Leone's diamond exports have almost quadrupled from some $26 million to $99 million in 2008. However, the recession in 2009 caused diamond exports to fall to $79 million that year, which also created a fall in diamond prices. Some of the laborers who were laid off from Koidu Holdings' mines have begun farming because food prices have sharply risen. Furthermore, other miners are following Koidu Holdings' profit-sharing example and investing in Sierrra Leone's other mineral operations such as gold, bauxite, and rutile. Hopefully these commercial operations will lead to diversification of the country's exports, raising incomes, better working conditions and social welfare for local labor, and greater political stability in the country.

QUESTIONS:

1) Who are the various stakeholders who have benefited from the socio-economic move away from the sale of "blood diamonds" to legal commercial diamond operations in Sierra Leone?
2) Evaluate the impact of Koidu Holdings' corporate social responsibility practices on Sierra Leone.

Source: "Digging in the Dumps," *The Economist*, May 30, 2009, pp. 49–50.

accept the use of child labor, unusual long work hours, below subsistence-level wages in the production of exports (e.g., the case of Nike in Vietnam), or working under dangerous conditions with toxic chemicals (e.g., manufacture of fire crackers in Sivakasi, India). Developed countries may restrict imports from developing countries that implement such policies. For instance, environmental degradation brought about through slash and burn policies in the Brazilian Amazon region in order to grow sugar cane for ethanol can be one reason why the European Union imposes a tariff on Brazilian ethanol of €0.19 per liter. The European Union hopes that this measure will force Brazil to change its environmental and labor practices.

Health and Safety Every country has the sovereign right to protect the health and physical safety of its citizens from contaminated imports. *Food safety measures* introduced to prevent the entry of harmful pests and diseases via imported foods, animals, and plants are a justifiable means to protect human life and physical health. For Japan, the world's largest net importer of agricultural products, food safety has been of particular concern. For example, when the first case of BSE-infected cattle was discovered in the United States in 2003, Japan's government quickly moved to halt U.S. beef imports. The two countries held several rounds of talks before Japan lifted the ban on U.S. beef in 2005. Similarly, the European Union has banned imports of genetically modified (GM) crops and processed goods from the rest of the world.

Geo-Political Rationale

There are several geo-political and strategic reasons why nations practice managed trade. The geo-political objective is to sacrifice some economic efficiency for the greater good of the country in terms of national security, protection of critical industries, and international commerce.

National Security For national security reasons, U.S. exports of certain types of high-technology defense equipment, instruments, devices, and components are generally restricted to allies and friendly countries; this applies to dual-purpose equipment (items that could be used for civilian and military purposes) as well. American firms that seek to tap China's huge market for these products can do so only if the U.S. government removes export controls, and if the firms guarantee that the sale of these products will not jeopardize U.S. national security. Because the need to receive government approval prevents the affected firms from openly competing and increasing sales, these firms receive special treatment and protection. They include companies like Raytheon, General Dynamics, and Boeing in the United States, and EADS (European Aeronautics and Defense Systems) in Europe.

Strategic Industries Some countries provide protection to *strategic industries* that have a significant employment impact on certain sectors of an economy—the so-called "national champions"—when these champions are unable to compete globally. In 2009, France and also the United States evoked this concept to protect their automotive sectors. Also, in 2011, legislation was introduced in Italy to designate some Italian companies as strategic in order to prevent their foreign takeovers, just as France invoked a similar sentiment in protecting Groupe Danone in 2007. The severe recession that began in 2008 with the collapse of United States investment bank Lehman Brothers, led several financial firms in the United States to seek massive federal bailout capital to survive and compete in the global marketplace.

embargoes
trade sanctions which are imposed upon a nation to restrict trade with that country

Embargoes When trade sanctions are imposed upon a country for political reasons, an embargo is in force, and trade will be restricted with that country. Embargoes, which may not be universally enforced, are meant to "punish" a country for perceived unacceptable international behavior. Trade embargoes have been used against several countries over time.

The United States has maintained a trade embargo against Cuba for almost 50 years. The United States wants to put pressure on the Cuban government to move toward democratization and bring greater economic and political freedom to its citizens. More recently, United States trade embargoes have been imposed upon Iran and Sudan.

REALITY CHECK LO-4

Boeing is the single largest exporter for the United States, yet it is restricted from exporting sensitive military equipment to all countries. What specific restrictions does the U.S government impose upon defense contractors such as Boeing?

SUMMARY

Trade has influenced culture, shaped history, affected living standards, and opened society to new ways of thinking. Open trade and investment creates "winners" and "losers," but the gains from open trade and investment are always greater than the losses. Trade enhances the quality of life of consumers, brings with it cultural and technological riches, and makes the world a more peaceful place because of national interdependence. Trade generates jobs both in the export and import sectors of an economy. The disruptive nature of trade can be softened by retraining and re-educating the negatively affected workforce and enabling workers to learn new skills in order to become more productive and gainfully employed.

Three major economic ideas comprise trade theory. Mercantilism, the oldest, was based upon the idea of wealth accumulation (i.e., countries striving to generate trade surpluses so that their holdings of gold and silver would increase, making them rich and powerful). Second, theories based on specialization in the production of goods and services include the theories of absolute and comparative advantage. Finally, H-O and factor price-equalization theories emphasize factor abundance as the fundamental reason behind exports and trade.

Porter's model of National Competitive Advantage is based upon the trade theories mentioned above. The robustness of Porter's model can be attributed to his integration of the theory and structure of a firm's behavior to trade theory. Porter looked more closely at the theory of firm and industry specifics to identify characteristics that made firms and industries in countries "winners" or "losers" in international trade. Porter's hybrid model was designed to operate within an environment of government actions and unforeseen external events—external shocks, positive or negative.

Trade policy refers to government actions that seek to alter the free flow of merchandise or services from and to a country. The primary instruments of trade policy include tariffs (specific, ad valorem, and GSP) and export subsidies; however, non-tariff barriers such as import quotas, voluntary export restraint, and domestic content provisions have become equally important.

Managed trade aims to replace free global-market forces with government actions to determine trade outcomes. Policymakers may use various socio-economic or geo-political rationales to protect specific companies, industries, or countries to achieve certain strategic objectives. Socio-economic rationale may include countertrade, export cartels, infant industry argument, or ethical considerations such as labor and environmental practices, and health and safety issues. Geo-political justification could include considerations of national security, strategic industries, and embargoes.

KEY TERMS

international business *p. 36*
trade, *p. 36*
foreign direct investment, *p. 37*
outsourcing, *p. 38*
mercantilism, *p. 40*
factors of production, *p. 40*
trade surplus, *p. 40*
absolute advantage, *p. 42*
comparative advantage, *p. 42*
trade policy, *p. 47*
tariffs, *p. 47*
custom duties, *p. 47*
specific tariff, *p. 47*
ad valorem tariff, *p. 47*
preferential duties, *p. 47*
generalized system of preferences (GSP), *p. 47*
export subsidy, *p. 47*
export taxes, *p. 47*
most favored nation (MFN), *p. 48*
import quotas, *p. 49*
voluntary export restraint (VER), *p. 49*
domestic content provisions, *p. 49*
managed trade, *p. 49*
countertrade, *p. 50*
export cartel, *p. 50*
infant industry argument, *p. 51*
embargoes, *p. 52*

CHAPTER QUESTIONS

1. How would you make a convincing case that open trade in goods and services as well as free flow of foreign direct investment will enhance the well being of (a) consumers, (b) producers, and (c) the government of countries? Give specific examples to prove your position.

2. What trade theories support the recent rise of China and India on the global stage? Explain your views in detail.

3. Some believe there is a disconnect between trade theory and trade policy. What rationale could the United States use to support its trade policies? Give specific examples.

4. When would a country such as France use socio-economic rather than geo-political reasons to support its trade policy? Can you provide some examples?

MINI CASE: ECONOMIC NATIONALISM

Buy American! Buy Spanish! British jobs for British workers! The ideology of economic nationalism seeks to implement trade policies that help to keep jobs and investment at home, while ignoring the advantages of open international trade and investment. Economic nationalism was popular during the Great Depression of 1929–33, when it served to protect domestic firms from international competition. However, this led to curtailing international business activity, making the global economic slowdown worse. Widely recognized as a myopic policy, economic nationalism nevertheless re-emerged during the global financial crisis that originated in the United States in 2008, prompting many analysts to wonder whether the public has learned anything from international business history.

Soon after the U.S. stock market crash of 1929, Willis Hawley and Reed Smoot, two Republicans in the U.S. Congress, sponsored a bill to raise import tariffs to the highest level in U.S. history.[21] Given the high rate of U.S. unemployment at that time, the bill was passed in order to keep jobs at home. This resulted in retaliation from other nations as they raised tariffs on exports from the United States and other countries. The net result was a ruinous fall in global trade and a worldwide depression.

In late-2008 and early-2009, when the United States faced the worst recession since the Great Depression, the call for a new round of trade barriers was being debated.

(continued)

MINI CASE: ECONOMIC NATIONALISM

However, this time, the focus was upon inserting non-tariff barriers on items in the American Recovery and Reinvestment Act of 2009, which was meant to give the floundering U.S. economy a boost. This legislation, commonly known as the "stimulus package," included a "Buy American" provision that restricted government spending to U.S. companies. As a result, public works such as infrastructure projects were required to use commodities such as iron and steel that was domestically sourced, despite that these products cost more than imports from countries such as China. Similarly, the development and delivery of computerized medical records would be restricted to domestic IT firms, even if such services could be sourced at a much lower cost from India.

Some experts argued that such protectionism may violate international trade rules, and U.S. exporters feared retaliation against their goods and services. Canada, in fact, soon threatened retaliation. Meanwhile, other countries moved in similar directions. The British prime minister talked of "British jobs for British workers," the French president urged French car companies to invest at home rather than elsewhere in the European Union, the government of Spain launched a "Buy Spanish" campaign. It may not be Smoot-Hawley, but the global implications could be the same.

QUESTIONS:

1) Is economic nationalism justified?
2) Is the Smoot-Hawley plan better or worse than "Buy American"? "Buy Spanish"? Or "British jobs for British workers"? Explain fully.

Should "Carbon Tariffs" be Imposed upon Greenhouse Gas-Producing Imported Goods?

In the aggregate, China is the world's largest emitter of greenhouse gases, primarily carbon dioxide, while the United States is the largest emitter of carbon dioxide on a per capita basis. The countries of the European Union fall somewhere in between. To control global warming and climate change, there has been a worldwide movement to regulate greenhouse gases caused by energy-intensive industries such as the manufacturing of aluminum and other metals, paper, chemicals, and cement. The question is: Will the imposition of "carbon tariffs" (i.e., dollars per ton of carbon dioxide emitted by, for instance, aluminum production) in a particular country lead to unfair competition?

POINT If an agreement can be reached on a global basis without exceptions, a WTO-negotiated carbon tariff could lead to reduction in worldwide demand for carbon dioxide-intensive materials as well as a move from coal-fired power plants to greener alternative-energy sources for electric power. Carbon tariffs could also lead to greater investment in research and development to conserve energy and to find more efficient ways in the manufacturing process so as to minimize greenhouse gas emissions.

COUNTER-POINT By imposing a carbon tariff on the exports of greenhouse gas-emitting industries, one would be exposing these firms to unfair competition from those that do not emit carbon dioxide. Also, the output of these industries (steel, paper, cement, etc.) is so basic (inelastic) for life that the net reduction in their demand may not have much impact on greenhouse gas emissions. Finally, a carbon tariff may be hard to implement. Customs officials would either need to assess the emissions embedded in imports or make arbitrary assumptions—the latter being a recipe for trade war.

What Do You Think?

Which viewpoint do you support, and why? Use the Internet to learn more about this issue and come up with your own argument.

INTERPRETING GLOBAL BUSINESS NEWS

The following relate to Chapter 2.

1) Health care costs, especially in the United States, have been skyrocketing in the recent past. This has led to a new trend, "internationalization of health care services." Countries as diverse as India, China, Thailand, and Cuba have developed export strategies to supply health care services to patients in wealthy countries. What are the implications of this development to both the developing and developed economies of the world? Describe who will benefit and who will lose from this growing trend.

2) Because of the rising price of food grains in the global market, the Argentine government introduced a new sliding scale of export tariffs in early-2008—up to 44 percent on grains and cereals—which they say protects local prices from following record rises on international markets. Argentine farmers staged a 21-day strike in March 2008 in protest. Why? Who are the beneficiaries and the disenchanted?

3) In pursuit of ethical international business practices, western retailers are trying to ensure that suppliers in the developing world meet international labor and environmental standards. Yet, critics argue that this approach risks marginalizing those most in need of jobs. Explain what each side of this argument means.

4) As the global recession bites, China's exporters are looking homeward and threatening multinational enterprises operating in the country. What do you think is the likely outcome?

PORTFOLIO PROJECTS

Explore Your Own Case in Point: Understanding the Nature of Your Company

After reading this chapter you should be prepared to find the answers to some basic questions about your favorite company.

1) Determine whether your company is a producer of goods or services. What are the major products and/or services provided by your company? Are those outputs sold only domestically or are they also exported?

2) If some or all of the output is exported, how much of it is exported? To where are they exported, and why?

3) Do these products and services face tariff or non-tariff barriers in the target export markets? What are the tariff rates or non-tariff barriers imposed on these items?

4) Does your chosen company fall within the framework of "managed trade" in the export market? If so, on what basis? How is the company trying to overcome this challenge?

Develop an International Strategy for Your Own Small Business: Your Idea for Exporting

Using the data sources listed earlier, as well as other sources you may find on your own, develop a strategy and make a convincing case for why you would like to produce a particular product or service and export it to a target country. It is important that you identify in detail the comparative advantage of sourcing the product or service in your home country. You should look into supply as well as demand for your product or service. You should focus sales to one target country and its currency. The following questions will help you define your objectives:

1) What product or service do you plan to produce at home and sell abroad? What is your rationale and what competitive advantages do you have?

2) What foreign country do you plan to target and why? What is its demand for your product or service?

3) Identify factors such as tariffs and quotas that can affect trade in goods or services between your home and the target country. Explain how they could affect the demand for your product or service, and how you could overcome those challenges.

CHAPTER NOTES

[1] A. Maddison, "The Rise of China," *The Wall Street Journal*, February 14, 2011.

[2] G. Das, *India Unbound* (New York: Anchor Books, 2002).

[3] The World Bank, *World Development Indicators* (2010), pp. 32–36.

[4] W. Michael Cox and R. Alm, "China and India: Two Paths to Economic Power," *Economic Letter*, Federal Reserve Bank of Dallas, August 2008.

[5] A.K. Gupta and H. Wang, *Getting China and India Right: Strategies for Leveraging the World's Fastest Growing Economies for Global Advantage* (San Francisco: Jossey-Bass, 2009).

[6] J. Bernstein, A *Splendid Exchange: How Trade Shaped the World* (Atlantic Monthly Press, 2008).

[7] P.T. Ellsworth, *The International Economy*, 3rd ed. (New York: Macmillan Co., 1964), pp. 1–80.

[8] J.E. Gaspar et al., *Introduction to Business* (Boston: Houghton-Mifflin Co., 2006), pp. 56–66.

[9] International Monetary Fund, *International Financial Statistics Yearbook* (2010), pp. 66–71.

[10] The World Bank, *World Development Indicators Database, and 2010 World Development Indicators*, pp. 394–397.

[11] D. Ricardo, *On the Principles of Political Economy and Taxation* (London: John Murray Publishers, 1817).

[12] M.E. Porter, *The Competitive Advantage of Nations* (New York: Free Press, 1990). For a good understanding of Porter's basic theory, read "Why Nations Triumph," *Fortune*, March 12, 1990, pp. 94–108.

[13] http://video.nytimes.com/video/2010/04/19/world/europe/1247467650320/volcano-set-to-cost-airlines-millions.html?ref=eyjafjallajokull

[14] D.R. Appleyard and A.J. Field, Jr., *International Economics: Trade Theory & Policy*, 2nd ed. (Boston: Richard D. Irvin, Inc., 1995).

[15] J. Mathews, "The End of the U.S. Ethanol Tariff" *The Globalist*, January 6, 2012 (The Globalist Research Center, Washington, DC).

[16] United States International Trade Commission, *Harmonized Tariff Schedule of the United States (1994)*, USITC Publication 2690 (Washington, DC: U.S. Government Printing Office, 1993).

[17] Section 421 of U.S. Trade Act of 1974 which was added to the U.S. China Relations Act of 2000 as a safeguard provision to China's accession to the World Trade Organization.

[18] www.wto.org/english/thewto_e/acc_e/acc_e.htm

[19] The World Bank, *Atlas of Global Development* (Glasgow, U.K.: HarperCollins Publishers, 2007).

[20] The communist nations closely allied with the Soviet Union, including Bulgaria, Cuba, Czechoslovakia, East Germany, Hungary, Poland, and Romania, whose foreign policies depended on those of the former Soviet Union.

[21] Formally called the United States Tariff Act of 1930, also called Hawley-Smoot Tariff Act raised import tariffs to protect American business and farmers that led to retaliation and adding considerable economic strain to the Great Depression.

CH 3

Regional Economic Integration

© C Miller Design/Getty Images

AP Photo/Tatan Syuflana

After studying this chapter, you should be able to:

LO-1 Explain regional economic integration, its evolution, and its benefits and costs.

LO-2 Identify how economic geography helps explain, promote, and segment regional integration blocs.

LO-3 Identify the primary reasons why countries are now seeking to pursue regional integration at the expense of multilateral trade liberalization.

LO-4 Explain why the European Union is seen as the most advanced regional integration bloc.

LO-5 Describe how NAFTA has affected U.S.-Mexico bilateral trade in goods and services.

LO-6 Explain the importance of ASEAN and indicate why Asia may become the most important free trade region for this century.

LO-7 Explain why regional integration in Latin America is challenging, and why there is potential for a grouping like MERCOSUR to become more predominant.

CULTURAL PERSPECTIVE

Mediterranean Union: Integrating North Africa and the Middle East into EU Markets?

When French President, Nicolas Sarkozy, assumed his six-month European Union (EU) presidency in July 2008, the first initiative that he launched was the Union for the Mediterranean. The union's goal was to enhance the political and economic relations between the European Union's 27 members and other countries surrounding the Mediterranean Sea (see Exhibit 3.1). While the EU has, since then, been able to integrate most of the Eastern European countries into its fold, it has not progressed much in political and economic integration of countries across the Mediterranean region. Tensions over issues such as trade, immigration, democracy, and human rights have been exacerbated by Europe's historical colonization of North Africa and the Middle East.

The key elements of the French initiative were cleaning up the Mediterranean Sea, promoting solar energy, and developing shipping and ports. However, it is unclear what contribution the new union will make to economic challenges such as immigration and lack of access to EU markets, especially for farm produce.[1]

The union's stated aims included offering co-ownership of the initiative to non-EU members in an attempt to avoid the impression that the EU is imposing its policy agenda on its new partners. The European Commission prepared a short list of economic projects, including the development of solar power in North Africa. However, businesses expressed concerns about issues such as inadequate support for foreign investment in North Africa and the Middle East. The initiative took a political twist when President Sarkozy initially wanted to include only EU members who bordered the Mediterranean Sea as part of the Mediterranean Union. Furthermore, Turkey voiced suspicions that the Mediterranean Union may be a way to undermine its plans to join the EU. Would it be possible for economics to overcome geo-politics to make the Mediterranean Union a reality?

EXHIBIT 3.1

Introduction

As described in the opening vignette, regional integration is an ongoing process, and the reasons for regional integration are many and varied; they may be purely economic, purely political, or a combination of both. While the biggest impact of a successful Mediterranean Union would be felt by member countries that surround the Mediterranean Sea, the broader effect would be on all EU members and other countries as well. The willingness of Mediterranean Union member states to come up with well-designed, pragmatic, economic policies that promote gradual increase in economic cooperation within its members is likely to determine the union's eventual success. Ideally, such a union could lead to increased sustainable economic growth in the Mediterranean region coupled with export specialization and converging living standards.

As this chapter discusses, regional integration can bridge barriers between national borders, and increase interdependence within a region and the rest of the world. It is always prudent to implement progressive economic policies (especially in trade and investment) that enable a country's neighboring countries to grow and prosper. Hence, one could argue that regional and global integration are not substitutes, but complements to developments of a particular region.

What Is Regional Economic Integration?[2]

LO-1

Explain regional economic integration, its evolution, and its benefits and costs.

Despite the fact that *global* trade and investment liberalization (discussed in Chapters 1 and 2) can lead to global benefits—greater volume of trade and investment across countries, faster economic growth, job creation, tax revenues, increased competition, and increased consumer welfare—some countries prefer to work more closely within a *regional* setting such as NAFTA and the European Union (discussed in detail later in the chapter). Furthermore, because the future of the Doha Round of trade liberalization (which began in 2001—see Chapter 1) is uncertain, there has been a sharp increase in the number of regional trade and integration agreements. A question needs to be asked: What are the motives for regional integration? Why do certain countries want to work more closely with one another while others do not? Are all regional trading blocs based on identical economic and/or geo-political principles?

Regional integration includes a multitude of economic and/or political steps that may be taken by member states of a union to increase their global competitiveness—not only preferential trade access. Regional integration helps countries—especially small and medium-sized countries—scale up their supply capacity through regional production networks and become more globally competitive. This development could take place through sector-wide transformations in agriculture, manufacturing, and services. For regional integration to be successful, member countries need to undertake **spatial transformations** and allow efficient geographic distribution of economic activities within and among countries. Furthermore, regional integration strategies need to be customized to the economic geography (to make the best use of the size and location) of the countries involved, and their openness to interaction with major world markets.

regional integration
implementation of a multitude of economic and/or political steps by member states to increase their global competitiveness, including preferential trade access

spatial transformations
the process of allowing efficient geographic distribution of business activities within and among countries

free-trade area
an area in which two or more countries agree to eliminate all barriers to trade such as tariffs, quotas, and non-tariff barriers like border restrictions, while at the same time keeping their own external tariffs (within WTO guidelines) against nonmembers

Stages of Regional Integration

Countries may have social, economic, security, or political reasons for regional integration. For the most part, countries generally begin working together with some form of economic integration in mind, for example, to promote trade and investment. Economic integration occurs when two or more countries join together to form a larger economic bloc. The primary objectives here are economic gain; that is, to work together rather than separately to increase economic growth and efficiency (through economies of scale in production to become globally competitive and tap world markets), to raise employment, skills, and the quality of life for the citizens of the region, and to promote peace and prosperity as well. As shown in Exhibit 3.2, while some groups of countries may be satisfied with regional trade and investment integration, others may seek greater economic and social unions so that members of those groups will have similar shared economic and social values. In some scenarios, countries that share similar economic and political systems may choose to form a union to fend off foreign aggression or threat.

Economic integration can take several forms, representing varying degrees of integration; however, if a logical progression could be outlined, it may appear similar to the following example. First, two or more countries may create a **free-trade area** by eliminating all barriers to trade such as tariffs, quotas, and non-tariff barriers like border restrictions, while keeping their own external tariffs (within WTO guidelines) on members not included in the free-trade

EXHIBIT 3.2 FORM AND STAGES OF REGIONAL INTEGRATION

Stage of Integration	Abolition of Tariffs and Quotas Among Members	Common External Tariff and Quota System	Abolition of Restrictions on Factor Movements	Harmonization and Unification of Economic Policies and Institutions
Free trade area	Yes	No	No	No
Customs union	Yes	Yes	No	No
Common market	Yes	Yes	Yes	No
Economic union	Yes	Yes	Yes	Yes

Source: From ROOT. *International Trade and Investment*, 7E. © 1994 South-Western, a part of Cengage Learning, Inc. Reproduced by permission. www.cengage.com/permissions

ArtisticPhoto/Shutterstock.com

County flags of some World Trade Organization members.

customs union
a group of free trade member countries that have adopted a common external tariff with nonmember countries

common market or single market
a market formed when member countries of a customs union remove all barriers to allow the movement of capital and labor within the customs union

economic and monetary union
a union formed when members of a common market agree to implement common social programs (on education, employee benefits and retraining, health care, etc.) and coordinated macroeconomic policies (such as fiscal and monetary policies) that would lead to the creation of a single regional currency and a regional apex central bank

political union
the union created when member countries of an economic and monetary union work closely with one another to arrive at common defense and foreign policies and behave as a single country

area. Second, when countries within a free-trade area have differential external tariffs, imports will primarily enter the free-trade area through the country that has the lowest external tariffs and trade restrictions, thereby causing other free trade member countries to lose import business. This may eventually lead to the creation of a **customs union**, in which all free trade member countries would need to adopt a common external tariff with nonmember countries. Third, within the member countries of the customs union, investment (hence business and job opportunities) will flow to countries that have the highest labor productivity and low capital cost. This, in turn, may encourage the removal of barriers to allow free movement of capital and labor within the customs union, thereby creating a **common market or single market**. Fourth, within the common market, the free movement of labor and capital may encourage member states to implement common social programs (on education, employee benefits and retraining, health care, retirement programs, etc.) and coordinated macroeconomic policies (e.g., similar fiscal and monetary policies) that could lead to the creation of a single regional currency and an **economic and monetary union**. Finally, because member countries of the economic and monetary union will work closely with each other on all major business and economic issues, the urge to have common defense and foreign policies may lead to the creation of a **political union** (i.e., a group of countries that will behave as a single country).

Pros and Cons of Regional Integration

The benefits and costs of regional integration crucially depend upon the level of integration the countries in the group achieve. These countries have a variety of motives for participating in the union: creation of greater business opportunities, global competitiveness, increased value for consumers (better choice, price, and service), shared values, peace within the region, common security against possible external threats, and more. While the countries' motives may be similar (though not identical), the degree of success of the integrated group will depend upon how well it implements the agreed-upon economic policies. The effect of regional integration will depend on the *net* impact of the benefits and costs.

The benefits of regional integration include:

- Creating a larger pool of consumers with growing incomes and similar culture, tastes, and social values.
- Encouraging economies of scale in production, increasing the region's level of global competitiveness, and enhancing economic growth through investment flows.
- Freeing the flow of capital, labor, and technology to the most productive areas in the region.
- Increasing cooperation, peace, and security among countries in the region.
- Encouraging member states to enhance their level of social welfare to match that of the most progressive states.

The costs of regional integration include:

- Undermining the most-favored-nation status rule (the lowest tariff applicable to one member must be extended to all members), an essential principle of the WTO.
- Imposing laws and regulations that are uniform, and that at times do not take into account national economic, cultural, and social differences.
- Eliminating jobs and increasing unemployment in protected industries.
- Losing sovereignty, national independence, and identity.
- Reducing the powers of the national government.
- Increasing the probability of rising crime associated with illegal drugs and terrorism because of ease of cross-border labor movement.

REALITY CHECK LO-1

Do you believe that increased regional integration will, overall, help or hurt the citizens of your city? Defend your position.

The Economic Geography of Regional Integration[3]

LO-2

Identify how economic geography helps explain, promote, and segment regional integration blocs.

The removal of tariff and non-tariff barriers across national borders can enable small and medium-sized firms to consolidate, specialize, and gain economies of scale in production that will help them achieve competitiveness on a regional and global scale. The World Bank's (2009) *World Development Report* (WDR), titled "Reshaping Economic Geography,"[4] analyzes trade and regional economic integration through the lens of **economic geography** (i.e., market size, location, and openness to trade). The WDR concludes that positive changes within these three categories are essential for successful regional integration. Hence, the policy instruments needed for successful integration include: institutions that unify the markets, infrastructure that efficiently connects these markets, and lower economic barriers to facilitate trade. Such a strategy will enable firms in regional trading blocs to increase their supply of goods and services

economic geography the study of principles that govern the efficient spatial allocation of economic resources and the resulting consequences

by taking advantage of economies of scale in production, and enhancing demand for their specialized products in global markets.

American economist Paul Krugman received a 2008 Nobel Prize for his insights on how economic geography affects international trade; for example, that free trade, (and, therefore, globalization) increased in the 19th century based on the theory of comparative advantage. In the 20th century, transportation costs decreased (e.g., use of railroads and container ships eliminated costly reloading) so much that trade in goods manufactured at home—beer, computers, or cars—made economic sense. Where transportation costs have decreased, companies have been able to increase economies of scale and specialization of production. Increasingly, sophisticated buyer-supplier networks in major world regions are becoming a key feature of the globalization process.

Steps to Regional Integration

One question often asked is: Can relatively small, poor countries benefit from the same economic forces that have transformed regions like Asia or Europe? If so, how? Individually, these small countries may not have efficient institutions, governance, policies, skilled workers, or the ability to sustain suppliers and complementary services. Regional integration could help overcome this challenge. The primary problem is to identify the roadblocks to regional integration so that appropriate institutions and policies can be put in place, which would eliminate the roadblocks and lead to economies of scale and specialization of production. Lowering or eliminating trade barriers between neighbors is important to achieving this goal.

Yet, regional integration is more than just cross-border trade liberalization. As the WDR emphasizes, a number of steps (such as regional infrastructure enhancement and labor market liberalization as a way to increase supply efficiently and move toward increasing demand in the global marketplace) must be taken. More specifically, the appropriate approach for countries could include the following three fundamentals: start small, think global, and compensate the least fortunate.

Start Small Regional integration should have clear goals and initially address a narrow, well-defined area of cooperation in which the costs and benefits are easily defined. For example, today's European Union started with an agreement called the "European Coal & Steel Community" in 1952. This initiative was started soon after World War II by six founding members who felt that the best way to avoid future wars within Europe was to increase cooperation between coal and steel production companies—which were regarded as "basic industries" and the major ingredients used in producing arms used in wars during that time.

Think Global Regional integration should not create unconnected or isolated countries. Instead, it should help countries gain access to world markets that they may not have access to otherwise. While larger countries may be able to choose between global integration and regional or bilateral (between two countries only) integration, small and landlocked countries need regional integration in order to achieve economies of scale, efficiency, and global integration. For example, shared transportation hubs or carriers (e.g., TACA airlines in Central America) could give access to previously unreachable world markets.

Compensate the Least Fortunate Concentration of economic activity generally follows regional integration, because firms will want to specialize by increasing the scale of production in fewer places. This is an inevitable and desirable part of the regional integration process, and will lead to increased efficiency and competitiveness; however, it also means that some regions will gain more than others, at least initially. As people migrate to the efficient regions, they will spread their benefits by sending remittances home. However, explicit

HABIB KOUYATE/AFP/Getty Images

Regional Integration Group. *The West African Economic and Monetary Union helps less fortunate members.*

compensation programs may be required to ensure access to social services and basic infrastructure in lagging areas. For example, the eight-member West African Economic and Monetary Union adopted a common, external, revenue-sharing tariff in 2000. The two more economically advanced countries of the union, Ivory Coast and Senegal, collected 60 percent of customs proceeds, but retained only 12 percent, and shared the remainder with the other member countries to help develop those regions[5].

Major Classes and Characteristics of Regional Integration

The merits of global versus regional trade agreements have been debated for many years. In global trade agreements, the tariff and non-tariff barriers that were discussed in Chapter 2 are reduced or eliminated using WTO's most favored nation (MFN) rules. Under regional trade agreements, conversely, tariff and non-tariff barriers are reduced only among regional member countries. When regional or bilateral trade pacts do not discourage trade with countries in other regions, they can help; otherwise, regional integration is not advisable. How countries can best gain access to markets within their neighborhoods and across the world becomes a lingering question. With the right combination of policy actions, countries that are the most geographically disadvantaged (e.g., landlocked countries) can overcome their challenges. This can be measured by determining whether or not market access noticeably improves with the implementation of new policies.

In general, countries within trading blocs that have significantly lowered trade barriers have done better economically than others. Cyprus, for example, decided to join the European Union in 1990 and started the process of lowering its tariff barriers to EU levels. By 2004, when Cyprus was officially admitted to the EU, economic growth had started to accelerate. Cyprus has been able to achieve efficiency through economies of scale in production as well as specialization with access to major European markets.

When the various regional integration blocs are analyzed from an economic geography perspective, they fall under three general categories—regional blocs close to major world markets, remote regions with large local markets, or remote regions with small local markets. According to the World Bank's WDR, what differentiates these three categories is their distance from large world markets, and whether or not there is a large country nearby.

Regional Blocs Close to Major World Markets Market access is essential for economic growth, and proximity to major world markets is an asset for just-in-time production, exports of perishable goods (fresh fruits, vegetables, and flowers), and tradable services such as marketing, research, and complex IT tasks. Countries close to major markets have the advantage of connecting to markets, suppliers, and ideas. In addition, developed countries seek these regional trading blocs to (1) expand their growth potential abroad as domestic markets mature, and (2) deliver low-cost manufacturing platforms for locally-based firms. Regional trading blocs that are close to world markets—such as the North American Free Trade Agreement (NAFTA), the Dominican Republic-Central America Free Trade Agreement (DR-CAFTA), the Caribbean Community (CARICOM), as well as the bilateral U.S. free trade with Chile and Colombia—have all benefited from privileged access to the U.S. market (See Exhibit 3.3).

Similarly, access to the rich European market has been a boon to Eastern European countries as they sought entry through eastward enlargement of the European Union. The Balkan states have also signed an intraregional free trade agreement, the Central European Free Trade Agreement (CEFTA), and the region's proximity to the EU permits close integration of its companies into pan-European production networks. The Association of South East Asian Nations (ASEAN) is intensifying its free trade relations with the huge markets in

EXHIBIT 3.3 REGIONS CLOSE TO WORLD MARKETS

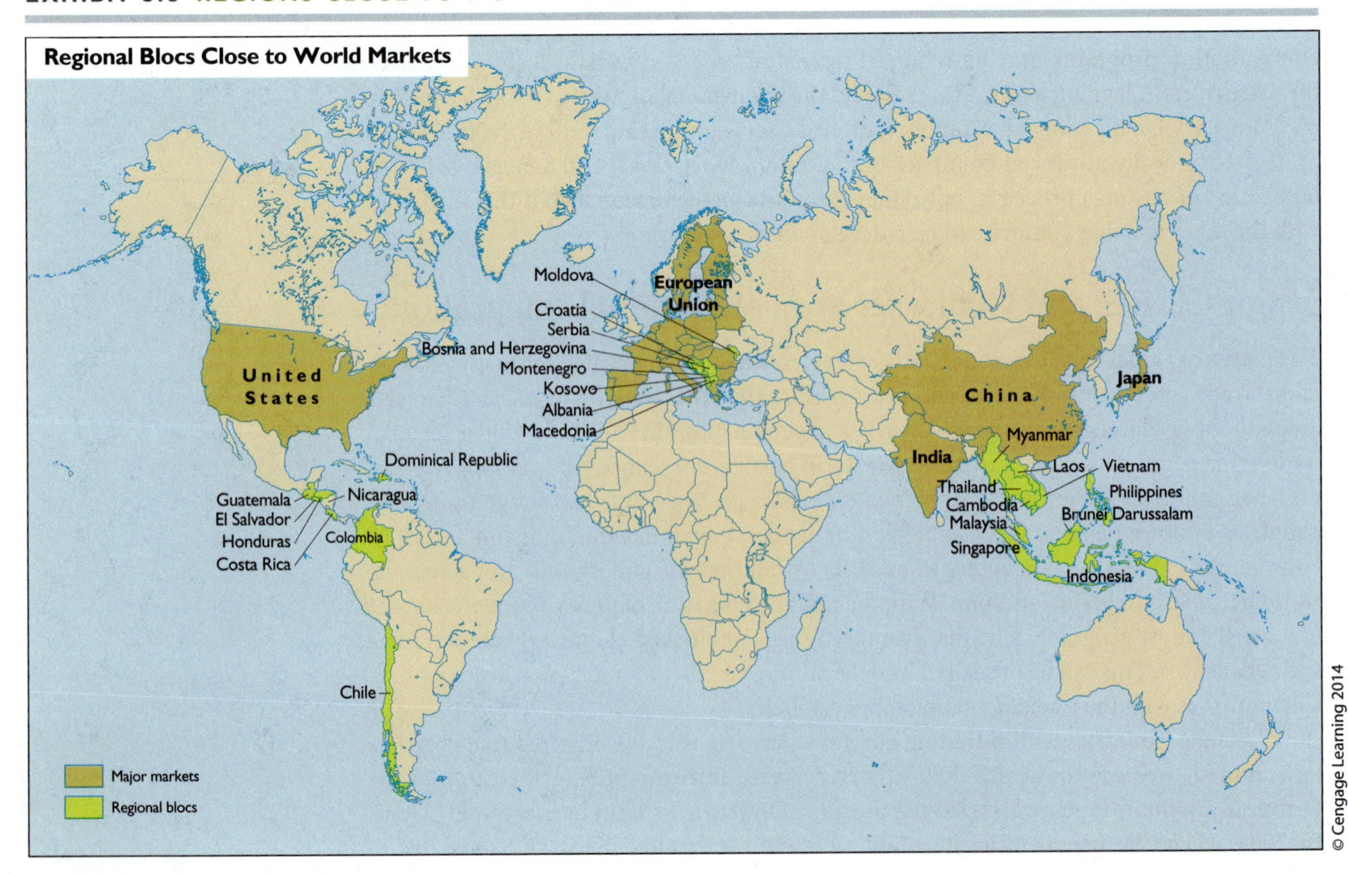

China, India, Japan, and South Korea, and India plays an important role in the South Asian Association for Regional Cooperation (SAARC). As indicated in Exhibit 1.2 in Chapter 1, this is "Asia's century" as China, India, and Japan are likely to be among the world's top four largest markets by 2020, with long-term benefits for all countries.

However, the oil-rich regional economy of the Middle East and North Africa, despite its close proximity to the European Union market, has been unable to grow fast enough to create jobs for its growing population. Governments in the region have started the transition from crude oil exports to manufacturing and services, but the region's investment climate (primarily because of economic and political suppression) is still weak. The Pan-Arab Free Trade Area (PAFTA) and the Arab Maghreb Union (AMU) have had little effect on non-oil export performance. Declining imports from the rest of the world, and an accompanying

ECONOMIC PERSPECTIVES The Ascent of the Maghreb Union

Change in politics and mutual economic need is making the Maghreb the next frontier for European investments. The Maghreb Union comprises the five North African countries of Algeria, Libya, Mauritania, Morocco, and Tunisia, and was formally created in 1989. The members of the Maghreb have quite different political systems, ranging from monarchy to authoritarian strongmen (the "Arab Spring" initiative of 2011 will hopefully lead to more democratic and stable economies over time), but share the same goal of forming an economic and political union of North Africa. These Muslim nations, with some of the world's lowest population density (almost three-fourth's of the region is covered by the Sahara Desert), are strategically located along the Mediterranean Sea across southern Europe. Major companies like Japan's Sumitomo Electric Industries, France's Renault and Groupe Safran, Europe's Airbus, and America's Boeing are all investing millions of dollars in the Maghreb in various manufacturing facilities to supply both the domestic and European markets. Yet, corruption and nepotism are serious challenges in the Maghreb. While Algeria and Morocco have made some progress in their efforts to eliminate those problems, other Maghreb countries have yet to institute effective reforms.

While the global financial crisis that originated in the United States in 2008, and the European sovereign debt crisis that started in 2010, has slowed investment flows to the Maghreb and delayed the startup of some projects, by late-2011 the prospects for the Maghreb looked relatively encouraging for several reasons. Algeria and Tunisia are rich in crude oil and natural gas; pipelines under the Mediterranean enable them to supply some of the much needed natural gas to Europe as an alternative to unreliable supplies from Russia. Wage rates in the Maghreb are less than half those in eastern European Union countries such as Romania and Bulgaria, where wages have been rising since those countries joined the European Union. Furthermore, the 44-hour workweek (five and a half days a week) in the Maghreb, as compared with 35 hours in the European Union, makes the Maghreb attractive as well. And, with Maghreb's non-unionized labor, it is easier for companies to match production with market demand. Employees in the Maghreb do not object to overtime work nor do they demand the luxury of the five week annual vacation that Europeans enjoy. Unlike countries of European Union periphery that have high sovereign debt (prior to the financial and sovereign debt crises) and are now facing severe debt service problems (and are unable to attract foreign investment), the Maghreb countries are relatively debt free and continue to attract foreign investment. When one analyzes the Maghreb as a whole, it appears that the global credit and European sovereign debt crises help the Maghreb Union at the expense of countries such as Portugal, Ireland, Greece, Spain, and Italy.

QUESTIONS:

1) Name some reasons why the countries of the European Union periphery may be losing their competitiveness against the Maghreb countries.

2) What are some of the major business reasons why investors find the Maghreb an attractive economic region for future investment?

Source: Based on Carol Matlack and Stanley Reed, "The Rise of the Maghreb," *BusinessWeek*, March 16, 2009, pp. 39–41.

increase in intra-PAFTA and intra-AMU exports suggest that the trade agreements have diverted trade rather than created trade. The region could take advantage of its proximity to Europe by exporting more high-value-added horticultural products, such as fresh vegetables and fruits, especially during the winter. It may be hoped that the Mediterranean initiative mentioned in this chapter's opening vignette will help move the Middle East and North Africa in the direction of increased trade with the European Union.

Remote Regions with Large Local Markets This second group of countries is far from world markets such as the U.S., EU, and large Asian economies like China, India, and Japan. A large local market gives countries the advantage of attracting industrial activities. If the country's infrastructure is also well connected to world markets, this advantage is reinforced. Brazil is farther than Central America and the Caribbean from the U.S., EU, and the big Asian markets. South Africa, another country with a large domestic market, and the leading economy in Africa, is also far from the major markets just mentioned. Australia is another example, as it is also far from the big markets (See Exhibit 3.4).

Effective institutions, good governance, and solid regional infrastructure can help resource-rich economies like Australia, Brazil, and South Africa to grow though increased production, specialization, and access to world markets. Each of these countries can complement its global integration with efforts to build stronger regional economic blocs focused upon its own growing economy. For the smaller economies of the regional bloc, modern infrastructure is especially important to reduce the distance to large neighboring countries, and to use those neighbors as a further conduit to world markets. Examples of such regional trading blocs are MERCOSUR (Mercado Común del Sur), the Southern African Development Community, and Australia-New Zealand cooperation.

EXHIBIT 3.4 REGIONS WITH SOME LARGE LOCAL MARKETS BUT LOCATED FAR FROM WORLD MARKETS

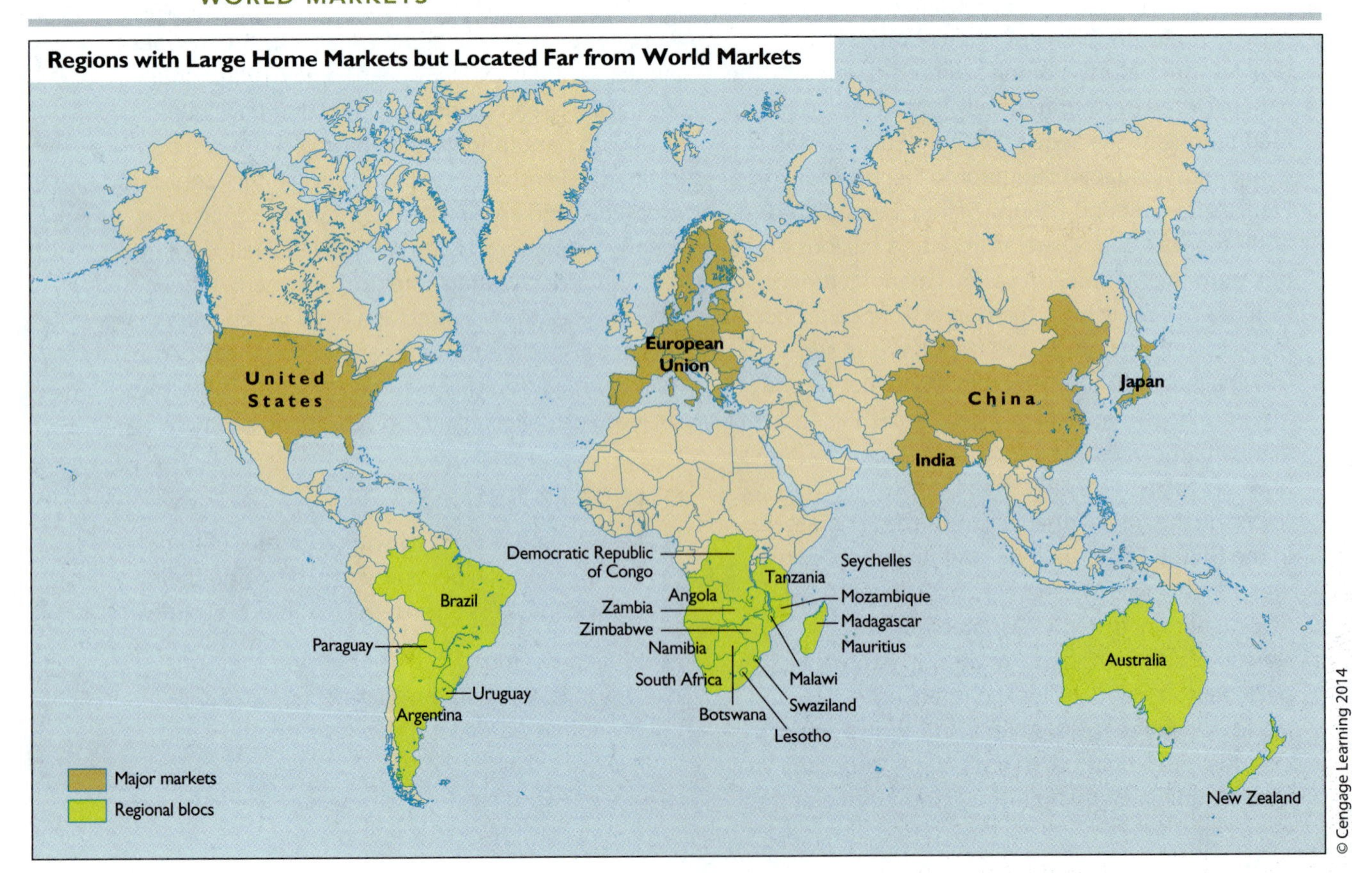

Remote Regions with Small Local Markets International integration is most difficult for countries in regions that are divided, far from world markets, and lack the economic size of a large local economy. These regions, which Paul Collier[6] (2007) calls the "bottom billion," are located in Central Asia; East, Central and West Africa; and the Pacific Islands. All of these regions could gain from effective regional cooperation. Central Asia (Kazakhstan, Kyrgyzstan, Tajikistan, Turkmenistan, and Uzbekistan) has the highest proportion of landlocked countries. In sub-Saharan Africa, there are also several landlocked countries, many with a small population and GDP, which are some of the world's poorest nations and those most prone to conflicts. The small Pacific Islands are the most geographically fragmented "sea-locked" countries.

Various regional integration blocs exist for such countries: (1) the Commonwealth of Independent States and the Shanghai Cooperation Organization, both focused on Central Asia; (2) the Central African Customs and Economic Union, the East African Community, the Economic Community of West African States, and the Economic Community of Central African States, all dealing with Africa; and (3) the Asia Pacific Economic Cooperation (APEC), which addresses Pacific Island issues as well as Asian Pacific Rim issues (See Exhibit 3.5).

The challenge for these three regions is to find ways to successfully integrate regionally and internationally. Many countries in these regions have minerals (including crude oil and natural gas) and other natural resources that are best exploited on a regional basis, since pipelines or railroads must pass through neighboring countries in order to reach the major global markets. Regional integration is paramount for resource-led economic growth and to more broadly spread the benefits of this growth. This will require institutional reform; increasing infrastructure investments to improve market access; and incentives such as preferential access to world markets, liberalized rules of origin, and skills development.

EXHIBIT 3.5 REGIONS WITH SMALL LOCAL MARKETS LOCATED FAR FROM WORLD MARKETS

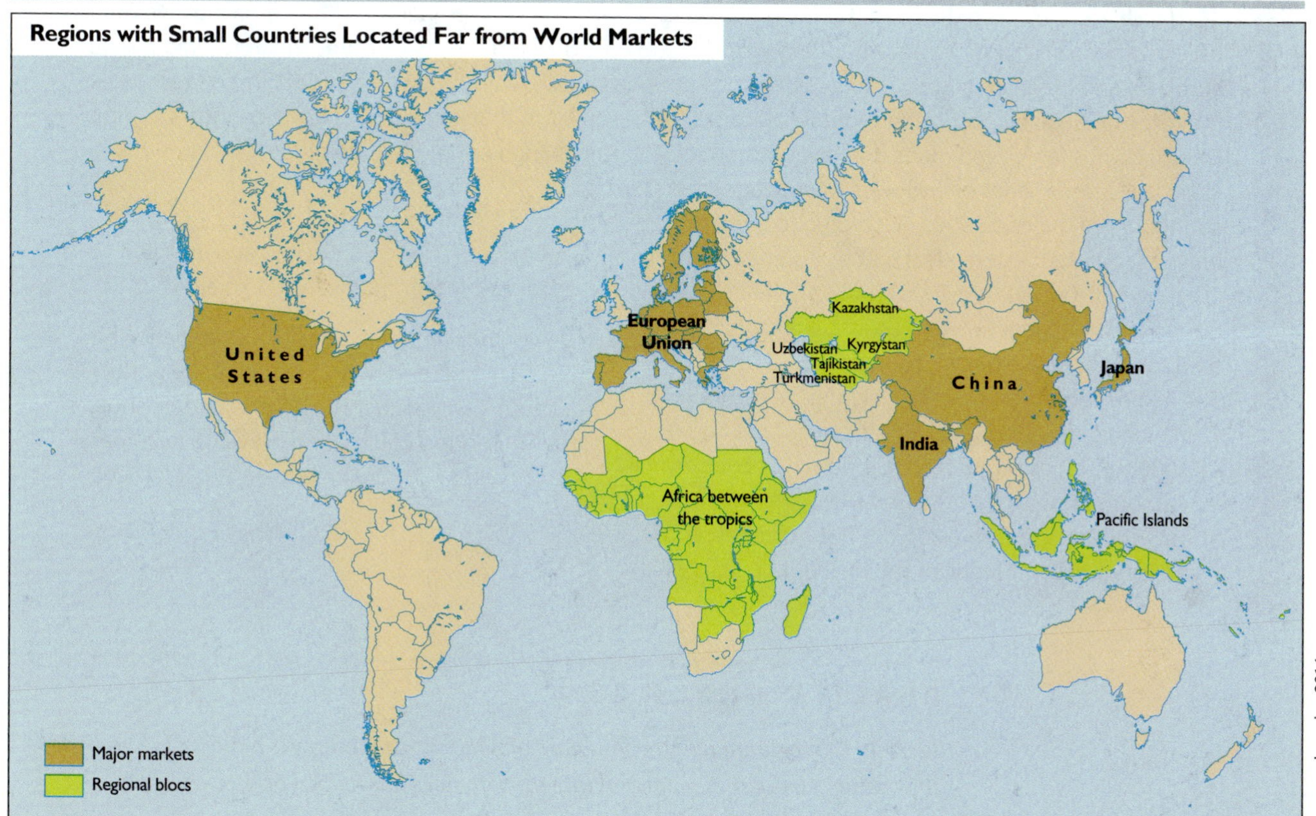

ETHICAL PERSPECTIVES

The Chinese Syndrome[7]

International integration is most difficult for countries in regions that are divided, far from world markets, and lack the economic size of a large local economy. This is the situation that the Democratic Republic of Congo (DR Congo) faces despite its size and rich mineral wealth. China's massive appetite for mineral resources has attracted it to DR Congo.

China's giant state-owned enterprises are in an enviable position because they are cash rich. Their increasing wealth means that they can afford to make eye-popping acquisitions as well as to undertake complex foreign investments with long-term objectives. But, they are increasingly regarded as unpalatable investors, especially in the West or by private sector-driven economies. China's state-owned firms have, therefore, preferred to conduct business in places such as Africa, where access to mineral resources can be negotiated with governments in ways that generate mutual benefits, whatever those benefits may be.[8] Third parties often wonder if African countries are getting the short end of the stick. A classic example is the $9 billion deal that was signed in 2008 between the DR Congo and China's massive state-owned enterprises, the China Railway Engineering Corporation (CREC) and SINOHYDRO.

The DR Congo, located in central Africa, is the largest country on the continent—larger than Western Europe—and is rich in mineral resources. Despite the fact that Belgians had colonized it for decades, DR Congo has few paved roads or railway systems, especially after a series of civil wars that ravaged the country since the mid-1990s. According to a BBC news report, the bilateral deal that was signed with CREC and SINOHYDRO in 2008 would provide DR Congo with "desperately-needed infrastructure: 2,400 miles of roads, 2,000 miles of railways, 32 hospitals, 145 health centers and two universities." In return, China would receive 10 million tons of copper and 400,000 tons of cobalt to feed its booming economy.

Although China characterized this barter deal as a "win-win" for both countries, the BBC commented that "the whole arithmetic of the deal unfairly favors the Chinese." A rights-advocate lawyer in DR Congo, Georges Kapiamba, concurred with this criticism. But the Monaco-based lawyer representing the DR Congo's state-owned mining company, Gécamines, argued that: "Without the Chinese, all this [the currently disused Kolwezi mine in DR Congo's Katanga Province] will be just scenery."

Kolwezi's proven mineral reserves were significant enough for the Chinese to release the first tranche of $3 billion to commence the DR Congo infrastructure projects. CREC and SINOHYDRO will invest another $3 billion before DR Congo's copper and cobalt mines become operational. When production began, in late-2011, the final $3 billion was disbursed for construction of roads, railways, and hospitals. The Chinese companies are expected to recoup their investment within 10 years. Thereafter, the joint venture—one-third DR Congolese-owned and two-thirds Chinese—will continue to exploit the mine.

Human rights groups are critical of the deal because the project details were not published. Indications are that the Chinese state-owned enterprises will be exempt from paying taxes on mining income and customs duties on imported machinery until all the infrastructure work is complete. Critics, such as attorney Georges Kapiamba, believe that the deal amounts to a licensed plundering by the Chinese majority owners of DR Congo's resources, similar to that carried out by the country's colonial ruler, King Leopold II of Belgium.

QUESTIONS:

1) Does the DR Congo-China venture make economic integration sense? Explain.
2) Do you believe that the Chinese are behaving ethically, or are they taking advantage of the DR Congo? Can you identify other strategic choices that DR Congo could use to develop its mineral resources?

Source: Tim Whewell, "China to Seal $9 billion DR Congo Deal," *BBC News*, April 14, 2008.

REALITY CHECK LO-2

Identify the regional integration blocs of which your country is a part. Do you think that being part of these regional integration blocs has helped or hurt your personal welfare? How?

Does Regional Integration Confound Global Trade?

LO-3

Identify the primary reasons why countries are now seeking to pursue regional integration at the expense of multilateral trade liberalization.

As was just discussed, groups of countries all over the world have formed various kinds of economic cooperation agreements, primarily to enhance issues of mutual interest—not solely trade. And, with uncertainty surrounding the outcome of the Doha Round of trade negotiations, countries (large and small) are clamoring for bilateral or regional trade agreements to meet their specific agendas. Economists are concerned that as a result of these negotiations, the prospects of creating a truly open *global* economic system that benefits all countries may recede.[9] Some governments may initiate regional pacts (such as the Mediterranean Union discussed at the beginning of this chapter) to cement diplomatic, environmental, or security ties and risk slowing the momentum behind multilateral (global) trade liberalization.

To further elaborate on this issue, the chapter will now look more closely at how four major diverse regional integration blocs are performing. These regional integration blocs will likely play a profound role during the coming century. Will they confound globalization?

REALITY CHECK LO-3

Are policymakers in your country pushing for more regional integration or global integration? Why? Will that benefit you personally? If so, how?

The European Union (EU)

LO-4

Explain why the European Union is seen as the most advanced regional integration bloc.

The EU, headquartered in Brussels, Belgium, is the most highly evolved example of regional integration in the world. It is already in the fourth stage of the economic integration process (see Exhibit 3.2) and is moving toward the final step, which requires political union with common defense and foreign policy institutions. After the devastation of infrastructure in Europe during World War II, the United States helped to rebuild Europe through the Marshall Plan. In addition, as discussed in Chapter 1, the World Bank Group (especially the International Bank for Reconstruction and Development) was established in 1944 to help rebuild and stabilize European economies. The objective of all of these initiatives was to create a strong, democratic, independent, and united Europe based on free-market principles and open economic systems.

The origins of the EU can be traced to the creation of the European Coal and Steel Community (ECSC), which established a common market in coal, steel, and iron ore among the six founding member countries: France, West Germany, Italy, Belgium, the Netherlands, and Luxembourg, in 1952. The objective of ECSC was to encourage member countries to cooperate in steel production, thereby preventing these countries from warring with each other. Thus, peace and prosperity were the primary reasons for the creation of ECSC.

The second major step was to approve the Treaty of Rome in 1957, establishing the European Economic Community (EEC) that called for free trade among members as well as a common external tariff for non-members. In 1960, the United Kingdom, Denmark, Sweden, Finland, Switzerland, Austria, and Portugal formed the European Free Trade Association (EFTA). Although the United Kingdom, Ireland, and Denmark applied to join the EEC in August 1961, these countries were not allowed to enter the EEC until 1973 (bringing total membership to nine). The delay occurred primarily because French president Charles de Gaulle showed resistance to the United Kingdom's joining the EEC; de Gaulle believed that the U.K. was a "Trojan horse" which, once admitted into the EEC, would try to cater to American rather than EEC interests. Greece joined the EEC in 1981, followed by Spain and Portugal in 1986, bringing the membership to 12.

EXHIBIT 3.6 THE EUROPEAN UNION

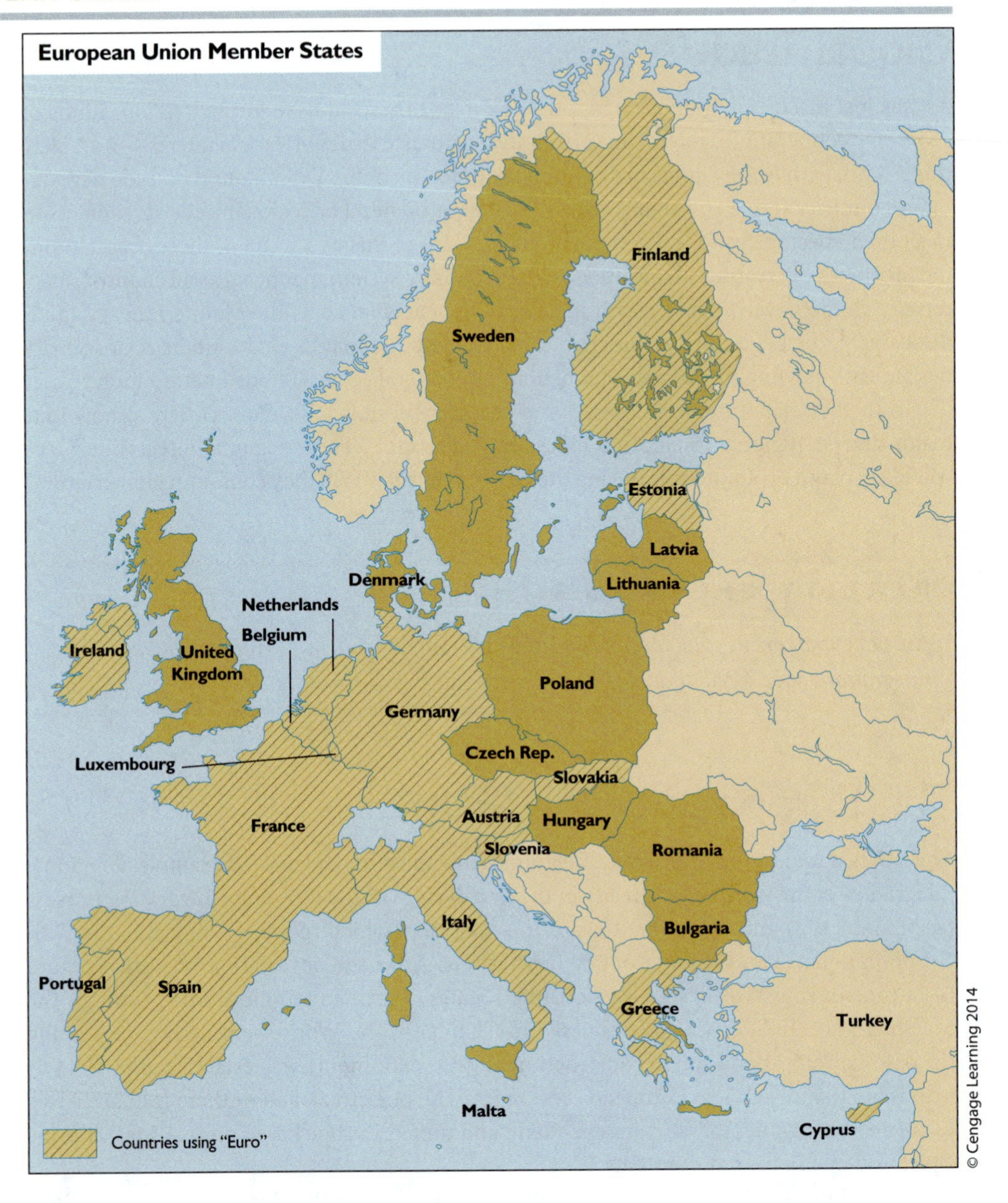

Until that time, the EEC focused upon the establishment of a common market with free movement of goods, services, and capital. However, in 1992 the Maastricht Treaty was signed and the EEC became a full economic union or single market with free movement of labor among member countries. The European Union (EU), began incorporating (harmonizing and unifying) the fiscal, monetary, and social policies of its member countries. In January 1995, Austria, Sweden, and Finland joined the EU, bringing membership to 15. In May 2004, 10 new countries (eight from the former Soviet bloc, Cyprus, and Malta) were admitted to the EU, bringing the membership to 25. Bulgaria and Romania were admitted to the EU in January 2007, thereby bringing the membership to 27 (see Exhibit 3.6 and Exhibit 3.7 for details). Croatia will become a member on July 1, 2013.

The EU's eastward enlargement reflects a common past. It also opens new business and investment opportunities for its members. The enlarged EU will offer tremendous challenges and opportunities for businesses in non-member countries that seek to become part of the EU. For instance, the global credit crisis has had a devastating effect on Iceland, and the country has since indicated its interest in joining the EU.

The EU is a regional bloc based on treaties. Through various treaties such as the Maastricht Treaty, the Copenhagen Treaty, the Treaty of Nice, and the Lisbon Treaty, the EU is deepening and strengthening its institutional (economic, political, social, and defense) linkages, which will hopefully enable it to act as one country that will effectively compete with the United States As Exhibit 3.7 illustrates, the EU is larger than the U.S. both in terms of gross national income (GNI) and population.

Turkey

As of now, the fate of EU candidate country Turkey is still uncertain, a case which has been highly controversial. Geographically, only about 5 percent of Turkey's land mass is in Europe. Furthermore, because of its relatively low per-capita income level, critics have warned that significant EU budgetary resources may need to be diverted to Turkey's infrastructure development soon after it joins the EU[10]. Another issue of concern to Europeans is the powerful role of the military in what (as some Europeans believe) is not a truly democratic nation—one with a questionable human rights record and inadequate rights for minorities, especially the Turkish Kurds. Turkey's population of some 74 million would be the second largest in the EU, after Germany's 82 million, and its growth rate is high. It is estimated that by 2020, Turkey's population will exceed Germany's declining population. Moreover, an issue not openly discussed, but which is a bigger EU concern, is that Turkey's population is predominantly Muslim. Consequently, if Turkey were admitted to the EU in the near future, then by 2020 it would be the largest member (based on population), with significant voting rights, which could potentially change the nature of the EU. Although Turkey applied to join the EU in 1987, and EU's consultation with Turkey has continued since 2004, and the issue of whether Turkey will be admitted to the EU continues to be controversial and questionable.

The Euro

As part of the Maastricht Treaty of 1992, the euro, EU's single currency, was introduced on January 1, 1999. Its performance (stability), until the start of the European sovereign debt crisis that originated with Greece (followed by Ireland and Portugal) in April 2010, was remarkable, and the euro was considered the crowning success of the EU's plans to integrate European economies.

Before the beginning of the European sovereign debt crisis in early-2010, the international role of the euro as a foreign exchange reserve currency (to be discussed in greater detail in Chapter 4) appeared to be gaining ground. That was further enhanced because of the 2008 global credit crisis—foreign governments have sought to diversify their holdings of foreign exchange reserves by moving more reserves away from dollars and toward euros. For example, some 30 percent of global foreign exchange reserves were kept in euros in 2009, up from 18 percent in 1999, while dollar foreign exchange reserves declined to 60 percent from 70 percent over the same period[11].

After meeting strict fiscal and monetary criteria, 17 of the 27 EU countries are allowed to use the euro as their currency. Exhibit 3.6 provides a graphic representation of countries that are part of the Eurozone (countries that are allowed to use the euro as their national currency). The world's most independent central bank, the European Central Bank (ECB), based in Frankfurt, Germany, is the apex central bank for the Eurozone countries, and maintains responsibility for Eurozone's monetary policy (implemented by the central banks of the 17 member countries) and the stability of the euro. The ECB tries to maintain the stability of the euro by keeping Eurozone inflation below, but as close as possible to, 2 percent annually.

While the U.K., Denmark, and Sweden have met the strict criteria to join the Eurozone, they have opted not to join, but to continue using their own respective national currencies. The other seven countries hope to join the Eurozone sometime in the future after the European sovereign debt crisis has been resolved, and new potential entrants have met the strict fiscal and monetary criteria set by the EU.

EXHIBIT 3.7 THE EUROPEAN UNION AND THE UNITED STATES: A COMPARISON

	Population (million)	Surface Area (thousand sq km)	Population Density (people per sq km)	Gross National Income ($ billion 2009)	Gross National Income per Capita ($ 2009)	PPP Gross National Income ($ billion 2009)	PPP Gross National Income per Capita ($2009)
Austria*	8.00	84	101	389	46,450	321	38,410
Belgium*	11.00	31	356	488	45,270	395	36,610
Bulgaria	8.00	111	70	46	6,060	101	13,260
Cyprus*	0.80	9	86	23	28,900	21	26,370
Czech Republic	10.00	79	136	182	17,310	251	23,940
Denmark	6.00	43	130	327	59,060	214	38,780
Estonia*	1.00	45	32	19	14,060	26	19,120
Finland*	5.00	338	18	245	45,940	188	35,280
France*	63.00	549	114	2,751	42,620	2,191	33,950
Germany*	82.00	347	235	3,476	42,450	3,017	36,850
Greece*	11.00	132	88	328	29,040	325	28,800
Hungary	10.00	93	112	130	12,980	191	19,090
Ireland*	4.00	70	65	197	44,280	147	33,040
Italy*	60.00	301	205	2,115	35,110	1,919	31,870
Latvia	2.00	65	36	28	12,390	40	17,610
Lithuania	3.00	65	53	38	11,410	58	17,310
Luxembourg*	0.48	3	185	36	75,880	31	64,400
Malta*	0.41	0.3	1281	6	15,310	9	20,990
Netherlands*	17.00	42	490	801	48,460	657	39,740
Poland	38.00	313	125	468	12,260	698	18,290
Portugal*	11.00	92	116	233	21,910	256	24,080
Romania	21.00	238	93	179	8,330	312	14,540
Spain*	46.00	505	92	1,476	32,120	1,447	31,490
Slovak Republic*	5.00	49	113	87	16,130	120	22,110
Slovania*	2.00	20	101	48	23,520	54	26,470
Sweden	9.00	450	23	454	48,840	354	38,050
United Kingdom	62.00	244	256	2,558	41,370	2,217	35,860
The current EU 27	496.69	4,318	115	17,129	34,485	15,560	31,326
Turkey	75.00	784	97	652	8,720	1,010	13,500
United States	307.00	9,832	34	14,234	46,360	14,011	45,640

* Eurozone countries

Source: World Bank. 2011. *World Development Indicators*, 2011, pp. 10–12. © World Bank. http://data.worldbank.org/data-catalog/world-development-indicators/wdi-2011 License: Creative Commons Attribution CC BY 3.0

REALITY CHECK LO-4

Using end-of-year annual data, identify how the value of the euro has changed (with respect to your national currency) over the past five years. In your opinion, has the euro been stable? Would this be the right time to visit the European Union? Explain.

The North American Free Trade Agreement (NAFTA)

LO-5

Describe how NAFTA has affected U.S.-Mexico bilateral trade in goods and services.

NAFTA is a comprehensive free-trade agreement among Canada, United States, and Mexico that addresses issues ranging from protection of workers' rights and the environment to phased reduction of tariff and non-tariff trade barriers, which were finally eliminated in 2009 (see Exhibit 3.8). Historically, Canada has always been the United States' largest trade partner, and Mexico has ranked either second, or third. With such close trade links to its northern and southern neighbors, it made sense for the U.S. to explore more formal trade agreements with its strategic neighbors, which later resulted in NAFTA. Ideas about integrating the U.S. and Canadian economies with the Mexican economy gained strength with the success of the Canada-U.S. Free Trade Agreement, which was signed in 1988, and became effective in 1989. NAFTA negotiations began in 1990; the agreement was signed by the three governments in December 1992, ratified by the legislatures of the three countries, and went into effect on January 1, 1994.

NAFTA has three major objectives. First is the expansion of trade in goods and services through the phased elimination of all trade barriers including tariffs, quotas, and licensing restrictions, among the parties. Second is the protection of intellectual property rights (enforcement of patent and copyright laws for software, music recordings, etc.). Third is the creation of institutions to address potential problems (unfair trade practices, disputes between companies or governments, environmental protection, worker's rights, competition policies, and the implementation of NAFTA rules and regulations). Two additional, peripheral agreements addressing Mexican labor laws and environmental quality were signed by the United States and Mexico to make sure that Mexico would not practice unfair labor laws and would enforce agreed-on environmental quality standards. The NAFTA and the additional agreements simultaneously became effective on January 1, 1994.

While the structure of NAFTA is detailed, its institutions are not as far-reaching as those of the European Union, which include coordination of European political, legal, foreign, and defense policies. Because Mexico has close economic ties with the United States, its economic prospects are heavily influenced by the performance of its northern neighbor. When the U.S. economy slides into a recession, the impact on Mexico is severe, as can be seen by the decrease in the volume of Mexican exports to the United States and the decrease in Mexican worker remittances from the United States As early as 1999, Mexico initiated steps to safeguard its economy against this risk by signing a free trade agreement with the EU. Since then, Mexican trade with the EU has been steadily increasing. Although the United States remains Mexico's largest trade partner, trade and foreign investment diversification (especially with the EU) will be necessary for Mexico to maintain economic growth as low-cost manufacturing becomes increasingly diverted to China from the Unites States.

Until 2004, the United States' top two trade (exports plus imports) partners were its neighbors, Canada and Mexico. In 2004, U.S. trade with Canada was $448 billion, and with Mexico $269 billion. However, since 2005, China has surpassed Mexico and has become the United States' second largest trade partner (see Exhibit 3.9).

EXHIBIT 3.8 NORTH AMERICAN FREE TRADE AGREEMENT

REALITY CHECK LO-5

If you are living in the United States, visit a local chain grocery store like Kroger or Safeway and investigate from where some of those fresh vegetables come. Is NAFTA at work?

EXHIBIT 3.9 UNITED STATES: EXPORTS AND IMPORTS OF GOODS TO AND FROM TOP TEN TRADE PARTNERS (BILLIONS OF U.S. DOLLARS)

Exports (fob)

	2004	2005	2006	2007	2008	2009	2010
World Total	819	907	1038	1163	1300	1057	1276
Canada	188	211	230	248	261	205	248
Mexico	111	120	143	137	152	129	163
China	35	42	55	65	72	70	92
Japan	54	55	60	63	67	51	61
United Kingdom	36	39	45	50	54	46	49
Germany	31	34	41	50	55	43	48
South Korea	26	28	33	35	35	29	39
Netherlands	24	27	31	33	40	32	35
Singapore	20	21	25	26	29	22	29
France	22	23	24	28	30	27	28

Imports (cif)

	2004	2005	2006	2007	2008	2009	2010
World Total	1526	1733	1919	2017	2166	1604	1968
China	211	260	306	340	356	310	383
Canada	260	292	308	318	340	228	280
Mexico	158	173	201	213	218	178	232
Japan	133	142	152	149	143	98	124
Germany	79	87	91	97	100	73	84
United Kingdom	48	52	55	58	60	48	51
South Korea	48	46	48	49	50	41	51
France	33	35	38	43	45	35	39
Venezuela	26	35	38	41	53	29	33
Saudi Arabia	23	29	33	37	57	23	33

Source: IMF: *Direction of Trade Statistics Database*, 2011.

Association of South East Asian Nations (ASEAN)

LO-6

Explain the importance of ASEAN and indicate why Asia may become the most important free trade region for this century.

ASEAN, headquartered in Jakarta, Indonesia, was established in August 1967 by five founding members: Indonesia, Malaysia, the Philippines, Singapore, and Thailand. ASEAN's current membership stands at 10; Brunei joined in 1984, Vietnam in 1995, Laos and Myanmar in 1997, and Cambodia in 1999 (see Exhibit 3.10). As of 2009, the ASEAN region had a population of 591 million (larger than the EU), a land area of 4.5 million square kilometers (slightly larger than the present EU), and a combined GDP of $1.5 trillion (about one-tenth of the EU). Exhibit 3.11 provides some key economic indicators for ASEAN.

EXHIBIT 3.10 ASSOCIATION OF SOUTH EAST ASIAN NATIONS (ASEAN)

ASEAN's two main objectives are: (1) to accelerate economic growth, social progress, and cultural development in the region; and (2) to promote regional peace and stability through the rule of law in relationship among countries in the region. In 2003, ASEAN leaders agreed to establish an ASEAN Community based on three pillars: ASEAN Security Community; ASEAN Economic Community; and ASEAN Socio-Cultural Community.

ASEAN Security Community (ASC)

Since ASEAN's establishment in 1967, tension has never escalated into armed confrontation among its member countries. ASC's objective is to ensure that countries in the region live in peace with one another and rely exclusively on peaceful processes in the settlement of intra-regional differences. In recognition of security interdependence in the Asia-Pacific region, ASEAN established the ASEAN Regional Forum (ARF) to discuss major security issues in the region, including relationships with the major powers, non-proliferation, counter-terrorism, and transnational crime.

ASEAN Economic Community

The goal is to create a stable, prosperous, and highly competitive ASEAN economic region, in which there is free flow of goods, services, investment, and capital; and simultaneously to reduce poverty and socio-economic disparities. Although the ASEAN Economic Community calls for the establishment of a single market and production base, unlike the EU it does not call for the free movement of labor across ASEAN. Launched in 1992, the ASEAN Free Trade Area has been in place since 2007. It aims to promote economies of scale and specialization in production by eliminating tariff and non-tariff barriers among member countries. Other major integration-related economic activities include: financial sector liberalization; road, railway, pipeline, seaport and airport connectivity, and modernization; interconnectivity of telecommunication services; and human resource development.

EXHIBIT 3.11 ASEAN SELECTED KEY ECONOMIC INDICATORS, 2009

	Population (million)	Surface Area (thousand sq km)	Population Density (people per sq km)	Gross Domestic Product (US$ billion 2009)	Gross Domestic Product per Capita (US$ 2009)	PPP Gross Domestic Product (US$ billion 2009)	PPP Gross Domestic Product per Capita (US$ 2009)	Total Trade (US$ billion 2009)
Brunei Darussalam	0.41	5.8	70.42	10.76	26,486	20.07	49,411	9.57
Cambodia	14.96	181.0	82.62	10.36	693	26.94	1,801	8.89
Indonesia	231.70	1860.4	124.55	546.87	2,364	967.22	4,180	213.34
Lao PDR	6.13	236.8	25.88	5.58	910	14.40	2,350	2.96
Malaysia	28.31	330.3	85.71	193.11	6,822	384.79	13,594	280.22
Myanmar	59.53	676.6	87.99	24.97	419	65.09	1,093	10.19
Philippines	92.23	300.0	307.42	161.36	1,750	325.11	3,525	83.87
Singapore	4.99	0.7	7,025.35	182.70	36,631	248.21	49,766	515.62
Thailand	66.90	513.1	130.38	264.32	3,951	540.05	8,072	286.27
Vietnam	86.03	331.1	259.85	96.32	1,120	267.61	3,111	125.92
ASEAN Total	**591.18**	**4435.7**	133.28	**1496.34**	**2,531**	**2,859.49**	**4,840**	**1536.84**

Source: ASEAN Finance and Macro-econommic Surveillance Unit Database. ASEAN Merchandise Trade Statistics Database (2010). (from www.aseansec.org)

ASEAN Socio-Cultural Community

The objective is to ensure that the ASEAN workforce is well prepared to benefit from the economic integration process that is under way. Programs are being put into place through investments in basic and higher education, training, R&D, and raising the standard of disadvantaged groups and rural population through better public health care and social protection.

The Future of ASEAN

ASEAN's Vision 2020 calls for aggressive outward-looking economic policies. Several bilateral Free Trade Agreements (FTAs) are currently being implemented. The ASEAN-Japan Comprehensive Economic Partnership (AJCEP) agreement covers trade in goods, services, and investment and economic cooperation that came to force on December 1, 2008. The ASEAN Australia-New Zealand FTA called AANZFTA was signed in February 2009, and the ASEAN-India FTA (AIFTA) was signed in January 2010 soon after the ASEAN-South Korea free trade agreement (AKTRA) was realized on January 1, 2010. The FTA with China, ASEAN-China Free Trade Agreement (ACFTA) is expected to become fully operational on January 1, 2015. If all goes as planned, the ASEAN inspired FTAs will create the world's largest free trade area that will comprise much of Asia.

A growing ASEAN concern is the economic ascendancy of China, which as a major low-cost manufacturing center, has been one of the world's most attractive destinations for foreign direct investment. China is embracing capitalism and flexing its political muscle as it strives to become the world's second superpower. For the first 18 of the past 20 centuries, China was the world's largest economy, and many Chinese elite see the past two centuries of underdevelopment and colonial occupation as an aberration that must—and will—be overcome. To prevent job losses (and the loss of exports to China) and also to tap China's growing domestic consumer market, members of ASEAN are hoping to develop a free trade agreement with China by 2015. For China, a free trade agreement with ASEAN would mean strengthening its regional influence.

REALITY CHECK LO-6

Identify the ASEAN country that is considered to be the regional hub for multinational corporations operating in Asia. How does that country's per capita income compare with the United Stateas and why?

LO-7

Explain why regional integration in Latin America is challenging, and why there is potential for a grouping like MERCOSUR to become more predominant.

Regional Integration in Latin America

Although the countries of Latin America have significant natural as well as human resources, the region has been a patchwork of constantly changing regional trade and investment agreements as will be discussed next. The first step toward free trade in Latin America was taken with the signing of the Treaty of Montevideo in 1960, creating the Latin American Free Trade Association (LAFTA). Seven countries—Argentina, Brazil, Chile, Mexico, Paraguay, Peru, and Uruguay—indicated their intention to create a free trade zone by 1972, but this was not completed because members were unable to agree upon the timetable and the phased lowering of tariff barriers. In 1969, frustrated by the lack of progress in LAFTA, Bolivia, Chile, Colombia, Ecuador, and Peru joined in creating the Andean Group, which aimed to create economic integration through reduced taxes, a common external tariff, and investment in the poorer industrial areas of their respective countries.

EXHIBIT 3.12 REGIONAL INTEGRATION IN LATIN AMERICA

Argentina and Brazil, on the other hand, began discussions on bilateral trade liberalization in 1985 that led to the signing of the Treaty of Asunción in 1991 among Argentina, Brazil, Paraguay, and Uruguay, creating the Southern Cone Common Market, or MERCOSUR (*Mercado Común del Sur*). That treaty called for progressive tariff reduction, the adoption of sectoral agreements, a common external tariff, and the ultimate creation of a common market by 2005. Much remains to materialize in MERCOSUR, given Argentina's economic uncertainties following its debt crisis and the crash of the Argentine peso in 2002.

Robin Laurance/Imagestate Media Partners Limited - Impact Photos / Alamy

DR-CAFTA. *Sugarcane farmers in the Dominican Republic increase sugar and bioethanol exports to the U.S.*

Issues such as these have undermined implementation of most Latin American trade agreements so far, forcing participating countries to repeatedly change their alliances, objectives, and approaches.

With the anticipated success of NAFTA, formal discussions to establish a Free Trade Area of the Americas (FTAA) began in 1994 under the Clinton administration. This idea was initiated at the Summit of the Americas, attended by 34 nations (all countries of Latin America excluding Cuba). If and when implemented, the FTAA would encompass 800 million people and a huge regional economy. The United States had hoped to meet a 2005 deadline for the agreement, but before 2005, there was dispute between the United States and Venezuela because of perceived U.S. interference in domestic Venezuelan politics. Venezuela's president, Hugo Chavez, expressed opposition to the FTAA in general—and the United States in particular—and was able to enlist some Latin American leaders to support his cause. Given these unresolved issues, FTAA is unlikely to begin any time in the near future.

As a means to push NAFTA south of Mexico, after formally signing a free trade agreement with Chile on June 6, 2003, the Bush administration began free-trade talks with the five Central American countries (Costa Rica, El Salvador, Guatemala, Honduras, and Nicaragua) and the Dominican Republic. The resulting agreement, DR-CAFTA (Dominican Republic and Central American Free Trade Agreement), became effective in 2005. Although U.S.-Central American bilateral trade is roughly 10 percent of U.S.-Mexico trade, the U.S. and Central American economies are relatively complementary; the United States has the competitive advantage in the production of grains, and Central America is a low-cost producer of coffee, tropical fruits (especially bananas), ornamental plants, and sugar (including bioethanol from sugar cane).

Based on the information about the various major regional trade blocs, it is apparent that if multilateral trade and investment liberalization fails to continue, regional integration blocs are likely to be the way of the future.

REALITY CHECK LO-7

Visit your local grocery supermarket and discover from where the various brands of premium coffee beans come. Which trade agreement do you think makes that choice possible?

SUMMARY

Two or more countries could join together to form a regional integration bloc. The main objectives for integration could be: economic; geo-political; social; and/or regional security.

When the goal is purely economic, then the unification process is called regional economic integration. In most cases, the primary reason is to increase efficiency and global competitiveness of member countries by using economies of scale in production and specialization. Although there are many types of economic integration blocs, which depend upon how closely member countries want to work with one another, there are five distinct degrees of progression that serious economic integration groups could follow. First, and most basic, is a free trade area, which essentially calls for the elimination of tariffs, non-tariff barriers and quotas among member countries. Second, is a customs union, in which a free trade area would impose a common external tariff on non-members. Third, is a common or single market that builds on a customs union by allowing free movement of labor and capital among member states. Fourth, an economic union calls for convergent social, economic and monetary policies among member states. And, finally a political union will call for common foreign and defense policies where the regional group of countries behaves as a single country.

The benefits of regional integration include: the creation of a large pool of consumers with growing income; increased supply of goods and services at globally competitive prices; enhanced flow of capital, labor, and technology; and increased cooperation, peace, and security among member countries. The major costs of regional integration are the move away from MFN status, loss of some sovereignty, and relative disregard for cultural and social differences.

Economic geography attempts to explain international trade flows as well as the degree of success and segmentation of regional integration blocs. The World Bank's 2009 World Development Report (WDR) identifies four factors that are crucial in the economic integration process: key global markets; location (proximity to these markets); degree of openness between countries of the regional bloc; and existence of large local markets within the regional bloc. With the Doha Round of trade negotiations at a standstill, countries that would like to benefit from continued globalization are resorting to regional economic integration as a means to achieve their economic growth objectives.

The European Union is the world's most advanced and largest (from the standpoint of GDP/GNI) form of regional integration bloc because it is totally integrated economically, and almost moving to a political union.

NAFTA, on the other hand, is only in the first stage (free trade) of the economic integration process and has a long way to go—if there is political will at all—to catch up with the EU. However, because of the size of the U.S. economy, NAFTA ranks a close second (in terms of GDP/GNI) to the EU and has significantly benefited Mexico.

The future could be quite different. As ASEAN expands its free trade agreements (FTA) to include, Australia, New Zealand, India, China, Japan, and South Korea, this enlarged FTA bloc will likely become the world's largest, reflecting that this is "Asia's century."

As a regional integration bloc, Latin America offers tremendous potential. It is rich in natural resources, and Brazil in particular has significant quality human resources as well. However, a lack of political unity, unsustainable economic and social policies, and external interferences in domestic politics create a challenge for Latin America to achieve its potential as an economic integration powerhouse. If multilateral trade and investment liberalization fails to continue, regional integration blocs are likely to be the way of the future.

KEY TERMS

regional integration, *p. 61*
spatial transformations, *p. 61*
free-trade area, *p. 61*
customs union, *p. 62*
common market or single market, *p. 62*
economic and monetary union, *p. 62*
political union, *p. 62*
economic geography, *p. 63*

CHAPTER QUESTIONS

1. Will countries be better off under a multilateral economic liberalization regime or under a system of regional economic integration? Why?

2. How useful is economic geography in explaining the success of regional economic integration blocs? Give examples.

3. Why are countries pushing to sign regional integration blocs?

4. Although the European Union is the most advanced form of regional integration, it is currently facing a challenging time. What are some of the major challenges facing the EU?

5. NAFTA has improved Mexico-U.S. trade and investment, yet, bilateral trade between the United States and China is greater than with Mexico. Why is this true?

6. It appears likely that a free trade area in much of Asia is likely by the end of 2020. What are the global implications for such a development?

7. Regional integration in Latin America offers tremendous potential. Yet, economic achievements are relatively modest so far. Why?

MINI CASE: THE EUROPEAN UNION SANS FRONTIÈRE?

A European Union without borders? After accepting ten new members in 2004, and another two in 2007, the EU is experiencing severe problems, especially since the beginning of the global credit crisis in 2008 and the related European sovereign debt crisis of 2010. Some EU taxpayers wonder if proper vetting was done before so many new members were admitted in haste. The massive bailout of the banking sector in Ireland and Portugal, followed by the painful restructuring of Greece's sovereign debt and chronic fiscal deficit problems has exposed the limits to which well-off EU members are willing to rescue other EU countries. The total failure of the financial sector among "star economic performers" of the recent past—the United Kingdom, Ireland, and Spain—clearly exposed the weakness of the deregulated Anglo-American capitalism that was practiced by some "market-oriented" member states. Public demand for tighter, more effective regulation of the financial sector that is being debated for legislation in the United States and Europe is evidence that taxpayers in the west are getting fed up with a "so-called capitalist system" that privatizes profits and socializes risk.

The scenario asks many questions:[12] (a) whether the EU has moved eastward too fast and too soon; (b) whether EU is resorting to "à la carte" membership that is straining the management of the union; (c) whether new members should be admitted any time soon; and (d) whether there ought to be a demarcation—referring to countries such as Turkey, Georgia, and Ukraine—beyond which the EU will not cross.

EU critics argue that just as the Soviets aggressively and forcefully took over neighboring states to keep communism safe, the EU is accepting new members to its fold—all the way to Russia's borders—to keep Europe safe for democracy. In this process, a number of countries have been (and are) in the course of being accepted into the EU without adequate vetting. The Russians are concerned because a large number of EU members are also members of NATO (the North Atlantic Treaty Organization), which has a policy stating that an attack on any one NATO member is an attack on all its members, therefore, a military incident would require a coordinated military response. Russia is watching the proposed EU and NATO memberships of Georgia and Ukraine very closely because of this. While Russia may not be very concerned about Georgia and Ukraine joining the EU, their membership in NATO may not be acceptable. It may be in Russia's interest to destabilize Georgia and Ukraine if they joined NATO as Georgia witnessed in 2009.

Although the EU has some exemplary value-based goals that all member countries must follow

(continued)

MINI CASE: THE EUROPEAN UNION SANS FRONTIÈRE?

(the so-called Copenhagen criteria of adherence to democracy, rule of law, rights of minorities, etc.), critics argue that member countries appear to be "cherry picking" aspects of EU goals they would like to follow. Hence, the EU essentially practices differentiated regional integration. For example, the U.K., Denmark, and Sweden have chosen to opt out of the euro after meeting euro-entry requirements. The Schengen open-border area (which dictates that once a person enters a EU country legally, that person can cross into other EU member states without other country's visas) extends to non-members such as Iceland, Norway, and Switzerland; while EU members such as the U.K. and Ireland remain outside of this agreement. The Lisbon Treaty exempts Britain and Poland from the Charter of Fundamental Rights although they violated human rights by rendi-tioning 9/11 terrorism suspects to third countries in order to extract confessions through torture. A lack of uniform enforcement of rule of law within the EU will only weaken the EU as monitoring the various permutations and combinations of membership policies could turn into a Brussels nightmare.

QUESTIONS:

1) Given the security concerns of both the EU and Russia, where should EU's eastern border end? Do you think the buffer states should become NATO members as well? Why or why not?

2) Should non-uniformity policies in the EU (i.e., cherry picking EU policies that members may choose to follow) be tolerated or encouraged? Make your case.

South American Oil Giant Looks Beyond Traditional Trade Partners

In 2009, Venezuela and China marked 35 years of diplomatic relations with a clear commitment to further strengthen ties amid a drastically different geopolitical and economic landscape. Venezuela has one of the largest reserves of oil in the world, and certainly the largest in the Western hemisphere; Venezuela is still a major supplier of crude oil to the United States. During the presidency of George W. Bush, Venezuela almost completely nationalized its oil industry and drove out U.S. multinational oil companies for political reasons. (President Hugo Chavez believed that the Bush administration was interfering in Venezuela's politics.)

The Venezuelan government is now looking further afield to China, ASEAN, and other Asian countries, and away from the traditional U.S. market to boost its oil exports and economy. Venezuela's trade with China now exceeds $10 billion. During a 2009 visit to China, President Hugo Chavez remarked, "We have no doubt that China is the main engine to drive the world past the [global credit] crisis." President Chavez has also said that China's presence in South America is vital to the development of the region. Talks are in the air about a potential trade agreement between China and some resource-rich South American countries.

POINT Supporters of regional trade agreement between China (and/or ASEAN) and Venezuela believe that President Chavez is doing nothing more than diversifying the market for his crude oil in order to avoid excessive dependence on the United States. The same argument, they claim, is made about other resource-rich Latin American countries. Furthermore, analysts believe that since this is Asia's century, with China leading the world in terms of growth and development, it only makes sense that Latin America should do just as American and European companies are doing—rushing to China and India.

COUNTERPOINT Opponents argue that this is nothing but an act of revenge by dictator Hugo Chavez. They believe that Chavez does not have the technology to

(continued)

South American Oil Giant Looks Beyond Traditional Trade Partners (continued)

extract the heavy Venezuelan crude. They believe that only Western oil companies (not even the Chinese) have the needed technology and financial resources to extract Venezuelan oil. They also add that from an economic geography standpoint, proximity to the always oil-hungry United States makes most sense.

What Do *You* Think?

Use the Internet or other sources to research this issue. Which argument would you support? Develop your own line of reasoning.

INTERPRETING GLOBAL BUSINESS NEWS

Financial news is everywhere in the popular press and media. How do you interpret the following examples of financial news related to the concepts in this chapter?

1) When you read business news, you will note that the Doha Round of trade negotiations have been stalled, partly reflecting the fact that both the United States and the European Union are unwilling to cut agricultural subsidies to their farmers. Unless the cuts are made, other countries, especially the emerging market economies, will be unwilling to further reduce tariff barriers in other sectors. The United States has decided to use bilateral (e.g., with Colombia) or other forms of regional trade instead. What do you think?

2) The ASEAN expanded its free trade agreements: with India and South Korea in 2010 and will do that with China by 2015. Yet, there is no talk of an ASEAN-U.S. free trade agreement. What do these developments mean to global business?

3) Iceland is making moves to join the European Union after the economic devastation it suffered in the global credit crisis. The EU is favorably considering its case, provided Iceland meets the basic requirements of becoming a member of the EU. Is Iceland's case different from Turkey's case?

4) The Democratic Republic of Congo, which is larger than the whole of Western Europe, is rich in a variety of mineral resources. Yet, press reports indicate the country is in dire straits. Although the DR Congo is part of a Central African Trade bloc, why has the country's economic development been stunted?

PORTFOLIO PROJECTS

Explore Your Own Case in Point: Understanding How Regional Integration Blocs Affect Your Chosen Company

After reading this chapter you should be prepared to answer some basic questions about your favorite company.

1) Identify regional trading blocs with which your chosen company operates. Identify the benefits that your company gains because it is part of those trading blocs. Is your company taking advantage of the situation?

2) Which trading bloc is most attractive for your company, and why? Explain the importance of that bloc in terms of economic geography (i.e., business density, distance and infrastructure, and intra-regional trade barriers).

3) If you could advise your company about the benefits of regional trading blocs, which trading bloc would you recommend that the company consider next? Why?

4) Would your company be better off under a system of multilateral trade liberalization like the WTO, or with bilateral or regional trading blocs?

Develop an International Strategy for Your Own Small Business: Targeting Your Business to a Specific Regional Trading Bloc

Identifying a target country for your company will be easier if you first seek a free trade area or regional economic zone that includes your target country. If your target country is part of a free trade area or regionally integrated community, you will receive preferential access to those markets. This could significantly lessen the burden of entering foreign markets and also make it easier for you to identify your target country. The following questions will assist you in this process:

1) First, research whether or not your home country is a member of any regional economic integration group(s). If yes, what are those regional economic integration group(s)?

2) Assume that your home country is a member of two or three different regional economic integration group(s). Your next job is to determine which of those groups most appeal to you. This could be based on factors such as proximity to your home country, cultural similarity, or market potential. Which regional group will you be most comfortable with from a business potential point of view?

3) Finally, after identifying the economic integration group of your choice, pick one country from that group as your target country. Again, your choice of country will require careful analysis. You will need to ask: Why country *A*, and not country *B*? The answer to this question will enable you to make sound international business decisions.

Data sources: The World Bank: www.worldbank.org; The World Trade Organization: www.wto.org; Transparency International: www.transparency.org; United States Department of State: www.state.gov/r/pa/ei/bgn/; United States Central Intelligence Agency: www.cia.gov/library/publications/the-world-factbook/docs/profileguide.html.

CHAPTER NOTES

[1] T. Barber, "Mediterranean Union: Skepticism Abounds over Value of New Club," *Financial Times*, July 11, 2008, p. 3.

[2] J. Gaspar, L. Bierman, R. Hise, J. Kolari, T. Arreola-Risa, and M. Smith, *Introduction to Business* (Boston: Houghton-Mifflin Co., 2006), pp. 67–76.

[3] U. Deichmann and I. Gill, "The Economic Geography of Regional Integration," *Finance & Development* 45, no. 4, December 2008, pp. 45–47.

[4] The World Bank, "Reshaping World Geography," *World Development Report 2009.*

[5] U. Deichmann and I. Gill, "The Economic Geography of Regional Integration," *Finance & Development* 45, no.4 (December 2008): p. 47.

[6] P. Collier, *The Bottom Billion: Why the Poorest Countries Are Failing and What Can Be Done About It,* (New York: Oxford University Press, 2007).

[7] T. Whewell, "The Chinese are Coming," BBC News, June 25, 2011.

[8] P. Lee, "China Has Congo Copper Headache," *China Business,* March 11, 2010.

[9] J. Bhagwati, *Termites in the Trading System,* (New York: Oxford University Press, 2008).

[10] D. Gros, "Turkey and The EU Budget: Prospects and Issues," First Annual LUISS-CEPS Workshop on "Turkey and the EU: What Prospects?", 2004.

[11] International Monetary Fund database (Washington DC).

[12] V. Schmidt, "A 'Menu Europe' Will Prove far More Palatable," *Financial Times*, July 22, 2008.

CH

4

The International Flow of Funds and Exchange Rates

Currencies around the world.

After studying this chapter, you should be able to:

LO-1 Explain the balance of payments for a country.

LO-2 Describe the foreign exchange market and its components.

LO-3 Discuss the development of international monetary systems.

LO-4 Explain exchange rate changes over time.

LO-5 Forecast exchange rates using different methodologies.

CULTURAL PERSPECTIVE

The Dollar as Safe Haven and Reserve Currency

The global economic and financial crises of 2008–2009 were the worst since the Great Depression of the 1930s. Collectively dubbed the "Great Recession," these crises were marked by crashing financial markets; wealth losses in the trillions of dollars; failures of banking, securities, and business firms; unprecedented government stimulus packages increasing deficit spending; record low government interest rates; rising unemployment; and declines in world trade. The credit bubble that inflated financial markets, and excessively expanded home lending in the United States and some European countries, had finally burst.

During the crises, the U.S. dollar rose substantially in value against most other currencies. As Exhibit 4.1 shows, the euro was steadily rising in value against the dollar from $1.30 per euro in early-2007 to $1.60 by mid-2008. But in August of 2008, the euro began to fall in value against the dollar; it reached a low of nearly $1.25 in October 2008 when financial markets collapsed. In 2007–2008 the dollar's value rose because investors around the world were selling stocks, commodities, and other risky assets, and, in turn, purchasing dollars.

The rationale for holding dollars in the recent crises was twofold. First, the dollar was perceived as an asset that could weather global financial storms due to the belief that the United States would endure the crises. In effect, the market was signaling that it had confidence in the U.S. dollar. Some experts question this confidence in view of the large U.S. trade deficits that have persisted for decades. U.S. imports exceed exports by an increasing margin, and borrowing from import nations financed the resulting deficits. Rising foreign debt will increase the U.S. debt burden, which will cause lenders to demand a risk premium for increasing credit risk. As a result, this higher risk should cause the dollar to decrease in value; however, because the crises caused falling world interest rates, which in turn would tend to lower the debt burden of the United States, the market perceived that the United States could tolerate its trade deficit debts at that time.

Second, the U.S. dollar is a reserve asset in many countries. Governments and financial institutions hold dollars to maintain liquidity, as they can be easily used to buy other assets around the world. Many products traded in global markets, such as gold, oil, and other commodities, are denominated in dollars. Furthermore, international bonds and bank loans are also often denominated in dollars, a practice that lowers debt costs in many instances. For these reasons, about two-thirds of total foreign exchange reserves of countries are held in U.S. dollars. Hence, the dual advantages of safe-haven and reserve-currency status explain the rising dollar value in the recent crises.

When will it be clear that the crises have subsided? One approach is to monitor the value of the dollar. As it returns to pre-crises levels, it can inferred that the crises have passed. Will the dollar continue as a safe haven and reserve currency in future crises? Some critics argue that large U.S. government deficits may

EXHIBIT 4.1 THE DOLLAR TO EURO EXCHANGE RATE: JANUARY 2007–JUNE 2009

Source: Data based on the website of the Pacific Exchange Rate Service (http://fx.sauder.ubc.ca/data.html).

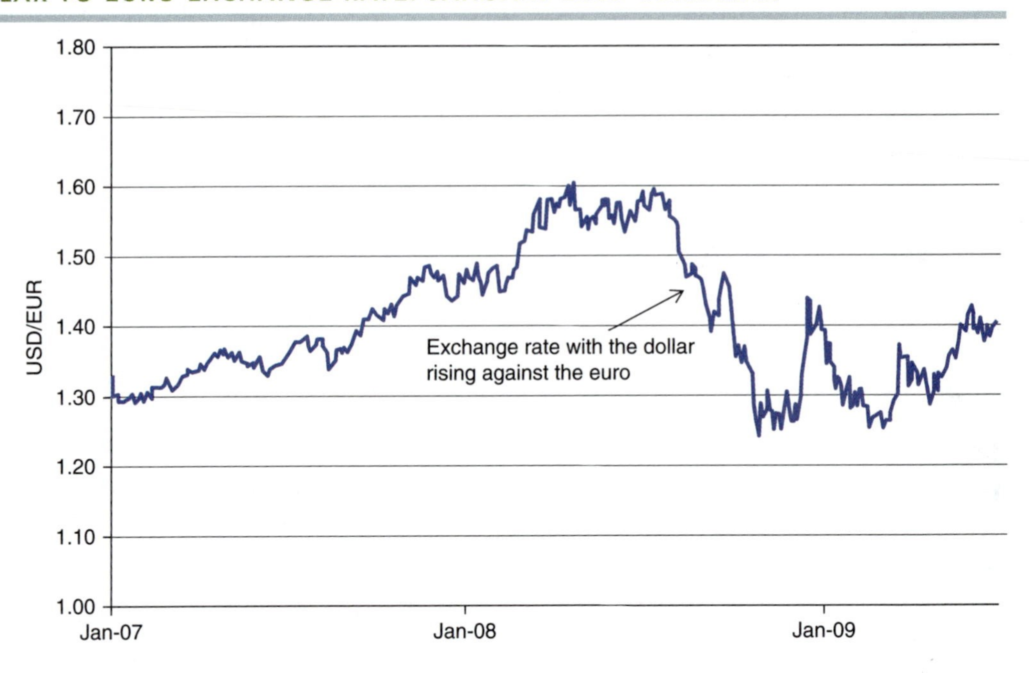

decrease others' willingness to accumulate dollars and lead to an end to its leadership in global currency markets. However, Congress has been actively debating ways to reduce the U.S. budget deficit in the future. The future of the dollar will be interesting to watch.

Introduction

World economic and financial markets have become increasingly integrated due to steadily expanding international trade over the past 100 years. Balance of payments accounts document trade and finance interactions between countries; they show exports, imports, trade finance, foreign investment, and other important trends in international activities between countries. In this regard, consumers, businesses, and governments must convert from one currency to another at market exchange rates to make payments for internationally traded goods, services, and financial instruments. For example, a firm in the United States would need to convert dollars to euros to purchase supplies from European firms.

Major changes in the world monetary system have had an impact on foreign exchange (also called forex) markets over the years. The gold standard for benchmarking or pegging currencies was replaced in 1973 by a flexible exchange rate system with freely floating currency values determined by market supply and demand.[1] Resulting currency fluctuations led to a variety of efforts by countries to manage currency values, including pegging, dollarization, and adoption of regional currencies such as the European euro.

Currency values can change for many reasons. One factor is different price levels in different countries for the same goods and services. Price imbalances could be due to mispricing or due to differential inflation across countries. Another factor is varying interest rates across countries. According to parity theories discussed later in this chapter, price levels and debt costs should be the same in different countries after considering exchange rates. If not, exchange rates should change to make prices more uniform across countries. Additionally, the economic prospects of countries can affect their currency values.

In this chapter we will discuss international trade patterns, examine the foreign exchange market, and discuss the behavior of international currencies; we will also explain how foreign exchange rates can be forecast.

The Balance of International Payments

LO-1
Explain the balance of payments for a country.

To fully appreciate the global nature of business, it is important to have a basic understanding of a country's balance of payments. **Balance of payments (BOP)** refers to a statement of account that summarizes all transactions between the residents of one country and the rest of the world for a given period of time, usually one year. A country's balance of payments is an objective standard that shows how well the country's economy and government policies are performing. Since BOP is based on a system of credits and debits, the balance of payments must always balance. BOP is generally split into two major components with major business implications: (1) the current account, and (2) the financial account.[2]

balance of payments (BOP) a statement of account that shows all transactions between the residents of one country and the rest of the world for a given period of time

Analyzing BOP statistics is based upon "flow of funds." In flow of funds analysis, money moving into a country is a credit (plus sign), while money leaving the same country is a debit (negative sign). Exhibit 4.2 provides a simplified version of U.S. BOP for the period 2000–2010 period; the signs on numbers indicate whether funds leave or enter the United States.

The Current Account

current account the activities of consumers and businesses in the economy with respect to the trade balance, services balance, income balance, and net transfers

The **current account** of the BOP is largely driven by activities of consumers and business. It consists of four subaccounts: (a) trade (or goods) balance, (b) services balance, (c) income balance, and (d) net transfers. These four components add up to give the current account balance.

EXHIBIT 4.2 U.S. BALANCE OF PAYMENTS (IN BILLIONS OF DOLLARS)

(Credits +; debits –)	2000	2001	2002	2003	2004	2005	2006	2007	2008	2009	2010
Current account											
Exports of goods and services and income receipts	**1,421**	**1,295**	**1,258**	**1,340**	**1,572**	**1,816**	**2,133**	**2,460**	**2,591**	**2,116**	**2,497**
Goods	771	718	685	715	806	892	1,015	1,138	1,276	1,046	1,289
Services	298	286	292	304	353	389	436	504	549	509	546
Income receipts	350	290	280	320	413	535	682	818	764	561	662
Imports of goods and services and income payments	**–1,780**	**–1,629**	**–1,652**	**–1,790**	**–2,115**	**–2,459**	**–2,846**	**–3,072**	**–3,168**	**–2,405**	**–2,829**
Imports of goods and services	–1,450	–1,370	–1,399	–1,515	–1,769	–1,996	–2,212	–2,344	–2,522	–1,933	–2,330
Goods	–1,226	–1,148	–1,168	–1,264	–1,477	–1,683	–1,863	–1,969	–2,117	–1,562	–1,936
Services	–223	–221	–230	–250	–291	–313	–348	–375	–405	–371	–394
Income payments	–329	–259	–253	–275	–346	–462	–634	–728	–646	–472	–499
Net transfers	**–58**	**–64**	**–64**	**–71**	**–88**	**–105**	**–91**	**–115**	**–128**	**–130**	**–137**
Statistical discrepancy	–59	–13	–39	–7	97	36	–1	64	200	225	235
Memoranda:											
Balance on goods	–454	–429	–482	–549	–671	–790	–847	–830	–840	–516	–647
Balance on services	74	64	61	53	61	75	86	129	144	138	151
Balance on goods and services	–379	–365	–421	–495	–609	–715	–760	–701	–695	–378	–496
Balance on income	21	31	27	45	67	72	48	90	118	89	163
Unilateral current transfers, net	–58	–64	–64	–71	–88	–105	–91	–115	–128	–130	–137
Balance on current account	**–417**	**–398**	**–459**	**–521**	**–631**	**–748**	**–803**	**–726**	**–706**	**–420**	**–470**

Source: U.S. Bureau of Economic Analysis (www.bea.gov).

The bottom of Exhibit 4.2 gives the U.S. BOP numbers for these four accounts in the period 2000 to 2010. As shown in the last line of Exhibit 4.2 ("Balance on current account"), the United States has typically run a large current account deficit over the past few decades, with a decrease in this deficit in recent years from $803 billion in 2006 to $470 in 2010.

Trade Balance The **trade balance** is the net of merchandise exports (+ sign as incoming dollars come in when merchandise, such as a Dell computer, is exported) and merchandise imports (– sign as dollars leave the country to pay for imports, such as Toyota brand cars).

The business news media pays a great deal of attention to the trade balance—more attention than may be warranted. When a country imports more than it exports, it has a merchandise trade deficit or **trade deficit.** The trade balance provides an indication of how competitive an economy is via its primary trade partners. In 2008, the U.S. goods trade deficit was $840 billion. Exhibit 4.3 lists the top ten countries that were our major export and import trade partners with the United States in the year 2011. It is worthwhile to know our major trade partners, as they are the countries with whom we conduct most merchandise trade business.

trade balance
the net of merchandise exports and merchandise imports

trade deficit
when merchandise imports exceed merchandise exports for a country

services balance
the net of exports of services and imports of services

income balance
the net of investment income from abroad and investment payments to foreigners

Services Balance The **services balance** (shipping, airlines, consulting, insurance, banking, tourism, software development, etc.) is the net of exports of services (+ sign when foreigners use services in a country) and import of services (– sign when foreign services are used). As in the case of the trade balance, a surplus in the services balance will indicate that a country is competitive in its service industry. What can be concluded about the overall competitiveness of the U.S. service sector from Exhibit 4.2? The United States is primarily a service economy, with intangible services provided for customers in other countries comprising more of its exports. Software companies like Microsoft (United States), SAP (Germany), and Infosys (India) are major exporters of software services, each contributing to their respective countries' net trade in services.

Income Balance The third subaccount in the current account of BOP is **income balance,** which is the net of investment income from abroad (+ sign reflects earnings from overseas investment) and investment income paid to foreigners (– sign indicates payments are sent overseas).

EXHIBIT 4.3 TOP TEN COUNTRIES TRADING WITH THE UNITED STATES

Dollar values of imports plus exports (year-to-date total; December 2011). These countries accounted for 62.8 percent of total trade with the United States

	Country	Billions of U.S. dollars
1.	Canada	597.4
2.	China	503.2
3.	Mexico	460.6
4.	Japan	195.0
5.	Germany	147.5
6.	United Kingdom	107.1
7.	South Korea	100.1
8.	Brazil	74.3
9.	France	67.8
10.	Taiwan	67.2

Source: United States Census Bureau www.census.gov/foreign-trade/statistics/highlights/top/top1112yr.html

Balance of Transfers Finally, the **balance of transfers** is the net of transfer payments between countries based on outflows (– sign means that a payment is going abroad as foreign aid, retirement benefits, etc.) and inflows (+ sign reflects repayment of foreign aid loans, etc.).

Current Account Balance The sum of these four subaccounts equals the current account balance, which is more important than the trade balance discussed earlier in the chapter. Whether the current account balance is positive (surplus) or negative (deficit) is important because it provides a measure of the financing needs of a particular country. A country with a current account surplus is called a capital surplus country. For example, China, France, Japan, Singapore, and Switzerland have consistently had current account surpluses over recent years. These countries maintain surplus funds, which they invest abroad. The United States, in contrast, has had large current account deficits each year, which implies that it will need to attract capital from abroad in order to finance current account deficits. If foreign capital will not be available to finance the U.S. current account deficit, it can be predicted that the dollar will become weaker and U.S. interest rates will increase in order to attract foreign capital. Countries with current account surpluses generally finance countries with current account deficits.

The Financial Account

The **financial account** describes the second half of a country's balance of payments, which shows how the country's current account balance is financed. Exhibit 4.4 shows that foreign-owned assets in the United States average around $1 trillion per year from 2000 to 2008. Hence, foreign capital finances the large U.S. current account deficit. Keeping current account deficits for long periods of time is unsustainable for most countries. Foreign countries (investors) will be less willing to continue investing in current account deficit countries for extended periods of time because of perceived risk of nonpayment of debt. In this case investors will require a **risk premium** that increases interest rates of the borrowing country.[3]

The financial account of the BOP consists of three subaccounts: (1) U.S.-owned assets abroad; (2) foreign-owned assets in the United States; and (3) net financial derivatives. Each of these accounts reports the inflow (+ sign) or outflow (– sign) of funds to and from the country being analyzed. The former two accounts—U.S.-owned assets abroad and foreign-owned assets—are greatly affected by **foreign direct investment (FDI)** and security investments across national borders.

TOBIAS SCHWARZ/Reuters/Landov

German Chancellor Angela Merkel and Former Greek Prime Minister George Papandreous resolving problems in the 2008–2009 financial crisis.

balance of transfers
the net of transfer payments going overseas and inflows from abroad

financial account
consists of domestic-country-owned assets abroad, foreign-owned assets in the domestic country, and net financial derivatives

risk premium
the added return required by investors for risk associated with a security or asset

foreign direct investment (FDI)
encompasses purchases of fixed assets (such as factories and equipment) abroad used in the manufacture and sales of goods and services

EXHIBIT 4.4 U.S. FINANCIAL ACCOUNT (IN BILLIONS OF DOLLARS)

(Credits + ; debits –)	2000	2001	2002	2003	2004	2005	2006	2007	2008	2009
U.S.-owned assets abroad	–560	–382	–294	–325	–1,000	–546	–1,285	–1,472	0	–238
Foreign-owned assets in the United States	1,038	782	795	858	1,533	1,247	2,065	2,129	534	435
Financial derivatives, net	n.a.	n.a.	n.a.	n.a.	n.a.	n.a.	29	6	–29	n.a.

Source: U.S. Bureau of Economic Analysis.

Foreign Direct Investment FDI encompasses the purchases of fixed assets (such as factories and equipment) abroad used in the manufacture and sales of goods and services for local consumption or exports. Acquisitions of a foreign company (including those being privatized), creation of new manufacturing or research facilities abroad, and expansion of an existing plant in a foreign country are all examples of foreign direct investments. The flow of FDI is dictated by opportunities to earn profit overseas.

There are thousands of examples of FDI that one can relate to in the world around us. In the automobile industry, for example, there has been significant FDI inflow into the United States. Mercedes Benz (Germany) has a plant manufacturing M-Class SUVs in Alabama; Honda (Japan) manufactures the Accord in Ohio; and Hyundai (South Korea) has a plant in Alabama. Similarly, General Motors and Ford have car-manufacturing operations in several countries overseas.

FDI decisions have important implications to consumers, businesses, government, and society. Consumers gain through greater choice of products (or services) at competitive prices, businesses face increased competition as well as profit opportunities, governments reap additional tax revenues, and society benefits through increased employment opportunities and corporate social responsibility.

Security Investments Security investments also have a significant impact on the BOP's financial account. Financial capital flows between countries in search of higher rates of return on foreign stocks and bonds. Often, individuals and firms hold foreign financial assets in order to diversify their investments beyond domestic stocks and bonds only. During the technology boom years of the mid- to late-1990s, massive inflows of funds for investment in U.S. stocks occurred as foreign investors tried to take advantage of the perceived profit opportunities. Capital flows generally represent investments for the long term (more than one year). Central banks, government agencies, and large financial institutions make other financial investments. Central banks (such as the U.S. Federal Reserve and Germany's Deutsche Bundesbank) hold foreign exchange, or currencies, of major countries (U.S. dollar, euro, yen, etc.) as part of their reserves in addition to their local currency. To earn interest on their foreign exchange reserves, central banks deposit some of their reserves with foreign central banks. Certain government agencies (e.g., Export Import Bank and USAID, which are involved in international lending activities) make foreign loans to pursue foreign policy objectives (e.g., economic and military). In addition, large financial institutions finance international trade, manage cash for international corporations, and make international loans to corporations and foreign governments. These security investment inflows and outflows of funds affect a country's BOP.

statistical discrepancy reconciles any imbalance between the current account and financial account to ensure that all debit and credit entries in the balance of payments statement sum to zero

Statistical Discrepancy Lastly, there is a **statistical discrepancy** line item in BOP statistics. While the financial account balance is intended to offset the imbalance in the current account, the offset is not complete. The statistical discrepancy line reconciles any remaining imbalance to ensure that all debit and credit entries in the BOP statement sum to zero. This line captures statistical inconsistencies in the recording of the credit and debit entries as well as illegal trade.

World Trade and the Balance of Payments

Exhibit 4.5 shows world trade patterns by selected region and economy during the years 2000–2008. According to this exhibit, Asian countries' exports are growing the fastest with China normally expanding its exports at a rate of about 20 percent per year (except for the decrease to 8.5 percent in 2007). India is second in export expansion at around 13 percent growth per year. The United States has slowed its import growth from 4 percent to only 0.5 percent and has increased its exports in recent years. This helps to explain its declining current account balance from 2006 to 2008. Nonetheless, the United States has typically been a net importer of goods and services in the past, which explains its recent, large, current account deficit. Europe is a net exporter with exports and imports growing at an average of 3.5 and 3.0 percent, respectively. Some countries such as Norway are net importers, but most European Union countries are net exporters. These world trade patterns help to explain the U.S. BOP accounts, especially which countries are lending funds to the United States to finance its growing current account deficit.

Over the past 65 years, the growth of international trade has been driven by world economic growth, as well as the elimination of barriers to trade such as tariffs, nontariff

EXHIBIT 4.5 GROWTH IN WORLD MERCHANDISE TRADE BY SELECTED REGION AND ECONOMY, 2000–2008 (ANNUAL PERCENTAGE CHANGE)

Exports				Imports		
2000–08	**2007**	**2008**		**2000–08**	**2007**	**2008**
5.0	**6.0**	**1.5**	**World**	**5.0**	**6.0**	**1.5**
2.5	5.0	1.5	North America	3.0	2.0	−2.5
0.0	2.0	−6.0	Canada	3.5	5.0	0.5
2.0	1.5	−5.0	Mexico	3.0	4.0	0.5
3.5	6.5	6.0	United States	3.0	1.0	−3.5
5.5	3.5	0.5	South and Central America	8.5	17.5	13.5
3.5	4.0	0.0	Europe	3.0	4.0	−1.5
3.5	3.5	−0.5	European Union (27)	3.0	3.5	−1.5
1.0	1.5	0.0	Norway	5.0	9.5	2.0
3.5	7.0	1.5	Switzerland	2.0	5.0	2.5
7.5	7.5	2.5	Commonwealth of Independent States (CIS)	17.0	20.0	16.5
10.0	11.5	5.5	Asia	8.0	8.0	4.5
2.5	2.5	5.5	Australia	9.0	11.0	10.0
20.5	19.5	8.5	China	16.0	14.0	4.0
−4.0	−20.5	−11.0	Hong Kong, China	3.0	7.0	−2.0
12.5	13.0	7.5	India	13.5	16.0	14.0
6.0	9.5	2.0	Japan	2.5	1.5	−2.0
8.0	8.5	4.5	Six East Asian traders[a]	5.5	5.0	4.0
5.0	**6.0**	**1.5**	**World**	**5.0**	**6.0**	**1.5**
2.5	5.0	1.5	North America	3.0	2.0	−2.5

[a] Hong Kong, China, Republic of Korea, Malaysia, Singapore, Taiwan, and Thailand.

Source: World Trade Organization International Trade Statistics, www.chinaglobaltrade.com/fact/growth-volume-world-merchandise-trade-selected-region-and-economy-2000-2008.

import and export quotas, and other restrictions. However, the World Trade Organization (WTO) observed that in 2009, world trade declined by 12.2 percent, the largest decline since World War II. In addition, global exports dipped 20 percent from their peak in 2008 to the lowest in 2009. The global economic and financial crises in 2008 and 2009 were primarily responsible for this sharp downturn in world trade activities. As economic recovery began, the WTO expected that world trade would rebound and grow by 9.5 percent in 2010. Forecasters anticipated that economic development in China, India, and other emerging market countries would dramatically boost world trade and thereby affect countries' BOP accounts in the years ahead.[4]

REALITY CHECK LO-1

Have you ever thought you had some money left over but did not? You started with $20 in cash that was gradually spent on coffee and a few everyday items you picked up at the store. When you went to see a movie at a local theatre, you unexpectedly did not have enough cash left to buy a ticket and had to borrow some cash from a friend. How was your current account and financial account affected by these transactions, specifically balance of payments? How can you explain the shortage of cash?

LO-2
Describe the foreign exchange market and its components.

The Foreign Exchange Market

There are almost 200 countries in the world, most of which are engaged in international trade, and about 150 different currencies that are used to make international payments for goods and services. Due to the central role of currencies in payments, we next turn our attention to the marketplace for buying and selling currencies.

RUNGROJ YONGRIT/EPA/Newscom

Trading in global forex markets.

The exchange of currencies takes place in **foreign exchange markets** (often referred to as **forex**), which consist of a network of international banks (who work with exporters and importers) and currency traders (who buy, sell, and speculate in currencies). Over $1.5 trillion dollars worth of currencies are traded daily. The three largest foreign exchange markets are in London, New York, and Tokyo followed by Hong Kong, Singapore, and Bahrain. Each of these centers caters to the foreign exchange needs of certain regions of the world. London is the largest foreign exchange market; it largely serves Europe and Africa, and handles over 30 percent of the world's daily transactions. New York City handles about 20 percent of transactions and meets the needs of the Western Hemisphere. Tokyo services about 8 percent of the transactions for Asia and Tokyo competes with Hong Kong and Singapore. Bahrain primarily covers the Middle East, and smaller foreign exchange markets exist in almost all countries.

The foreign exchange market is a 24-hour market with international financial institutions connected by means of sophisticated telecommunications systems that enable instant, real-time exchange rate quotations. The largest 20 banks in the world handle about 50 percent of all forex transactions; the largest forex traders are Citibank, JP Morgan Chase (United States) and Deutsche Bank (Germany). The function of the foreign exchange market is to facilitate international trade (in goods and services) and investment (FDI, security investment, and short-term money market flows). Hence, there is a close relationship between the balance of payments and foreign exchange markets.

foreign exchange markets
a global network of international banks and currency traders that trade different countries' currencies

exchange rate
the price at which one currency can be converted to another currency

independent floating exchange rate system
system that sets the values of major currencies based on their demand and supply in world currency markets

managed floating exchange rate system
system that determines the value of some currencies partly by demand and supply in the foreign exchange market, and partly by active government intervention in the foreign exchange market

fixed exchange rate system
system in which the country pegs its currency at a fixed rate to a major currency or basket of currencies, while the exchange rate fluctuates within a narrow margin around a central rate

spot market
exchange that trades currencies on a real-time basis for immediate delivery

The Exchange Rate

An **exchange rate** is nothing more than a price at which one currency can be converted to another currency. A U.S. company making sales in Europe and being paid euros will normally convert euros to dollars for deposit in its U.S. bank account. In a free-market-oriented foreign exchange market, major currency values are determined by the demand for and supply of currencies; this is called the **independent floating exchange rate system**. For example, exchange rates between the U.S. dollar, euro, and yen are market determined. The values of some currencies (e.g., Indonesian rupiah, Thai baht, Russian ruble, Indian rupee, and Singapore dollar) are determined by the **managed floating exchange rate system**. In this system, the currency's value depends partly upon demand and supply in the foreign exchange market, and partly on active government intervention in the foreign exchange market (by means of central bank purchases and sales of its own currencies to manage currencies).

Some countries conduct the bulk of their international transactions with a few major trade partners and for this reason link their currencies to those of the major trade partners (e.g., Chinese yuan, Malaysian ringgit, and Saudi Arabian riyal). This system, called the **fixed exchange rate system**, is one in which the country pegs its currency (formally or informally) at a fixed rate to a major currency or basket of currencies and the exchange rate fluctuates within a narrow margin around a central rate.[5]

Components of the Foreign Exchange Market

The forex market consists of spot, forward, and futures markets. The **spot market** trades currencies on a real time basis for immediate delivery. For example, a British firm may need dollars to pay for U.S. imports. It can work with banks in London to exchange pounds for dollars to make this payment. Large banks normally carry an inventory of frequently-used currencies in international transactions and can make electronic payment transfers.

Banks earn a transaction fee for forex services. If one travels to another country and converts local currency to a foreign currency, the bid (buy) and ask (sell) prices of the foreign currency will be posted in banks. The difference between bid and ask prices for

ETHICAL PERSPECTIVES

Is the Chinese Renminbi Undervalued?

Many countries, particularly in the West, have complained that China's currency—the renminbi (RMB), or yuan—is undervalued. Since 1995, the RMB has been pegged within a narrow band at 8.28 RMB per USD. How could a fixed exchange rate policy be an ethical issue?

The famous Scottish philosopher and political economist Adam Smith in the 18th century coined the term "beggar-thy-neighbor," meaning to implement economic policies that benefit one country at the expense of other countries. Many business firms, policymakers, and others in the United States and Europe, have voiced concern that the undervalued yuan is decreasing their competitiveness in world trade markets. It is argued that China's huge trade surplus is driven by underpriced exports, which causes exports in the United States and Europe to be overpriced. These price imbalances help to explain the massive current account deficits between Chinese and Western industrial economies. Who gets disadvantaged? Not only exporting firms in the United States and Europe, but also people who lose their jobs to Chinese workers.

The trillions of dollars held by the Chinese government due to exports to the West are largely recycled into purchases of treasury securities and government bonds in the United States and other countries, too. These inflows of funds have kept interest rates low in the West. In turn, some critics suggest that the housing bubble in the United States and Europe was fueled by low interest rates and large flows of bond funds, and that the housing bubble led to the 2008 and 2009 financial and economic crises. In response to these crises, interest rates in the United States and other developed countries sank so low that there was no room for central banks to cut rates and stimulate their sluggish economies—a predicament known as a liquidity trap.

Contrary to these arguments, China contends that lower wage rates, rapid economic growth, and other factors have contributed more to its competitiveness in world trade than potential undervaluation of the yuan. Moreover, foreign investors have been pouring capital into China to invest in its economic growth, which had accumulated in China's holdings of international reserves of dollars, euros, and other currencies. Lower interest rates and wage rates have reduced worldwide inflation and lowered operating and financing costs of business firms, thereby increasing profits. Moreover, consumers in the West have benefited from low-cost consumer products exported from China. If the yuan was floated in world currency markets, these advantages would be reversed.

Accusing China of "unfair trade" practices, some U.S. politicians have proposed imposing tariffs on Chinese imports if the country does not change its currency policy. However, protectionist proposals of this kind are a two-edged sword, as China could retaliate with tariffs against U.S. imports. In general, it is likely that all parties will lose in a trade war such as this. The U.S. current account deficit may not change due to increased imports from other emerging market countries, China's economic growth may be slowed to some degree due to falling exports, and, China might decide to maintain its fixed exchange rate policy to further exacerbate the situation.

According to some experts, the most favorable outcome would be a gradual revaluation of the yuan with an eventual goal of a managed floating exchange rate system. In this way, both China and the United States would stand to gain. Revaluation of the yuan would reduce the overly rapid growth of the Chinese economy. In the United States, reining in government deficit spending and increasing saving would help to reduce the risk of inflation that could trigger further current account deficits due to high domestic prices. In these ways, the two countries could work together to ease trade tensions and currency parities.

QUESTIONS:

1. Why is an undervalued Chinese yuan an ethical issue? Who benefits? Who suffers?
2. What would be a workable solution to the yuan valuation debate? Is there a solution that would allow all parties to benefit?

Sources:

Gene Hsin Chang, and Qin Shao, "How Much Is the Chinese Currency Undervalued? A Quantitative Estimation," *China Economic Review* 15 (2004), pp. 366–371;
Dilip K. Das, "The Evolution of the Renminbi Yuan and the Protracted Debated on Its Undervaluation: An Integrated Review, *Journal of Asian Economics* 20 (2009), pp. 570–579;
Morris Goldstein, and Nicholas Lardy, "China's Exchange Rate Policy Dilemma," American Economic Review 96 (2006), pp. 422–426;
Anthony J. Makin, "Does China's Huge External Surplus Imply an Undervalued Renminbi?," *China and the World Economy* 15 (2007), pp. 89–102.

a currency, or **bid-ask spread**, represents the transaction fee earned by the bank. **Direct quotes** give the prices of a foreign currency in dollars (or the number of dollars per one unit of foreign currency). **Indirect quotes** are the reciprocal of the direct quote, or the prices of a dollar in foreign currency terms.

As an example, the spot rate for the euro may be quoted at 1.40 EUR/USD, which is a direct quote indicating that €1 = $1.40 (i.e., one euro costs 1.40 dollars). The indirect quote would be 1/1.40 = 0.71 USD/EUR, or $1 = €0.71 (i.e., one dollar costs 0.71 euros). Assume that the spot rate increased from 1.40 EUR/USD a few weeks ago to 1.45 EUR/USD today. This change means that each euro can now buy more dollars than it could a few weeks ago. That is, the euro appreciated in value against the dollar, or conversely the dollar depreciated in value against the euro. In addition, if the bank sells euros for 1.40 EUR/USD (ask price) and buys euros for 1.35 EUR/USD (bid price), the bid/ask spread in percentage terms is $(1.40 - 1.35)/1.40 \times 100 = 3.6$ percent. Hence, the bank converting the currency is earning 3.6 percent on EUR/USD trades to cover its expenses and required profit margin.

The **forward market** enables purchases and sales of currencies in the future with prices (known as the **forward rate**) established at a previous time. The forward market is an informal over-the-counter (OTC) market run by banking institutions. For example, suppose that a European firm has contracted to pay for some imported goods from a U.S. firm in dollars. The European firm is not responsible to make payment until the goods arrive in Europe in one month via ship. It can use a forward contract with a bank to lock in the EUR/USD exchange rate. In this way the European firm can know what its expenses are in euros, and not be exposed to exchange rate risks associated with fluctuating exchange rates over time. Exchange rate quotations can be checked daily in newspapers, a bank will have the latest spot and forward rates. Forward rates are regularly quoted for 30, 90, and 180 days in the future.

The difference between forward and spot exchange rates reflects expectations by investors about future exchange rate movements. For instance, if the spot rate for the euro is 1.40 EUR/USD and 60-day forward rate is 1.50 EUR/USD, the market expects that the dollar will depreciate against the euro in the next 60 days. Because the dollar is selling for less in the forward market per euro than in the spot market, foreign exchange dealers say that the dollar is selling at a **discount** in the 60-day forward market (relative to the spot market). If the dollar was expected to appreciate in the 60-day forward market against the euro, it would be selling at a **premium**. Again, firms use the forward market to lock in future exchange rates and ensure against uncertain future currency movements. This insurance reduces their future exchange rate risk and, therefore, is considered a **hedge** that lowers risk. Because it is likely that the actual future spot rate will not exactly equal the earlier forward rate, a hedge is not precise.[6]

bid-ask spread
the difference between bid and ask prices of a currency; the transaction fee earned by the bank

direct quotes
prices of a foreign currency in dollars, or the number of dollars per one unit of foreign currency)

indirect quotes
the reciprocal of the direct quote, or the prices of a dollar (for example) in foreign currency terms

forward market
exchange that enables purchases and sales of currencies in the future with prices (or the forward rate) established at a previous time

forward rate
the price at an earlier time of a currency in terms of another currency established for future delivery in the forward market

discount
in the forward market, the selling of a currency at a spot rate that is less than the forward rate

premium
in the forward market, the selling of a currency at a spot rate that is more than the forward rate

hedge
insurance that reduces future risk

REALITY CHECK LO-2

Browse the Internet and find the spot rate for EUR/USD. If the one-month forward rate was 1.50 EUR/USD, would the dollar be selling at a discount or premium relative to the spot rate?

International Monetary Systems

LO-3
Discuss the development of international monetary systems.

Over time, various international monetary systems have developed to facilitate international trade. In this regard, governments around the world have worked together to promote stable exchange rates and world trade.

Money and Inflation

inflation
an increase in the prices of goods and services caused by the supply of money exceeding the demand for goods and services

gold standard
monetary system that pegs currency values to the market value of gold

Bretton Woods Agreement
the 1944 decision to establish a global currency system with the U.S. dollar pegged at a fixed rate of exchange to gold, and the currencies of 43 other countries fixed to the dollar

Many governments have used money to meet political goals of stimulating economic growth and providing employment for citizens. Printing more money could increase economic activity. With more money on hand, people can purchase more goods and services and the economy can benefit, at least for a while. This political use of money was not without its pitfalls, however; excess supplies of money could cause **inflation**. That is, when the supply of money exceeds the demand for goods and services, the prices of goods and services can rise. For example, if the amount of money in a country doubled, but the production of goods and services stayed the same, the price of all goods and services would rise by about twofold, assuming that other factors, such as external trade, were constant.

The Bretton Woods System

In 1944, the **Bretton Woods Agreement** established a global currency system based on a **gold standard** with the U.S. dollar pegged at a fixed rate of exchange to gold in an effort to control inflation. After World War II, the U.S. dollar became a standard of value for all world currencies, and the currencies of 43 other countries were fixed to the dollar. If a country's currency changed by more than 1 percent from its pegged level against the dollar, government intervention was initiated to restore fixed exchange rates.

Brooks Kraft/Corbis

Gold is a popular world currency.

The **International Monetary Fund (IMF)** was established under the Bretton Woods Agreement to help ensure the stability of the international monetary and financial system. It seeks to foster smooth functioning of the international monetary system, provide emergency funds as a lender of last resort to countries with balance of payments problems, and offer financing to countries conditional on recommended economic changes. Member countries contribute to the Fund in return for temporary access to pooled resources to correct balance of payments difficulties when needed.

Over time, the U.S. dollar became overvalued, with negative consequences to its export competitiveness in world markets. This problem forced the United States to stop buying and selling gold for the settlement of international transactions on August 15, 1971. Subsequently, major nations met to consider abandoning the Bretton Woods Agreement, including pegging the dollar to gold. Under the resulting **Smithsonian Agreement** on December 17–18, 1971, the United States devalued the dollar against other countries' currencies. The IMF implemented a temporary regime of central rates and wider margins of 2.25 percent above or below these central rates. On April 24, 1972, the European Monetary System established a managed float exchange rate system with a range of 2.25 percent around central rates for six currencies, known as the "snake-in-the-tunnel," an exchange rate precursor to the euro. On August 15, 1974 the United States closed the gold window and relinquished the dollar-gold exchange standard.

Then, in January 1976, IMF members adopted the **Jamaica Agreement**, which ushered in a reformed international monetary order. Some of the key principles in the Jamaica Agreement were: (1) members could adopt their own exchange systems; (2) a system of global fixed exchange rates (as under Bretton Woods) would only be implemented if approved by a vote of 85 percent of membership; (3) gold would no longer be a common denominator of the monetary system; and (4) the **special drawing right (SDR)** created by the IMF was recommended as the primary reserve asset of the international monetary system.

Today, the SDR is a basket of currencies consisting of dollars, euros, pounds, and yen, with relative weights set by the IMF based on trade patterns. While the dollar has continued to be important in denominating the value of other currencies, many countries have allowed their currencies to float, or vary, in world markets to some extent. Due to the breakdown of the Bretton Woods world monetary system in 1971, some developing countries have experienced periodic episodes of volatile currency values, high inflation, and economic stagnation. To promote stability in the international monetary system, the IMF in cooperation with the World Bank work to assist member countries with exchange rate, liquidity, economic development, and structural issues.

International Monetary Fund (IMF)
financial authority established under the Bretton Woods Agreement in 1944 to help ensure the stability of the international monetary and financial system

Smithsonian Agreement
the 1971 decision allowing the United States to devalue the dollar against other countries' currencies, thereby beginning the breakdown of the 1944 Bretton Woods Agreement

Jamaica Agreement
the 1976 international monetary order that allowed countries to adopt different exchange rate systems including floating their currencies in world markets

special drawing right (SDR)
a basket of currencies consisting of dollars, euros, pounds, and yen created by the International Monetary Fund (IMF) for use as a benchmark to value the currencies of different countries

clean float currency
monetary system with minimal government intervention; largely market determined

dirty float currency
monetary system with varying degrees of government intervention to maintain a range of acceptable values against other currencies

dollarization
the practice of using the dollar or some other foreign currency together with, or instead of, a domestic currency in a country

The Flexible Exchange Rate System

After 1971, a flexible exchange rate system began to emerge with market forces of supply and demand determining the prices of different currencies. Currency values can be affected by a variety of forces, including current account balance, economic conditions, inflation and interest rates, and other factors. At times, central banks intervene in the forex market by buying or selling currency to prevent its value from going too high or low.

A **clean float currency** has minimal government intervention, and with few exceptions, is market determined. A **dirty float currency** has varying degrees of government intervention to maintain a range of acceptable values against other currencies. Hence, currencies that freely float in forex markets on a daily basis may be subject to a managed float at times. Some emerging market countries practice managed float due to potential problems with liabilities denominated in foreign currencies and assets denominated in local currency. A large depreciation of the currency could cause difficulties in making debt payments denominated in foreign currencies and thereby damage the domestic financial system and economy.

Of course, some countries do not float their currencies for these reasons. For example, some countries practice **dollarization**, which means to use the dollar or some other foreign currency together with, or instead of, a domestic currency. Dollarization can be unofficially adopted by citizens in a country or officially approved by a country as legal tender in transactions (e.g., the sole domestic currency). Countries such as Ecuador (2000), El Salvador (2001), and Panama (1904) have adopted the U.S. dollar. Other currencies frequently used in dollarization are the euro, New Zealand dollar, Swiss franc, and Australian dollar. Less frequent usage exists for the Turkish lira, Israeli new shekel, Russian ruble, and Indian rupee.

The European Euro

In many ways, the aforementioned exchange rate problems set the stage for the emergence of the European euro (€). The European community established the European Exchange Rate Mechanism (ERM) in 1979. Under the ERM, a weighted basket of European currencies known as the ECU (European Currency Unit) was defined based on a managed-float system with fixed exchange rates varying within 2.25 percent margins. The ERM nearly fell apart in 1992 due to economic imbalances arising from the unification of East and West Germany as well as economic disparities among different countries in Europe. Laying the groundwork for the euro, 12 European nations formed European Monetary Union (EMU) in 1999. The EMU introduced the euro as a new currency to replace the currencies of the member countries in the Eurozone, which has since grown to 17 members.

In 2002, euro coins and notes were distributed. The euro was an immediate success; it quickly became the second most important currency in the world, ahead of the Japanese yen. For countries using the euro, problems of currency fluctuations, inflation, and related economic downturns were substantially reduced. For individual European consumers and businesses, the euro put an end to the expensive and time-consuming need to convert one currency to another as goods and services are purchased, or as business is conducted between countries.

By 2009, 17 countries had joined the Eurozone (i.e., Austria, Belgium, Cyprus, Estonia, Finland, France, Germany, Greece, Ireland, Italy, Luxembourg, Malta, the Netherlands, Portugal, Slovakia, Slovenia, and Spain) encompassing 327 million Europeans.[7]

The European Central Bank (ECB) and Eurosystem of central banks in Eurozone countries maintain responsibility for managing the euro. They print and distribute euros and oversee the Eurozone payments system. Under the 1992 Maastricht Treaty, Eurozone members are required to meet certain monetary and budgetary requirements. These requirements have caused some of the 27-member European Union (EU) countries, such as Sweden, Norway, Denmark, and the United Kingdom, to reject the euro. However, some countries outside the Eurozone, including some Eastern European micro states, have adopted the euro as their sole currency.

It is expected that the Eurozone will continue to expand in the future as a way to eliminate exchange rate risks associated with uncertain currency movements, improve macroeconomic stability, and contribute to price parity across countries competing in world trade. Interestingly, some countries in Africa, South America, and Southeast Asia are discussing the possibility of creating regional currencies similar to the euro.[8]

Hard and Soft Currencies

hard currencies
leading world currencies of developed industrialized countries, including the U.S. dollar, European euro, Japanese yen, and British pound sterling

soft currencies
emerging market countries' currencies that are less stable in value than hard currencies and are sometimes pegged to hard currency values

Together, the dollar, euro, and yen account for around 60 percent of the world economy. The dollar, euro, and yen describe three currency areas of the world that lend monetary stability to each respective regional economy. The British pound sterling is another example of a leading world currency. These **hard currencies** are used by emerging market countries to peg the values of the **soft currencies**. For example, Argentina for many years pegged its peso's value to the U.S. dollar, wherein the value of the peso was kept within a set range of values per dollar. Thus, currency pegging is a way for emerging market countries to enhance their monetary stability.

However, it should be recognized that, even though each hard currency is fairly stable within its own region of the world, its value can considerably fluctuate against its counterparts around the world. Thus, exchange rate risk remains a major factor in international trade and finance even among large industrial countries.

REALITY CHECK LO3

China's currency, the "renminbi," is denominated in yuan units. The yuan is pegged to a basket of world currencies. What if China freely floated the yuan? How would the dollar to yuan exchange rate be affected? In evaluating this possibility, take into account that the U.S. imports large quantities of Chinese exports.

LO-4
Explain exchange rate changes over time.

International Flows of Goods and Capital

World trade and foreign investment have expanded tremendously over the past 100 years. International movements of goods and capital tend to integrate economic and financial markets. The use of the Internet allows anyone to shop for a bicycle in any country and purchase the bike

David R. Frazier Photolibrary, Inc./Alamy

Pharmaceuticals trade in global markets.

at a competitive price. According to the **law of one price**, identical goods should sell for the same price in different countries according to the local currencies. Suppose one is located in the United States and could purchase a bike for \$150 in the United States, but it sells for €100 in Europe. If the exchange rate were \$1.40 per euro, then the cost of the bike in Europe, in dollars, would be \$140 (i.e., €100 x \$1.40/€). This comparison shows that it is cheaper to purchase the bike from the European supplier. Because it is likely that shipping costs would be higher from Europe to the United States than within the United States, the \$10 difference in price may be attributable to shipping costs. If the law of one price holds, this comparison should be true. If not, one could make **arbitrage** profits by purchasing bikes in Europe and selling them in the United States for less than U.S. bike vendors. Over time, the price of European bikes would rise in price due to higher (arbitrage) demand, and U.S. bike prices would fall due to lower demand; eventually prices in Europe and the United States would converge.

Purchasing Power Parity

The law of one price is the underlying principle of **purchasing power parity (PPP)** theory. By comparing the prices of identical goods in different countries, assuming efficient markets that arbitrage away price differences, the real or PPP exchange rate can be computed. Of course, markets are not perfectly efficient due to imperfections such as trading costs (e.g., the bicycle's shipping costs in the above example) or other costs. Given that these imperfections are not large, and markets are fairly efficient, a basket of goods should have approximately the same prices across different countries. If the prices of goods change in one country but not in other countries, the exchange rate of the country's local currency should likewise change with foreign currencies to maintain PPP.

The Big Mac Index In 1986, *The Economist* began publishing the **Big Mac Index** based upon McDonald's restaurant sandwich consisting of a number of goods. What if the Big Mac costs \$3.80 in the United States but €2.50 in France? Given an exchange rate of \$1.40 per euro, the French Big Mac in dollars costs \$3.50. *The Economist* computes the parity ratio of foreign cost (in dollars) to U.S. cost, or \$3.50/\$3.80 = 0.92.[9] Since this ratio should be 1 under PPP, in our example the euro is undervalued by 8 percent against the dollar. Again, market

law of one price
principle stating that identical goods should sell for the same price in different countries according to local currencies

arbitrage
buying goods in a lower priced market and selling them in a higher priced market to make profits

purchasing power parity (PPP)
theory stating that a basket of goods should have approximately the same prices across different countries

big mac index
calculation using the cost of a McDonald's restaurant sandwich to assess the relative values of currencies

imperfections such as transportation costs, taxes, and the like could explain all or part of this difference. Differential costs of the Big Mac over time and across nations should be related to changes in currency values as PPP tends to push prices up or down to one price.

According to *The Economist*[10], on January 11th, 2012 the average dollar price in major U.S. cities for a Big Mac was \$4.20. At that time, the average euro price was €3.49, which translates to \$4.43 given an exchange rate of \$1.27. Again, the actual PPP ratio is computed as foreign cost (in dollars) to U.S cost (in dollars), which equals \$4.43/\$4.20 = 1.05. Because this ratio is greater than 1 by 5 percent, the euro was 5 percent overvalued.

Based on the cited Big Mac Index, Norway's kroner was overvalued by 63 percent, and Switzerland's franc by 58 percent; but other countries' currencies were undervalued against the dollar, such as Malaysia's ringgit by 57 percent, South Africa's rand by 53 percent, and Hong Kong's dollar by 52 percent. The Brazilian real and Israeli new shekel were near parity and neither over- nor undervalued. While it would not be practical to purchase Big Macs in undervalued currency countries and sell them in overvalued currency countries to earn arbitrage profits, it is possible to buy and sell the basket of ingredients required to make a Big Mac. Consequently, if price differentials like these existed in traded goods markets, short-run differences should be reversed over time.

Inflation and PPP Consider what would happen if inflation caused the prices of U.S. goods to increase 10 percent over the next year, but no inflation occurred in Europe. Higher U.S. prices would motivate consumers to purchase European goods. To do this, consumers would sell dollars and buy euros, resulting in a decline in value of the dollar (due to increased supply) against the euro (due to increased demand). This would continue over time until PPP was once again achieved. We can compute how much the dollar will decline by using the following PPP equation:

$$P_{US}(1 + I_{US}) = (1 + p)P_E(1 + I_E),$$

where P_{US} = price index of U.S. goods in dollars
P_E = price index of European goods in dollars
I_{US} = inflation rate in the United States in dollar terms
I_E = inflation rate in Europe in euro terms
p = percentage change in the euro, which equals the forward premium $[(F - S)/S] \times 100$ with F the forward dollar/euro exchange rate and S the spot dollar/euro exchange rate.

Given an exchange rate of \$1.40 per euro, an initial PPP with P_{US} = \$140 and P_E = €100 or \$140, and 10 percent U.S. inflation and 0 percent European inflation, we have

$$\$140(1.10) = (1 + p)\ \$140(1),$$

such that the forward premium $p = [(\$154 - \$140)/\$140] \times 100 = 10$ percent. Hence, the value of the euro will increase by 10 percent against the dollar over the next year due to U.S. inflation. After this adjustment in exchange rates, the purchasing power of buyers will be the same for both U.S. and European goods.

An important lesson here is that, if one country's inflation rate exceeds other countries' inflation rates, then it will experience depreciation of its currency relative to foreign currencies. A simple way to write this idea (approximately at least) is: $X = I_{Domestic} - I_{Foreign}$, where X gives the rate of depreciation of the domestic currency relative to the foreign currency (i.e., X = 10 – 0 = 10 percent in the above example).

Problems with PPP PPP posits that exchange rate changes are explained by relative prices across countries. However, empirical tests of PPP have found mixed results. While PPP appears to hold in the long run for periods exceeding five years, it may not hold in shorter periods. For countries with large price disparities due to inflation or other reasons, PPP is predictive of exchange rate movements. But for other countries with little difference in inflation rates, PPP is less reliable.[11]

A variety of problems could explain the failure of PPP for shorter durations of time. Earlier in the text, it was noted that transportation costs and trade barriers cause some discrepancies in prices between countries. Other potential problems include government intervention in trade and exchange rates (e.g., trade restrictions and prohibitions on conversions of local currencies for foreign currencies), multinational firms with pricing power on a global basis (e.g., Microsoft sets prices of its software in different countries), and goods that are not traded but affect internal prices in a country (e.g., rental costs of equipment and property). Moreover, the value of a country's currency is probably attributable to more than differences in price levels between countries. Market expectations about the economic growth, global competitiveness, monetary and fiscal policy, and many other factors could possibly affect a country's currency value in world forex markets. Indeed, a nation's currency is a financial asset of its own, with its complex pricing factors, including relative prices.

Interest Rate Parity

Relative interest rates on financial securities are another possible determinant of exchange rate changes. Under the law of one price, if an investor purchases government bonds in the United States and comparable maturity and risk government bonds in Europe, the rates of return on both should be the same for an individual investor.[12] For example, assume that the one-year United States Treasury bond rate is 4 percent and the similar European government bond rate is 6 percent. It is worth noting that U.S. bonds pay earnings in dollars and European bonds pay in euros. An investor from the United States would view the higher interest rate European bond as attractive. But, to purchase the European bond, the U.S. investor would need to convert dollars to euros, purchase the European bond with the euros, and then later convert euro earnings on the European bond back to dollars. (The investor could, for example, use forward contracts at the time the bond is purchased to lock in the future dollar to euro exchange rate.) For comparison purposes, the U.S. investor would compute the dollar interest rate on the European bond. According to **interest rate parity (IRP)** theory, the dollar interest rate on the U.S. and European bonds should be the same. Otherwise, there would be arbitrage opportunities for investors to purchase the higher interest rate bond and sell the lower interest rate bond to make riskless profits. If **covered interest rate parity** holds with no arbitrage profits, we have the following IRP equation:

$$(1 + i_{US}) = (F/S)(1 + i_E), \tag{4.2}$$

where i_{US} = interest rate on European bond paid in euros
i_E = interest rate on U.S. bond paid in dollars
F = forward dollar to euro exchange rate
S = spot dollar to euro exchange rate.

This equation says that a dollar invested in a U.S. bond earns the same dollar return as a dollar converted to euros and invested in European bonds with euro returns later repatriated to dollars. If S is fairly stable over time, this IRP can be approximated with the following well-known formula:

$$(i_{US} - i_E) = (F - S)/S = p, \tag{4.3}$$

with p = forward premium as before in the PPP equation. Note that in our previous example, we have (0.04 – 0.06) = –0.02, which implies that F < S. If S was $1.40 per euro, then F would

interest rate parity (IRP)
theory stating that interest rates on bonds in different countries should be the same, as investors would buy and sell these bonds to make arbitrage profits until this condition holds

covered interest rate parity
principle implying that forward exchange rates and spot exchange rates set interest rates on bonds in different countries equal to one another

be $1.37 = [–0.02 + 1]$1.40. Consequently, the dollar should appreciate in value by 2 percent over the next year against the euro, as dollars sell at a premium in the forward exchange market. Alternatively, the expression $(F - S)/S < 0$ suggests that the euro will depreciate in value against the dollar, as it simply gives the rate of return on the euro expressed in dollars.[13] If the forward rate is not $1.37, then arbitrage opportunities are available for currency and bond traders. Arbitrage by these market participants would tend to change the difference in interest rates as well as the difference between forward and spot exchange rates until the IRP equation held again.

According to the **uncovered interest rate parity** theory, it is possible that the expected future spot rate is not equal to the forward exchange rate. This difference is possible if a risk premium exists in expected future spot rates due to risk adverse investor behavior. Uncertainty about whether future spot rates will equal previous forward rates may cause currency traders to demand a premium for this risk. In this case, neither covered nor uncovered IRP hold. If investors are risk neutral, no risk premium exists and the expected future spot rate equals the current forward exchange rate, such that covered and uncovered IRP are the same. Since market expectations cannot be exactly measured, the uncovered IRP theory can only be indirectly tested. While the covered IRP focuses on spot and forward rates, the uncovered IRP utilizes spot and expected future spot rates in comparing interest rates across countries.[14]

In sum, IRP argues that the interest rate earned on assets in different countries will tend toward equality after taking into account exchange rate changes. If IRP does not hold, global capital flows will take place to arbitrage away excess profit opportunities in international investments.

Problems with IRP Like the PPP, empirical evidence on IRP theories is mixed.[15] Transactions cost is one possible impediment to IRP. As the investment time horizon increases, deviations from IRP may be more likely due to political risk (e.g., government controls of capital flows), legal restrictions, tax effects, managed-float exchange rate regimes, and other unpredictable circumstances that can occur over time and disrupt traders' ability to arbitrage away profit differentials. In addition, market psychology can play a role in exchange rate movements, as forex traders speculate in currencies. Herd behavior can cause large purchases or sales of a particular currency that drive currency values beyond their normal bounds, resulting in problems such as currency crises.

While IRP may not strictly hold at all times, market efficiency due to traders seeking arbitrage profits would tend to cause relative interest rates and exchange rates between countries to change in integrated financial markets. When interest rates change in the United States, foreign interest rates and exchange rates should also change under IRP. However, foreign central banks may seek to counteract interest rate and exchange rate fluctuations by changing policy goals or targets. Thus, central bank intervention is another reason that IRP may not hold at all points in time.

Finally, international investors may globally diversify their investments and behave passively toward arbitrage activities. Higher or lower earnings on bonds in different countries would average out over time, thereby reducing investors' desire to move capital in response to unpredictable interest rate differentials.

While there are a number of reasons why IRP may not hold, it remains a puzzle in financial economics why empirical evidence only weakly supports IRP theories.[16] It is relatively easy for market participants to arbitrage profitably in integrated global financial markets on similar bonds in different countries with unequal interest rates.

uncovered interest rate parity
principle implying that expected future spot exchange rates and spot exchange rates set interest rates on bonds in different countries equal to one another

ECONOMIC PERSPECTIVES The Asian Currency Crisis

In the 1990s Asian economies, including those in Thailand, Indonesia, Malaysia, Philippines, Hong Kong, Singapore, Taiwan, and South Korea, were growing more rapidly than other countries around the world. With the fall of Communism in Russia in 1991, many emerging market countries in Southeast Asia began to open up to foreign investment. Foreign capital inflows surged and created a new optimism about the future of the region. Asian banks jumped on the bandwagon and aggressively expanded their lending to business firms.

While the future looked bright for the Asian economies, troubles in Thailand triggered problems throughout the region. Excessive credit expansion in Thailand had led to unwise investments in high-risk commercial developments and business firms. Many corporations had family or personal relations with banks that resulted in self-dealing loans known as "crony capitalism." To foster economic development, the Thai government heavily borrowed funds by issuing sovereign bonds into world financial markets to build up the infrastructure of the country. Huge credit demands kept interest rates relatively high. Large amounts of debt by firms, banks, and the government were in foreign currencies accumulated in world financial markets.

The Thai baht was pegged to the dollar, which caused it to become overvalued. Recognizing this overvaluation, investors and speculators began to sell the baht in July 1997. When the Thai government removed the peg, the currency plunged 20 percent in one month. The central bank attempted to intervene and purchase bahts to support its value, but failed. Market forces were simply too great due to the sudden exodus of foreign capital that had inflated the economy earlier.

The bubble had burst—the banks, firms, and government could not pay back many loans denominated in appreciating foreign currencies. The stock market fluctuated and then collapsed. The economic and financial downturn had reversed the earlier strident gains.

Unfortunately, the panic in Thailand spread to other Asian countries. Currency values in dollars in a number of Asian countries collapsed in concert with the Thai baht. Currency contagion swept through the Indonesian rupiah, Malaysian ringgit, Philippine peso, Hong Kong dollar, Singapore dollar, Taiwan dollar, and South Korean won, in addition to their stock markets. Some central banks attempted to stem the tide by intervening via local currency purchases, but could not maintain their currency values at fixed pegs and had to let their currencies float. Foreign investors lost confidence in Asian markets and rushed to sell off stocks, bonds, real estate, and other capital assets. This capital flight caused lower currency values as investors sold Asian currencies to buy other currencies. The speed and magnitude of the regional currency crisis was unprecedented.

The IMF and other countries responded by putting together rescue packages of loans. What began as a relatively small problem in Thailand, which received $17 billion in total loans, had swelled to much larger proportions with $42 billion and $58 billion in bailouts for Indonesia and South Korea, respectively. Some lessons from the Asian currency crisis include:

- Overvalued currencies with pegged exchange rates at artificially low levels can lead to problems. If a peg cannot be defended from speculative attack by the government, a currency panic can occur.
- Large foreign flows of capital into an emerging market country can be dangerous. Market psychology among foreign investors can cause herd-like behavior, withdrawing funds from a country, and thereby devastating its financial markets.
- A fast-growing economy is not necessarily healthy. A bubble economy driven by credit expansion and foreign capital inflows will reverse at some point, and lose excessive gains in a sharp economic contraction. This principle applies to both developing and developed industrial economies, as seen in the U.S., Japanese, and European 2008–2009 global economic and financial crises.
- The stability of the government and economy in developing countries are critical components in currency crises.

Due to differences across countries, and because many factors potentially promote such stability, the causes and cures for currency crises differ across countries. After a currency crisis, major structural reforms are needed in the macroeconomy to address imbalances that led to the crises. Financial sector, private and public governance, and transparency are other areas of needed reform in most cases.

(continued)

QUESTIONS:

1) What were the major causes of the economic bubble in Thailand? What lessons can be learned from this bubble?

2) Why did problems in Thailand contagiously affect other Asian countries? Why does the fall in a country's currency affect its stock market?

Sources:

Steven Radelet and Jeffrey Sachs, "The Onset of the East Asian Financial Crisis," in Paul R. Krugman, Ed., *Currency Crises*, National Bureau of Economic Research, (Chicago: University of Chicago Press, 1998), pp. 105–162.

Craig Burnside, Martin Eichenbaum, and Sergio Rebelo, "Prospective Deficits and the Asian Currency Crisis," *Journal of Political Economy* 109 (2001), pp. 1155–1197.

REALITY CHECK LO4

Browse the Internet and find the latest Big Mac Index data. What does the data show in terms of the value of the dollar relative to the euro, pound, and yen? Are these currencies over- or undervalued relative to the dollar?

LO-5

Forecast exchange rates using different methodologies.

Forecasting Exchange Rates

The PPP and IRP theories can be used to forecast future exchange rates. The PPP approximation $X = I_{Domestic} - I_{Foreign}$ suggests that forecasts of relative inflation rates in two countries can be used to estimate the future exchange rate X of domestic currency to foreign currency. Inflation forecasts are readily available from private and public sources to implement this forecasting strategy. Another approach is to use the forward rate in the covered IRP to forecast future spot rates also.[17] In this respect we can write:

$$F = S(1 + p) \tag{4.4}$$

where (as defined above) F = forward rate, S = spot rate, and p = forward premium. The forward premium is the expected percentage change in the exchange rate. If the spot rate is \$1.40 per euro, and forward rate is \$1.50, and the forward premium is 7 percent (\$1.50/\$1.40 – 1). Here the euro is anticipated to appreciate in value against the dollar.

Another forecasting approach is to use a multiple regression model to estimate the relationship between changes in spot rates and fundamental factors. An example of such a fundamental model for changes in spot rates on the dollar/euro exchange rate (denoted ΔX) is as follows:

$$\Delta X = b_{0+} b_1(I_{US} - I_E) + b_2(i_{US} - i_E) + b_3(Y_{US} - Y_E), \tag{4.5}$$

where $\Delta(I_{US} - I_E)$ = difference in inflation rates
$\Delta(i_{US} - i_E)$ = difference in interest rates
$\Delta(Y_{US} - Y_E)$ = difference in GDP growth rates.

Historical data can be collected, for example, on a monthly basis for the dependent variable (ΔX) and independent variables (on the right-hand side), and the regression model fitted to the data series to estimate the b-coefficients. Given these estimated b-coefficients, the most recent values of the independent variables can be put into the equation to estimate the change in future dollar to euro exchange rates (or ΔX). This kind of fundamental model of exchange rates needs to be updated and revised over time to adjust for changing relationships between exchange rates and independent variables. Private firms routinely produce and sell exchange rate forecasts using fundamental models.

REALITY CHECK LO5

Some observers believe that the large U.S. government deficits will lead to higher inflation in the future. If this did happen, how could the PPP theory be used to forecast the impact of this higher inflation on the value of the dollar?

SUMMARY

The balance of payments (BOP) account provides details about the flows of funds over time between a country and the rest of the world. The current account in the BOP provides information on the trade balance, service balance, income balance, and net transfers. The financial account in the BOP shows how the current account is financed, with U.S.-owned assets abroad, foreign-owned assets in the United States, and net financial derivatives. It is affected by foreign direct investment (FDI) and security investments across borders. The financial account balances the current account for the most part, with any remaining differences attributable to statistical discrepancy.

As world trade has expanded over time, an international monetary system has developed to enable payments to be made in multiple national currencies. The foreign exchange market is a global network of international banks and currency traders that trade currencies around the clock. Exchange rates give the price of a currency relative to another currency. With the breakdown of the 1944 Bretton Woods Agreement gold standard for money in 1971, a flexible exchange rate system emerged with independent floating exchange rates for many currencies and a managed floating exchange rate system for others. Spot rates of exchange rates now and forward rates in the future are available to trade currencies, with discounts and premiums on currencies based on the difference between these two rates.

Money evolved over time from coins made of precious metals to paper money issued by countries as a national symbol of sovereignty and identity. A major event is the creation of the euro in 1999 that is used by 16 European countries today. The euro has reduced currency fluctuations, inflation, and related economic downturns in Eurozone countries. Due to the success of the euro, countries in Africa, South America, and Southeast Asia are considering the adoption of regional currencies of their own.

Two well-known theories based upon the law of one price that help to explain exchange rate movements over time are purchasing power parity (PPP) and interest rate parity (IRP). PPP states that the prices of similar goods in different countries should be same after converting one currency into another currency. Differences in prices will be eliminated by traders that buy and sell goods between countries to make arbitrage profits. The Big Mac Index is a widely-used PPP test. Differences in Big Mac costs across countries give insights into which currencies are overvalued and undervalued relative to the dollar. Such currencies should change in value over time to restore PPP; however, differences may persist due to market inefficiencies, such as trading costs, trade barriers, tax effects, government intervention, and other possible imperfections.

Similarly, IRP says that interest rates on bonds across countries should be the same after converting currencies at exchange rates over time. The covered IRP theory uses spot and forward rates, while the uncovered IRP employs spot and expected future spot rates, which may differ from forward rates due to risk. A puzzle in financial economics is that, despite the ease with which investors can buy and sell bonds in different countries due to integrated financial markets, empirical evidence only weakly supports IRP theories. Nonetheless, PPP and IRP theories can be used to forecast exchange rates, and more complex multiple regression models based on fundamental factors related to exchange rates.

KEY TERMS

balance of payments (BOP), *p. 91*
current account, *p. 91*
trade balance, *p. 92*
trade deficit, *p. 92*
services balance, *p. 92*
income balance, *p. 92*
balance of transfers, *p. 93*
financial account, *p. 93*
risk premium, *p. 93*
foreign direct investment (FDI), *p. 93*
statistical discrepancy, *p. 94*
foreign exchange markets, *p. 97*
exchange rate, *p. 97*
independent floating exchange rate system, *p. 97*
managed floating exchange rate system, *p. 97*
fixed exchange rate system, *p. 97*
spot market, *p. 97*
bid-ask spread, *p. 99*
direct quotes, *p. 99*
indirect quotes, *p. 99*
forward market, *p. 99*
forward rate, *p. 99*
discount, *p. 99*
premium, *p. 99*
hedge, *p. 99*
inflation, *p. 100*
gold standard, *p. 100*
Bretton Woods Agreement, *p. 100*
International Monetary Fund (IMF), *p. 101*
Smithsonian Agreement, *p. 101*
Jamaica Agreement, *p. 101*
special drawing right (SDR), *p. 101*
clean float currency, *p. 101*
dirty float currency, *p. 101*
dollarization, *p. 101*
hard currencies, *p. 102*
soft currencies, *p. 102*
law of one price, *p. 103*
arbitrage, *p. 103*
purchasing power parity (PPP), *p. 103*
big mac index, *p. 103*
interest rate parity (IRP), *p. 105*
covered interest rate parity, *p. 105*
uncovered interest rate parity, *p. 106*

CHAPTER QUESTIONS

1. In the balance of payments (BOP) accounts, what are the four basic components of the current account? How can information about the financing of a country's current account be obtained?

2. What is the difference between independent floating, managed floating, and fixed exchange rate systems? Provide an example of a direct quote of an exchange rate.

3. Briefly describe the international monetary systems implemented under the Bretton Woods, Smithsonian, and Jamaica Agreements.

4. How can the Big Mac Index be used to make purchasing power parity (PPP) comparisons between countries? Using such comparisons, what can be learned about the future possible direction of exchange rates between countries?

5. Assume that the one-year U.S. Treasury bond rate is 3 percent and the similar European government bond rate is 5 percent. Comparing these inflation rates, could it be expected that the dollar will appreciate or depreciate against the euro over the next year? If the spot rate is 1.50 dollars per euro, what would be the forward rate?

MINI-CASE: ICELAND'S ECONOMIC WOES

In 2008 and 2009, international financial markets suffered large declines in stock, bond, and real estate prices that caused a slowdown in global economic growth. Many emerging market countries were adversely affected. As economic woes deepened, developing countries around the world suffered from falling currency values. Because leading industrial nations typically make loans to developing countries denominated in the lender's currency, developing countries' debt burdens rapidly rose as their foreign debt was denominated in dollars, euros, and other stronger currencies.

A prominent example is the case of Iceland, which privatized its banking system in 2000, and proceeded to binge on credit. Borrowing large sums of money at home and abroad, the banking sector moved onto the global stage as an international lender. When the global interbank lending market seized in October 2008, the Icelandic banking sector collapsed due to huge foreign debts that could not be paid. Normally, Iceland's króna traded at about 90 króna per euro. The banking crisis ignited a currency crisis that pushed the króna's value down to 340 króna per euro before the country intervened to suspend trading. In 2009, Iceland was considering three options: retaining the króna as the national currency, changing its national currency to the euro without joining the European Union (EU); or joining the EU and adopting the euro.

QUESTIONS:

1) What advantages would Iceland gain if the euro was adopted? Disadvantages? Explain your answers.

2) What advantages would Iceland gain if the country joined the EU? Disadvantages? Explain your answers.

Source: Based on Stijn Claessens, Giovanni Dell'Ariccia, Deniz Igan, and Luc Laeven, "Cross-Country Experiences and Policy Implications from the Global Financial Crisis," *Economic Policy* 25 (2010): pp. 267–293.

Point Counter-Point: What Caused the Asian Currency Crisis?

The Asian currency crisis was remarkable for the fact that it affected multiple countries in a region of the world. Prior to the crisis in 1997, the region had enjoyed enviable growth and massive inflows of foreign capital to finance an economic boom. A stable, pegged exchange regime encouraged foreign capital and investment. What went wrong? Some economists point to fundamental economic imbalances as the root cause of currency crisis, while others argue that financial panic was what instigated the event.

POINT Macroeconomic imbalances were the underlying forces responsible for the Asian currency crisis. Exchange rates were pegged and therefore unable to allow the economy to adjust to internal and external forces. Current account imbalances led to an overvalued currency. Domestic and foreign investments exceeded reasonable limits and resulted in high-risk business projects being undertaken. The excessive expansion of credit to finance these investments led to an unsustainable bubble in financial market and the real economy. When the financial crisis erupted, markets overreacted and spread throughout the region, causing a panic.

COUNTER-POINT Fundamental economic imbalances existed but were not commensurate with the damage incurred by the currency crisis. The currency crisis was triggered by a financial crisis instead. Massive foreign capital inflows, risky bank loans, corruption, and financial fraud created an explosive mix that later led to what amounted to a bank run in terms of sudden capital outflows. Foreign and domestic capital flight put tremendous pressure on Asian currencies as currency conversion surged. Foreign currency reserves held by the governments were quickly depleted, instigating panic in currency markets.

What Do *You* Think?

Was the main problem the economic crisis? Or the financial crisis? If both were a problem, which problem was most crucial in explaining the Asian currency crisis? Explain your answers.

INTERPRETING GLOBAL BUSINESS NEWS

Financial news is everywhere in the popular press and media. How do you interpret the following examples of financial news related to the concepts in this chapter?

1) In the 2008 and 2009 global economic crisis, the value of the British pound considerably decreased against the euro. How would this currency news affect Chinese students contemplating university studies at a British university versus one in a Eurozone country? How would it affect exports from Britain?

2) Up until the 2008 and 2009 economic crisis, the Japanese yen carry trade was popular. To implement this carry trade, investors would borrow funds from Japan at low interest rates and lend these funds in the United States or in Europe at higher interest rates. The recent economic crisis mostly caused lending to cease. Unwinding carry trade loans involves paying off Japanese loans. What do you think would happen to the supply and demand for dollars and yen as this happens? What would happen to the value of the yen against the dollar?

3) Between 2002 and 2005, the U.S. dollar depreciated against the Canadian dollar and the European euro. Despite the falling dollar, trade deficits increased between the United States and these countries in this same period. Why is the United States importing so much?

4) Interest rate parity suggests that high (low) interest rate countries will experience currency depreciation (appreciation). In 2008 and 2009, low interest rate countries like the United States and Japan had currency appreciation, which agrees with IRP theory. Were there additional reasons for the dollar and yen to appreciate in these years of global economic crisis?

PORTFOLIO PROJECTS

Explore Your Own Case in Point: How Currency Movements and Purchasing Power Parity Affect Your Company

After reading this chapter you should be prepared to answer some basic questions about your favorite company.

1) Volatile currency movements can have important affects on your company. Historically speaking, were there any currency crises in different countries that would have affected your company's costs or revenues? What about the recent 2008 and 2009 global economic crisis period?

2) How can your firm lower its debt costs by tapping global credit markets in the future? Will it cost less to borrow from low interest rate countries?

3) How does purchasing power parity affect your firm's purchases of goods and services from other countries? Will it cost less to buy identical supplies from other countries that have lower prices?

Develop an International Strategy for Your Own Small Business: Using the Big Mac Index for Exporting

Use the Big Mac Index to evaluate how currency changes could affect your firm. Focus on a target country to export your products or services. Some questions to evaluate are as follows:

1) What does the Big Mac Index say about the value of the foreign currency? Is it over- or undervalued?

2) If the foreign currency is overvalued, as it falls in the future, how will exports be affected?

3) Is there any chance of a currency crisis in your target country? How did you evaluate this risk? If there was a currency crisis, how would it affect your exports to that country?

CHAPTER NOTES

[1] F. Caramazza, and J. Aziz, "Fixed or Flexible? Getting the Exchange Rate Right in the 1990s," *Economic Issues*, International Monetary Fund, (Washington, DC, 1998).

[2] For an excellent overview of the BOP, see James E. Meade, *The Balance of Payments*, (London: Oxford University Press,).

[3] For more information on the causes and consequences of BOP problems, see articles by: Graciela L.Kaminsky, and Carmen M. Reinhart, "The Twin Crises: The Causes of Banking and Balance-of-Payments Problems," *American Economic Review* 89, pp. 473–500; and P. Krugman, "A Model of Balance-of-Payments Crises," *Journal of Money, Credit and Banking* 11 (1979), pp. 311–325.

[4] For example, see: Yongzheng Yang, "China's Integration into the World Economy: Implications for Developing Countries," *Asian-Pacific Economic Literature* 20 (2006), pp. 40–56.

[5] For further discussion of exchange rate systems, see Stanley Fischer, "Exchange Rate Regimes: Is the Bipolar View Correct?, *Journal of Economic Perspectives* 15 (2001), pp. 3–24; and Milton Friedman, *Essays in Positive Economics*, "The Case for Flexible Exchange Rates," (Chicago: University of Chicago Press, 1953).

[6] For more in-depth discussion of exchange rates, see *Exchange Rate Theory and Practice*, National Bureau of Economic Research Conference Report, edited by John F. Bilson and Richard C. Marston (1984).

[7] "Economic and Monetary Union of the European Union" at http://en.wikipedia.org/wiki/Economic_and_Monetary_Union_of_the_European_Union.

[8] For discussion of regional currencies, see Ariel M. Viale, James W. Kolari, Nikolai V. Hovanov, and Mikhail V. Sokolov, "Computing and Testing a Stable Common Currency for Mercosur Countries," *Journal of Applied Economics* 11 (2008), pp. 193–220.

[9] L. L. Ong, "Burgernomics: The Economics of the Big Mac Standard," *Journal of International Money and Finance* 16, (1997) pp. 865–878.

[10] *The Economist*, "Big Mac Index," web-only article, January 14, 2012, www.economist.com/node/21542808

[11] For an in-depth review of the PPP debate, see Kenneth Rogoff, "The Purchasing Power Parity Puzzle," *Journal of Economic Literature* 34 (1996), pp. 747–668.

[12] For an excellent overview of interest rate parity, see Robert P. Flood and Andrew K. Rose, "Uncovered Interest Rate Parity in Crisis," *IMF Staff Papers* 49 (2002), pp. 252–266.

[13] Similarly, the rate of return on any asset is expressed as $R_t = (P_{t+1} - P_t)/P_t$, where P is the price at time t. For example, for a bond we have R_t = (dollars/bond$_{t+1}$ – dollars/bond$_t$)/dollars/bond$_t$, which is comparable to (F – S)/S = (dollars/euro$_{t+1}$ – dollars/euro$_t$)dollars/euro$_t$, where the euro is the asset rather than a bond.

[14] For more discussion on how expectations affect exchange rates, see Dornbusch, Rudiger, "Expectations and Exchange Rate Dynamics," *The Journal of Political Economy* 84 (1976), pp. 1161–1176.

[15] F. S. Mishkin, "Are Real Interest Rates Equal Across Countries? An Empirical Investigation of International Parity Conditions," *The Journal of Finance* 39 (1984), pp. 1345–1357.

[16] For further discussion as well as an historical review of interest rate parity, see James R. Lothian, and Liuren Wu, "Uncovered Interest-Rate Parity over the Past Two Centuries," CRIF Working Paper No. 6-1-2005, Fordham University.

[17] For example, see Peter Hansen, and Robert J. Hodrick, "Forward Exchange Rates as Optimal Predictors of Future Spot Rates: An Econometric Analysis," *The Journal of Political Economy* 88 (1980), pp. 828–853.

ii

Global Business Environment

sandar Todorovic/ terstock.com · Ricardo De Mattos/iStockphoto.com · ArtisticPhoto/Shutterstock.com · Noel Hendrickson/Blend Images/ Jupiter Images · Jorg Hackemann/Shutterstock.com

CHAPTER 5

The Cultural Environment

CHAPTER 6

The Legal and Political Environment of Global Business

CHAPTER 7

Corruption and Ethics in Global Business

CH 5

The Cultural Environment

© C Miller Design/ Getty Images

Noel Hendrickson/Blend Images/Jupiter Images

After studying this chapter, you should be able to:

LO-1 Define culture and identify the four characteristics of culture which companies doing business abroad need to recognize.

LO-2 Name several elements of culture.

LO-3 Name and distinguish among the cultural dimensions proposed by Hofstede and Trompenaars.

LO-4 Identify the primary and secondary sources that can be used to learn about foreign countries' cultures.

LO-5 Describe the cultural aspects of doing business in various countries, including East Asian countries, Arab countries, and Latin America.

LO-6 Explain why culture is important in global management and marketing.

Teaching Business Abroad

An American business professor was hired to teach a seven-week course in one of France's graduate business schools. In preparation for this assignment, he consulted various secondary sources to learn about France's history, economy, politics, and culture. One letter from the school's director indicated that his apartment would be located on *Rue Jules Massenet*. Not knowing who Jules Massenet was, he consulted an encyclopedia and learned that Monsieur Massenet was France's leading opera composer in the last half of the 20th century; the most important of his 20 compositions are *Manon* and *Thaïs*.

After arriving at the business school, the professor attended a welcoming dinner where he and several other invited lecturers were the guests of honor. His hosts were surprised and pleased to find out that he knew about Monsieur Massenet. The professor's stay at the French business school turned out to be most pleasant and productive.

The same professor later gave a five-day workshop for the Kuwait Institute of Banking studies. His hosts provided him with a business-class ticket on Kuwait Airlines, and during the flight he was treated to a sumptuous dinner of salad, fish, dessert, cheese, and wine. At the end of the meal, coffee was served. Although he was not ordinarily a coffee drinker, he decided to drink a cup because he believed that it might be a common beverage consumed in Kuwait. The coffee, served in a small cup, was Turkish coffee that proved to have a very strong taste—completely unlike any he had ever tasted.

In Kuwait, he was asked to give an evening talk to the Inter-Arab Investment Guarantee Corporation (IAIGC), the organization that underwrites exports and investments among Arab nations. Upon his arrival, nearly a dozen Arab businessmen, who were nicely attired in three-piece business suits, cordially greeted him. Shortly before his talk, he was led to a table, which contained many delicious pastries. After eating one, he was offered coffee. After his experience on the plane, he was tempted to decline but, not wanting to offend his hosts, he accepted. After drinking two cups and thanking his hosts, he began the presentation. The audience appeared to be receptive to his remarks, and a lively 15-minute question-and-answer session followed.

Introduction

culture
learned behavior; a way of life for one group of people living in a single, related, and independent community

Cultural understanding plays a major role in global business success. It is true that a company selling its products or services in foreign countries must contend with various aspects of the external environment in addition to culture. These include the business market, competition, technology, economy, and the legal and political climate. This chapter will discuss the cultural dimension of companies' international environment.

LO-1
Define culture and identify the four characteristics of culture that companies doing business abroad need to recognize.

Defining Culture and its Characteristics

Culture is a concept that can be challenging to define. Perhaps one reason is that there are so many and different components of culture, such as manners, power, face saving, names and titles, language, religion, gift giving, and risk taking. Culture involves how a group of people behave, what the people value and appreciate, what the people believe is right and fair, and many other aspects of life. Perhaps the best definition of **culture** is "learned behavior; a way of life for one group of people living in a single, related, and independent community."[1]

There are four characteristics of culture which are important for global companies to recognize. First, culture is not inherited; rather it is learned, usually through one's parents, friends, schools, and other influences. Second, it is nearly impossible to change an entire country's culture; culture is relatively static and not easily modified—especially by external forces. Third, it is the responsibility of the global firm to ascertain the level of importance of various aspects of culture in the foreign markets it serves, and recognize these aspects when doing business overseas. For example, Mexican business executives who buy business-to-business products from U.S. suppliers indicate that "knowledge of Mexico's business climate and conditions" and "enthusiasm" were the most important cultural variables determining from which supplier they purchased.[2] Fourth, companies' operations, chiefly marketing and management, need to recognize and adjust to the cultural environment existing in the countries the global company serves. The ability to do so often means success in international markets. **Acculturation** is the term used to describe the ability of a firm to adjust to a culture different from its own.

acculturation
the ability of a firm to adjust to a culture different from its own

REALITY CHECK LO-1

Think of some foreign products that are marketed in the United States Have the foreign manufacturers used marketing that is sensitive to U.S. culture? Provide some specific examples.

LO-2
Name several elements of culture.

Elements of Culture

As shown in Exhibit 5.1, culture affects numerous aspects of a society. These include, language, religion, values and attitudes, manners and customs, material elements, aesthetics, education, and social institutions.[3] The following text will now examine these individually.

Language

Verbal and non-verbal communication are the two primary types of language. **Verbal communication** refers to the message's actual content (what it says), whereas **non-verbal communication** involves tone of voice as well as the gestures, body position, facial expressions, eye contact, and any other body language that accompanies verbal communication.

verbal communication
a message's actual contents (i.e. what the message says)

Language is important to managers when evaluating employees, communicating on an intra-company basis with overseas divisions, and helping to interpret the circumstances (context) in which language occurs.

Language is also crucial when providing access to local markets through advertising. There are numerous examples of how language mistakes have cost marketers in international markets. Several mistakes have occurred, for example, because companies did not understand how slogans for products would be interpreted. In Taiwan, the Pepsi slogan: "come alive with the Pepsi generation," was translated to "Pepsi will bring your ancestors back from the dead." The Kentucky Fried Chicken slogan: "finger-lickin' good," was translated in China as "eat your fingers off." Salem cigarettes' slogan: "Salem—feeling free," translated into Japanese as "When smoking Salem, you feel so refreshed that your mind seems to be free and empty." Exhibit 5.1 provides another example of mishaps that can occur when a company is unfamiliar with the local language.

One way to eliminate such gaffes is to use **backward translation**. In this technique, a message is translated from English into another language, then someone skilled in that foreign language translates it back into English; this second translation can then be compared to the original English version.

non-verbal communication
tone of voice, gestures, eye contact, body positions, facial grimaces, and other body language that accompanies verbal communication

backward translation
translating a message from English into a foreign language, then translating it back into English to check for accuracy

Religion

Religion is a powerful cultural aspect that must be recognized as companies manage their overseas operations and market their products in foreign cultures. In Muslim countries, for example, American companies cannot anticipate employing women because they are not encouraged to work outside the home. Also, different religions observe different holidays, which must be recognized. Muslims observe Ramadan, which is a month-long celebration

EXHIBIT 5.1 THE IMPORTANCE OF LANGUAGE IN FOREIGN COUNTRIES' CULTURES

"Chuck" had been sent by the president of Parker Pen Company to visit the firm's trading company in Buenos Aires, Argentina. This was the first time he had been outside the United States, and he did not know how to speak Spanish.

Upon arriving after a 14-hour flight from Chicago, Chuck went to a bank of telephones to call the trading company and arrange for transportation. Because he could not read the instructions for use, he prevailed upon a good-natured passerby for help. Then, he had to figure out the Argentinean money system to decide which coins to insert. While talking with the trading company, he was asked to take a taxi to the office as they were tied up with important customers.

Upon finding the taxi pickup area, Chuck was dismayed to find that all of the licensed taxi drivers were on strike; he was hoping that the "regular" drivers would know enough English to compensate for his lack of Spanish skills. After an extended length of time, he was able to convey to the driver where he needed to go.

After an hour of working with the people at the trading company, he was invited to accompany them to lunch. Because the menu was in Spanish, he was in a quandary about what to order. He thought that the word "bistec" might mean beef steak, so he ordered it. He was right. The waiter proudly presented Chuck with a two-pound steak. Chuck found out later that Argentina is justifiably proud of its world famous, Pampas beef cattle.

Chuck and his colleagues worked another four hours at the headquarters of the trading company. About six o'clock, he was invited to accompany a group of customers to dinner. Although it was a different restaurant, it was the same problem: The entire menu was in Spanish. Fortunately, or unfortunately, there was one item that Chuck could read: "bistec." Chuck ate his second 32 ounces of prized Argentinean steak.

Around eleven o'clock, Chuck had returned to his hotel where he was greeted in the lobby by Parker Pen's president who said: "Chuck, I just arrived. The food on the flight was terrible. Let's go get something to eat." Chuck ate his third two-pound steak with his boss.

Herbert Scholpp/Westend61 GmbH / Alamy

Religious celebrations are very important in Mexico.

with varying dates year to year. Jews observe a number of annual holidays, including Purim, Passover, Shavuot, the Day of Atonement, and Hanukkah; these dates also vary from year to year.

Weekends and work hours can vary according to different religions. In Kuwait, weekends are Thursday and Friday, not Saturday and Sunday as they are in most Western nations. When one author of this text was in Kuwait, he was intrigued that the workday was divided into two segments: 8:00 a.m. to noon, and 4:00 p.m. to 8:00 p.m. When questioned about this, one of his hosts replied that this arrangement was made so that there could be "four traffic jams a day instead of two" in Kuwait City. (The author assumed the real reason was to avoid work during the hottest part of the day.)

Companies marketing food products overseas must be aware of religious differences. Jews and Muslims are prohibited from eating pork, and their food must be prepared in a particular way, kosher for Jews and halal for Muslims.

Values and Attitudes

Values are basic beliefs or philosophies that are pervasive in a society. In some countries, such as the United States, a high value is placed upon foreigners and foreign items, as they are associated with sophistication—French wines, for example, or Swedish automobiles. In other countries, such as Japan and Korea, there is a subtle resistance to foreigners and things foreign. This is reflected in an aversion to purchasing foreign products and their resistance to accepting employment with foreign firms operating in these countries.

Attitudes are feelings or opinions. Attitudes toward change must be considered by international businesses. In many societies, proposed change is viewed with suspicion—especially if it is suggested by foreigners.

values
basic beliefs or philosophies that are pervasive in a society

attitudes
Feelings or opinions

manners and customs
the way a society does things

Manners and Customs

International companies must understand the **manners and customs**, the way a society does things that prevail in foreign countries. Manners and customs affect both the management and marketing operations of a company.

ECONOMIC PERSPECTIVES Attitudes Toward Work

A country's culture affects the attitudes toward work that members of its labor force hold. These attitudes can have an impact on workers from other cultures who come into the country to work, as well as on employers in the country, and are often legally sanctioned by government. The resulting policies regarding hours, pay, and vacations will influence various aspects of a nation's economic performance, such as total hours worked, GDP achieved, costs per worker-hour, and productivity.

In France, a newly hired worker, even one without a higher education degree, expects to have a protracted tenure with his or her employer, to not work excessive hours per week, to be paid a high hourly rate, to receive generous fringe benefits, and to receive long vacations annually. Concessions such as these were encouraged and often legally guaranteed by the French government; as a result, they had to be accepted by French companies. When the government raised the retirement age in 2010 from 60 to 62, riots and strikes ensued.

A similar attitude toward work was noted in Greece in 2010. Government workers were compensated at unsustainable levels, and as a result, the nation had incurred massive debts and deficits. When the Greek government announced austerity measures, these workers violently demonstrated. The International Monetary Fund and other EU nations contributed billions of dollars to rescue the Greek economy.

In Arab countries, business executives will often digress from the primary purpose of the meeting, then eventually return to the topic initially discussed. Mexican business executives will want to gauge the interest of American salespeople in Mexican history and architecture. Russian negotiators tend to be abrupt and change demands at the last minute. They may also ply foreigners with vodka, as one author of this text discovered when meeting with the general director of one of St. Petersburg's largest department stores. Japanese negotiators will frequently engage in long periods of silence, or may have peripheral discussions among one another while ignoring foreign business people in the room.

Campbell's Soup failed in Brazil because the company did not realize that Brazilian housewives customarily add their own ingredients to a basic stock, rather than buying a fully-prepared soup. Knorr, on the other hand, was successful in this large market because it only sold basic soup stocks. In some countries, doughnuts are viewed as a snack item that can be consumed throughout the day, instead of only at breakfast, as is customary in the United States. In China, consumers drink soup, which usually contains rice, and do not use a spoon—customs not recognized when a direct-selling firm was entertaining important Chinese politicians and lawmakers in the United States, and soup was served with a spoon and without rice. In Japan, soup is typically consumed at breakfast.

Gift-giving is one aspect that describes manners and customs. In general, small gifts are appropriate, whereas large gifts may be viewed as a bribe, which contravenes international law. In Muslim countries, for example, it would be inappropriate to bring a gift for another man's wife. Types of wrapping paper, ribbons, and colors are other elements of gift giving that are important, as is knowing when to give a gift.

Material Elements

Material culture in a society is often a direct result of technology. It is perhaps best demonstrated by a country's infrastructures; that is, the basic economic, social, financial, and marketing frameworks that enable the society to function. Economic infrastructure involves transportation, energy, and communications. Social infrastructure refers to housing, medical services, and educational institutions. Financial infrastructure consists primarily of banks, and marketing infrastructure refers to marketing research and advertising firms.

material culture
a direct result of technology; best demonstrated by economic, social, financial, and marketing infrastructures

Without the availability of these forms of infrastructure, international businesses will not be able to obtain funds to finance their operations, transport their products to market, or draw upon the expertise of local marketing research and advertising firms.

In Africa, and some parts of Asia, there is a growing movement toward "leapfrog" technology—technological advances that bypass intermediate stages industrialized nations experience. For example, people who have always written with a pencil on paper, and never had access to a typewriter, are now leapfrogging over typewriter technology to use a laptop computer.

Aesthetics

Color, form and music are the major components of **aesthetics** (i.e. taste and beauty as perceived by a society).

Color is an important packaging variable. Companies plying international markets must carefully choose colors, as colors often represent different things in different countries. For example, black in the United States indicates mourning, but in Japan white is the color of mourning. Green is an acceptable color in Muslim countries; all flags of those countries contain green. Korean aesthetics tend to emphasize dark shades of color, while pastels are popular in many Western countries. Opera and symphonic music tend to be more revered in European countries, such as Italy and France, than they are in the United States.

Education

The level of education held by people in foreign countries is a major factor in explaining economic growth. Education must be considered when expatriate managers hire host-country personnel to work on complicated production machinery, place them in training programs, staff office positions, and so on. The level of education must be such that high-tech products can be accepted because the market knows how to use them. The content of advertisements must recognize a nation's level of education.

Some countries emphasize different educational specialties. South Korea and Japan stress education in the sciences and engineering. Russia is strong in mathematics and computer programming; India emphasizes engineering and software development.

France, Japan and India, and to some extent, Great Britain, have a tiered system of higher education, which features prestigious colleges and universities. Foreign companies operating in these nations may be tempted to recruit only from these universities but should, instead, hire the best-qualified individuals regardless of academic pedigree.

Social Institutions

Social institutions refer to the way people relate to one another within group settings in a society. Families, churches, work places, and friends are primary examples. Sociologists refer to groups that are important to individuals as **reference groups**. Reference groups can be those of which people are already a member, or those to which people aspire to belong.

Some counties have a high level of **social stratification**, meaning that groups at the top of the social pyramid exert a great deal of control over others at lower levels of the pyramid. India is usually cited as having a high degree of social stratification, whereas the Scandinavian countries are considered to be very egalitarian or "middle class."

REALITY CHECK LO-2

Indicate what reference groups are most important to you. How important are these reference groups when conducting business in foreign countries? Why?

aesthetics
what is perceived as taste and beauty in a society

social institutions
the way people in a society relate to one another within group settings

reference groups
groups that are important to individuals

social stratification
the extent to which groups at the top of the social pyramid exert control over others at lower levels of the pyramid

Clustering Countries and Regions by Culture

LO-3
Name and distinguish among the cultural dimensions proposed by Hofstede and Trompenaars.

There have been several attempts to group countries and regions of the world together according to their cultural dimensions and similarities. The purpose is to provide international managers with cultural clusters that would allow for similar marketing and management strategies.

Hofstede's Research

Dutch researcher Geert Hofstede pioneered research into cultures with a study focusing upon IBM employees in 64 countries; this research was later extended to many more countries and other groups of subjects. Hofstede's findings led him to identify clusters of countries and regions according to five cultural levels, or dimensions.[4]

Individualism vs. collectivism involves the worth of the individual versus the worth of the groups of which that person is a member ("me versus the group"). Japan and Mexico, for example, are societies that are highly collectivistic, or group oriented, whereas the United States and Great Britain are highly individualistic.

Power distance refers to egalitarianism (equality) versus authority. High power distance countries are those where superiors and elders are treated with deference and respect, in contrast to low power distance countries, where relationships are more egalitarian. For example, in a high power distance culture, one would not address one's boss by his or her first name. Australia and the United States, for example, are low power distance countries, whereas Russia and Venezuela are high power distance countries.

Masculine vs. feminine is another of Hofstede's dimensions. It is important to note that this dimension does not refer to the position or role of women in society. Instead, it is the extent to which a society values traditionally masculine attributes (assertiveness, competition) or traditionally feminine ones (modesty, caring for others). Japan, Greece, Belgium, and Mexico have been described as highly masculine cultures; Denmark, Sweden, and Norway have been described as more feminine.

Uncertainty avoidance examines the extent to which societies tolerate risk or are risk averse. Finland, Sweden, Norway, and Greece, for example, were found to be less tolerant of risk than were countries such as Portugal, Brazil, Spain, Yugoslavia, and Turkey.

Time orientation is the final cultural variable Hofstede examined. It is the extent to which a society emphasizes short-run or long-run time horizons. China and Japan, for example, have much longer time horizons than do most Western nations.[5] When Japanese firms enter a foreign market, they are willing to wait four or five years to make a profit; U.S. firms expect to generate profits in new overseas markets in a year or less.

individualism vs. collectivism
the worth of an individual versus the worth of a group

power distance
the level of egalitarianism (equality) in a society

masculine vs. feminine
the extent to which a society minimizes gender inequality

uncertainty avoidance
the extent to which societies tolerate risk or are risk averse

time orientation
the extent to which a society emphasizes short-run or long-run time horizons

Trompenaars's Cultural Dimensions

Building on the work of Hofstede, Fons Trompenaars added a number of cultural variables to the theory.

Universalism vs. particularism refers to the importance of rules versus relationships in a society. It has been illustrated by the story of a person riding in the passenger seat of a car with a best friend, who is driving. The driver has a "fender bender" while driving ten miles over the speed limit. Should the passenger admit to police that the friend was speeding (rules) or say that the driver was not (relationship)?[6]

The **neutral vs. emotional** variable involves the extent to which persons within a society emotionally express themselves. South American countries, like Brazil and Argentina, are considered to be more emotional than the United States.

The **specific vs. diffuse** variable refers to the compartmentalization of roles. For example, are men in a society depicted in multiple roles (diffuse), such as business executive, father, husband, or president of a social club? Or are men generally depicted on only

universalism vs. particularism
the importance of rules versus relationships

neutral vs. emotional
the extent to which a society expresses itself emotionally

specific vs. diffuse
the degree to which a society compartmentalizes roles

Robert Fried/Alamy Limited

South American men are usually more demonstrative than are men in other cultures.

one dimension, such as businessman (specific)? Are women who work and have children depicted in both roles, mother and manager, or in one, mother?

Achievement vs. ascription refers to how "rewards" in a society are handed out. Are they based on performance (achievement), as is typical in mainstream U.S. culture? Or are they based on ascription, such as one's place in society because of birthright, or what university one attended? The latter is more typical in many Latin American cultures.[7]

The GLOBE Project

The Global Leadership and Organizational Behavior Effectiveness (GLOBE) project has involved surveying thousands of business executives from 61 different countries about nine cultural dimensions. These cultural dimensions are indicated in Exhibit 5.2, along with the specific questionnaire item used to measure each cultural dimension. Notice that some of these items are based on Hofstede's work, while others were added to obtain what the developers of the instrument believed to be a more comprehensive and richer portrait of the cultural dimension of doing business.

Exhibit 5.3 shows the result of the GLOBE research on the nine cultural variables for six different regional clusters. Germanic Europe (Austria, Germany, The Netherlands, and German Switzerland) has emerged as the group that was the most in favor of uncertainty avoidance (risk averse); Eastern Europe (Albania, Georgia, Greece, Hungary, Kazakhstan, Poland, Russia, and Slovenia) was the least risk averse culture. The Germanic cluster was the one with the most futuristic outlook, Eastern Europe the least forward-looking. Southern Asia (India, Indonesia, Iran, Malaysia, Philippines, and Thailand) was ranked first on power distance, closely followed by the Arabic group (Egypt, Morocco, Turkey, Kuwait, and Qatar) and Latin Europe cluster (France, French Switzerland, Israel, Italy, Portugal, and Spain).

The Anglo group (Australia, Canada, England, Ireland, New Zealand, South Africa, and the United States) evidenced the highest level of institutional collectivism ("Collectivism I"), followed closely by Southern Asia and the Arabic groups. The lowest level for institutional collectivism existed for Eastern Europe. The Southern Asia bloc had the highest level of family collectivism ("Collectivism II"), the Germanic and Anglo clusters had the lowest.

achievement vs. ascription
how rewards in a society are handed out: performance vs. place in society

EXHIBIT 5.2 GLOBE CONSTRUCTS AND CORRESPONDING QUESTIONNAIRE ITEMS

Culture Construct Definitions	Specific Questionnaire Item
Power Distance: The degree to which members of a collective expect power to be distributed equally.	Followers are (should be) expected to obey their leaders without question.
Uncertainty Avoidance: The extent to which a society, organization, or group relies on social norms, rules, and procedures to alleviate the unpredictability of future events.	Most people lead (should lead) highly structured lives with few unexpected events.
Humane Orientation: The degree to which a collective encourages and rewards individuals for being fair, altruistic, generous, caring, and kind to others.	People are generally (should be generally) very tolerant of mistakes.
Collectivism I: The degree to which organizational and societal institutional practices encourage and reward collective distribution of resources and collective action.	Leaders encourage (should encourage) group loyalty, even if individual goals suffer.
Collectivism II: The degree to which individuals express pride, loyalty, and cohesiveness in their organizations or families.	Employees feel (should feel) great loyalty toward this organization.
Assertiveness: The degree to which individuals are assertive, confrontational, and aggressive in their relationships with others.	People are (should be) generally dominant in their relationships with each other.
Gender Egalitarianism: The degree to which a collective minimizes gender inequality.	Boys are encouraged (should be encouraged) more than girls to attain a higher education.
Future Orientation: The extent to which individuals engage in future-oriented behaviors such as delaying gratification, planning, and investing in the future.	More people live (should live) for the present rather than for the future.
Performance Orientation: The degree to which a collective encourages and rewards group members for performance improvement and excellence.	Students are encouraged (should be encouraged) to strive for continuously improved performance.

Source: Robert House, Mansour Javidan, Paul Hanges, and Peter Dorfman, "Understanding Cultures and Implicit Leadership Theories Across The Globe: An Introduction To Project GLOBE," *Journal Of World Business* 37 (2002): pp. 3–10. Reprinted with permission from Elsevier Limited via the Copyright Clearance Center.

Southern Asia scored highest on humane orientation; the lowest score on this construct was found for Germanic Europe. Germanic Europe, Anglo, and Southern Asia scored highest on performance orientation, whereas Eastern Europe contained the lowest level. Eastern Europe ranked first on gender egalitarianism, the Arabic bloc lowest. Germanic Europe had the highest score on assertiveness; Eastern Europe had the lowest.[8]

Gannon's Cultural Metaphors

Martin Gannon believes that it is extremely difficult for executives of companies conducting business overseas to learn much about the cultures of a number of countries through "do's" and don'ts". He suggests that it would be more productive for international executives to gauge a specific culture by using an image ("metaphor") that depicts how people in a specific culture think and behave. Some examples of his metaphors are:

- French wine—Purity; classification; composition; compatibility; maturation
- German symphony—Orchestra; conductors; performance; society; education and politics
- British house—Laying the foundation; building the brick house; living in the brick house[9]

EXHIBIT 5.3 GLOBE RESULTS ON NINE CONSTRUCTS FOR SIX REGIONAL GROUPINGS (CONSTRUCT = SCORES ON A SIX-POINT SCALE)

Regional Clusters	Uncertainty Avoidance	Future Orientation	Power Distance	Institutional Collectivism	Family Collectivism	Humane Orientation	Performance Orientation	Gender Egalitarianism	Assertiveness
LATIN EUROPE (SPAIN, PORTUGAL, ITALY, FRENCH SWITZERLAND, FRANCE, AND ISRAEL)	4.18	3.68	5.21	4.01	4.80	4.09	4.10	3.37	4.14
EASTERN EUROPE (ALBANIA, GEORGIA, GREECE, HUNGARY, KAZAKHSTAN, POLAND, RUSSIA, AND SLOVENIA)	3.57	3.37	4.08	3.84	5.53	3.84	3.71	3.84	3.51
GERMANIC EUROPE (AUSTRIA, GERMANY, THE NETHERLANDS, AND GERMAN SWITZERLAND)	5.12	4.40	4.95	4.03	4.21	3.55	4.41	3.14	4.55
ARABIC (EGYPT, MOROCCO, TURKEY, KUWAIT, AND QATAR)	3.91	3.58	5.23	4.28	5.58	4.36	3.90	2.95	4.14
ANGLO (AUSTRALIA, CANADA, ENGLAND, IRELAND, NEW ZEALAND, SOUTH AFRICA, AND THE UNITED STATES)	4.42	4.08	4.97	4.46	4.30	4.20	4.37	3.40	4.14
SOUTHERN ASIA (INDIA, INDONESIA, IRAN, MALAYASIA, PHILIPPINES, AND THAILAND)	4.10	3.99	5.39	4.35	5.87	4.72	4.33	3.28	3.86

Source: Special Issue on GLOBE, *Journal Of World Business* 37 (2002): pp. 1–89.

REALITY CHECK LO-3

Choose a country with which you are unfamiliar and research its rankings on Hofstede's dimensions. What specific business practices would you expect to find in that country based on the rankings? Read some business literature about that country and see whether your expectations are fulfilled.

Sources of Cultural Information

LO-4
Identify the primary and secondary sources that can be used to learn about foreign countries' cultures.

Companies considering conducting business overseas, and those already doing business abroad, have a number of sources they can access to learn more about the culture of various foreign countries. Some of the primary sources are talking to employees who have lived or worked abroad, executives who have traveled to other countries, training programs, and consulting firms. Persons who may be about to undertake an international assignment can be exposed to cultural idiosyncrasies in which they are asked how they would handle various cultural traits that might occur in their assigned countries.

Various secondary sources are very helpful. These include:

- *The U.S. Department of Commerce Country Commercial Guide*—Provides cultural information for 133 countries.
- *The Economist's* Intelligence Unit contains the same type of information on 180 countries in its *Country Reports.*
- *Culture Grams,* from Brigham Young University's Center for International and Area Studies, describes customs existing in 174 countries.
- *Craigshead's International Business, Travel and Relocation Guide to 84 Countries* gives cultural information for these nations.
- *Price Waterhouse Coopers Doing Business in 118 Countries*—Contains useful information about 118 countries.

REALITY CHECK LO-4

Choose one of the above sources and read the write-up on any five countries of your choice. How much information is provided about their cultures? Are there any similarities among your choices?

Cultural Dimensions of Conducting Business in Individual Countries

LO-5
Describe the cultural aspects of doing business in various countries, including East Asian countries, Arab countries, and Latin America.

Although it has been emphasized that it is more important to have an overall flexible and open attitude about foreign cultures than to memorize lists of "do's and don'ts," individual countries have specific business customs that are worth learning. In this section we highlight a few countries and cultures where many U.S. firms may aspire to do business.

Cultural Dimensions of Doing Business in Japan

A business entrepreneur, "Mr. Jones," who owns and manages a software and computer company, has made more than 20 trips to Japan, his most important international market.

This experience enabled him to develop a series of business strategies that recognized the cultural aspects of doing business in Japan.

Mr. Jones noticed that most flights from the United States to Tokyo—about 14 hours in length from the United States' West Coast—arrive late in the afternoon. Upon being greeted by his Japanese hosts, he would typically go to dinner, and stop in various Tokyo bars. Mr. Jones soon believed that these "welcoming" activities were designed to take advantage of his severe case of jet lag so that he would be more likely to grant concessions at the next day's meetings. After gaining some experience in this practice, Mr. Jones decided to fly into Tokyo, getting several days of rest to eliminate jet lag, and thereafter alerting the Japanese business representatives that he had arrived.

On several occasions during his meetings, the Japanese executives would engage in lengthy periods of silence. Mr. Jones believed that this was a tactic to get him to speak first in hopes that he would make concessions. Eventually, Mr. Jones decided to wait out these periods of silence and allow the Japanese executives to speak first. In one instance, it took 30 minutes of silence, but the strategy worked.

Mr. Jones also noticed that not much had happened during negotiations until the evening before he was scheduled to return to the United States. Then, he was under pressure to accomplish a lot in negotiations, with the hope that he would "give the store away." Mr. Jones countered this ploy by arranging for his return ticket after all negotiations and agreements had been made.

Mr. Jones also learned about other cultural aspects of doing business in Japan, which have included the following:

- Upon meeting a Japanese executive, a slight bow and handshake are appropriate.
- Business card etiquette is important. On one side of the card, the information should be in English; the other side should have the same information in Japanese.
- It is not appropriate to look directly into the eyes of your Japanese hosts.
- It is important for your Japanese hosts to know your title and rank. They prefer to do business with high-ranking individuals.
- Japanese business has a group orientation, rather than an individualistic one. "The peg that stands out gets hammered down" is an old Japanese saying.
- They expect foreign business representatives to arrive prepared and to have decision-making authority.
- New potential business partners must have been referred to Japanese business representatives through a third party.

Cultural Dimensions of Doing Business in Korea

Korea has a rich cultural tradition with which foreign business representatives should be acquainted. Here are some highlights of Korean values, attitudes, and customs:

- Older generations are respected for their knowledge and wisdom. Gray hair is viewed positively.
- The number *1* is good, whereas the number *4* signifies death or failure.
- Children are not supposed to say their parents' names, even when used with a title.
- Younger brothers and sisters are not allowed to use the names of their older siblings.
- "Yangban" refers to the noble class. Its culture is honor, reputation, and dignity. It is illustrated by never begging, even when one is hungry, and never running, even when it rains.

- "We" is more important than "I."
- At the dinner table, older generations, superiors, or parents will start to eat earlier than subordinates, younger generations, or children.
- It is important not to show your backside when meeting with a colleague. Thus, you will back out of his office instead of turning around to leave.
- Teachers are so revered that walking in their shadows is viewed as impolite.
- Rocks, trees, clouds, and skies are important elements of Korean culture.
- Adults who are married with their own children will often live with their parents.
- **"Inwa"** involves harmony among unequals: loyalty is owed to parents and authority figures, yet superiors are responsible for the well-being of their subordinates.
- A personal relationship needs to occur before business matters can be discussed with foreigners.[10]

Cultural Dimensions of Doing Business in China

The overriding cultural aspect of doing business in China is **guanxi** ("*gwanshe*"). Foreign business representatives who ignore *guanxi* are less likely to be successful in the Chinese market.

Guanxi refers to the relationship between subordinates and superiors. It denotes friendship among unequals involving unlimited exchanges of favors; thus, it is not based upon sentiment. It is utilitarian, not emotional. It has an individual orientation, not a group one.

Exchanges are often uneven, working to the advantage of weaker members in the *guanxi* relationship. Thus, claims of modesty and inadequacy should be viewed as subtle demands for generosity, reminding the more powerful individual of his or her obligation to be more magnanimous. This concept also applies to relationships with more powerful and wealthy foreigners who are expected to cede certain points to Chinese business representatives during business dealings.

Floresco Productions/OJO Images Ltd/Alamy

Korean family showing respect for the grandfather.

inwa
korean philosophy stressing harmony among unequals, loyalty to parents and authority figures, and superiors being responsible for the well-being of subordinates

guanxi
chinese philosophy denoting friendships among unequals and unlimited exchanges of favors; it is not based on sentiment, emotions, or a group orientation

Persons of low rank may be powerful and influential due to *guanxi* relationships with superiors. Therefore, foreigners who want to conduct business in China may need to seek out these lower level persons and obtain their favor in order to gain access to the more powerful superiors who are the decision makers.[11]

Cultural Dimensions of Doing Business in Arab Countries

There are a number of "don'ts" that business representatives must recognize when doing business in Arab countries:

- Avoid sitting so that the sole of one's shoe is shown.
- The left hand is viewed as "unclean." (After returning from conducting a five-day workshop for the Kuwait Institute of Banking Studies, one author of this text realized that he had used his left hand when distributing all of his handout materials!)
- Good posture is imperative.
- Foreign business representatives should not inquire about the wives of Arab business representatives.
- Do not be overly effusive when praising the possessions of Arab hosts, as this could create a perception that you expect they give these possessions to you.
- Arab business representatives will probably be reluctant to do business with women. If a woman is accepted, modest dress is appropriate.
- Arab business representatives may frequently divert from the topic initially discussed, then return to it.

Cultural Dimensions of Doing Business in Latin America

Latin America is an attractive market for foreign companies. Brazil, Mexico, Argentina, and Colombia are populous countries (Brazil, 201 million; Mexico, 112 million; Argentina, 41 million; and Colombia, 44 million) and they have reached viable per capita GDPs: Brazil

Gal Schweizer/CON/Getty Images

Dancing is an important cultural dimension in Latin America.

ETHICAL PERSPECTIVES

Right or Wrong? It Depends on the Culture

Cultures around the world have different paradigms describing what is ethical or unethical when conducting business in overseas markets.

Foreign companies that want to promote their products in France are often surprised that the French consider it unethical for advertisements to disparage competitors and/or their products. This cultural norm has been incorporated into legislation outlawing such practices.

Ethical considerations permeate contractual agreements. Whether agreements will be reached by a handshake or by signed contract, businesspeople in some countries believe that it is ethical to unilaterally modify the terms if "conditions have changed."

When Americans do business in Latin America, they often find that their hosts spend a lot of time discussing cultural matters, such as the art, history, architecture, and music that is pertinent to his or her home country before "getting down to business." The American business people, on the other hand, believe that such matters are unimportant, they detract from closing the deal, or they should be discussed only after an understanding and agreement has been made.

In Muslim countries, it is considered unethical to charge interest on business loans. In non-Muslim nations, it is accepted that interest will be charged and must be paid.

Paying bribes to foreign officials deciding upon who should be awarded infrastructure contracts is an ethical conundrum of doing business overseas. American companies complained that when they would not pay bribes, they would not get contracts because companies from other countries did pay them. In order to cope with this problem, the Advocacy Center was created in the U.S. Department of Commerce. This enabled high-ranking U.S. government officials, such as the Secretary of Commerce, to accompany American executives in efforts to secure some of these lucrative accounts.

$10,200; Mexico, $13,200; Argentina, $13,400; and Colombia, $9,200. Chile is small (16.7 million people) but has per capita GDP of $14,600. Uruguay is similar, with 3.5 million people and a per capita GDP of $12,600.[12]

When doing business in Latin America, it is important to understand that potential customers want to develop a personal relationship before doing business with foreign executives. Dinner meetings and lunch meetings provide a good time for executives to get to know one another better. Often, conversations about buying and selling, and contracts and terms will be relegated below discussions about the particular Latin American country's culture, history, architecture, current economic conditions, and similar topics. Dinners often occur late in the evening, at 9:00 p.m. or 10:00 p.m. Formal manners and appropriate business attire are appreciated.

Latin Americans are not as conscious about time as are North Americans. They are not as rushed as workers from the United States. If something does not get done today, there is always the next day—or the day after that. Companies that want to do business in Latin America will need to be flexible about meeting times, dates, and deadlines.

Latin Americans are not as immersed in their work as the business people in the United States. Their motto is: "We work to live," not "We live to work."

REALITY CHECK LO-5

Find someone who is a native of a foreign country and now works in the United States (or your home country). Ask that person about customs and business practices in the United States, and how these compare with customs and business practices in his or her native country. How easily do you think you would adapt if you worked in that person's country?

LO-6

Explain why culture is important in global management and marketing.

The Importance of Culture For Managing and Marketing in Overseas Markets

When managing people and resources in a foreign country, close attention to host-countries' cultures is critical. Failure to do so can severely damage a company's performance in these markets. In recent years, a number of companies have addressed the cultural aspects of managing their overseas operations. Not infrequently, a key factor in global management success has been communication.

Management Styles

U.S. companies have management styles that frequently conflict with the management styles preferred in other cultures. For example, a young executive whose age and impetuous nature did not jibe with Japan's management culture headed PepsiCo's initial foray into Japan.[13] As another example, McDonald's uses a decentralized model to give its international managers, who are almost 100% foreign, more decision-making authority.[14]

Microsoft discovered that businessmen in India's knitted cotton industry carried sensitive information about inventory, customers, cost estimates, proposals, and orders, in their heads or noted them in various ledgers. Often, these highly significant data were lost—or were compromised—when managers would quit on short notice. Microsoft recommended an order tracking system that the knitting companies could access over the web by text message.[15]

Tata is an Indian conglomerate, which specializes in automobile manufacturing and recognizes the importance of using several management styles. Tata recently acquired Jaguar and Land Rover, and also purchased Britain's Tetley Tea, and Corus, a European steel company (for $12 billion). Analysts are bullish on Tata because of its "Indian origin, which makes it more sensitive to cultural differences than many of its peers in developed countries."[16]

Lenovo is a Chinese manufacturer of PCs. In an effort to become a truly global company, the firm decided to eliminate headquarters; instead it holds rotating meetings for senior managers at its various locations around the world. The company has made a concerted effort to integrate the different management styles existing in its various international decisions through the following philosophy: "In all situations, assume good intentions; be intentional about understanding others and being understood; respect cultural differences."[17]

Hyundai, the Korean car manufacturer, has not met its sales goals in the U.S. market because of its failure to recognize U.S. management styles in its U.S. operations:

- Headquarters sends out "coordinators," who are responsible for keeping an eye on American managers. Coordinators closely monitor American managers' decision making and the results of those decisions. Hyundai's international organization is highly centralized; it is much more authoritarian than the environment to which its U.S. managers are accustomed.
- Sales goals are established with little input from U.S. executives. Instead of basing goals upon projected demand, they are driven by production quotas. This has resulted in an unsold inventory of 32,000 Sonatas stored at Hyundai's Montgomery, Alabama plant.
- There is an over-management of details; headquarters rarely listens to advice from its American managers, and little, if any, dissent is permitted.[18]

The above examples provide some in-depth glimpses into the ways in which management styles can give rise to challenges or lead to success. While it is difficult to draw overarching conclusions from various companies' experiences with management styles, some attitudes and beliefs that drive various management styles can be noted, and some comments and cautions can be offered:

- "Master of destiny" philosophy: the idea that workers and companies can influence the future. Hard work, a commitment to company goals, and effective time management are important aspects of this managerial orientation.
- A company is an independent enterprise. It is a vital social institution. Workers will do what is best for the company instead of what is best for their government or their families.
- Rewards are based on merit. This management style may be problematic in other cultures, where friendships and family ties may be more important.
- Decisions are based upon objective analysis. Accurate information and its timeliness are important aspects of decision-making. In some cultures, judgment and intuition may be viewed as being more vital.
- Wide-sharing in decision-making. Effective decisions are often viewed as the primary way to evaluate subordinates. Decision-making, thus, is decentralized and delegated to lower levels of management. In other cultures, such as the Middle East, only top executives will make the most important decisions.
- An internal quest for improvement. This often involves a company's need to adjust to change in its environment in order to achieve higher sales, profits, and market shares. This style may be problematic in other cultures that are more interested in maintaining the status quo.
- Competition is necessary. This is reflected in competition among workers and competition among companies. In China and Japan, however, cooperation is emphasized over competition.[19]

Product Development and Management

When developing new products, management styles must be considered along with many other aspects of marketing expertise. Products that are wildly successful in home-country markets may need to be modified for an international market. The Barbie doll (Mattel Inc.), for example, was a smash hit in the United States, but did not achieve much popularity in Japan until the doll's legs were shortened and its chest made smaller. Automobiles that were exported to Japan from the United States were not accepted until the steering wheels were placed on the right side instead of the left side.

Not surprisingly, there can be different cultural groups within countries of which organizations need to be aware. In China, for example, there are marked differences among consumer preferences from one city to another. Women in Shanghai are considered cosmopolitan and sophisticated, so Proctor & Gamble markets Oil of Olay skin cream in this area. But in Urumqi, the largest city in China's Uighur region, Safeguard soap and Crest toothpaste are primarily sold in the female market.[20]

Half of McDonald's sales are overseas, and the growth rates overseas exceed that in the United States. This performance is largely attributed to McDonald's tailoring its products to comply with local tastes. Here are some examples:

- "The Big Tasty" (a giant hamburger) was developed in test kitchens in Germany and then launched in Sweden. It has been a huge success in Latin America and Australia.
- The "Croque McDo" (France) is based on the traditional *croque-monsieur*, a grilled sandwich of ham and melted cheese on toast.

- A "McKroket" in the Netherlands is a deep-fried patty of beef ragout, based on the traditional deep-fried meat *kroket*.
- Porridge is available on McDonald's breakfast menus in Great Britain.
- India's "Maharaja Mac" consists of two chicken patties with smoke-flavored mayo.
- A "Rice Burger" in Taiwan contains shredded beef between two rice patties.
- South Korea's "Bulgogi Burger" is a pork-patty sandwich marinated in soy bean sauce.

New wrappers, boxes, and bags, to better promote the company were developed in Europe, and introduced by McDonald's into the United States in 2008. At the same time, McDonald's announced that "artisan breads," baguette-style sandwich rolls popular in France, would enter the U.S. market as a premium product.[21]

There are many examples of American brands that have been unsuccessful in foreign markets because their names were not culturally acceptable. Colgate was chagrined to discover that its toothpaste, "Cue," in France was the name of a notorious pornographic magazine. In Italy, Schweppes Tonic Water was interpreted as "Schweppes Toilet Water." Coca-Cola in Chinese was originally read as "Ke-Kow-Ke-La" which, unfortunately was translated as "bite the wax tadpole" or "female horse stuffed with wax." The name was changed to "Ko-Kou-Ko-Le" meaning "happiness in the mouth." When Chevrolet introduced the Chevy Nova into Latin America, the company quickly realized that "no va" meant "it won't go" in Spanish. The name was changed to "Caribe." In 2012, IKEA was chagrined to learn that in Thailand, its Jattebra plant pot was interpreted by shoppers as a crude term for sex.[22]

Advertising Campaigns

Like brands, advertising campaigns must be carefully tailored to local cultures. The list of failed campaigns rivals the one for misnamed brands (see previous examples under "Language"). Parker Pen's ads in Mexico were supposed to read, "It won't leak in your pocket and embarrass you." Unfortunately, the ad people believed that the Spanish word, "embarazar," meant "embarrass." The ad in Spanish read, "It won't leak in your pocket and make you pregnant." When a large Japanese tourist agency entered English-speaking markets, it was mystified when it received numerous requests for unusual sex tours. The explanation: the company's name was Kinki Nippon Tourist Company. Nike's Chamber of Fear ads featured NBA star, LeBron James, defeating a computer-generated Kung Fu master. Chinese viewers were disturbed by the ad and it was cancelled. Toyota had an ad in China showing a Land Rover Cruiser SUV towing a military truck; another featured a stone lion, a symbol of power in China, bowing down to Toyota's Prado GX. Chinese consumers were insulted by the negative portrayal of their military, as well as bowing down to anything Japanese. Nike's "Just Do It" campaign did not work in China because it emphasized individual, youthful irreverence. Because Muslims view dogs as unclean, Taco Bell did not use Gidget, a talking Chihuahua mascot, in its ads in Singapore.[23]

Communication

Communication is a key function in business, and culture has an impact on communication styles whether a firm is small or large, multinational or domestic. Companies with foreign personnel running their overseas operations must be especially careful to clearly communicate.

The use of jargon is usually inappropriate, as it greatly increases the risk of misunderstanding. Exhibit 5.4 gives some examples. Abbreviations like CAD, CAM, COO, CEO, and CFO may not be understood by personnel in foreign countries, nor will Latin and French phrases.

EXHIBIT 5.4 EXAMPLES OF U.S.-BASED BUSINESS JARGON THAT WOULD NOT BE UNDERSTOOD BY FOREIGN BUSINESS REPRESENTATIVES

1. "Flying by the seat of my pants."
2. "On the same wave length."
3. "Shotgun approach."
4. "Run it up the flag pole."
5. "100 k."
6. "Belly up."
7. "Overview."
8. "If it ain't broke, don't fix it."
9. "Let's throw it on the wall and see if it sticks."
10. "Let's see how it plays out."
11. "It ain't over until the fat lady sings."
12. "Reinvent the wheel."

Managers attending business functions in person may not have the opportunity to find words in a dictionary. In such cases, the old saying that "a little knowledge is a dangerous thing" can be true. One of the authors of this text was in Mexico having lunch with a group of faculty from another university. Although he is somewhat knowledgeable about the Spanish language, he was having difficulty reading the menu, which was completely in Spanish. Finally, he recognized the word "cordero" (lamb), so he ordered "sesos de cordero."

After the waiter had taken their orders, one of the other diners who was fluent in Spanish asked, "Do you know what you ordered?"

"Sure; I ordered chunks of lamb."

"No, you ordered *brains* of lamb."

REALITY CHECK LO-6

Choose three or four ads from a U.S. magazine or website and describe the cultural factors to which each ad appeals. Do you think the ads are successful from a cultural standpoint? Why or why not?

SUMMARY

Companies conducting business overseas need to be in harmony with the prevailing cultures in those countries. Culture is learned, and is almost impossible for a foreign company to change.

The major elements of culture include language, religion, values and attitudes, manners and customs, material elements, aesthetics, education, and social institutions.

Hofstede (individualism vs. collectivism, power distance, masculine vs. feminine, uncertainty avoidance, and time orientation), Trompenaars (universalism vs. particularism, neutral vs. emotional, specific vs. diffuse, and achievement vs. ascription) and Gannon (country metaphors) have used various constructs to capture the cultures of world nations. The GLOBE project was perhaps the most aggressive effort to examine the cultures of countries and regions of the world on nine different dimensions; it involved surveying thousands of business executives in 61 countries.

Along with various consulting firms, there are a number of secondary sources available for learning about cultures of other countries. Some examples include the *U.S. Department of Commerce Country Commercial Guide*, Country Reports from *The Economist's* Intelligence Unit, and Price Waterhouse Coopers' *Doing Business in 118 Countries*.

When doing business in foreign countries, there are certain specifics to keep in mind. Japanese firms tend to make group decisions; they want to deal with people of high rank who have decision-making authority and have been referred by third parties. Korean culture stresses a reverence for older people, a group orientation rather that an individualistic one, inwha (harmony among equals), superiors' responsibility for the well-being of subordinates, and the development of personal relationships before business relationships can occur. *Guanxi* is the most important cultural aspect of doing business in China; it denotes friendships among unequals. Because low-ranking people in Chinese firms may have a *guanxi* relationship with superiors who have decision-making authority, foreign businessmen may need to cultivate the favor of lower-echelon personnel in Chinese companies.

In Arab countries, business visitors need to be aware that the left hand is unclean, that asking about Arab business representative's wives is inappropriate, that Arab businessmen are generally reluctant to deal with women, and that they have a tendency to divert from primary items under discussion.

Latin American executives want to develop a personal relationship before doing business with foreign executives. They are not as time oriented or as immersed in their work as are North Americans.

Management of overseas personnel and resources, product development, and advertising are significantly affected by foreign countries' cultures. Clear communication can improve the outcomes of management decisions in these three areas.

KEY TERMS

culture, *p. 118*
acculturation, *p. 118*
verbal communication, *p. 118*
non-verbal communication, *p. 119*
backward translation, *p. 119*
values, *p. 120*
attitudes, *p. 120*
manners and customs, *p. 120*
material culture, *p. 121*
aesthetics, *p. 122*
social institutions, *p. 122*
reference groups, *p. 122*
social stratification, *p. 122*
individualism vs. collectivism, *p. 123*
power distance, *p. 123*
masculine vs. feminine, *p. 123*
uncertainty avoidance, *p. 123*
time orientation, *p. 123*
universalism vs. particularism, *p. 123*
neutral vs. emotional, *p. 123*
specific vs. diffuse, *p. 123*
achievement vs. ascription, *p. 124*
inwa, *p. 129*
guanxi, *p. 129*

CHAPTER QUESTIONS

1. What are the four characteristics of culture that global marketers must recognize?

2. Name four elements of culture and briefly indicate why they are important when marketing products and services internationally.

3. How do Gannon's cultural metaphors differ from how Hofstede uses culture to classify countries?

MINI-CASE: ADVISING CLIENTS ABOUT CULTURAL ASPECTS OF EXPORTING TO ECUADOR

After graduation, you have been employed by a large consulting firm which specializes in advising U.S. clients on exporting to various overseas markets. Your firm has specialized in European and Asian markets, but now sees opportunities for advising clients about the Latin American market. You and seven of your colleagues have each been assigned a specific country in Latin America. Yours is Ecuador.

You start your research by obtaining some basic facts about the country. Its name is Spanish for "Equator," obviously derived from the fact that it is located on the equator. Its capital, Quito, is 9,300 feet above sea level; it has a fairly constant year-around temperatures of 75° (high) and 55° (low).

Ecuador's population is 15 million, or 138.4 people per square mile. Sixty-six percent live in urban areas. Spanish is the official language and 95 percent of its people are Catholics. Its land mass is about 109,000 square miles.

Major industries in Ecuador include oil, food processing, textiles, wood products, and chemicals. Its chief crops are bananas, coffee, cocoa, rice, potatoes, manioc, plantains, and sugar cane. Its GDP was $115 billion in 2010, with a per capita GDP of $7,800. Its currency is the U.S. dollar. Twenty-seven percent of its imports come from the United States; 34.4 percent of its exports go to that nation.

Your boss wants you to develop a cultural map of Ecuador so that your firm can include this in its prospectus to potential clients. You begin by noting that its official language is Spanish and 95 percent of its people are practicing Catholics.

QUESTIONS:

1. What sources about Ecuador should you consult to obtain cultural information about this country that will need to be included in your cultural map?
2. What other aspects of Ecuadorian culture, other than its predominant religion and language, might affect that country's culture?

Should You Defend Your Country from Criticism of its Culture Even Though it May Cost Your Company a Major Sale?

You are about to close a major sale in a foreign market when, suddenly, the individual who will make the final decision lashes out with a diatribe against the culture of the United States. Music, art, abortions, and pornography are specifically named.

POINT Upholding one's country and its culture should take precedence over the possibility of making a sale—even a large and important one. You should vigorously defend the United States, indicating that while there may be some aspects of the U.S. culture that deserve censure, on the whole, it has a rich culture, one that has developed because the freedom to make choices exists. You should also counterattack by pointing out that the host country's culture has its faults.

COUNTER-POINT Everyone is entitled to his or her own opinion, so you should not object to the potential customer's criticism of the U.S. culture. In fact, you should agree with what is being said and give some additional examples to support the criticisms. Why jeopardize a major sale over something as trivial as what a foreigner thinks about the United States?

What Do *You* Think?

Which argument do you believe is the most valid? Why? Is there a diplomatic middle ground?

4. What are some important secondary sources that companies can consult to learn about the cultures of other countries?

5. What are some cultural factors that U.S. companies must recognize when doing business in Latin America?

6. What types of managerial decisions in foreign countries are driven by cultural factors?

INTERPRETING GLOBAL BUSINESS NEWS

Financial news is everywhere in the popular press and media. How do you interpret the following examples of financial news related to the concepts in this chapter?

1. France has a central office for the fight against traffic in cultural goods. Why is this office needed?[24]

2. Critics have charged that the economic and financial problems experienced by the United States in 2008-2010 were largely caused by a government belief that every American should be able to own a home. Is this belief culturally compatible with what exists in other countries?

3. Swiss banks, like UBS and Credit Suisse, have a culture of secrecy for their depositors, and this culture has been supported by Swiss government policy. What problems has this policy caused for the banks and their depositors, especially American ones?

PORTFOLIO PROJECTS

Explore Your Own Case in Point: How Your Company Manages Foreign Cultures

After reading this chapter you should be prepared to answer some basic questions about your favorite company.

1. Examine the countries where your company does business according to where they rank on the Hofstede cultural dimensions. Think of some examples of how a U.S. manager would need to modify his or her behavior when communicating with associates from one or more of these foreign countries.

2. If you were visiting a foreign country to negotiate a transaction on behalf of this company, what cultural knowledge would you need to gain before the visit? How and from where would you get the information?

3. If a representative from a foreign country where your company does not currently conduct business contacted you with a proposal, how would you evaluate the proposal in light of cultural characteristics of that country?

Develop an International Strategy for Your Own Small Business: Exporting Cookies to Europe

You have worked hard to achieve success in your baked goods company. So far, you have marketed your products only to U.S. and Canadian markets. Your marketing specialist has decided that the company needs to explore the possibility of exporting to Europe. You need to prepare a preliminary assessment of the cultural aspects of the European market that must be considered if the company moves forward with this exporting strategy.

1. What major aspects of culture should you consider in your assessment?

2. Do these aspects need to be identified with specific countries or regions in Europe?

3. Do you expect that the cultural landscape affecting the consumption and sale of cookies will be the same or different than what prevails in the United States?

CHAPTER NOTES

[1] V. Terpstra, R. Sarathy, and L. Russow, *International Marketing* (Cleveland, Ohio: North Coast Publishers, 2006).
[2] R. Hise, R. Solano-Mendez, and L. Gresham, "Doing Business in Mexico," *Thunderbird International Review*, March-April 2003, pp. 211–224.
[3] M. R. Czinkota and I. A. Ronkainen, *International Marketing* (Mason, Ohio: Thomson South-Western, 2004).
[4] V. Terpstra, R. Sarathy and L. Russow, *International Marketing*. Cleveland, Ohio: North Coast Publishers, 2006.
[5] Ibid.
[6] Barbara Wilson, presentation to Texas A&M University Study Abroad Class, Nice, France, May 2006.
[7] J. K. Johansson, *Global Marketing* (New York, New York: Mc-Graw-Hill, 2003).
[8] Special Issue On GLOBE, *Journal Of World Business*, 37 (2002), pp. 1–89.
[9] Johansson, J. K., *Global Marketing* (New York, New York: McGraw-Hill, 2003).
[10] The authors thank Jong-Kuk Shin, Pusan National University and Young-Tae Choi, University of North Florida, U.S.A. for the material in this section.
[11] J. K. Johansson, *Global Marketing*. New York, New York: Mc-Graw-Hill, 2003.
[12] *World Almanac*, 2011 (New York, New York: World Almanac Books, 2011).
[13] F. Balfour and D. Kiley, "Ad Agencies Unchained," *Business Week*, April 25, 2005, pp. 50–51.
[14] P. Gumbel, "Big Mac's Local Flavor," *Fortune*, May 5, 2008, pp. 115–121.
[15] M. Bahree, "Microsoft in India," *Forbes*, September 29, 2008, pp. 74–77.
[16] "A Special Report on Globalization," *The Economist*, September 20, 2008, pp. 8–10.
[17] Ibid.
[18] D. Welch, D. Kiley, and M. Ihlwan, "My Way or the Highway at Hyundai," *Business Week*, March 17, 2008, pp. 48–51.
[19] Johansson, *Global Marketing*. New York, New York: Mc-Graw-Hill, 2003.
[20] Balfour and D. Kiley, "Ad Agencies Unchained," pp. 50–51.
[21] Gumbel, P., "Big Mac's Local Flavor, pp. 115–121.
[22] J. Hookway, "IKEA'S Products Make Shopper's Blush in Thailand," *The Wall Street Journal*, June 5, 2012, pp A1, A16.
[23] Balfour and D. Kiley, "Ad Agencies Unchained," pp. 50–51.
[24] *Financial Times*, May 21, 2010.

CH 6

The Legal and Political Environment of Global Business

© C Miller Design/ Getty Images

Reuters/HANNIBAL HANSCHKE

After studying this chapter, you should be able to:

LO-1 Provide an overview of the different global political systems and their potential impact on international business.

LO-2 Explain the differences among communism, capitalism, and socialism and how these different economic ideologies affect the conduct of international business.

LO-3 Discuss the key political and economic risks and the role of corruption when conducting global business.

LO-4 Analyze the different types of legal systems, and some key principles involving criminal, contract, tax, product safety, and dispute settlement law.

LO-5 Discuss the importance of intellectual property protections in today's global business environment, and the major types of intellectual property protections including patents, trademarks, and copyrights.

Penalties That Fit the Crime

Oh no, a person has been caught speeding! This person was driving about 80 miles per hour in a 60-mile-per-hour speed zone, and a police officer had pulled them over and written them a ticket. The ticket is for $103,000—yes, one hundred and three thousand dollars!

Welcome to Finland! In Finland, traffic fines are generally based on two factors: the driver's income and the severity of the offense. If a college student with a very low income is caught speeding, he or she will pay a minimal fine (maybe around $100), but if the speeding driver is the CEO of Nokia Corporation earning over, say, $30 million per year, the fine for the same offense may well be over $100,000.

Until 1999, offenders were on the "honor system" to accurately report their income, but since then all tax records have been made available online as public records. The police can instantly enter a speeder's identification into their patrol car's computer, obtain the driver's reported income, and compute the accurate speeding fine.

Finland and some other Scandinavian countries have progressive (income linked) systems of fines for a wide range of civil and criminal offenses, including securities laws violations and shoplifting. The idea is that fixed money fines have a disproportionate impact on the less wealthy, and fail to be an adequate deterrent to those with very high incomes. For example, is an $80 speeding ticket truly going to deter a CEO making $30 million a year from speeding? But once a wealthy executive has gotten a $100,000 speeding ticket, might he or she drive a little more carefully in the future?[1]

Introduction

As the example of traffic fines in Finland demonstrates, different countries throughout the world have different legal and political systems. The progressive Scandinavian penalty system metes out punishment according to the offender's financial resources. More typically, various kinds of laws are stricter in some countries and more lax in others. What might be a heavily punished crime in one country may be a very lightly punished crime in another one—or perhaps not a crime at all. Some countries, for example, such as Switzerland, have traditionally put considerable legal weight on corporate and individual privacy rights, while other countries (such as Finland) have regulations requiring personal information to be publicly available.

Doing business in some countries is fraught with legal and political risks. The recent fall of governing regimes that had been in power for decades in countries such as Egypt and Libya illustrates this point. Widespread corruption and governmental expropriation of assets frequently occurs in some countries, notably in the developing world, while the legal and political situation in other nations is very stable. This chapter will provide an overview of political and legal environments throughout the world and how such environments affect the conduct of global business.

Political Systems

Democracy vs. Totalitarianism

LO-1

Provide an overview of the different global political systems and their potential impact on international business.

Different countries throughout the world have different political systems. The country of Finland, which was discussed earlier, is a democracy. **Democracy** is Greek for "rule by the people"; it refers to a form of government in which all citizens have the right to vote. In the United States, for example, all citizens over the age of eighteen are eligible to vote for the election of the President of the United States, and the President is elected for a four-year term in office, with a limit of two consecutive terms. The purest form of democracy existed in the city-states of ancient Greece, particularly Athens, and is known as **Athenian democracy**. Developed around 500 BCE, the Athenian system provided for all adult citizens to assemble periodically and vote on matters affecting the community.

democracy
greek for "rule by the people"; form of government in which all citizens have the right to vote

athenian democracy
a pure form of democracy, in which all adult citizens vote directly on matters affecting the community

representative democracy
form of government in which citizens vote to elect given individuals to serve as their representatives for a certain period of time

totalitarian government
system of government in which individuals govern without the support or consent of the citizenry; for example, a military dictatorship

Over time, as cities (and nations) throughout the world have grown much larger, most, if not all, democracies today are what are known as **representative democracies**. Because it would be nearly impossible to gather all citizens together to vote on all matters, democratic nations have developed a system of electing representatives (such as members of the U.S. Congress, members of state legislatures, state governors and, the President of the United States) to serve as their representatives in conducting the affairs of state. Elections in representative democracies are always conducted by secret ballot, with legal protection afforded to citizens' rights to freedom of speech and expression. By definition, democracies are to some extent unstable, because elections are held at periodic intervals and new representatives of the people come into political power at that time.

Some countries with strong representative democracies, such as Great Britain, Japan, Spain, South Korea, and Norway, also have ceremonial monarchs (kings and queens) that serve as permanent heads of state but have no real political power. Monarchs of this kind help provide a degree of stability to the overall political system. Countries following this kind of model are, of course, not pure representative democracies; they are referred to as constitutional monarchies.

Opposite democracies are totalitarian countries. A **totalitarian government** is a system in which individuals govern without the support or consent of the citizenry. A country run by a military dictatorship, for example, would represent a totalitarian regime. The dictatorships that prevailed in Eastern Europe during the Cold War are another example. Other countries are primarily theocratically totalitarian in nature, meaning that non-elected religious leaders have considerable political control of the country. This situation exists in the country of Iran today where religious "Ayatollahs" hold principal sway. Another totalitarian variant is the absolute monarchy, in which the king or queen holds iron-clad political power. King Henry VIII who ruled England in almost a tyrannical fashion from 1509 to 1547 was an example of an absolute monarch.

Many kinds of governments also exist between the extremes of democracy and totalitarianism such as today's China where party rulers share some rights with citizens. It should be noted, though, that the openness of democratic countries like Finland, and the protections such countries tend to generally provide for property rights and freedom of expression, usually make those countries more hospitable places to conduct global business than countries with totalitarian or semi-totalitarian political regimes. However, this is not always the case, particularly where such regimes take strong pro-business approaches. For example, while property and other rights in totalitarian countries are completely under the control of the ruling regime, the political systems in such countries may actually be more "stable" than in democratic countries because a dictator in such a country may be in power for many decades. For example, the House of Saud family has had a king with strong political power firmly ruling Saudi Arabia's pro-business economy since 1931. As another example, Singapore historically has had a highly pro-business political system in a parliamentary model context, with one ruling party, in power since 1959. The stability of that system has enabled international business to flourish in Singapore. It is important to remember that power and regulations inherently change periodically even in democratic regimes, and they sometimes change in ways that are not favorable to business.

REALITY CHECK LO-1

Have you ever lived in a country without a representative democracy? If not, find someone who has and talk to them about their experiences.

Asia File/Alamy

Singapore has had a highly pro-business political system. Tharman Shanmugaratnam is Singapore's Deputy Prime Minister as well as the chairman of the International Monetary and Financial Committee, the policy advisory committee of the IMF.

LO-2
Explain the differences among communism, capitalism, and socialism and how these different economic ideologies affect the conduct of global business.

National Economic Ideologies

A country's political system plays on important role in the conduct of international business in that country, but the economic ideology that prevails in that country has a greater role in business. For example, two given countries might both be "representative democracies," but if one is more socialistic in its economic ideology, and the other more capitalistic in economic ideology, the conduct of business in these countries will differ considerably from one another. In today's complex economic world, very few countries purely follow one economic ideology or another. For example, the United States is primarily a capitalistic country with an economic ideology that strongly supports free markets, individual initiatives, and private ownership. However, the United States has had a federal minimum wage, a federal income tax system, and a federal retirement plan (Social Security) since the 1930s; since the 1960s it also has had a welfare "safety net" to reduce poverty and a government-run health care program (Medicare) for the elderly. The following sections provide a general overview of the basic economic ideologies that prevail in the world today.

Communism

communism
an economic ideology whereby the government or state owns and controls all major factors of production and is philosophically an economically classless society

Communism represents an economic ideology whereby the government or state owns and controls all the major factors of production. Employee labor unions exist in such countries, but are controlled by the state. Under Communist economic ideology, individual rights give way in the extreme to collectivistic rights—under Karl Marx's classic view, a communist country is at heart an economically classless one. The past two or three decades have brought a considerable decline in communist economic ideology throughout the world, the shift of the old Soviet Union away from communism as the most notable.

ECONOMIC PERSPECTIVES Family Planning in China

Beginning in 1979, the communist government of China formally adopted a "one child" family planning policy. This policy officially restricted the number of children that married Chinese couples could have, although exceptions have been allowed for couples outside urban areas (i.e., rural couples), parents without any siblings themselves, and so forth. The goal of the program has been to help alleviate China's over-population problem. While the program has achieved this goal, it has also resulted in "gendercide"; Chinese couples have regularly aborted or killed female babies because of a strong cultural preference for sons. In China today, the ratio of males born to females born is significantly higher. Ethical or moral issues aside, the Chinese one child policy has also had considerable economic impact.

Because of China's skewed sex ratios, young Chinese men are finding it very difficult to get married. These rootless young men, known in China as "bare branches," have increasingly become involved in criminal activities, and thus has led to extra costs for law enforcement. Moreover, China's ultra-competitive marriage market has led parents with single sons to save more money in order to help them with dowries and to otherwise attract mates. Indeed, observers have attributed about 50 percent of the increase in China's saving rate over the past 25 years to its one child policy. This sharp increase in China's saving rate has helped offset other Chinese governmental efforts to try and boost Chinese consumer consumption. Less consumption by Chinese consumers means fewer exports to China by U.S. consumer product companies such as Coca Cola, Proctor & Gamble, and Colgate-Palmolive, and fewer profits (and U.S. jobs) for these companies.

QUESTIONS:

1. What types of crimes do you think Chinese bare branches might most likely be involved with?
2. What kinds of impacts does China's one child rule have on retirement policies in that country?

Sources: "Gendercide", *The Economist*, March 6, 2010, p. 13; "The Worldwide War on Baby Girls," *The Economist*, March 6, 2010, pp. 77–80.

China is currently the largest nation in the world with a communist economic ideology, and it is emerging as one of the most economically powerful countries in the world. But to achieve this success, China has found that it needs to very slowly move away from a 100 percent communist economic ideological approach. For example, today some private (or foreign) ownership of certain major Chinese businesses is permitted, although these businesses still generally remain 80 percent or more government owned and controlled. Moreover, there has been some relaxation of state control of labor unions.

Socialism

Socialism involves an economic ideology in which the government or state plays a strong role in the economy and may own stakes in certain businesses. Unlike communist countries, however, countries with socialist economies do not aspire to be "classless." That said, such economies tend to be somewhat more collectively than individualistically oriented, with disparities in income and wealth less extreme than in capitalistic countries. Many European countries (e.g., France, Great Britain, and Spain) have strong socialistic orientations, with governments in those countries historically owning stakes in various businesses such as major airlines and oil companies.

Socialistic economies put a high degree of importance upon worker and labor rights, and upon the existence of strong free labor unions. Not surprisingly, labor union membership and participation rates in economically socialistically oriented countries such as Sweden, Norway, and Denmark tend to be among the highest in the world. These countries also have traditionally had the highest per-capita net incomes in the world, and have been very hospitable places to conduct global business from a number of perspectives.

Capitalism

Capitalism refers to an economic system where businesses are privately owned with a strong individualistic profit orientation. Very little role for government exists in a purely capitalistic or "free market" economic system. Individual gains and losses of wealth can be very large, as the government pursuant to this ideology is primarily uninvolved in the economic system and, therefore, the individual successes and failures that occur. Individual incentives are at the core of capitalistic economic ideology.

The United States, with its strong individualistic, entrepreneurial, free-market spirit, historically has been viewed as the leading economically capitalistic economy in the world. However, as noted earlier, even in the United States, the federal government has taken a role in the economic sector. More recently, through its Troubled Asset Relief Program (TARP) and other programs, the government has held major ownership stakes in a number of the country's largest automobile manufacturers, insurance companies, and banks. Moreover, a host of long-standing U.S. government programs—including food stamps, Medicaid, farm subsidies, flood insurance, and scholarships and research grants—continue to help smooth out individual income disparities and economic successes and failures. While economic ideologies vary widely in countries throughout the world, and many countries today have economic ideologies that are to some extent "mixed," the existence of these ideologies clearly affects the conduct of international business in given jurisdictions.

socialism
an economic ideology in which the government plays a strong role in the economy and may own stakes in certain businesses

capitalism
an economic ideology where businesses are privately owned, strong individual incentives exist, and the government plays very little role in the economy

REALITY CHECK LO-2

What is your opinion of the United States' economic ideology? Would you advocate a purely capitalistic economic ideology, or one involving much more government intervention and ownership? Explain the reasons for your opinion.

LO-3
Discuss the key political and economic risks and the role of corruption when conducting global business.

Economic Risks, Political Risks, and Corruption

Economic Risks

Engaging in global business inherently poses **economic risks**. Economic risks include economic problems or mismanagement in a given country that will have a meaningfully negative impact on the conduct of business in that country.

What are some such economic risks? One such risk, for example, might involve restrictions on the transfer or exchange of a given foreign country's currency or the devaluation of that currency. What if, for instance, a major international corporation conducting business in Russia spent $50 million U.S. dollars to purchase 50 million rubles, and the currencies were trading at a "par" 1:1 exchange rate? Then, because of a severe economic downturn in Russia, the ruble sharply declined in value from par (one ruble per dollar) to only ten cents on the dollar, so that the $50 million dollars was now only worth $5 million dollars? Moreover, the currency devaluation may perhaps have been accompanied by some limitations on the ease of converting the ruble back to dollars. For example, a company may be limited to converting no more than 100,000 rubles back into dollars each day. Therefore, the company's initial investment of $50 million dollars to purchase Russian rubles is now worth only $5 million dollars, and the company can only now redeem its rubles for dollars at a rate of 10,000 dollars per day. This is a hypothetical situation in which the company has fallen victim to an economic risk of doing business in Russia.

Currency devaluation and conversion restrictions are only some of the many economic risks companies take when engaging in international business. In many countries in the world, the repayment of any loans the company makes to others may be questionable, in part because of weak legal structures with respect to the enforcement of contractual obligations. (Legal structures will be discussed later in the chapter.)

Other potential economic risks might involve human resources and labor relations. A country, for instance, may have particularly militant labor unions known for frequent unplanned or wildcat strikes, or perhaps for holding corporate executives hostage until their demands are met. Another potential economic risk companies face doing business internationally is inflation. Some countries, such as Brazil and Peru, have experienced hyper-inflation in recent decades; this can dramatically increase the costs of doing business. Corruption is also a very important economic (and political) risk that companies face in global business, and because of its critical importance a special section is devoted to it next.

Two final key points can be made about the economic risks companies face in engaging in international business. First, there are many ways companies can potentially avoid, or at least mitigate, such risks through careful planning and research. For example, research exists regarding the stability of currencies throughout the world, and companies can take advantage of this research by primarily doing business in countries known to have stable currencies. Switzerland, for example, is widely viewed as one of the most economically stable countries in the world, in part due to the very high degree of stability of its currency—the Swiss franc. Moreover, there are sophisticated financial hedging and other techniques which companies can, if they plan ahead, engage in to protect themselves from currency risks. Similarly, the United Nations' International Labor Organization and other agencies have considerable information about labor militancy throughout the world, which businesses can use in their planning.

Second, economic risks are not independent of political risks, which are discussed in the next section. Economic problems such as hyper-inflation often lead to political unrest and related civic problems. Conversely, political changes such as a military junta's overthrow of a democratically elected regime, can quickly impact a country's economic situation. Businesses engaging in (or intending to engage in) enterprise overseas need to plan for both economic and political risks.

economic risks
the risks that economic problems or mismanagement in a given country will have a meaningful negative impact upon the conduct of business in that country

Political Risks

Political risks are the risks that political forces or problems in a given country will have a meaningfully negative impact upon the conduct of business in that country. Political risks can be both micro and macro in nature. A **micropolitical risk** refers to a political risk that only affects a certain industry or set of firms in a given country. For example, a country's potential nationalization of companies in the oil industry would represent a micropolitical risk.

A **macropolitical risk** refers to a political risk that affects all businesses in a given country. For example, the potential overthrow of a democratically elected political regime by a military junta, as mentioned above, is likely a macropolitical risk; such a dramatic change in a nation's political governance will likely affect all businesses and firms in that country. As noted earlier, the recent regime changes in Egypt and Libya have created considerable economic risks for multinational oil and other companies doing business in these nations.

Potential changes in government, civil wars, social unrest, and possible government confiscation of assets are all examples of the types of political risk that companies face in global business. Rankings of countries throughout the world by potential political risks typically place Scandinavian and European countries such as Norway, Sweden, Switzerland, Luxembourg and Denmark near the top of the list, meaning that companies engaging in business in these countries face the least number of potential political risks. Countries such as Russia, Croatia, and Brazil tend to anchor the other end of the list—companies doing business in those countries face considerable political risks.

In recent years, and especially since September 11, 2001, terrorism and other threats to physical safety such as piracy of shipping vessels, have become increasingly significant political risks worldwide. **Terrorism** involves unlawful acts of violence threatening the physical safety of others. The aircraft attacks on the World Trade Center and the Pentagon on September 11, 2001 by foreign extremists represented an unprecedented act of global terrorism. Moreover, the threat of possible future terrorism of this kind has considerably increased the political risks of doing business in the United States.

That said, however, the United States is still a relatively safe place to conduct business. A recent survey of the world's most dangerous countries found Somalia, with its considerable

PJF News/Alamy

Piracy has posed an increasingly serious threat to safety and the stability of international political relations.

political risks
the risks that political forces or problems in a given country will have a meaningful negative impact upon the conduct of business in that country

micropolitical risk
a political risk that only affects a certain industry or set of firms in a given country

macropolitical risk
a political risk that essentially affects all businesses in a given country

terrorism
involves unlawful arts or violence threatening the physical safety of others

EXHIBIT 6.1 MOST DANGEROUS COUNTRIES IN THE WORLD – 2009

1. Somalia
2. Afghanistan
3. Iraq
4. Democratic Republic of Congo
5. Pakistan
6. Gaza, Palestinian Territories
7. Sri Lanka
8. Yemen
9. Sudan
10. Zimbawe
11. Cote d'Ivoire
12. Haiti
13. Algeria
14. Nigeria
15. Georgia/Caucasus, Russia

Source: Zack O'Malley Greenburg, "World's Most Dangerous Countries," March 4, 2009, www.Forbes.com.

piracy and general unrest, to be the most dangerous country in the world. The "top 15" most dangerous countries in the world ranked in this recent study are set forth in Exhibit 6.1.

As part of its response to the September 11 attacks, the U.S. Congress passed the **Terrorism Risk Insurance Act of 2002,** which President George W. Bush signed into law on November 26 of that year. This law provides for (after a certain deductible) U.S. government insurance coverage for the risk of a U.S. business or property being attacked by a "foreign person or foreign interest." Thus, the U.S. government is providing businesses with insurance from events of terrorism.

Terrorism Risk Insurance Act of 2002
a United States law that after a certain deductible provides U.S. businesses government insurance coverage for the risk of terrorism

Moreover, in terms of the general political risks that U.S. companies face when doing business overseas, a U.S. government agency called the **Overseas Private Investment Corporation (OPIC)** sells insurance to interested businesses. This insurance protects them against political risks such as insurrections, revolutions, political violence, and nationalization. OPIC has very specific premium rates for its insurance. For example, companies in the oil and gas exploration business pay an annual rate of $0.65 to $0.85 per $100 of "political violence" risk insurance when conducting business overseas. Thus, an oil company wishing to purchase $10 million of this insurance would pay annual premiums to OPIC of $65,000 to $85,000 per year, depending on various different criteria. It should be noted, however, that such OPIC insurance is limited to firms that operate in countries with which the United States has already signed a bilateral investment treaty. In other cases, companies may be able to purchase political risk insurance from private insurance firms or insurance sold through the World Bank.

Overseas Private Investment Corporation (OPIC)
a U.S. government agency that sells political risk insurance to U.S. businesses operating in countries with which the United States has a bilateral investment treaty

Corruption

As noted earlier in this chapter (as well as in earlier chapters) the existence or lack of existence of corruption in a country, state, or province has a very significant and special impact on the ability of companies to conduct global business in that jurisdiction. **Corruption** is a situation where businesses are able to illegally alter relevant private and/or public decision-making through bribes, kickbacks, blackmail, extortion, and similarly related activities.

corruption
a situation where businesses are able to illegally alter relevant private and/or public decision making by way of bribes, kickbacks, blackmail, extortion, and related activities

There are essentially two kinds of business corruption: private corruption and public corruption. **Private corruption** is business corruption involving other private businesses, individuals, or groups. For example, paying "protection money" or giving sales kickbacks to an organized crime group (e.g., the Mafia) would represent an example of private corruption.

private corruption
business corruption involving other private businesses, individuals, or groups

Similarly, a supplier paying a bribe to an officer of a company that purchases its products to help "facilitate" the purchase of said products is another example of private corruption. Private corruption can often be very difficult to detect, and in some countries in the world, government officials charged with enforcing anti-corruption laws simply ignore the laws (or they too, may be receiving bribes! See "Public Corruption," next). For example, the prevalent role of the "Russian Mafia" in Russia, and its ability to extort protection money from businesses widely unhindered by government authorities, existed in that country until Vladamir Putin became Russia's President in 2000.

Moreover, private corruption can at times be difficult to define. For example, if a supplier of Target Corporation were to pay a top Target executive a $10,000 cash bribe to obtain business, this would be a clear example of private corruption. But, what about simply lavishly entertaining this Target executive in the supplier's box seat at the Super Bowl? Or, on a more general scale, the practice of paying business lobbyists and making business campaign contributions to elected officials in hopes of achieving legislation favorable to a company's business interests?

In addition, definitions of private corruption may vary widely across the globe. For example, a 2010 survey asked individuals whether they or someone in their household had paid a bribe in the last 12 months. The survey found a 1 percent bribery rate in Norway, a 5 percent rate in the United States, a 13 percent rate in Italy, a 22 percent rate in Peru, a 33 percent rate in Turkey, and a somewhat astounding 84 percent rate in Cambodia.[2]

On December 8, 2008, Transparency International, released a comprehensive study of corporate bribery in developed countries throughout the world, ranking countries on a "Bribe Payers Index." The study's ranking, shown in Exhibit 6.2, found Belgium, Canada, the Netherlands, and Switzerland to have the highest scores, or least corporate bribery, and Russia, China, Mexico, and India had the highest scores, or most corporate bribery, among 22 of the world's most economically developed countries. (Note that less-developed countries like Cambodia were excluded from the study.) The results are shown in Exhibit 6.2 (and the work of Transparency International is further discussed in Chapter 7).

Public corruption The practice of making illegal payments to government officials or engaging in blackmail, extortion, or other related activities to obtain government contracts or governmental approval for business activities encompasses corruption. For example, paying a bribe to a government official to obtain a license to conduct a certain kind of business in a particular country also constitutes public corruption. Blackmailing a government official to obtain a government business contract is also considered public corruption.

In 1977, the **Foreign Corrupt Practices Act (FCPA)** became law in the United States. This law prohibits U.S. companies from bribing or otherwise corrupting foreign government officials to win foreign government contracts or obtain other foreign government assistance for their businesses. Recently, the U.S. Justice Department has enforced this law more aggressively. For example, on May 10, 2011 the U.S. Justice Department won a federal court conviction against the Lindsey Manufacturing Co. of Azusa, California for FCPA violations in connection with that company's sale of electric transmission towers to a government-owned utility company in Mexico. In connection with obtaining $19 million in sales contracts from the Mexican Government's *Comisión Federal de Electricidad (CFE)* Lindsey Manufacturing bought one electric commission official a $300,000 Ferrari Spider automobile, sent $500,000 in cash to the brother and mother of another CFE official, and bought another CFE official a $1.8 million yacht. Various top Lindsey Manufacturing Company officials face potential jail time in federal prison for their actions.[3]

It is important to note that not every country has stringent laws in this regard like the United States does, and even if they do, such laws may not be aggressively enforced—or enforced at all. Indeed, in many countries and cultures throughout the world, bribes are simply an expected part of compensation. This can be particularly true in totalitarian regimes where the individuals in command can accumulate considerable personal wealth in this manner. Clearly, different standards regarding the regulation of corruption exist around the world.

public corruption
the practice of making illegal payments to government officials or engaging in blackmail, extortion or other related activities to obtain government contracts or governmental approval for business activities

Foreign Corrupt Practices Act (FCPA)
a United States law that prohibits U.S. companies from bribing or otherwise corrupting foreign government officials to win foreign government contracts or obtain other foreign government assistance for their businesses

EXHIBIT 6.2 TRANSPARENCY INTERNATIONAL BRIBE PAYERS INDEX 2008

(Scores range from 0 to 10. The higher the score for the country, the lower the likelihood of companies from this country to engage in bribery when doing business abroad. Based on Transparency International's 2008 Bribe Payers Survey of 2,742 senior business executives from 26 developed and developing countries, selected on the basis of the size of their imports and foreign direct investment inflows.)

Likelihood of bribes being paid ("10" means "very least"/highly unlikely).

1	Belgium	8.8
1	Canada	8.8
3	Netherlands	8.7
3	Switzerland	8.7
5	Germany	8.6
5	Japan	8.6
5	United Kingdom	8.6
8	Australia	8.5
9	France	8.1
9	Singapore	8.1
9	United States	8.1
12	Spain	7.9
13	Hong Kong	7.6
14	South Africa	7.5
14	South Korea	7.5
14	Taiwan	7.5
17	Brazil	7.4
17	Italy	7.4
19	India	6.8
20	Mexico	6.6
21	China	6.5
22	Russia	5.9

REALITY CHECK LO-3

Do you know anyone who has ever paid someone else a bribe? Where would you draw the line between business "favors" and bribery, kickbacks, or "protection money"?

The Legal Environment

LO-4

Analyze the different types of legal systems, and some key principles involving criminal contract, tax, product safety, and dispute settlement law.

Legal Systems

There are three primary kinds of legal systems in countries throughout the world: civil law legal systems, common law legal systems, and theocratic law legal systems. A **civil law legal system** is a legal system based on a comprehensive listing of legal rules in sets of written codes of law. For example, a code in a civil law country could specifically list the different types of pornography that were permissible in the given society, along with which types of pornography were impermissible or illegal.

In a civil law country, power lies with the legislative branch of government, which enacts specific laws or rules, which are, in turn, set forth in written legal codes. Judges in civil law countries have relatively little power, as the codes set forth specific rules and the role of the judge is simply to enforce these specific rules. There is little room in civil law countries for judicial "interpretation" or changing legal regulations; the rules are specifically and comprehensively set forth in given written codes, and only the legislative branch of government can change these rules by passing new laws and altering the given codes.

From a cultural perspective, civil law systems provide considerable clarity regarding the rules people in the given society need to follow. Citizens clearly know the given rules and judges straightforwardly enforce these codified rules. It is not surprising that countries like Germany, with strong cultural preferences for uncertainty avoidance, are civil law countries. Indeed, Germany's Civil Code of 1896 and its general civil law system have diffused not only into most other European countries (e.g., Switzerland, and Austria), but also into Asia. Japan, for instance, was heavily influenced by Germany's 1896 civil code, and adopted a similar civil code later that same year. In turn, Japan's civil legal system has been adopted in good measure by other Asian countries such as China, South Korea, and Taiwan. Companies and individuals planning on doing business in civil law legal system countries need to carefully review existing rules and codes which apply to the nature of business that they are going to be conducting. Over 80 countries in the world are currently civil law legal system countries.

In contrast to countries with a civil law legal system, the United States follows a common law legal system. A **common law legal system** is one in which legislative bodies generally enact less specific legal rules, so that judges and courts are given considerable authority with respect to interpreting these rules based upon precedent and other factors. For example, a common law legal system might afford its citizens the right to be free from government interference with "free speech." It would then be up to judges to interpret the term "free speech" based on precedent, other evidence, and considerations (e.g., is a certain type of citizen mass protest permissible "free speech?").

Common law legal systems originated in England in 1066 when William the Conqueror assumed the English throne. King William believed in a strong, centralized judicial and court system. Today, the major common law legal system countries are Great Britain and its former colonies (i.e., the United States, Australia, India, and Canada).

One key advantage of a common law legal approach is that judges have a fair amount of flexibility to change their interpretations of the law based on changing societal developments, without waiting for the legislative branch to pass new rules or amend a constitution. For example, the development of the Internet and its increasingly widespread usage since the 1990s has already considerably altered judicial interpretations of "free speech," intellectual property rights, and other issues in the United States and other common law countries.

One possible downside of a common law approach, however, is that it gives much power to the courts and judges. Rather than just enforcing specific codified rules, judges in common law countries often have considerable opportunities to interpret the law as they see fit. This leads some to criticize that in common law countries it is often appointed judges who "make the law" rather than elected legislators.

A **theocratic law legal system** is a legal system based on a religious document and religious teachings. In the world today, Islamic law, as followed in countries such as Iran and Saudi Arabia, is the primary example of theocratic law in operation. In these countries, the religious teachings of the prophet Muhammad, particularly as set forth in the holy religious book of Islam, *The Koran*, form the basis of the national legal system. For example, because *The Koran* views either the payment or receipt of interest as unlawful usury, banks in a country like Iran cannot charge formal interest on loans they make, or pay interest on deposits they receive.

civil law legal system
a legal system based on a comprehensive listing of legal rules in sets of written codes of law

common law legal system
a legal system where legislative bodies generally enact less specific legal rules giving judges or courts considerable authority in interpreting these rules based on precedent and other factors

theocratic law legal system
a legal system based on a religious document and religious teachings

David Levenson/Alamy

Common law legal systems, such as the supreme court of the United Kingdom, allow for legal interpretation by judges and courts.

Criminal Law

Criminal law establishes which violations of a nation's laws are crimes punishable by possible incarceration. It should be noted that actions that constitute crimes may widely differ in countries throughout the world, depending upon the nature of that nation's legal system. For example, a woman's committing adultery is not a crime punishable by incarceration in the United States, but may be in certain countries following Islamic theocratic law.

Moreover, the definition of what constitutes a crime in a given country may change considerably over time as changes in a nation's social mores and social norms evolve. Thus, for example, during the Prohibition Era of the 1920s and 1930s it was unlawful to sell liquor in the United States. Historically in the United States, the possession and sale of marijuana was a crime punishable in many cases by jail time. Today, several states in the United States (i.e., California, Colorado, Oregon, and Michigan) have legalized the sale and use of marijuana for medical treatment. What this means in practical terms is that medical doctors in these states are free to prescribe marijuana for a wide range of medical problems such as

criminal law
law that establishes which violations of a nation's laws are crimes punishable by possible incarceration

anxiety, headaches, and insomnia; as well as for relieving the side effects of cancer treatments. As a result, by 2009 there were approximately 400,000 medical marijuana patients filling their prescriptions at about 700 medical marijuana pharmacies and dispensaries in California (some call these pharmacies "pot shops"!). A report from that same year found that the City of Los Angeles had more medical marijuana pharmacies than Starbucks coffee shops![4] Thus, the criminal laws in the State of California appear to have changed so that the sale of marijuana is now "legal."

Contract Law

Contract Law is the body of law governing legally enforceable agreements between parties to engage in economic exchange. For example, a party wishing to sell a given piece of commercial real estate to another party would enter into a real estate contract with the other party. In civil law countries, contracts tend to be relatively short and unspecific because many of the relevant issues are already covered in the given civil code. In common law countries, however, judges have more flexibility to interpret contracts in different ways than in civil law countries, which means that contracting parties need to have long and very specific contractual language if they want to avoid judicial construction of their contractual document.

Contracts are nearly meaningless unless they can be successfully enforced. Because of overcrowding in courts throughout the world, increasing numbers of contracts today have provisions allowing them to be enforced outside the judicial process by way of alternative dispute resolution methods such as arbitration (discussed further, later in this chapter).

Companies and individuals engaging in global business (or planning to do so) need to become familiar with the idiosyncrasies of contract law in the different countries where they may operate. For example, in some countries certain groups of citizens (e.g., females) may not have full "capacity" to enter into contracts. In other countries, the rules regarding what legally represents "offer" and "acceptance" or contractual "mutual agreement" may differ considerably from the rules which exist in the United States. In general, it is advisable to retain local attorneys to help write any contracts involving foreign jurisdictions.

Tax Law

Tax law refers to the body of law addressing governmental levying of taxes upon individuals and corporations. Tax rates and regulations vary widely throughout the world and play a considerable role in decisions by global businesses when deciding where to locate. Sometimes, however, the benefits of conducting business in a certain location are so great that a business will want to operate there despite high tax rates or complex tax regulations. For example, despite that the United Kingdom recently raised the top individual tax rate in that country to 50 percent, and has a very complex set of tax laws and regulations, very few financial and other firms want to leave their bases of operations in London, England. These businesses simply believe that London's advantages, both "personal and professional," outweigh the tax costs.[5]

But London, England may represent a special situation for many companies. High tax rates and highly complex tax structures in many countries, including the United States, have led a number of major corporations to seek out more tax-friendly locations for operations. For a number of major U.S. companies, the country of choice in this regard has been Switzerland. With its highly stable political system and relatively less complex tax structure, Switzerland has been able to attract a number of major U.S. corporations to re-incorporate and redomicile in its jurisdiction. For example, Transocean Corporation, a multi-billion dollar U.S. oil company, announced its "redomestication" to Switzerland in October 2008. At that time Transocean's CEO Robert Long stated: "Switzerland has a stable and developed

contract law
the body of law governing legally enforceable agreements between parties to engage in economic exchange

tax law
the body of law dealing with governmental levying of taxes on individuals and corporations

tax regime and a network of tax treaties with most countries where we operate."[6] Indeed, the corporate tax rate in Switzerland can be as low as about 9.5 percent for companies that do most of their business outside of Switzerland, versus the 25.9 percent average global corporate tax rate, and the 30 percent or higher corporate tax rates that prevail in the United States.

It should be pointed out that the move by Transocean Corporation and a number of other American companies to Switzerland is completely legal, and may benefit the shareholders of these companies. Transocean's finances in Switzerland will be completely transparent or open to its shareholders and the general public. That said, some companies in the United States and other developed countries engage in the practice of establishing operations in **tax haven countries**, countries with little or no tax transparency, as a way of attempting to illegally avoid United States or other taxes. For example, the infamous Enron Corporation had 43 subsidiaries in Mauritius, a tiny island nation off the East Coast of Africa, and in this manner was able to dodge the U.S. Internal Revenue Service for many years.[7] Other tax haven countries that are favorites of tax evaders include Belize, the Cayman Islands, Antigua and Barbuda, and the Isle of Man (a favorite of U.K. businesses).

Antitrust Law

Antitrust laws refer to laws designed to promote "fair competition" among businesses. For example, antitrust laws typically prohibit companies from engaging in **collusion** (i.e., acting in a manner which secretly thwarts competition among one another). One example of collusion could be an agreement between companies to divide up certain markets to avoid competition with one another in specific geographic markets or locations. For instance, two major European natural gas companies, E.ON AG of Germany and GDF Suez SA of France, were recently fined $1.53 billion by the European Union (EU) for violating EU antitrust laws that prohibit this kind of collusion. The companies had secretly and illegally agreed not to sell natural gas in each others' home markets (i.e., GDF Suez of France agreed not to sell any natural gas in E.ON's home country of Germany, and vice versa), therefore thwarting free and fair competition in the energy markets in these countries.[8] Another rather common example of unlawful antitrust collusion could include the practice of collaborating and fixing prices on certain goods, products, or services (e.g., certain airlines fixing prices on specific air travel routes to diminish competition for air travel dollars on those routes).

Antitrust laws are also known as "anti-monopoly laws." A **monopoly** is a situation where there is only a single seller of a product in an industry, and where there are very high barriers to enter this industry. In the United States, for instance, at the turn of the 20th century there was primarily only one major oil company—John D. Rockefeller's Standard Oil Company. The company's dominance of the oil industry was considered by many to be a monopoly, or "trust." Over a lengthy period, beginning with the passage of the Sherman Antitrust Act in 1890, state and federal regulators sued Standard Oil and eventually forced the company to dissolve into many smaller companies (e.g., the East Coast operations of the original Standard Oil became Standard Oil of New Jersey, which today is Exxon Mobil Corporation; the West Coast operations became Standard Oil of California, which today is Chevron Corporation). Since that time U.S. antitrust regulators have forced similar breakups in other U.S. industries. The original AT&T telephone company has been the most notable recent example; in the 1980s the monopoly was broken into numerous "Baby Bell" corporations including Bell Atlantic, Bell South, and Pacific Bell. It should be noted that some U.S. political administrations in Washington, DC tend to interpret the Sherman Act more strictly than others.

On the global level, antitrust regulators in many countries have been far less aggressive than in the United States. In Mexico, for example, an individual named "Carlos Slim" has become the second richest man in the world by establishing quasi-monopolies in two different telecommunications companies with little interference from the Mexican

tax haven countries
countries with little or no tax transparency

antitrust laws
laws to promote "fair competition" among businesses

collusion
practice of companies acting in a manner which secretly thwarts competition amongst themselves

monopoly
situation where there is only a single seller of a product in an industry and there are very high barriers to enter this industry

government heretofore. Carlos Slim's "Telmex Corporation" has approximately an 80 percent share of the fixed-line and broadband telecommunications industry in Mexico, and his "Telcel Corporation" has about a 75 percent share of the mobile communications industry in that country. In the past, other major telecommunications companies such as MCI, WorldCom, and AT&T have spent billions of dollars to try and establish a beachhead of business in Mexico with little success, given Slim's dominance of the market and his connections to the Mexican government. In June, 2008 the Mexican Government brought an $18 million U.S. dollar antitrust fine against some of Carlos Slim's operations, but to the multi-billionaire Slim, this was roughly the equivalent of a very small traffic ticket. Antitrust laws may be illegal in most developed countries in the world, but they are not always meaningfully enforced.[9]

Product Safety Law

Product Safety law establishes the standards of product safety to which the manufacturers and sellers of products are to be held. These standards vary considerably in countries around the world. Some countries place relatively lax safety standard obligations upon product manufacturers and sellers, operating under a regime of **caveat emptor** or "buyer beware." In such jurisdictions, the burden is placed upon the buyers of products to determine their levels of safety. For example, in more developing countries such as Sri Lanka, Ukraine, and Pakistan, tobacco companies are free to sell tobacco products (cigarettes, etc.) without governmental interference or regulation. It is up to the buyers of such products to be aware of any health or other risks that might result from using these products.

Other countries, including the United States, have nearly moved to the opposite end of the product safety law spectrum, adopting a regime of **caveat venditor,** or "seller beware." In such countries, the burden is placed upon the manufacturers and sellers of products to ensure the products they sell are safe; or they must clearly and explicitly warn consumers about the potential safety risks of their products. Thus, in the United States, for instance, sellers of tobacco and other products are required to explicitly warn consumers about the potential health risks associated with tobacco use. Manufacturers and sellers of products must be clearly aware of the different product safety law standards that exist in the specific countries where they operate.

SHAWN THEW/EPA/Newscom

Recalls due to product safety concerns. *Product safety laws vary among countries requiring sellers to be keenly aware of the standards within the countries they sell to.*

product safety law
the law which establishes the standards of product safety to which the manufacturers and sellers of products are to be held

caveat emptor
"buyer beware"; involves placing the burden of determining product safety on consumers

caveat venditor
"seller beware"; involves placing on manufacturers or sellers of products the burden of making sure products are safe or at least clearly and explicitly warning consumers about the potential safety risks of said products

Dispute Settlement Law

Dispute settlement law refers to the law that governs how disputes that arise in global business will be settled. For example, suppose two major international corporations such as IBM Corporation in the United States and Nokia in Finland enter into a contract. There is then an alleged breach of this contract by IBM, and Nokia wants to obtain redress for this breach. There are two primary ways to potentially resolve this dispute: a public option and a private option.

The public option will resolve the case through **litigation**, which means bringing the case to a public- or government-run court of law to settle the dispute. Contracts between major international companies like IBM and Nokia likely contain clauses which specify the specific court(s) that will hear any disputes that arise out of the contracts (e.g., the contract might state that any relevant disputes will be heard in the courts of New York State in the United States, because that is where IBM Corporation is headquartered). One significant problem, however, with attempting to resolve disputes of this kind to the courts is that courts throughout the world generally have considerable backlogs; it may take a year or more before the court can hear the case. Moreover, court cases, with their formal procedures, often take many months to try even after the dispute process has begun. Consequently, many global businesses have chosen to resolve their disputes via a private process called arbitration.

Arbitration is an alternative dispute resolution process agreed to by the relevant parties, whereby a neutral private party hears the case and renders a decision. For example, the contract between IBM and Nokia may have a provision stating that any disputes arising under that contract will, instead of being tried in court, be heard and decided upon by an independent private arbitrator. Indeed, the contract may also specify that a special arbitrator (e.g., a prominent former jurist) will hear any disputes. Arbitration cases tend to be heard and decided upon rather quickly—an advantage given the time sensitivity of international business contracts. Moreover, unless clear misconduct on the part of the arbitrator occurs (e.g., taking a bribe from one of the parties), arbitration decisions are almost always deemed final and binding on the parties—meaning that they cannot be appealed to the courts. Given the finality and binding nature of arbitration decisions, however, it is very important for parties to ensure they have full confidence in the arbitrator they agree upon to hear their dispute(s).

dispute settlement law
the law governing how disputes arising in the conduct of global business are settled

litigation
involves bringing a dispute to a publicly or governmentally run court of law for resolution

arbitration
an alternative dispute resolution process whereby the parties designate a neutral private person or group of persons to hear and decide the case

intellectual property
property that is the product of intellectual rather than physical activity

REALITY CHECK LO-4

Visit a hardware store, grocery store, or discount store and read the product safety warnings printed on the packaging of several different products. To what extent do you believe these warnings are necessary and appropriate? If possible, talk to someone who has lived in another country about product safety warnings in that country.

LO-5

Discuss the importance of intellectual property protections in today's global business environment, and the major different types of intellectual property protections including patents, trademarks, and copyrights.

Intellectual Property Protections

Intellectual property is property that is the creative product of an individual's intellectual, rather than physical, activity. Examples of intellectual property include the chemical formula for a new drug to cure colon cancer, a new biography of President Barack Obama, a new computer software video game, and the musical score to a new movie.

In today's "knowledge economy," intellectual property is more important than ever. Such property, though, is usually very hard to make or conceive, but relatively easy to copy. For example, a pharmaceutical company might spend hundreds of millions of dollars in research and development to come up with a new chemical formula for a drug to cure colon cancer. Once the chemical formula is discovered, however, it may, absent restrictions, be possible for other pharmaceutical companies to copy it and manufacture a similar drug. Likewise, it may take a lot of effort and money to conceive of and develop a successful new computer software video game, but once it is developed the given computer software can be copied by others for a fraction of the cost.

To protect the creation of intellectual property and to encourage innovation, creativity, and investment in this domain, most nations have laws that afford certain intellectual property special protections. **Intellectual property protections** encompass limited monopoly rights legally granted by a nation to the creator of intellectual property. Patents, trademarks, and copyrights are all examples of intellectual property protections.

Patents

A **patent** is the right granted to the inventor of a product or process that excludes others from selling, making, or using the invention for a certain period of time. Patent rights generally remain enforcable for 5-20 years, depending on the invention and the country. Typically, the inventor of the product is granted a monopoly over it for the given period of time (i.e., no one else can copy, make, or sell this invention for the specified time period). Thus, a pharmaceutical company developing a new drug in the United States will generally be given a 17-year patent or monopoly on the sale and production of that drug. This 17-year monopoly rewards the particular pharmaceutical company for its innovation and for its considerable research and development costs. After 17 years, the pharmaceutical drug's chemical formula becomes available to the general public, allowing other companies to manufacture so-called "generic" versions of the drug.

During most of the latter part of the 20th century, Japan and the United States were the world's patent powerhouses, issuing far more patents than any other countries. China did not have formal patent protection laws until 1985. But since that time, China has experienced an intellectual property and patent "boom"! Today, China issues approximately 30,000 patents annually, and ranks as the third busiest patent office in the world. By the year 2015, it is expected to rank number one in the world, pulling firmly ahead of both Japan and the United States.[10]

Trademarks

A **trademark** is a distinctive phrase, name, word, picture, symbol or design, or combination of these, that identifies a given business' service or product, and is owned by said business. "Coca-Cola" is perhaps the most famous trademarked name in the world, and its distinctive logo very clearly identifies the beverage being sold by the company that produces it nearly anywhere in the world. The famous Nike "swoosh" logo is trademarked, as are McDonald's well-known "golden arches" and "Ronald McDonald" symbols.

Ironically, companies try assiduously through public relations campaigns, celebrity endorsements and the like (e.g. all the star athletes that have endorsed Nike products) to make them as popular as possible, while at same time not so popular that trademarks become genericized. A **genericized trademark** is a trademark that has become so well known or colloquial that it describes a general class of product or service, rather than a specific product or service as intended by the trademark's owner. A good example of genericization are the words "aspirin," "escalator," and "zipper" (originally trademarks of Bayer AG, Otis Elevator, and BFGoodrich, respectively), which became common English words through widespread usage. Products such as Post-It® brand notes (3M) and Pull-Ups® potty training pants (Kimberly-Clark) have retained their trademark status in spite of their popularity because their manufacturers have vigilantly enforced trademark protections for the brand names.

In addition to the possible risk of trademarks becoming genericized, trademark holders also face the constant risk of imitation—or sometimes outright copying or counterfeiting of their trademarked products or services. For example, Starbucks Corporation recently successfully defended its coffee house trademark in China, where a Shanghai coffee house had opened with the name "Xingbake." In the dialect of Chinese spoken in Shanghai, *Xing* means star, and "bake" is pronounced "bah-kuh" and sounds like "bucks." Starbucks had

intellectual property protections
the limited monopoly rights legally granted by a nation to the creator of intellectual property

patent
the right granted to the inventor of a product or process that excludes others from selling, making, or using the invention for a certain period of time

trademark
a distinctive phrase, name, word, picture, symbol or design, or combination of these, that identifies a given business' service or product and is owned by said business

genericized trademark
a trademark that has become so well known or colloquial that it now describes a general class of product or service, as opposed to a specific product or service as intended by the trademark's owner

MACIEJ NOSKOWSKI/Bim/iStockphoto.com

McDonald's Corporation's "Golden Arches" are an important trademark for it throughout the world.

successfully registered its trademark in China in 1996, and the copycat Shanghai coffee house was ordered to pay Starbucks $62,000 U.S. dollars in damages.[11]

McDonald's Corporation, however, was not as successful when it recently tried to prevent a family-run restaurant in Kuala Lumpur, Malaysia from calling itself "McCurry." The highest court in Malaysia ruled that McDonald's does not have a monopoly on the prefix "Mc," and that other restaurants in Malaysia could also use that prefix so long as they

ETHICAL PERSPECTIVES

Get Rid of Ronald McDonald?

As noted earlier in the text, Ronald McDonald is a very important trademark symbol for the McDonald's Corporation. People around the world associate the fun Ronald McDonald clown with McDonald's food, but recently, representatives from an advocacy group called Corporate Accountability International argued that this positive representation may have some negative consequences.

One retired physician volunteering with the group said "Ronald McDonald is a pied piper drawing youngsters all over the world to food that is high in fat, sodium, and calories." Thus, the Boston, Massachusetts organization in 2010 began a campaign to "Retire Ronald."

In response to this campaign to dump Ronald, however, McDonald's CEO Jim Skinner has answered a forceful "No." Skinner said that Ronald McDonald "does not hawk food," but is a "force for good" serving as an ambassador for the McDonald's brand and the Ronald McDonald House charities. Moreover, McDonald's CEO stated that Ronald McDonald "communicates effectively with children and families around balanced, active lifestyles." In response, however, the "Retired Ronald" group representatives argue that while on the "surface" Ronald is there to give children toys and enjoyment, he actually sends "insidious" messages to young people.

QUESTIONS:

1. Do you think Ronald McDonald should go the way of Joe Camel and the Marlboro Man (i.e., old symbols and trademarks of Camel and Marlboro cigarettes), and be retired?

2. Are there ways McDonald's Corporation can make Ronald McDonald a somewhat less controversial symbol?

Sources: Ashley M. Heher, "McDonald's Says No Way Ronald Will Retire," *Yahoo News,* May 20, 2010; Ashley M. Heher, "Dump Ronald: No Way CEO Says," *Houston (TX) Chronicle,* May 21, 2010, p. D3.

clearly distinguished their food from that of McDonald's.[12] It seems clear based on these examples that global companies like McDonald's and Starbucks face different kinds of trademark enforcement throughout the world.

Copyrights

The final major category of intellectual property protection is copyright. A **copyright** is the exclusive legal right that authors, playwrights, publishers, artists, composers, performers, photographers, and other creators have to publish and disseminate their work as they see fit. This textbook and other textbooks used in college classes are, for example, copyrighted. These copyrights thus limit the extent materials from them can be copied or distributed without the authors' consent.

Copyright law in the United States generally gives the originator of a creative work the exclusive right to sell, exhibit, and publish it for her or his lifetime plus 70 years. The duration of copyright in many, if not most, other developed countries is similar. Over 90 countries throughout the world have signed a document called the Berne Convention, which provides international copyright protections.

It is fair to say, however, that despite the Berne Convention, copyright infringement is a major problem in the world today. The problem is particularly extreme for computer software technology. Indeed, in a number of countries today, the majority of software installed on computers was "pirated" or illegally acquired. Similar problems also exist with respect to certain web-based information such as photos and text, which are often copied without permission.

REALITY CHECK LO-5

Next time you go to the supermarket, look for some famous trademarked brands (think, "Green Giant"). Consider the confidence consumers have in various brands, and how this confidence would be affected if intellectual property protections did not exist.

SUMMARY

The legal and political environments that global businesses face play a major role in how they conduct business. Politically, countries with democratic systems of government pose different challenges and offer different advantages than do countries with totalitarian or semi-totalitarian systems.

Different economic ideologies (communism, socialism, and capitalism), also impact how business is conducted in different locations around the world. Moreover, political risks, economic risks, and corruption are important factors to evaluate when conducting business in foreign locations. Some countries (e.g., Myanmar, Somalia, Iraq, and Afghanistan) may be dangerous places to conduct business operations, and corporations need to evaluate the relevant risks and rewards before opening manufacturing plants or other facilities in these locations. The standards for what defines "corruption" also vary widely in different countries.

Rules of law, such as the ability to enter into a binding and enforceable contract, also represent a key global business consideration. Legal considerations include whether the country uses civil law or common law. Global businesses need to be sure they are aware of the legal structures in all places they operate, such as the relevant tax and antitrust laws.

copyright
the exclusive legal right that authors, playwrights, publishers, artists, and composers have to publish and disseminate their work as they see fit

Finally, in today's knowledge economy, the role of intellectual property protection is becoming increasingly important, with intellectual property protection infringement and piracy on the rise throughout the world. Thus, global businesses need to be very familiar with patent, trademark, and copyright regulations in the countries where they operate.

KEY TERMS

democracy, *p. 142*
athenian democracy, *p. 142*
representative democracy, *p. 142*
totalitarian government, *p. 142*
communism, *p. 144*
socialism, *p. 145*
capitalism, *p. 145*
economic risks, *p. 146*
political risks, *p. 147*
micropolitical risk, *p. 147*
macropolitical risk, *p. 147*
terrorism, *p. 147*
Terrorism Risk Insurance Act of 2002, *p. 148*
Overseas Private Investment Corporation (OPIC), *p. 148*
corruption, *p. 148*
private corruption, *p. 148*
public corruption, *p. 149*
Foreign Corrupt Practices Act (FCPA), *p. 149*
civil law legal system, *p. 151*
common law legal system, *p. 151*
theocratic law legal system, *p. 151*
criminal law, *p. 152*
contract law, *p. 153*
tax law, *p. 153*
tax haven countries, *p. 154*
antitrust laws, *p. 154*
collusion, *p. 154*
monopoly, *p. 154*
product safety law, *p. 155*
caveat emptor, *p. 155*
caveat venditor, *p. 155*
dispute settlement law, *p. 156*
litigation, *p. 156*
arbitration, *p. 156*
intellectual property, *p. 156*
intellectual property protections, *p. 157*
patent, *p. 157*
trademark, *p. 157*
genericized trademark, *p. 157*
copyright, *p. 159*

CHAPTER QUESTIONS

1. Do you think, overall, that countries in the world are becoming more democratic, or less democratic, in nature? Why?

2. Are there any places in the world, today, where "pure," "free market" capitalism exists? If so, what is it about these locations that permits this ideological approach to thrive?

3. What are some arguments *in favor* of permitting at least some level of "corruption" in the conduct of business throughout the world?

4. Criminal laws vary widely throughout the world. What may be a "crime" in one country, may represent permissible conduct in another locale. Why do you think there are such vast global differences in this regard?

5. What are some steps countries can take to better enforce intellectual property rights in their jurisdictions?

MINI CASE: BECOMING A KING?

The country of Ghana in Western Africa is a representative democracy. Nevertheless, many of its towns and regions continue to be allowed to have tribal chiefs, known as "kings" and "queens," that have considerable power in those given locales. One such town is that of Otaum, Ghana, located on the southern tip of the country about an hour from the capital, Accra. In 2008, the 90-year-old King of Otaum died, and town elders performed a traditional ritual involving considerable prayer and liquor, by which they decided who among the deceased king's 25 living relatives would become the new king.

They reached a decision, and at 4 a.m. Eastern Standard Time in the United States they called Peggielene Bartels, a 55-year-old single secretary living in Silver Spring, Maryland with the news. Bartels, a distant relative of the deceased king, had been chosen as the new King of Otaum! Bartels would have the power to resolve disputes in the town, appoint elders, and manage more than 1,000 acres of royal land.

Bartels initially thought the call was joke, and then said if anything she should be named "Queen"! The response was "times are changing" and that women in Ghana can now be "kings." Bartels pondered the situation for three months, and then decided to accept the job offer, but (at least initially) on her own terms. After flying to Ghana for her coronation ceremony, she returned to the United States to her job as a secretary. For the next five or six years until retirement, she plans to be a "commuting king," using her vacation time to spend a number of weeks per year in Otaum fulfilling her royal duties. After retirement from her secretarial job, she will plan to move to Ghana and fulfill her role of king full time. When recently interviewed by a major U.S. newspaper, she stated "[n]ot everyone gets to become King . . . [p]erhaps it is my destiny."[13]

QUESTIONS:

1. Why do you think the democracy of Ghana continues to permit local towns or regions to have tribal chiefs, kings, and the like? Do you think this tradition will continue into the future?
2. Would you have made the same decision as King Peggielene Bartels to accept the royal position? Would you have waited five or six years until retiring as a secretary in the United States to move to Ghana and become king full time?

Mini Case based on Paul Schwartzman, "Secretary by Day, Royalty by Night," *Washington Post*, September 16, 2009, www.washingtonpost.com.

Should the U.S. Outlaw Offshore Relocations for Tax Purposes?

As noted in the chapter, a number of major corporations are re-incorporating and moving their corporate headquarters to countries like Switzerland for tax purposes. The question is: Should the U.S. Congress intervene and pass a law strictly limiting the ability of U.S. corporations to re-incorporate elsewhere if they want to continue the majority of their operations in the United States?

POINT Moves of this kind by major U.S. corporations cost U.S. workers jobs and the U.S. government considerable amounts of taxes. Some of these transactions are structured as "sales of stock" which also means that the companies' shareholders are faced with unexpected taxes. If these companies want to continue to significantly operate in the United States, they need to remain headquartered and incorporated in the United States.

COUNTERPOINT The United States' corporate tax rate of 30 percent (or more) is much higher than tax rates in many other developed countries like Switzerland, and can put U.S. incorporated businesses at a competitive disadvantage in today's global economy. A company's primary duty is to its shareholders, and lower tax rates will help increase corporate earnings and thus inure to the benefit of shareholders long term, even if shareholders face some short-term tax liabilities related to the move. A law of this kind may face challenges under the U.S. Constitution.

What Do *You* Think?

What are your thoughts about such re-incorporation moves by the U.S. companies?

INTERPRETING GLOBAL BUSINESS NEWS

1. While the U.S. government rails against Switzerland and other places providing U.S. corporations with tax advantages or benefits, the Mexican government has similar complaints about the U.S. government. It appears that the U.S. government permits U.S. banks to take deposits and pay interest to nonresident foreign nationals from Mexico without reporting the interest paid to either the Mexican government or the U.S. Internal Revenue Service. Mexico wants an income and tax information exchange program with the United States in part to help fight drug lords who do not report taxable income. Do you agree with the Mexican government's position on this matter?

2. Luxembourg, the European nation wedged between the borders of Belgium, France, and Germany, is the only country in the world that continues to have a "Grand Duke." The Grand Duke of Luxembourg has continued to have far more power than most other European monarchs, including the power to approve or disapprove on bills passed by Parliament, and to serve as Commander in Chief of the Luxembourg army. There have, however, been recent calls in Luxembourg to considerably reduce the Grand Duke's power. What do you think might be some advantages and disadvantages in this regard?

3. Counterfeit goods continue to enter the United States in massive numbers. Indeed, in recent years the U.S. Customs and Border Protection Service has seized over 15,000 different shipments of counterfeit goods per year, including clothing, watches, and handbags. What are some ways the U.S. government can make its anti-counterfeiting actions more effective?

4. In 1985, China had only 5,000 lawyers serving a population of more than 1 billion. Today China has more than 150,000 lawyers and that number is growing exponentially. What are some of the benefits and costs of this dramatic increase in the number of lawyers in the country of China?

PORTFOLIO PROJECTS

Explore Your Own Case in Point: Legal and Political Factors Affecting Your Company

After reading this chapter, you should be prepared to answer some basic questions about your target company.

1. Does your company operate in any countries that are considered very politically or economically risky?

2. Does your company primarily operate in civil law or common law countries? What are some of the implications of this?

3. Has your company purchased any insurance from the U.S. Overseas Private Investment Corporation (OPIC)?

4. What are some key intellectual property protections, if any, that your company possesses? When do these protections (e.g., patents) expire? How does your company intend to recoup lost revenues due to any patent or other intellectual property protection expirations?

Develop an International Strategy for Your Own Small Business: Using "OPIC"

Small businesses can sometimes be nimble and take risks that larger businesses are afraid to take. In terms of venturing overseas and doing business in countries where there's "political risk," the U.S. Overseas Private Investment Corporation (OPIC) sells reasonably priced insurance to companies to protect them in this regard. Identify high possible return business ventures in politically risky countries, and then analyze the cost of OPIC insurance to protect against these risks. Develop a plan to purchase OPIC insurance which offsets the given risks.

CHAPTER NOTES

[1] S. Stecklow, "Finnish Drivers Don't Mind Sliding Scale, but Instant Calculation Gets Low Marks," *Wall Street Journal,* January 2, 2001, online.wsj.com.

[2] Global Corruption Behavior Index accessed at "Corruption Realities Index 2010, www.sublimeoblonon.com/2011.

[3] B. Wolf, "U.S. Wins Corporate–Conviction in Bribery Act Trial," Reuters, May 11, 2011, www.reuters.com.

[4] R. Parloff, "How Pot Became Legal," *Fortune Magazine,* September 28, 2009, pp. 140–162.

[5] C. Bryan-Low, "Despite Taxes, London Still a Fund Home," *Wall Street Journal,* September 8, 2009, p. C1.

[6] S. Cage, "Corporate Oil Booms in Law-Tax Switzerland," Reuters, April 9, 2009, www.reuters.com.

[7] T. Carlson "Artful Dodgers," *Reader's Digest,* September, 2002, pp. 47–48.

[8] C. Forelle, "EU Slaps $1.53 Billion Fine on Alleged Gas Cartel," *Wall Street Journal,* July 9, 2009, p. A9.

[9] G. Smith, "Cracking Down on Carlos Slim," *Business Week,* July 27, 2009, p. 57.

[10] T. Glocer, "A Boost From Professionals," *Business Week,* August 24 & 31, 2009, p. 61.

[11] P. Chaudbry, A. Zimmerman, J. Peters, and V. Cordell, "Preserving Intellectual Property Rights: Managerial Insight into the Escalating Counterfeit Market Quandary," *Business Horizons,* vol. 52 (2008): pp. 57–66.

[12] J. Hookway, "McCurry Wins Big McAttach in Malaysia," *Wall Street Journal,* September 9, 2009, p. B5.

[13] P. Schwartzman, "Secretary by Day, Royalty By Night," *Washington Post,* September 16, 2009, www.washingtonpost.com.

CH 7

Corruption and Ethics in Global Business

© C Miller Design/ Getty Images

Hand-out/ROYAL LEPAGE SHELTER FOUNDATION/Newscom

After studying this chapter, you should be able to:

LO-1 Explain briefly the meaning of ethics.

LO-2 Describe how ethics and economic progress are connected.

LO-3 Describe briefly the function of corporate social responsibility (CSR).

LO-4 Recount the events in some of the more famous corporate financial scandals.

LO-5 Explain how ethics can be taught.

LO-6 Explain how internal controls can facilitate ethical behavior and help prevent financial impropriety.

Reminding People About What is Right Leads to Positive Outcomes

As an economics professor at the Massachusetts Institute of Technology, Dan Ariely studies human behavior. As part of his research, he set up an experiment in which participants would receive cash for correct answers on a test. At the same time, the participants were given the impression that it would be possible to cheat without getting caught. Participants were unaware that Ariely was trying to determine whether they would choose to cheat—not trying to assess their knowledge.[1]

Before taking the test, one group of participants was asked to write down as many of the Ten Commandments as they could recall. Remarkably, not one person from this group cheated. All other groups had some cheaters. Ariely's experiment demonstrates that being reminded of a moral benchmark can have a profound impact on people's behavior; people need ethical guidance to make the right choice.

In business, employees derive their ethical perspective from their company's top management. For example, the Institute of Internal Auditors publishes a newsletter for senior management and boards of directors, titled "Tone at the Top," and one of its goals is to provide cutting-edge information on ethics. "Tone at the Top" will significantly affect the ethical perspectives of all persons in organizations that subscribe to it. If a company's leadership establishes and adheres to a well-designed ethics code, then this will have a positive impact upon the behavior of people in the company. If, on the other hand, a company's leadership sends the message to employees that making money is the only thing that matters, then employees will be tempted to sacrifice their personal integrity and the company's integrity for the purpose of making a profit.

While making a profit is an appropriate and worthy goal, companies must simultaneously fulfill their ethical responsibilities: making quality products and services, treating people within and outside the company with respect and dignity, taking care of the environment, and being good corporate citizens in the communities and nations where the company operates. Reminding people in a company to do what's right is a good way to keep a company on track, profit-wise and otherwise.

Introduction

Ethics refer to the guidelines by which people relate to the world, including how they conduct business, how they treat other people, and how they care for the environment. People develop their ethical perspectives from a study of history and literature, from religious principles, and from personal experiences and observations. Ethics define how people view the world. Three philosophical principles regarding ethics include the imperative principle, the utilitarian principle, and the generalization argument.[2] These can be summarized as follows:

- *Imperative Principle:* Do what is right. Act according to absolute moral rules, such as "lying is wrong." Under the imperative principle, ethics is a function of moral rules and principles and does not involve a situation-specific calculation of consequences.
- *Utilitarian Principle:* Do what produces the greatest good. For example, this is how the government justifies the concept of eminent domain. The government can force an individual to sell his or her land so that a road can be built for the benefit of the public as a whole. Thus, the good of the many outweighs the good of the one.
- *Generalization Argument:* This is a combination of the imperative principle and the utilitarian principle: do what is right, but filter the action by consideration of the consequences. Following the generalization argument, one would make a decision by considering the consequences if everyone made the same choice under similar circumstances. For example, some people consider it ethical to purchase clothing items with the intent to wear them one day and return them the next day for a refund. Yet, would stores be able to provide a return policy if everyone wore clothes one day and then returned them? One would conclude that taking a one-day "free rental" on clothes is unethical.

LO-1
Explain briefly the meaning of ethics.

What Is Ethics?

Ethics can be defined as the branch of philosophy that addresses the values pertaining to human behavior, with specific regard to the "rightness" and "wrongness" of actions and to the "goodness" and "badness" of the intent and results of such actions. An ethical problem, or dilemma, occurs when one must make a choice among alternative actions and the right choice is not absolutely clear. Often that choice affects the well-being of others.

ethics
the branch of philosophy that addresses the values pertaining to human behavior, with regard to the "rightness" and "wrongness" of actions and to the "goodness" and "badness" of the intent and results of such actions

integrity
adherence to moral and ethical principles; soundness of moral character; honesty. As a practical matter, a person of integrity knows what is right and has the courage to do it

Closely related to ethics is the concept of integrity. **Integrity** can be defined as adherence to moral and ethical principles; soundness of moral character; honesty. As a practical matter, a person of integrity has two essential characteristics. First, one must have knowledge about what morally constitutes the right thing to do. Second, one must have the courage to do what is right, and carry out the action. Unethical behavior is rarely the result of not knowing the right thing to do, but it is often the result of lacking courage to do what is right. On some occasions, however, a person may be in a situation where the right course of action is not clear, the so-called "gray" area. If the person has integrity, he or she will seek to find out what to do and not remain in a "gray" area.

Essentially there are only four basic steps in ethical decision-making. First: define all the facts and circumstances. Second: identify the people affected. Third: determine the alternative decisions and consequences. And fourth: make the decision, which is comprised of two parts; determine the right action; and carry out the right action. The four steps in ethical decision-making are summarized in Exhibit 7.1.

When one evaluates goals and objectives, a vital question must be asked: What is one's highest aspiration? Possible answers include wealth, fame, knowledge, popularity, or integrity. But, if integrity is second to any of these possibilities, then it is subject to sacrifice

EXHIBIT 7.1 BASIC STEPS IN ETHICAL DECISION-MAKING

1. Define all the facts and circumstances, including who, what, where, when, and how.
2. Identify the people affected by the situation and their rights and obligations.
3. Identify the alternative decisions and consequences.
4. Make the decision: determine the right thing to do and then do it.

in situations where a choice must be made. Such situations will inevitably occur in every person's life. When a choice must be made, courage will be required to give up wealth, fame, popularity—or anything else—that is required to maintain integrity.

In the business world, the purpose of ethics is to direct business men and women to abide by a code of conduct that facilitates and encourages public confidence in their products and services. Many companies have an ethics code to guide their employees in how they conduct business. In addition, business and accounting organizations, such as the Better Business Bureau (BBB), American Institute of Certified Public Accountants (AICPA), and Financial Executives International (FEI), recognize their professional responsibilities by providing ethical guidelines to their members.

Key components of the ethics code of the BBB are summarized in Exhibit 7.2. The BBB Code of Business Practices signifies good advertising, selling, and customer service practices that build customer trust and confidence in business. The Code is based upon the BBB Standards for Trust, which includes eight values that summarize the essential elements of creating and maintaining trust in business. Companies based in the United States and Canada that meet these standards and complete application procedures will be accredited by BBB.

EXHIBIT 7.2 THE BBB CODE OF BUSINESS PRACTICES

1. Build Trust: Establish and maintain a positive track record in the marketplace.
2. Advertise Honestly: Adhere to established standards of advertising and selling.
3. Tell the Truth: Honestly represent products and services, including clear and adequate disclosures of all material terms.
4. Be Transparent: Openly identify the nature, location, and ownership of the business, and clearly disclose all policies, guarantees, and procedures that influence a customer's decision to buy.
5. Honor Promises: Abide by all written agreements and verbal representations.
6. Be Responsive: Address marketplace disputes quickly, professionally, and in good faith.
7. Safeguard Privacy: Protect any data collected against mishandling and fraud, collect personal information only as needed, and respect the preferences of customers regarding the use of their information.
8. Embody Integrity: Approach all business dealings, marketplace transactions, and commitments with integrity.

Source: Better Business Bureau, www.bbb.org/us/bbb-accreditation-standards/.

REALITY CHECK LO-1

Search the Internet for articles on business ethics. Look for guidance on how to conduct business. Some people cynically say that business ethics is an oxymoron. Why do people make that statement?

LO-2
Describe how ethics and economic progress are connected.

Ethics in Business and Society

Ethics and economic progress are tightly intertwined. For business activity to occur, trust is essential. If people did not ethically behave, trust would be impossible. Consider the millions of business transactions taking place daily that require mutual trust. Would anyone go to a job if they did not trust their employer to pay them? How many people would shop on the web if they did not trust that their financial information would be secure?

The classical economists, such as Adam Smith, considered economics a branch of ethics. In their view, business activity would grind to a halt without trust, fair dealings, and honest communication. Many of today's economists still hold this view. In his 1995 book, *Trust: The Social Virtues and the Creation of Prosperity*, Johns Hopkins professor Francis Fukuyama writes: "One of the most important lessons we can learn from an examination of economic life is that a nation's well being as well as its ability to compete, is conditioned by a single, pervasive cultural characteristic: the level of trust inherent in the society."[3]

Ethics and Economics

A civilized society is built upon a foundation of commonly accepted ethical values. Without that foundation, the civilization collapses. The 1987 movie *Wall Street* portrayed the unscrupulous dealings of people involved in securities trading based upon nonpublic (inside) information. In a dramatic scene, one of the film's major characters, a wealthy executive portrayed by actor Michael Douglas, delivers a speech to a large audience of business colleagues declaring, "Greed is good!" The scene implied that greed is an acceptable motivation and that business people will do anything to make money—including unethical behavior. In reality, greed is unacceptable, and unethical behavior will ultimately destroy a company's ability to make money. While a goal of any company should be to increase its owners' wealth, to do so requires the public's trust. In the long term, trust depends upon ethical business practices.

In free societies such as the United States, people usually have the freedom to make their own decisions about the "right" thing to do. Before the American republic was founded, a common belief was that where there was liberty, anarchy would result because people would be unable to govern themselves. Yet, U.S. citizens were free and well behaved. How could this be? In the early 20th-century, the great English writer G. K. Chesterton observed that America was the only nation in the world founded upon a creed. He said that creed was set forth with dogmatic and even theological lucidity in the Declaration of Independence. Chesterton was referring to the second paragraph of America's founding document: "We hold these truths to be self-evident, that all men are created equal, that they are endowed by their Creator with certain unalienable rights, that among these are life, liberty and the pursuit of happiness." The American society was founded upon ethical values regarding respect for individuals, their lives, their property, and their freedoms.

A culture or society will be on the edge of disaster when its people lack integrity. No nation can survive very long without citizens who share common values such as courage, devotion to duty, respect for other people's lives and property, and a willingness to sacrifice personal interests for a greater cause. When a society's ethical values begin to deteriorate, people often look to government for help. Unfortunately, government has limited ability to maintain a society, especially a free society, when ethical values are collapsing. In a famous address to Harvard University in 1978, the Russian dissident Aleksandr I. Solzhenitsyn stated the following:

> *Destructive and irresponsible freedom has been granted boundless space. Society has turned out to have scarce defense against the abyss of human decadence, for example against the misuse of liberty for moral violence against young people, such as motion pictures full of pornography, crime, and horror. This is all considered to be part of freedom and to be counterbalanced, in theory, by the young people's right not to look*

and not to accept. Life organized legalistically has thus shown its inability to defend itself against the corrosion of evil.[4]

Solzhenitsyn concludes that government cannot save a free society from its own citizens. If the people do not live according to positive ethical values, then laws and regulations will be unable to maintain the society. The laws and regulations will be circumvented. In such a society, economic activity will be unsustainable.

The Corruption Perceptions Index and Transparency International

How can a company assess the level of corruption in places where the company is considering doing business? Each year the advocacy organization Transparency International, which was also mentioned in Chapter 6, publishes the **Corruption Perceptions Index (CPI)**. The CPI, which was first released in 1995, provides a measurement of the potential corruption risk per country. The CPI ranks 180 different countries by their perceived levels of corruption, as determined by expert assessments and opinion surveys. The index, ranging from "0-10," assigns a lower CPI to those countries with a perceived high corruption risk.

Corruption Perceptions Index (CPI)
a report published each year by Transparency International, providing metrics to the potential corruption risk for 180 countries

EXHIBIT 7.3 FCPA VIOLATIONS AND CORRUPTION PERCEPTIONS INDEX FOR SELECTED COUNTRIES

Country	Number of Reported Violations (2002 - 2007)	Corruption Perceptions Index
Iraq	8	1.3
China	5	3.6
Indonesia	4	2.6
Nigeria	3	2.7
Kazakhstan	2	2.2
Russia	2	2.1

Transparency International is an international organization that includes 90 locally established national chapters and chapters-in-formatin; TI publishes annually a ranking of countries according to the Corruption Perceptions Index (CIP).

Violations of laws such as the Foreign Corrupt Practices Act (FCPA), which will be discussed later in this chapter, are more likely in countries with high corruption risk. Criminal investigations by the U.S. Securities and Exchange Commission (SEC) and the U.S. Department of Justice often involve countries with a low CPI (high corruption risk). Exhibit 7.3 shows the number of FCPA violations in selected countries with low CPI scores. When planning to begin business operations in a country, examining that country's CPI is a good starting point for risk assessment.

Corruption is not limited to countries with low CPI scores (i.e., high risk of corruption). Not long ago, Siemens, a Munich-based multinational corporation, settled a case involving a bribe of the Norwegian Department of Defense under a contract for the delivery of communications equipment. Interestingly, Norway would not be regarded as a country with high corruption risk. Norway's CPI index at the time was 8.7, representing a very low perceived risk for corruption. Based upon this example, limitations of CPI risk assessment must be kept in mind; that is, a low-risk country does not guarantee that there will be no corruption. Risk assessment should be thorough and focused upon operations in high-risk countries, without ignoring low-risk countries.

REALITY CHECK LO-2

Have you ever done business with someone you did not entirely trust, or who did not trust you? Describe your experience. How would the transaction have been different if trust was present?

LO-3
Describe briefly the function of corporate social responsibility (CSR).

What Is Corporate Social Responsibility?

Corporate financial scandals at the beginning of the millennium have reminded people of the importance of a positive corporate reputation. When a business firm loses its reputation, word spreads quickly due to electronic communications. Inevitably there is a loss of trust, which is fundamental to business activities involving the firm's customers, suppliers, lenders, investors, and others. A positive corporate reputation connotes management's commitment to ethical accounting and principled business practices. A key factor in corporate reputation is acting responsibly, such as fairly treating employees and taking care of the environment. Other factors related to corporate social responsibility include wise use of assets, financial soundness, and investment value, all of which depend upon honest financial reporting.

Corporate social responsibility (CSR) refers to a company's obligations to society, including the welfare of a wide range of stakeholders: people and places affected by company activities. People include customers, employees, suppliers, creditors, lenders, investors, and anyone who interacts with the company and its products or services. Places include the communities and countries in which the company does business. CSR also includes the responsibility to take care of the environment (land, air, and water) so as to minimize or eliminate pollution.

Corporate social responsibility is nothing new. At the beginning of the industrial age, concerns about morally questionable business practices such as hazardous working conditions, low pay, excessive work hours, and child labor were presented to the British public in some of Charles Dickens' classic novels *Oliver Twist*, *A Christmas Carol*, and *David Copperfield*. In *A Christmas Carol*, first published in 1843, and made into a Hollywood movie starring Jim Carrey in 2009, the book's protagonist, Ebenezer Scrooge, is metaphysically confronted by the consequences of self-centered, miserly business practices, that is, he receives a visit from the ghost of his deceased business partner, Jacob Marley:

corporate social responsibility (CSR)
a company's obligations to society, including the welfare of people and places affected by company activities

> *"But you were always a good man of business, Jacob," faltered Scrooge, who now began to apply this to himself.*

> *"Business!" cried the Ghost, wringing its hands again. "Mankind was my business. The common welfare was my business; charity, mercy, forbearance, and benevolence, were, all, my business. The dealings of my trade were but a drop of water in the comprehensive ocean of my business!"*[5]

While Scrooge may have been a successful businessman, he failed in his responsibilities to his community. Among his failures were lack of concern for the working conditions of his employees and refusal to provide help to the poor. *A Christmas Carol* portrays the religious holiday of Christmas, with ethical responsibility at the center of the story. The Judeo-Christian religious ethic offers moral imperatives such as: be honest, respect other people's lives, respect other people's property, be kind to others, and so forth. The major world religions, including Christianity, Judaism, Islam, Hinduism, and Buddhism, all offer guidance on many key ethical values. Religion is arguably the broadest basis that society has for ethics and provides the internal justification for many ethical acts such as providing safe working conditions, treating employees fairly, and protecting the environment.[6] A widely reported study by researchers at the Mays Business School of Texas A&M University found that higher levels of religiosity lead to less likelihood of financial fraud.[7]

Whether ethical values are derived from a study of history and literature, religious principles, or personal experience and observation, there are some basic values upon which everyone must agree. Corporate social responsibility mandates that a company strive to:

- provide a quality product or service to its customers;
- provide an appropriate return on investment to the company's stockholders;
- treat its employees with dignity and respect;
- take care of the environment;
- meet its legal obligations; and
- fairly deal with suppliers, lenders, and other business parties.

Rules, Policies, and Guidelines

Following legal rules is a starting point for making an ethical choice. For example, if in the course of business you wish to use a software product for a specific application, you can apply existing copyright protection laws to decide whether permission or payment is required.

A second way to resolve an ethical question is to apply the formal policies of your company or of an appropriate professional organization. For example, the Code of Ethics and Professional Conduct of the Association for Computing Machinery includes provisions for respecting the privacy of others and honoring confidentiality. While members of the association could legally ignore this code, they might use the provisions to help determine ethical courses of action.

A third way to make an ethical choice is to follow an informal guideline such as moral intuition. A person might consider the following personal questions:

- What would your mother or father say if you acted in that way?
- How would you feel if you saw your situation described in the newspaper?
- Does the situation "smell bad?"
- Would you use your behavior as a marketing tool?

Two principles that can help when making an ethical decision are the principle of consistency and the principle of respect. To apply the principle of consistency, which is derived from the generalization argument presented earlier, ask: "What if everyone did it?" and examine what the consequences would be if everyone who faced a similar decision made the same choice. For example, if one believes that copying software rather than purchasing it is ethical, examine the implications of every consumer copying the software.

To apply the principle of respect, one would make the choice that treats people with the greatest respect. This implies that one would act toward others in the same way it would be hoped they would act in return. This principle is referred to as the "Golden Rule": Do unto others as you would have them do unto you. This was the guiding principle followed by Mr. J.C. Penney when he started his company. The J.C. Penney company partners with the Points of Light Foundation each year to bestow upon exceptional people the Golden Rule Award, which recognizes excellence in volunteer commitment. Awards are given in four categories: Adult, Youth, Group Volunteer, and Education Volunteer. Winners receive crystal trophies, with cash prizes awarded to the nonprofit agency which was the recipient of the volunteer hours.

Ethics Codes at Selected Companies

Many companies have established a corporate ethics code. In ExxonMobil's Standards of Business Conduct, company guidelines state that "No one in the ExxonMobil organization has the authority to make exceptions to these policies [on business conduct]. Regardless of how much difficulty we encounter or pressures we face in performing our jobs, no situation can justify their willful violation."[8] Business people need formal standards upon which to base decisions regarding ethical issues such as information security, personal privacy, use of company resources, care for the environment, and professional behavior. Further steps taken by ExxonMobil to ensure integrity are listed in Exhibit 7.4.

Founded in 1919, Halliburton is one of the world's largest providers of products and services to the oil and gas industries. In just two operating groups, Halliburton employs nearly 70,000 people in 80 countries. Components of Halliburton's Code of Business Conduct, although not limited to, include expectations that all directors and employees:

- observe the highest form of personal ethics in all business transactions;
- aspire to fairness in dealings with shareholders and stakeholders alike, and;
- never allow company loyalty or drive for profit to result in illegal behavior.

Well-designed corporate ethics codes, which are monitored and enforced by top management personnel, will help employees to do the right thing in difficult circumstances. Ethics codes cannot guarantee that people will always make the correct choice. Yet, ethics codes and ethics training will help minimize unethical behavior. Further, ethical dilemmas

EXHIBIT 7.4 STEPS TO ENSURE INTEGRITY AT EXXONMOBIL

- A substantial majority of the Board of Directors are non-employees.
- The Board Audit Committee is empowered to investigate any matters brought to its attention and has 100 percent non-employee membership.
- An independent internal audit staff assesses compliance with policies and procedures, and evaluates control effectiveness in about 300 audits conducted annually around all business units.
- Steps are taken to assure the independence of both internal and external auditors.
- Employees regularly review and discuss expectations, and are encouraged to raise questions or concerns.
- Violations are promptly reviewed, communicated upward, and acted upon.

Source: ExxonMobil, www.Exxonmobil.com.

ECONOMIC PERSPECTIVES Walmart Canada's Environmental Stewardship

By exercising good corporate social responsibility (CSR), also called corporate citizenship, a company can engender high regard from its customers, who in turn want to give their business to the company. CSR operates as a type of corporate self-regulation incorporated into business operations. Economic activity flourishes in a business environment where businesses responsibly operate and have good relations with their customers and other constituents.

In Spring 2010, Walmart Canada received the CSR Award for the Environment from the Retail Council of Canada. Headquartered in Mississauga, Ontario, Walmart Canada operates more than 300 retail stores throughout Canada, and serves more than one million customers daily. Walmart Canada's goals include providing environmental leadership by reducing the ecological impact of its operations via corporate-wide programs focused upon waste, energy, and products, as well as outreach programs that protect and enhance local environments. The corporation's global goal is to produce zero waste, to be powered one hundred percent by renewable energy, and to provide customers with products that sustain people and the environment.

Walmart Canada was selected to receive the CSR Award for the Environment as a result of its environmental demonstration store in Burlington, Ontario. The Burlington store features a first-of-its-kind application of geothermal technology and energy-conserving lighting innovations in a large Canadian retail operation.

In a press release, Walmart Canada described its new supercentres as 60 percent more energy efficient as previously existing store structures, with roughly 85 percent of its waste being diverted from typical waste locations, such as landfills. The company stores modeled after the supercentre prototype aim to improve existing energy efficiencies by 30 percent.

David Cheesewright, CEO and President of Walmart Canada, in his acceptance of the award, stated that his company is committed to contributing to the community and to making the shopping experience easier and more affordable.

The Retail Council of Canada (RCC) started in 1963. RCC is a not-for-profit, industry-funded association representing more than 40,000 store fronts of all retail types across Canada, including department, specialty, discount, and independent stores, and online merchants.

QUESTIONS:

1) Is Walmart Canada taking care of the environment? Do you think Walmart's customers care if the company is a good corporate citizen?
2) Do you think it is appropriate for industry organizations such as the Retail Council of Canada to give awards for corporate social responsibility? Do you think awards like these motivate companies to act more responsibly?

Source: Karin Campbell, "Walmart Canada Awarded Two Excellence in Retailing Awards," CNW, www.newswire.ca/en/releases/archive/June2010/01/c8808.html, June 1, 2010.

occur in all functional areas of the firm, including accounting, finance, human resources, marketing, and production. Everyone occasionally faces decisions and situations requiring ethical judgment.

REALITY CHECK LO-3

Do corporate stockholders have a right to expect that the companies in which they invest will act in the best interests of people within and outside the business, the communities where the business operates, and the environment? Or should these concerns be bypassed if the corporation finds it necessary to do so to achieve a reasonable return on investment?

LO-4

Recount the events in some of the more infamous corporate financial scandals.

Financial Scandals

Corporate financial scandals are nothing new; they are as old as corporations. The East India Company, chartered in 1600 by Queen Elizabeth I, was involved in financial controversies regarding its occasional inability to clearly identify corporate profits and losses associated with its expeditions.[9] More recent scandals have often led to investors' loss of confidence in the stock market and in the reliability of corporate financial reports. In some countries, the legislatures have enacted new laws concerning fraud and corporate financial reporting. Some of the most infamous corporate financial scandals of the recent past decade include Enron, WorldCom, Vivendi, and Parmalat. These and others are briefly described next.

Enron

Enron Corporation is considered by many to be the most infamous financial scandal in United States history. The Enron scandal caused people to question the reliability of the financial reporting practices of publicly traded corporations. Enron was a key event leading the U.S. Congress to pass a new federal securities law, the Sarbanes-Oxley Act of 2002, often referred to as SOX. (SOX will be discussed in more depth later in the chapter.) Before its collapse in late-2001, Enron was a highly regarded energy company located in Houston, Texas. The company's bankruptcy, which was the largest in U.S. history at the time, resulted in 20,000 individual job losses. Many of these employees also lost their life savings, which had been invested in Enron stock.

AP Photo/David J. Phillip

The Enron financial scandal was a key event leading the U.S. Congress to pass a new federal securities law, the Sarbanes-Oxley Act of 2002.

Prior to bankruptcy, Enron was a major global provider of electricity, natural gas, pulp and paper, and communications services. In 2000, corporate revenues exceeded $100 billion. *Fortune* magazine had identified Enron as "America's Most Innovative Company" for six years in a row. By the end of 2001, however, Enron had proven to be mostly innovative at "cooking its books." As explained in the 2005 documentary film *Enron: The Smartest Guys in the Room,* a great number of the company's assets and profits were overstated—or in some cases completely fraudulent and nonexistent. Many of the company's financial obligations and losses were created "offshore" and were not disclosed in the company's financial statements. Using technically complex accounting transactions between Enron and related companies, Enron was able to remove unprofitable operations from the company's financial records.

Enron's former CEO, Kenneth Lay, presided over the financial scandal that led to the downfall of Enron Corporation. Lay notoriously sold massive amounts of his Enron stock in late-2001 as the company stock price fell, while at the same time urging company employees to purchase the stock, assuring everyone that the stock price would surge again. The company's former president, Jeffrey Skilling, led Enron to abuse an accounting practice known as mark to market accounting.

Mark to market accounting generally refers to accounting practices that update the value of an asset to its current market levels. Mark to market accounting ideally should give investors, lenders, and others more useful information for decision making. However, as with any accounting practice, it is subject to abuse and manipulation by unscrupulous business managers. Enron recorded expected future profits immediately as if those profits were already earned. As a result, Enron booked gains that, in some cases, would eventually show up as losses. The company leadership decided to disguise the company's actual financial situation, which was declining, and to deceive Wall Street analysts and investors. As a result, the company's stock price continued to rise.

After several years of deception, the truth about Enron was finally revealed in 2001. A number of Enron employees were charged with crimes, including the company's top two former managers. In 2004, former CEO Kenneth Lay was indicted by a grand jury on 11 counts of securities fraud and related charges. In the same year, former president Jeff Skilling was indicted on 35 counts of fraud, insider trading, and other crimes. In 2006, Lay was found guilty of 10 counts, which could have resulted in 20 to 30 years in prison. Lay was not incarcerated, however, as he died from a heart attack before he could be sentenced. In 2006, Skilling was found guilty of 19 counts, which included conspiracy, insider trading, false statements to auditors, and securities fraud. In December 2006, Skilling began serving a prison sentence of 24 years and four months.

WorldCom

WorldCom began in 1983 as Long Distance Discount Services, Inc. (LDDS), located in the United States in a middle-sized town, Hattiesburg, Mississippi. Bernard Ebbers had become the company's CEO in 1985. In subsequent years, the company name had been changed to LDDS WorldCom, and later WorldCom. From 1999 to 2002, the company had manipulated earnings by using fraudulent accounting methods, thereby presenting a false image of economic growth and prosperity. As a result, the company's stock price continued to climb, when it should have been falling.

Two techniques were used to cook the books. The first was underreporting "line costs" by recording them as assets on the balance sheet instead of correctly expensing each one on the income statement. The second was overstating revenues through recording fraudulent transactions regarding "corporate unallocated revenue accounts." During 2002, a small group of internal auditors at WorldCom worked together, frequently in the evening and in secret, to explore and reveal $3.8 billion in fraud.

WorldCom filed for Chapter 11 bankruptcy in 2002, which was, at the time, the largest in U.S. history. WorldCom emerged from Chapter 11 bankruptcy in 2004 with about $5.7 billion in debt and $6 billion in cash. Approximately $3 billion of the cash was intended for settling assorted financial obligations. For example, prior bondholders eventually received $0.357 on the dollar in bonds and stock in the new MCI company. Prior stockholders lost all of their investment, as the old WorldCom stock was worthless. In 2005, Bernie Ebbers was found guilty of fraud and conspiracy, and for filing false documents with regulators. He was sentenced to 25 years in prison.

Vivendi

Vivendi (formerly Vivendi Universal), a French-based multinational corporation, has operations in music, television and film, publishing, telecommunications, the Internet, and video games. The company is headquartered in Paris. Between October 2000 and April 2002, the company cooked its books to make its financial performance appear better than it was, for the purpose of making a number of acquisitions. When the company's board of directors discovered CEO Jean-Marie Messier's actions, Messier was forced to resign.

mark to market accounting
accounting practices that update the value of an asset to its current market levels

In an out-of-court settlement with the U.S. Securities and Exchange Commission in 2003, Vivendi agreed to pay a fine of $50 million, and Messier was required to pay a fine of $1 million and to forfeit his $25 million severance package. Messier was also barred from serving as a director of a publicly traded company for ten years. Later Messier was fined 1 million euros by the Autorité des Marchés Financiers, the French equivalent of the U.S. Securities and Exchange Commission (SEC).

In the civil fraud case which was settled out of court, the SEC demonstrated that a series of repeated actions had been used to hide Vivendi's cash flow and liquidity problems; improperly adjusted accounting reserves were used to meet earnings before interest, taxes, depreciation, and amortization targets; and material financial obligations were not disclosed. In an effort to enhance Vivendi's stock price, during 2002, Messier had clandestinely used money from company accounts to repurchase shares of the company's stock. The stock repurchases led to a cash shortage that almost caused Vivendi to become insolvent.

Parmalat

Parmalat, an Italian-based multinational corporation, specializes in dairy and food products. The company became the world's leading company in production of UHT (Ultra High Temperature) milk—milk that remains safe to consume for up to 9 months at room temperature, provided the container remains sealed. European consumers typically use smaller refrigerators than their counterparts in the United States, so Parmalat's UHT milk gained immediate popularity in Europe.

In the late 1990s, Parmalat entered into world financial markets in a significant way, financing several international acquisitions, especially in the Western Hemisphere, with debt. However, by 2001, a number of the new operations were losing money. As a result, the company began extensively using derivatives for financing. This facilitated efforts to disguise the extent of the company's financial liabilities and losses. Parmalat cooked its books by purchasing its own credit-lined notes, thereby creating an asset that did not really exist.

By 2003, the company was no longer able to pay off debts and make bond payments: a 14 billion euro shortfall led to the company's collapse, which became Europe's biggest bankruptcy. Prior to Parmalat's collapse, the company's former CEO, Calisto Tanzi, had become a symbol of great economic success and a business hero of sorts. Italians were amazed how a company that was once very powerful could suddenly disintegrate. In the aftermath of the company's demise, Tanzi was charged with financial fraud and money laundering. He was sentenced to ten years in prison for fraud.

When the company officially entered bankruptcy, the Italian government used the legal means, or *commissariamento* (i.e., management of a company by a commissioner) to save the trademark. In the aftermath of the bankruptcy, Parmalat began anew and expanded its global operations throughout Europe, Latin America, North America, Australia, China, and South Africa.

Other Financial Scandals

The Teapot Dome scandal occurred in the United States during the 1920s. Teapot Dome was an oil field owned by the U.S. government and located in Wyoming. Albert Fall, while serving as Secretary of the Interior under President Warren G. Harding, secretly leased Teapot Dome oil reserves to a businessman who paid Fall hundreds of thousands of dollars in zero-interest loans. Eventually Fall was indicted and convicted. He became the first U.S. cabinet member to be sent to prison.

During the 1930s, Samuel Insull, who had once served as president of the Edison power company, became the head of a massive utility holding company. The stock market declined and Insull's holding company collapsed in 1932. Total losses to investors amounted to approximately $700 million, a record at the time. Insull was charged with mail fraud and

PACO SERINELLI/Stringer/Getty Images

Parmalat, of Italy, cooked its books by purchasing its own credit-lined notes and thereby creating an asset, which was in reality worthless.

embezzlement but fled the country. After spending some time as a fugitive from justice, Insull returned and was tried and acquitted. The courts determined that a holding company was not accountable for the acts of the companies it controlled. Insull later died virtually penniless.

Financial scandals have occurred throughout history in all countries in the world. Sometimes the name of the person committing the fraud becomes so notorious that the fraudster's name identifies that type of fraud. Such is the case of Charles Ponzi, who committed one of the most infamous frauds of all time. He tricked thousands of New England residents into investing in a postage stamp speculation scheme during the 1920s. Ponzi was swamped with money from investors, as he guaranteed a 40 percent return in three months.

Ponzi achieved this remarkable rate of return by using money received from later investors to provide early investors with returns on their investment, thus giving them an appearance of a profitable investment. Eventually, of course, Ponzi was unable to keep up the appearance of profitability and his fraud was discovered. This type of fraud is referred to as a pyramid scheme or simply **Ponzi scheme**. Ponzi schemes have occurred numerous times since the first one committed by Charles Ponzi.

Between the early-1990s and 2008, money manager Bernard Madoff perpetrated a Ponzi scheme amounting to an estimated $65 billion. In March 2009, a U.S. Department of Justice press release stated that Madoff was charged with federal offenses including securities fraud, wire fraud, mail fraud, money laundering, making false statements, perjury, theft from an employee benefit plan, and making false filings with the SEC.[10] Because he pleaded guilty to the charges, Madoff was not required to testify and reveal the details of how his investment firm defrauded its customers, where the money went, or who else was involved in the scheme. He was sentenced to a statutory maximum of 150 years in prison and began serving in June, 2009, at the age of 70.

Ponzi scheme
a type of fraud, also called a pyramid scheme, in which money received from later investors is used to provide returns to earlier investors, thus giving an appearance of a profitable investment

REALITY CHECK LO-4

Unethical people who try to gain your confidence are called "con" men. Charles Ponzi is among the most infamous con men. Have you ever been tempted by an offer that seemed too good to be true? Was it?

LO-5
Explain how ethics can be taught.

Can Ethics Be Taught?

Academic research shows that ethics classes affect people's actions in a positive manner. Thinking about the consequences of not teaching ethics, U.S. President Theodore Roosevelt observed, "To educate a person in mind and not in morals is to educate a menace to society." Teaching ethics does not mean that every student taught will become proficient in the subject matter. Nonetheless, teaching ethics will have at least some impact upon the ethical perspectives and behavior of those being taught.

The Association to Advance Collegiate Schools of Business (AACSB) stated in the early-2000s that the time has come for business schools to renew and revitalize their commitment to the centrality of ethical responsibility. In preparing business leaders for the 21st century, they suggest the following five fundamentals of ethics education:

- Personal integrity
- Responsibility of business in society
- Ethical decision-making
- Ethical leadership
- Corporate governance

Acting upon high ethical standards in business can be challenging. Some people will ask, "If everyone else is cheating, then how can an ethical person possibly succeed?" This is the wrong question. The real question is: How do you measure success? Exhibit 7.5

EXHIBIT 7.5 HOW DO YOU MEASURE SUCCESS?

A popular story recounts a meeting that may have taken place at the Edgewater Beach Hotel in Chicago in 1923. There is debate whether the meeting occurred, but what has been confirmed is the rise and fall of the men featured in the story, who were nine of the richest men in the world at that time: (1) Charles Schwab, President of the world's largest independent steel company; (2) Samuel Insull, President of the world's largest utility company; (3) Howard Hopson, President of the largest gas firm; (4) Arthur Cutten, the greatest wheat speculator; (5) Richard Whitney, President of the New York Stock Exchange; (6) Albert Fall, member of the President's Cabinet; (7) Leon Frazier, President of the Bank of International Settlements; (8) Jessie Livermore, the greatest speculator in the Stock Market; and (9) Ivar Kreuger, head of the company with the most widely distributed securities in the world.

Twenty-five years later: (1) Charles Schwab had died in bankruptcy, having lived on borrowed money for five years before his death; (2) Samuel Insull had died virtually penniless after spending some time as a fugitive from justice; (3) Howard Hopson was insane; (4) Arthur Cutten died overseas, broke; (5) Richard Whitney had spent time in prison in Sing-Sing; (6) Albert Fall was released from prison so he could die at home; (7) Leon Frazier, (8) Jessie Livermore, and (9) Ivar Kreuger each died by suicide. Measured by wealth and power these men achieved success, at least temporarily. Making a lot of money may be an acceptable goal, but money most assuredly does not guarantee a truly successful life.

Many people think of fame and fortune when they measure success. However, at some point in life, most people come to realize that inner peace and soul-deep satisfaction come not from fame and fortune, but from having lived a life based upon integrity and noble character. President Lincoln put it this way: "Honor is better than honors." At a Congressional Hearing on ethics in July 2002, Truett Cathy, founder of Chick-Fil-A, quoted Proverbs 22:1: "A good name is more desirable than great riches; to be esteemed is better than silver or gold." In the final analysis, living an honorable life really is more satisfying than fame and fortune. How do you measure success?

Adapted from: L.M. Smith and K.T. Smith. 2009. Business and Accounting Ethics, http://goo.gl/ThAor.

provides a poignant essay on the foolishness of measuring success by the accumulation of wealth or power.

The world is made up of many individuals, each of whom can make a difference for good. Never underestimate the power that one person can have in standing up for what is right. There are many examples of individuals who made a difference, such as environmental consultant Erin Brockovich, who sued Pacific Gas & Electric for poisoning a town's water supply; or consumer advocate Ralph Nader, whose 1965 book *Unsafe at any Speed* exposed the automobile industry's resistance to safety features. One person's courage has sometimes altered the course of history. The success of a nation, a profession, or a business, depends upon each individual doing his or her part. Whether individuals do their parts depends on their personal integrity.

Many people have made observations about ethics and personal integrity over the years. A few selected quotations regarding ethics in business and society are shown in Exhibit 7.6.

Eugene Ashton Perry / Library of Congress

Can ethics be taught? President Theodore Roosevelt said, "To educate a person in mind and not in morals is to educate a menace to society."

EXHIBIT 7.6 ETHICS IN BUSINESS AND SOCIETY: SELECTED QUOTATIONS

- "Associate with men of good quality, if you esteem your own reputation; for it is better to be alone than in bad company." (George Washington)
- "Honor is better than honors." (Abraham Lincoln)
- "To educate a person in mind and not in morals is to educate a menace to society." (Theodore Roosevelt)
- "A good name is more desirable than great riches; to be esteemed is better than silver or gold." (King Solomon)
- "To see what is right and not to do it is want of courage." (Confucius)
- "It has become dramatically clear that the foundation of corporate integrity is personal integrity." (Sam DiPiazza, CEO of PricewaterhouseCoopers)
- "A people that values its privileges above its principles soon loses both." (Dwight D. Eisenhower)
- "It is high time that the ideal of success should be replaced by the ideal of service." (Albert Einstein)
- "With malice toward none; with charity for all; with firmness in the right, as God gives us to see the right, let us strive on to finish the work we are in." (Abraham Lincoln)
- "O beautiful for spacious skies, . . . O beautiful for heroes proved In liberating strife, Who more than self their country loved, And mercy more than life! America! America! May God thy gold refine, Til all success be nobleness And every gain divine!" (Katherine Lee Bates)
- "Seven deadly sins: politics without principle; wealth without work; pleasure without conscience; knowledge without character; business without morality; science without humanity; and worship without sacrifice." (E. Stanley Jones, Methodist missionary)
- "If we want to produce people who share the values of a democratic culture, they must be taught those values and not be left to acquire them by chance." (Cal Thomas, syndicated columnist)
- "You must be the change you wish to see in the world." (Mohandas K. Gandhi)
- "For what will it profit a man, if he gains the whole world and forfeits his life? Or what shall a man give in return for his life?" (Jesus of Nazareth)
- "The reputation of a thousand years may be determined by the conduct of one hour." (Japanese proverb)

Source: "Ethics in Business & Society: Selected Quotations," http://goo.gl/Hi4gj.

ETHICAL PERSPECTIVES

Human Trafficking

One of the great social problems of the 21st century is the global slave trade, also called human trafficking. It is estimated that the human trafficking business earns more than $30 billion per year and involves up to 27 million victims, about 80 percent of which are women and 50 percent are minors.

About 200 years ago, William Wilberforce, a member of the British Parliament, led the movement that ended the slave trade in his country. Launched on a political career when he was only 21 years old, Wilberforce initially had little interest in religious matters or social justice. He had lots of money and lots of friends. Social events, dinners, balls, and highjinks with friends were the focus of his attention. Advancing in politics was his chief ambition.

Influenced by his friend and tutor, Isaac Milner, Wilberforce began to rethink the merits of religious faith. This led to a spiritual rebirth, after which Wilberforce lamented how he had wasted precious time, opportunities, and talents in selfish pursuits. He was determined to spend the rest of his days making the world a better place. Although he considered retiring from public life on the grounds that religion was incompatible with politics, his friend and fellow Member of Parliament William Pitt, and others such as John Newton, a former slave-ship captain turned Anglican minister, urged Wilberforce to continue serving in government.

Wilberforce was greatly affected by the biblical story of the Good Samaritan, which teaches that people have a responsibility to aid others who are found in need. As a result, Wilberforce observed, "It is evident that we are to consider our peculiar situations, and in these to do all the good we can." After considering his circumstances and personal abilities, Wilberforce decided that he would remain in public life. "It would merit no better name than desertion," he wrote, "if I were thus to fly from the post where Providence has placed me." Yet, there was a notable change in what he did. Rather than being driven by selfish ambition, Wilberforce now focused his career upon working for causes such as prison reform, restricting capital punishment, the prevention of animal cruelty and, above all, abolishing the slave trade.

Given the substantial business and economic interests involved with slave labor, abolishing this trade was easier said than done. After nearly 20 years of unsuccessful attempts to garner support for an antislavery bill, Parliament voted to end the international slave trade in 1807 and to abolish slavery throughout the British Empire in 1833. Sadly, Wilberforce's lifelong friend William Pitt did not live to see this victory.

What would have happened if Wilberforce had left public life? Without his influence, slavery might have continued for generations. Further, the effect would not be limited to people in Wilberforce's country. Britain played a major role in fighting the slave trade worldwide. From 1808 to 1860, the Royal Navy's West Africa Squadron seized approximately 1,600 slave ships and set free 150,000 African slaves.

During the American Civil War, the Confederacy made efforts to forge a military alliance with Great Britain, appealing to mutual economic interests. This was to no avail because the British government would not go against British public opinion and aid the Confederates who maintained the right to own slaves. If Britain had not previously abolished slavery within its empire, then it may have come to the aid of the Confederacy and perhaps altered the outcome of the American Civil War.

One person, William Wilberforce, made it his life's ambition to come to the aid of those in need. He made a difference for good in his own country, which in turn affected people throughout the world. Like Wilberforce two centuries earlier, abolitionists in the 21st century find it difficult to get the attention of people who feel they are too busy taking care of their own lives to get involved in an international social problem.

Today's global slave trade involves far more people than the transatlantic slave trade of Wilberforce's day. Among the modern-day abolitionists are organizations such as the Polaris Project and Women of Vision. In 2010, New York Mayor Michael Bloomberg began a city-wide campaign to combat human trafficking, which included posters and a website to educate New Yorkers about modern-day slavery.

QUESTIONS:

1) On what other matters might Wilberforce have spent his time and energy, rather than upon ending slavery? How much effort should a politician or any person spend, in Wilberforce's day or the present, to advance a noble cause?

(continued)

2) Can one person still make a difference in politics?

3) Can history be repeated and the global slave trade be stopped once again?

Sources: Kevin Belmonte, *William Wilberforce: Hero for Humanity*, Grand Rapids, MI: Zondervan Press, 2007; Charles Colson, "Our Peculiar Situations," BreakPoint Commentary, Radio Broadcast, November 14, 2002; Rebecca Migirov, "Human Trafficking: Our Global Slave Trade," Virtual Village, http://my.hsj.org/Schools/Newspaper/tabid/100/view/frontpage/articleid/363723/newspaperid/101/Human_Trafficking_Our_Global_Slave_Trade.aspx, May 25, 2010; Liz Rhoades, "Campaign to End Human Trafficking, *Queens Chronicle*, www.zwire.com/site/news.cfm?newsid=20432189&BRD=2731&PAG=461&dept_id=574902&rfi=8, May 27, 2010.

REALITY CHECK LO-5

Most people begin learning about ethics at an early age. What is one of the first lessons you learned about ethical behavior?

Internal Controls

LO-6

Explain how internal controls can facilitate ethical behavior and help prevent financial impropriety.

Internal controls comprise a system of rules and procedures designed to ensure the accuracy and reliability of financial and accounting information. The concept of internal control has very old historical roots; ancient Egyptians and Romans applied procedures of internal control. For example, families in Ancient Rome often depended upon an account-keeper, also called dispensator or procurator, to maintain stewardship of financial matters. The Bible also describes internal control procedures such as the use of accounting reports to monitor a steward's performance and dual custody of assets.[11] The Apostle Paul wrote, "We want to avoid any criticism of the way we administer this liberal gift. For we are taking pains to do what is right, not only in the eyes of the Lord but also in the eyes of men."[12] Paul recognized that internal controls prevent dishonest persons from doing wrong, but just as importantly prevent honest persons from being the subject of suspicion and false accusation.

Only a few generations ago, businesses mostly were owned and operated by one person. For this simple form of business, the control structure also can be very simple. The owner-operator maintains firsthand knowledge of all activities of the business. He or she monitors the business so that goods are not stolen or lost.

Today, in contrast, the dominant form of business is the corporation in which the owners (i.e., the stockholders) rely upon professional managers to operate the firm. Professional managers rely upon the accounting information system to supply them with the financial information they need to make effective decisions. Consequently, good information leads to good decisions. For example, if accounting records reveal that spending is exceeding what has been budgeted, then managers can take appropriate steps to reduce spending.

Internal control procedures fit into two categories. The first: preventing accidental errors and intentional misrepresentations—also called irregularities—from occurring. Second: identifying errors and irregularities after they occur so that corrective action may be taken. Thus, internal controls can be categorized as either preventive controls or feedback controls. Both categories of accounting controls are essential to a company's control structure. Preventive controls include hiring competent and ethical employees, having (and following) written policies and procedures, providing for the physical security of firm assets, and keeping adequate documents and records. Examples of feedback controls include production quality control and internal auditing.

internal controls
a system of rules and procedures designed to ensure the accuracy and reliability of financial and accounting information

jorisvo/Shutterstock.com

Concepts of internal control have ancient origins, such as the Apostle Paul's writing about the dual custody of assets and how it protects an honest person from suspicion and false accusation.

Foreign Corrupt Practices Act

In recent years, the Foreign Corrupt Practices Act has been garnering more attention and corporations are under increased scrutiny. Congress passed the Foreign Corrupt Practices Act (FCPA) in 1977 in response to corruption and bribery of foreign government officials by managers of U.S. companies. People might expect that an old law such as the FCPA would not have a large current impact upon U.S. companies, but recent events show otherwise. During the past five years both the SEC and the U.S. Department of Justice (DOJ) have increased their investigation and prosecution of companies and individuals for violation of the FCPA.

The **Foreign Corrupt Practices Act** consists of two parts: an anti-bribery provision and a requirement to maintain an adequate internal control system over financial books and records. With regard to bribery, the FCPA prohibits any U.S. firm, including any officer, director, or employee, from using "the mails or any means or instrumentality of interstate commerce corruptly in furtherance of an offer, payment, promise to pay, or authorization of the payment of any money, or offer, gift, promise to give, or authorization of the giving of anything of value to":

(1) a foreign official;

(2) a foreign political party;

(3) an official of a foreign political party;

(4) a candidate for foreign political office; or

(5) any person who will in turn give the money or any item of value to one of the aforesaid individuals or entities for purposes of influencing a decision or act in order to assist in obtaining or retaining business or directing business to a person.

Penalties for conviction of such acts include fines and imprisonment.

With regard to internal controls, the FCPA amended the Securities Exchange Act of 1934 by requiring public companies to devise and maintain a system of internal accounting control. This internal control must be sufficient to provide reasonable assurance for the following:

(1) that transactions are executed in accordance with management's general or specific authorization;

(2) that transactions are recorded as necessary to permit preparation of financial statements in conformity with generally accepted accounting principles or any other criteria applicable to such statements, and to maintain accountability for assets;

(3) that access to assets is permitted only in accordance with management's general or specific authorization; and

(4) that recorded accountability for assets is compared with the existing assets at reasonable intervals and appropriate action is taken with respect to any differences.

Foreign Corrupt Practices Act (FCPA)
a U.S. federal law that consists of two parts: an anti-bribery provision and a requirement to maintain an adequate internal control system over financial books and records

The intent of Congress was to use the internal control provisions of the law to strengthen the anti-bribery provisions. Yet, the internal control provisions are not limited to the detection or prevention of foreign bribery, and they affect all public companies whether or not they are involved in international trade.

A few people complain that the FCPA puts American firms at a disadvantage against non-U.S. competitors. This complaint misses the point. If bribery is wrong, then bribes should not be given. If succeeding in business required unethical behavior, then not to "succeed" is better. Of course, genuine success is not based upon profits but upon being a person of character, a person who does what is right regardless of the consequences. The argument to do whatever it takes to win is a premise that leads corporate managers to use questionable accounting practices and sometimes to commit fraud to maintain impressive financial statements. While this unethical strategy may increase stock prices in the short term, the truth ultimately will be discovered.

As the FCPA is a U.S.-based law, it is enforced on U.S.-based companies, and therefore does not apply to foreign companies that fall outside the statute definition. The law does apply, however, to any entity that is an issuer under the U.S. securities laws, any foreign entity with subsidiaries in the United States and any act in furtherance of a bribe occurring in the United States. While more than 30 countries have enacted laws comparable to the FCPA, many are not as aggressively enforced and the provisions of the statutes do not have the substance of the FCPA.

Corporate financial scandals occurring in the early 2000s have led to new regulatory measures, including the especially significant Sarbanes-Oxley Act, often referred to as "SOX," which was enacted in 2002. Investors had lost billions of dollars due to scandals at companies such as Enron, WorldCom, Tyco International, Adelphia, and Global Crossing. As a result, investors had lost confidence in the reliability of the securities markets. After all, why would people purchase stock in a publicly traded corporation if the financial information is unreliable?

SOX established new and more rigorous standards for corporate boards of directors, corporate management, and public accounting firms. SOX increased the potential prison sentence for fraud to 25 years. SOX established new crimes with potential 20-year sentences for destroying, altering, or fabricating records in federal investigations, or any scheme or attempt to defraud shareholders. SOX requires that the Chief Executive Officer and Chief Financial Officer of a publicly traded corporation must certify in each periodic report containing financial statements that the report fully complies with the Securities Exchange Act of 1934 and that the information fairly presents the company's financial condition and results of operations.

As a result of the FCPA and later SOX, some people might have anticipated that strong corporate governance would be implemented and that companies would become models of corporate social responsibility. Unfortunately, news media continue to report bribery allegations in distant locations, increasing fines, and lots of money spent on control enhancements. To expand market share, many companies work to grow markets in developing countries,

Jorg Hackemann/Shutterstock.com

Images of Roman Goddess, Justitia, are often seen in courtrooms and courthouses. Justitia usually carries scales in one hand, which measures the strength of opposing sides of a case, and a sword in the other hand, which represents the power of reason and justice.

which indeed have some of the highest growth and potential, but also have additional challenges related to the FCPA.

Computer Security of Accounting Information

Advances in technology have revolutionized business and other aspects of society. Electronic business, or e-business—the exchange of goods or services using an electronic infrastructure—began with the early computers of the 1950s. However, e-business did not become commonplace until the development of the world wide web in the 1990s. Technology facilitates business activities, but there are some downsides. Business managers must beware of potential problems associated with e-business. A business must take precautions to avoid becoming a victim of computer crime.

A computer crime involves the use of computers to perpetrate or facilitate illegal activity. The average computer crime has been estimated to cost almost $200,000, whereas the average armed robbery involves far less money: only $250. Statistics show that the higher the dollar amount of a crime, the lower its probability of prosecution.[13]

Increased use of computers to maintain financial records has led to more opportunities for computer crime. Estimates of computer fraud losses are several billion dollars per year. One of the most highly publicized computer crimes was the Equity Funding fraud, in which nonexistent insurance policy records were added to the customer master file of the firm over a nine-year period from 1964 to 1973. Allegedly this was done by a large number of employees claiming to be carrying out "unscheduled" file updating which was not part of the normal data processing operations.

Based on movies and television shows, you might think that the biggest threat to computer security is intentional sabotage or unauthorized access to data or equipment. For most organizations this is not true. The five basic threats to security are:

- natural disasters;
- dishonest employees;
- disgruntled employees;
- persons external to the organization; and
- accidental errors and omissions.[14]

Accidental errors and omissions cause the great majority of the problems concerning computer security. Errors and omissions are especially prevalent in systems of sloppy design, implementation, and operation. However, if the system's development process is implemented properly, errors and omissions will be minimized. At the same time, better computer security will protect against intentional misrepresentation of data by employees and persons external to the company. An effective internal control structure, which includes computer security, is an integral part of any reliable information system.

REALITY CHECK LO-6

Preventive controls can keep a worker from being tempted to do wrong. While an individual is ultimately personally responsible for his or her own behavior, isn't it better for a company to set up controls that help people do what's right? How could such controls be created and implemented?

SUMMARY

Ethics provide guidance by which people interact with the world, including how they conduct business, how they treat other people, and how they care for the environment. Ethical perspectives can come from history and literature, religious principles, and personal experiences and observations. Integrity is defined as adherence to moral and ethical principles, soundness of moral character, and honesty. A person of integrity has two essential characteristics: knowledge of what is right, and courage to do what is right.

Ethics and economic progress are tightly intertwined. Millions of business transactions take place daily that require mutual trust. Classical economists considered economics a branch of ethics. Business activity would grind to a halt without trust, fair dealings, and honest communication.

Corporate social responsibility (CSR) is the idea that companies have obligations to society that include the welfare of stakeholders, such as customers, employees, and suppliers, and the communities and countries where the company does business. CSR also includes environmental responsibility.

Corporate financial scandals are nothing new. Some of the more recent scandals have led to investor's loss of confidence in the stock market and in the reliability of corporate financial reports. In some countries, the legislatures have enacted new laws concerning fraud and corporate financial reporting. Some of the most infamous recent corporate financial scandals include Enron, Worldcom, Vivendi, and Parmalat.

Ethics classes affect people's actions in a positive manner. Teaching ethics does not mean that everyone taught will become ethical. Nonetheless, teaching ethics will have at least some impact on the ethical perspectives and behavior of those being taught.

The concept of internal control refers to rules and procedures designed to ensure the accuracy and reliability of financial and accounting information. Business managers rely upon the accounting information system to supply them with the financial information needed to make effective decisions.

KEY TERMS

ethics, *p. 166*
integrity, *p. 166*
Corruption Perceptions Index (CPI), *p. 169*
corporate social responsibility (CSR), *p. 170*
mark to market accounting, *p. 175*
Ponzi scheme, *p. 177*
internal controls, *p. 181*
Foreign Corrupt Practices Act, *p. 182*

CHAPTER QUESTIONS

1) What do you consider the key characteristics of a person of integrity?

2) Why is ethical character of people so important to business and society?

3) How does corporate social responsibility (CSR) contribute to successful business operations?

4) Briefly describe the financial scandals at Enron, Worldcom, Vivendi, and Parmalat; what other scandals have happened in recent years or months?

5) How can ethics be taught?

6) Why are internal controls important to successful company operations?

MINI CASE: EXXONMOBIL CORPORATION: WHY ARE CORPORATE ETHICS CODES SO IMPORTANT?

What if someone is an excellent plumber, but often overbills his customers for the hours he works? This plumber will not be in business very long. ExxonMobil believes that the way the company conducts business is as important as the results obtained. For nearly 40 years, the companies now known as ExxonMobil have promoted business ethics and integrity through a 12-page booklet titled "Standards of Business Conduct." Some of the topics included in this booklet are ethics, antitrust, conflicts of interest, environment, product safety, and alcohol and drug use.

In 1999, Exxon and Mobil merged to form the ExxonMobil Corporation, a multinational giant in almost every aspect of the energy and petrochemical business. With oil and gas explorations on six of seven continents, the company is the largest non-government gas marketer and reserves holder. Fuels are marketed under the Exxon, Mobil, and Esso brands. ExxonMobil regards a well-founded reputation for scrupulous dealing as a valuable company asset.

QUESTIONS:

1) Why is ethics so important to doing business?
2) If all companies established a corporate ethics code, would that eliminate company financial scandals? Why or why not?

Point Counter-Point: What is the Right Way to Decide Where to do Business?

When a company is looking for ways to improve profitability and thereby increase returns on investment to its stockholders, the company will often seek new places to do business, including countries where it is not currently doing business. Assume that the company has decided to start business operations in one additional country but has not decided which country. The company is deciding between Country A and Country F. Setting up operations will cost about the same in either country. Country A has a very low risk of corruption; its CPI is 8.5. On the other hand, Country F has a very high risk of corruption; its CPI is 1.4. Country A is a smaller market than Country F. Projected sales revenue in Country A is $1 billion. Projected sales revenue in Country F is $2 billion.

POINT A business has an obligation to its owners to make a profit, and thereby provide the owners with a return on their investment. Because Country F offers the potential of twice the revenues of Country A, the company should set up operations in Country F.

COUNTER-POINT While Country F offers the possibility of twice as much revenue as Country A, the risk of corruption in F is several times higher. If the company establishes business in Country F and later becomes involved in corruption, the company could lose all its extra profits settling court cases and paying fines. The safer route would be to establish business in Country A, where the risks of corruption are much lower.

What Do *You* Think?

Which argument for selecting a country in which to do business is the right one? After considering the risks of corruption, where would you do business, Country A or Country F? Why?

INTERPRETING GLOBAL BUSINESS NEWS

1) A news article described a fraud that occurred at a small company. A lower-level manager had been embezzling money for many years. The manager said that she was justified in embezzling the money because the company had not paid her what she was worth. In addition, she said that the company would not miss the money, as it had made huge profits thanks to her efforts. What do you think? Do you think the company will miss the money? Assuming the manager was underpaid, was she justified in committing fraud?

2) A news story criticized corporate ethics codes, saying that they had no impact upon corporate behavior. Do you think ethics codes affect or do not affect the behavior of corporations and their employees?

3) In a news article about the Foreign Corrupt Practices Act (FCPA), the writer said that the FCPA hurt the ability of American firms to compete with non-U.S. firms. The writer said that the time had come for Congress to repeal the FCPA so that American firms would be better able to compete in the global marketplace. What do you think?

PORTFOLIO PROJECTS

Explore Your Own Case in Point: The CPI

Find the Corruption Perceptions Index (CPI) score for two countries where your selected company does business, one country with a relatively high score and one country with a relatively low score. Search for news stories about corporate financial scandals in these two countries. Prepare a short summary of news stories about financial scandals in these countries. Briefly describe what you perceive are the risks of corruption, such as paying bribes, that your selected company might face in these countries.

Questions:

1. Do you think the CPI score accurately identifies the probability of a financial scandal occurring in the two countries you selected?

2. In addition to people identified in the new stories, who else might have been hurt by the scandals?

3. What are some steps that could be taken to reduce the likelihood of recurrence of the scandals in the news stories?

Develop an International Strategy for Your Own Small Business: Corporate Ethics Codes

Research the corporate ethics codes of several major companies. Identify what you consider are key aspects of those ethics codes. Based on your findings, prepare an ethics code that you would use for your own small business.

CHAPTER NOTES

[1] D. Ariely, *Predictably Irrational: The Hidden Forces That Shape Our Decisions*, New York: HarperCollins Publishers, 2010.

[2] T. Louwers, R. Ramsay, D. Sinason, J. Strawser, and J. Thibodeau, *Auditing and Assurance Services*, 4th ed., New York: McGraw Hill 2011.

[3] F. Fukuyama, *Trust: The Social Virtues and the Creation of Prosperity*, New York: Simon & Schuster, 1995.

[4] A. Solzhenitsyn, "A World Split Apart," Address Given at Harvard Class Day Afternoon Exercises, June 8, 1978.

[5] C. Dickens, *Oliver Twist*, 1838, Electronic Text Center, University of Virginia Library, http://etext.lib.virginia.edu/toc/modeng/public/DicOliv.html.

[6] A. Craig Keller, K. T. Smith, and L.M. Smith, "Do Gender, Educational Level, Religiosity, and Work Experience Affect the Ethical Decision-Making of U.S. Accountants?" *Critical Perspectives on Accounting*, 18, no. 3, 2007, pp. 299–314.

[7] AACSB International, "Religion Curtails Financial Fraud," *BizEd Magazine*, accessed November 1, 2010, www.bizedmagazine.com/research/religion.asp.

[8] R. W. Tillerson, "Standards of Business Conduct," ExxonMobil, accessed January 2006, www.exxonmobil.com/corporate/about_operations_sbc.aspx.

[9] P. Lambe, "Accounting for Knowledge Management," Green Chameleon, accessed September 21, 2004, http://greenchameleon.com/thoughtpieces/account.pdf.

[10] United States Attorney, Southern District of New York, "Bernard L. Madoff Pleads Guilty to Eleven-count Criminal Information and is Remanded into Custody," Press release, March 12, 2009, accessed September 18, 2010, www.justice.gov/usao/nys/pressreleases/March09/madoffbernardpleapr.pdf .

[11] L.M. Smith and J. R. Miller, "An Internal Audit of a Church," *Internal Auditing*, 5:1, 1989, pp. 34–42.

[12] Paul the Apostle, 2 Corinthians 8:20–21, *The Guideposts Parallel Bible, New International Version*, Grand Rapids, Michigan: Zondervan, 1956.

[13] D. Larry Crumbley, L.M. Smith, and L. DeLaune, *Trap Doors and Trojan Horses, an Auditing Action Adventure,* Durham, NC: Carolina Academic Press, 2009.

[14] S. H. Kratchman, J. Lawrence Smith, and L.M. Smith, "Perpetration and Prevention of Cyber Crimes," *Internal Auditing* 23, no. 2, March-April, pp. 3–12.

Global Business Strategy and Organization

andar Todorovic/ erstock.com Ricardo De Mattos/iStockphoto.com ArtisticPhoto/Shutterstock.com Noel Hendrickson/Blend Images/ Jupiter Images Jorg Hackemann/Shutterstock.com

CH 8

Entry Strategies in Global Business

© C Miller Design/ Getty Images

STR/AFP/GETTY IMAGES/Newscom

After studying this chapter, you should be able to:

LO-1 Summarize the major entry strategies used by companies, especially those from emerging-market economies, in the globalization process.

LO-2 Explain the evolution of multinational enterprises (MNEs).

LO-3 Explain the major strategic reasons why MNEs invest abroad.

LO-4 Explain the pros and cons of foreign direct investment (FDI) from a host country perspective.

LO-5 Describe what countries can do to successfully attract FDI.

India, Inc. Goes Global

On March 31, 2010, Bharti Airtel, India's biggest cell-phone operator, announced that it was acquiring 100 percent of Kuwait-based Zain Group's African assets excluding those in Morocco and Sudan, for $10.7 billion. This was the largest acquisition between two multinational companies in the developing world, thereby propelling Bharti Airtel to become a world-class multinational corporation. This acquisition created the world's seventh largest cell phone operation company, with some 179 million fixed and wireless subscribers across 18 countries. Such types of overseas acquisitions are becoming commonplace among other cash-rich Indian companies as well. According to Dealogic, a research firm, between 2000 and 2008, Indian companies announced over 1,000 international mergers and acquisitions (M&A), worth over $72 billion.[1]

As part of the economic liberalization process that began in 1991, India's regulators gradually increased the amount of foreign exchange available to Indian companies for expanding their operations abroad. Overseas investment, once considered a drain on India's scarce foreign exchange reserves and a diversion of domestic investment, has given way to supporting India's national champions as they try to compete in the global marketplace. In fact, borrowing abroad in international financial markets has allowed Indian firms to finance their foreign acquisitions. Indian companies did borrow—within strict regulatory limits—given the low global interest rates starting in 2000 (post-dotcom era). Tata Steel (part of India's oldest and largest conglomerate, Tata Group) borrowed heavily to purchase Anglo-Dutch steel-maker Corus in 2007 for $12 billion. Tata Motors, another division of Tata Group, took a loan of $3 billion to acquire prestigious Jaguar Land Rover from Ford Motor Company in 2008. Hindalco, India's biggest aluminum manufacturing company, borrowed $3 billion to buy Novelis, a manufacturer of aluminum products in Canada.[2] Suzlon, an Indian manufacturer of clean energy wind turbines, sold convertible bonds to acquire Germany's REpower.

Are all of these acquisitions fundamentally sound? Time will tell. While these acquisitions may seem daring, in many cases they were defensive strategies. With ongoing globalization and because India opened its economy to foreign competition, many people in corporate India believe that the best way to protect their domestic turf, and grow as well, was to venture overseas with the primary motive of acquiring new technologies, specializing, and gaining scale economies. If acquisition of foreign firms hadn't occurred, then Indian companies would face increased foreign competition at home or be acquired by another company. Because Indian corporations are often seeking foreign know-how and technology, they often retain the managers and key personnel of acquired firms.

Introduction

In this chapter we will explore the reasons why and how firms engage in international business, and also study international movements of factors of production (i.e., land, labor, capital, and technology). Traditionally, we would consider factors of production to be mobile only within a country, but as we have seen with the advent of international organizations such as the IMF, World Bank, and WTO (all discussed in Chapter 1), factors of production have become relatively mobile. This is especially true within regional economic integration blocs (discussed in Chapter 3).

By observing what is going on in the world, one can see the importance of international business. Entrepreneurs from all over the world purchase goods, services, real estate, or even mines and technology in other countries. For example, in 2010, Chinalco, a Chinese, state-owned aluminum manufacturing company bought a bauxite mining interest in Australia. That same year, Donald Trump, an American real estate magnate, bought real estate in Scotland to build a billion-dollar golf course and resort there. Also, when global export of services are analyzed, it can be shown that there are millions of Asians working in the Middle East just as there are millions of Mexican and Central American workers in the United States. In addition, thousands of management consultants and engineers from the United States, Japan, and Europe export their services by working outside their respective countries—as their services are outsourced to foreigners. Next, the chapter will show how export of technology is relatively easy provided it is done legally. Finally, this chapter will closely examine foreign direct investment (FDI), which is a major focus of international business (and briefly discussed in Chapters 2 and 3). FDI describes the motives behind the movement of capital from one country to another to purchase foreign assets and it also involves ownership, management, and control of those foreign assets (manufacturing facilities, branch office, etc.). This is done through multinational enterprises (MNEs), sometimes referred to as multinational corporations (MNCs), transnational corporations (TNCs), or transnational enterprises (TNEs).

As mentioned in earlier chapters, globalization was formerly used to imply, largely, that businesses had expanded from developed to developing economies. The opening vignette, however, reinforces that mergers and acquisitions (M&A) activity now flows in both directions, and increasingly also from one developing country to another. Emerging-market MNCs are now competing furiously against those from rich countries. There has been a sharp increase in the number of emerging-market companies acquiring established businesses and brands in the West, starkly demonstrating the fact that globalization is a two-way street (see Exhibit 1.3). Furthermore, several U.S. financial institutions avoided bankruptcy in the Global Credit Crisis of 2008-09 only by obtaining financial support from sovereign-wealth funds (state-owned investment funds) of various Persian Gulf states and the Chinese government.

LO-1

Summarize the major entry strategies used by companies, especially those from emerging-market economies, in the globalization process.

Strategy Choice and Implementation: Going International[3]

There are several ways that domestic businesses can participate in and profit from international operations, and much depends on the amount of risk (ownership, operation, or transfer) that entrepreneurs are willing to take. A fundamental consideration that must be made in business is the risk-return trade-off. In general, the greater the risk (loss of capital invested) entrepreneurs are willing to take, the greater the rewards (profit) they are likely to reap. The converse is also true. Thus when firms decide to go international, as indicated in Exhibit 8.1, a wide range of opportunities may be available and entrepreneurs can choose the approach that suits their **risk profile**, (i.e., the amount of potential financial loss they are willing to take).

risk profile
the potential financial loss that entrepreneurs are willing to take in a business

EXHIBIT 8.1 ENTRY STRATEGIES IN GLOBAL BUSINESS

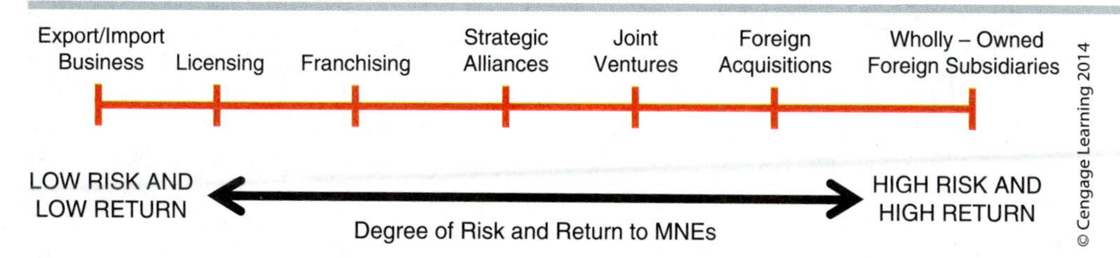

When domestic firms refrain from entering overseas markets because of concerns such as uncertainty and unfamiliarity with foreign cultures, foreign firms may take that opportunity to enter our domestic market. Global competition in a free enterprise system cannot be avoided and businesses must simultaneously seek to explore opportunities both at home and abroad in order to succeed. Conducting business internationally can be rewarding both financially and emotionally. In the ensuing approaches to going international, the amount of business risk that firms will need to take increases as described in Exhibit 8.1. But, as was just mentioned, with increased risk the opportunity to make greater profit also increases. It is important, therefore, that these firms have well thought-out exit strategies in place before their entries into the host countries, and not after foreign entry has taken place.

Export-Import Business

As described in Chapter 2, Exhibit 2.2 on page 38, the total value of global merchandise trade (exports plus imports) in 2010 was approximately $30 trillion. International trade therefore offers tremendous opportunities to firms interested in penetrating foreign markets (by exporting) or importing merchandise at competitive prices for domestic consumption. The **export-import business** is a relatively low-risk operation given the fact that capital is not tied up and it is relatively easy to enter or exit out of this business.

Furthermore, there are well-established techniques for financing trade (called trade finance) that are aimed at facilitating trade and minimizing financial risk. Simply stated, in trade finance, the exporter is assured payment will be received soon after the importer receives the stated merchandise in good condition. This is accomplished with the help of agreed-upon documents (export invoice, insurance on goods, shipping documents, customs clearance documents at foreign ports, etc.) that are made available to the importer's bank after which payment is immediately made. Next, when the importer receives the stated documents, she or he can take delivery of the merchandise only after making payment to the bank. There is, therefore, hardly any commercial risk in this business, and banks play an important role in facilitating international trade.

Firms can conduct export-import business with as little as three or four employees, as in the case of importing spices, groceries, or handicrafts from abroad. Large trading companies (especially Japanese trading firms like Mitsui & Co.) may employ hundreds or thousands of workers, because they trade in high-cost and high-volume consumer durables (cars, washing machines, appliances, etc.) and industrial products (chemicals, crude oil, etc.). In the United States, companies like Cargill, Archer Daniels Midland (ADM), and ConAgra Foods are major exporters of agricultural products. Furthermore, very large corporations like Boeing, General Electric, and Intel conduct their own import-export businesses. Still, some 20 percent of U.S. international trade is conducted by small business.

The opportunity to participate in export-import business is significant (as seen in Exhibit 2.2), and various governmental and nongovernmental agencies offer specialized seminars and programs on how to identify markets overseas and sell merchandise there. For example, certification from the U.S. Department of Commerce can be obtained for individuals enrolling in the Global Market Series Export Certificate Program. In order to facilitate and

export-import business
a relatively low-risk business operation that involves penetrating foreign markets (by exporting) or importing merchandise (of all kinds) at competitive prices for domestic consumption

Andrew Holbrooke/Corbis

Export-Import Business: ConAgra Foods–a major international trader in agricultural commodities.

encourage small- and medium-size firms to penetrate emerging overseas markets, the U.S. government (U.S. Agency for International Development) has set up the Global Technology Network, which is a network of domestic and international partners. Furthermore, the U.S. government provides a wealth of information on business conditions in various countries that can help entrepreneurs identify potential overseas business opportunities.

With the rise of the Internet, conducting international trade has become even easier and more exciting. Companies, big and small, have created websites that detail all the products and services that they provide. Product catalogs with detailed specifications, pictures, prices, shipping details, and so on, are made available on websites for all to see and from where patrons can order. Websites can be instantly updated so that interested customers are made fully aware of what is currently available. The Internet has largely eliminated the need for printing brochures, which invariably become outdated the moment they are printed. Once orders are placed, both the buyer and seller can readily identify the location of the product as it moves along the supply chain. Because it is relatively easy to participate in the export-import business, competition is generally keen and the profit margins may not be high.

Licensing

In international trade, the relationship between the exporter and importer is at arm's length; that is, the two parties may not even know or meet with one another. Merchandise is shipped and payment is received; it is that straightforward. The relationship with the overseas partner is closer with licensing. The company that is providing the license (i.e., the licensor) must properly evaluate, understand, and trust the overseas partner, because relationships such as this generally last for years. Licensing involves slightly more risk to the licensor than those in pure international trade business. In **licensing**, a company or individual provides the foreign partner with the necessary means (patented technology, copyright, process, trademark, etc.) to manufacture and sell its products in the target country for an annual license fee. The license fee could be based upon a percentage of final sales revenue of the product, or the number of units sold.

licensing
the practice in which a company or individual provides the foreign partner with the technology (patented technology, copyright, process, trademark, etc.) to manufacture and sell products or services in a target country for an annual license fee

When a product is licensed, the foreign partner will use the licensor's patented technology as agreed to manufacture and sell products that meet the licensor's standards (i.e., to avoid sales of substandard products, which could ruin the licensor's global reputation). For example, pharmaceuticals manufacturers such as Sanofi-Aventis, Merck, and Takeda frequently license their technology to foreign firms (e.g., Cipla in India) for a fee to produce certain drugs and sell them in the local market.

Why do firms license their technology to foreign partners rather than export the drug to that country, or manufacture the product overseas? The reason is quite simple. If the market for a particular drug in a target country is huge, it may make sense to manufacture the product in that target country to take advantage of lower transportation, labor, and raw material costs. Also, the licensor may not have the financial resources needed for making the overseas investment in plant and equipment, or the licensor may have better uses for those resources. In some cases, a firm may provide its license to a foreign partner to manufacture and sell the patented product in the target country and also in other countries in the region.

However, because a major point of concern to the licensor is the need to trust the licensee, a common approach to protect the licensor is to incorporate penalty clauses in the contract with the licensee. Such actions could also work as an exit strategy from the host or target country. Unscrupulous licensees have been known to manufacture licensed products and sell them under different brand names. In this case, the licensor will lose some of the patent fees because of sales diversion.

Franchising

In franchising, the parent firm assumes relatively more risk than with licensing. **Franchising** obligates the parent firm to provide specialized equipment and/or services to the franchisee (e.g., product specification and adaptation, pricing, promotion, and distribution strategies), and sometimes to fund some startup costs. In return, the franchisee pays an annual fee, which is generally based upon sales generated and seed money provided for the venture.

The fast-food industry is best known for franchises, domestically and internationally. Some of the well-known international fast-food franchises include McDonald's, Burger King, Pizza Hut, KFC, Subway, Starbucks, and Domino's. Most of the franchises are owned and operated by local residents who generally obtain local capital to start their business.

As with licensing, franchising typically leads to the penetration of international markets without significant capital investment abroad by the parent company. In return for the franchise fee, the franchisee receives technical assistance starting with the location and layout of the outlet, maintenance and use of equipment required to run the operation, and training in how to serve customers efficiently and manage the franchise hygienically.

The parent company's objective is to make sure that when a customer visits its franchisee in any country, the quality of products and services provided are similar. Thus, customers visiting a McDonald's outlet in Sydney, Australia for example, can expect to receive the same quality product and service that they would receive in the United States, Germany, Singapore, or Saudi Arabia. Yet, the menu and service offered at McDonald's outlets in different countries of the world are adapted to meet local cultural norms. For example, in India where most people are vegetarians and cows are considered sacred animals, McDonald's does not serve beef hamburgers at all, instead their "McVeggie" and "Maharaja McChicken" burgers are very popular. Similarly, if you visit a McDonald's outlet in Dhahran, Saudi Arabia, a conservative society, you will notice that females and families are served in a separate section from the "singles" (all male) section, and their menus do not contain any pork items.

With the spread of MTV culture and also because of convenience and standardization, fast-food and related franchises have spread all over the world. For example, Yum! Brands, which is based in Louisville, Kentucky, is organized around its five core constituents: KFC, Pizza Hut, Taco Bell, A&W All American Food Restaurants, and Long John Silver's. International profits have been the key to Yum! Brands' success. China is Yum! Brands' fastest-growing and most profitable market outside the United States.

franchising
the practice in which the parent firm is obligated to provide specialized equipment and/or service (e.g., product specification and adaptation, pricing, promotion, and distribution strategies), and sometimes to fund some startup costs, to franchisees in return for an annual fee

Strategic Alliances

Strategic alliances are marriages of convenience between two or more firms that stand to gain revenues (or market share) through cooperation with each other for specific reasons and for a given period of time. Thus, one could consider strategic alliances as cooperative ventures. Although similar in many ways to joint ventures (which will be described in the next section), strategic alliances differ from joint ventures in one major characteristic: they involve non-equity arrangements, meaning that strategic alliances do not involve the creation of a separate entity with joint ownership.

Strategic alliances are primarily aimed at enhancing revenues. And, because strategic alliances are based on cooperative arrangements, there are numerous ways in which firms from different countries can cooperate to form them. For example, firms could form a strategic alliance in marketing when each alliance partner has a niche market. The global airline industry is a good illustration of this type of strategic alliance. There are three major strategic alliances in this industry:[4] the Star Alliance, with a 2011 revenue of $161 billion and 25 members (largest carriers by revenue are Lufthansa and United); SkyTeam, with a 2011 revenue of $152 billion and 15 members (largest carriers by revenue are Delta and Air France-KLM); and OneWorld, with a 2011 revenue of $106 billion and 12 members (largest carriers by revenue are American and JAL). Members within each alliance code-share flights (e.g., Lufthansa Flight #11 could be designated as United Flight #2011); this enables each member airline to make reservations on the other's flight.

This strategic airline alliance helps passengers in a couple of ways. First, passengers traveling between two cities (in different countries) could complete some of their flight segments using United Airlines and the remaining segments by flying Lufthansa Airlines. Although United may not have flights to the final destination, Lufthansa will. Second, passengers who are members of United's frequent-flyer program will receive mileage credit for the Lufthansa segment as well. The same applies to members of Lufthansa's frequent-flyer program. Star Alliance members also stand to gain, since they can better use their seating capacity and hence maximize revenues. Strategic alliance in the global airline industry is aimed at maximizing seating capacity utilization on all flights with the ultimate goal of maximizing airline revenues and profits.

A challenge strategic alliances face is that any member could prematurely quit the alliance, thereby negatively affecting some or all of the other partners. For example, when the merger of Continental Airlines and United Airlines was completed in 2011, Continental had moved from SkyTeam to Star Alliance. This has serious implications to competition as the industry consolidates and becomes more concentrated. Choosing the right alliance partner is the key to the success of strategic alliances. Similarly, companies could form strategic alliances in production, where each partner manufactures a specialized component and swaps those components with other partners (e.g., automobile component manufacturers). Here again, the primary objective would be to maximize production capacity utilization and enhance revenues and profits.

International Joint Ventures

When domestic markets become saturated (reflected by the high degree of domestic competition and low profit margins) and opportunities for sales and profits overseas are significant, some domestic firms may consider making major investments abroad to expand their businesses. Since the profit potential is large, these firms may be willing to take on more financial risk. Yet these firms may not yet be willing to take on the risk of completely owning and operating a plant overseas. They may prefer to share the increased risk as well as the return with a local corporate entity—this is what joint ventures aim to accomplish. The ultimate objective of most joint ventures is to use joint production and sales distribution networks to generate increased revenue (also market share) and profits.

strategic alliances
an agreement between two or more firms that do not involve the creation of a separate entity with joint ownership and in which the firms stand to gain revenues and maximize profits through cooperation for a given period of time

An **international joint venture** refers to a business that is jointly owned (implies shared equity) and operated by two or more firms (usually one from the host country and the other from another country) that pool their resources (labor, capital, technology, and management) to penetrate a host country as well as foreign markets, generate and split profits, and share the commercial risk. In July 2011, for example, Dow Chemical of the United States and Saudi Aramco of Saudi Arabia announced plans to build a $20 billion petrochemical complex—one of the world's largest—in Jubail, Eastern Saudi Arabia to produce high value-added plastics for packaging, automotive, and other industries in high-growth markets of Asia, the Middle East, and Eastern Europe. When completed in 2016, the joint venture, to be called Sadara Chemical will have seven billion dollars in equity that will be shared by the two partners.[5] A similar project (Qatar Gas) to produce liquefied natural gas (LNG) has been in effect in the Persian Gulf state of Qatar.

The highly capital intensive automobile industry provides an excellent example of international joint ventures. Shanghai GM, General Motors' joint venture with the Shanghai Automotive Industry Corporation (SAIC) that was created in 1997, is GM's fastest growing operation worldwide.[6] As another example, Coca-Cola has built 41 bottling plants and two concentrate manufacturing plants with three separate joint venture partners in China since 1979! With over $2 billion already invested in China, Coca-Cola plans an additional $2 billion investment by 2012. Together with its bottling partners, Coca-Cola employs some 40,000 workers there and has been profitable for the past 12 years.[7]

The formation of a joint venture makes sense because the capital investment needs are so large (billions of dollars) that no single company would be willing to come up with all the needed funds. Furthermore, even if a company had the capital to invest, it would be unwilling to risk that much capital in one venture; that is, firms will want to diversify to reduce risk. International joint ventures also enable each partner to use its comparative advantage for the betterment of the joint operation.

In most cases, international joint ventures will include at least one local firm (a firm that is from the host country). The reason is simple. The local partner will be most knowledgeable about the domestic economic, cultural, and political environments. Hence, the local partner will be able to help efficiently overcome country-specific logistics and bureaucracy.

Chen Jianli Xinhua News Agency/Newscom

International Joint Venture: One of serveral Coca Cola bottling plants in China.

international joint venture
a business that is jointly owned and operated by two or more firms (usually one from the host country and the other from another country) that pool their resources (labor, capital, technology, and management) to penetrate host country markets, generate and split profits, and share commercial risk

International joint ventures with local firms often lead to the transfer of management and technical expertise in the long term. In addition, some of the corporate profits generated by these ventures will remain in the domestic economies.

Cross-Border Mergers and Acquisitions

Domestic companies with clearly identified core competencies or competitive advantages may enter foreign markets by merging with or acquiring (buying) well-established firms overseas. Bharti Airtel's acquisition of Zain's African assets indicated in the opening vignette is a good example. The advantages are obvious; an existing firm in a host or target country may already have a well-established production or marketing operation along with a good distribution network or valuable technology. By merging the strengths of the home company with those of the host country firm, the new firm will become more competitive internationally.

ECONOMIC PERSPECTIVES Medical Tourism

The United States spends just over 15 percent of its GDP on health care, yet some 45 million Americans do not have health insurance and an estimated 30 million are underinsured. Health care costs $2.3 trillion dollars in the United States (or roughly $7,600 per capita), the most expensive in the world. Health care inflation in the United States has consistently exceeded consumer price inflation as well as income growth. That means an increasing amount of an American family's monthly budget goes toward paying for health care costs—something that is unsustainable at the current rate.

Medical tourism, which combines medical treatment in a foreign country with rest and recreation, has been in place since the late-1990s. This promises to be an alternative yet competitive market force that will likely reduce costs and improve quality of health care in the United States. Service from foreign medical facilities, especially in Asia (India, Singapore, Thailand, etc.), is likely to bring greater price competition to the inefficient American system that is riddled with special interest groups, oligopolies, and perverse incentives such as the "fee-for-service" system that rewards providers for performing procedures, not for achieving better health outcomes.

Medical tourism is not about exporting patients to Asia, but importing competition from Asia that could serve as a catalyst for health care reforms in the United States. The number of Americans traveling abroad for treatment is expected to soar from 750,000 in 2007 to ten million by 2012, and will be worth some $21 billion a year to developing countries. An increasing number of Americans are seeking health care abroad at their own expense for joint replacements, cosmetic surgery, hysterectomies, and other non-emergency procedures. They do so for reasons of cost, and because the hospitals under consideration in Asia are as good as those in the West.

Asian hospital chains could be the biggest winners. Chief among them are India's Wockhardt and Apollo Hospital chains, Singapore's Parkway Health, and Thailand's Bumrungrad Hospital. These hospitals meet the stringent requirements for accreditation by the Joint Commission International, a non-profit organization that assesses the quality and safety of healthcare providers worldwide. The benefits to these hospitals include earnings from American patients and raising service and hygiene quality to international levels to attract foreigners as well as local upscale patients.

QUESTIONS:

1) How has the health care crisis in the United States affected the globalization of health care? Explain what you think can be done to reduce health care costs in the United States.

2) It appears that Asia will be a net exporter of health care services to the West, especially the United States. Are there opportunities for U.S. firms to venture into this field? How?

Source: "Globalization and Health Care," *The Economist*, August 16, 2009, pp. 74-76.

In **acquisitions**, the home country firm will purchase the host country firm and implement its own international business strategy (deciding what products and services to produce, how to price and market them, how to manage the new company, etc.). However, in the case of mergers, the management of both companies will play an active role in business development and execution. Well thought-out cross-border mergers and acquisitions will enable the new firm to have instant access to foreign markets that fit its global strategy.

Goodwill and market share come with mergers and acquisitions. For example, in 1993 when Coca-Cola acquired major assets of Parle Exports in India, it instantly received access to Parle's huge national bottling and distribution network. In India, some 70 percent of the 1.1 billion consumers live in rural areas, so access to these consumers was vital for Coca-Cola's success. Coca-Cola had to upgrade existing production and distribution facilities in India and introduce and market Coca-Cola's global products. Similarly, when Lenovo of China acquired IBM's personal computer business, it received access to IBM's global supply chain and distribution network along with China's huge 1.3 billion consumer market.

The company being acquired should be well established and have a good reputation in the local market. As compared with other types of foreign market entry discussed so far, mergers and acquisitions are relatively risky because a significant amount of capital may be needed to acquire and upgrade foreign facilities. Moreover, corporate cultural differences may inhibit smooth integration of the two organizations of different nationality, customs, and values.

If for some unfortunate reason (e.g., labor problems) the new firm performs poorly, an exit strategy should be in place that enables the home company to leave the host country and dispose of the foreign venture at a reasonable price without incurring significant loss. It is important to remember that an exit strategy must always be in place at the time of entry into the host country and not after the merger or acquisition has taken place.

acquisition
purchase of established firms abroad with the goal of using the existing production, marketing, and distribution networks and of having instant access to foreign markets that fit the purchasing firm's global strategy

Wholly-Owned Subsidiaries

As an alternative to foreign acquisitions, a domestic or home country firm may decide to build and operate its own new facilities (also called "green field" plants) overseas. These wholly-owned **subsidiaries** of home country firms generally require large capital investment. Hence the risk and rewards in such ventures are high. Yet, the new subsidiaries will most likely be modern, efficient, environmentally sound, and designed to contemporary international standards, which will enable them to handle the latest in supply chain management. For these reasons, subsidiaries are sometimes preferred to acquisitions.

However, subsidiaries will require major marketing efforts to penetrate the international market because of cultural differences and because the entrant is new and relatively unknown. A subsidiary will need to establish a new customer base through a well-orchestrated marketing campaign.

subsidiaries
new facilities built and operated overseas that require large investment of capital because these new establishments are tailored to the exact needs of the home country firm

multinational enterprises (MNEs)
firms that are headquartered in one country, but own and control manufacturing, services, R&D (research and development) facilities, or other business entities on foreign soil

REALITY CHECK LO-1

Identify the types of international business activities that are being conducted in the city or region where you live. Which type is most popular and why?

Multinational Enterprises (MNEs)

LO-2
Explain the evolution of multinational enterprises (MNEs).

Multinational enterprises (MNEs) are firms that are headquartered in one country, but own and control manufacturing, services, R&D (research and development) facilities, or other business entities on foreign soil. General Electric (United States), Microsoft (United States), Sony (Japan), Toyota (Japan), BMW (Germany), Siemens (Germany), Shell (United

Kingdom-Netherlands), Hyundai (South Korea), Lenovo (China), Tata (India), and Petrobras (Brazil) are just a few of the hundreds of large MNEs that are based in one country but own and operate establishments in other countries.

In general, MNEs are large corporations with significant amounts of resources (capital, management talent, and technology) at their disposal. Given these assets, MNEs are willing and able to take on huge risks needed to globally operate. Exhibit 8.2 provides a list of the top ten MNEs in the world (year end 2010) in terms of market value or capitalization (company stock price times the total number of shares outstanding in the world market). MNEs from the United States and China dominate the top ten rankings.

The *Financial Times* annually publishes the list of the 500 world's largest companies. Historically, and also in 2010 year end, U.S. MNEs dominated the *Financial Times* Global 500 list with 160 (down from 240 in 2003) companies ranked in the top 500, followed by the United Kingdom with 34 companies. A recent (since 2000) strategic development is the rise of emerging-market MNEs—MNEs from China (27), India (14), Brazil (11), Russia (11), South Korea (9), and South Africa (6) in the FT Global 500 list.[8] With the growing importance of these countries in the global economy and the crucial role they are expected to play in the 21st century, emerging-market MNEs are a force to be reckoned with as they are likely to play a pivotal and more dominant geopolitical role in the future.

While the emergence of MNEs can be traced to the early part of the 20th century, their growth—led by U.S. MNEs—greatly accelerated only after World War II, when various international organizations (and international rules of the game) were established and international trade and investment rules and regulations began a process of liberalization (as discussed in Chapter 1). At that time, most of the MNEs were primarily from industrialized or developed countries of Europe and North America that were in search of raw materials like crude oil and other minerals (iron ore, copper, bauxite, gold, coal, etc.), which were largely to be found in developing regions such as the Middle East, Africa, Asia, Latin America, and Australia.

In the manufacturing sector, with the introduction of assembly line production by Ford Motor Company in 1903, U.S. companies such as Ford and General Motors sought to actively penetrate the European market by acquiring some of the numerous small-scale

EXHIBIT 8.2 THE WORLD'S TEN LARGEST COMPANIES (YEAR END 2010)

Multinational enterprises from the United States and China dominate the world business scene

Rank	Company	Nationality	Market Value ($ billion)	Sector
1	Exxon Mobil	United States	417	Oil & Gas
2	PetroChina	China	326	Oil & Gas
3	Apple	United States	321	Technology Hardware/ Equipment
4	Indl & Coml Bank of China	China	251	Banking
5	Petrobras	Brazil	247	Oil & Gas
6	BHP Billington	Australia/U.K.	247	Mining
7	China Construction Bank	China	233	Banking
8	Royal Dutch Shell	UK/Netherlands	228	Oil & Gas
9	Chevron	United States	216	Oil & Gas
10	Microsoft	United States	213	Software & Computer Services

Source: "FT Global 500 Companies", From the Financial Times,

car companies there. By the early-1950s, assembly line production had spread beyond the auto industry to include the manufacture of almost all consumer durables like appliances (washing machines, refrigerators, stoves, etc.) and consumer electronics (radio and television sets, phonographs, etc.). In recent decades, aircraft manufacturing and even iPhone assembly operations have started implementing manufacturing techniques like just-in-time and just-in-sequence manufacturing, supply chain management, and ERP (enterprise resource planning) systems across national borders.[9]

Although U.S., European, and Japanese MNEs still play a dominant role in the world economy, they are and will continue to be challenged by the rise of MNEs from emerging-market economies, especially from China, India, Brazil, Russia, South Korea, and South Africa. The rise of emerging-market MNEs will be the distinctive feature of foreign direct investment for the 21st century.

REALITY CHECK LO-2

Identify an emerging-market MNE that has operating facilities in your neighborhood or state. Determine the national origin of that company and its motive for choosing your state.

MNEs and their Global Strategic Motives

LO-3
Explain the major strategic reasons why MNEs invest abroad.

The text has discussed that MNEs could enter foreign markets as exporters, licensors, franchisors, joint venture or strategic partners, through mergers and acquisitions, or as wholly-owned subsidiaries. Now the text will provide information on what motivates MNEs to go international. The strategic motives of China's MNEs are quite different from those of U.S. MNEs or their European counterparts. And, within a foreign country, each MNE may have a specific reason for wanting to go abroad. All of them, however, would like to use their respective competitive advantages and core competencies to achieve specific national or corporate objectives.

In a free enterprise system, the overriding objective of firms wanting to invest abroad is to **maximize shareholder wealth** (i.e., to maximize the net present value of future cash flows of foreign investment adjusted for exchange rate movements). Or, to put it in simpler terms, companies go abroad to maximize profits so that shareholders can receive larger dividends and allow share prices to rise over time.

So, how do companies try to maximize profits when investing abroad? How do they choose the country or countries in which to invest? The answer to these two questions is embedded in the following three strategic motives: companies seek to go abroad to increase revenues, to cut costs, and/or to diversify operations to minimize risk (i.e., to reduce the impact of business cycles or political changes on a firm's cash flows). Or, companies may try to accomplish all three goals together. Let's discuss these three strategies in some detail.

maximizing shareholder wealth
to maximize the net present value of future cash flows of foreign investment adjusted for exchange rate movements or to maximize profits so that shareholders could receive larger dividends and see their share prices rise over time

Revenue Maximizing Strategies

When MNEs go abroad to maximize revenue, they generally do so for two major reasons. First, there could be massive competition in the home market that will be reflected in decreasing profit margins and market saturation for their products or services. Second, firms may genuinely identify new business opportunities abroad based upon the their competitive advantages in production, technology, and management. Now we will try to identify and segment the potential markets abroad.

Entering High-Growth Markets Countries with high-growth potential will witness rising per-capita income and a growing middle class with high demand for goods and services. Investors from abroad will want to take advantage of this development by entering these high-growth and profitable markets. Exhibit 1.2 on page 7 in Chapter 1, as noted at the beginning of that chapter, provides growth projections developed by the author for the world's ten largest economies. Particularly close attention needs to be paid to Brazil, Russia, India, and China, the so called BRIC countries—a term coined by Jim O'Neil, chief economist with the U.S. investment banking company Goldman Sachs—which are expected to become the fastest growing economies in the 21st century. Also, as you can see from Exhibit 2.3 in Chapter 2, the rate of increase in net foreign investment inflow into BRICs has accelerated as foreign companies try to enter these profitable markets. China and India each have a population of over a billion with a high consumption "middle class" which is estimated to be larger than total U.S. population. However, both China and India also have a large population of poor who outnumber the middle class and are often referred to as the "bottom of the pyramid" with regard to per-capita income. According to the late Professor C. K. Prahalad of the University of Michigan who coined this phrase, even this segment of population offers profitable business opportunities as consumers of lower level differentiated products—something that MNEs cannot and should not ignore.[10]

Entering Stable, High-Income Markets Stable, high-income economies (see Exhibit 2.3 on page 39) include the United States, Japan, and Canada, as well as regions such as the European Union. While economic growth rates in these stable economies may be low compared with emerging-market economies like BRIC, their high per-capita-income levels translate to high consumption that could prove to be a stable source of revenue and profits for MNEs wanting to enter these markets. A close look at Exhibit 2.3 will show that the majority of foreign investment flows each year has been to these stable developed market economies despite the fact that the growth rate of foreign investment flows is much larger to emerging-market economies.

Entering Countries with Monopolistic Market Structures Market structure refers to the degree of competition in specific industries within a country. Monopolistic market structure refers to cases where there are few players in a particular industry in a country.

Ricardo De Mattos/iStockphoto.com

BRIC: Brazil is expected to be one of the fastest growing economies in the 21st Century, along with Russia, India, and China.

What does this imply? In industries that reflect monopolistic market structures (such as monopoly, duopoly, or monopolistic competition), profit margins are generally high because there are few competitors. For example, when Motorola, Inc., a major U.S. company in the semiconductor and cell phone business, entered the China market in the 1980s, there were no significant competitors in China's semiconductor industry. Motorola nearly had China's market to itself and was able to set high prices for its products. In the process, it generated solid revenues and profits for a long time period until the late-1990s, when competitors like IBM, Intel, Nokia, Samsung, and Toshiba entered China. In the meantime, Motorola established itself firmly in China where it has been more profitable than in the United States for a long time.

Entering Trade Restricted Sectors As we discussed earlier, countries often impose various types of trade barriers like tariffs, quotas, and subsidies to protect certain high-profile industries from global competition. These trade barriers lead to decreased competition from abroad, and raise prices and profits of domestic firms. Such protection over time will often lead to lesser-quality domestic products and services.

The only profitable way for foreign firms to enter these trade-restricted markets is through FDI rather than through exports. So, a foreign firm that wants to enter the protected market will need to determine whether that host country market is so large and profitable that it is willing to make long-term commitments and investments in that country.

A good example is the voluntary export restraint agreement that the governments of Japan and the United States entered together in the early-1980s, soon after the Iranian Revolution of 1979 that led to a curb in Iranian oil exports and a more than doubling of crude oil prices. Per this agreement, Japan limited its car exports to the United States to about 1.6 million units a year for three years. The objective was to protect Detroit's "Big Three" auto makers (GM, Ford, and Chrysler) and provide them three years time to retool and manufacture fuel-efficient small cars.

Japanese car manufacturers knew that they could effectively compete against Detroit both in quality and price. Furthermore, the Japanese manufacturers did not want to give up on the world's largest and most lucrative car market. Therefore, the Japanese car companies needed to decide between two options: (1) manufacture cars at home (in Japan) and export a maximum of 1.6 million cars a year to the United States; or (2) circumvent trade restrictions by establishing manufacturing plants in the United States to produce and sell as many cars as possible there.

Honda was the first Japanese firm to pursue the option of assembling cars in the United States beginning in 1982. By 1987, six other Japanese automakers were also operating, or announcing plans to build, U.S. assembly plants. This was the beginning of Japanese car transplants in the United States. Today, Toyota manufactures and sells more cars in the United States than General Motors, which, since declaring bankruptcy in 2009, has been successfully downsizing and restructuring its U.S. operations.

Cost Minimizing Strategies

Another reason why MNEs go abroad is to minimize costs. For example, if the domestic market for a product is highly competitive, then the MNE may not make much profit. The only alternative for the MNE in such an environment will be to cut costs. When the MNE finds that it is unable to domestically cut costs for various reasons, then it would decide to move production abroad or outsource some of its components from abroad in order to show a decent profit to its shareholders. Thus, when the cost of domestic factors of production (i.e., land, labor, capital, and technology) increases, MNEs feel the pressure to seek lower factor costs abroad to maintain or increase corporate profit margins. There are several important strategic ways of minimizing costs on a global scale as discussed next.

Economies of Scale in Production Most manufacturing operations exhibit economies of scale in production, meaning that as a firm continues to increase output, the average cost per unit will decrease until it reaches an optimum level because the firm will be using its fixed assets (plant and machinery) most efficiently. This implies that for a given sales price, unit profit (profit margin) will continue to rise until production reaches that optimum level and economies of scale are achieved.

In the 1890s, Britain's Lever Brothers found that it could achieve economies of scale in production by entering into both America's and India's huge soap and detergent markets. Similarly, Procter & Gamble of the United States entered the Chinese market in the 1980s to take advantage of economies of scale in production there. Hence, if the target foreign market is large, MNEs may decide upon the basis of economies of scale to use FDI as a mode of entry to that market—and potentially export from there as well.

Minimizing Factor Input Cost The unit cost of factors of production (i.e., land, labor, capital, and technology) vary from country to country because of factor endowments and productivity. A country such as Brazil is rich in agricultural and mineral resources and also has relatively inexpensive productive labor. For these reasons, Brazil is one of the world's lowest cost producers of ethanol and soybeans. Japanese corporations have heavily invested in Brazil to lease large tracts of land to grow soybeans for export to Japan, where they are used to derive products like tofu (soybean curd), soy sauce, soy milk, soybean oil, and chicken feed.

Similarly, U.S. MNEs such as General Motors and Walmart have heavily invested in China to take advantage of that country's low cost productive labor in manufacturing; and General Electric, IBM, Microsoft, and others have heavily invested in India to use that country's productive, low cost, English-speaking educated labor for service sector jobs.

Reacting to Exchange Rate Movements When the currency of a particular country is expected to strengthen over time, FDI may flow into that country to buy assets like plant and equipment at current, relatively inexpensive prices. This way, when profits are generated in future years, the MNEs that had made the initial investment will receive higher income when those profits become converted into home currency.

For example, U.S. corporations have been pouring investments into China to build manufacturing facilities to produce goods for the local and export markets. Since economists expect the Chinese yuan to appreciate against the dollar in the future, the forthcoming Chinese yuan profits of U.S. MNEs when converted to U.S. dollars will be high. If this happens as expected, the U.S. firm and their investors will be handsomely rewarded.

Risk Minimizing Strategies

Another way for MNEs to maximize profits apart from maximizing revenues and minimizing costs is to minimize risk. A key approach to minimizing risk is through diversification abroad. The following text will first discuss in detail what diversification means, and then describe two important ways how MNEs could identify the approach to global diversification.

Diversification A major reason why MNEs establish operations abroad is to diversify and minimize risk so that *global* corporate cash flows and earnings will be relatively stable. Growth-oriented or forward-looking MNEs generally do not want to have all their investments in the local or domestic market. They do not want to put "all their eggs in the domestic basket." They would like to invest overseas because all countries do not grow at the same rate, nor do they follow the same business cycle. Thus, companies want to diversify so that when there is an economic downturn at home, the economies of foreign countries where investment has been made (e.g., China, India, Brazil, Indonesia, and South Africa) may do well. This way, the aggregate profits that the company generates worldwide would be stable.

The Coca-Cola Company, for example, has operations in more than 140 countries and generates more than 55 percent of its profits from its overseas operations. Coca-Cola's annual profits are, therefore, more stable than those of a firm that focuses upon the U.S. market alone. Hence, if a firm is trying to maximize long-term profits, diversification is the key. Because international diversification is an important MNE objective, businesses must determine how to efficiently diversify.

Correlation of Returns A relatively simple approach to diversification is to identify overseas projects that have performance levels (annual after tax cash flows adjusted for exchange rate movements or return on investment) that are not highly correlated to domestic cash flows or project returns over time. This can be accomplished through simulations that develop annual cash flows of projects over time to determine the after tax cash flow and return on investment, and then compare them with those of domestic operations. If the correlation coefficient is one or close to one, the international project's returns are very highly correlated to those of the domestic project. This implies that risk is not diversified, and one might as well invest or expand domestically and discontinue considering the international project. On the other hand, if the correlation coefficient is low or negative, the international and domestic projects complement one another and risk can be reduced.

Product Life Cycle Theory Another approach to diversification can be explained with the help of product life cycle theory. Almost all manufactured products in an established market go through a life cycle starting with the birth of the product and ending with the death of the product. The **product life cycle theory** explains what happens to a product at the different stages: introduction (purely domestic market); growth (along with exports); maturity (emphasizing outsourcing and overseas production); and decline—before the product is discontinued.

Consider the example of the video cassette recorder (VCR) when Sony first introduced it to the Japanese market. During the introduction stage (the 1970s), both revenues and profits were low (although prices were set high to recoup R&D costs) because Japanese consumers were not sure about the utility value of the product. In the second stage, the growth phase (the 1980s), the product gained acceptance (and exports commenced), revenues rapidly increased, and profits were maximized. In the third phase (the 1990s), the product became mature and competition from other manufacturers heated up (leading to production abroad to cut costs). Japanese consumers found the need to purchase multiple units for different rooms in their homes. During this stage, revenues were maximized and profits started to decline because of competition. In the final stage (2000 and later), both revenues and profits declined further as a new product, DVD, entered the market and replaced the VCR.

How does product life cycle relate to diversification? According to Raymond Vernon's product life cycle theory, MNEs facing competition at home during the third phase (maturity) will be forced to become efficient. The MNE will, therefore, want to diversify through investment abroad and stabilize corporate cash flow. Thus, the MNE will manufacture the product abroad for foreign consumption as well as for exports to the home country to maximize overall corporate profits. Otherwise, the domestic firm will have to go out of business.

Dunning's Eclectic Theory of Foreign Direct Investment[11]

In Chapter 1, this text analyzed how well-functioning institutional structure and good governance facilitate globalization. In Chapter 2, various theories of international trade were discussed. And, in Chapter 3, the text described how economic geography influences trade and investment flows and facilitates the creation of regional economic blocks. This chapter analyzes how firms, especially MNEs, behave in a global economy with the objective of maximizing shareholder wealth and profits.

product life cycle theory explains what happens to a product's revenue and profits at the different stages –introduction, growth, maturity, and decline—before the product is discontinued

After considering all these theories of international economics, British economist John Dunning arrived at his eclectic theory of FDI in 1980. Dunning synthesized these theories (theory of comparative advantage, Heckscher-Ohlin theorem, factor price equalization theorem, Porter's "Diamond" model of national competitive advantage, and the effectiveness of governance and institutions in an economy) to answer the question: Why do firms invest in international production? That is, what core competencies or advantages should a firm have that will motivate such a firm to participate in FDI or other modes of foreign entry?

The bedrock of the eclectic theory is the structure and core competency of firms that seek to locate production abroad. In addition, Dunning identified the three key economic "advantages" that firms should have for FDI to occur: (1) ownership advantages or firm-specific advantages; (2) location advantages or country-specific advantages; and (3) internalization advantages.

Ownership, or *firm-specific, advantages* are internal to the firm that can be transferred at a very low cost within a MNE regardless of location: brand name, trademark, or patent; supply chain and production process; entrepreneurial and management skills; and financial strength. These advantages must exceed those of competitors located in the foreign target countries for the MNE to maximize revenues or minimize cost—or both—to increase profits. For example, a firm that has a patent for manufacturing a particular brand-name drug will have monopoly rights to use that brand name abroad to produce goods profitably.

Locational, or *country-specific, advantages* relate to the economic, political, and social systems of a particular country. As discussed earlier in the chapter, this could include the cost of production factors (i.e., labor quality and productivity, land and resources beneath them, cost of capital, and quality of infrastructure) as well as the political environment (i.e., well-functioning institutions, rule of law, and transparency of governance). For example, a democratic country such as India, which has a large and well-qualified English-speaking workforce, attracts a significant amount of FDI from companies such as GE and IBM. In fact, these two MNEs have their second largest R&D facilities in India.

Finally, *internalization advantages* refer to the mode of entry abroad. For example, a firm may conclude that the only way it can operate abroad will be through full control of its foreign operations. This may relate to concern over the costs of monitoring contractual obligations or concern over misappropriation of technology or trade secrets. Hence, FDI may be more appropriate than giving a foreign company the license to manufacture. In essence, when the cost of negotiating and monitoring a foreign partner is high, FDI will be the preferred route. For example, Coca-Cola prefers to follow the FDI route in most countries to prevent loss of its secret cola formula.

As is shown by the above analysis, Dunning's eclectic theory offers a comprehensive approach to explaining why MNEs, regardless of whether they are from developed or emerging markets, have international operations.

REALITY CHECK LO-3

Identify a foreign MNE that is operating in the state or region where you live. Determine which of the three strategies discussed above is the principal motive of the foreign investor for choosing to do business in your state?

LO-4
Explain the pros and cons of foreign direct investment (FDI) from a host country perspective.

Host Country Perspective of Foreign Direct Investment

Host countries generally consider foreign direct investment (FDI) to be a complement or substitute for domestic investments. Investments take many forms—buildings, plant and equipment, technology, improvements to property, and inventories. These investments are generally financed through domestic savings, and in countries with high saving's rates such as those in much of Asia, this is likely to lead to high rates of economic growth.

Because all investments need not be financed through domestic savings alone, some countries have created a favorable investment climate to proactively attract FDI as an important alternative source of funding domestic growth. A good investment climate is one in which government policies encourage entrepreneurship, employment generation, sustainable economic growth, and poverty reduction to benefit society as a whole. FDI is also stimulated by the availability of efficient physical infrastructure such as in China, and investment in people, through better education and health care. Investment produces growth, but investment also chases sustainable growth, as seen in Exhibit 2.3 on page 39 with BRIC countries, the United States and the United Kingdom.

Benefits of Foreign Direct Investment

Along with significant financial inflows, FDI creates new jobs, allows access to new technologies, and facilitates transfer of important management (and employee) skills; it also increases domestic competition and choice. In addition, FDI generates tax revenues (corporate, income, and sales taxes) needed for government services, reduces poverty, and accelerates economic development.

If it were not for the huge amount of FDI inflow from abroad, especially since the mid-1990s, job creation and economic growth in the United States would have been a lot slower. As was discussed in Chapter 4, the United States has been running a large current account deficit in the balance of payments each year. The size of the current account deficit indicates the financing needs of a country, or how much a country needs to attract or borrow from abroad. Fortunately for the United States it's relatively open and flexible economic system has enabled it to attract sizable FDI from abroad. In fact, the United States consistently has been the world's largest recipient of FDI capital in the world, averaging some $200 billion a year in net FDI inflows since 2005. The United States has been made more globally competitive as a consequence of such FDI flows. A more specific example is the FDI made by foreign automobile companies that forced Detroit automakers to change their ways and manufacture cars acceptable to the American consumer.

Costs of Foreign Direct Investment

Although FDI has tremendous positive effects on countries as indicated above, developing countries in particular are concerned that they may become exploited by MNEs. Some host countries are concerned that in the rush to exploit natural resources, foreign MNEs may sacrifice the environmental quality, health, and social fabric of host countries.

For example, environmentalists in Canada have been concerned that in the push to extract crude oil from the tar sands of Alberta, foreign oil companies have degraded the pristine Canadian landscape and also polluted the water in the region. Similarly, environmentalists have complained that since the signing of NAFTA, some U.S. companies have moved their polluting facilities and operations across the border into Mexico where enforcement is lax.

Human rights organizations have accused multinational firms of exploiting the labor force in host countries, thereby preventing human capital development and tarnishing the image of the countries concerned. For example, in the 1990s Nike Corporation was found guilty of using child labor at its production facilities in several countries, including Cambodia, Indonesia, and Pakistan. In each case, Nike subsequently announced that it had rectified the situation.

A third concern of local governments in host countries is the lack of corporate social responsibility on the part of MNEs. As was discussed in Chapter 7, the concept of corporate social responsibility refers to the premise that corporations should seriously consider the social consequences of their business decisions if they are to have a long-term mutually productive relationship in a country or region. Foreign MNEs often work with host government leaders at the national level and, in the process, sometimes fail to consider and contribute to the welfare of local citizens where resources are being exploited.

Shell Oil Company's crude oil exploration and production operations in the Niger Delta of Nigeria denote a good example. For decades, the local Niger Delta population has seen very little trickle-down benefit from the billions of dollars of revenue that the Nigerian federal government earns from Shell's operations. They have also complained about pollution of the land and water from numerous large and small oil spills. Rebel groups have, therefore, evolved over time in the Niger Delta who regularly sabotage crude oil pipelines running through the area, disrupting petroleum supplies on the world market. As one of the largest contributors to Nigeria's economy, Shell could negotiate a better deal with the Nigerian government to serve the interests of the Niger Delta population and prevent environmental degradation, thereby decreasing the motivation of local people to join the rebel groups.

Finally, host countries have also been concerned about political interference by MNEs in their country's affairs when things do not go the way the foreign company wants. For example, in early-2000, fearing that Venezuelan President Hugo Chávez was becoming too socialist as he ran for re-election to the presidency, the United States government provided moral support to Mr. Chávez's opponent. Unfortunately for the United States, Mr. Chávez won re-election because he was able to mobilize Venezuela's poor, who form the majority of voters, by providing various forms of subsidies. In 2002, when a coup attempt briefly ousted Chávez and installed a conservative official as president, the United States was one of the very few countries to recognize the new government (which lasted only 2 days). As a result, after his return to power Mr. Chávez became strongly anti-American, banning all U.S. oil company operations in Venezuela and instead inviting European, Russian, and Chinese companies to operate in what is the western hemisphere's largest pool of oil reserves. Mr. Chávez has indicated, in his own defense, that he was simply trying to diversify his country's crude oil market.[12]

REALITY CHECK LO-4

Identify a foreign multinational company, big or small, that is operating in your area. Of the concerns outlined in this section, what is your biggest concern about that MNE's operation?

Asmaa Waguih/Reuters

Human rights organizations monitor the exploitation of host countries' labor forces by multinational firms, including such issues as child labor.

Improving Host Country's Investment Climate

LO-5

Describe what countries can do to successfully attract FDI.

Countries that have been successful in attracting FDI generally have been those that have improved their investment climate through proper economic reforms, transparent governance structure, and rule of law (see Chapter 1). A good investment climate is one in which government policies enable firms (domestic and MNEs) and entrepreneurs to invest profitably, create jobs, contribute to economic growth, and reduce poverty. The goal is to create a sustainable investment climate that benefits the whole society for the long term.

Yet, countries significantly differ upon how they regulate the entry of new businesses, both domestic and foreign. Governance, as was discussed in Chapter 1, describes how countries exercise authority and how efficiently bureaucrats deliver basic infrastructure services—water, sanitation, roads, electricity, security, and the like—for public as well as private firms. Good governance also calls for transparency and a proper system of checks and balances as well as accountability of public officials. The level of corruption—using public office for private gain—in a country can be a good indicator of the degree of weak governance.

ETHICAL PERSPECTIVES

Chaebols: Too big to fail?

South Korea's *chaebols* (corporate conglomerates) are accused of sticking to the past and not adapting to globalization. Globalization would require these world-famous MNEs to become more transparent in their governance structures, promote employee advancement based upon performance rather than on loyalty or nepotism, and support supplier concerns.

South Korea's *chaebols* are huge, diversified business conglomerates like Japan's *keiretsus* and are responsible for the country's stellar industrialization since the 1960s, thereby making South Korea the fourth largest economy in Asia. That growth was made possible because the South Korean government facilitated the conglomerates' access and control over various segments of the economy by removing the barriers to entry into various industrial sectors. Hence *chaebols* like Samsung, Hyundai, LG, SK Group, and Hanwa Co. now dominate South Korea's economy with their sprawling empire by using authoritarian governance structures, tradition, and preference for employee loyalty rather than creativity or competence. Although some 80 percent of South Korea's working population is tied to small and medium-size companies, a significant number of them are beholden to the conglomerates as suppliers of goods and services. Because of a lack of transparency in governance, the *chaebols* are accused of squeezing profits and stealing innovations of small and medium-size suppliers.

Mr. Lee Myung-bak, the president of South Korea since 2008, has his origins in Hyundai Construction Company and is credited for transforming the operations of that conglomerate. However, the South Korean people really wonder whether President Lee will be able to reform the *chaebols* and make them more open and stake-holder friendly in a globalized economy. Of concern to many is the level of corruption at the top of these MNEs, and the unwillingness of the government to meet out justice to these officials.

For example, in 2007 the chairman of Hyundai Motors, Mr. Chung Mong-koo, was convicted of misappropriating some $100 million from the company, but the sentence was squashed since the government felt that he was needed to run the company. In early 2008, the chairman of Samsung was accused of trying to pass his chairmanship to his son with the help of slush funds. Events such as these call into question the role of corporate governance, transparency, and justice in South Korea and how the *chaebols* can be reformed to compete more effectively, domestically, and globally to achieve South Korea's growth potential.

QUESTIONS:

1) Are the *chaebols* too big to fail? Should they be exempt from corporate social responsibility?
2) Discuss what could be done to make the *chaebols* more competitive and ethical.

Source: Anna Fifield, "Korea's Bulldozer Must Clean up the Chaebol," *Financial Times*, March 28, 2008.

Jacobs Stock Photography/Photodisc/Jupiter Images

Governance: Singapore, with a transparent system of proper checks, balances, and accountability, ranks among the least corrupt countries.

Governance has an impact upon the provision of social service investment such as education and health, which in turn will have an effect on labor productivity, the cost of doing business, and the investment climate in a country. As described earlier, Transparency International annually ranks countries according to the level of corruption with a rank of one reflecting the least corrupt. New Zealand, Denmark, Finland, Sweden, and Singapore that have a transparent system of government with high penalties for violations of law were ranked between 1-5 as least corrupt in 2011, while the United States was ranked 24, and China and India were ranked 75 and 95, respectively.

governance
describes how countries exercise authority and how efficiently they deliver basic infrastructure services like water, sanitation, roads, electricity, security, and the like for public as well as private firms

REALITY CHECK LO-5

Visit the Economic Development Board or similar organization in your county or city and find out what actions are being taken to make the local investment climate attractive to foreign businesses.

SUMMARY

Entrepreneurs worldwide constantly seek ways to grow their businesses, and going international is one such option. Economic reforms have freed and vitalized companies in emerging-market countries and encouraged them to take risks and compete in the global economy. The net result is a significant increase in the acquisition of developed country companies by firms from emerging-market economies. Depending upon the risk profile of individual companies, the opportunities to conduct global business will vary from low risk (and low return) export and import business to licensing, franchising, strategic alliances, joint ventures, cross-border mergers and acquisitions, and wholly owned subsidiaries (most risky with highest return).

Multinational enterprises have played an important role since the early 20th century, but their role accelerated after World War II along with global trade and investment liberalization brought about multilaterally through international organizations such as the World Bank, IMF, and the WTO. The rise of emerging-market MNEs, especially those from China and India, is phenomenal as indicated in their rankings in the *Financial Times* Global 500 companies, as well as in the ranking of the 10 largest companies in the world by value.

Firms invest abroad primarily to maximize shareholder wealth. Three major strategies that MNEs use to achieve this objective include: revenue maximization, cost minimization, and risk minimization through diversification abroad.

From a host country's point of view, although FDI does bring along with it significant financial inflows, new jobs, access to new technologies, important management (and employee) skills, and increases in domestic competition and choice, it also has major drawbacks. Some host countries have been concerned that in their rush to exploit resources foreign companies may sacrifice a host country's environmental quality and exploit their labor force. Host countries are also concerned that foreign firms may not practice proper corporate social responsibility and may interfere in a host country's domestic politics. Countries that have been successful in attracting foreign direct investment have been those that have improved their investment climate through proper economic reforms and transparent governance structures.

KEY TERMS

risk profile *p. 192*
export-import business, *p. 193*
licensing, *p. 194*
franchising, *p. 195*
strategic alliances, *p. 196*
international joint venture, *p. 197*
acquisition, *p. 199*
subsidiaries, *p. 199*
multinational enterprises (MNEs), *p. 199*
maximizing shareholder wealth, *p. 201*
product life cycle theory, *p. 205*
governance, *p. 210*

CHAPTER QUESTIONS

1. It is anticipated that emerging-market multinationals will play a greater role in international business during this century. What choice of international business operations do you think they would choose? Why?

2. What is a recent development in the evolution of multinational enterprises and how does that development affect globalization?

3. MNEs try to maximize profits. How could MNEs maximize profits and minimize profit volatility at the same time?

4. Quite often, host countries have a love-hate relationship with MNEs. Why?

5. To partially overcome its current account deficit, the United States needs to attract FDI that could spur economic growth. What policy measures should the United States take to keep attracting FDI into the country?

MINI CASE: ARCELORMITTAL: A STATELESS CORPORATION?

ArcelorMittal,[13] the world's largest steel company, has some 274,000 employees working in 60 countries. It ranks 124th on the *Financial Times* Global 500 2011 list. The company's registered headquarters is located in Luxembourg City, its operational and financial headquarters are in London, and its marketing and distribution centers are worldwide through its "Steel Solutions and Services" network. With 2010 crude steel output of 90.6 million tons (representing some 8 percent of world steel output), ArcelorMittal produces almost three times the amount of steel as the second largest producer, Nippon Steel of Japan. The largest regional market for ArcelorMittal steel is Europe (49 percent of total sales) followed by North America (25 percent), South America (12 percent), Africa (5 percent), and rest of the world (9 percent). While the mature European and North American markets form the basis of revenues for ArcelorMittal, future growth is more likely in such emerging markets as China, India, and Brazil where the company is making significant new investments. Fifty-seven percent of ArcelorMittal employees are located in Europe, 16 percent in Asia, 12 percent in North America, 9 percent in South America and 6 percent in Africa. ArcelorMittal is a highly vertically integrated steel company: it owns iron ore and coal mines that provide a significant amount of raw material input that is needed in steel making. It also owns steel mills in several countries in four continents of the globe that manufacture everything from basic steel rebars for the construction industry to fine steel used in the manufacture of appliances and cars. Also, because of its strong presence in Africa, the Americas, and Europe, ArcelorMittal has been able to consolidate its global operations (manufacturing, finance, and sales), which makes it one of the most efficient steel producers in the world for others to emulate. The Mittal family, who are originally from India, owns 41 percent of the company and the balance of shares is publically held.

Arcelor came to existence in 2002 through the merger of three European companies (Arbed of Luxembourg, Aceralia of Spain, and Usinor of France) to create a global leader in the steel industry, producing some 47 million tons of high quality steel annually.[14] Mittal Steel, on the other hand, was formed when two sister companies of the Mittal family, LNM Holdings and ISPAT International were merged in 2004 to produce some 63 million tons of steel with the key objective of being a low cost global competitor. The merger of Arcelor and Mittal was consummated in 2007, thereby creating ArcelorMittal, the world's largest steel company. The key to Mittal Steel's success is its proven expertise in acquiring steel companies (especially privatized ones in countries like Kazakhstan, Romania, and Ukraine) and restructuring these under-performing assets. This was done by successfully stripping non-performing assets, integrating the acquired companies, and implementing a "best practices" approach in operations management to enhance profitability. The size, scale, and product mix of ArcelorMittal's integrated operations gives the company the flexibility to produce what the global market needs. Ownership of coal and iron ore mines (e.g., in Kazakhstan and Liberia) enables the company to keep raw material costs under control, thereby stabilizing ArcelorMittal's cash flows and profitability.

QUESTIONS:

1) Is ArcelorMittal a "stateless" corporation or a MNE? Where is its home country?

2) What is Mittal Steel's core competency, and what was its strategic motive for global business?

The Human Cost of Mining in DR Congo[15]

The eastern province of South Kivu in the Democratic Republic of Congo borders Burundi, Rwanda, and Uganda in East Africa. South Kivu is rich in coltan and cassiterite, key minerals that are used by major multinational enterprises for making components used in cell phones and similar consumer electronic durables. In the decades since civil unrest began to plague the area in the 1970s, commercial mine operators moved out of South Kivu and "freelance" miners (poor men with minimal equipment working on their own) took their place. Initially, local militias taxed and controlled the mines worked by the freelancers. Then the Congolese government decided to move in the National Army and control the mines by pushing the militias out. In the process, as the Army and militias engage in conflict, the civilians are caught in the middle. Both the predatory militias and the Army demand a cut from what the freelance miners dig. When they are unable to exact taxes, these gunmen move into the villages and terrify the local population—stealing, killing, and raping.

With the high and rising global demand for cell phones and consumer electronics, MNEs now face uncomfortable questions: Are they unintentionally supporting criminal behavior by sourcing minerals from militarized zones? Should an agreement similar to the "Kimberly Process" (which prevents the sale of "blood" diamond mining) be negotiated to make it illegal for multinational enterprises to source minerals like coltan and cassiterite from militarized zones?

POINT Given the sordid nature of mining in South Kivu, MNEs should take the initiative to work with international organizations like the WTO and ILO (International Labor Organization) and the Council of Europe to quickly come up with a policy framework that will prevent further human rights violations.

COUNTER-POINT This is essentially a Congolese problem. The DR Congo government needs to take action and professionalize its military so that they do not prey upon their own citizens. Non-performing institutions and poor governance are the root causes for the failure of law and order in the Congo. Although MNEs feel empathy toward the poor Congolese civilians, there is little that they can do as they are dealing with mineral dealers and not the miners (since they do not have any organized mines).

What Do *You* Think?

Use the Internet to learn more about this issue. Which argument would you support? Give reasons and cite data for your position.

INTERPRETING GLOBAL BUSINESS NEWS

Financial news is everywhere in the popular press and media. How do you interpret the following examples of financial news related to the concepts in this chapter?

1) A 2009 survey conducted by Roland Berger, a British consulting company, finds that large international pharmaceutical companies plan to focus on global strategic alliances and licensing as a way to boost sales and productivity. "Big Pharma" is also moving away from expensive, centralized R&D by emphasizing mergers and acquisitions abroad to invigorate R&D and product innovation at a lower cost because health care systems worldwide are becoming less willing to reimburse companies for high-priced therapies. What do you think of this approach?

2) An article in the June 22, 2009 issue of *Business Week* indicated that automobile production in the United States now comprises less than 2 percent of U.S. GDP, versus 5.1 percent in the early-1970s. Moreover, Americans buy more cars from Japanese and European manufacturers than from the Big Three U.S. auto makers. What are the Big Three doing, domestically and globally, to improve their prospects?

3) Chinese companies, from oil refiner Sinopec to appliance giant Haier, have invested or plan to invest or acquire oil fields in Iraq, New Zealand's appliance maker Fisher & Paykel, and Argentina's oil company YPF. Is China, Inc. trying to "buy the world"?

4) "Medical tourism" is a big and growing business in India and it is expected to annually expand at a double-digit rate for the foreseeable future. India's private hospitals provide modern facilities staffed by skilled doctors and can offer international patients—a growing number from the United States—quality care at affordable prices (e.g., $6,000 for cardiac surgery that might cost $100,000 in the United States). Is there an opportunity for international strategic alliances or joint ventures?

PORTFOLIO PROJECTS

Explore Your Own Case in Point: Identify the Appropriate Global Entry Strategy for Your Chosen Company

After reading this chapter you should be prepared to answer some basic questions about your target company.

1) Analyze and determine your company's mode of entry into foreign markets. This should be based upon a serious analysis of your company's risk-return tradeoff. In your opinion, has your company taken the right approach?

2) Does your company have an exit strategy? Recall that exit strategies are to be determined before entry into the foreign market rather than after entry.

3) What is the host country's attitude toward your company? At the government level? At the customer level? How receptive and appreciative is the host country toward your company's business?

4) Critically and objectively evaluate how ethical your company's global operations are and determine if they are good corporate citizens (i.e., do they have a well thought-out corporate social responsibility program for the long term?).

Develop an International Strategy for Your Own Small Business: Achieving the Right Global Mode of Entry

Now that you have identified the target regional economic zone and country where you would like to conduct business, your next step will be to determine the mode of entry into that foreign market. The following questions will assist you in identifying the right strategy:

1) First, determine how much risk you are willing to take in international business (i.e., How much capital can you afford to lose based on a worst case scenario?). As you know, the least risky method of entry overseas will be through export and import business. Exhibit 8.1 will help.

2) If your ambition is to generate high returns through international business, you will need to (a) determine what your company's competitive advantage is, and (b) identify why you would want to have an overseas operation. To maximize revenue? To minimize cost? Both? Or to diversify risk?

3) Now that you have a good idea of how much risk you are willing to take, and also why you would want to invest in an overseas operation, it is relatively easier for you to determine the entry mode into the international marketplace. Use Exhibit 8.1 to determine your mode of entry abroad.

CHAPTER NOTES

[1] "Gone Shopping," *The Economist,* May 30, 2009, pp. 65–66.
[2] "The Challengers–A New Breed of Multinationals has Emerged," *The Economist,* January 12, 2008, pp. 62–64.
[3] J. E. Gaspar et al., *Introduction to Business* (Boston: Houghton-Mifflin Co., 2006), pp. 76–85.
[4] J. Baer, "Ties in the Skies," *Financial Times*, September 10, 2009, p. 7.
[5] A. Allam and J. Lemer, "Dow Chemical and Aramco in $20bn Nenture," *Financial Times,* July 25, 2011.
[6] "G.M., Eclipsed at Home, Soars to Top in China," *The New York Times,* July 22, 2010, p. A1.
[7] The Coca-Cola Company, *"2008/2009 Sustainability Review,"* p. 4; Press Release, *Coca-Cola Continues Strong Investment in China: Three New Plants in Hohhot, Luohe and Sanshui Underscore China Commitment,"* October 29, 2010.
[8] A. Dullforce, "FT Global 500 2011 Companies," *Financial Times*, June 24, 2011.
[9] A. Batson, "Not Really 'Made in China'", *The Wall Street Journal,* December 16, 2010, p. B1–2.
[10] C. K. Prahalad, *"The Fortune at the Bottom of the Pyramid: Eradicating Poverty through Profits,"* (Wharton School Publishing, 2004).
[11] J. H. Dunning, "Toward an Eclectic Theory of International Production: Some Empirical Tests." *Journal of International Business Studies,* 11 (1) (1980): pp. 9–31.
[12] D. Molinski and J. Lyons, "Hugo Chavez Moves to Diversify Sale of Venezuelan Oil Away from U.S. Refineries," *The Wall Street Journal,* April 19, 2010.
[13] P. Marsh, "Mittal Hedges His Bets on Prospects for Steel," *Financial Times,* October 5, 2009.
[14] www.arcelormittal.com
[15] K. Allen, "Human Cost of Mining in DR Congo," *BBC News, South Kivu,* September 2, 2009.

CH 9

Control of Global Business

© C Miller Design/ Getty Images

AP Photo/April L. Brown

After studying this chapter you should be able to:

LO-1 Discuss the importance of mission statements in general corporate strategy formulation.

LO-2 Explain tactical versus operational plans in implementing corporate strategy, and Miles' and Snow's four basic types of longer-term strategic implementation.

LO-3 Analyze various impediments to the coordination of strategic implementation that might exist for global businesses, and the positive role knowledge management and systems can play in this regard.

LO-4 Discuss and analyze various types of control systems utilized by global businesses including bureaucratic controls, interpersonal controls, and output controls and measurement systems such as Six Sigma initiatives.

LO-5 Analyze the role that organizational culture plays in controlling organizational activities, and how, when necessary, organizational cultures can potentially be changed.

Walmart and Girl Scout Cookies

Walmart, the world's largest retailer, has recently started selling private label "Great Value," "Fudge Mint," and "Fudge Covered Peanut Butter Filled" cookies that to many consumers taste almost identical to the Thin Mints™ and Tagalongs™ cookies sold by the Girl Scouts of the U.S.A. (GSUSA). The Walmart cookies, however, sell for $2.38 a box, while the same Girl Scout cookies sell for $3–4 per box. Is Walmart trying to strategically compete with the Girl Scout organization through offering its "Fudge Mint" and "Fudge Covered Peanut Butter Filled" alleged Girl Scout cookie "knock-offs"? Is such competition fair?

Traditionally, Walmart has supported GSUSA through the Walmart Foundation, but the Girl Scouts net nearly half a billion dollars each year through cookie sales—far more than they receive from Walmart's corporate social responsibility support. In a sense, Walmart's cookie sales present a tension in its strategic goals between making profits and being a socially responsible corporation.

Interestingly, Walmart has decided not to sell "knock-off" cookies in Canada, where Girls Scout cookies are an even greater part of the national fabric than in the United States. But this could change: the multi-million-dollar-per-year Girl Scout cookie market in Canada may be too tempting for Walmart to resist![1]

Introduction

While the opening vignette regarding Girl Scout cookies may be a somewhat simple example, it refers to a number of important aspects regarding the "control of global business." As discussed further in this chapter, global corporations in their strategy formulations often need to define their commitments to corporate shareholders vis-a-vis stakeholders like community groups such as the Girl Scouts. Is the company's critical role making profits for shareholders? Or does it have other equally important duties toward it employees, customers, and other stakeholders, as well as to the larger community? Moreover, while "success" in dollar profits may be relatively easy to manage and control, how is success measured in other areas such as corporate social responsibility? What does the sale of inexpensive "knock-off" Girl Scout cookies indicate about Walmart's organizational culture?

Finally, it is important to note that when Walmart began selling these cookies in the United States, it made a strategic decision not to sell them in its stores in Canada. Formulating different strategic approaches and control mechanisms for different countries where they operate in the world is an important challenge facing successful global businesses.

LO-1

Discuss the importance of mission statements, and the difference between shareholder and stakeholder orientations in such statements, and in general corporate strategy formulation.

Strategy Formulation

In formulating strategy, global businesses define their overall goals. Often this is initially done in a corporate mission statement. One major strategic goal formulation is whether to adopt an overall shareholder or stakeholder orientation. Shareholders are the owners of the given business or corporation. Stakeholders are individuals or groups that have a vested interest or "stake" in the business or corporation despite that they are not owners. Typical stakeholders include the company's employees, customers, and the communities where the business operates.

Mission Statement

Most global businesses have a concept of their general purpose, which they express in a **mission statement**. This written statement outlines why the company exists and what it strives to accomplish. Mission statements provide general guidelines for the company's strategy formulation and decision-making processes. For example, is the company focused very highly upon making profits for shareholders? Or perhaps on achieving other goals such as corporate social responsibility? Does the company wish to remain independent, or perhaps be acquired by another company? How international or global does the company intend to be? What emphasis does the company put upon product quality versus offering the lowest possible prices?

As an example, Walmart's mission statement says: "[i]n everything we do, we're driven by a common mission: saving people money so they can live better."[2] Viewed in this context, its decision to sell "knockoff" Girl Scout cookies at $2.38 a box makes a lot of sense. By selling such cookies at this price, Walmart enables its customers to "live better" by having the opportunity to buy these high-quality cookies for roughly a dollar per box less than they would pay for brand name Girl Scouts cookies. Similarly, Walmart's website "walmart.com" recently announced a special deal on the sale of selected best-selling hardcover books; it will be selling them for only $8.99 each! This is less than one-half of the retail price of books by famous authors such as Stephen King and Barbara Kingsolver at traditional bookstores like Barnes and Noble. Walmart executives commented that the company wishes to establish "price leadership" in this area.[3]

mission statement
a written statement of why a company exists and what it plans to accomplish

In contrast, Starbucks Corporation's mission statement takes a much broader quality-oriented stance. It states that Starbucks' mission is "to inspire and nurture the human

Customers of this Starbucks Coffee shop can expect being able to buy a high-quality cup of coffee.

spirit—one person, one cup, one neighborhood at a time" and that with respect to its coffee "it has been, and always will be about quality . . . sourcing the finest coffee beans."[4] Thus, Starbucks strongly cares about the communities it serves around the world, and about providing customers in those communities with the highest quality cup of coffee.

Notice, however, that neither Starbucks' nor Walmart's mission statements address company shareholders or fiscal responsibility. Many corporate mission statements, however, do emphasize such priorities. For example, the mission statement of Anadarko Petroleum Corporation, a $13 billion-per-year global oil exploration firm, states: "our mission is to deliver a competitive and sustainable rate of return to shareholders by developing, acquiring and exploring for oil and gas resources vital to the world's health and welfare." Anadarko's mission has both a global orientation and a strong focus upon providing a solid and continuing "rate of return" to shareholders.[5] Finally, and somewhat similarly, the mission statement of Altria Group, Inc. (the manufacturer of Marlboro, Benson & Hedges, and other cigarettes) says that company's mission "is to own and develop financially disciplined businesses that are leaders in responsibly providing adult tobacco consumers with superior branded products."[6]

In sum, corporate mission statements provide a blueprint for companies in their strategy formulation and control functions. As the company conducts business, its executives can monitor performance against its stated mission and goals. One critical difference among mission statements of different companies is the extent to which they express an orientation toward shareholders versus stakeholders or vice versa.

Shareholders versus Stakeholders

The **shareholder model of strategy formulation** operates from the premise that the key strategic purpose of a business is to maximize financial returns for its owners or shareholders. The late Nobel Laureate economist, Milton Friedman, a proponent of this viewpoint, summarized it by once stating that the over-riding strategic goal of corporate officers should be "to make as much money for their shareholders as possible."[7] A shareholder model of strategy formulation is set forth in Exhibit 9.1.

shareholder model of strategy formulation
strategy formulation model that operates from the premise that the key strategic purpose of a business is to maximize financial returns for its owners/shareholders

ECONOMIC PERSPECTIVES The E-Book Revolution

While Walmart's mission statement has been fulfilling its "low price" mission by selling hardcover books for less than they are sold at traditional bookstores, even Walmart is having trouble keeping up with technological developments in the bookselling arena and the economic impacts of these developments. By 2014, it is predicted that at least 20 to 25 percent of books being sold will be digital "e-books"! E-books don't require paper, printing presses, delivery trucks or storage space, and thus can be sold even more cheaply than Walmart sells hardcover books in its stores. New inventions such as Apple's "iPad" make e-books more and more accessible to the general public; e-books may have a negative impact on Walmart. The economic impact of e-books may be even greater on bookstores such as Barnes and Noble. Without question, digital books will have a huge impact on the book publishing industry, in much the same way that digital music downloads have had on the music industry and music stores.

QUESTIONS:

1) Have you ever purchased an e-book?
2) What are some advantages to purchasing a traditional hardcover book over an e-book?

Source: Jeffrey A. Trachtenberg, "E-Books Rewrite Bookselling," Wall Street Journal, May 21, 2010, p. A1.

EXHIBIT 9.1 SHAREHOLDERS MODEL OF STRATEGY FORMULATION

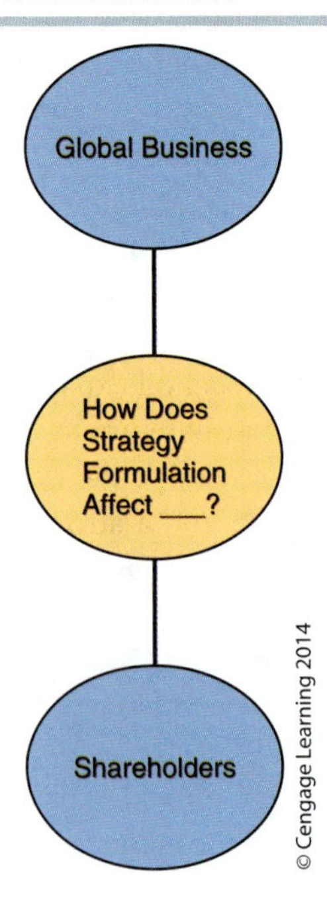

stakeholder model of strategy formulation strategy formulation model that believes businesses exist to benefit not just their shareholders, but also all the various groups such as employees and customers that have a meaningful stake in their operations

In contrast, the **stakeholder model of strategy formulation** believes businesses exist to benefit not just their shareholders, but also all the various groups that have a meaningful stake in their operations. Such groups, for example, might include a company's employees, its customers, and the community where it operates. It could even be argued that a business should treat banks and other institutions that lend it money (i.e., creditors) as stakeholders, because such entities also have a clear vested interested in and relationship with the business. A stakeholder model of strategy formulation is set forth in Exhibit 9.2.

Starbucks Corporation takes a stakeholder approach toward strategy formulation, because it places considerable emphasis upon how its business decisions affect its customers

EXHIBIT 9.2 STAKEHOLDER MODEL OF STRATEGY FORMULATION

How Does Its Strategy Formulation Affect ___?

Global Business

Employees

Consumers/ Customers

Shareholders

Communities Where It Does Business

Creditors

Suppliers/ Vendors

and the neighborhoods and communities where it does business, in addition to how decisions affect its shareholders. In contrast, the large oil exploration company, Anadarko Petroleum Corporation, takes more of a shareholder approach, placing a very clear emphasis in strategy formulation upon how its business decisions will help deliver an ongoing and competitive rate of return to its shareholders.

Understanding the differences between shareholder and stakeholder orientations in strategy formulation is important in determining appropriate "control systems" for the given global business, as will be discussed later in this chapter. For example, if contributing to the communities where the company does business is an important strategic goal pursuant to a stakeholder approach, a company's charitable contributions and other corporate social responsibility ("CSR") indicia will be important to measure and review on an annual basis. However, if the given global business takes a shareholder approach, CSR-related outputs will be relatively unimportant.

REALITY CHECK LO-1

Find and read the mission statements of some of the companies with which you regularly interact. How would you characterize each mission statement? Are some more oriented to profits and others more to CSR?

Strategy Implementation

LO-2

Explain tactical versus operational plans in implementing corporate strategy, and Miles' and Snow's four basic types of longer-term strategic implementation.

Suppose that a global company has successfully formulated a strategy. Now what? The next step would be to put that strategy into action. We call this strategy implementation, meaning that the global business must now implement this strategy.

An Example of Strategic Implementation: Walmart

If Walmart uses a strategy that offers its customers the lowest possible prices on products, how does it achieve this strategy? Does it, for example, buy more apparel from Chinese manufacturers than can be produced, and sold for lower prices than from American manufacturers? Does it vertically integrate its operations by purchasing a Chinese textile manufacturing company, or by setting up its own textile manufacturing operations in

China? Can Walmart leverage its tremendous buying power to get suppliers of products such as soap, detergent, and paper towels to sell these products in bulk at somewhat lower prices than they are sold to other retailers? Should Walmart open new stores in locations where the cost of doing business (e.g., the cost of labor) is relatively cheap?

When putting its strategies to work, Walmart will implement both operational and tactical plans in the short term. **Operational plans** are very short-term (less than one year) plans formulated for implementing strategic goals. For example, to achieve its longer-term "low price" strategic objectives, Walmart could, as discussed above, have an operational plan to buy more apparel products from lower-priced Chinese manufacturers (rather than from somewhat more expensive apparel manufacturers in the United States) during the next six months. Walmart will also develop **tactical plans**, which are one- to three-year plans formulated for implementing strategic goals. A tactical plan for Walmart might be to build and open a textile manufacturing plant in China within the next two-and-one-half years.

It is important to note that the operational and tactical plans being potentially implemented by the Walmart may fit Walmart's strategic formulation, but perhaps not the strategy formulation of another corporation. For example, a retailer that places an emphasis on the highest quality rather than the lowest prices might prefer to purchase women's and men's apparel from countries known for high quality apparel, such as Italy and the U.K.

Finally, operational and tactical plans involve quite short-term strategy implementation—zero to three years. Longer-term strategy implementation involves global companies deciding whether they want to be "prospectors," "defenders," "reactors," or "analyzers." In the next section we will explore this decision-making process.

Prospectors, Defenders, Reactors, and Analyzers

In a classic 1978 book titled *Organization Strategy, Structure and Process,* Professors Raymond E. Miles and Charles C. Snow developed a four-part typology describing how global (and other) businesses engage in strategy implementation on a longer-term basis. Miles and Snow characterized firms to be: 1) prospectors, 2) defenders, 3) reactors, or 4) analyzers. **Prospectors** are organizations that have basic strategic implementations involving extending their successes through global expansions, and finding new market opportunities. Anadarko Petroleum Corporation, for example, may decide that the best long-term way to implement its strategic goal of providing financial returns to its shareholders could be to explore for oil in parts of the world where it has not yet explored, such as Africa. In such a situation, Anadarko will be "prospecting" for oil in a new part of the world, and after implementing shorter-term operational and tactical plans, will likely set up permanent operations on the African continent.

Defenders, in contrast, implement basic market strategies of concentrating upon existing operations and defending their home turfs. Altria Group, Inc., for instance, may feel that the importance of "fiscal discipline" in its stated mission mandates that it reduce its operations and concentrate upon making its existing U.S.-based Marlboro, Benson & Hedges, and other tobacco operations as efficient and profitable as possible. In short, Altria will be mostly concentrating upon "defending" its existing strategic position. (It should be noted that Altria Group recently split off all of its more prospector-oriented international operations into a separate corporation, allowing it to concentrate on its existing U.S. brands. The existing Altria shareholders received all the shares in the new company.)

Companies that are **reactors** are those that have strategic implementation processes that respond to strategic actions initiated by competitors. At times this approach can be seen as inconsistent and unstable. For example, some have criticized the Target Corporation of being a "reactor" to its competitor Walmart's lowest-price-oriented strategic actions. Target was the principal competitor involved in the "price war" (mentioned earlier), in which Walmart's

operational plans
very short-term (less than one year) plans formulated for implementing strategic goals

tactical plans
one to three year plans formulated for implementing strategic goals

prospectors
organizations that have basic strategic implementations involving extending their success through global expansions, and finding new market opportunities

defenders
organizations that implement basic market strategies of concentrating upon existing operations and defending their home turfs

reactors
organizations that have strategic implementation processes that respond arbitrarily to strategic actions initiated by competitors

Bruce Coleman/Photoshot

The Hershey train symbolizes one of the world's predominant chocolate companies—The Hershey Corporation.

online plans to sell highly popular hardcover books at a discounted price surpassed the competition by offering the books at $8.99 apiece. Unlike some other retailers (e.g., Costco), however, Target's primary strategy is somewhat different from that of "lowest price." If Target starts matching Walmart's prices on some products, but not others, a potentially unstable situation for Target could be created; Target may be viewed as the "low price" retailer. This could potentially result in fewer "up-scale" customers deciding to shop at Target.

Finally, **analyzers** are companies that take a middle ground between being prospectors and defenders. Companies implementing the analyzer strategy take some steps to extend their markets, while simultaneously putting a lot of emphasis on avoiding excessive risk and defending existing operations. The Hershey Corporation, maker of Hershey chocolate bars and other confectionary treats, is one global business that has strategic implementation policies that fall into this category. Hershey Corporation has assiduously expanded and extended its business by developing new products and increasing global reach, but has done so in a very careful manner, avoiding undue risks and protecting its existing business operations.

Part of the reason Hershey has taken this approach relates to the company's somewhat unusual corporate social responsibility obligations. Company founder Milton Hershey and his wife Catherine had no children, and thus decided to leave their controlling Hershey Corporation stock to a trust which supports the Milton Hershey School in Hershey, Pennsylvania. The Milton Hershey School provides an extremely high-quality elementary and secondary education and medical care to very low income students from throughout the United States. The school currently has about 1,800 students, and one reason the Hershey Corporation has taken an "analyzer" strategic implementation approach is due to its ongoing financial obligation to this school and its students. Hershey Corporation avoids taking undue business risks so that it will always have funds available to generously support the Milton Hershey School and continually protect the legacy of its founder Milton Hershey. The Hershey Corporation is constantly analyzing and balancing its strategic business needs in the context of the corporation's obligations to the Milton Hershey School.

analyzers
organizations that take a middle ground between being prospectors and defenders

After formulating strategic goals, global businesses must put them into action. Businesses need to weigh all the pros and cons regarding different possible approaches that can be taken. Businesses also need to consider how different strategic actions are likely to impact relevant shareholder and stakeholder (e.g. the Milton Hershey School) groups. Once a corporate strategy has indeed been implemented, however, the next step determines how best to coordinate it—a topic discussed next.

REALITY CHECK LO-2

Do you think one of these four strategic approaches is safer than another? Or do they all carry risks? What do you see as the key risks a company faces by taking each of these approaches to strategy formulation?

LO-3

Analyze various impediments to the coordination of strategic implementation that might exist for global businesses, and the positive role knowledge management and systems can play in this regard. In particular, discuss the role of tacit versus explicit knowledge, and that of the Internet.

Coordination

Just as an athlete needs to coordinate his or her movements to achieve the goal of running faster, throwing more powerfully, or striking a target, businesses need to coordinate their actions to attain the goals set forth in their mission statements. As discussed earlier in the text, businesses may need, for example, to coordinate the various legal, political, and economic risks of doing business in foreign countries. Moreover, they may, for instance, need to coordinate the impact of new technologies or new events on their business model.

Impediments to Coordination

Coordinating strategy formulation and implementation may sound relatively easy in theory, but in practice it is usually not very easy at all. Once in practice, impediments to coordination of strategic implementation tend to abound. Legal, political, economic, technological, and other impediments may all abound in today's highly complex global business environment.

Anadarko Petroleum Corporation presents a good example. Many may not know that Anadarko has already been prospecting for oil in Africa! More specifically, Anadarko owns a sizeable stake in the Jubilee Oil Field located in the off-shore territorial waters of the African country of Ghana. Jubilee is one of the world's most important recent oil discoveries, holding an estimated 1.8 billion barrels of oil. A rough total valuation of the Jubilee field is about U.S. $17 billion.[8]

Unfortunately for Anadarko Petroleum Corporation, it does not own 100 percent of the Jubilee field. As frequently happens in big-dollar global business, it was able to take advantage of this opportunity only by joint venturing with other enterprises. Anadarko's partners in this joint venture have included various private equity funds, other oil companies, and the Ghana National Petroleum Corporation (GNPC), which is owned by the Ghanaian government. Anadarko owns about a 23.5 percent stake in Jubilee.

What are some coordination problems Anadarko faces with respect to its (albeit highly successful) investment in Ghana? First, Ghana is a long distance away from Anadarko's headquarters outside Houston, Texas. Second, people in Ghana speak a different language than people in Texas. Third, while Anadarko is one of the larger owners of the Jubilee oil field, its stake is still very much a minority one (i.e., only about 23.5 percent). The other owners of the field may have different interests than Anadarko; for example, they may want to exploit the field's resources more slowly or more rapidly than Anadarko wants to proceed. Simply put, Anadarko has a lot of "eggs" (its Jubilee stake is worth around $4 billion) in a basket very far away from Texas.

Most important, Anadarko must keep its relationship with the Ghana National Petroleum Corporation (GNPC) as positive as possible. While the GNPC only owns 13.8 percent of the

Jubilee field (compared to Anadarko's 23.5 percent stake) all of the Jubilee joint venture parties have been going out of their way to make sure they coordinate their activities with the GNPC. Why is this especially important? Anadarko wants to avoid any political risks or impediments that might result from conflict with the Government of Ghana. At the extreme, for example, there is also the risk that the government there could expropriate Anadarko's multi-billion dollar investment in that country.

The Anadarko-Jubilee example illustrates just a few of the numerous impediments that may exist when a global business endeavors to coordinate its strategic initiatives. That said, and as discussed further in the text, the Internet and other technological advances have made coordination easier today than it was just 20 years ago.

Knowledge Management and Systems

A U.S. multinational corporation such as Anadarko Petroleum Corporation doing business in a place like Ghana just 20 years ago was much different than today. In order to monitor and control operations in Ghana 20 years ago, Anadarko would have had to rely upon telexes and faxed reports—assuming that phone lines between the United States and Ghana were properly functioning (which wasn't always the case). Any "in person" supervision would have been impossible without executives flying from Houston to Ghana on a frequent basis. Today, the Internet and other "world is flat" advances in technology such as long-distance videoconferencing have enabled companies like Anadarko to have much better day-to-day knowledge about what is happening at their African operations. For example, emails with attachments can be continuously exchanged between the U.S. headquarters and Ghana.

New technologies are also making it easier for companies to more widely disseminate both tacit and explicit knowledge to their subsidiaries and other global affiliates. **Tacit knowledge** is knowledge that is informal and difficult to communicate, such as a special cake recipe from a family member that calls for a "pinch of this" and "pinch of that." In an industrial context, tacit knowledge may involve manufacturing a car in the specially nuanced Toyota Motor Corporation "way." In contrast, **explicit knowledge** is knowledge that is codifiable and easy to specify or write down with little loss of richness. Organizational control often hinges upon the ability to convert tacit knowledge into explicit knowledge so that foreign operations have a full understanding of what is expected of them.

Traditionally, making necessary transformations of tacit knowledge into explicit knowledge has presented major challenges for global businesses. Historically, for example, Toyota Motor Company has frequently sent hundreds of workers hired at a plant it is opening in a new country to Japan for months of training in the special "Toyota way" of auto manufacturing. Today, though, web videos and other Internet-based training tools make an expensive approach to knowledge transfer less necessary. Moreover, if someone at the Toyota plant outside Huntsville, Alabama has a question to ask someone who is in Japan, they are just an email away! In short, new technologies have made it much easier for Toyota and other global companies to transmit relevant tacit knowledge around the world, and where appropriate, transform it into more explicit knowledge.

Finally, new technologies such as the Internet have aided global businesses **absorptive capacity**, which is the ability to recognize the value of new knowledge, as well as assimilate and apply it. This is particularly relevant to corporate research and development ("R&D") efforts. Traditionally, an R&D discovery in one part of the company would not necessarily mean that it would be openly "absorbed" (i.e., used) by another part of the company, especially if the different parts of the company (e.g., subsidiaries) were in different countries. The ability to exchange new knowledge and information over the Internet and via other new technologies has somewhat ameliorated such situations. R&D discoveries in the United

tacit knowledge
knowledge that is informal in nature and difficult to communicate

explicit knowledge
knowledge that is codifiable and easy to communicate or write down

absorptive capacity
the ability of organizations to recognize, assimilate, and apply new knowledge

States operations of Anadarko Petroleum Corporation can, for example, be easily communicated to and absorbed by the Anadarko operations in Ghana.

REALITY CHECK LO-3

What's an example of some tacit knowledge you've learned on a job you've held? How would you communicate this knowledge to a newcomer?

LO-4
Discuss and analyze various types of control systems used by global business including: bureaucratic controls, interpersonal controls, and output controls and measurement systems such as Six Sigma initiatives.

Control Systems

To coordinate or control their operations, businesses rely upon several kinds of control systems. These include bureaucratic controls, interpersonal controls, and output controls and measurements. For example, a company might have specific financial or other goals it wishes to achieve and systems for carefully monitoring and controlling the achievement of those goals.

Bureaucratic Controls

Bureaucratic controls describe systems of rules and regulations that are promulgated within a global business. Such controls are often implemented to help maintain consistent procedures within an organization. For example, a rule that all employees in the organization (including the CEO!) must fly coach when they travel on commercial airlines represents a consistent bureaucratic control within an organization. A company may also have a rule that employees can spend no more than $50 per person for a business-related company-reimbursed dinner. Similarly, a company may have rules regarding personal usage of company telephones.

Bureaucratic controls can play an important role within organizational risk management. A bank, for instance, may have a strict rule that any loans above the amount of $50,000 must be approved by at least two bank officers, and that one of the approving officers must hold the rank of vice president or higher. Such a bureaucratic control is designed to ensure that larger financial risks (i.e., loans over $50,000) will be taken only with appropriate scrutiny. While it is possible that two bank officers could—intentionally or unintentionally—approve a loan whose borrower is insufficiently qualified, the likelihood of this happening is much less than it would be if only one officer's approval were needed.

Financial budgets, which are implemented within a global business, are a quintessential type of bureaucratic control. An organizational unit's financial budget represents an allocation rule with respect to how much that unit can spend. In some situations, the business's top management team may simply allocate a total annual budget for a particular organizational unit. For example, the R&D (research and development) unit might receive a budget of $85 million for a given year and have considerable flexibility upon how to spend this money. In other cases, however, the top management team may be much more specific with respect to budget allocations. For example, it might tell the R&D department that of the $85 million annual budget, at least $12 million of it must be spent on R&D for a particular new product. This approach involves the use of greater bureaucratic control by the company's top managers.

bureaucratic controls
systems of rules and regulations promulgated within a global business

Interpersonal Controls

Interpersonal controls involve executives engaging in personal contact with subordinates as a way of managing an organization. Michael Dell, the founder of Dell Computer Corporation, interacted directly with every single employee during the early days

interpersonal controls
involves executives engaging in personal contact with subordinates as a way of managing an organization

vario images GmbH & Co.KG / Alamy

Dell Computer Corporation founder Michael Dell has always maintained a very "hands on"/direct contact style of management.

of the company. In this way, Dell had direct interpersonal control over everything that was happening at the company. Such complete interpersonal control works best in smaller organizations; with over 40,000 employees in Dell Computer today, it would be nearly impossible for any one executive to have direct ongoing in-person contact with each employee in the organization. However, many CEOs make a major effort to meet one-on-one on a regular basis with all senior managers and business unit heads. Former General Electric Corporation CEO Jack Welch was well known for this. In addition, many are using Internet technology, email and other similar ways to maintain direct communication lines with all employees on an ongoing basis. While communication may not be two-way (i.e., not every employee is invited to directly reply to the CEO), it is still a direct way for lower-level employees to receive input from the CEO. Company town-hall meetings and other methods may also be used to make sure important managerial personal contact exists within an organization.

Output Controls and Measurement

Another aspect of organizational control is output and measurement. **Output controls and measurement** involve establishing specific goals on given metrics and then measuring to what extent these goals have been achieved at certain time intervals (e.g., quarterly, annually). There are several areas where output controls and measurement can be put into practice, including profits, growth, productivity, market share, quality control, and corporate social responsibility.

Profits Financial profits and specific financial goals are one kind of output control and measurement used by global businesses. For example, Smithfield Foods Company, the world's largest pork producer, has set the clear organizational goal of getting $0.10 profit for each pound of its processed pork products (like Armour smoked bacon) that is sold. The company's CEO C. Larry Pope has coined the phrase "[i]t's time for the dime," and put bumper stickers with the slogan everywhere in the organization. Smithfield CEO Pope recently stated that because his industry doesn't "have a lot of Harvard people," it's important to keep the profitability message "simple and deliverable."[9]

output controls and measurement involves establishing specific goals on given metrics and then measuring to what extent these goals are being achieved at certain time intervals

While the Smithfield Foods "it's time for the dime" goal to all of the organization's processed pork sales, it does not apply to its sale of whole pigs and other unprocessed products, especially in China. Chinese citizens love pork, and indeed they consume about half the world's supply of this product. To date, however, Smithfield Foods has not had much of a presence in China. In the following section, the text will discuss some output control metrics that Smithfield might be interested in with regard to China.

Growth Smithfield Foods is looking for "growth" in China. CEO C. Larry Pope says his focus upon what happens with the company's Chinese operations is on "five or ten years" from now.[10] Smithfield may now be willing to lose some money with respect to its unprocessed pork sales in China in order to gain a toe-hold in that country's huge pork market.

Las Vegas hotelier MGM Mirage is another company focused upon growth. In a huge gamble (pun intended), MGM Mirage recently spent $8.5 billion on a new CityCenter Resort which adds more than 4,800 new rooms to a hotel room market that some argue is already saturated. The new venture leaves MGM Mirage with around $12 billion in debt—billion, not million. Critics caution that MGM's development of the huge CityCenter project is simply a long-term wager by the company on the future of Sin City. It is measuring its current output not upon how financially profitable it could be, but on how much successful growth it could accomplish. In gamblers' parlance, MGM Mirage is doubling down on Vegas![11]

As the Smithfield and MGM examples demonstrate, growth is an important control metric. Global businesses are constantly examining whether their companies are growing or not. In certain business contexts, if a business is not successfully growing, it may end up closing. Thus, measuring and controlling effective growth can be extremely important in today's global business environment.

Productivity Another output control measure frequently used by global businesses is productivity or efficiency. In the banking industry, for example, a particular bank's efficiency ratio (i.e., how little expense or overhead is needed to produce a given amount of income) is a closely monitored metric. If one bank can achieve a profit of $2 million per year with 90 employees, and another bank needs to employ 200 employees to achieve the same level of profits, the first bank's employees are more productive or efficient than the second. This may signal that the first bank is a better run organization.

Technology continues to play a very important role in increasing employee and general corporate productivity. Computers and telephone answering machines have made workers more productive and efficient to a great extent. Before telephone answering systems, for example, employees were hired specifically to answer phones and take phone messages. Moreover, sometimes written phone messages were lost or misplaced. Today's phone answering systems often keep permanent records of calls. In sum, global businesses that put a strong emphasis upon productivity are also likely to be willing to heavily invest in the technological advances necessary to increase employee and other corporate productivity.

Market Share The key output metric for some global businesses is market share, or the percentage of the business in a certain market that is captured by a product or service that the organization provides. Market share may be an independent business goal, apart from growth. For example, Smithfield Foods may not only want to grow its overall sales of pork products, but may instead have a specific market share goal it wishes to attain for the unprocessed product pork market in China. If this is the case, then Smithfield managers in charge of Chinese operations (and the employees they supervise) are likely to be measured and rewarded (i.e., controlled) with respect to how well they achieve the company's market share goals.

Annette Shaff/Shutterstock.com

Google Corporation has an astounding market share of the Internet search-engine market worldwide.

One company that has traditionally put a great deal of emphasis upon attaining market share goals is Google Corporation. In its early years, Google was so intent upon capturing search-engine market share that it didn't care about making any profits. Google's efforts in this area (in contrast to many other start-up Internet companies) have been very successful. Today it has about a 66 percent share of the search-engine market in the United States, and close to an astounding 70 percent share worldwide. In this way, Google has left competitors such as Microsoft and Yahoo-AOL in the dust.[12]

ETHICAL PERSPECTIVES

Privacy Rights, Google, and Facebook

In addition to economic power concerns, Google and other cutting-edge Internet sites (such as Facebook) have also come under recent attack with respect to their arguable infringement upon people's privacy rights. In 2010, for example, Google was widely criticized by privacy regulators for inadvertently collecting data about people as part of its worldwide project to capture images of streets around the world. More specifically, as part of this street scanning it had recorded personal communications sent over Wi-Fi data networks in some 30 countries. Also in that same year, it was alleged that Google's "double click" digital marketing and advertising division had been receiving data from social networking sites such as Facebook. Such data included consumers' names and other personal details, despite that these individuals had not given their consent to the social networking sites to release this data to Google. Google's double click division could then potentially release this information to its various advertising clients such as the Ford Motor Company. Google has been able to obtain considerable personal information about people around the globe through various means.

QUESTIONS:

1) Would you mind if the Ford Motor Company obtained information about you from Facebook and/or Google regarding your usage of those Internet sites?

2) Have you ever looked at a Google map picture of your family's home or apartment?

Sources: Emily Steel and Jessica E. Vascellaro, "Sites Confront Privacy Loophole," The Wall Street Journal, May 21, 2010, p. B1; "Lives of Others," The Economist, May 22, 2010, p. 67; "Dicing with Data," The Economist, May 22, 2010, p. 16.

There is, however, one very important concern that global businesses need to remember when establishing high market-share output control measurements: antitrust law. As discussed in Chapter 6, antitrust law is concerned about anti-competitive concentrations of business power (e.g., monopoly or oligopoly power) and very high business market shares can be one indicator of such power. Indeed, because of its extraordinary success in capturing market share, the Google Corporation was the subject of various U.S. Department of Justice and Federal Trade Commission antitrust investigations in 2009. Therefore, if a global company decides to make market share an important output measure, it's very important for that company's attorneys to provide it with a clear understanding of the potential antitrust implications associated with a particular approach.

Quality and Six-Sigma Initiatives Many global businesses place a very strong emphasis upon quality, and then seek to measure and control for this output. Quality may apply to products, customer service, or both. For example, and as noted earlier in the chapter, the Starbucks Corporation cares a lot about the quality of its coffee and the cups of coffee it sells to the general public around the globe.

Six Sigma initiatives are one interesting type of quality control function that have received a good deal of attention in recent years. These are organizational initiatives that seek to limit defects or problems to 3.4 per million (or less than one thousandth of one percent). Statistically, the term "sigma" measures how far a given problem deviates from a given norm, and a Six Sigma procedure is one that barely deviates from perfection.

Let's say, for example, that a major international airline handles three million pieces of passenger luggage per year, and has about 50,000 pieces of lost or temporarily misplaced luggage per year. It could adopt quality control measures that reduce lost or misplaced luggage to only about 20,000 pieces per year, but the airline is not happy with this—it wants to do more. An effective Six Sigma program would reduce the number of lost or misplaced pieces at the international airline to about ten per year! Is this a realistic goal? And if it can't be achieved, what are some reasonable alternatives (e.g., a successful initiative that would reduce lost or misplaced luggage at the global airline to about 2,000 pieces per year)?

Corporate Social Responsibility As discussed earlier in the chapter, some global businesses take a stakeholder approach to strategy formulation; giving back the communities where they do business is an important output they may want measure and control. For such companies, corporate social responsibility (CSR) is an important output control. Google Corporation's corporate motto is "Don't Be Evil," and the company has committed literally hundreds of millions of dollars, from both its initial public stock offering and its ongoing profits, to a variety of CSR initiatives in individual communities and on the global stage. In particular, Google has been very active in contributing funds to public health and environmental programs and causes.

Of course, not every global business is as active as Google on the corporate social responsibility front. That said, a wide variety of annual survey and award lists have emerged in recent years that rank companies according to the level of their activities and contributions to communities, to the environment, and the like. For a number of global businesses, achieving a higher ranking on these surveys has become an important and measurable output goal.

Moreover, in some industries government entities formally score businesses with respect to their CSR activities. For example, pursuant to a United States banking law called the Community Reinvestment Act (CRA), all banks in the United States receive annual grades ("excellent," "satisfactory," or "unsatisfactory") from federal banking regulators according to their community reinvestment and CSR activities. These activities include placing bank branches in low-income areas and making loans to low-income individuals. They may also involve bank monetary donations to charities and charitable activities in the communities in which they operate. Banks work hard to receive at least a "satisfactory" CRA grade, because banks with lower grades may face negative regulatory consequences.

REALITY CHECK LO-4

What do you think is a good output control and measurement for the professor in this class?

Organizational Culture and the Change Control Function

LO-5

Analyze the role that organizational culture plays in controlling organizational activities, and how, when necessary, organizational cultures can potentially be changed.

Organizational culture, represents the "personality" of a given organization, its shared norms, and values. Organizational culture can be a very effective control mechanism for an organization, particularly when the norms of a given business's culture are fully accepted by that organization's workforce. Very often, however, such norms are not fully accepted, and this can pose a challenge to organizational control. To meet this challenge, an organization may seek to change its culture.

Types of Organizational Culture

If a global business has a strong and accepted cultural norm that employees do only the highest quality of work, it may not be necessary for supervisors to constantly monitor employees' work quality. As an example, for generations there has been a cultural norm of "highest quality journalism" at the *New York Times* newspaper.[13] In this organizational context, the newspaper's reporters don't require close supervision to do great journalistic work. The reporters' pride in being journalists at arguably the best newspaper in the United States will operate as an automatic kind of internal control mechanism motivating them to do very high quality work.

organizational culture the personality of a given organization, its shared norms, and values

Similarly, Google Corporation's "Don't Be Evil" motto contributes to the organizational culture by creating an overall norm for ethical behavior at that company. Put another way, there's social pressure on Google Corporation's employees to act in an ethical manner, and this social pressure acts as a control system apart from any formal rules and regulations.

On a less positive note, convicted financial swindler Bernard Madoff created a cocaine-fueled "culture of sexual deviance" at the "BMIS" (Bernard Madoff Investment Services) company he once lead, according to a lawsuit filed in October 2009 by former Madoff investors. From the mid-1970s until the company's demise over thirty years later, Madoff allegedly sent employees (with company money!) to purchase drugs for company use. Cocaine usage was so prevalent at BMIS that industry insiders regularly referred to the company as the "North Pole"! Madoff allegedly also hired topless entertainers for company parties, encouraged employee affairs, and used company money to pay for sexual "escorts" and masseuses. Ironically, this organizational culture also operated as something of a control mechanism, and helped to prevent Madoff from being caught for many years. In part, employees feared that if they "ratted on" Madoff, he could also potentially "rat" on them and their activities.[14] For many decades, what went on at BMIS stayed at BMIS.

TIMOTHY A. CLARY/AFP/Getty Images/Newscom

Convicted financial swindler Bernie Madoff coordinated a deviant culture at BMIS.

While the New York Times, Google, and (historically) BMIS appear to have clear and uniform organizational cultures, the creation of cultural norms of this kind is often very difficult to accomplish, especially in a multinational or global company. Many large companies have very different types of operating divisions and business units, which make it difficult to have a uniform culture throughout the organization. For example, in 1986 the General Electric Company, the well-known maker of light bulbs, power turbines, and aircraft engines, bought NBC (National Broadcasting Company). According to most observers NBC was a cultural "odd fit" with its parent company. The "glitz and glamour" culture of a television broadcasting company with its various "celebrity" employees is so different from that of an aircraft engine manufacturing company that one inside observer pointed out that "a TV network had no business inside a company like GE."[15] Indeed, GE recently divested its NBC operation. Somewhat similar dynamics have applied to the Washington Post Company and its 1984 purchase of (Stanley) Kaplan Educational Centers, the SAT test preparation company. The cultural differences between a newspaper with "star" reporters and daily reporting requirements, and a slower-moving testing company which employs graduate students to help high school students prepare for the SAT have become rather poignant in recent years. This has been particularly true as the financial success of the Washington Post newspaper has declined precipitously while the financial success of the Kaplan Centers has steadily risen. Indeed today, Kaplan is the key profitability center for the entire Washington Post Corporation.[16]

Where there are clashes within a given organization's culture, or if there are threats to this culture in the future, it typically will not work as an effective organizational control system. In such situations, it may be advisable to try and implement some sort of organizational change.

Organizational Change

Organizational change represents the implementation of a different business or cultural path for an organization. There will often be considerable resistance to such change, despite that change may be very necessary. For example, employees of BMIS likely wouldn't have wanted to change its "free cocaine culture" despite that it was illegal and counterproductive. If effective change had occurred in the 1990s at the Madoff firm, billions of dollars of other people's savings might well have been preserved, and the company might still be an ongoing concern.

Many times, organizational change in a business is most effective when pushed from the top by the company's CEO and other executives. In an important recent book titled *The CEO Within*, Harvard Business School Professor Joseph L. Bower argued that the types of CEOs who most effectively instigate positive organizational change are those that he termed "inside-outsiders." This describes CEOs who rise internally within the company, but who have followed a non-traditional path to the executive suite. For example, Bower cites the famous former CEO of General Electric Corporation, Jack Welch, as a classic "inside-outsider," because Welch was a chemical engineer in a company of electrical and mechanical engineers, and came from GE's plastics business, which was traditionally viewed as a peripheral operation. Jack Welch engendered considerable positive organizational change at GE over time.[17]

More recently, Nancy McKinstry, another classic "insider-outsider," was named CEO of the giant Dutch publishing company, Wolters Kluwer. McKinstry, who advanced through the ranks of Kluwer's North American operations, became both the first woman and first American to run the venerable 200-year-old Dutch company. Since assuming the top post in 2003, McKinstry has already brought considerable positive organizational change to the company, in particular, by moving the publishing company to an "open global culture" and appointing a Spaniard to lead the firm's operations in France—something unheard of

organizational change involves implementation of a different business or cultural path for an organization

historically![18] In sum, a CEO who is both a trusted insider and someone who brings an "outside" or different perspective to the operations may be the type of individual who can most effectively engender positive organizational change.

REALITY CHECK LO-5

Describe the organizational "cultures" of companies where you've been employed.

SUMMARY

Strategic control is at the center of all global business. Corporate mission statements often provide an excellent initial blueprint with respect to the given corporate setting. The shareholder versus stakeholder models of strategy formulation represent two different approaches to the conduct of global business. The latter model purports that businesses have obligations to their employees, customers, communities, and other relevant stakeholders, while the former model views the role of global business as one of maximizing financial returns for its shareholders.

After formulating strategic goals, global businesses then need to put those goals into action. Short-term strategic implementation generally takes the form of implementing operational and strategic plans. In the longer term, companies tend to adopt a more overall typology for strategic implementation. In their classic work, Miles and Snow categorize companies in this regard as either prospectors, defenders, reactors, or analyzers.

Regardless of the approach, global businesses must navigate around various impediments to coordination using technology and global knowledge management systems as effectively as possible. They must also use a variety of different control systems, including bureaucratic, interpersonal, and output controls.

Organizational culture can be an extremely potent type of control system, particularly where cultural norms are fully accepted by an organization's workforce. Unfortunately, though, the establishment of strong, clear, and uniform organizational norms can often be a very difficult thing to achieve. Where clashes exist within organizational culture and norms, it may be advisable for the company to try and implement organizational change.

KEY TERMS

mission statement, *p. 218*
shareholder model of strategy formulation, *p. 219*
stakeholder model of strategy formulation, *p. 220*
operational plans, *p. 222*
tactical plans, *p. 222*
prospectors, *p. 222*
defenders, *p. 222*
reactors, *p. 222*
analyzers, *p. 223*
tacit knowledge, *p. 225*
explicit knowledge, *p. 225*
absorptive capacity, *p. 225*
bureaucratic controls, *p. 226*
interpersonal controls, *p. 226*
output controls and measurement, *p. 227*
organizational culture, *p. 231*
organizational change, *p. 232*

CHAPTER QUESTIONS

1. In what ways are corporate mission statements more than just "public relations"?
2. Do you think global businesses should place more emphasis upon operational or tactical plans? Why or why not?
3. In what positive and negative ways has the Internet changed the conduct and coordination of global business?
4. Do you think Six Sigma quality control initiatives really work?
5. In what ways did the organizational culture at Bernard Madoff Investment Services (BMIS) company help lead to Madoff's success for so many years?

MINI CASE: BERKSHIRE HATHAWAY'S INVESTMENT STRATEGY

The Berkshire Hathaway Inc. has almost a "personality cult" organizational culture which essentially revolves around one man and his investing prowess. The man's name is Warren Buffett, the "Oracle of Omaha." Historically, Berkshire Hathaway's business model has been to purchase insurance companies. One great thing about insurance companies is the "cash float," which works as follows. Suppose that a person purchases a $100,000 whole life insurance policy from Berkshire Hathaway and pays premiums of $4,000 per year to Berkshire for this policy. The Berkshire Hathaway company is obligated to pay the $100,000 death benefit when the person dies; in the meantime it gets to invest the $4,000 per year "float." Warren Buffett, who has been a very savvy investor, has made a huge fortune from investing this "float" money. But recently, Berkshire Hathaway has been amoving away from purchasing insurance companies with large "floats" and has been buying major industrial businesses instead. In 2010, for example, it completed a $44 billion purchase of one of the nation's largest railroads, Burlington Northern Santa Fe (BNSF). Berkshire paid for this acquisition with $15.8 billion in cash it had available, and the remainder in Berkshire Hathaway stock. Mr. Buffett, who was born in 1930, is now well beyond the age when most workers retire.

QUESTIONS:

1) How does Mr. Buffett's age affect Berkshire Hathaway's recent strategic moves such as buying Burlington Northern Railroad instead of another large insurance company?
2) What does Berkshire Hathaway's purchase of Burlington Northern Santa Fe Railroad say about where Buffett thinks the price of energy—oil and gasoline—is going to be in the future? (Hint: How does the energy efficiency of shipping goods via rail compare with shipping goods via truck or airplane?)

Point Counter-Point: Milk Prices and Starbucks

Recently, a decline in milk prices has been helping the Starbucks coffee chain. Lower milk prices will contribute around $0.05 to Starbucks Corporation's recent annual earnings of about $1.00 per share. Should Starbucks hedge the price of milk in the commodities market in order to lock in this important nickel-per-share in extra "dairy" related annual earnings?

(continued)

POINT Starbucks should definitely hedge the price of milk on the commodities markets to the greatest extent possible in order to lock in the extra nickel-per-share in annual earnings. Starbucks' stock traditionally has traded at a very high price-to-earnings ratio, at times over a 40 price-to-earnings, so a nickel-per-share in extra annual earnings does a lot for its stock price. Higher prices for milk will hurt Starbucks' profits unless it hedges the cost of milk in the commodities markets, just as it currently hedges the costs of coffee. Hedging is an important strategic control mechanism for Starbucks.

COUNTERPOINT While commodities speculators can hedge the type of milk used to make cheese, there isn't currently a well-developed futures market for "drinkable milk." Thus, unlike pizza companies which use "cheese milk," Starbucks does not have a perfect hedge for its drinkable milk needs. Moreover, there continues to be a surplus of dairy cows in the United States, making it unlikely that the price of dairy milk will surge upward any time soon. In addition, the cost of drinkable milk is still a relatively small part of the cost of Starbucks' products, and as such any small increases in the cost of milk may be effectively passed on to the consumer (i.e., Starbucks customers). The bottom line is that the benefits of Starbucks trying to hedge its milk costs are probably not worth the costs involved.

What Do *You* Think?

Use the Internet and other sources to research these issues and formulate a better understanding of hedging and commodities markets. Do you ever think about the costs of milk when you visit Starbucks?

INTERPRETING GLOBAL BUSINESS NEWS

1. Reynolds American Inc. is the second largest cigarette maker in the United States. It manufactures well-known brands such as Camel, Pall Mall, and Kodiak (smokeless tobacco). Reynolds American recently purchased a Swedish company called Niconovum AB, which makes products that help people *stop* smoking. Niconovum's products are primarily related to nicotine-replacement therapy and include nicotine replacement chewing gum. How would you characterize this strategic move by Reynolds American (e.g., prospector, defender)? Why?

2. Leaders that are successful in effecting positive organizational change often rank extremely high on "emotional intelligence" ("EQ") rather than more basic analytical intelligence of the type measured by "IQ." What "EQ" traits do you think are most important in making leaders successful change agents?

3. Not two long ago *Fortune* magazine ran a cover article titled "Obama & Google (A Love Story)." A number of executives from Google have taken jobs in the Obama Administration, and President Obama regularly meets with Google founders Sergey Brin and Larry Page, as well as with Google CEO Eric Schmidt. Why, given what you know from this chapter about Google, do you think President Obama likes the Google Corporation and its executives so much? What concerns might you have about the "cozy" relationship between Google and President Obama?

4. Fears over future sharply rising energy, oil, and gasoline prices (as noted earlier in this chapter's "Mini-case") have prompted many businesses to shift their energy needs from traditional oil and gasoline to cheaper and more plentiful natural gas. AT&T, for example, recently replaced 8,000 of its regular service vans with natural gas-powered vehicles. It believes the shift to natural gas service vans will save it the cost of about 49 million gallons of regular gasoline over the next decade. What are some of the negatives of this cost control measure? Does the fact that less than 1,500 of the United States' 162,000 vehicle service stations currently sell natural gas have any implications on AT&T's strategic moves in this regard?

PORTFOLIO PROJECTS

Exploring Your Own Case in Point: Control of Global Business

After reading this chapter you should be prepared to answer some basic questions about your favorite company.

1) What is the corporate mission statement of your target company, assuming it has one? If the company does not have a mission statement, how would you go about writing one for it? How well do the company's actions adhere to its stated mission?

2) With respect to its strategy formulation, would you categorize your company as a shareholder model or a stakeholder orientation? Why?

3) What are some current or short-term operational and tactical plans that your company is pursuing? How do these plans fit in with the company's longer-term strategic goals?

4) Describe any quality control and Six Sigma-type initiatives in which your company is currently involved. If it is not involved in any such initiatives, should it be? Why or why not?

Develop an International Strategy for Your Own Small Business: Strategic Control in Your Business

Strategic control issues are very important for all businesses, but can have particular consequences for small businesses with international business operations or aspirations. The following questions will help deepen your understanding of these concerns as they may apply to your own small business:

1) Is your small business currently involved in any joint ventures with other companies? Is it planning any joint ventures? If so, what type of positive control mechanisms do you have, or plan to have, in order to protect your business' interests vis-a-vis those of your joint venture partner(s)?

2) What role is the Internet playing, or can it potentially play, in helping to coordinate your small business' global operations?

3) Is your small business active in your community through charitable or other corporate social responsibility activities? If so, how are you measuring the effectiveness of your business' activities in this regard?

4) How would you characterize the organizational culture or "personality" of your small business? Do you feel good about this culture, and does it act as a positive control mechanism for your organization? If not, what about your culture would you like to change?

CHAPTER NOTES

[1] C. Gulli, "The Girl Scout Cookie Skirmish," Maclen's Magazine, August 31, 2009, p. 57.
[2] Wal-Mart Stores, Inc., www.walmartstores.com.
[3] G.A. Fowler and M. Bustillo, "Walmart, Amazon Gear Up for Holiday Battle," The Wall Street Journal, October 19, 2009, p. B3; M. Bustillo and J.A. Trachtenberg, "Walmart Strafes Amazon in Book War," The Wall Street Journal, October 16, 2009, p. A1.
[4] Starbucks Coffee Company, www.starbucks.com.
[5] Andarko Petroleum Corporation, www.anadarko.com.
[6] Altria Group, Inc., www.altria.com.
[7] M. Friedman, Capitalism and Freedom, Chicago: University of Chicago Press, 1962, p. 133.
[8] J. McCracken, R. Gold and W. Connors, "NOOC, Exxon Vying for Stake in Ghana Field," October 12, 2009, p. B1.
[9] N. Byrnes, "Smithfield! Not Living So High on the Hog," Business Week, November 9, 2009, p. 52.
[10] Ibid.
[11] C. Palmer, "The Biggest Gamble In Sin City, *Business Week*, November 9, 2009, p. 56.
[12] K. Auletta, Googled: The End of the World As We Know It, Penguin Books, 2009.
[13] J. K. Glassman, "Media's Bright Spots," Kiplinger's Personal Finance Magazine, December 12, 2009, p. 18.
[14] C. Melas, "Lawsuit: Madoff's Workplace Was Rife with Cocaine, Sex," www.cnn.com, October 22, 2009.
[15] P. Glader and Jeffrey McCracken, "NBC Has Been Something of an Odd Fit with Its Parent," The Wall Street Journal, October 2, 2009, p. A4.
[16] "Look Past the Washington Post Flagship," The Wall Street Journal, October 19, 2009, p. C10.
[17] J.L. Bower, "The CEO Within: Why Inside–Outsiders Are The Key To Succession Planning," Boston: Harvard Business School Press, 2007.
[18] J.S. Lublin, "Inside Outsiders' Bring Knowledge, Objectivity," The Wall Street Journal, October 12, 2009, p. B5.

CH 10

The Organization of Global Business

After studying this chapter, you should be able to:

LO-1 Discuss the concept of stateless corporations.

LO-2 Describe the importance of organizational structures for global businesses.

LO-3 Discuss the role that export departments and international divisions play in the organization of global businesses.

LO-4 Define functional, divisional, hybrid, and matrix structures, and illustrate their advantages and disadvantages for global business.

Organizational Restructuring at Royal Dutch Shell

In the Summer of 2009, Royal Dutch Shell PLC announced to its staff that its organizational restructuring plans would be accelerated, and that the result would be substantial job cuts. These cuts would represent a broadening of the cost-reduction program that Shell's Chief Executive Peter Voser implemented in May 2009. The primary objective of the cost-reduction program would be to help the Anglo-Dutch oil and gas company adjust to lower oil prices.

Shell made this announcement via an internal email to mid-managers in its upstream business which said "the coming days will bring more information about Shell's organizational restructuring." Shell's upstream business includes the following: exploration and production, oil sands, and gas and power. A separate statement was posted on the company's intranet, and Mr. Voser stated that "ongoing changes will result in significant staff reductions." In July 2009, Shell had already reduced its top management positions by 20 percent.

Mr. Voser announced the shakeup before becoming Chief Executive on July 1, 2009, which included the merger of the three upstream units into two new geographically focused divisions: Upstream International and Upstream Americas. The organizational restructuring will also expand Shell's downstream division, which primarily refines and markets oil products, and includes trading, biofuels, and solar energy. A new division, Projects and Technology, will also be created to manage the design of all major projects upstream and downstream.

Shell's profits, like those of most major oil companies, experienced a significant decrease due to the reduction of oil prices from a peak of $147 per barrel in July 2008, to approximately $70 per barrel in the summer of 2009. A comparison of the net profit in the second quarter of 2008 to the net profit in the same quarter of 2009 shows a decrease of 67 percent. To compensate for this drop, Shell's organizational restructuring will cut several layers of management, paralleling Exxon Mobil Corporations's centralized model and emulating a similar effort launched at BP (British Petroleum) p.l.c. two years ago.

ExxonMobil's centralized model is organized by global functions such as refining, exploration, and transportation. BP's organizational structure, in contrast, was dominated by individual business units that operate big oil fields or other assets and enjoy a large degree of autonomy, which often led to waste because business-unit leaders sometimes duplicated one anothers' initiatives. In 2007, five months after taking the job, BP p.l.c.'s new boss, Tony Hayward, announced the move to a centralized model similar to ExxonMobil's model. This move came as BP attempted to recover from a string of mishaps and problems that some blamed on an excessively complex organizational structure. According to some experts, the organizational restructuring at BP led by Mr. Hayward was an effort to distance himself from John Browne, BP's former chief executive, who was largely responsible for the company's prior organizational structure. Mr. Hayward was elected to succeed Lord Browne when Browne resigned due to personal legal problems. Due to problems of his own, in October 1, 2010, Tony Hayward was replaced as BP's CEO by Bob Dudley.

Shell has been heavily criticized for slow decision making, cost overruns, and delays in several of its high-profile oil-and-gas ventures. By simplifying its organizational structure, Shell could avoid some of these maladies.[1]

Introduction

To achieve sustainable competitive advantage on a worldwide scale, global businesses have resorted to one of the most basic weapons in their arsenals, namely, the ability to organize people and resources. This ability is reflected in an *organizational structure*. Global businesses such as Shell, General Motors, Procter & Gamble, and PepsiCo have used different types of organizational structures in order to achieve a sustainable competitive advantage. In this chapter, the concept of stateless corporations, which constitutes a futuristic vision of how global businesses are organizing people and resources around the world, will be introduced. Next, the notions of organizations and organizational structures will be formally introduced. We also argue that organizational structures can help companies fail or succeed.

This chapter will describe different types of organizational structures that global businesses have used. The text will also look at companies that have an export department and use exports as an initial step toward globalization. This initial step is usually followed by an organizational structure that includes international efforts, which concentrate upon an international division. Once a firm becomes a global business, organizational structures will likely be functional and divisional, and the divisions could be related to products, markets, or geographical regions. Hybrid structures and matrix structures are also included as important variations of the functional and divisional structures. The characteristics of all these organizational structures are listed, along with their advantages and disadvantages. The organizational structures of global real-world firms are used as examples throughout this chapter.

LO-1
Discuss the concept of stateless corporations.

The Stateless Corporation

Some companies are global and so well integrated into the countries where they have a presence, that it is difficult, if not impossible, to identify one country as the home country for these corporations. For this reason, firms like these that transcend international boundaries are called **stateless corporations**. Consider, for example, Lenovo, the Chinese computer manufacturer, which became a global brand in 2005 when it purchased IBM, one of America's best known companies, for $1.75 billion. To help with the integration of Chinese and American workers, the chairman of Lenovo, Yang Yuanqing, moved with his family to North Carolina in order to increase his knowledge of American customs and culture. As part of the purchase agreement, Lenovo obtained the right to use the IBM brand for five years, however, Lenovo used it for only three years due to the confidence it had in its own brand. In 2007, Lenovo was included in the exclusive *Fortune 500* list, occupying the 499th place, due to worldwide revenues of $16.8 billion. Lenovo's chairman says: "This is just the start. We have big plans to grow." Consider now the company Arcelor Mittal and Lakshmi Mittal, its London-based Indian boss, who says that his firm has no nationally, but is "truly global," and that his multinational team of high-level executives get along so well that when the team meets, Mittal sometimes forgets there are different nationalities in the room.[2 3]

stateless corporation
a new phase in the evolution of the multinational corporation, where work is sourced wherever it is most efficient and the corporation transcends nationality altogether

Lenovo and Arcelor Mittal are two examples of the newest phase in the evolution of global business: stateless corporations. Businesses can become global starting with an export department, followed by overseas sales offices, in order to promote the export of goods that are domestically made. Building manufacturing facilities around the world to cater to local demand may follow. Today businesses aim to create what Sam Palmisano, the CEO of IBM, referred to as the "globally integrated enterprise"—a business organization that sources the work from the most efficient location. For business leaders, building a firm that can seamlessly integrate across different cultures and time zones represents a major challenge. For instance, how can virtual teams of multinational workers bond? One answer may be that they must spend a lot of time talking. And how does one work with awkward cultural differences? Lenovo, for example, has had to encourage its shy Chinese workers to speak candidly in meetings with American colleagues.[4]

While many major corporations have a global presence, stateless corporations are different because they attempt to transcend nationality altogether. C.K. Prahalad, an expert in the field and a professor at the University of Michigan Business School, postulates that stateless corporations represent the fourth stage of globalization. In the first stage, global companies produce goods in one country and export them to other countries. In the second state, global businesses establish foreign subsidiaries to handle the exports from their home countries. In the third stage, global firms set up operations in other countries. In the fourth stage, stateless corporations locate their core corporate functions and top executives in different countries in order to achieve competitive advantage via access to talent, capital, low costs, or proximity to their most important customers. For example, the software company Trend Micro has financial headquarters in Tokyo, where it went public; has product development in Taiwan, where there is an abundance of workers with PhD degrees; and has sales in Silicon Valley, giving it access to the giant American market. When stateless corporations organize this way, they are no longer limited to the strengths nor constrained by the weaknesses of a single country. "This is very new, and it is important," says Prahalad. "There is a fundamental rethinking about what is a multinational company," he says. "Does it have a home country? What does headquarters mean? Can you fragment your corporate functions globally?" Prahalad asks.[5]

REALITY CHECK LO-1

More and more global business firms are becoming stateless corporations. Do you think this may benefit to the world economy? Why or why not?

organization
a tool that people use to coordinate their actions to obtain something they seek or value

Organizing Global Business

LO-2
Describe the importance of organizational structures for global businesses.

Organizations exist to enable a group of people to effectively coordinate their efforts in order to achieve a goal. In turn, the structure of an organization refers to the pattern of organizational roles, relationships, and procedures that enable such coordinated action by its members. Consequently, an **organization** can be defined as a tool that people use to coordinate their actions to obtain something they seek or value. At the same time, an **organizational structure** can be defined as the formal system of task and authority relationships that control how people coordinate their actions and use resources to achieve organizational goals. The organizational structure serves the following purposes:[6 7]

organizational structure
the formal system of task and authority relationships that control how people coordinate their actions and use resources to achieve organizational goals

- It allows the members of the organization to perform a wide variety of activities based upon a division of labor that leads to the departmentalization, standardization, and specialization of functions and tasks.

- It permits to the organization members the coordination of their activities by integration mechanisms such as hierarchical supervision, formal rules and procedures, and training and socialization.
- It determines the boundaries of the organization and regulates its interfaces with the environment and its interactions with other organizations.

Organizational structures can allow a company to fail or succeed. In fact, it has been argued that one of the reasons why GM filed for Chapter 11 bankruptcy protection was due to the disastrous reorganization of GM in the 1980s by then-CEO Roger Smith. Under Smith's organizational structure, eight business units were clustered into two divisions: a big-car division and a small-car division. It was intended that these two divisions would increase productivity and promote unity throughout the company, but unfortunately the result was internal conflicts and lookalike automobiles marketed under different brands. For example, it was hard to differentiate between a $25,000 Cadillac and a $9,000 Pontiac. The luxury market was most severely affected because GM opted for cosmetic and decorative differences such as bumper extensions and exotic colors, rather than real competitive advantages such as better engines and mechanical systems, electronics, safety, and fuel efficiency. When GM's market share plummeted, its plants were left with significant excess capacity. By 1989, the newly restructured GM was incurring losses of more than $2,000 on every car it sold. When new models were more quickly pushed into production, the quality levels of the new models became substandard.

Smith's successor, Rick Wagoner, was also criticized for maintaining a faulty organizational structure with too many divisions. A **division**, or a business subunit consists of a collection of functions or departments that share responsibility for producing a particular product or service. At GM, some of the divisions include North American Operations, GM Acceptance Corporation, International Operations, and Hughes Electronics. Wagoner was CEO of GM when the firm was forced to declare bankruptcy and was taken over by the U.S. government. Wagoner will likely be remembered as the man who lost GM.[8]

As another example of how organizational structures can affect the success of a company, consider the following edited excerpt of an interview with Carol Bartz, who took over as chief executive of Yahoo, Inc. in January 2009 after a tumultuous year that saw a hostile takeover bid from Microsoft Corp. and the departure of the previous CEO, the company's

division
a business subunit that consists of a collection of functions or departments that share responsibility for producing a particular product or service

AP Photo/Paul Sancya

The General Motors Renaissance Center headquarters building in downtown Detroit, Michigan. The future of General Motors looks bleak.

co-founder, Jerry Yang. This interview by Kara Swisher of *The Wall Street Journal*[9] shows that Ms. Bartz believes that Yahoo!'s organizational structure prohibited innovation.

Ms. Swisher: I want to ask you: What is Yahoo!?

Ms. Bartz: We are the place that millions and millions of people come every day to check in with the people and things they are interested in. Seventy-six percent of the audience in the United States comes to Yahoo!. Fifty percent of the world-wide audience comes to Yahoo. It is where people find relevant and contextual information.

Ms. Swisher: About?

Ms. Bartz: About what they care about, whether it is their friends, their associates. It is news, it is sports. We have 11 leading sites: news, sports, finance, home page, mail—twice the number of mail accounts as the next competitor.

Ms. Swisher: What did you think of Yahoo! before you came, and how did you get there?

Ms. Bartz: Jerry (Yang) said, will you please come to my house and talk to me? I want to offer you the Yahoo! CEO job. And I said, Jerry, OK, fine. Upon arrival, I asked Jerry to draw me an organizational chart. He pulls a flip chart out of the closet and starts drawing the organizational structure of Yahoo!. I am looking at this thing and I go, is that really the organizational structure of Yahoo!?

Ms. Bartz: I said, why don't you show me who on this organization would make the big decision—the big CEO search decision. So he started drawing arrows. And it was like a Dilbert cartoon. It was very odd. I said, you need a better organizational structure here. I could not figure out who was in charge of anything, and he did not explain that part very well. I walked out and said, uh, maybe I am a little bit, 10 percent interested in your job offer.

Ms. Bartz: Yahoo! is such an important property and such a great name, and it needed some structure. And since I am actually quite good at that, I decided to take the CEO job.

Ms. Swisher: Which organizational structure do you think Yahoo! needs?

Ms. Bartz: Organizational structures can get in the way of innovation, because if people are all bound up, and if they do not know if they get to make the decision or somebody else, and if they do, what happens to them, and so on and so forth. There is a freeing when you organize around the idea that you are clearly in charge and go for it.

Note: Yahoo's board ousted Ms. Bartz as CEO in September 2011.

Eliza Snow/iStockphoto.com

Yahoo headquarters in Sunnyvale, California. Yahoo has averaged one CEO a year for the last five years.

In the next sections, the various organizational structures that global businesses use as they evolve from domestic firms to stateless corporations will be presented.

REALITY CHECK LO-2

Do you think that there is an "optimal" organizational structure for each company? If no, why not? If yes, how can the company find its optimal organizational structure?

ECONOMIC PERSPECTIVES Inflated Figures at Mahindra Satyam

Mahindra Satyam, formerly known as Satyam Computer Services Ltd., was founded in 1987 by B. Ramalinga Raju. The company offers consulting and information technology services spanning various sectors, and is listed on the New York Stock Exchange, the National Stock Exchange (India), and Bombay Stock Exchange (India). In January 2009, then company Chairman B. Ramalinga Raju resigned after notifying board members and the Securities and Exchange Board of India (SEBI) that Satyam's accounts had been falsified. B. Ramalinga Raju confessed that Satyam's balance sheet of September 30, 2008 contained inflated figures for cash and bank balances of $1.07 billion. B. Ramalinga Raju and his younger brother B. Rama Raju, Satyam's former managing director, are in jail awaiting trial on fraud and other offenses. Ironically, *Satyam* means "truth" in Sanskrit.

In June 2009, the company unveiled its new brand identity "Mahindra Satyam" after being purchased by the Mahindra Group's IT arm, Tech Mahindra. The new managers have redesigned the company's organizational structure, which was based upon B. Ramalinga Raju's system of silos. The system was intended to motivate the leaders of each division by allowing them to function as separate businesses. However, the system was used by B. Ramalinga Raju to prevent anyone but him from getting a complete overview of the firm operations. In consequence, it is believed that the organizational structure helped B. Ramalinga Raju to mask his alleged fraud and inflict major economic damage to the company.

QUESTIONS:

1) Do you agree that the organizational structure under B. Ramalinga Ragu was conducive to fraud?
2) How would you propose to change the organizational structure to prevent fraud in the future?

Source: Eric Bellman, "Mahindra Satyam's New Owner Tries to Move Beyond Disgraced Founder," The Wall Street Journal, July 23, 2009.

LO-3
Discuss the role that export departments and international divisions play in the organization of global businesses.

Export Departments and International Divisions

When one looks at how global businesses around the world are organized, one finds a wide variety of organizational structures. The early stages of a company's process toward becoming globalized are represented by export departments and international divisions.

Creating an Export Department

The first step a domestic firm takes when entering the global arena is usually to export some of its products. This is typically done by one or two sales representatives, although sometimes the employees handling the exports may primarily work within another function such

EXHIBIT 10.1 AN ORGANIZATIONAL STRUCTURE WITH AN EXPORT DEPARTMENT UNDER SALES

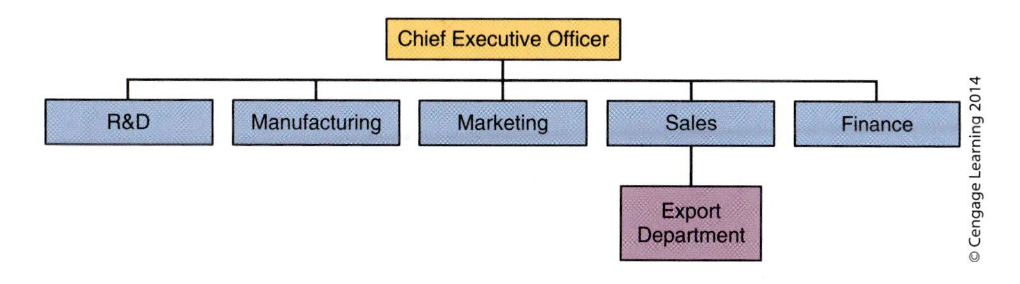

as Marketing or Operations. As the demand for the exported products grows, the number of people needed to handle the job increases as well, which leads to the formation of an export department.

An organizational structure with an export department is presented in Exhibit 10.1, which denotes the export department as part of the Sales function. Examples of companies with an export department are B.N.W. Industries, Zippo Manufacturing Company, Mack Trucks, and Maglite.

International Division

As the volume of exports grows, it may become feasible for the firm to manufacture and sell the products in the countries where the exports are being shipped. It may also be viable to adjust the product to local tastes and culture. Expertise in foreign markets becomes important as well. As a consequence, the export department becomes the international division.

An organizational structure with an international division is presented in Exhibit 10.2. Walmart is an example of a global business with an international division. The organizational structure of Walmart is presented in Exhibit 10.3.

An international division is advantageous because it permits global businesses to concentrate all international efforts and expertise in one location. For this reason, many global companies have used the international division as a stepping stone in their worldwide expansions. If the international division is at the same organizational level as domestic operations, it signals to international customers their importance to the company. A third advantage of the international division is that it fosters a global mindset in the people working within the division, and facilitates the key process of designing products that cater to local tastes and cultures.

However, an international division can also have disadvantages. One major disadvantage is the potential conflict between domestic and international operations. That is, managers

EXHIBIT 10.2 AN ORGANIZATIONAL STRUCTURE WITH AN INTERNATIONAL DIVISION

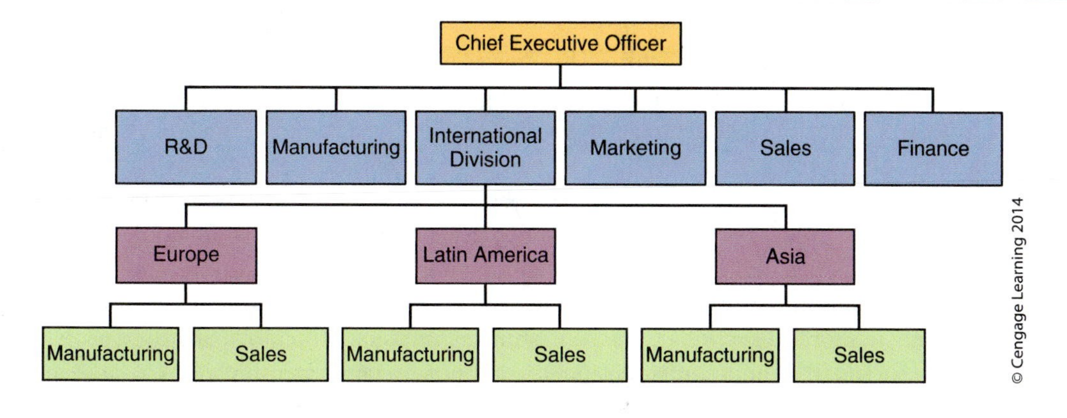

EXHIBIT 10.3 THE ORGANIZATIONAL STRUCTURE OF WAL-MART

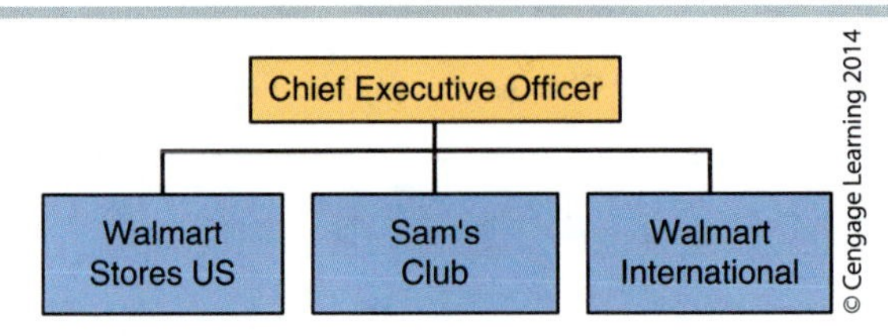

in the international division may feel like "second class" citizens if they are not at the same hierarchical level as managers in domestic operations. For example, in Exhibit 10.2, the manufacturing manager for Europe would be at the fourth tier in the organizational structure, while the manager for domestic manufacturing is at the second tier. This internal situation would contradict the importance of global business to the firm. Other disadvantages of the international division come from separating domestic and international operations, resulting in a lack of communication and coordination. Specific drawbacks of separating domestic and international operations may include the following:

- preventing the design of products with both domestic and international appeal;
- precluding the sharing of core competencies and knowledge; and
- complicating the capture of learning-curve savings resulting from consolidating production in manufacturing plants around the world.

REALITY CHECK LO-3

Find a company with an export department and a company with an international division. How are these companies similar and how are they different?

LO-4
Define functional, divisional, hybrid, and matrix structures, and illustrate their advantages and disadvantages for global business.

Four Organizational Structures for Global Business

When a company evolves beyond its need for an international division, it may be considered a global enterprise. At this stage in its development, it may have any of several organizational structures. Four common structures and their relative merits are examined next.

Functional Structure

functional structure
an organizational structure that groups people together because they hold similar positions in a company, perform similar tasks, or use the same kinds of skills

Most domestic firms start with a functional organizational structure. When a company grows beyond the affairs that can be handled by a single group of people and one boss, it usually adopts a functional structure. This creates an initial division of labor with regard to the main activities that must be performed by the organization to continue conducting business. In a functional structure, activities are grouped by a common function, from the bottom to the top of the organization. All purchasing agents, for example, are part of the Purchasing function, and the purchasing manager is responsible for all purchasing activities. Employees are committed to achieving the goals of their respective functional areas. Planning and budgeting is conducted by function and reflects the cost of resources used in each functional area. Careers are normally defined on the basis of experience within the function.[10] In short, a **functional structure** is an organizational structure that groups people together because they hold similar positions in a company, perform a similar set of tasks, or

EXHIBIT 10.4 A FUNCTIONAL ORGANIZATIONAL STRUCTURE FOR A GLOBAL BUSINESS

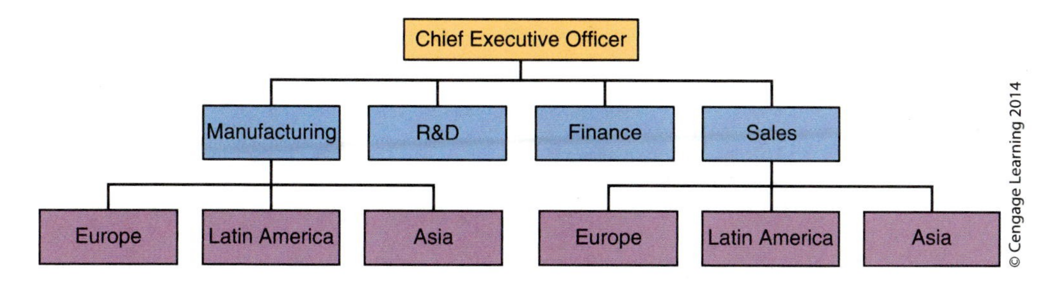

EXHIBIT 10.5 THE ORGANIZATIONAL STRUCTURE OF BOEING COMMERCIAL AIRPLANES

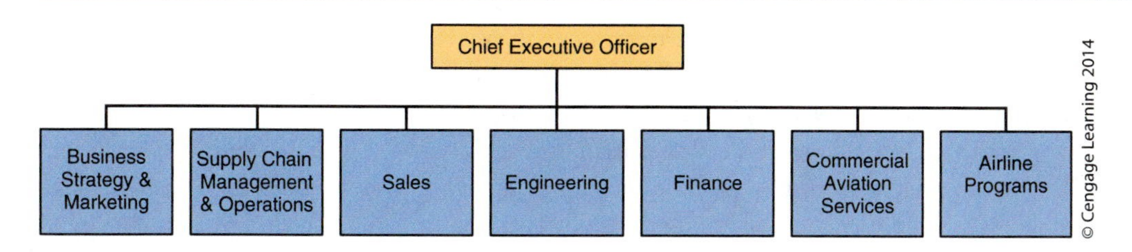

use the same kinds of skills. Exhibit 10.4 presents an example of a functional structure for a global business.

Global businesses that use a functional structure typically have a narrow product line or a highly integrated product mix, such as aircraft manufacturers or oil and gas firms. Boeing Commercial Airplanes provides an example of a global business with a functional structure. Exhibit 10.5 presents the organizational structure of Boeing Commercial Airplanes. Global businesses in the mining and energy industries also tend to have functional structures.

The functional structure has several advantages. First, the functional structure promotes economies of scale. Manufacturing all products in one single plant, for instance, enables the organization to acquire the latest and most scale-intensive machinery. Constructing only one production facility instead of a separate facility for each product line reduces duplication and waste. Second, the functional structure promotes in-depth skill development of employees by providing a well-defined career ladder that allows employees to be exposed to a range of activities within their own functional expertise. Third, the functional structure encourages collaboration, efficiency, and quality within the function.

Although the functional structure offers advantages to the global business, some businesses do not adopt this structure because it is not appropriate for them due to several reasons. First, there can be an inability to respond to environmental changes that require coordination between the functional areas. In these cases, the coordinating mechanisms across functions can become overloaded. Tasks become backlogged and top management cannot respond fast enough. This lack of speed in decision-making has proven fatal for several global businesses, as indicated in the opening vignette of this chapter "Organizational Restructuring at Royal Dutch Shell." Second, each employee has a restricted view of the organization's primary goals. This can lead to local optimization at the expense of global optimization. In other words, employees may make decisions that optimize a given function (e.g., sales), but not the global business as a whole. Third, accountability is diffused because profit and loss accounts are calculated for the entire firm rather than for each function.[11]

Divisional Structure

A **divisional structure** refers to one type of organizational structure in which functions are grouped together to serve the needs of products, markets, or geographical regions.

divisional structure
an organizational structure in which functions are grouped together to serve the needs of products, markets, or geographical regions

EXHIBIT 10.6 A DIVISIONAL STRUCTURE FOR A GLOBAL BUSINESS WITH THREE DIVISIONS

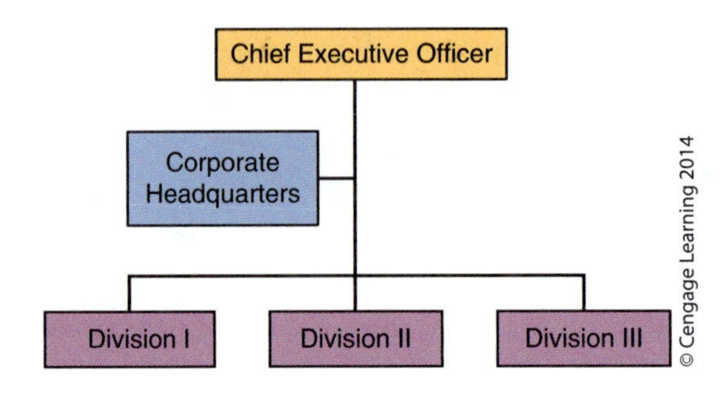

While the functional structure is organized according to the various inputs that enable an organization to produce its goods and services, the divisional structure is instead organized according to the various outputs of the global business. A divisional structure for a global business with three divisions is presented in Exhibit 10.6.

Note that although each division is managed as a separate business, coordination across the divisions is overseen by a group of managers at corporate headquarters who are responsible for allocating resources among divisions and deciding upon the long-term strategy of the firm. Corporate headquarters is also included in Exhibit 10.6. One of the primary issues in a divisional structure is the degree of autonomy granted to the divisions when making decisions that are strategic, and which involve a significant amount of resources.

One advantage of the divisional structure is that functions are able to focus their activities upon a specific kind of product, market or geographical region. This narrow focus helps a division to create high-quality products and provide high-quality customer service. Second, divisions develop a common identity and approach to problem solving, which increases cohesiveness and results in improved decision making and performance. Third, because each division has the full complement of functional resources, it can respond to the requirements of individual products, markets, or geographical regions and quickly adapt as these needs change. In addition, each division can be held fully accountable for its performance and this enables better control. One more advantage of the divisional structure is that employees' identification with their division increases their commitment, loyalty, and job satisfaction.

The primary disadvantage of the divisional structure is that it requires high operating and managing costs, which is a consequence of each division having its own set of functions, in addition to the corporate headquarters adding a new management level for which to pay. Because divisional structures normally have more managers and more levels of management than functional structures, communication problems may arise as various managers in various divisions attempt to coordinate their activities. A third disadvantage of divisional structures is that divisions may start to compete for organizational resources and may start to pursue divisional goals at the expense of the goals of the global business as a whole.

A **product structure** is a particular kind of divisional structure that groups products into separate divisions according to their similarities or differences. Exhibit 10.7 presents product structure for a global business with four product divisions.

product structure
a special case of the divisional structure where products are grouped into separate divisions according to their similarities or differences

ExxonMobil is an example of a global company with a product structure. Its product divisions include Upstream, Downstream, and Chemical. The Upstream division includes exploration, development, production, and gas and power marketing. The Downstream division includes refining and supply, fuels marketing, and lubricants and specialties. Honda is another example of a global company with a product structure; its product divisions are automobiles, motorcycles, and power products. A third example of a company with a product structure is IBM; its five IBM product divisions include the following:

EXHIBIT 10.7 A PRODUCT STRUCTURE FOR A GLOBAL BUSINESS WITH FOUR PRODUCT DIVISIONS

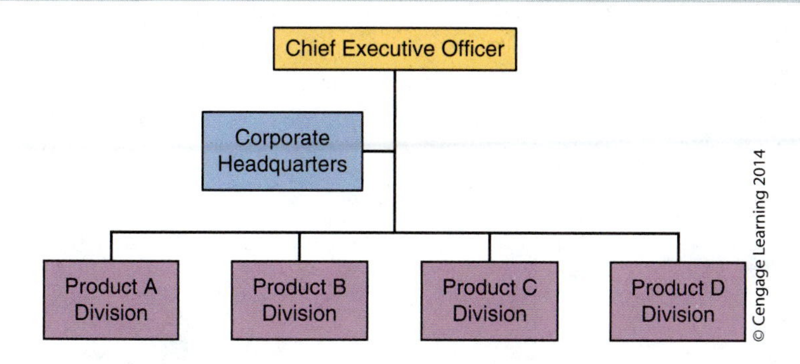

- Global Technology Services, which provides information technology infrastructure services and business process services;
- Global Business Services, which provides professional services and application outsourcing services;
- Software, which consists of middleware and operating systems software. Middleware software enables clients to integrate systems, processes and applications across a standard software platform. Operating systems are the software engines that run computers;
- Systems and Technology, which supplies clients with business solutions requiring advanced computing power and storage capabilities; and
- Global Financing.

market structure
a special case of the divisional structure where products are grouped into separate divisions according to the needs of different customers

geographical region structure
a special case of the divisional structure where products are grouped into separate divisions according to the needs of the different geographical regions the company serves

A **market structure** is a particular kind of divisional structure that groups products into separate divisions according to the needs of different customers. The market structure is also called *customer structure* or *customer class structure*. Exhibit 10.8 illustrates a product structure for a global business with three market divisions.

Hilton Hotels Corporation is an example of a global business with a market structure. It is organized around the following divisions, which serve different markets or customer classes around the world: Hilton, Hilton Garden Inn, Doubletree, Embassy Suites, Homewood Suites by Hilton, Hampton, Scandic, Conrad, and Timeshares. Hilton Hotels Corporation manages approximately 3,000 properties totaling about 500,000 rooms in 80 countries and territories.

A **geographical region structure** is a particular kind of divisional structure that groups products into separate divisions according to the needs of the different geographical regions the company serves. The geographical region structure is also called *area structure*.

EXHIBIT 10.8 A MARKET STRUCTURE FOR A GLOBAL BUSINESS WITH THREE MARKET DIVISIONS

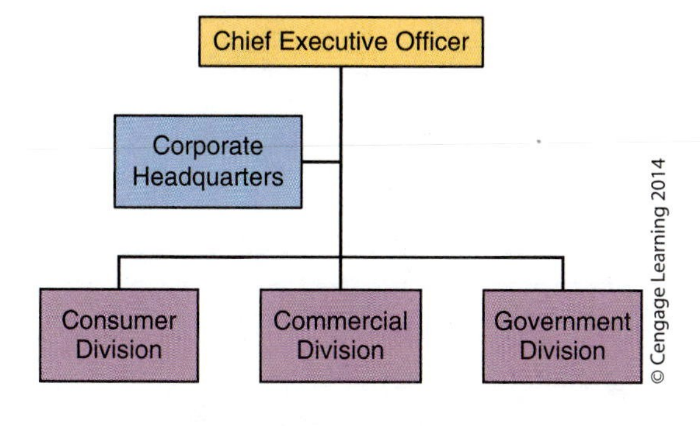

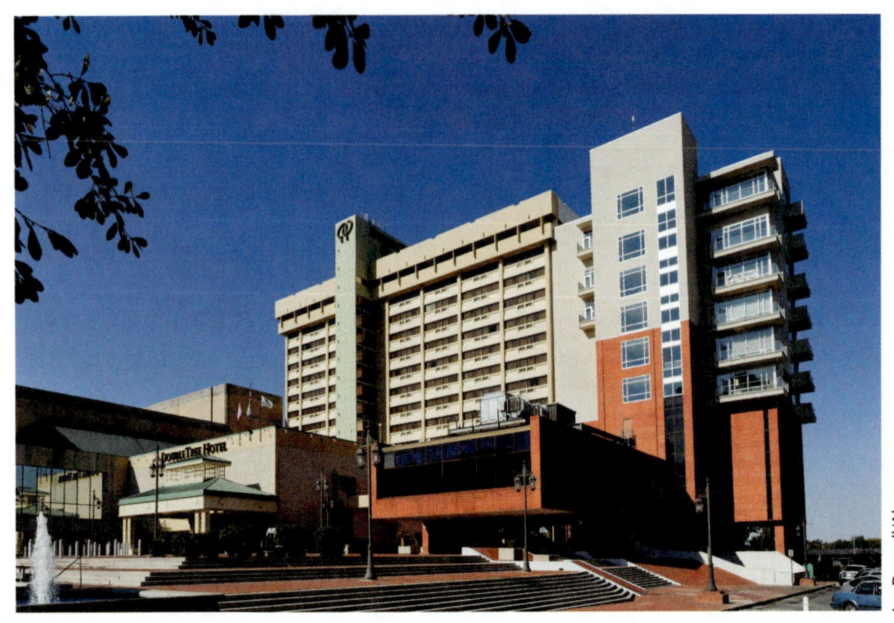

Ian Dagnall/Alamy

A Hilton Hotel. The first hotel to bear the Hilton name was the Dallas Hilton, a high-rise that opened in Dallas, Texas in 1925.

Exhibit 10.9 illustrates a product structure for a global business with three geographical region divisions.

Cementos Mexicanos S.A.B. de C.V. (CEMEX) is an example of a global business with a geographical region structure. Its three divisions include: 1) North America; 2) South America and the Caribbean; and 3) Europe, Asia, and the Middle East. Each regional manager supervises and is responsible for all the business activities undergoing in the countries comprising the region. These activities include production, distribution, marketing and sale of cement, ready-mix concrete, and aggregates. CEMEX's corporate headquarters evaluates the results and performance of each geographical region, and allocates economic resources according to this data. CEMEX is the world's largest building materials supplier and third largest cement producer. The company has a presence in more than 50 countries.

Hybrid Structure

hybrid structure
a combination of different organizational structures

As global businesses grow in reach and depth, sometimes they adopt a combination of organizational structures that best fit their needs. This combination of organizational structures is called a **hybrid structure**. Global businesses with hybrid structures are said to be organized by more than one dimension at the top level. A global business with a hybrid structure is presented in Exhibit 10.10.

EXHIBIT 10.9 A GEOGRAPHICAL REGION STRUCTURE FOR A GLOBAL BUSINESS WITH THREE DIVISIONS

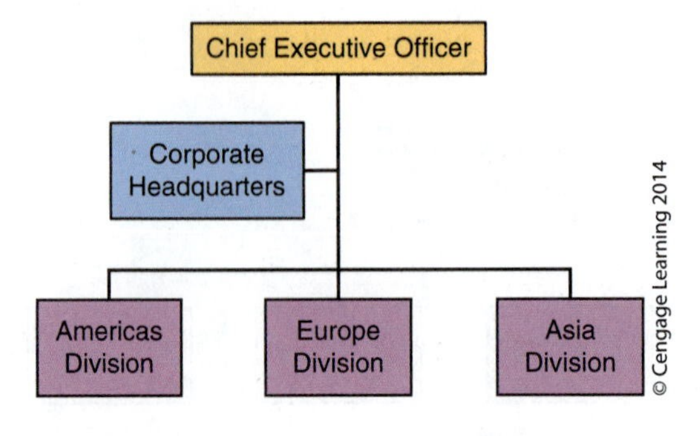

EXHIBIT 10.10 A GLOBAL BUSINESS WITH A HYBRID STRUCTURE

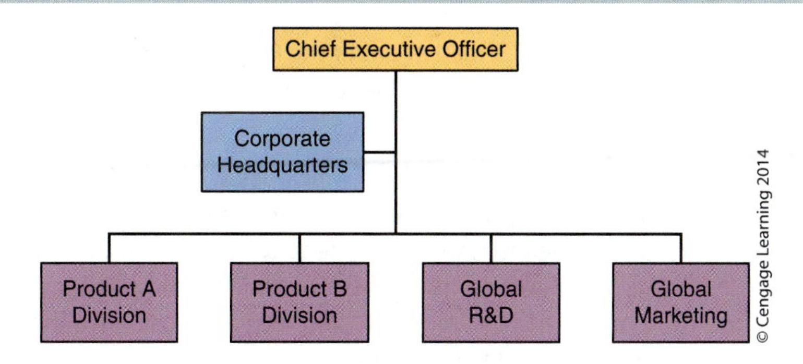

As the reader can see on Exhibit 10.10, this global business is using a mix of product structure (Product A and Product B Divisions) and functional structure (Global R&D and Global Marketing).

PepsiCo is an example of a company that uses a hybrid structure, which is organized into three business units:[12]

- PepsiCo Americas Foods, which includes Frito-Lay North America, Quaker Foods North America, and all of its Latin American food and snack businesses such as Sabritas and Gamesa in Mexico;
- PepsiCo Americas Beverages, which includes PepsiCo Beverages North America and all of its Latin American beverage businesses;
- PepsiCo International, which includes all PepsiCo businesses in the United Kingdom, Europe, Asia, Middle East, and Africa. Hence Pepsi uses a combination of a product structure and a geographical region structure;

Another example of a global business with a hybrid structure is Procter & Gamble (P&G). This company is organized along the following divisions:[13]

- *Beauty.* P&G is a global market leader in beauty products, with retail sales estimated at $230 billion. In hair care, P&G has more than 20 percent of the global market share. In skin care, the Olay brand is the top facial skin care retail brand in the world, and P&G owns this brand. In prestige fragrances, P&G competes with the Gucci, Hugo Boss, and Dolce & Gabbana brands.
- *Grooming.* This division is comprised of blades and razors, face and shave preparation products (such as shaving cream), electric hair removal devices, and small household appliances. P&G is a global market share leader in the manual blades and razors market. P&G is also a global market share leader in almost all of the world regions where P&G has a presence. P&G sells its electric hair removal devices and small house appliances under the Braun brand in several markets worldwide, where P&G faces competition from both global and regional companies.
- *Health Care.* This segment consists of oral care, feminine care, pharmaceuticals, and personal health products. In oral care, P&G holds the second market share position at approximately 20 percent of the global market. In feminine care, P&G is the global market leader with about one-third of the global market share. In pharmaceuticals and personal health, P&G is the market leader in nonprescription heartburn medications and in respiratory treatments behind Prilosec OTC and Vicks, respectively. At the same time, P&G holds approximately one-third of the global bisphosphonates market for the treatment of osteoporosis under the Actonel brand.
- *Snacks, Coffee, and Pet Care.* In snacks, P&G competes worldwide against both international and local competitors, and has a global market share of approximately 10

percent in the potato chips market via the Pringles brand. In the coffee business, P&G mostly competes in North America, where it occupies a leadership position with approximately one-third of the U.S. market under the Folgers brand. The vast majority of P&G's pet care business is also in North America, where the firm has about 10 percent of the market share.

- *Fabric Care and Home Care.* This P&G segment includes a variety of fabric care products, such as laundry cleaning products and fabric conditioners; home care products, such as dish care, surface cleaners, and air fresheners; and batteries. In fabric care, P&G is the global market leader with approximately one-third of the global market share, and P&G has the number one or number two market share position in the markets where the company competes. In home care products, P&G's global market share is about 20 percent across the categories in which the company competes. In batteries, P&G competes primarily behind the Duracell brand and has over 40 percent of the global alkaline battery market share.
- *Baby Care and Family Care.* In baby care, P&G has more than one-third of the global market share and mostly competes in diapers, training pants, and baby wipes. P&G's largest brand in baby care is Pampers with annual net sales of approximately $8 billion. P&G is the number one or number two baby care competitor in most of the key markets where the firm competes. In family care, P&G mostly focuses in North America supported by the Bounty paper towel and Charmin toilet tissue brands, with U.S. market shares of over 40 percent and over 25 percent, respectively.
- *Market Development.* This segment is responsible for developing go-to-market plans at the local level. Market Development includes dedicated retail customer, trade channel, and country-specific teams. The division is organized along seven geographic regions: North America, Western Europe, Northeast Asia, Central & Eastern Europe/Middle East/Africa, Latin America, Australia/India, and Greater China.
- *Global Business Services.* This P&G segment provides information technology, processes, and data tools to help the other segments listed above to gain a better understanding of the business and improve customer service. Global Business Services is responsible for providing world-class solutions at minimum cost and capital investment.

After looking at a detailed description of P&G's organizational units, it should now be clear to the reader that P&G offers a great variety of products, serves diverse markets, and has a world-wide presence. As a result, P&G decided that the most appropriate organizational structure for the company is the hybrid structure.

Matrix Structure[14]

For most firms, hybrid structures, which result from combining functional and divisional structures, provide them with enough flexibility to achieve the goals of the organization. However, in special cases, companies need the simultaneous benefits of both the functional and the divisional structures: the technological expertise within functions and the horizontal coordination across functions. For example, a defense contractor may need deep functional skills as well as the ability to coordinate across the functions for each contract or project. Similarly, a global company may need to coordinate across the demands of functions, products, and geographic locations. For these special cases, the answer is the **matrix structure**, which is an organizational structure in which people are grouped simultaneously by function and by division. A global business with a matrix structure is presented in Exhibit 10.11.

matrix structure
an organizational structure in which people are grouped simultaneously by function and by division

The functional managers and the division managers have equal authority within the organization, and employees report to both managers. For example, a sales person may be assigned to work in a particular product division. Hence the sales person has the Sales

EXHIBIT 10.11 A GLOBAL BUSINESS WITH A MATRIX STRUCTURE

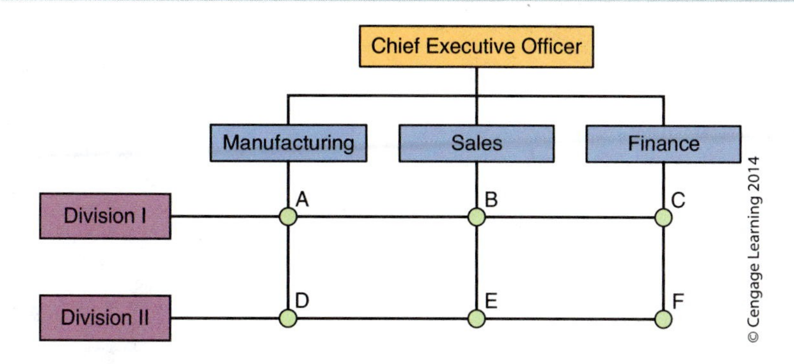

function as a primary location, but works full time on the product division. The reporting relationship is dual: The sales person reports to both the sales manager and the product division manager. In Exhibit 10.11, node *A* represents all manufacturing employees working on Division I, while node *D* represents all manufacturing employees working on Division II.

The matrix structure is advantageous because it allows the company to meet multiple demands from the environment. Resources can be flexibly allocated and the firm can adapt to changing external conditions. It also provides employees the opportunity to acquire both functional and division-related skills. One more advantage of the matrix structure is that it facilitates innovation and creativity and provides a work setting in which employees with different functional expertise can cooperate to solve non-programmed decision-making problems.

A basic problem of the matrix structure is determining the responsibility and authority relationships between the functional and divisional managers. By design, there is role ambiguity. Two bosses making conflicting demands on the employee can cause role conflict. Matrix structures also limit opportunities for promotion because most employees move laterally, from division to division, and not vertically to upper management positions.

The extent of these problems explains why matrix structures are used only by companies that depend upon rapid product development for their survival, or by firms that manufacture products designed to meet specific customer needs. When the matrix structure fails, it is usually because one side of the authority structure (function or division) dominates, or because employees did not learn to work in a collaborative way. Matrix structures are especially common in high-tech and biotechnology companies.

Bayer AG, a chemical and pharmaceutical company founded in Barmen, Germany in 1863, is well-known worldwide for its original brand of aspirin. In 1984, Bayer announced major changes to its organizational structure in response to significant sales gains, especially overseas, in the early-1980s. Until that time, Bayer had been successfully using a functional structure. Due to the changing conditions, Bayer was looking for a new organizational structure that would allow the firm to achieve the following three primary objectives: 1) Switch management control from the then-West German parent company to its foreign divisions and subsidiaries; 2) Rearrange its business divisions to more clearly define their duties; 3) Empower lower level managers by giving them more responsibility, freeing top executives to concentrate upon strategic matters.

The new organizational structure that Bayer adopted was a matrix structure, which clustered all of its business operations into six groups under an umbrella company called Bayer World. Each of these six groups have included several subgroups comprised of product categories such as dyestuffs, fibers, or chemicals. At the same time, each of its administrative and service functions were placed under Bayer World into one of several functional groups, such as marketing, human resources, plant administration, or finance. In addition, top executives who had headed functional groups in the past, were given authority over different geographical regions, which, like the product groups, were supported by and intertwined

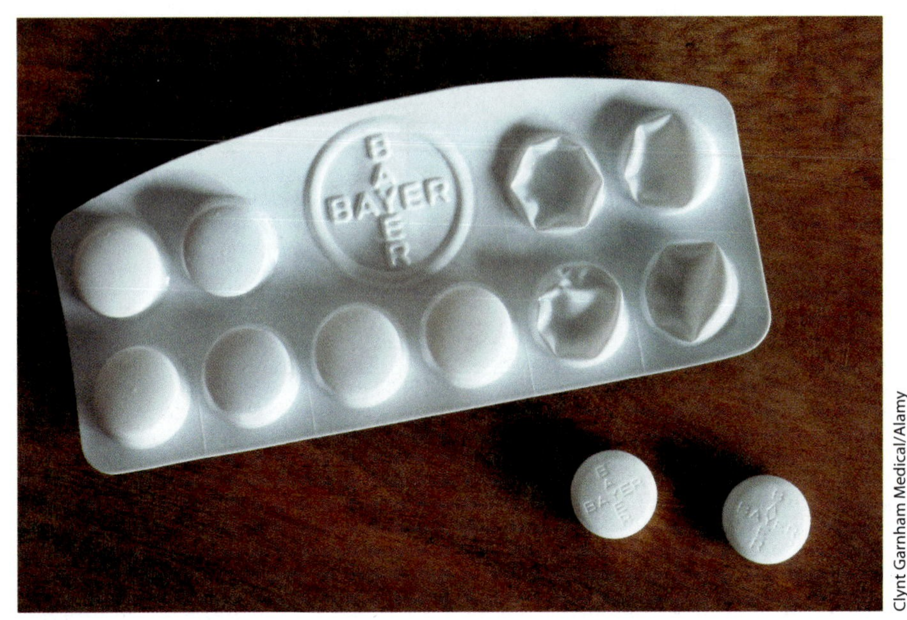

Aspirin, Bayer's first major product, was invented in 1897.

with the functional groups. The final result of the new organizational structure divided the original nine functional areas into 19 multidisciplinary, interrelated business groups.

By 1985, Bayer proclaimed that the new matrix structure was a great success because it allowed the company to get closer to its three primary objectives. In addition, Bayer learned that the new matrix structure helped the firm to be more responsive to market changes and new business opportunities while streamlining plant administration and service division activities.[15]

ETHICAL PERSPECTIVES

Ethics at ConocoPhillips

ConocoPhillips Company is an international energy corporation with headquarters located in Houston, Texas. ConocoPhillips is a Fortune 500 Company, and one of the six oil and gas "supermajors." ConocoPhillips was created through the merger of Conoco Inc. and the Phillips Petroleum Company on August 30, 2002.

Business organizations are often faced with the dilemma of where to place the ethics office in the organizational structure. Frequently, the ethics officer is considered a staff position and could be part of the Human Resources function, a member of the legal department, or located in a separate ethics office. Businesses should aim to incorporate ethics within the staff, rather than in a line position, so that it can operate in an advisory capacity.

ConocoPhillips decided to take a different approach and place the ethics office in the audit and finance department. This way, ethics can operate as a division of the firm that has a reach extending into all other areas of the firm. ConocoPhillips named Steve L. Scheck as the General Auditor and Chief Ethics Officer, reporting to the board of directors rather than to top management. According to Mr. Scheck, it helps that the ethics function is connected to the traditional internal audit function: "It is critically important for ethics to have the same force as internal audit. My charter says that I can go and my staff can go and look at anything in the company. We have free and unfettered access to anything in the company."

QUESTIONS:

1) Do you think that ethics should be part of a staff position, a line position, or both?
2) What are some of the advantages and disadvantages of placing ethics in the audit and finance area?

Source: Vanessa Hill et al., "Implementing Ethics in a Corporate Environment: A Conversation with Steve L. Scheck," The Journal of Applied Management and Entrepreneurship 11, no. 1, 2006.

REALITY CHECK LO-4

Locate in the business press a recent case of a company changing its organizational structure. Identify the former and later organizational structures.

SUMMARY

Global businesses have been using organizational structures as a basic source of sustainable competitive advantage. For example, as described in the opening vignette of this chapter, when Shell simplifies its organizational structure, its three upstream units will be merged into two geographically focused divisions, which is expected to speed up decision-making processes and avoid delays and cost overruns in their most important projects. In this chapter, we described the importance of organizational structures for business firms, and the different organizational structures that global businesses use when evolving from domestic companies to stateless corporations—a futuristic vision of how global businesses will organize people and resources around the world.

The first step in the path toward globalization is the creation of an export department, followed by the export department becoming an international division. Once a company outgrows its international division and becomes a global enterprise, it may adopt one of four common organizational structures: functional structure, divisional structure, hybrid structure, or matrix structure. In turn, the divisional structure has three specific structures: product structure, market structure, and geographical region structure. The advantages and disadvantages of each type of organizational structure were analyzed. The chapter also illustrated the different organizational structures via real-world global businesses.

KEY TERMS

stateless corporation, *p. 240*
organization, *p. 241*
organizational structure, *p. 241*
division, *p. 242*
functional structure, *p. 246*
divisional structure, *p. 247*
product structure, *p. 248*
market structure, *p. 249*
geographical region structure, *p. 249*
hybrid structure, *p. 250*
matrix structure, *p. 252*

CHAPTER QUESTIONS

1. Why are global businesses evolving toward stateless corporations?

2. Organizational structures can help a company fail or succeed. Why do you think that is the case?

3. What is the difference between export departments and international divisions?

4. Compare and contrast the following organizational structures: functional structure, product structure, market structure, and geographical region structure.

5. Which type of companies often adopt hybrid structures?

6. A matrix structure may provide the advantages of the functional and divisional structures, but it may also provide the disadvantages of these two structures. Argue in favor of or against this assertion.

MINI CASE: WHAT IS THE BEST ORGANIZATIONAL STRUCTURE FOR THE ROYAL DUTCH/SHELL GROUP?

Royal Dutch Shell p.l.c. commonly known as "Shell" is one of the six "supermajor" oil and gas companies. Shell is the second-largest energy company and the fifth-largest company in the world according to *Forbes* magazine list for 2011. Shell's revenues were $470 billion in 2011 and it employs more than 90,000 workers. Shell began in a unique way compared with other oil and gas supermajors. Royal Dutch Shell PLC was founded in February 1907 when two companies merged: The Royal Dutch Petroleum Company (which had the legal name Koninklijke Nederlandsche Petroleum Maatschappij) and the "Shell" (the quotation marks were part of the legal name) Transport and Trading Company Ltd of Great Britain.

The merger was an effort to globally compete with the then predominant petroleum company Standard Oil, owned by John D. Rockefeller. Under the terms of the merger, the Dutch group owned 60 percent and the British group owned 40 percent of the new company (the ratio is the same today). Shell is the world's biggest and oldest joint venture. The Royal Dutch Petroleum Company was a Dutch company created in 1890, and the "Shell" Transport and Trading Company was a British company founded in 1897.

Shell is also unique for its organizational structure and its global presence. Shell has been characterized as one of the world's three most international organizations; the other two, the Roman Catholic Church and the United Nations. At the same time, Shell's organizational structure is far more complex than the Roman Catholic Church or the United Nations. From an ownership and legal perspective, Shell comprises four types of company: The parent companies, the group holding companies, the service companies, and the operating companies. This formal structure of Shell is presented in Exhibit 10.12.

During the early 1960s, with the help of McKinsey & Company, Shell created a tri-dimensional matrix structure known as the Shell Matrix, which had functions, regions, and sectors. The Shell Matrix is presented in Exhibit 10.13. This matrix organization continued into the 1990s.

Shell was the only major oil company that did not undergo radical restructuring between 1985 and 1993. The absence of restructuring at Shell appeared to reflect two factors: 1) Shell's flexibility had meant that Shell had been able to adjust to a changing oil industry environment without the need for discontinuous change; and 2) because of Shell's management structure, in particular the lack of a CEO with autocratic powers, Shell was much less able to initiate the kind of top-down restructuring driven by powerful CEOs such as Larry Rawl at Exxon, or Jim Kinnear at Texaco. In contrast, managerial control of Shell was vested in the Committee of Managing Directors (CMD).

On March 29, 1995, Cor Herkströter, Shell's Chairman of the CMD, gave a speech to Shell's worldwide employees outlining the principal aspects of a radical reorganization

EXHIBIT 10.12 THE FORMAL STRUCTURE OF SHELL

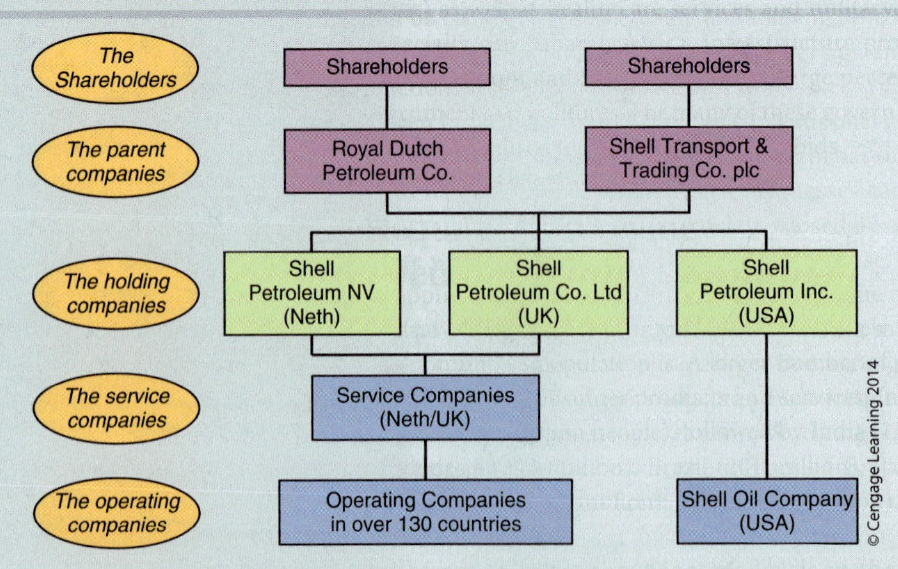

(continued)

MINI CASE: WHAT IS THE BEST ORGANIZATIONAL STRUCTURE FOR THE ROYAL DUTCH/SHELL GROUP?

EXHIBIT 10.13 THE SHELL MATRIX

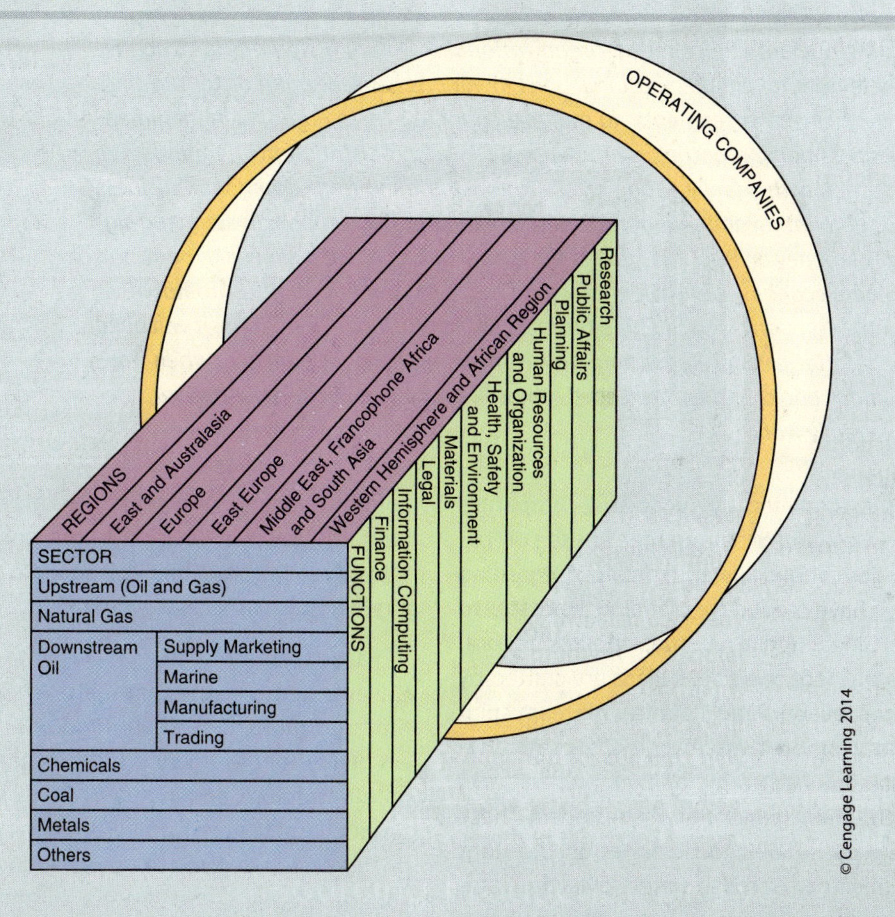

of the company, which were to be implemented at the beginning of 1996. Four years later, Shell finalized what would be the most ambitious and far-reaching organizational restructuring since the start of the company. The new structure represented a move from a geographically-based company to a business sector-based firm. The restructuring also included the elimination of more than 1,000 corporate positions, the sale of a vast majority of its headquarters in London, and the redesign of its coordination and control systems.

At the same time, because Exxon, Shell's biggest competitor, was merging with Mobil, Shell was no longer the world's largest energy company. In addition, several other major oil and gas companies were joining the trend of mergers and restructurings. For example, two of Shell's state-owned European rivals were being re-energized by mergers and privatizations. In 1999, the merger of Total, Fina, and Elf Aquitaine created the world's fourth oil and gas supermajor, after ExxonMobil, Shell, and BP. Also in the 1990s, the Italian multinational oil and gas company Eni S.p.A. was transformed from a public corporation into a joint stock company when most of Eni's share capital was put on the market in four successive public issues. Lastly, as described in the opening vignette to this chapter, 2009 brought another wave of organizational restructuring to Shell.

QUESTIONS:

1) What are some advantages and disadvantages of the Shell Matrix?
2) Why do you think Shell has undergone so many organizational restructurings?
3) How would you decide what would be Shell's best organizational structure?

Source: Robert M. Grant "Organizational Restructuring within the Royal Dutch/Shell Group," Cases to Accompany Contemporary Strategy Analysis, 5th ed., Hoboken, New Jersey: Blackwell Publishing, 2005.

A Matrix Organization May or May Not Be the Best Way to Restructure a Business

For many firms, the obvious choice for an organizational structure is the matrix structure. These firms need to operate multiple business units in various countries and distribute their products to different customer segments via multiple channels. These organizational dimensions such as business units, countries, customer segments, and distribution channels, have champions that speak with equally strong voices to those coming from traditional business functions such as accounting and manufacturing. For example, if a company is spending significant amounts of money on R&D, the head of the global business unit will need to be strong to achieve the global economies of scale that would make investment on R&D profitable. At the same time, if the company is conducting business in Mexico, India, and China, it will need a country manager that can develop strong government relations. In principle, when both strong business and strong countries are needed, a matrix structure is necessary. However, does a matrix structure really work?

POINT Yes, as exemplified by successful companies such as Nokia, Cisco, and Schlumberger. These companies are no longer caught in sterile debates regarding dotted lines, and have productive planning processes to amicably settle. Global optimization, as opposed to local optimization, is their common goal. Plans are crafted by teams working in collaboration. People with team spirit are rewarded and promoted, while traditional command-and-control managers opt out. For example, at Cisco, 20 percent of the management group resigned. These departures were considered to be a step in the right direction, and a victory of collaborators over the command and controllers. In the matrix structure, the organization defines roles and responsibilities and then holds people accountable. To prevent myopic approaches and functional silos, the matrix structure promotes the rotation of managers between units. Moreover, businesses with a successful matrix structure, have top executives that instill a one-company culture and settle internal disputes via strong leadership teams. For firms with global business, the matrix structure is the way to go

COUNTER-POINT The surest way to slow down a firm is to adopt a matrix structure. The key factor in the success of a company is leadership, and to make sure that leadership is effective, the company needs *organizational clarity*: very few committees, short decision paths, and unambiguous allocation of resources and responsibilities. Unfortunately, matrix structures possess the exact opposite of organizational clarity, resulting in endless committees and unproductive agreement processes, long and unclear decision paths, and especially, non-transparent responsibilities leading to confusion regarding "who owns successes and failures."

Past examples, such as those of the ABB Group and Unilever demonstrate that matrix structures can sometimes do more harm than good. ABB, the world's largest builder of electricity grids, was nearly ruined by the matrix structure, and in 2010, ABB was reorganized as a product structure with five divisions (power products, power systems, discrete automation and motion, low voltage products, and process automation). Unilever is an Anglo-Dutch multinational corporation that owns many of the world's consumer product brands in foods, beverages, cleaning agents, and personal care products. Unilever has been oscillating between various organizational structures since 1996.

Although the matrix seems to be a logical organizational structure, as indicated by Goold and Campbell, "most managers have not found it to be an easy structure. Managers have struggled with ambiguous responsibilities and reporting relationships, been slowed down by the search for consensus decisions, and found it hard to get all the different units to work constructively together. Many companies are now deeply suspicious of matrix structures, and even leading proponents of it, such as Shell and ABB, have concluded that such structures are no longer working for them."

What Do *You* Think?

Which viewpoint do you support and why? Could it be the case that the matrix structure is the best for some global businesses but not for others?

Source: Jay R. Galbraith and Guido Quelle, "Matrix is the Ladder to Success," BusinessWeek, www.businessweek.com/debateroom/archives/2009/08/; Michael Goold and Andrew Campbell, "Making Matrix Structures Work: Creating Clarity on Unit Roles and Responsibility," www.ashridge.org.uk, June 2003.

INTERPRETING GLOBAL BUSINESS NEWS

Business newspapers and magazines such as the *Financial Times*, *The Wall Street Journal*, *The Economist*, and *BusinessWeek*, are filled with news on organizational structures. After reading this chapter, you should be able to interpret the relevance of the notes being published. The following lines will ask you to do so for a sample of news:

1) Westpac Banking Corporation is a multinational services company and one of the Australian "big four" banks. Gail Kelly, the Chief Executive of Westpac plans to redesign the organizational structure of the corporation. Under the new organizational structure the chief-facing consumer and business financial services will merge into a new division, to be called Westpac Retail and Business Banking. Peter Hanlon will lead the new division and will be responsible for all consumers, small-to-medium enterprises, and commercial customers. A second new division will be led by Peter Clare and will be named Product & Operations, which will help to redesign Westpac's products and processes with emphasis on streamlining and simplifying the company's business. A third new division with a tentative name of "Westpac Technology" is in the works.

   (Source: "Westpac Banking to Overhaul Structure" *The Wall Street Journal,* July 18, 2008, page B7.)

   Describe what type of organizational structure Westpac is adopting.

2) Eli Lilly and Company is a global pharmaceutical company that had sales of $23 billion in 2010. Lilly is making changes to its organizational structure to reduce the number of layers of management in order to minimize bureaucracy. Under the new organizational structure, Eli Lilly will combine global regulatory, medical, and patient safety business units into a new division called Lilly Research Labs. Eli Lilly has also consolidated and streamlined its European infrastructure and global marketing business units.

   (Source: "Lilly Alters Structure" *The Wall Street Journal,* May 22, 2008, Jenny Park.)

   What type of organizational structure will Eli Lilly use in the future?

3) Starbucks is the largest coffeehouse company in the world, with 17,133 stores in 49 countries, including 11,068 in the United States, nearly 1,000 in Canada, and more than 800 in Japan. The CEO of Starbucks announced the expansion of the company's matrix structure in order to improve customer satisfaction. The company will now operate in the United States under four divisions: Western/Pacific, Northwest/Mountain, Southeast/Plains, and Northeast/Atlantic. Starbucks believes that with the new organization structure, it will be able to develop products faster and with more appeal to customers. A second phase of the Starbucks organizational restructuring is the creation of centralized support functions that will help the United States and international divisions.

   (Source: "The Organizational Structure of Starbucks, Unilever, and Wal-Mart" *www.associatedcontent.com/article/782963/ the organizational structure of starbucks.html,* May 28, 2008.)

Do you agree that with the expansion of its matrix structure Starbucks will get the listed advantages?

4) Merck & Co., Inc. is one of the largest pharmaceutical companies in the world. Merck was restructured into five divisions after it completed the buyout of rival Schering-Plough in 2009 for $41.1 billion. The five divisions are Global Human Health, Animal Health, Consumer Health Care, Merck Research Laboratories, and Merck Manufacturing. "The Organizational structure for the new Merck was designed to capture the opportunities in the broader and deeper in-line pharmaceutical franchises that would be created through the integration of Merck and Schering-Plough products," Merck said in a statement.

   (Source: "Merck to Form 5 Divisons after Schering Buyout," BusinessWeek, August 31, 2009.)

Draw the organizational structure of the new Merck. What type of organizational structure is it?

PORTFOLIO PROJECTS

Exploring Your Own Case in Point: Global Organizational Structure

After reading this chapter, you should be prepared to answer some basic questions about your favorite global company.

1) Is the company a stateless corporation? If not, is the company on its way to becoming a stateless corporation?

2) What type of organizational structure is the company currently using?

3) Are competitors using the same organizational structure or a different one? Why do you think competitors are using the same or different organizational structures?

4) Do you think the company may benefit from a hybrid or matrix structure?

Developing an International Business Strategy for Your Own Small Business: Choosing an Organizational Structure

From an organizational structure perspective, the first major decision that you have to make is to determine the best organizational structure for your firm. The following questions will help you to make this decision:

1) Would an export department or an international division be appropriate for your company?

2) If you adopted a functional structure for your company, what would it look like?

3) If you adopted a division structure for your company, what would it look like?

4) If you adopted a hybrid structure for your company, what would it look like?

5) If you adopted a matrix structure for your company, what would it look like?

6) What would be the most appropriate organizational structure for your company? Why?

CHAPTER NOTES

[1] Benoit Faucon et al., "Shell Plans Further Reductions in Jobs," The Wall Street Journal, September 5, 2009; Guy Chazan, "BP Readies for a Shake-up," The Wall Street Journal, October 11, 2007.
[2] "In Praise of the Stateless Multinational," The Economist, September 18, 2008.
[3] "A Bigger World," The Economist, September 18, 2008.
[4] Ibid. (i).
[5] S. Hamm, "Borders are So 20th Century," BusinessWeek, September 22, 2003.
[6] N. Nohria, "Note on Organization Structure," Harvard Business School, June 30, 1995.
[7] G. R. Jones, Organizational Theory, Design, and Change, 6th ed., (New Jersey: Prentice Hall, 2010).
[8] J. A. Sonnenfeld, "How Rick Wagoner Lost GM," BusinessWeek, June 1, 2009.
[9] K. Swisher, "A Question of Management: Carol Bartz on How Yahoo's Organizational Structure Got in the Way of Innovation," The Wall Street Journal, June 2, 2009.
[10] Ibid. (v).
[11] Ibid. (v).
[12] PepsiCo, Inc., 2008 Annual Report.
[13] The Procter & Gamble Company, 2008 Annual Report.
[14] Ibid. (v).
[15] "Matrix Management and Structure," Encyclopedia of Business, 2nd edition, www.referenceforbusiness.com/encyclopedia.

Managing Global Business

ndar Todorovic/ erstock.com

Ricardo De Mattos/iStockphoto.com

ArtisticPhoto/Shutterstock.com

Noel Hendrickson/Blend Images/ Jupiter Images

Jorg Hackemann/Shutterstock.com

CH 11

Global Human Resource Management

© C Miller Design/Getty Images

Nathan Benn/Alamy

After studying this chapter, you should be able to:

LO-1 Explain the basic cultural and regulatory issues involved in global human resource management including outsourcing and offshoring.

LO-2 Describe the challenges involved in staffing foreign operations, assessing needs for training and development, and designing appropriate strategies to meet those needs.

LO-3 Discuss performance appraisals and employee compensation issues around the world, including cultural differences, cost of living, and how expatriate issues are handled.

LO-4 Explain the interplay between international labor standards and free trade, the free trade and labor concerns presented by NAFTA, as well as the functions of labor unions.

Breaking the Political "Glass Ceiling" in Japan

The 2008 election of Barack Obama as the first African-American president of the United States was a sad moment for Hiromu Nonaka in Japan. By 2001, Mr. Nonaka had risen through Japanese political ranks to become the Chief Cabinet Secretary, generally considered the second government office in Japan and a traditional step before becoming Prime Minister. Mr. Nonaka, however, had decided not to seek the position of Prime Minister—in large measure because he belonged to the *buraku*, a feudal class of Japanese outcasts that still faces considerable social discrimination today.

Although ethnically indistinguishable from other Japanese, the *buraku* are descendants of individuals who performed unclean tasks, such as working as undertakers or animal slaughterers, during feudal times. Although the *buraku* were officially liberated under Japanese law in 1871, considerable discrimination continues to exist against them, especially in the upper reaches of Japanese society. Mr. Nonaka worked very hard and, unlike most Japanese politicians, never tried to hide his *buraku* roots. Nevertheless, when he was a very strong contender to become Prime Minister of Japan in 2001, a rival, Taro Aso (Japan's previous prime minister) was quoted as a saying at a closed-door meeting "are we really going to let those people take over the leadership of Japan?"

Today, at 83, Mr. Nonaka's chances of becoming Japanese Prime Minister have probably passed him by, however, he hopes for the day that a *buraku* will attain Japan's highest office, just as an African-American has attained the highest office in the United States.[1]

KO SASAKI/The New York Times/Redux Pictures

Japanese government official Hiromu Nonaka's "buraku" roots probably prevented him from becoming Japan's Prime Minister.

Introduction

In the book, *The World Is Flat*,[2] Thomas L. Friedman talks about how the Internet has helped "flatten" the world of work throughout the globe. For example, a company called NightHawk Radiology employs medical doctor radiologists in foreign countries such as Australia. Because of global time zone differences, these radiologists can be working while radiologists in the United States are asleep. U.S. hospitals can send patient X-rays to these doctors over the Internet at two o' clock in the morning, and then in return receive fairly expeditious readings and reports of these X-rays through the Internet. Moreover, because radiologists in many foreign countries get paid less than U.S. radiologists, hospitals are often able to have X-rays read more cheaply than before—and there's less need to have U.S. radiologists "on call" 24 hours per day. Today there is a world market for labor and human resources in many ways.

Technological changes have had a number of other important implications on human resource management throughout the world. First, companies based in the United States are far more likely to have at least some operations in other countries than in the past. The Internet, computers, easy air travel, cell phones and the like, have made it much easier for U.S. companies to conduct business in other countries. In staffing operations in these other countries, U.S. companies will face a multitude of cultural issues and staffing decisions. In addition, technological advances have helped create what some have called a "knowledge economy," with machines now performing jobs that were previously completed by people, while people move into jobs requiring higher levels of knowledge. For example, computers now handle many routine corporate tasks such as basic tax reporting, payroll administration, and employee time-keeping. As a result, corporate accountants and human resource managers now fulfill more strategic, higher level knowledge-based functions such as advanced tax and executive succession planning. In this respect, the role of human resources and those who manage such resources has become increasingly important in today's global economy.

Global Strategic Human Resource Management

LO-1

Explain the basic cultural and regulatory issues involved in global human resource management including outsourcing and offshoring.

The conduct of human resource management (HRM) differs markedly throughout the world, and U.S. companies conducting business in different countries face markedly different human resource environments. Many of these differences are related to cultural factors that vary from country to country. Other differences derive from regulations such as labor and tax laws, immigration and border security. Global strategic HRM also involves outsourcing and offshoring.

Statistical Overview

One way to gain an understanding of strategic HRM on a global scale is to examine recent statistical analyses. For example, reflecting cultural and other differences, the percentage of female participation in the workforce varies widely in different countries. Scandinavian countries such as Sweden and Norway have very high female labor force participation rates, with 76.1 percent of eligible females working in each country. In contrast, the female labor force participation rate in Turkey is only 27.3 percent. Moreover, this rate has declined considerably over the past decade, a change largely attributed to religious considerations in this predominantly Muslim—but politically secular—nation. The female labor participation rates in Mexico, Poland, and the United States are about 46.7 percent, 56.5 percent, and 69.9 percent respectively.[3]

The types of work people do throughout the world also differ considerably. For instance, only 1.3 percent of the civilian workforces in the United Kingdom and 1.5 percent of the civilian workforce in the United States work in the agriculture, forestry, and fishing sector of the economy, while 14.1 percent of the labor force is employed in this sector in Mexico, and 15.8 percent of the population in this sector in Poland. International trade rules and treaties such as NAFTA, which have an impact upon agricultural trade barriers and subsidies, can strongly influence the growth or decline of employment in this sector. In fact, the percentage of Mexican workers employed in the agricultural sector has declined considerably since the ratification of NAFTA.

Statistics also reflect how immigration laws and the ability of foreign-born individuals to work in a given country vary widely throughout the world. For example, 25.7 percent of the labor force in Australia is foreign born, but in Japan this figure is less than one percent. Self-employment and entrepreneurship also varies widely; 36.3 percent of workers in Greece are self-employed versus only 8.5 percent in Norway. Norms also differ widely regarding the prevalence of part-time versus full-time employment. In the Netherlands, 36.1 percent of all employees work on a part-time basis in contrast to only 3.5 percent in the Czech Republic.

Finally, although the global economic recession that began in 2008 increased unemployment rates throughout the world, some countries have faced persistently higher rates of unemployment than others. For example, unemployment rates in Eastern European countries such as Poland and the Slovak Republic consistently have been in the 15 percent range, with unemployment rates for young workers in those countries (age 24 and under) in the 20 percent range. These unemployment rates have been more than twice those in European countries such as Denmark and the Netherlands.[4]

What does all of the above mean in terms of global strategic human resource management planning? Perhaps a lot. A business in need of a plentiful, available labor supply of young workers, for example, might find Poland a great place to open a business. If the business is seeking a location where workers are interested in part-time employment, however, the Netherlands (with a 36.1 percent part-time employment rate) might be a far better race than Poland (10.1 percent part-time employment rate) and also better than the Czech Republic (only a 3.5 percent part-time employment rate). Global human resource statistics provide helpful information about establishing and running operations in various countries, as well as about national cultures.

Cultural Issues and Differences

As discussed earlier, considerable cultural differences exist among countries—differences that have a profound impact upon the practices of international human resources management. For example, in certain Asian and other countries the general expectation is that women will not be full-time participants in the workforce, while in certain Scandinavian countries the exact opposite is true. In some countries, certain jobs are highly respected and remunerated while in other countries this not the case; for example, medical doctors hold very high status in the United States, but much more moderate status in Russia. In some countries, a large premium is put upon long-term employment (and other) relationships, while in other countries much shorter-term relationships are expected.

As discussed in Chapter 5, in a classic study, Dutch social scientist Geert Hofstede identified five major dimensions of national culture as they apply to human resource management throughout the world.[5] They are: power distance, uncertainty avoidance, individualism vs. collectivism, masculinity vs. femininity, and long-term and short-term orientation.

Power Distance This dimension refers to the degree of equality of authority distribution in a given society and its workplaces, and employee expectations related to the same. In countries with more egalitarian (low power distance) cultures, employees may address their bosses by their first names, and efforts may be made to eliminate overt workplace hierarchical differences such as special parking spaces reserved for senior managers. In low power distance countries, such as Denmark and the Netherlands, it is also common for workplace employee committees or other mechanisms to be established that give employees some direct input into the management of the organization. In contrast, workplaces in high power distance countries such as Mexico, Japan, and Russia tend to have more centralized, hierarchical—and perhaps even autocratic—workplace decision-making structures. Relationships between bosses and subordinates are likely to also be more formal in such situations.

Uncertainty Avoidance This dimension relates to a culture's desire for predictability, or the lack of predictability in the workplace and elsewhere. In countries such as Germany and Austria, which rank high on uncertainty avoidance, people want clear rules, procedures, and structures. They value orderliness and predictability—"free spirit" employees may have difficulty fitting into the workplace culture. Countries with low uncertainty avoidance scores such as Jamaica have a more "hang loose," live-and-let-live attitude about things. For example, human resource managers in Germany are more likely to take an employee's tardiness very seriously, as opposed to those in Jamaica.

Individualism vs. Collectivism This dimension relates to the extent that people think of themselves as members of a group or collective, rather than discrete individuals. For example, in highly individualistic cultures such as the United States, employees tend to be evaluated and rewarded in great measure for their individual achievements and performances. People are expected "to make it on their own" and society places a high value upon individual success. By contrast, many Asian countries such as South Korea, Japan, and Taiwan rank high on collectivism. In these countries, people tend to think of themselves as part of a group or collective and measure their success according to the success of the group. In such countries, it may be more common for workers to be paid based upon the performance of their work team or group, rather than upon their individual job performance. Workers in such countries may expect the community to help take care of them, just as they expect to contribute to the care of others.

Masculinity vs. Femininity This dimension should not be confused with male dominance or women's rights; instead it relates to values that are traditionally associated with one gender or the other. Highly masculine cultures place a high value on things such as competition, assertiveness, and achievement. Japan, Austria, and Mexico are among the most masculine cultures. Other countries, such as Sweden and Norway, are more feminine, and place high value upon things like care for the weak and relationships. Human resources practices and policies in more feminine countries, for example, may likely be more liberal with respect to sick days, disability pay, and parental leave than those in more masculine countries.

Long-Term vs. Short-Term Orientation This factor involves the extent to which members of a given society value long-term and future planning as opposed to a more immediate short-term perspective. Many Asian countries such as China and Japan have this kind of orientation. In contrast, a much shorter-term orientation exists in the

United States and Britain. Human resource practices in longer-term-oriented countries may place greater emphasis upon worker retirement savings programs and pensions than those in the United States.

When these dimensions of cultural differences are considered, it is easy to see how they have a general overall impact upon the conduct of international HRM and the appropriateness of HRM practices in certain countries. For example, it may be difficult to implement highly stratified compensation packages tied to individual performance in more collectivist-oriented countries. In such countries, compensation structures based upon team performance or seniority may be far more effective. Multinational corporations managing operations around the globe must be keenly aware of these issues, particularly with regard to moving employees from one country to another. For example, an executive who grew up and worked most of his or her life in a high power distance country such as Mexico or Japan will be used to being addressed as "Mr." or "Ms." This executive may have difficulty adjusting to an executive role in a low power distance country like Denmark or the Netherlands where all employees address one another by first name. At the very least, good strategic HRM ensures that executives making transitions are well trained regarding the cultural values in their new home countries.

Regulatory Issues Including Immigration and Border Security

Countries around the globe have vastly different regulatory legal-political systems and structures which govern the conduct of HRM. As shown later in this chapter, some of these regulations pertain to the ability of employees to form labor unions and engage in collective bargaining. In Canada, for example, labor relations are regulated at the provincial level (e.g., by the province of Ontario) rather than at the national level. Such provincial regulations generally make it easier for employees to join labor unions than the federal regulatory system pertaining to labor relations, which exist in the United States.

France, for example, instituted its well-publicized 35-hour work week in 1998. France began its experiment with a shorter work week believing that it would help lead employers to hire more workers, thus reducing the country's chronically high unemployment rate.[6]

Gary Moon/Age Fotostock

The U.S. Immigration Border Fence Between the U.S.-Mexico Border in Arizona.

There was some evidence that job creation did initially take place, and that other countries began in part to emulate the French experiment; for example, Belgium cut its work week to 38 hours in 2003. More recent evidence related to French job creation and the 35-hour work week, however, has been mixed, and a recent law now allows companies to negotiate more than 35 work week hours from their employees. Still, employees in France are likely to continue to work less than the approximately 42 hours per week averaged by workers in the United States.

Governmental regulations related to immigration and border security are among the most important in the field of international HRM. Some countries, such as Singapore, have somewhat flexible immigration policies, making it easy for workers from other countries to legally work there on a semi-permanent or permanent basis. In recent years, for example, many U.S. scientists have found work in Singapore.[7]

Somewhat similarly, Great Britain, a member of the European Union (EU), opened its doors to workers from Poland, the Czech Republic, and six other Eastern European countries as soon as these countries obtained "accession" status in the EU (meaning that they began the application process) in 2004. Since that time, more than 500,000 workers from those countries have been granted legal entry into the U.K.—a huge number for an island nation of 60 million people.[8]

In contrast, the United States has more restrictions related to foreign worker entry into its borders. A sizeable number of individuals, however, have ignored U.S. government regulations and have entered the United States illegally. It has been estimated that there may be as many as 20 million illegal immigrants in the United States, with many of these individuals historically working in the service and construction industries. While hiring illegal immigrants is unlawful under U.S. federal law (as well as under some state laws), effectively enforcing such legal regulations has proven to be extremely difficult.

Outsourcing and Offshoring

Outsourcing involves the process of a company subcontracting a certain production function to a third party. As noted elsewhere in this chapter, many companies are outsourcing

outsourcing
the process of a company subcontracting a certain production function to a third party

REUTERS/Henry Romero

Virtually all the U.S. automobile companies have off-shored auto manufacturing to Mexico and other countries.

a part of their job recruitment process to Internet-based recruiters such as Careerbuilder.com. **Offshoring** involves the process of transferring an organizational function to another country, regardless of whether this function is outsourced or stays within the same company or corporation. For example, a U.S. company that hires another U.S. company, such as Automatic Data Processing Corporation (ADP), to process all of its corporate payroll functions would represent outsourcing. General Motors transferring manufacturing of its Saturn automobiles from a GM plant in Detroit, Michigan to a GM plant in Monterrey, Mexico would represent an example of offshoring. If a sneaker company such as Reebok transferred the manufacturing of its sneakers to a third-party company in Vietnam or Thailand, that would represent an example of both outsourcing and offshoring. The NightHawk Radiology example mentioned earlier in this chapter, which involved U.S. hospitals subcontracting radiology services to radiologists in countries such as Australia, represents another example of this practice.

Offshoring and outsourcing practices have been extremely controversial among U.S. workers and labor unions because these practices involve transforming U.S. corporate jobs into jobs with other companies overseas. Why do companies engage in this activity? One reason is cost. Salaries for sneaker manufacturing workers in countries such as Vietnam or Thailand are far lower than those in the United States, especially compared with recent increases in the U.S. minimum wage. Moreover, there may not be significant differences in the quality of work completed by workers in the two countries. For example, NightHawk Radiology has highly qualified radiologists in Australia, who earn lower salaries than U.S. radiologists. If companies can have quality work at a lower price completed by overseas workers, they can charge less for these products than if U.S. workers were hired for the same job. Lower-priced, high-quality X-rays or Reebok sneakers inure to the benefit of U.S. consumers and hospital patients. Thus, while such practices hurt U.S. workers, arguably, they may be beneficial for the overall U.S. economy by providing high-quality goods and services at a low price.

The counterarguments to the above analysis, however, have various dimensions. First, the "quality" of outsourced or offshored goods and services may not always be comparable to products manufactured or services provided by the company's own U.S.-based workers. Workers at an outsourced airline reservation call center in India may not work as well as call center workers directly employed by the airline in Sioux City, Iowa. It is much harder for an airline (or any company) to monitor quality at a subcontractor's operation in India (or elsewhere) than at its own domestic operation. Moreover, there have been allegations of unethical behavior (e.g., very unsafe working conditions) in some outsourced offshore operations serving U.S. corporate customers. Nevertheless, increasing globalization, technological advances, and consumer pressure for lower prices insure that the outsourcing and offshoring trend by U.S. corporations is here to stay.

offshoring
involves the process of transferring an organizational function to another country whether outsourced or not

REALITY CHECK LO-1

Do you know anyone who has lost a job because his or her position has been outsourced or offshored?

LO-2
Describe the challenges involved in staffing foreign operations, assessing needs for training and development, and designing appropriate strategies to meet those needs.

Staffing Policies

A key initial decision a company will have to make is how to staff the office. Should it to the extent permissible under British accounting profession regulations, staff the office with accountants from its U.S. home "parent" offices, or should it hire British licensed accountants to do the work? Alternatively, given Britain's rather open immigration policies vis-à-vis other European Union countries, should the company try to recruit accountants from Poland, France, and Spain for its new London office? More specifically, headquarters or parent country employees who are being sent to work overseas for their companies are known as **parent country nationals**. Workers already living in the foreign or host country where the U.S. company is opening operations and being employed by the U.S. company are known as **host country nationals**. Finally, employees from other countries (i.e., neither the parent nor the host country) who are employed by a U.S. company in a foreign country are known as **third country nationals**. Because they are working in countries other than their native countries, both parent country nationals and third country nationals are known as **expatriates**.

Virtual Staffing

Technological advances such as the exchange of X-rays over the Internet mentioned earlier in the chapter have made it possible for someone to work as a virtual expatriate today. Such an individual could, for example, potentially help manage the London office of the aforementioned U.S. accounting firm without actually relocating to London. This might be accomplished via trips to the London office, supplemented by extensive ongoing emailing, videoconferencing, web-based collaboration, and so forth. With increasing technological advances, however, arrangements of this kind have their drawbacks. For example, it's very difficult for virtual expatriates to build strong and trusting relationships with people in the foreign office; they are virtually managing. Consequently, companies in nearly all global situations require expatriates to live in the place of their foreign assignments. The pros and cons of hiring expatriates to staff operations in other countries are very important considerations for many international HR managers.

Expatriate Issues in Staffing

What drives a company to hire expatriates for foreign country assignments? What are the potential risks involved in making staffing assignments of this kind? What are the potential benefits? How "long term" should expatriate assignments be? The answers to these questions depend largely upon the particular situation and the particular corporation involved.

Despite the inherent cost and cultural advantages that often exist for hiring locally (i.e., host country nationals), a local labor market may not have enough qualified workers. For example, if Microsoft Corporation has a computer programming operation in Monterrey, Mexico, it may not be able to find enough qualified local computer programmers to adequately staff the operation.

One reason for hiring expatriates that are parent country nationals relates to control. Staffing foreign operations with workers from the parent country will help impose the values and structures of the headquarters and the parent country upon the foreign operation. Japanese multi-national companies are especially known for staffing their foreign operations, especially at the managerial level, with parent country national expatriates. These Japanese multi-nationals are traditionally concerned about the imposition of Japanese cultural norms and values upon their foreign operations.

The risks of an expatriate staffing policy, however, are many. First, rates of **expatriate failure**, or when the expatriate does not complete his or her assignment and returns home early, have traditionally been 30 percent or more. Not infrequently, family issues play a part in this, either because the expatriate's family does not adjust well to the overseas assignment, or because the expatriate takes the assignment without bringing his family along, engendering marital and other problems. Because of this, there appears to be an increasing trend toward shorter-term expatriate assignments.[9]

parent country nationals
employees from the home countries who are sent to work for their companies overseas

host country nationals
workers already living in the foreign or host country where the parent company is opening operation

third country nationals
employees from a new parent or host country who are being employed in a given foreign country

expatriates
employees who are working in countries other than their native countries

expatriate failure
when an expatriate does not complete his or her full expatriate assignment

Repatriation, the process that takes place when an expatriate employee returns home, can also present a multitude of problems. There is some evidence that the "culture shock" that employees face upon repatriation can be greater than the culture shock they initially faced when first going to work in a foreign country.

But, given the widespread use of expatriate staffing throughout the world, the benefits of this practice often strongly outweigh its costs and risks. Expatriate workers, as mentioned above, can bring skill sets that are unavailable in the local workforce, or that are complementary to what the local workforce has to offer. Third-country national expatriates, in particular, may represent a cheaper source of labor than other alternatives. Finally, expatriate assignments may provide very useful career development opportunities for employees, especially in today's increasingly global environment. To allow for further development, many large multinational corporations have been taking care to ensure that all interested employees (including female employees, who, as a group, have often been denied assignments of this kind in the past) are given expatriate opportunities.

What Are Training and Development?

Training involves providing employees with skills specific to the jobs they will be doing. For example, a U.S. company sending an employee to work for a few years in its Madrid, Spain office would likely ensure the employee receives training that includes Spanish language lessons. **Development** involves preparing employees for new future assignments or higher level positions. For instance, a company that has identified an employee with future managerial potential might send that employee to a three-week university-sponsored program to help develop the individual's decision-making and leadership skills.

Needs Assessment

Assessing company training and development needs in the international HRM context is directly related to company international strategic planning. For example, if General Motors Corporation is planning a new car manufacturing operation in Spain and intends to send executives from the United States to work in that location, it must be sure its executives have received some training in Spanish language and culture. If cultural norms and pension systems in a certain part of the world encourage relatively early managerial retirements (e.g., at age 55), the company must ensure it has developed a strong cadre of younger employees to step into these positions.

Moreover, corporations establishing operations in foreign countries, or thinking about doing so, must also focus on the potential training and development needs of the host country nationals it may employ. Interestingly, the Marriott Corporation, for example, that opened operations in former communist countries such as Poland, Hungary, and Romania, found that local host-country employees needed a lot of training in customer service and satisfaction. The free-market concept of pleasing customers in order to gain more future business and profits was never a part of business thinking in the former centrally-planned, communist economic structures. In sum, companies engaging in international operations must assess their employee training and development needs from a wide variety of perspectives.

Types of Training and Development

The types of training and development the company provides will differ depending upon the given situation. In some situations, for example, Internet-based training might be sufficient, while in other situations, more formal, in-person training and development programs may be required.

repatriation
process that takes place when the expatriate employee returns home

training
providing employees with skills specific to the job they are going to be doing

development
preparing employees for new future assignments or higher level positions

It is also important to note that training and development instructional styles differ considerably throughout the world. For example, in Japan, a lot of training and development is focused upon improving the group, with instruction addressed to small groups and testing focusing upon group questions and answers. In contrast, training and development programs in the United States typically center upon the individual, with individual assignments, readings, testing, and so forth. In some countries, such as the United States, it is often acceptable for different levels of employees to train together in a particular training and development program (i.e., to have upper- and mid-level managers together in the same program). Other countries are much more status conscious, and would find it inappropriate for employees from different levels of the organization to train together. Thus, in most Arab countries, for example, it would not be acceptable for upper and middle managers to train together in the same program.

Expatriate Needs in Training and Development

As mentioned earlier, special training and development needs are likely necessary for expatriates. A U.S. accounting firm sending accountants to London must ensure the accountants know about British accounting standards; perhaps the firm may prepare them to take a British licensing examination. It is also important for companies to realize that their foreign employees working in the United States may need training and preparation. Foreigners often expect life in the United States to resemble what they see in Hollywood movies or television shows, and are, therefore, not adequately prepared for the fact that life in the United States is different from what they've seen in television shows or movies.

ECONOMIC PERSPECTIVES Expatriates in Qatar

Qatar, a Middle Eastern Peninsula jutting into the Persian Gulf, is one of the richest countries in the world, and its citizens are among the wealthiest. Oil and gas revenues have made Qatar the second highest per-capita income country in the world. All Qataris receive first class government-provided health, educational, and other social benefits. That said, Qatari citizens are not generally a happy group.

Why are Qataris unhappy? They are unhappy because they have become second-class residents in their own land. Because of Qatar's incredible economic growth, it has had to import workers (expatriates) by the hundreds of thousands from all over the world. Today, Qatari citizens make up only 15 percent or about 240,000 people of the 1.6 million individuals living in Qatar. This demographic oddity has made nationals a minority in their own country, creating a sense of both victimization and privilege.

While Qatari citizens are very well "taken care of" financially, many complain that the best jobs and professional career opportunities are given to expatriate foreigners. Or, as a leading political science professor at Qatar University recently put it, "[t]he foreigners are crowding us out." Qatari citizens are becoming increasingly angry about a social contract that provides them financial and material comfort for not working, so long as they don't question the government's economic decisions about hiring multitudes of foreign workers.

QUESTIONS:

1. Why are Qatari citizens complaining about receiving a lot of material benefits without needing to work?
2. What are some possible solutions that Qatar's government can implement to provide more career opportunities for its citizens?

Source: Michael Slackman, "Affluent Qataris Seek What Money Cannot Buy," The New York Times, May 13, 2010, www.nytimes.com.

Robert Harding World Imagery/Alamy Limited

The bustling capital of Qatar, the city of Doha.

Performance Appraisal and Compensation

LO-3

Discuss performance appraisals and employee compensation issues around the world, including cultural differences, cost of living, and how expatriate issues are handled.

Performance appraisal involves the process of assessing employee performance. It has multiple purposes and repercussions for the individual and the organization. Perhaps most importantly (at least in the minds of many employees), a direct link between performance appraisals and compensation usually exists. Employees who perform well should receive higher rewards and compensation than those who poorly perform. While this concept may seem straightforward, determining compensation for workers in a variety of countries and cultures can be very complex.

Assessing Performance

One key purpose of performance appraisal is to provide employees with performance feedback. Performance assessment also helps identify areas for potential training and development. For example, if an employee's performance is negatively impacted by a lack of foreign language skills, it may behoove the company and the employee to ensure he or she gains more language skills.

In some jobs, performance is relatively easy to measure: a salesperson, for instance, has clear sales goals and they are either met or not met. In other jobs, however, measuring overall job performance might be much more difficult. For example, evaluating the performance of a research scientist working on a speculative multi-year cure for cancer may be extremely complicated. Other relevant issues include who conducts the performance appraisal ratings, and how feedback is presented. These and related issues may have considerable cultural dimensions affecting them.

Cultural Differences in Performance Appraisal

As mentioned earlier, cultural norms, rules, and legal differences help to influence how performance appraisals are conducted around the world. In Mexico, for example, the norm is not to give bad feedback at the outset, but instead to focus first upon something positive

performance appraisal
the process of assessing employee performance

and then tell employees how to improve.[10] In other countries, including the United States, it is not uncommon for employers to be much more direct with negative feedback than they are in Mexico.

Given the United States' strong individualistic (as opposed to collectivistic) culture, performance reviews are primarily conducted at the individual level, and emphasize individual strengths and weaknesses. Not surprisingly, however, in a more collectivistic culture like Japan, performance appraisals or reviews tend to focus upon group performance and upon how increased group harmony might be achieved. Japan, as mentioned earlier in the chapter, also has a strong future or long-term orientation. Reflecting this, it is not uncommon for Japanese performance reviews to focus upon how employees and groups can improve over the long term, and upon developmental training that might help improve the long-term productivity of the employees and groups.

Finally, it should be noted that in high power distance countries such as Russia, strict hierarchies are maintained in the performance appraisal system, and managers evaluate subordinate employees. In contrast, lower power distance countries such as Denmark and the Netherlands, may have more full-circle or 360-degree performance appraisal systems. In these systems, subordinates may evaluate managers along the same lines that managers evaluate subordinates.

Compensation and National Differences in Cost of Living

Compensating employees around the world presents a major challenge to today's multinational corporation because the cost of living dramatically differs around the globe. A 2008 survey using New York City, the most expensive city in the United States, as a benchmark receiving 100 index points, found 21 other cities in the world to be more expensive. For example, Moscow, Russia had 142.4 cost of living index points, meaning that it cost over 42 percent more to live in Moscow than in New York City. London, England had 125 points; Geneva, Switzerland had 115.8; and Beijing, China had 101.9. Major world cities that had an index lower than New York City included Berlin, Germany, which had 93.0 points and Mumbai, India, which had 90.3 points. Such differentials in cost of living are important factors considered by corporate HR and other executives when determining where to establish foreign operations, and the compensation necessary to provide employees with livable wages in different locations throughout the world.[11]

Moreover, there are also national differences in the forms of compensation employees receive in different parts of the world. In some countries, for example, a significant part of the compensation package may be in year-end bonuses. Generous housing allowances are not uncommon parts of the compensation package in certain parts of the world. Employee retirement benefits, and how much employees contribute to those benefits, also differ widely around the globe. International HR managers must make sure that the compensation packages they offer in a particular country are compatible with compensation in that country.

Expatriate Issues in Compensation

When it comes to establishing compensation packages for expatriate employees, a number of complicated special issues can arise. For example, should a computer programmer from the company's Mumbai, India office assigned to work in London, England receive as a base pay the rate for computer programmers in London? Or the potentially much lower rate for programmers in Mumbai? How do taxes, which may vary considerably between countries, figure into compensation levels? Should expatriate employees be paid in the currency of their home country, the currency where they are now living, or a mix of the two? (An employee from Mumbai, India living in London, England may have additional expenses at home in India which need to be paid in local currency.)

In compensating expatriates, most multinational companies use some variation of the **balance sheet approach**, which involves keeping the expatriate on the home country's salary structure (balance sheet) and also providing various additional allowances so that the expatriate can essentially maintain a home country standard of living while working elsewhere. Moreover, an increasing number of countries now split expatriate compensation between the home and current country of residence currencies. Thus, for example, the aforementioned computer programmer from India would continue to receive his or her Mumbai, India base salary and be kept on the Indian operation's balance sheet. The company will then add various allowances for cost of living, housing, education, taxes, and the like to this base salary so that the employee's overall standard of living while working in the company's London, England office will be in parity with his or her standard of living in Mumbai.

Executive Pay

Executive compensation has recently become a hot-button issue in countries throughout the world, as the global economic crisis that began in 2008 has heightened scrutiny of compensation differences between workers versus top managers. Such heightened scrutiny has also emanated from recent increased reporting requirements with respect to total top executive compensation through the world. For example, beginning in 2006, publicly traded German companies have been required to release to the public very detailed compensation information regarding top managers, and this information has fueled recent calls in that country to curb top executive pay.[12]

Moreover, the United Nations International Labor Organization's recent *World of Work Report* also focused on the internationally widening gap between executive and employee pay. Throughout the industrialized world, the *World of Work* report noted that pay disparities were far greater in some countries than others. For example, while the average CEO in the United States was paid 183 times more than the average employee, CEOs in the Netherlands earned only 73 times average employee wages, and in Australia 135 times.[13] In response to such concerns and recent global financial conditions, a number of major corporations throughout the world have recently frozen top executive salaries for the immediate future.

balance sheet approach
keeping an employee on the home country's salary structure and also providing additional allowances

REALITY CHECK LO-3

Have you received and/or given a performance appraisal in your job? In what ways did you think the appraisal was fair? Are there ways in which its fairness could have been increased?

International Trade, Labor Relations, and HRM

LO-4
Explain the interplay between international labor standards and free trade, the free trade and labor concerns presented by NAFTA, as well as the functions of labor unions.

As described in Chapter 1, certain countries such as China have a comparative advantage relative to a country such as the United States when it comes to abundant low-wage workers. Because of this, China is able to manufacture certain products at a much lower cost than other countries, and then export these products. As a result, U.S. consumers are able to enjoy relatively low prices at stores like Walmart and Target on certain Chinese manufactured products such as electronics and toys.

But, as also described in Chapter 1, ethical and other managed trade concerns have arisen, specifically regarding the abuse of workers in other countries around the world. For example, in Myanmar (Burma) it has been estimated that the military has forced as many

GFC Collection/Alamy

The headquarters of the United Nation's International Labor Organization in Geneva, Switzerland.

as 800,000 citizens to work as laborers—a condition equivalent to slavery. Paying many workers in this country almost nothing gives products a low cost advantage, but is it ethically acceptable for a country such as the United States to allow products of this kind to be sold within our borders? Would you be willing to pay slightly more for a shirt not manufactured under sweatshop or slave-labor circumstances?

The United Nations International Labor Organization (ILO), in particular, has engaged in considerable efforts to develop a set of minimal labor standards for all United Nations members as well as other countries. Such minimal standards involve prohibitions against slave or forced labor, restrictions on the use of child labor, certain basic job safety protections, and the right of workers to form labor unions, among other things. These United Nations global labor standards, however, have been very difficult to enforce. Instead, there has been a growing trend to try and establish labor standards for countries that have entered into bi- or multi-national free trade agreements such as the North American Free Trade Agreement (NAFTA), as discussed next.

The North American Agreement on Labor Cooperation (NAALC)

As discussed in Chapter 3, the North American Free Trade Agreement (NAFTA) established free trade between the United States, Canada, and Mexico. During the negotiation of this agreement there was considerable discussion about the low wages given to workers in Mexico, and the overall perceived lack of enforcement of labor rights in that country. Because of this situation, U.S. labor unions feared that companies would move American manufacturing jobs to Mexico. In the 1992 presidential election, Texas businessman Ross Perot ran as a third-party candidate predicting that NAFTA would create a "giant sucking sound" of U.S. jobs to Mexico.[14]

To address these concerns, proposals were raised during the NAFTA negotiations regarding a trilateral (United States, Canada, and Mexico) labor commission which would establish and regulate minimum labor standards for all three countries. All three countries, however, expressed considerable concern about the delegation of national sovereignty to a commission of this kind. The compromise was a special labor side agreement (i.e., an agreement outside the main NAFTA agreement), which would require each of the three countries to strongly enforce its own existing labor laws and regulations. Moreover, this labor side agreement, the NAALC, has an unusual enforcement mechanism whereby parties in any of the NAFTA countries can approach the labor department in their own country and file a formal complaint about labor standards in another NAFTA country. A formal complaint would then trigger intense mediation efforts among the countries to try and get better enforcement of the complained-about labor standards.

A major complaint about the NAALC process, however, is that it lacks any real "teeth." The issue was an important one during the 2008 U.S. presidential campaign, when Senator (now President) Obama pledged to try and renegotiate better labor standards in NAFTA, if elected.

International Labor Relations

As noted earlier in this chapter, a central tenet of the United Nations International Labor Organization's global labor standards is the right of workers to have freedom of association, form labor unions, and engage in collective bargaining. The idea is that individual workers, especially those who are less educated or skilled, are frequently relatively powerless vis-à-vis their employers and thus are potentially subject to unfair treatment. However, if these employees can group together and form a **labor union**, or a formal organization representing a group (or groups) of employees, these employees collectively may have the ability to stand against the employers, if necessary.

The primary goal of labor unions is to engage in negotiations with employers to attempt to reach **collective bargaining agreements**—agreements which comprehensively set forth employee terms and conditions of employment at a workplace or group of workplaces. Collective bargaining agreements or contracts typically establish work policies including rates of pay, amounts of vacation time, and seniority rights of employees. Agreements typically last three years, after which a new round of negotiations results in a new contract. Collective bargaining agreements also typically have extensive grievances procedures whereby employees with complaints regarding the administration of the labor contract can have their grievances effectively heard.

Jim West/Alamy

Leaders of the Ford Motor Company and the United Autoworkers Union shake hands on reaching a new collective bargaining agreement.

labor union
a formal organization representing a group or groups of employees

collective bargaining agreement
a contract comprehensively setting forth employee terms and conditions of employment at a given workplace or group of workplaces

Comparative Labor Relations

As pointed out earlier in the chapter, relations between labor and management are governed and conducted very differently around the globe. In Canada, as discussed earlier, labor relations primarily are regulated not by the national government, but rather by provincial governments such as the Province of Ontario. In contrast, in the United States, nearly all private sector labor relations activities are regulated by the federal government—specifically by the National Labor Relations Board (NLRB).

Canadian provincial regulations generally make it much easier for employees to form and join unions, and more difficult for employers to replace workers who go on strike, than federal regulations in the United States. Not surprisingly, labor unions have been considerably more successful in recent years in Canada than in the United States, and far more employees are covered by collective bargaining agreements in that country. Nevertheless, the relatively pro-union nature of Canadian labor regulations pales in comparison to their counterparts in Scandinavian countries. In Sweden, for example, union membership and collective bargaining participation rates are over 80 percent, compared to less than 10 percent for private-sector workers in the United States.

multi-employer bargaining negotiations in which a number of employers jointly bargain with a given labor union

co-determination employee representation on corporate boards of directors

Perhaps the most interesting labor relations system in the world exists in Germany. In Germany, **multi-employer bargaining**, or a situation in which a number of employers join together to bargain with a given labor union, is much more common than in the United States. **Co-determination**, however, the most prominent feature of German labor relations, allocates seats for employees on corporate boards of directors. Within larger German companies (those with more than 2,000 employees), employees and unions are allowed to select one-half of the members of German corporate boards of directors or supervisory boards. This allows workers a choice regarding corporate management—far greater than in any other country in the world.

ETHICAL PERSPECTIVES

Stranded by a Volcano

In mid-2010 Iceland's Eyjafjallajökull Volcano erupted, halting all air travel to and from Europe for about one week, and stranding thousands of air travelers. More than 40,000 Americans were stranded in Great Britain alone. Of those 40,000 plus stranded Americans that were members of a labor union, and covered by a collective bargaining agreement, their jobs were likely still very secure when they got home. Most collective bargaining agreements, as noted above, have employee grievance procedures, and also protect employees from discharge or discipline unless the employer has "good cause." Taking any action against an employee who has missed work due to a natural disaster would not fall into that category, but would be something the employee could "grieve" via the labor contract. The vast majority of American workers, however, are not covered by collective bargaining contracts or represented by labor unions. Instead, they are subject to the doctrine of "employment at will" that states they can be fired or disciplined by their employer for any reason and at any time. While one U.S. employment expert said she hoped employers "would do the right thing" under this "very compelling circumstance," there was nothing illegal about employers firing or disciplining employees who didn't show up to work because of the Icelandic volcano, particularly because many employers were looking to down-size their workforces due to the ongoing global recession.

QUESTIONS:

1. Why is refraining from disciplining employees the arguable "right thing" or ethical thing to do? Argue the opposite.
2. How does new technology such as remote email and skype impact stranded employees in different ways than twenty years ago?

Source: Liz Wolgemuth, "Why Stranded Workers Could Get Burned by the Volcano," April 20, 2010, Yahoo News, http://news.yahoo.com/s/usnews.

PaKos Photography/Alamy

The Eyajafalljokull Volcano in Iceland erupts.

SUMMARY

The deployment and management of human resources on a global scale has become an increasingly important part of international business. Cultural differences around the world play a critical role in how international HRM is conducted, as do legal and regulatory contexts such as a country's rules regarding immigration. Offshoring and outsourcing involve critical corporate decisions to move an organizational function to another country. This can be done via subcontracting a certain production function to a third party, or not. The market for human resources today is a global one, with employers facing strategic decisions regarding where to hire and where to deploy employees.

These and related factors directly affect how employees are paid, evaluated, and trained in different countries throughout the world. For example, today it may be possible for companies to use the Internet to "virtually staff" various operations. Special compensation packages may be necessary for employees who move houses in order to work in countries other than their native ones. Moreover, employee training and development styles differ in various countries. For example, training and development in the United States focuses upon the individual, while in Japan it focuses on the group. Performance appraisal systems vary widely in different national cultures as well.

In addition, there are considerable cultural differences in performance appraisal schemes throughout the world. In Mexico, for example, employers tend to be very gentle when providing employees with negative feedback. Also, there are different cultural norms throughout the world regarding executive pay, including offsetting worldwide costs of living.

International trade accords such as NAFTA are also having an increasing impact on the conduct of HRM in the United States. Finally, labor unions play a more prominent role in many countries around the world than they do in the United States. Germany, for example, is notable for allowing labor union officials to directly represent workers on corporate boards of directors.

KEY TERMS

outsourcing, *p. 270*
offshoring, *p. 271*
parent country nationals, *p. 272*
host country nationals, *p. 272*
third country nationals, *p. 272*
expatriates, *p. 272*
expatriate failure, *p. 272*
repatriation, *p. 273*
training, *p. 273*
development, *p. 273*
performance appraisal, *p. 275*
balance sheet approach, *p. 277*
labor union, *p. 279*
collective bargaining agreement, *p. 279*
multi-employer bargaining, *p. 280*
co-determination, *p. 280*

CHAPTER QUESTIONS

1. What are some of the potential problems global businesses face when they outsource or subcontract their manufacturing work to companies in other countries (e.g., a U.S. sneaker company outsourcing the manufacturing of its sneakers to a separate company in China or Vietnam)?

2. What are the pros and cons of using the Internet for the "virtual staffing" of corporate operations?

3. Why is it often very difficult for supervisors in any culture to provide employees with a negative performance appraisal?

4. If you were President of the United States and trying to negotiate better labor standards for NAFTA, what new provisions might you try and negotiate (at least from the U.S. perspective)?

MINI CASE: SICK LEAVE IN BELGIUM

Europe has had far more employees take time off as sick leave than the United States. In recent years, the average European worker annually took 11.3 days of sick leave, compared to an average of 4.5 days annually for the U.S. worker. Belgium, for example, is where employees in some sectors average as many as 35 days of sick leave per year.

Belgium also has the highest suicide rate in Western Europe, and about half of all Belgians on sick leave say they are suffering from clinical psychological depression. Belgium's sick leave compensation structure involves full pay for the first month, and then 80 percent of one's salary indefinitely. This generous policy also likely contributes to the proclivity of Belgian employees to take sick leave.

Recently, the Belgian government has been examining ways to cut down on the amount of sick leave employees are taking. Doing this, however, is proving difficult because only about 5 percent of the people who take sick leave can be proven to be "cheating" (i.e., people with absolutely no medical basis for missing work).

QUESTIONS:

1. Do you think Belgium's compensation structure for employee sick leave is too generous? If so, what could better compensation involve?

2. What are the difficulties in categorizing mental illness such as depression to constitute illnesses meriting sick leave compensation vis-à-vis more physically diagnosable illnesses such as the flu or cancer?

Mini Case based on John W. Miller, "Belgians Take Lots of Sick Leave, and Why Not, They're Depressed," The Wall Street Journal, January 9, 2009, p. A1, A6.

Point Counter-Point: Should Employees or Labor Union Representatives Have the Right to Seats on Corporate Boards of Directors?

As noted earlier in the chapter, German labor unions have the right to appoint one-half the members of corporate boards of directors or supervisory boards in large German corporations. In the United States, some collective bargaining contracts provide for a union representative (usually one out of fifteen board members) on corporate boards. Should union and/or employee representatives be allowed on corporate boards of directors?

POINT Union and employee representation on corporate boards helps companies better address their employees. Employees' grievances are heard, and employees with such representation are likely to be more sensitive to corporate needs for flexibility such as perhaps, the need to move some corporate operations to a lower cost location. Employee representation of this kind allows corporations to address the concerns of, perhaps, its most significant stakeholder group—its employees.

COUNTERPOINT Corporations should primarily be managed for the benefit of their owners and shareholders, not for the single stakeholder group of employees. Union and employee representatives on corporate boards have an inherent conflict of interest because they are seeking benefits for workers more than benefits for shareholders. Representatives that are on corporate boards should be there by way of the company's consent, as in a consensual labor contract, rather than being forced by the government to be included on the board, as in Germany.

What Do *You* Think?

Which viewpoint do you support, and why? Find several articles in nonpartisan publications that assess the effects of employee representation and/or the lack of representation.

INTERPRETING GLOBAL BUSINESS NEWS

1) Various governments recently have been considering placing limitations on top corporate executive pay and/or taxing corporate executive bonuses very highly (e.g., at a 70 percent tax rate). Will such limitations make it more difficult for corporations in those countries to attract top executive talent?

2) Recently, China adopted new workplace protection legislation known as the Labor Contract Law. This law makes it more difficult for businesses to dismiss employees. How do you think the recent economic global downturn has affected the enforcement of this new law in China and the protections it gives to China's 700 million workers?

3) When first elected President in 2008, Barack Obama appointed a strongly pro-free-trade U.S. Trade Representative, but also a U.S. Secretary of Labor who had expressed strong concerns about the impact of free trade on workers and labor. Why do you think he appointed cabinet officials with such opposing views? What positions do you expect each took during cabinet meetings?

4) Recent global economic slowdowns have caused many companies to cut back or consider cutting back their training and development budgets. What might the implications of such actions be, both in the short term and the long term?

PORTFOLIO PROJECTS

Explore your Own Case in Point: Understanding the Nature of your Company

After reading this chapter, you should be prepared to answer some basic questions about your favorite company.

1) Are any employees of your company represented by labor unions or covered by collective bargaining agreements? Are any of these employees working outside of the United States?

2) Does your company have any operations in places with collectivist cultures such as Taiwan, South Korea, or Latin America? How are its performance appraisal and compensation packages in these locations different from those in countries with individualistic cultures such as the United States and Britain?

3) Does your company employ expatriates in any overseas operations it might have? If so, what resources does the company provide to train expatriates before they go to the foreign location? Does the company also provide training or support for expatriates during the repatriation phase?

4) To what extent, or in what ways, does your company use the Internet for employee training and development?

Develop an International Strategy for Your Own Small Business: Hiring Employees Overseas

Assume that eventually you will need to hire employees to work in operations in your target country. Identify the types of employees that might work best for you in these operations: host-country nationals, parent-country nationals, or third-country nationals. Develop a plan that will identify and recruit employees, and then provide them with needed training and development.

CHAPTER NOTES

[1] Story based on Norimitsu Onishi, "Japan's Outcasts Still Want for Society's Embrace," New York Times, January 16, 2009, p. A1.
[2] T. L. Friedman, The World Is Flat: A Brief History of the Twenty-First Century. New York: Farrar, Straus & Giroux, 2005.
[3] OECD statistics, 2008, "www.oecd.org.statsportal."
[4] R. Schwartz, "Job Losses Pose a Threat to Stability Worldwide," The New York Times, February 14, 2009, p. A1; OECD Statistics, 2008, pp. 30–37.
[5] G. Hofstede, Culture's Consequences: International Differences in Work-Related Values. Beverly Hills, CA: Sage Publications, 1984.
[6] G. Keller, "French Businesses Loath to End 35-Hour Work Week," www.usatoday.com/news/world/2008-09-03-3294170250_x.htm, Associated Press, September 3, 2008.
[7] P. Saffo, "A Looming American Diaspora," Harvard Business Review, February 2009, p. 27.
[8] S. Fitch, "New Brittania," Forbes Magazine, May 21, 2007, pp. 136–138.
[9] R. L. Minter, "Preparation of Expatriates for Global Assignments: Revisited," Journal of Diversity Management 3, second quarter, 2008, p. 37–42.

[10] M. Gowan, S. Ibarreche and C. Lackey, "Doing the Right Things in Mexico," Academy of Management Executive 10 (1996), pp. 74–81.
[11] Mercer Cost of Living Survey, Worldwide Rankings, 2008, www.finrank.ie/costofliving.
[12] M. Walker and M. Esterl, "Germany Weighs Executive-Pay Curbs," The Wall Street Journal, November 13, 2008, p. A6.
[13] International Labour Organization, World of Work Report 2008: Income Inequalities in the Age of Financial Globalization, Geneva: International Labor Office, 2008, p. 17.
[14] The 1992 Campaign, Transcript of 2d Debate Between Bush, Clinton and Perot, The New York Times, October 16, 1992, p. 2, www.nytimes.com.

CH 12 Global Marketing

© C Miller Design/Getty Images

matt griggs/Alamy

After studying this chapter, you should be able to:

LO-1 Distinguish between marketing research and marketing intelligence systems.

LO-2 Distinguish between standardization and adaptation.

LO-3 Describe how new products are developed and how existing products are managed for international markets.

LO-4 Explain the four different methods of promoting international marketing products, and provide some advantages and disadvantages of each.

LO-5 Define channels of distribution and physical distribution, and indicate the role of each of these for marketing products internationally.

LO-6 Discuss the objectives and decisions involved in international pricing.

LO-7 Discuss aspects of customer service required for goods and services that are globally marketed.

CULTURAL PERSPECTIVE

Vinchel Must Learn to Market its Wines Internationally

Vinchel, a winery located in Chelyabinsk, Russia, in the southeastern part of the Ural Mountains, was founded in 1969. Anatoly Bondarev is Vinchel's current general director.

For its first two decades of business, the firm was owned by the state because Russia was a communist republic. Under the Soviet system, state planners determined how much and which types of wine the company could produce. The government decided which markets would be used for the company's output, so there was no need for Vinchel to design a marketing plan.

Then, in the early-1990s, Russia threw off Communism and the government no longer controlled companies. Bondarev and Vinchel's other executives were forced, for the first time in the firm's history, to develop a comprehensive program to market its wines in Russia, Western Europe, and the United States.

Bondarev realized that the focus upon marketing would require Vinchel to obtain more information about the wine market and the new environment in which the company now had to operate. He and his executive team would have to develop appropriate marketing strategies to achieve their sales goals. Understanding the basic concepts of effectively managing Vinchel's international customers was an additional responsibility that would now have to be assumed.[1]

Introduction

Companies need to engage in various marketing activities when serving their international markets. Marketing activities in international and domestic markets are often the same, but they are not usually performed in the same manner. The marketing efforts required for companies entering foreign markets for the first time can be daunting: they must begin to perform marketing activities in different ways to succeed in new and different locations.

Analyzing International Markets

Companies must conduct research on their foreign markets to decide in which countries to conduct business, and in which market segments in those countries they should target. In making these decisions, companies will often use market potentials and sales potentials. **Market potential** refers to the total number of units of a product that could possibly be sold by all companies doing business in a specific international market. For example, a company may arrive at a market potential for personal computers in Brazil by first assuming that 50 percent of 60 million households will purchase a computer within five years. Then, it might project that it could obtain five percent of this market potential, arriving at a **sales potential** of 1.5 million units (30 million × 5 percent = 1.5 million). Similar calculations could be made for individual market segments in foreign markets, such as by age, gender, income, and so on.

Kinds of Markets

There are three major markets within each foreign market that can purchase products and services and need to be analyzed: consumer markets, the industrial market, and government markets. Consumer markets in developed countries often account for over 50 percent of those nations' GDPs (gross domestic products) and purchase a wide variety of products, such as food, clothing, transportation, banking services, credit services, and entertainment. The industrial market includes companies that purchase products and services such as equipment and machinery, supplies, lubricants, consulting services, cleaning services, advertising, marketing research, raw materials, semi-finished products, and so on. Government markets often involve many of the same products and services as industrial markets, but are likely to emphasize major infrastructure projects (roads, bridges, dams, airports, ports, communication services, clean water) as well as health care services and military operations. In many emerging markets, especially sub-Saharan Africa, infrastructure projects have taken the lead. In countries, such as Belgium and the Netherlands, a large percentage of the national GDP is devoted to government expenditures. For many of these government outlays, foreign and domestic companies are required to submit competitive bids.

Information Required: Surveying International Demographics

Companies need to collect a wide variety of information about their foreign markets. It is important to know what a country's population is. A larger number of people usually means higher market potentials for many consumer products and services. In 2010, China was the world's most populous nation (1.3 billion people), followed by India (1.2 billion), the United States (310 million), Indonesia (243 million), Brazil (201 million), Pakistan (184 million), Bangladesh (156 million), Nigeria (152 million), Russia (139 million), Japan (127 million), and Mexico (112 million).

Marketers also will want to know about income levels in their proposed foreign markets. GDP is frequently used as an overall measure of a nation's income; it represents the total purchasing power in a nation. The United States had the world's highest

market potential
the total number of units of a product that could possibly be sold by all companies doing business in a specific international market

sales potential
the percentage of a market potential that a specific company expects to sell in a specific international market

EXHIBIT 12.1 PER CAPITA GDPS, 2010 (ESTIMATE)

Nation	Per Capita GDP
1. Quatar	$179,000
2. Liechtenstein	141,000
3. Luxembourg	83,000
4. Singapore	62,000
5. Norway	55,000
6. Brunei	52,000
7. United Arab Emirates	50,000
8. Kuwait	49,000
9. United States	47,000
10. Andora	46,000
11. Switzerland	43,000

Source: *2012 World Book Almanac.*

GDP in 2010 ($14.1 trillion), ahead of China ($8.7 trillion), Japan ($4.1 trillion), India ($3.6 trillion), Germany ($2.8 trillion), United Kingdom ($2.1 trillion), Russia ($2.1 trillion), France ($2.0 trillion), Brazil ($2.0 trillion), and Italy ($1.7 trillion).

GDP per capita is a frequently deployed measure of a nation's purchasing power. Exhibit 12.1 shows the ten nations with the highest per-capita GDPs. In contrast, there are many poor nations where GDPs per capita are less than $1,000 annually. Some of these include Somalia, Malawi, Burundi, Afghanistan, Tanzania, Liberia, and Sierra Leone.[2] Despite that many African countries are among the poorest in the world, some Indian companies believe that African markets will experience sizable growth in the next 15 years. These companies are looking to expand in this region because they are not discouraged by the continent's corruption, bureaucratic red tape, and large and poor populations. Indian companies are aggressively introducing inexpensive products to the African market.[3]

A measure of countries' incomes, which has become increasingly important in recent years, compares the average incomes of the wealthiest 20 percent of people in a nation to the average incomes of the poorest 20 percent. In general, the disparities between these two measures have been becoming larger.

Goldman Sachs estimates that the world's middle class—those with $6,000 to $30,000 in annual income—is growing by seven million per year and that, by 2030, another two billion people will be termed "middle class." And yet, some companies are beginning to target low-income people around the world. The late marketing consultant, C. K. Prahalad, observed in 2008 that "poor people, once mobilized and provided with value, can create tremendous wealth for business."[4]

The age of a nation's population is another important measure of interest to international marketers. Increasing life spans in many countries such as Japan and in Western Europe have resulted in aging populations, which have greater needs for such products and services like prescription drugs and health care facilities. In contrast, Gerber, a subsidiary of Switzerland's Nestlé, has been launching convenience foods, such as cheesy pasta and chicken and vegetables, for preschoolers (two- to four-years of age) in foreign markets.[5]

International marketers are also interested in ethnicity as another market variable. Strategic Global Communication developed long-distance telephone packages for immigrants in the United States who wanted to call their home countries. Some examples include Ecuadorians in New York City, Asians in San Francisco and Los Angeles, Mexicans in Los Angeles, and Filipinos in San Francisco.

Dinodia Photos/Alamy

A busy street in India where cows are allowed to roam freely because they are revered.

Whether a market is located in a rural or an urban area is another way of analyzing overseas markets. In most countries, urban dwellers have a higher per-capita income than those in rural areas. Urban dwellers typically purchase a greater level of non-subsistence products, while their rural counterparts are more concerned with buying subsistence products like food, clothing, and shelter. Urban dwellers usually are considered to be more "worldly" and "sophisticated." In some nations, such as Singapore, Hong-Kong, and Bermuda, 100 percent of its inhabitants are considered to be living in urban areas.

For some products, such as food, religion is an important discriminator. Muslims and Jews, for example, do not eat pork or pork products, and follow a number of other dietary restrictions. Hindus and followers of other religions in India do not eat beef or beef products. Among Christians, Roman Catholics avoid meat on Fridays during Lent, and Seventh-Day Adventists follow a vegetarian diet.

LO-1

Distinguish between marketing research and marketing intelligence systems.

Marketing Research vs. Marketing Intelligence Systems

Marketing research collects information at one specific time in order to help marketers make better decisions about their overseas markets. Personal interviews, mail surveys, and focus groups are commonly deployed methods to collect this type of information. Often, a marketing research study is prompted by information that a company's **marketing intelligence system** (MIS) provides. For example, a study analyzing why households have stopped purchasing a company's products (marketing research) may be initiated because a company's MIS has revealed that its market share has decreased in a particular foreign market. Thus, marketing intelligence systems collect information regularly over time about the overseas environment in which the company operates.

marketing research
information collected at one particular time

marketing intelligence system (MIS)
information collected regularly over time

One key component that determines which specific types of information are needed from an MIS are based upon the decisions marketing managers need to make in overseas markets. For example, the five most important executives for Mary Kay Cosmetics' European operations identified the following types of information as required from its marketing intelligence system for that part of the world:

1. The lay of the land with respect to packaging, marketing, and labeling.
2. Psychographic information about European women.
3. Socio-demographic information about European women.
4. Industry data-sales, trends by product category.
5. Specific perceptions of Mary Kay products and career opportunities.
6. Aspirations of women including career, family, learning, and other goals.
7. Employment opportunities for women and salary comparisons.
8. Success of other direct selling companies and specific details about their marketing and commissions plans.
9. Usage of skin care and makeup products.
10. Demographic profile of women by country.
11. Country market information (i.e. income, population, female population).
12. Daily financial information including sales, expenses, and so on.
13. Political risk analysis and its impact upon current business and start-up operations.[6]

Exhibit 12.2 provides an overview of the sources that could be used to give these Mary Kay executives the information they need to carry out their responsibilities and make decisions for the company's European operations.

REALITY CHECK LO-1

Visit a department store and identify some products that may indicate that foreign suppliers have done marketing research to serve the customers who frequent the store.

EXHIBIT 12.2 TYPOLOGY OF INFORMATION SOURCES FOR MARY KAY COSMETICS MARKETING INTELLIGENCE SYSTEM—EUROPE

TYPE OF INFORMATION	LOCATION OF INFORMATION	
	INTERNAL	EXTERNAL
SECONDARY	Financial/accounting data and reports Operating reports Salesforce's call reports and other sales reports	Periodicals Newsletter and bulletins Published reports Syndicated reports Databases Organizations Books, directories, encyclopedias, and handbooks
PRIMARY	Studies conducted by a company's marketing research department Company's salesforce and other employees Marketing databases	Trade shows, exhibits, and fairs Conventions and meetings Company's advertising agencies Company's channels of distribution Consultants

Source: Richard T. Hise and Richard Bartlett, "Developing a Marketing Intelligence System for Companies' European Operations: Mary Kay Cosmetics Experience," paper presented to Academy of Marketing Science Cultural Perspectives on Marketing Conference, Puebla, Mexico, September 2004.

LO-2
Distinguish between standardization and adaptation.

Making the Standardization and Adaptation Decision

The first and most important decision that a firm must make when entering foreign markets is the degree to which its marketing strategies for those international markets will be the same or different from those already being deployed in its domestic markets. A **standardization** approach signifies that the marketing strategies used in its international operations will be the same as those being used domestically. An **adaptation** approach means that the strategies will be different.

Standardization has an advantage related to cost. Because the existing domestic production, research and development (R&D), and marketing strategies can be employed, standardization avoids the expense of establishing new operations. Another benefit is that the standardization strategy can be quickly implemented because companies will not need to spend time developing new ways to market their products to foreign markets. While the adaptation strategy will be more costly than standardization, it has the advantage of obtaining higher sales because it recognizes the needs and wants of customers in non-domestic markets.

There are product and market factors in overseas markets that require U.S. firms to pursue an adaptation strategy. For example:

- Most of the world uses the metric system of measurement while the United States uses the English system.
- Electrical voltages differ in many countries than those that exist in the United States.
- Brazilians use doughnuts as a snack item whereas Americans tend to associate doughnuts with breakfast.
- French families tend to purchase smaller quantities of products, such as one or two cans of a soft drink, whereas Mexican families purchase in larger quantities (6-packs or 12-packs of soft drinks) because their families are larger in size than are those in France.

All aspects of the international marketer's marketing strategy are subject to the standardization and adaptation decision. This includes the product (physical properties, brand name, package, quality, warranty, etc.), promotion (personal selling, sales promotion, advertising, and publicity), distribution (channels of distribution and physical distribution), and pricing (initial price, price changes, and dealer margins).

Many companies do not use either a standardization or adaptation strategy but rather a compromise called **glocalization**. Glocalization involves standardizing when possible, and adapting when necessary.

standardization
marketing strategies used in international markets by a company that are the same as those used in its domestic market

adaptation
marketing strategies used in international markets by a company that are different from those used in its domestic market

glocalization
the marketing strategy which involves pursuing a standardization strategy in foreign markets when possible and an adaptation one when necessary

REALITY CHECK LO-2

Visit a supermarket, chain drugstore, or discount store (e.g., Target or Walmart) and examine several products from a foreign supplier. Do you see evidence of standardization, adaptation, or glocalization?

LO-3
Describe how new products are developed for and how existing products are managed in international markets.

Developing the International Product Mix

Companies have four options to consider when marketing their products overseas. They can sell the same domestic product overseas. They can modify products for different countries and regions. They can develop new products for foreign markets. Or, they can incorporate all product differences into one design and develop a **global product** suitable for most world markets.

Ford reintroduced its Fiesta economy car into the U.S. market in 2010; it was first marketed there in the late-1970s, but production was ceased after only two years because it was not selling well. Encouraged by the 12 million Fiestas sold in Europe, Asia, and Latin America, Ford decided to target the United States again. After a great deal of discussion, the company decided that the name "Fiesta" would be used around the world, while such alternatives as "Verve" were rejected. At $14,000, the Fiesta remains one of the cheapest cars on the U.S. market.[7] Meanwhile, the Indian firm, Tata Motors, has launched the "Nano," which will sell for $2,500 and offer 50 miles to the gallon.[8] The Nano is likely to have great appeal in areas of the world where average incomes are low: Latin America, Africa, and Asia. Whether the Nano will be sold in the United States has not yet been determined.

Developing New Products for International Markets

Most companies follow a defined set of steps when developing new products for overseas markets. First, they have to decide upon the sources of new product ideas that will be used, including internal sources (R&D, sales force, marketing research, employee suggestions, etc.) and external sources (customer suggestions, independent inventors, marketing consultants, etc.). From these sources, new product ideas will emerge and be evaluated against a set of variables the company feels are related to new product success. The most important of these variables are captured in Exhibit 12.3.

Those product ideas that are not rejected in this step are then subjected to **concept testing**, and the idea is presented to a small sample of the intended market to gauge its reaction. Ideas that succeed in this process are then moved to the **business analysis** step, where projections of potential revenues and profits are made. If these numbers are acceptable, the physical product is then developed.

One very important aspect of the development step is product design. Chrysler, for example, has used design as a way to differentiate its offerings from those of competitors. Design ideas are borrowed from art, architecture, fashion, and furniture. Some top designers make over $1 million annually and have access to the executive suite.[9]

global product
a product that can be sold in most world markets

concept testing
the step in the new-product development process in which the new product idea is presented to a small sample of the international market to gauge its reaction

business analysis
the step in the new product development process in which projections of potential revenues and profits for a potential new product are made

EXHIBIT 12.3 CHARACTERISTICS AFFECTING RATE OF ADOPTION & LEVEL OF ADOPTION FOR NEW PRODUCTS

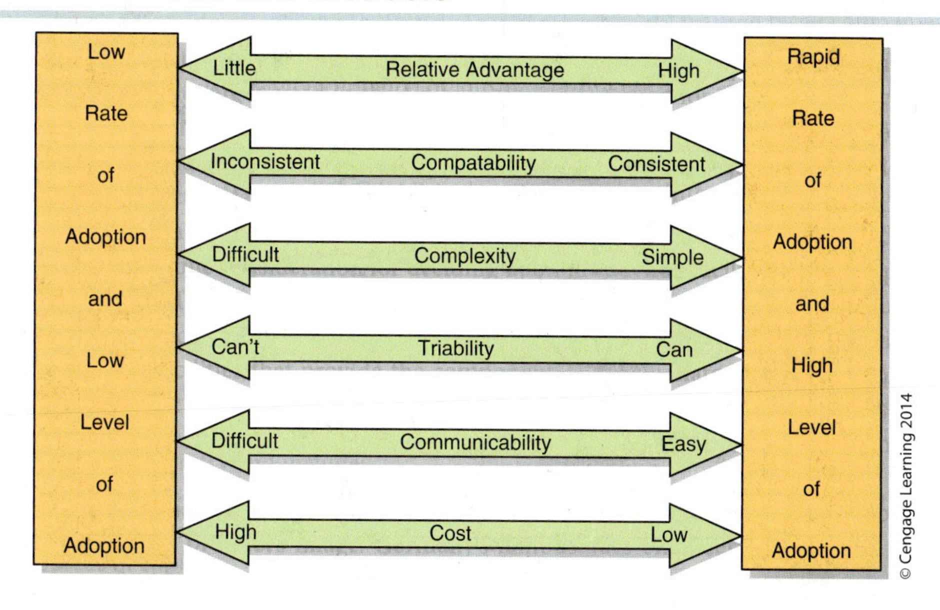

Following development, new products are subjected to **market testing**, the major purpose of which is to develop the most appropriate marketing mix for the new offering. In the last step, **commercialization**, the new product is manufactured, the marketing strategy is finalized, and the product is introduced to the foreign market.

Managing Existing Products

The **product life cycle (PLC)** is a useful tool for managing products after they have been introduced to foreign markets. Exhibit 12.4 shows that the lifetime of a product can be divided into four stages. In the introduction (first) stage, sales gradually increase, as do profits, which often are losses in the early part of the first stage. Sales and profits rapidly increase in the growth (second) phase; profits reach a maximum during the latter part of the growth stage, then begin to taper off. In the maturity (third) stage, sales reach a peak and then begin to decline as profits continue to decline. The decline (fourth) phase is aptly named because both sales and profits have continuously declined.

The PLC helps international marketers decide when to modify their marketing strategy. For example, prices will usually need to be reduced in the maturity phase because of the large number of additional competitors. Promotion will need to be increased during the growth and maturity stages because of a desire to begin reaching mass markets and the influx of more competitors.

Once products reach the decline phase, they need to be considered for elimination. Companies generally do a poor job of **product elimination (PE)**. Many do not have formal PE programs, putting together crash programs only when products get into trouble. Companies that have PE efforts usually have not put it in writing and eliminate too few products, leaving many poorly-performing products to drag down sales and profits. Products that have not achieved company-established goals of sales, profit, and market share become primary candidates for elimination.

market testing
the step in the new-product development process in which a company will develop the marketing mix for a new product

commercialization
the last step in the new-product development process in which the new product is manufactured, the marketing mix is finalized, and the product is introduced to the foreign market

product life cycle (PLC)
a depiction of the sales and profits for a new product over its life time

product elimination
a formal, written procedure to determine which of a company's products should be dropped

Where to Locate Research and Development Facilities

Companies have two options where they may locate their research and development (R&D) facilities: having one facility in the home country, or one facility in the home country and one or more additional facilities in the foreign markets.

With one location in its home country, a firm can reduce R&D costs and exert more control and coordination over the R&D program. However, there are several advantages of locating R&D facilities in foreign countries.

EXHIBIT 12.4 THE PRODUCT LIFE CYCLE

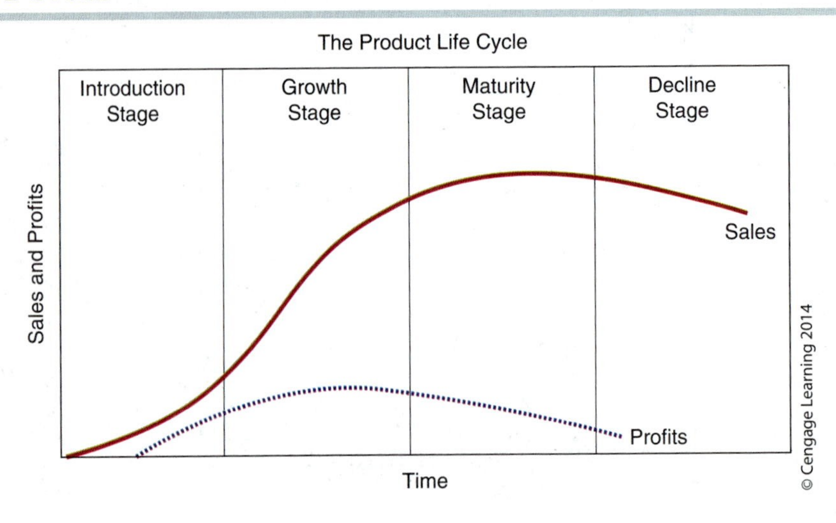

One advantage is that the multinational corporation (MNC) can use the intelligence of foreign scientists and engineers. For example, many of the Nobel Prize winners in physics, chemistry, physiology, and medicine have come from the United Kingdom, Germany, Switzerland, France, Sweden, Norway, and Japan. Another advantage is that new products developed overseas are more likely to be attuned to the company's overseas markets. Often, the technology developed overseas can be transferred back to the home country; Ford's European R&D operations, for example, have been credited with the technology that was used in the Fiesta when it was sold in the United States.

Increasingly, companies are finding that products originally developed for emerging markets can be successfully sold in developed markets. This strategy is the reverse of the traditional model, in which products originally developed and marketed in developed countries are then sold in emerging markets. General Electric, for example, first developed a low-cost electrocardiograph machine for doctors in India and China. These machines are now being sold for $250,000 in the United States to primary-care doctors, rural clinics, and visiting nurses. Nestlé had success with its Maggi noodles in South Asia; subsequently they were introduced in Australia. Microsoft, Nokia, and Procter & Gamble are also adapting this **reverse strategy**.[10]

The United States has several geographical areas well known for technology, including the Research Triangle in North Carolina, the I-28 corridor in Massachusetts, and Silicon Valley in northern California. Such areas exist in foreign countries, too; France, for example, has the Sophia Antipolis research park near Nice as well as the Polygone Scientifique and many other high-tech centers in the area around Grenoble.

Sam Dao/Alamy

Street vendors are common in Asia, the Middle East, and Latin America. In some cases, they sell counterfeit products.

Product Counterfeiting

One sinister aspect of product development is the practice of counterfeiting. U.S. companies lose billions of dollars in revenues each year because companies in foreign countries copy U.S. products and sell them as "American" products without the U.S. marketer receiving any compensation. In addition to the lost revenue, there is the possibility that the "knock-off" will be so inferior to the U.S. product that the U.S. firm's image will be tarnished in locations where the counterfeit has been sold.

For example, Chinese counterfeiters have cut into Sara Lee's sales of Kiwi shoe polish by 20 percent in Africa. Sara Lee switched labels in order to combat the problem, but they were quickly matched by the counterfeiters. New package sizes were duplicated in six months. A package with a deeper rim was copied in six months.[11]

As another example, authorities in Southeast Asia and other developing countries have been frustrated in their attempts to stop the trade in counterfeit prescription drugs. Packaged to look identical to legitimate drugs, these formulations are ineffective in treating the diseases and conditions (e.g., malaria) for which they are sold. What is worse, some contain small amounts of the actual drug which, over time, can build drug resistance in the organisms that cause or spread the disease.[12]

REALITY CHECK LO-3

Visit a grocery supermarket, chain drug store, or discount store (such as Walmart or Target) and choose 15 different products. Check the labels to see where they have been made. How many were manufactured in foreign countries?

reverse strategy
development of a new product first for emerging markets then selling it to developed markets

LO-4

Explain the four different methods of promoting international marketing products, and provide some advantages and disadvantages of each.

Developing the International Promotion Mix

The international marketing manager has four major methods that can be used to promote products and services in international markets: advertising, personal selling, sales promotion, and publicity. Each has advantages and disadvantages, which must be considered by the marketing manager when deciding upon the promotion strategy. Each option must be evaluated with regard to how likely it will achieve various promotion objectives, such as generating sales, increasing awareness of the product or service, reminding customers to purchase the product or service, or increasing the number of purchases.

Advertising

Major advertising media frequently used in international markets include television, radio, newspapers, magazines, and direct mail. In general, advertising reaches large audiences at low cost per contact.

Television advertising is being used more frequently because more people own television sets, especially in emerging markets. International marketers must be aware of legal restraints that regulate television advertising in host countries. For example, in some European nations, ads disparaging competition are not allowed.

Radio is an effective medium in countries such as the Philippines where television set ownership is low and a large percentage of the population lives in rural areas distant from major cities.

Residents of some countries are very avid readers of newspapers. In China, for example, men gather daily in tea shops, share various newspapers with each other, and discuss the news. Some business newspapers, such as *The Wall Street Journal*, have different editions for different parts of the world (Europe and Asia). One major advantage of newspaper ads is that they have a low cost per contact.

Magazines can be directed to consumers and business audiences, and are directed to more focused markets than newspapers. While some magazines for business audiences are general in nature (*Forbes, Fortune*, and *BusinessWeek*), others are targeted to specific industries (**vertical publications**) or to specific jobs existing in a number of industries (**horizontal publications**).

Direct mail is the most focused of advertising media; it can be directed to very specific target markets, like retirees over 70 years of age who live on the Costa del Sol in southern Spain.

Personal Selling

Personal selling is considered a very effective method to generate sales in international markets, especially with business audiences. Because it involves direct, face-to-face contact with foreign business persons, it encourages active participation and feedback from the prospects in the selling process. One disadvantage of personal selling is its high cost per contact: by some estimates, a sales call on an international prospect may have an average cost of $2,000.

One major decision that sales managers must make is whether to use expatriates or locals as sales personnel. Vivek Gupta, who lives in a Delhi, India suburb with his wife and two children, is an example of the latter. A graduate of an engineering college in India, Mr. Gupta works as a sales rep for IBM in India. One of his biggest sales involved convincing the telecommunications company, Vodafone, to allow IBM to handle everything from its customer service to finances—a $600 million contract.[13]

vertical publication magazine that target specific industries

horizontal publication magazine that target a specific job in various industries

Sales Promotion

Contests and sweepstakes, coupons, end-aisle displays in stores, sponsorships, and trade shows are examples of the most widely-used sales promotion techniques in foreign markets.

In the United States, companies spend approximately twice as much on sales promotion as on advertising. A similar pattern is occurring in other developed countries.

Several reasons explain the increasing popularity of sales promotion. Perhaps most significant, sales promotion can produce tangible benefits (such as increased sales dollars) in short periods of time. Because brand managers tend to be compensated for results achieved in the short term, they favor sales promotion over advertising because the results from an advertising campaign are often more difficult to measure and may take several years to be realized.

Sponsorships are increasingly important. In the United States, Anheuser-Busch, PepsiCo, General Motors, Coca-Cola, McDonald's, and Ford are some of the big spenders for sponsorships. European countries also have been placing more emphasis upon sponsorships, which has become more apparent in sports such as soccer and automobile racing. However, the financial and credit crisis that began in late-2008 has led to many companies trimming their sponsorship budgets.

Trade shows are an extremely popular tool for marketing products in foreign countries, especially in Europe and Asia. Hong Kong recently added millions of additional square feet of exhibit space. The largest and most well-known trade show in the world annually occurs in Hannover, Germany. However, not all trade shows require huge amounts of space and are dominated by large companies.

Companies that exhibit their products at trade shows overseas enjoy several benefits. Products are available for visual inspection and trial by foreign companies that may be interested in purchasing them. Exhibit-booth personnel are available to answer questions. Competitors can be monitored. Many visitors to trade shows are specifically interested in viewing new products. Exhibitors often can sell thousands, or even millions, of dollars' worth of their products at one trade show. In order to benefit the most from trade shows overseas, companies must notify customers and prospects in advance where and when they will be exhibiting. At the trade show, an effort should be made to attract visitors to the booth. One graphic arts company would make popcorn at its international trade show booth; the smell would draw companies to the booth—and they would be given a free bag while the exhibitor pitched its services. It is important for companies to collect information from visitors to the exhibit, including industry and company name, names of the individuals and their titles, contact information, potential interest in purchasing

ciapix/Shutterstock.com

Auto racing sponsorships are common in the United States, Europe, and Asia.

the exhibited product, price that might be paid, and possible quantities that might be purchased. Then, after the trade show, the exhibiting company's sales force should call upon the best prospects.

Publicity

Publicity refers to stories about a company, its products or services, and its executives that appear in media such as newspapers, magazines, television, radio, and on the Internet. While no direct payment is made to the media, large companies that conduct business overseas have public relations departments that attempt to influence media to positively report about them. Companies do not exert direct control over media, especially those in overseas countries, so success is not always guaranteed. In fact, it is not unusual for media to report negatively about foreign companies conducting business in host countries, as occurred during the BP Deepwater Horizon oil spill in the Gulf of Mexico in 2010. When this happens, companies' public relations departments must combat these stories if they are false. If they are true, firms need to take immediate, remedial actions in order to cope with the problem, and decide how their public relations departments will inform the media about solutions.

Publicity provides a number of benefits. It helps firms to prospect for new customers, paves the way for sales calls (a favorable press release being sent to prospects ahead of a sales call), helps sell minor products, and stretches the promotional budget. The most important benefit is that favorable stories provide objective, unbiased, third-party endorsement for a company. This is highly desirable in the eyes of foreign customers and prospects who may be skeptical of doing business with an overseas vendor.

REALITY CHECK LO-4

Look at the advertisements in an issue of a business magazine (e.g., Forbes, BusinessWeek*) or newspaper (e.g.,* The Wall Street Journal*). How many of them are from companies based in foreign countries? How well do the ads appeal to potential customers in the United States?*

LO-5
Define channels of distribution and physical distribution, and indicate the role of each of these for marketing products internationally.

Developing the International Distribution Mix

International distribution includes two major aspects: channels of distribution and physical distribution. Each needs to be effectively performed if the international marketer wants to be successful.

Channels of Distribution

indirect strategy
the use of channels of distribution to market products and services to international markets

direct strategy
bypassing channels of distribution by using marketing and sales offices located in foreign countries

Companies that conduct business in overseas markets have two options when it comes to channels of distribution. They can use distribution channels that are located in foreign markets, which is called an **indirect strategy**; or they can bypass those channels of distribution and market their products and services through marketing or sales offices that they establish and maintain in the foreign markets served, called **direct strategy**.

The indirect strategy, using channels of distribution existing in the foreign location, offers several advantages. Channels can introduce products into international markets more quickly than the company can by using a direct strategy. Channels often have excellent knowledge of foreign markets. Unlike the direct strategy, which requires recruiting and training a sales force for the marketing or sales office, the indirect strategy does not require an up-front investment. If channels of distribution are paid on commission, such as 10 percent of sales, the firm does not incur a cost until the channel sells the marketer's product.

There are, however, some disadvantages in using channels of distribution. Channels frequently carry competitive products, meaning that they may not devote much attention to the marketer's products. Using channels means that the company relinquishes control over much of the marketing effort, whereas a direct strategy allows a firm to maintain control over the marketing effort—the major reason why firms elect the direct strategy.

A company that is beginning to sell to overseas markets will often elect to use channels of distribution. As its business grows, it may conclude that the indirect approach may be more costly than a direct one. In order to find out, it will calculate the sales volume above which the total cost of an indirect approach will exceed that of a direct strategy. Suppose a company is paying a channel company a 10 percent commission on sales. If it believes that its investment cost for the direct option will be $200,000 and that the sales force would be paid a commission of six percent of sales, the fo1lowing formula can be used to calculate the level of sales at which the channel should be supplanted by the company's own sales force:

$$0.10X = \$200{,}000 + .06X$$
$$X = \$5 \text{ million}$$

At a sales volume exceeding $5 million, it would be less expensive to employ a direct strategy; under $5 million of sales, the direct strategy would be more costly. For example, at a sales volume of $6 million, the cost of the direct strategy would be $560,000 ($200,000 + 0.06 × $6 million), whereas the cost of the indirect strategy would be $600,000 ($6 million × 0.10).

Agents and distributors are the two major kinds of channels of distribution that international marketers can use. An **agent** acts on behalf of a company in a foreign market, and will be compensated by a commission on the volume of sales achieved. The agent makes a profit if the commission is greater than the costs incurred in selling the client's products.

A **distributor** purchases products from the company doing business in international markets and, in turn, resells them to other buyers. Distributors make a profit if they can sell the product at a price higher than what was paid for the products, plus the costs involved in reselling them.

Physical Distribution

Physical distribution refers to a company's storage and transportation operations used in moving its products to their foreign markets. Storage involves the use of warehouses for a company's products, either while they are retained in the home country or until they are transported to overseas markets. Sometimes products will also be stored in warehouses in the host country until purchased by international customers.

When a company decides to begin selling its products overseas, it encounters a new set of variables that affect its physical distribution operations. In some countries, such as Italy and Japan, there will be more distribution layers than in the United States. Often, the wholesalers and retailers constituting these layers will be small, inefficient operations. These factors result in more complicated and costly physical distribution operations. Poor logistics infrastructures are another challenge in many foreign countries: bridges, tunnels, roads, ports, railroads, and airports may be of inferior quality. Foreign buyers are more likely to accept longer delivery times than domestic customers, but once the buyer and seller agree upon delivery dates, buyers expect deliveries to be on time. Because buyers may be separated from sellers by thousands of miles—making it difficult to address the various problems that may arise—international buyers demand that orders received be complete (no items missing), accurate (the correct products are received), and in good condition (not damaged).

agent
a channel of distribution that represents a company in a foreign market and is paid by commission

distributor
a channel of distribution that purchases products from a company doing business in a foreign market and then resells them to other buyers

physical distribution
storage and transportation operations that are used in moving products to a foreign market

The greater distance required for international shipments requires sellers to place more emphasis on the package designed to protect products in transit. The greater distances also increases the logistics costs for international shipments. Whereas truck and rail shipments dominate domestic shipments, air and water are the most important for international shipments. Shipments by air account for only 1 percent of all international shipments, but represent 20 percent of their value. High-value perishable items and those that need to reach customers quickly, such as cut flowers, personal computers, and machine parts, are examples of goods that are typically transported on airplanes. Giant-sized container ships and oil tankers move large quantities of products to international buyers at low per-unit costs but at a much slower pace than shipment by air. Cargo ships have frequently been seized by pirates in the Gulf of Aden and the Indian Ocean, which has been a growing problem and cause of concern for businesses. The International Maritime Organization reported "a total of 135 attacks [in this region] during 2008, resulting in 44 ships having been seized by pirates and more than 600 seafarers having been kidnapped and held for ransom."[14]

Companies selling products overseas often must engage the services of a **freight forwarder**. Freight forwarders act as agents for companies shipping products to international customers. They arrange for moving products to domestic ports or airports, negotiate with ships or airlines to transport products, expedite clearing customs in both the home country and the host country, negotiate storage arrangements and, most importantly, complete all the confusing and time-consuming documentation (paper work) needed for an overseas shipment.

An important development in international physical distribution is **containerization**, in which shipments are placed in trailer-sized containers (usually 40×8×8 feet), which can be moved from one type of transportation (truck, train, airplane, or oceangoing vessel) to another type without needing the contents to be unloaded and reloaded (**intermodal transport**). Huge container cranes allow heavy containers to be loaded on or off ships without capsizing them. Containerization reduces handling costs, spoilage, and pilferage.

Physical distribution is a key component in a company's international operations. Didier Chenneveau was hired in 2008 by LG Electronics, the giant-sized, global South Korean electronics firm, "to deal with the company's chaotic physical distribution system." Mr. Chenneveau was attempting to merge LG's 10 warehouse-management systems, five transportation operations, and four computer program's inventory tracking systems into one global system.[15]

freight forwarder
agents for companies shipping products overseas who are chiefly involved with physical distribution activities and documentation

containerization
shipping products to overseas markets in trailer-sized containers

intermodal transport
international shipments using different modes of transportation

s_oleg/Shutterstock.com

Containers facilitate the use of intermodal shipments to overseas customers.

REALITY CHECK LO-5

Observe traffic on a major interstate highway or freight rail line near where you live or work. If you can, also visit the docks at a major ocean, lake, or river port, and observe the unloading and loading operations on cargo ships. Pay particular attention to the movement of containerized freight. Can you tell if any shipments are from overseas?

Developing the International Pricing Mix

LO-6

Discuss the objectives and decisions involved in international pricing.

Developing pricing objectives for international markets, setting prices in international markets, addressing the issue of dumping, and setting transfer prices are the major aspects of a company's international pricing strategies. These are important decisions because they affect companies' sales, costs, and profits obtained in overseas markets.

Pricing Objectives

Determining a company's international pricing mix involves consideration of four major objectives (see Exhibit 12.5).

Performance objectives involve bottom-line goals such as net profit, return on investment (ROI), market share, and penetration.

Prevention objectives can be used to keep competitors out of a foreign market—usually by low prices which competitors have difficulty matching—or deterring scrutiny by home and host-country governments. Both low and high prices can cause governments to analyze what prices are being set in foreign markets.

Maintenance pricing objectives are designed to keep the status quo: maintaining the same competitive landscape or maintaining favorable dealer relations (the margins dealers receive, the effort they put into selling products, etc.).

The fourth pricing objective is a survival objective. Sometimes a pricing strategy must be used in order to allow a company to survive in an international market. Mazda, for example, encountered this situation when its cars were first introduced into the U.S. market in the 1970s. Because its innovative rotary engine was not performing well, Mazda's sales

EXHIBIT 12.5 PRICING OBJECTIVES FOR INTERNATIONAL PRODUCTS AND SERVICES

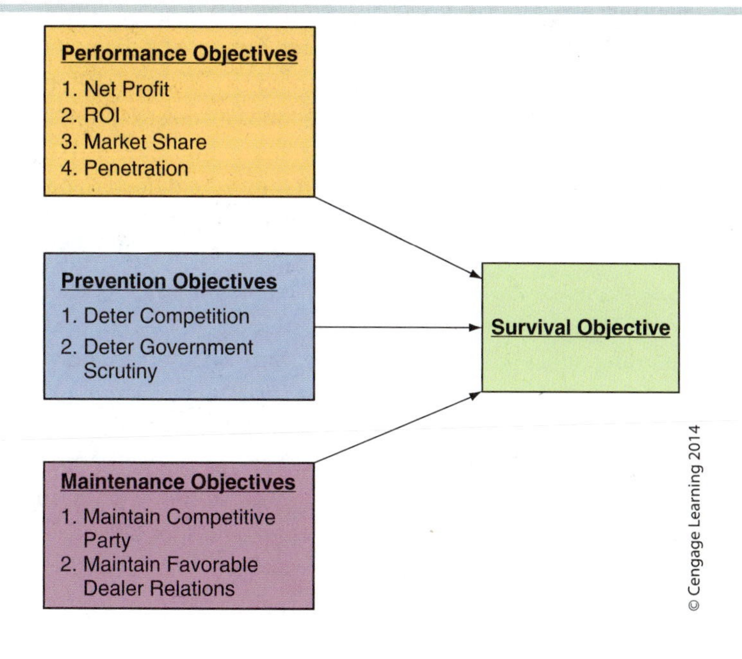

were so disappointing that its survival in the largest auto market in the world was doubtful. Mazda used steep price cuts, in the form of rebates, to both dealers and consumers, to buy time to retool the faulty engine. This pricing strategy worked as Mazda remained in the U.S. market, the engine was revamped, and reintroduced. Today, Mazda, has a strong position in the United States.

Setting Prices in International Markets

Once pricing objectives have been established, a company will be faced with the task of setting specific prices in its various international markets. Factors that must be considered include:

- costs;
- attractiveness of competitive products and their prices;
- how competitive the product is;
- how much marketing support (promotion budget, level of customer service, number of sales people selling the product, etc.) the product will get; and
- what the demand will likely be.

dumping
a price in a foreign market that undercuts the prices of companies competing there

gray marketing
unauthorized importers reselling a manufacturer's product in the manufacturer's domestic market at a price less than what the manufacturer charges in that domestic market

One approach to setting prices is to charge the same price in the foreign market as in the domestic market. This approach recognizes the fixed and variable costs associated with products. Often, a price will be set that includes these costs and the marginal costs (transportation, storage, and promotion) required to market the product overseas. A market differentiation approach also recognizes costs, but places a greater emphasis upon the demand that exists for products at various prices.

Dumping

A company that sets a price in a foreign market that undercuts the prices of competitive companies (especially host-country firms) may be accused of **dumping** (see Exhibit 12.6).

ETHICAL PERSPECTIVES

Gray Marketing Involves Ethical Issues

Gray marketing (also called "parallel importation") refers to unauthorized importers reselling a manufacturer's product in the manufacturer's domestic market at a price less than what the manufacturer charges in that domestic market. Although consumer products are most likely to be involved, there are instances where high-cost capital goods, such as machinery, have been re-imported into domestic markets.

Assume a U.S. manufacturer of men's shirts sells them in the U.S. market for $20 but charges $14 in Asian markets. A distributor not in the manufacturer's channels of distribution system buys the shirts for $14, then resells them in the United States for $18, thus causing the U.S. manufacturer to lose sales in its home market while the gray marketer makes a profit if the costs of selling in the manufacturer's domestic market is less than $4 ($18 - $14).

Gray marketers justify their actions in a number of ways. They claim that the opportunity for them to make a profit would not occur if the manufacturer was not overcharging its domestic customers. They argue that their actions increase competition and that the purchaser in the domestic market enjoys a lower price than they would need to pay if they bought from the manufacturer.

Manufacturers object to gray marketing stating that their images can be tarnished because their products are sold at lower prices, and the importers may not offer the same guarantees and warranties as the manufacturers. Another argument is that the gray marketer is getting a "free ride" on the manufacturer's investments in R&D and promotion. Manufacturers also allege that gray marketing often occurs because distributors in foreign countries "divert" some of the manufacturer's products to gray marketers.

EXHIBIT 12.6 FUJI FILM ACCUSED OF DUMPING IN THE U.S. MARKET

In the late 1990s, Kodak was attempting to recover from poor operating results. The company, led by George M.C. Fisher, appeared to be on the right track until it had to confront steep price cuts in the U.S. domestic market unveiled by its major competitor, Japan's Fuji Film. Fuji cut prices as much as 25 percent to 50 percent compared with what it charged in Japan—resulting in an increase of sales for Fuji and a drop in sales of 11 percent for Kodak in the U.S. market. Additionally, Kodak's market share dropped on its home turf, a situation made worse by the size of the market in the United States, which decreased due to heavy purchases by consumers of disposable cameras. Industry analysts predicted that within two years, Fuji's success in the United States would enable it to wrest the Number 1 spot from Kodak. In 1997, Kodak's global market share was 40 percent, compared with 35 percent for Fuji.

Kodak responded to Fuji's pricing strategies by accusing the Japanese firm of dumping. Fuji had already lost a dumping case in 1994, when Kodak convinced the U.S. government that Fuji was selling photo paper in the United States at one-fourth of the price it charged in its home market. Fuji invested $1 billion in new manufacturing facilities in Greenwood, South Carolina, consisting of a paper plant operation and a color film plant that started production in late 1997.

Kodak maintained that Fuji's dumping strategy was aided by Fuji's near monopoly in the Japanese market, where it had a 70 percent market share, giving it solid control of distribution and pricing.

Fuji countered Kodak's claims with the explanation that it does not compete in the U.S. market solely on price; it emphasized its high quality film that was increasingly successful with professional photographers, and the heavy use of free samples.

Source: Geoffrey Smith, "A Dark Kodak Moment," BusinessWeek, August 4, 1997, pp. 30–31.

A complaint may be lodged with the World Trade Organization because firms bringing the charge feel that they are losing sales and market share so badly that the dumper will be able to force them out of the market. Sometimes dumping is facilitated by the home country providing subsidies to companies that are dumping. For example, bricks from Iran have flooded Iraq, selling for about one-third less than Iraqi-made bricks. Iran subsidizes its brick manufacturers by providing low-priced fuel and electricity as well as substantial tax breaks.[16]

Two pricing strategies will often trigger allegations of dumping: (1) if the home-country firm sets a price in the foreign market below what it charges the domestic market; and (2) if the price is above what it domestically charges, but below the marginal cost needed to move the product overseas and sell it there.

Transfer Pricing

Many firms, especially large MNCs, have overseas subsidiaries to which they will sell products; the subsidiary, in turn, will resell the product. The prices a company charges its overseas subsidiaries, known as **transfer prices**, come under close scrutiny by taxing authorities in both the home country and the host country. These bodies often allege that a transfer price is set not to maximize profits but to minimize taxes. In order to deal with this possibility, taxing authorities often stipulate that the prices charged must be an **arms length price**, that is, a price that the overseas market is willing to pay.

REALITY CHECK LO-6

Using the Internet, research the prices of several products in one or more foreign countries and compare them to their prices in the home country where the goods are produced. What factors do you think determine the foreign prices? Do you think any of the prices are artificially high or low in one country or another?

transfer price
a price a company charges its overseas subsidiaries

arms length price
a price that an overseas market is willing to pay

LO-7

Discuss aspects of customer service required for goods and services that are globally marketed.

Developing the International Customer Service Mix

Providing greater levels of customer service to foreign customers is becoming a more important responsibility for international marketers. Companies that are considering purchasing from a vendor located in a foreign country will often make a choice based upon their perceptions of the vendor's willingness and ability to perform various services for them. And, for the same reason, current foreign customers are likely to become more loyal.

The emphasis that foreign companies place upon customer service is largely driven by the fact that there may be thousands of miles between them and their overseas vendors. In addition, as products and prices have become more similar, foreign prospects and customers will look at other factors to make a purchase decision. Often, the deciding variable will be the customer service that will be provided.

What kind of customer service is important to overseas buyers? Examples include deliveries (on-time and accurate), installation of equipment and machinery, problem solving, explaining and honoring warranties, repairs, accepting returns, providing emergency shipments, shipping products that are already assembled, handling documentation for exports and imports, and consistency of the order-cycle length.

How important is customer service compared to products and prices? According to extensive research by the Forum Corporation, "When the all-important issue of customer service is examined, it has been estimated that customers are five times more likely to switch vendors because of perceived customer service problems than for price or product

ECONOMIC PERSPECTIVES Toyota's Safety Recalls

In 2009-2010, Toyota was forced to recall millions of its automobiles from around the world due to significant safety problems. Its president, Akio Toyoda, and other executives were required to appear before the U.S. Congress to explain how they would deal with the situation in the United States. Many reasons have been offered to explain Toyota's problems. It had veered away from its focus upon customer satisfaction and emphasis on making improvements and, instead, pushed to increase its worldwide market share from 11 percent to 15 percent.

Most experts pointed to problems Toyota experienced with its suppliers, which can be divided into three categories. Tier-one suppliers, such as, Bosch, Delphi, and Tenneco, deliver large integrated systems directly to Toyota. Tier-two suppliers provide parts and components to Toyota and the tier-one vendors. Tier-three suppliers provide Tier-one suppliers with a single component.

Toyota had deviated from usual industry practice by naming favored Tier-one suppliers as the sole source of particular components. This resulted in close collaboration and a sense of mutual benefits. (Western manufacturers, on the other hand, award short-term contracts through bidding processes.) Such collaboration was largely responsible for the company's successful implementation of its famed "just-in-time" manufacturing strategy, in which component parts were received exactly when they were needed to enter the production process, which significantly reduced inventories and their attendant costs.

When Toyota began an aggressive expansion program in 2008, it needed to rely upon Tier-two and Tier-three suppliers, many of whom were located outside Japan. These suppliers were not subject to the same control that Toyota had over its Tier-one suppliers, and quality issues arose as a result.

QUESTIONS:

1. What should Toyota do about the recall problem?
2. Are there other possible reasons why these automobiles had to be recalled?

Source: "The Machine That Ran Too Hot," The Economist, February 27, 2010, p. 74.

issues." In addition, by having a higher standard of customer service, a **share of wallet** (the percentage of purchases in a category a buyer gives to one vendor) may be increased by as much as 80 percent.[17]

Companies must guard against providing too high a level of service, however. When customers do not respond in some desirable way (such as giving a vendor more business), or when the costs associated with providing a higher level of customer service are very high, firms may be over-committing resources. They also need to be sure that their customer service is reliable. **Reliability** includes receiving shipments on time; order accuracy, completeness and condition, getting repairs done on time; consistency of product quality, and so on.

An important aspect of customer service is how customer complaints are handled. Often, it takes only a single poorly-handled complaint to result in a lower level of satisfaction, thereby increasing the probability that the customer will choose another company. The astute company welcomes complaints, because if they are handled properly, they will prevent customer defection, increase loyalty, improve sales, and result in customers spreading favorable word-of-mouth comments. Jay Narivaha, senior vice president of the customer service consultancy, Technical Assistance Research Programs, says that customers who have problems resolved are more loyal than those who don't have problems.[18] Companies should fear non-complainers. These are customers who don't make their concerns known but simply defect to another vendor, leaving the previous supplier with less business and no information as to why.

When complaints from customers arise, the most effective strategy is to deal with them immediately. The importance of immediately responding to complaints is emphasized at British Airways. Sir Colin Marshall, British Airways' chairperson, says, "We try to make it clear to employees that we expect them to respond to customers on the spot—before a customer writes a letter or makes a phone call."[19] And British Airways follows another important tenet: even if the effort to immediately take care of a problem is not perfect—some mistakes occur—"it is better to make the effort than do nothing."[20]

Another rule of thumb: employees should be granted **empowerment** to immediately address problems. They should not be forced to consult with a distant superior, and

Feature Photo Service/Newscom

Customer service is an important component of companies international marketing programs.

share of wallet
the percentage of purchases in a category a buyer gives to one vendor

reliability
performance of various aspects of customer service that meets customer expectations

empowerment
aspect of customer service that allows employees to take care of customer problems immediately, without having to consult superiors

they should be given enough resources so that they can make an adjustment that will be meaningful to the aggrieved customer. Employees at Ritz Carlton International Hotels, for example, have the leeway to spend up to $2,000 to address a guest's grievance on the spot.[21]

REALITY CHECK LO-7

Talk to a friend or acquaintance who has traveled or lived overseas. Ask them to compare the quality of customer service they found when shopping in department stores in foreign countries to that which they experience when shopping in U.S. department stores.

SUMMARY

Companies will perform the same activities in their international markets as they do domestically, but may have to perform them differently. Analyzing international markets is necessary if companies want to be successful in those locations.

Standardization involves a company employing the same marketing strategies in its international markets as it does in its domestic market. Adaptation signifies that those strategies are different.

When companies develop new products for overseas markets, they usually employ a number of steps. Once products are introduced to foreign markets, the product life cycle (PLC), can be used to help marketers decide how to modify the product's marketing mix over time. Products in the decline stage are usually considered for elimination due to their poor performance.

There are several advantages to locating R&D facilities only in domestic locations and there are some positives in having R&D operations in foreign countries. Counterfeiting of U.S. products costs companies billions of dollars annually and may hurt their reputations.

There are four elements in a company's international promotion mix. Advertising reaches large audiences at low costs-per-contact. Personal selling is very effective, but at a high cost per contact. Sales promotion consists of a number of approaches to reaching international markets. One of the most important of these are trade shows which provide several benefits, such as, drawing interested prospects to the exhibit booth and the possibility of a large sales volume being attained. Publicity involves stories (negative and positive) about a company, its products and its executives that appear in various media such as newspapers, magazines, and on television.

A direct channel of distribution strategy refers to an international marketer not using channels to reach foreign customers; an indirect approach employs channels of distribution, such as agents and distributors. Physical distribution is storage and transportation that are used to move products to host-country purchasers. Freight forwarders are important in facilitating companies' overseas physical distribution programs.

Companies' costs, the attractiveness of competitor products and their prices, and how much marketing support is given to products, among others, are factors that must be considered when prices are set for products and services in international markets. Charges of dumping can be brought against companies whose prices under cut competitors' prices in foreign markets. When companies set a transfer price for their international subsidiaries, they need to be aware of tax policies in both the home country and the host country.

Customer service is an increasingly important responsibility for international marketers; it is a major factor in determining why customers switch to other vendors and how vendors can increase their business.

KEY TERMS

market potential, *p. 288*
sales potential, *p. 288*
marketing research, *p. 290*
marketing intelligence system (MIS), *p. 290*
standardization, *p. 292*
adaptation, *p. 292*
glocalization, *p. 292*
global product, *p. 293*
concept testing, *p. 293*
business analysis, *p. 293*
market testing, *p. 294*
commercialization, *p. 294*
product life cycle (PLC), *p. 294*
product elimination, *p. 294*
reverse strategy, *p. 295*
vertical publication, *p. 296*
horizontal publication, *p. 296*
indirect strategy, *p. 298*
direct strategy, *p. 298*
agent, *p. 299*
distributor, *p. 299*
physical distribution, *p. 299*
freight forwarder, *p. 300*
containerization, *p. 300*
intermodal transport, *p. 300*
dumping, *p. 302*
gray marketing, *p. 302*
transfer price, *p. 303*
arms length price, *p. 303*
share of wallet, *p. 305*
reliability, *p. 305*
empowerment, *p. 305*

CHAPTER QUESTIONS

1. Why do companies need to research their international markets?
2. What are the three major markets that exist in all foreign markets?
3. What is the difference between standardization and adaptation?
4. How can use of the product life cycle assist international marketers?
5. What are the advantages of using trade shows to promote products in international markets?
6. What are some of the disadvantages that can result when companies use channels of distribution to market their products overseas?
7. What are the advantages of using freight forwarders?
8. How can companies competitively set international prices while avoiding allegations of dumping?
9. How should companies deal with international customers who complain?

MINI CASE: MARKETING EQUINE-RELATED PRODUCTS TO INTERNATIONAL MARKETS

The Horse Place is a retailer that sells horse tack (saddles, saddle pads, bridles, reins, etc.) and supplies (grooming products, vitamin supplements, leg wraps, etc.). The Horse Place does not have a storefront. Its promotional strategy relies upon Internet and classified ads and one-third page ads in publications such as *Horse and Rider, Horse Illustrated*, and *Dressage Today*.

Until 2010, its products were exclusively sold in the U.S. domestic market. Its suppliers were primarily located there, but the retailer's owner, Mary Jones, had recently begun sourcing from suppliers in India. She considered their products to be excellent quality at about half the price she was paying domestic vendors.

The interaction with her Indian vendors prompted Mary to consider selling her merchandise in foreign markets. She believed that these had excellent potential for the kinds of products carried by The Horse Place. A cursory analysis of secondary sources resulted in the conclusion that Argentina, Brazil, Mexico, France, the U.K., Russia, and Germany represented the most promising opportunities.

Mary decided that she would use the Internet, classified ads, and one-eighth page ads to promote her products overseas. But she intuitively felt that these options would not be enough. Although her experience with her Indian vendors would provide some insight, she realized that selling to international markets would require her to think creatively.

Mary knew that she did not have the required funds to establish an overseas manufacturing facility. Even if she did, she was concerned about the risk involved. For the same reason, she was reluctant to open up a sales office. Eliminating these alternatives left her considering two strategies: licensing and exporting.

QUESTIONS:

1. What are the advantages and disadvantages of using licensing and exporting?
2. Will Mary need to use the services of a freight forwarder? If so, what specific services?
3. Are there any other countries, besides those mentioned, that might be important markets for The Horse Place's products?

Should Companies Marketing Their Products to International Markets Charge Lower Prices in Developing Markets than They Do in Developed Markets?

This question has become more important in recent years as developed nations reach out in a variety of ways to lesser-developed ones. Examples include the G-20 nations providing the International Monetary Fund with $1 trillion in April of 2009 to assist developing nations experiencing economic problems, and the United States supplying greater levels of economic aid to developing nations in Africa.

POINT Companies in developed nations have a noblesse oblige to improve the standard of living for people in developing countries that are less fortunate than people in developed countries. Aside from this argument, if the standard of living in poorer nations is improved, there would be more income to purchase more products from companies in developed nations that are charging the lower prices. If the products include prescription drugs, life expectancies in developed countries will also be improved.

COUNTER-POINT Companies have the major obligation to their stockholders, not to individuals in developing countries. Stockholders benefit if the prices of the stocks they hold increase in value. This is most likely to occur if profits are increased. Charging lower prices may jeopardize a company's profits; lower prices may lead to allegations of dumping. Another option may be to give the products away. With the tax savings achieved, the company's profits may exceed those obtained by selling the products at lower prices in developing markets.

What Do You Think?

Which viewpoint do you support, and why? Use the Internet to learn more about this issue and come up with your own argument.

INTERPRETING GLOBAL BUSINESS NEWS

For many countries, international tourism is big business. As globalization continues, total tourism dollars in the world's economy will significantly increase and both large and small nations will benefit from increased expenditures by visitors. Specific industries, such as lodging, airlines, restaurants, souvenir shops, and international attractions, including museums, art galleries, theme parks, wildlife preserves, and musical and concert venues, will strive to gain larger shares of tourist expenditures.

In 2009, worldwide tourism receipts reached $852 billion. The United States led the world with $94 billion in international tourism revenues, followed by Spain ($53 billion), France ($49 billion), Italy ($40 billion), China ($40 billion), Germany ($35 billion), United Kingdom ($30 billion), Australia ($26 billion), Turkey ($21 billion), and Austria ($19 billion). France drew the most visitors (74 million), with the United States (55 million), Spain (52 million), China (51 million), and Italy (43 million) rounding out the top five. The United Kingdom, Turkey, Germany, Malaysia, and Mexico ranked sixth through tenth, respectively.

Some international travelers will spend more than others when visiting other countries and are, therefore, prime targets for countries' marketing programs. For example, the average expenditure in 2009 for visitors to the United States was $2,206. China, India, Australia, Brazil, Venezuela, and Argentina were well above the average figure. Major reasons why people visit foreign countries can help marketers to target their promotional efforts. These include leisure, recreation and holidays, visiting friends or relatives, business, studying or teaching, attending conventions or conferences, and religious and pilgrimage reasons.

Galeries Lafayette, the large French department store headquartered in Paris, makes a concerted effort to get tourists to shop in the Paris store. Literature about the store is available through foreign travel agents and on flights into Paris. Brochures, which offer a 15 percent discount, are located in hotel lobbies. Executives estimate that tourists represent 10 percent to 15 percent of its revenues.

Source: Travel data are found in the *2011 World Almanac.*

PORTFOLIO PROJECTS

Explore Your Own Case In Point: What Marketing Strategy Does Your Company Use in its International Markets?

After reading this chapter, you should be prepared to answer some basic questions about your favorite company:

1. What products are sold in the company's international markets? Do they vary by country or by region?

2. What types of promotion does your favorite company emphasize in its international markets? Do they differ from those used in its domestic market?

3. What kinds of distribution channels are being employed in your company's international markets?

4. Does your company appear to be charging the same prices for its products that are being marketed to specific countries? How can you address that the prices may be quoted in different currencies?

Develop an International Strategy for Your Own Small Business: Collecting Information About the Mexican Market for Educational Products

You are the market analyst for a small company that sells educational programs for improving the mathematics skills of high school students in both domestic and international (European) markets. The company is considering marketing these same products to Mexico. An assessment of the Mexican market needs to be completed before a final decision to enter this market is made. Your boss asks you to give him "the numbers."

1. What preliminary data should you collect about the Mexican market?

2. How will you proceed to collect these data? What secondary sources could you use?

3. What critical data do you need to provide your boss so that he can decide if the company should expand into Mexico?

CHAPTER NOTES

[1] Case, "Vinchel Contemplates Market Expansion Strategies," Developed by Richard T. Hise and David Barcan, Support provided by USAID and The Eurasia Foundation.
[2] C. Alan Joyce, ed., 2011 World Almanac and Book of Facts, New York: The Rosen Group, 2008.
[3] M. Kripalani and D. Rocks, "India Plays Catch-Up in Africa," BusinessWeek, May 26, 2008, p. 55.
[4] C. K. Prahalad, "A Special Report on Globalization," The Economist, September 20, 2008, p. 10.
[5] A. McConnon, "Gerber is Following Kids to Preschool," BusinessWeek, August 18, 2008, p. 64.
[6] R. T. Hise and R. Bartlett, "Developing a Marketing Intelligence System for Companies' European Operations: Mary Kay Cosmetics Experience," paper presented to Academy of Marketing Science Cultural Perspectives on Marketing Conference, Puebla, Mexico, September 2004.
[7] D. Kiley, "One World, One Car, One Name," BusinessWeek, March 24, 2008, p. 63.
[8] I. Rowley and M. Srivastava, "Tata's Nano Hits a Speed Bump," BusinessWeek, August 11, 2008, p. 30.
[9] G. Edmondson and K. Kervin, "Stalled," BusinessWeek, September 29, 2003, pp. 54–56; G. Edmondson, C. Dawson, and K. Kervin, "Designer Cars," BusinessWeek, February 16, 2004, pp. 56–61; G. Edmondson, "Daimler Fumbles Are Firing Up Europe's Shareholders," BusinessWeek, April 19, 2004, p. 56.
[10] R. Jana, "Inspiration from Emerging Economies," BusinessWeek, March 28 & 30, 2009, pp. 36–38.
[11] D. Rocks and A. Halperin, "Stalking the Copycats," BusinessWeek, August 18, 2008, pp. 62–63.
[12] A. Marshall, "The Fatal Consequences of Counterfeit Drugs," *Smithsonian*, October 2009. Accessed 9/19/10 at www.smithsonianmag.com/people-places/Prescription-for-Murder.html.
[13] J. Hempel, "IBM's All-Star Salesman," Fortune, September 29, 2008, pp. 110–118.

[14] International Maritime Organization, "Piracy in the Waters off Somalia." Accessed 9/19/10 at www.imo.org/home.asp?topic_id=1178.
[15] M. Ihlan, "The Foreigners at the Top of LG," BusinessWeek, December 22, 2008, pp. 56–57.
[16] G. Chon, "Iran's Cheap Goods Stifle Iraq Economy," BusinessWeek, March 28 & 30, 2009, pp. 36–37.
[17] R. Whiteley, The Customer Driven Company, Boston: Addison-Wesley, 1991.
[18] R. Jacob, "Why Some Customers Are More Equal Than Others," Fortune, September 19, 1995, pp. 215–224.
[19] S. E. Prokesch, "Competing on Customer Service: An Interview with British Airways' Sir Colin Marshall," Harvard Business Review, November-December 1995, pp. 110–112.
[20] Prokesch.
[21] Jacob.

CH 13

Global Operations and Supply-Chain Management

© C Miller Design/ Getty Images

Kim Steele/Photodisc/Jupiter Images

After studying this chapter, you should be able to:

LO-1 Explain what global operations management is and how it operates.

LO-2 Describe the advantages and disadvantages of global procurement, and compare the reasons why companies outsource and insource.

LO-3 Identify the advantages and disadvantages of global production.

LO-4 Discuss the considerations for locating and relocating production facilities.

LO-5 Illustrate the benefits of global supply-chain management, and describe how the Internet and enterprise resource planning systems are affecting global supply chains.

CULTURAL PERSPECTIVE

Global Supply-Chain Management at Lenovo

Lenovo Group Limited is a multinational computer technology corporation based in the People's Republic of China. Lenovo develops, manufactures, and markets desktop and notebook personal computers, workstations, servers, storage drives, and information technology management software. In 2005, Lenovo acquired the former IBM PC Company Division, which marketed the ThinkPad line of notebook PCs, for approximately $1.75 billion. In 2009, Lenovo was the fourth largest vendor of personal computers in the world.

Lenovo recently decided to invest $30 million in new manufacturing plants in Mexico and India, as part of a strategy to compete with rivals Hewlett-Packard and Dell in major markets outside China. Lenovo will assemble computers at a new factory in Monterrey, Mexico, approximately 150 miles from the Mexico-U.S. border, and in close proximity to customers in the United States—the world's largest PC market. The Monterrey plant will be Lenovo's largest manufacturing investment outside of China, and will employ 750 people to assemble desktop and notebook computers for key markets in the Americas region, including the United States, Canada, and Brazil.

Lenovo will also open a smaller manufacturing facility in the northern Indian state of Himachal Pradesh in order to gain better access to customers in India, one of the PC industry's fastest-growing markets. This plant will be Lenovo's second facility in India and will employ 350 people.

Chief Executive Bill Amelio proposed the new manufacturing plants in Mexico and India in order to improve Lenovo's supply chain. Mr. Amelio joined Lenovo after working several years for Dell, where he served as senior vice president of the Asia-Pacific and Japan region. Dell is well-known for the speed of its supply chain. In turn, Mr. Amelio hired Gerry P. Smith, a supply-chain expert from Dell, to map Lenovo's global distribution network and identify inefficiencies. The network "looked like spaghetti," said Mr. Smith.

Locating manufacturing plants closer to customers helps get products into buyers' hands faster by reducing shipping times, and will also reduce shipping costs. Shipping a computer from China to the United States can take 30 days, while shipping a computer from Monterrey to the United States would take three to four days. The shipping cost would decrease proportionally to the decrease in shipping time. Although Lenovo had previously subcontracted manufacturing to third-party companies in Mexico, the majority of its products were still made in China.

Lenovo is very motivated to increase its presence into the United States, where it depends upon sales of ThinkPad laptops to business customers. The company now aims to tap into the U.S. consumer market by selling Lenovo-branded products through retail stores in the United States. While Lenovo controls more than 10 percent of the global PC market, its U.S. market share is less than 5 percent, and Lenovo does not rank in the top five U.S. PC firms.[1]

Introduction

In an endless quest to achieve a sustainable competitive advantage, businesses such as Lenovo, Boeing, Volkswagen, and Sony have increasingly used global operations and supply-chain management as competitive weapons. In this chapter, global operations management and its associated business functions—procurement, production, logistics, and research and development—are defined.

The factors that firms take into account when considering whether to procure domestically or globally, including outsourcing and insourcing decisions, are analyzed in detail. Interrelated strategic decisions—which production facilities to own and where to locate the facilities—are also discussed. In addition, the relocation of production facilities is explored.

Next, global supply-chain management is also discussed. In the current business environment, the level of competition has been elevated from "company A versus company B" to the supply chain of company A versus the supply chain of company B. The benefits of improving global supply-chain management are illustrated using a real-world company. The coordination and collaboration required in successful supply chains has been made possible by information technologies such as the Internet and enterprise resource planning systems. The impact of these two information technologies in global supply-chain management is also explained in the last section of this chapter.

LO-1
Explain what global operations management is and how it operates.

Global Operations Management

Businesses exist to create goods and services. Goods include automobiles, airplanes, and computers. Services may include health care, entertainment, and consulting. It is important to note that most firms produce and sell products that involve a combination of goods and services. In some products, the value of the goods dominates the value of the services, for instance, buying a car (the good) with a warranty (the service). In other products, the value of the services dominates the value of the goods, for example, spending a night at a hotel. In this example the service entails the use of the room and hotel facilities, while the goods include the consumed electricity, water and toiletries, and food (if breakfast is included). For brevity, this chapter will use the word *product* to encompass the combination of goods and services that the customer receives.

A **production system** is a system that businesses use to create the goods and services, or to produce the products. When the goods dominate the value of the product, the production system is typically called a **manufacturing system**. When the services dominate the value of the product, the production system is commonly called a **service system**. The production systems of Honda Motor Company, the Boeing Company, and Toshiba Corporation, would be called manufacturing systems. In contrast, the production systems of the Fred Hutchinson Cancer Research Center, the Walt Disney Company, and the consulting firm Accenture, would be called service systems. Sometimes the product value is not clearly dominated by the goods or the services provided; for example, a fine restaurant which could be considered both a manufacturing system and a service system.

production system
the system that businesses use to produce products

manufacturing system
a production system in which goods dominate the value of the product

service system
a production system in which services dominate the value of the product

A production system can be modeled as a system that begins with inputs and creates from them outputs via a production process. Exhibit 13.1 illustrates this model.

In this model, the *inputs* may include materials, land, labor, machines and equipment, energy, and information. The *outputs* represent the desired goods and services. And the *production process* may consist of one or more transformations which could be:

- physical, as in manufacturing;
- locational, as in transportation;

- informational, as in consulting;
- psychological, as in entertainment;
- physiological, as in health care;
- exchange, as in retailing;
- storage, as in warehousing.

EXHIBIT 13.1 A PRODUCTION SYSTEM MODEL

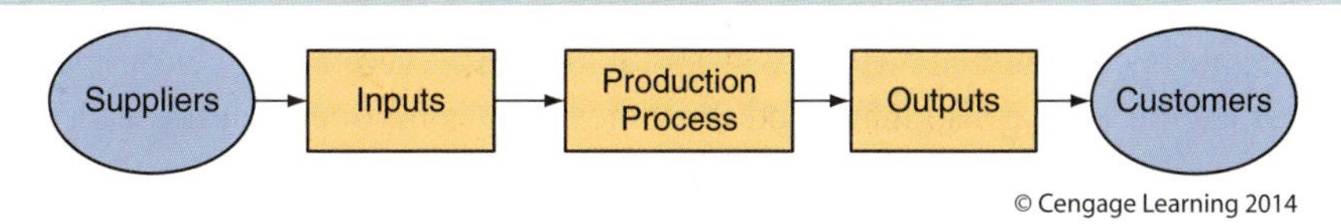

At Boeing, the transformation is physical and the outputs are airplanes. At the Fred Hutchinson Cancer Research Center, the transformation is physiological and the outputs are healthy patients. Some of the inputs for Boeing include aluminum, titanium, glass, engines, buildings, machines, engineers, and workers. Some of the inputs for the Fred Hutchinson Cancer Research Center are medical supplies and drugs, buildings, doctors, nurses, staff, medical equipment, and laboratories. In both examples, additional inputs include energy and information—airplane designs for Boeing, and medical protocols for the Fred Hutchinson Cancer Research Center. The sites where production takes place are called **production facilities**. For Boeing, production facilities include manufacturing and assembly plants, and for the Fred Hutchinson Cancer Research Center, production facilities include hospitals and clinics.

Products can be conceptualized as being integrated by several goods and services called **components**. For instance, two components of a car that are goods could be the engine and the tires, and two components that are services could be the inspection of the car prior to delivery and the transportation of the car from the factory to the dealership. In turn, the components will need to be produced from **raw materials**. The raw materials may include

A parade in Disneyland's Magic Kingdom. The Walt Disney Company employs more than 150,000 people.

production facility
the site where production takes place

components
goods and services that integrate a product

raw materials
materials used to produce components

goods and services, too. For example, two raw materials of the engine that are goods could be stainless steel and aluminum, and two raw materials that are services could be the quality control engineers that will inspect the engine as it is being assembled, and the logistics personnel that will move the engine around the factory from work station to work station. If the product is mostly comprised of services—for instance, taking a Caribbean cruise or spending a day at Disneyland—although it is not necessarily straightforward, it could also be possible to identify the components and raw materials in these products.

When a production process involves several steps, these steps are called **production stages**. Depending upon the complexity of the production process, different production stages may need to be assigned to different production facilities. Consider Boeing which assembles commercial airplanes at its Renton and Everett production facilities in Washington state. Boeing also manufactures some of the components of those airplanes at its Auburn and Frederickson production facilities in Washington state, its Portland production facility in Oregon, its Winnipeg production facility in Canada, and its Sydney and Melbourne production facilities in Australia. Production stages can also be present at businesses with service systems. A patient arriving at an emergency room, for example, may be taken first to radiology, then to surgery, and lastly to intensive care, all of which represent production stages.

Operations management refers to the management of the direct resources that are involved in the production system of a business organization. Until recently, operations management was mostly applied in manufacturing firms, and was called *manufacturing management* or *production management*. To include applications in service industries, the name was changed to *production and operations management*, or *operations management*. Following current practice, the text will use the term *operations management* to include the management of both manufacturing systems and service systems. In addition, when all of the production system direct resources originate from and reside in only one country, the term *domestic operations management* will be used. In contrast, when one or more of the production system direct resources originate from or are located in more than one country, the term *global operations management* will be used. Companies with global operations management include Boeing, Volkswagen, Lenovo, the Walt Disney Company, Accenture, and Cemex S.A.B. de C.V. The emphasis in this chapter is specifically upon global operations management.[2]

Most of the activities in operations management can be grouped into four business functions: procurement, production, logistics, and research and development. Procurement is responsible for the acquisition of goods and services. Production is responsible for the transformations required by the production process. Logistics is responsible for the movement of materials in the production system. Research and development (R&D) is responsible for the design of new products. Note that procurement, logistics, and R&D are service functions in both manufacturing and service systems. Within operations management, these four business functions can be classified as domestic or global. One example is Boeing, which buys from thousands of suppliers in more than 100 countries, but only has production facilities in the United States, and thus practices global procurement and domestic production. As a second example, Dell, which has manufacturing plants in Brazil, Ireland, Poland, and the United States, and R&D centers in China, India, Singapore, Taiwan, and the United States, practices global production and global R&D.

production stages
steps in the production process

operations management
the management of the direct resources that are involved in the production system of a business organization

REALITY CHECK LO-1

Select a product that you recently purchased. Do some research to establish whether the company that produced the product practices global operations management.

Global Procurement

LO-2

Describe the advantages and disadvantages of global procurement, and compare the reasons why companies outsource and insource.

Business enterprises face the strategic decision to determine the organizational boundaries of the firm. In operations management this entails deciding for the production system which components and raw materials should be produced in-house and which components and raw materials should be acquired from suppliers. This decision traditionally has been called the **make-or-buy decision**. Beginning recently, the term "sourcing decision" has been used as a synonym for this process. As an example of the sourcing decision, should Boeing make the engines of its commercial airplanes or buy them from suppliers such as General Electric, Rolls Royce, and Pratt & Whitney?

The term "make" not only applies to production but to logistics and R&D as well. As an example of a logistics sourcing decision, should Dell own ("make") a fleet of trucks to deliver its computers to customers, or should Dell contract ("buy") the delivery service from UPS and FedEx? As an example of a R&D sourcing decision, should a pharmaceutical company perform all clinical trials in-house ("make"), or should the pharmaceutical company contract ("buy") with university hospitals or other external entities to perform the trials? Moreover, the sourcing decision applies to service systems as well. Consider the Hilton Hotels Corporation with more than 500 Hilton branded hotels across the world. Should Hilton provide ("make") its own maid services or should Hilton contract ("buy") maid services from one or more suppliers?

A related strategic decision that business firms face is whether or not the making or buying processes should be global. Consequently, the following four alternatives are possible: make domestically, make globally, buy domestically, and buy globally. When a company buys globally, it is said that the company is practicing **global procurement**. When a firm globally produces goods or services, it is said that the firm is practicing **global production**. The same can be said for global logistics and global R&D. The remainder of this section will present the advantages and disadvantages of global procurement.

Bloomberg/Contributor/Getty Images

A display of Dell computers. Michael Dell started Dell, Inc. in his college dorm room.

make-or-buy decision determining which components and raw materials should be produced in-house and which components and raw materials should be acquired from suppliers; also called the sourcing decision

global procurement when a firm buys components and raw materials globally

global production when a firm globally produces goods and services

Advantages of Global Procurement

One advantage of buying is that the firm does not need to invest the money that is associated with making. For instance, Boeing avoids the multi-million dollar investment that would be required to produce the engines by buying the engines for its commercial airplanes from General Electric, Rolls Royce, and Pratt & Whitney.

A second advantage of buying is that the firm can focus upon the production stages and components with the most value added. Dell, which concentrates on the design and manufacturing of its servers and buys the delivery service from FedEx and UPS, represents a good example.

A third advantage of buying is that the firm can maximize its flexibility by allocating its orders among the suppliers in a dynamic way. This is particulary important with global suppliers when factors such as exchange rates, political changes, trade barriers, or the occurrence of catastrophic events such as hurricanes, earthquakes, or tornados, can alter the attractiveness of a supplier. One year the lowest-cost suppliers may be found in China and Vietnam, and the next year the lowest-cost suppliers may be found in Mexico and Honduras. Moreover, by procuring globally, as opposed to domestically, the firm has access to more suppliers, and these global suppliers usually can provide lower costs than domestic suppliers.

One more advantage of global procurement is that if global suppliers are selling to many companies in the same industry but in different countries, these suppliers can achieve economies of scale and lower costs. Ford, Honda, and BMW spends less buying tires from global suppliers (e.g., Michelin, Firestone, and Goodyear) than it does making the tires in-house.

The buying firm does not need to learn a new business, avoiding the business risks that the supplier is taking, and simplifying its own production process, thereby creating an advantage. For example, by buying the jet engines from suppliers, Boeing does not have to develop an expertise in jet engine production, and at the same time, the production process of Boeing is greatly simplified, because designing and producing jet engines is an engineering feat.

Lastly, sometimes global procurement is required as a result of a business practice known as *offsets*, which originated in international defense procurement, but is now common in all industries. To secure a contract, a foreign vendor (e.g., Boeing selling commercial airplanes to China Airlines) must "offset" the financial impact of the product acquisition by *direct* local procurement in China of goods and services relating to the acquired product, and *indirect* support of other local priorities in China through direct investment, technology transfer, and job creation. In other words, if Boeing wants to sell planes in China, due to offsets, Boeing is being enticed to buy from Chinese companies any goods and services that may be required to produce Boeing planes.

Disadvantages of Global Procurement

When a firm buys goods and services, it is relying upon suppliers on important dimensions such as quality, delivery, and cost. For instance, coordinating the deliveries of suppliers to meet a final assembly schedule is more difficult when suppliers are on the other side of the world, than when the goods and services are produced in-house. Furthermore, with foreign suppliers, if something goes wrong it may be difficult, perhaps even impossible, to enforce the contract that the company may have with the supplier. If the supplier goes bankrupt, the firm could lose that source of goods and services entirely.

Under global procurement, the business may also need to compete for the attention of suppliers. Consider the situation where Airbus, Boeing's only competitor in the commercial airplanes industry, places a big order of jet engines with GE, Rolls Royce, and Pratt & Whitney. Boeing will now have a huge disadvantage when negotiating prices and delivery times with any of those suppliers.

Another disadvantage of global procurement is that the profits that the company could earn by producing the goods and services in-house now go to the suppliers. This could affect the profitability of the buying company. Similarly, perhaps the company could produce the goods and services more efficiently than the supplier, and hence at a lower cost.

Buying may also tip the balance of power in favor of suppliers. When IBM's PC Division first decided to buy microprocessors from Intel and operating systems from Microsoft, IBM had the negotiation advantage. By choosing Intel's microprocessors and Microsoft's operating system, IBM made these products the industry standard. Consequently, as more software and peripherals were developed for the Intel-Microsoft standard, it became increasingly difficult for PC manufacturers, including IBM, to seek alternative sources of supply for microprocessors and operating systems.[3]

Buying from suppliers could unintentionally lead to suppliers becoming competitors. This is the case of SAP and Oracle. Several decades ago SAP, the largest provider of enterprise resource planning software in the world, was buying 80 percent of its databases from Oracle. When Oracle realized how profitable SAP's business was, Oracle created its own brand of enterprise resource planning software, to become a direct competitor of SAP. After Oracle's expansion, SAP has only purchased 20 percent of its databases from Oracle.

Procuring goods and services from suppliers can also carry the risk of suppliers providing those same goods and services to the competition. This is the case for IBM with regard to its suppliers Intel and Microsoft. Intel and Microsoft are now selling their products to Dell and Hewlett-Packard, which were IBM's competitors in the PC business until 2005, when Lenovo acquired IBM's PC Division.

Outsourcing and Insourcing

In Chapter 11, the text discussed outsourcing and offshoring from the Global Human Resource Management perspective. In this section, the text will revisit outsourcing and offshoring from the global procurement perspective.

When a firm has been "making" goods and services in-house, and then decides to "buy" these goods and services from suppliers, it is said that the firm has **outsourced** these goods and services. As in the case of the business functions procurement, production, logistics, and R&D, outsourcing can be domestic or global.

Domestic outsourcing means that the firm doing the outsourcing, and the supplier that will provide the outsourced good or service are located in the same country. **Global outsourcing** means the firm and the supplier are located in different countries. Moreover, in some business circles, global outsourcing is also called **offshoring**. In general, outsourcing is a term that can be used to describe almost any corporate activity that is managed by an outside vendor, from the running of the company's cafeteria to the provision of courier services.[4]

Consequently, the type of outsourcing considered in this chapter should be understood as "operations outsourcing"; however, for brevity it will simply be called outsourcing.

Outsourcing can have strategic implications for some business organizations. The Sony Corporation, for example, has recently been affected by outsourcing. When Sony Chief Executive Howard Stringer announced that he was considering drastic cost-cutting steps for Sony's core electronics division, outsourcing topped his to-do list. This shift marked a minor victory for Stringer. After more than three years leading the company, Stringer finally has appeared to be breaking the company's addiction to manufacturing ("make"). To show that he is serious, the Welsh-born American CEO has said he will close five or six of Sony's 57 global plants and reduce the company's budget for factories and chipmaking equipment by one-third over the next fiscal year. "We have to move very, very quickly and control our costs," Stringer told journalists in Tokyo. He appears to have made up his mind about outsourcing one specific product: television sets. What will Stringer's outsourcing strategy look like? That has not been determined, but experts predict that Sony will continue to make the ultra-thin,

outsourcing
when a firm has been making goods and services in-house, and then decides to buy these goods and services from suppliers

domestic outsourcing
when the firm doing the outsourcing and the supplier that will provide the outsourced goods and services are located in the same country

global outsourcing
when the firm doing the outsourcing and the supplier that will provide the outsourced goods and services are located in different countries; also called offshoring

offshoring
when a firm and the supplier are located in different countries

Reuters/Kim Kyung Hoon

A Sony monitor. Its founders, Akio Morita and Masaru Ibuka, derived the Sony name from sonus, the Latin word for sound, and from the English slang word "sonny."

high-end TVs in-house. Small and midsize sets, however, may be produced by one or more manufacturers in Taiwan or Hong Kong.[5]

Outsourcing is a practice that has rapidly grown in recent years. According to one estimate, in the 1940s only 20 percent of a typical American manufacturing company's value-added in production and operations came from outside sources; 50 years later the proportion had tripled to 60 percent. In the automobile industry, firms with the biggest profit per car, such as Toyota, Honda, and Chrysler, were also the biggest outsourcers, sourcing around 70 percent to various suppliers during the 1990s. Those car companies that outsourced the least (e.g., General Motors, which outsourced only 30 percent of its value-added operations) were the least profitable.[6]

The nature of outsourcing contracts has changed over time as well. What began as a straightforward arm's-length agreement between a buyer and a supplier has become structured more like a partnership agreement. Any increase in the client's volume of business is reflected in the outsourcer's scale of charges, and both parties in some way also share the risks and rewards of the outsourced activity. Some firms have taken the idea of outsourcing to such an extreme that they have left themselves with little to do. An American company named Vizio, Inc. produces LCD TVs, and only has 85 employees, but its sales are in the billions of dollars. Vizio uses modules to assemble its own brand of TVs, and because the major components of TVs are now readily available as commodities, Vizio can design the TV, buy the components, hire a contract manufacturer, and market the TVs with very little cost.[7] Similarly, the sports gear company Nike can be characterized as owning and making little beyond concepts and designs.[8] Companies like Nike, which focus only on product design and outsource all other production process functions are called **hollow corporations**.

When a firm has been buying goods and services from suppliers, and then decides to "make" these goods and services in-house, it is said that the firm has **insourced** these goods and services. Similar to its outsourcing counterpart, businesses can use insourcing for strategic purposes. For example, after two years of delays caused by outsourced suppliers, Boeing plans to do more work on its new 787 Dreamliner in-house. Plagued by repeated problems with some suppliers, Boeing has been forced to delay the delivery of its 787 by several months. and is now reconsidering its global outsourcing model that, according to experts, has been responsible for most of these delays. Boeing engineers report that in order to solve several design and production crises, they have frequently sent employeess to visit with suppliers, and Boeing's top executives are now relying less upon their outside suppliers as a result. If this change takes place, the impact on suppliers would be huge, since they account for approximately 70 percent of the 787 in cost—a far larger share than Boeing has outsourced on earlier planes. Outsourcing the majority of the work on the new 787 has been part of a strategy to share financial risk, to contain costs, and to allow foreign customers and their governments who are interested in manufacturing some of

hollow corporation
a company that only completes product design and outsources all other production process functions

insourcing
when the firm has been buying goods and services from suppliers, and then decides to make these goods and services in-house

Evolution1/Dreamstime.com

The Boeing 787 Dreamliner, whose development and production has involved a large-scale collaboration with numerous suppliers around the globe.

the components of the planes they are buying (which were defined earlier in this chapter as offsets) in their countries. As mentioned earlier, Boeing has thousands of suppliers in more than 100 countries. The Japanese companies Mitsubishi, Kawasaki, and Fuji produce the wings, forward fuselages, and center wing boxes, respectively. The Swedish company Saab makes cargo doors and the Italian company Alenia Aeronautica produces horizontal stabilizer and central fuselages. Boeing also has suppliers in Britain, France, Germany, and South Korea. Boeing Engineering Vice-President Mike Denton has said, "We will probably do more of the design and even some of the major production for the next new airplane ourselves as opposed to having it all out with suppliers.[9]

ECONOMIC PERSPECTIVES Outsourcing Production of TVs

Although demand continues to increase for flat panel liquid-crystal display televisions, major manufacturers of televisions such as Sony, Toshiba, and LG Electronics, must reduce their manufacturing costs due to sharp price declines. As a result, these companies are relocating production from South Korea, Japan, and Mexico to contractors such as Taiwan's Hon Hai Precision Industry Co., Ltd. and Hong Kong's TPV Technology Limited. "Rapidly declining profit margins have forced TV makers to outsource a certain percentage of their production to companies such as Hon Hai," said Santosh Kumar, an analyst at California-based consulting firm Frost & Sullivan.

J.P. Morgan predicts that the LCD TV outsourcing market will more than double in revenue over the next several years. As an example of the outsourcing trend among the major TV manufacturers, Sony plans to increase its percentage of television manufacturing outsourcing to more than 50 percent in its current fiscal year, from 20 percent in the past fiscal year. This will include transferring its plants in Tijuana, Mexico and Nitra, Slovakia, to Hon Hai, said George Boyd, a spokesman at the company.

QUESTIONS:

1) What are some of the advantages for Sony, Toshiba, and LG Electronics to move outsourcing TV manufacturing from South Korea, Japan, and Mexico to plants in China and Taiwan?
2) Under which conditions do you think Sony, Toshiba, and LG Electronics may decide to insource from plants in China and Taiwan, the manufacturing of TVs to companies in South Korea, Japan, and Mexico?

Source: Lorraine Luk, "China Takes Leading Role in TVs," The Wall Street Journal, June 10, 2010.

REALITY CHECK LO-2

Do you or does anyone you know work for a company that is outsourcing goods and services? Describe some of the pros and cons of outsourcing for the company involved and for the world economy.

LO-3

Identify the advantages and disadvantages of global production.

Global Production

Just as there are pros and cons of buying components and raw materials, there are advantages and disadvantages of making components and raw materials in-house. As was explained earlier in this chapter, locating all production facilities in only one country is known as *domestic production*, and locating production facilities in several countries is known as *global production*.

In some business circles, relocating a production facility from one country to another is called offshoring. Note that as indicated earlier in this chapter, in some other business circles, offshoring is also used to denote global procurement. Sometimes it is possible for a firm to produce the components and raw materials in-house or in partnership with another company.

Advantages of Making

One advantage of making components and raw materials in-house is cost. Because the producing firm is making the product it has designed, knowledge of the product may provide efficiency advantages over potential suppliers. For example, a car manufacturer may be in a better position to make the engines for its cars, because the car manufacturer designed both the car and the engine. A closely-related advantage of in-house production is cost control. If the company is making both the component and raw materials, there will not be any surprising price increases from suppliers.

A second advantage of producing components and raw materials is control over quality. If the supplier does not have an intimate knowledge of how the component or raw materials will be used in the product, final assembly may suffer due to decreased quality. This is the reason why Boeing maintains a production facility in Portland, Oregon, which manufactures precision machined parts.

Making components and raw materials in-house also allows the company more control over deliveries. Boeing, for example, learned of this advantage the hard way. Due to late deliveries from suppliers that have delayed production, Boeing's original plan to put its first 787 Dreamliner into the air in August 2007 had to be changed to January 2010. Consequently, as described earlier in this chapter, Boeing is now insourcing many of the 787 components in order to exert more control.

In-house production is sometimes the only option for components and raw materials that are highly specialized, particularly as a matter of trust. A hospital that is deciding to "make" or "buy" some highly specialized medical equipment provides a good example. This medical equipment is a component of a service, for instance, a medical procedure, that only this hospital can offer. The making means that the hospital would buy and operate the equipment, and the buying means that the hospital would contract the services from a supplier that would own the equipment. In this example, if the hospital buys the services from a supplier, then the hospital and the supplier are totally dependent on each other. Because of this dependency, the hospital will have a difficult time locating a supplier, and at the same time, if the hospital were lucky enough to find one supplier willing to take the risk, the hospital would still be afraid of being taken hostage by the supplier, because the supplier knows that it would be extremely difficult for the hospital to find another supplier. In short, because of a lack of mutual trust between the hospital and any potential suppliers, the hospital will have no choice but to invest in this highly specialized medical equipment.

In-house production is advantageous because it secures the supply source. In March 2000, lightning hit a power line in Albuquerque, New Mexico. The strike caused a massive surge in the surrounding electrical grid, which in turn started a fire at a local plant owned by Philips Electronics, and damaged millions of microchips. As a result, the mobile phone company Ericsson, which purchased the microchips from Philips and had no alternative source, encountered production problems that lasted for months and caused a loss of $400 million in sales.[10]

When components and raw materials involve intellectual property, making affords complete protection of the intellectual property. For example, an oil and gas company that is deciding whether to make or buy a new technology for oil extraction from unconventional sites. If two of the major technological components include intellectual property, it is likely that the oil company will produce these two components in-house.

Disadvantages of Making

The primary disadvantage of making is that it requires the company to have expertise in the production of the component or raw materials that will be made. Moreover, by making, the company may be missing out on the technological advances that the suppliers may have. If Ford decided to make the tires for its automobiles, for example, Ford would need to acquire expertise in tire production, which may not be a good strategy. In fact, Henry Ford's vision was to make as many components and raw materials as possible. However, he quickly realized that this was inefficient and began to outsource many components and raw materials. Ford could be assured of getting access to the latest technology in tire production by buying the tires from manufacturers such as Michelin and Firestone.

A second disadvantage of making is that the people producing the component or raw material, sometimes called internal suppliers, may not have the incentive to improve their product since they do not face competition. Companies sometimes resort to what is called **dual sourcing**, or producing in-house and purchasing from suppliers the components and raw materials they need. This provides the motivation to the internal suppliers to be as efficient as the external suppliers. Boeing, for example, has considered dual sourcing some work for the 787 Dreamliner, relying upon Boeing workers and upon suppliers to provide some components.[11] An added advantage of dual-sourcing is that the firm has internal expertise by which to judge the quality of work being done by suppliers.

Another disadvantage of making is that the firm may not be able to gain the economies of scale that can be gained by a supplier that is able to pool the activity of a large number of firms. Any tire company such as Goodyear or Goodrich should be able to enjoy economies of scale much greater than those of Nissan or Mercedes-Benz, for instance, if they were making tires for their automobiles.

By making, a firm could increase the complexity of its production process, and this could prove detrimental. If Dell decided that it would own and operate its own fleet of trucks instead of using UPS and FedEx to deliver computers to customers, attention would be taken away from Dell's main business of designing and assembling computers.

Lastly, a strategic disadvantage of making is that the firm would incur both fixed and variable costs, while when buying, the firm would only incur variable costs. This financial flexibility may prove crucial, especially when fixed costs are considerable. If the demand for the product, and hence the component, decreases, then the firm would need to financially absorb both a decline in sales and a higher cost per component produced because fixed costs would be allocated over a smaller number of units.

dual sourcing
when components and raw materials are produced in-house and purchased from suppliers

REALITY CHECK LO-3

Dual sourcing has been used by some companies to manage business risks. Identify a company that has used dual sourcing, and the risks that were managed.

LO-4
Discuss the considerations for locating and relocating production facilities.

Location Decision

Once a business organization has decided which components and raw materials will be made in-house, a **location decision** will need to be made. This consists of determining if the making will be done at one or more production facilities, and if these facilities should be located in one or more countries. Businesses face the one-versus-many production facilities decision when making location decisions.

Location of Production Facilities for Components and Raw Materials

One consideration for the one-versus-many production facilities decision is fixed costs. When fixed costs are high, one production facility will be favored. Conversely, when fixed costs are low, several production facilities may be justified based upon other factors.

A second consideration for the one-versus-many production facilities decision is the notion of the minimum efficient scale and its comparison to demand. As volume increases, unit costs decrease due to economies of scale and learning curve effects. Learning curves capture the following observed experience: the more times a task is performed, the less time and cost it will take on each subsequent repetition. However, there is a volume value, called *the minimum efficient scale*, or the point at which unit costs stabilize. When demand is equal or lower than the minimum efficient scale, one production facility location is preferred. When demand is higher than the minimum efficient scale, several production facilities are economically feasible.

The *value-to-weight ratio* is another consideration for the one-versus-many production facilities decision. Goods with high value-to-weight ratios are expensive but do not weigh very much; examples are microchips and jewelry. Examples of goods with low value-to-weight ratios are cement and oil. Because transportation costs will constitute a higher percentage of total unit costs for goods with a low value-to-weight ratio, the way to go in this situation is to have many production facilities in order to be close to the places where the components are needed. Conversely, goods with high value-to-weight ratios favor a single location to use the advantages of centralized production.

Companies also need to consider where to locate the single or multiple production facilities. A first consideration is the Heckscher-Ohlin (H-O) Model presented in Chapter 1. According to this model, countries will have comparative advantage according to their factor endowments such as land (quantity, quality, and mineral resources beneath the land), labor (quantity and skills), cost of capital, and technology quality. Consequently, a company would locate the production facilities in those countries that offer the best comparative advantage. If the component to be produced is labor intensive, then the company would locate the production facilities in countries such as China, Vietnam, and Mexico, among others, that offer a labor comparative advantage. As a second example, if the raw material to be produced consumes vast quantities of minerals, then the company would locate the facility in a country rich in minerals such as Australia.

location decision
determining if products made in-house will be produced in one or more facilities, and if these facilities should be located in one or more countries

A second location consideration is the infrastructure that the country offers, such as sea ports, airports, roads, electricity, and water access. Most developing countries offer very competitive labor costs and availability, but many lack the infrastructure of developed countries. Basic necessities of a production facility, such as a reliable power network, which one takes for granted in developed countries, may present a challenge in developing countries.

Trade policies such as those discussed in Chapter 1 (tariffs, preferential duties, and non-tariff barriers), which can vary greatly from country to country, also must be considered in the location decision. For example, as described in the opening vignette of this chapter, Lenovo's decision to open a manufacturing plant in Monterrey, Mexico, reflects a strategy to take advantage of NAFTA signed by Canada, the United States, and Mexico.

Financial considerations such as transactions risk, translation risk, and economic risk, which are analyzed in Chapter 14, play a major role in location decisions as well. Another location decision consideration involves government incentives in the form of tax breaks or low corporate taxes. For instance, due to its low 12.5 percent corporate tax rate, Ireland was able to attract numerous production facilities in the 1990s. In contrast, the corporate tax rates of countries such as the United Kingdom, Germany, France, the United States, and Japan are approximately 25 percent to 45 percent.

Political considerations such as social stability, form of government (democracy, dictatorship, etc.), and public attitudes toward foreign investment, are all important in the location decision. The presidency of Hugo Chávez in Venezuela makes that location an unattractive place for most countries to locate new businesses. The political reforms initiated by Deng Xiaoping in the early-1980s, however, have made China a favorite location of production facilities. Since the early-1990s, China has been the world's largest recipient of foreign direct investment among developing countries. In recent years, foreign direct investment to China accounts for one-fourth to one-third of total foreign direct investment inflow to developing countries.

Location of Production Facilities for Products

Companies also must decide where to locate the production facilities for their products. The products of BMW are automobiles, and it has production facilities in Germany, Great Britain, the United States, and South Africa, where cars are assembled. How is the location decision for products different from the location decision for components and raw materials? In short, there is not much difference. Most of the considerations for components and raw materials also apply to products. However, there are three major considerations that only pertain to products.

If a product can serve the needs of all customers around the world, then the company may locate all production facilities in one country. If the product must be customized for different countries, then multiple production facilities will be needed.

Harley-Davidson has four production facilities where its motorcycles are assembled, and all four facilities are located in the United States One reason for this location decision includes serving the world market with its standard motorcycle designs. This is not the case for Nestlé, whose products require regional customization; consequentially, Nestlé has established production facilities for its products all over the world.

Because products are sold to customers, and most of the time components and raw materials are not, one consideration for deciding upon production facility location is proximity to markets. This may explain BMW's decision to locate its assembly plants in Europe and America, which are its two biggest markets. Proximity to suppliers, and proximity to the production facilities that provide the components and raw materials is an important consideration, too. A company locating a production facility for oil and gas products may be attracted to the states of Texas and Louisiana, where there is an abundance of refineries and oil rigs.

The third consideration in deciding upon production facility location for products relates to the product's image. Germany's famous auto engineering has made it an

Philippe Lissac/Godong/Corbis

The Harley-Davidson company was founded in 1903 by William Harley and Davidson brothers Arthur, Walter, and William.

attractive country for car manufacturers. Italy would be of interest to firms with products in the leather industry, such as coats and shoes, because of Italy's historical supremacy in leather products. That is, customers would prefer to buy cars made in Germany and shoes made in Italy.

Relocation of Production Facilities

The location of a production facility is a long-term decision, and because this decision is such a significant cost driver, the consulting firm McKinsey believes that location has the power to provide a company success. As new opportunities appear around the world, sometimes it will become desirable for a company to relocate a production facility. In early-2009, Dell identified such an opportunity and announced that it would be moving its Irish manufacturing operations to Poland in the next year. This was part of a company-wide initiative to cut costs by $3 billion, which would result in the loss of 1,900 Irish jobs, or approximately 50 percent of the computer maker's workforce in Ireland. Dell established a manufacturing facility in Limerick, Ireland in 1990, and since then has become the second-largest foreign employer in Ireland—and one of its biggest exporters. However, in 2006, Dell was dethroned as the world's largest manufacturer of personal computers, when its rival Hewlett-Packard surpassed it. One major difference between Dell and Hewlett-Packard is that Dell owns the plants around the world where its computers are produced, whereas Hewlett-Packard decided years ago to outsource most of its production to contract manufacturers in Asia. "This is a difficult decision, but the right one for Dell to become even more competitive," said Sean Corkery, the vice president of the Dell's Europe, Middle East, and Africa operations, in a statement.[12]

REALITY CHECK LO-4

Locate in the business press a recent case of a company relocating its production facilities. Identify the winners and losers in that relocation decision.

Global Supply-Chain Management

LO-5

Illustrate the benefits of global supply-chain management and describe how the Internet and enterprise resource planning systems are affecting global supply chains.

The firm, its suppliers, and its customers comprise the traditional unit of business analysis. However, in recent years, the unit of business analysis has been extended to include the supply chain. A **supply chain** encompasses all the activities associated with the flow and transformation of goods and services from raw material to the end user, including the corresponding flows of monetary funds and information. These activities are typically performed by different business organizations identified as suppliers, manufacturers, distributors, and retailers.

An example of a simple supply chain is presented in Exhibit 13.2.

When the companies in a supply chain have locations in more than one country, the supply chain is considered a global supply chain. Examples of global supply chains are those of Boeing, Ford, United Airlines, and the pharmaceutical companies Merck and Pfizer.

Supply-chain management refers to the management of all the activities in the supply chain, in order to minimize the total costs of the supply chain, and to maximize the value of the product to the end user. The management of global supply chains is called global supply-chain management. In the current business landscape, supply-chain management has become a new source of competitive advantage. Dell, for example, is no longer competing against Hewlett-Packard, but the supply chain of Dell is competing against the supply chain of Hewlett-Packard.

Improving Global Supply-Chain Management

Motorola provides a good example of a company trying to improve its global supply-chain management. Recently, Motorola announced that in the next two years it will invest $60 million in Singapore to manage its global supply chain. Ed Zander, Motorola's chairman and CEO, during the launch of Motorola's global supply chain (which he called the "control tower"), said that the $60 million investment would allow the company to better manage its supply chain across different divisions such as mobile devices, networks, and connected home products. It is estimated that the volume of Motorola's supply chain operations such as manufacturing and distribution, exceeds $10 billion. Zander stated that Motorola realized several years ago that in order to stay competitive, the company needed to develop world-class supply chain capabilities. "Your cost structure, quality of manufacturing, and the way you compete in the next decade is through your supply chain," he noted. Zander added, "it is not just about saving money, it is also about faster time to market and improving product quality. The best-run companies usually have the best supply chain." Stu Reed, Motorola's executive vice president of integrated supply chain, stated that prior to the new Singapore investment, the worldwide supply chain operations of the firm were uncoordinated. "This is the first time that we are driving centralization. There was no 'control tower' of supply chain activities before this," he said. Reed noted that improving supply chain operations can typically

supply chain
all activities associated with the flow and transformation of goods and services from the raw material stage to the end user, together with the corresponding flows of monetary funds and information

supply-chain management
the management of all activities in the supply chain, in order to minimize the total cost of the supply chain, and to maximize the value of the product to the end user

EXHIBIT 13.2 A SIMPLE SUPPLY CHAIN

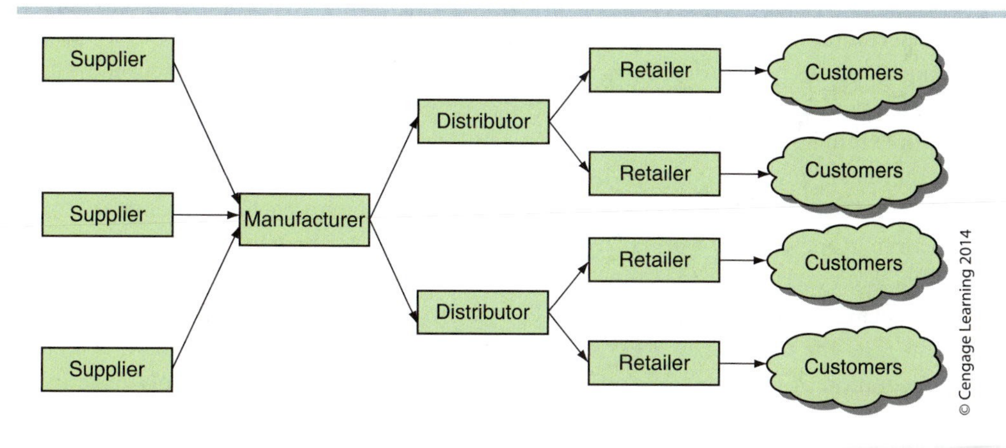

rein in "double-digit" productivity growth, and it can also reduce product cycles by 30 to 40 percent, thus allowing a faster response to customers.[13]

Like Motorola, other companies are also trying to improve their global supply-chain management, however, some have been more successful than others. As a result, major consulting companies around the world such as Accenture, The Boston Consulting Group, McKinsey & Company, Booz & Company, and IBM, have developed global supply-chain management consulting practices. IBM's supply-chain practice includes 7,500 consultants worldwide, and the company recently opened a supply-chain research facility in China to help a growing number of companies manage their ever expanding global trade networks. Sanjeev Nagrath, IBM Global Services' supply-chain management head, said that the supply-chain research facility is located in Beijing due to China's increasing relevance in supply chains around the world. "China is a key link in the global supply chain, from being a major procurement center for sourcing activities to a manufacturing center to now even an R&D center," he explained. The opening of the supply-chain research facility was welcomed by the Chinese government, especially after several scandals regarding Chinese products, such as tainted food and toys as well as unsafe drugs. Since then it has been discovered that many of the problems that led to the scandals originated in substandard supply chains, because some companies in the supply chain could not trace back to suppliers the faulty components in the defective products. Nagrath said that what happened in China caught the attention of many global companies, particulary of those firms in the pharmaceutical industry supply chains, due to the safety risks implicit in their products. Recently, concerns regarding the visibility of all aspects of supply chains and the traceability of materials along supply chains were focused upon during a two-day supply-chain summit organized by IBM. "They want to see into the supplier's supplier's supply chains," Nagrath stated.[14]

David J. Green - technology/Alamy

Motorola's wireless telephone handset division was a pioneer in cellular telephones.

telecommunication networks
collections of computer hardware and software arranged to transmit information from one place to another

internetworking
the linking of separate networks into an interconnected network, where each network retains its own identity

enterprise resource planning (ERP) systems
software packages designed to integrate the majority of a firm's business processes, execute all transactions related to the firm's business processes being integrated, store each piece of data only once in an enterprise-wide database, allow access to data and information in real time, and operate in a client-server environment, traditional or web-based

The Role of Information Technologies

The integration and coordination of global supply chains would not be possible without information technologies such as the Internet and *enterprise resource planning systems*. This section will describe these two information technologies and the roles they play in global supply-chain management.

Telecommunication networks include collections of computer hardware and software arranged to transmit information from one place to another. For brevity, telecommunication networks will simply be called networks. **Internetworking** refers to the linking of separate networks into an interconnected network, while each network remains independent. The Internet is an international network of networks containing hundreds of thousands of private and public networks in more than 150 countries. The Internet is an example of internetworking, and it is the world's largest and most widely used network, with an estimated 1,600 million users.

Enterprise resource planning (ERP) systems refer to software packages designed to integrate the majority of a firm's business processes, execute all transactions related to integration of the firm's business processes, store each piece of data only once in an

ETHICAL PERSPECTIVES

Supply Chain Disruptions

A popular proverb states "a chain is only as strong as its weakest link." Supply chains are no different. When a company member of the supply chain halts its production, the entire supply chain may collapse as a result. Recently, Honda faced that scenario when striking workers in the Foshan factory paralyzed Honda's automobile assembly facilities in China, forcing it to shut down, due to the lack of a key component produced in the striking workers factory. After offering a 24 percent increase in pay and benefits to the striking workers, Honda has hoped to restart operations in their four joint-venture final-assembly plants.

The strike made a weakness in Honda's China supply chain become evident. Due to the stable labor environment in China, Honda decided to open just one source of transmissions in that country, the Foshan factory, which would supply approximately 80 percent of demand, and to bring the remaining 20 percent from Japan. Interestingly, in all other parts of the world where Honda has production facilities, it is company policy to have at least two suppliers for each major component, like transmissions, to protect against catastrophic events, such as the strike in the Foshan factory, that may interrupt production.

Labor experts say that the Chinese central government has since been debating what to do about the strike in the Foshan factory. Higher wages are better for Chinese workers; however, higher wages may also reduce the attractiveness to foreign investors that would like to include China in their global supply chains.

QUESTIONS:

1) If you worked for Honda, how would you determine fair wages for workers in the Foshan factory?
2) What should the Chinese central government do regarding wages at Honda?

Source: Norihiko Shirouzu, "Honda Offers Strikers in China 24 percent Pay Boost," *The Wall Street Journal*, June 1, 2010.

enterprise-wide database, allow access to data and information in real time, and operate in a client-server environment, either traditional or web-based. ERP systems aim to:

- Store all information in a single database;
- Represent each business function by a module; and
- Design the system as a collection of business processes, and not functions.

The anatomy of an ERP system is presented in Exhibit 13.3.

EXHIBIT 13.3 ANATOMY OF AN ERP SYSTEM

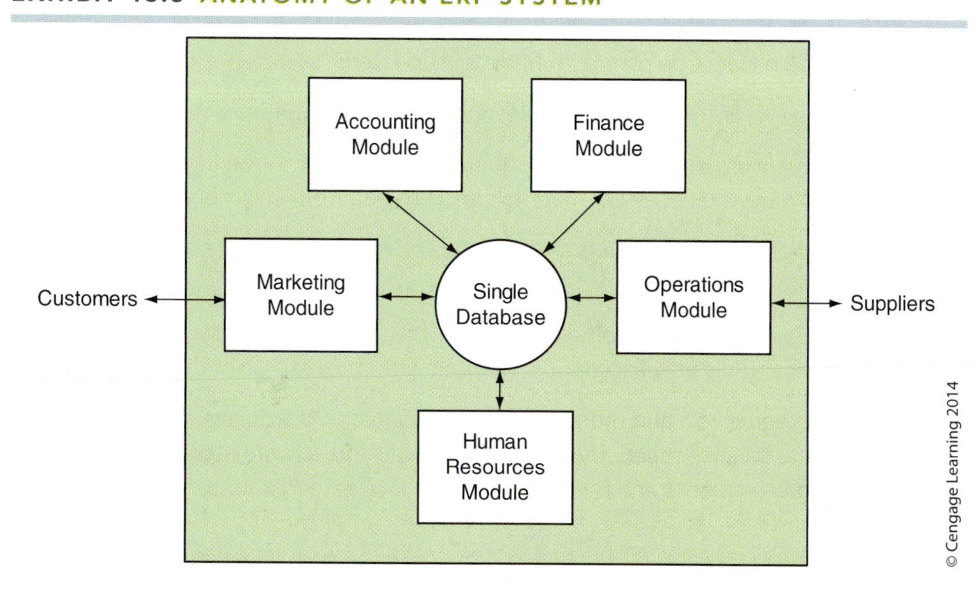

To serve the needs of global supply chains, ERP systems are *multi-language*, *multi-national*, and *multi-currency*. **Multi-language** refers to the property of ERP software to be in multiple languages. For example, one company sells an ERP system that can simultaneously operate in more than 30 different languages. When the user launches the ERP system, he or she has the option of selecting the language in which he or she will interact with the system. **Multi-national** refers to the property of ERP software to handle the accounting standards of multiple countries. Ford's ERP system follows the American accounting standards in its U.S. subsidiaries, and follows the Mexican accounting standards in its Mexico subsidiaries. **Multi-currency** refers to the property of ERP software to handle multiple currencies. A Japanese user of Sony's ERP system is able to view the company's profit & loss statement in Japanese yen, while an American user of Sony's ERP system is able to see the same statement in U.S. dollars. ERP systems are now being used in more than 100 countries, and by nearly all major industries, which include:

- Oil and gas;
- Automotive;
- High-tech and electronics;
- Consumer products;
- Public sector; and
- Health care.

ERP systems have been used with enormous success to integrate most business processes within a company. In turn, ERP systems in combination with the Internet, have become the backbone in the coordination and collaboration of global supply chains.

ERP systems integrate business processes within a company and along the supply chain, as illustrated in the example included in Davenport (1998).[15] A Paris-based sales representative for a U.S. computer manufacturer is preparing a quote for a customer using an ERP system. The salesperson enters some basic information about the customer's requirements into the ERP system using a laptop computer (let's assume that the ERP system resides in the United States and that the salesperson is accessing the system from Paris via the Internet). The ERP system then automatically produces a formal contract, in French, specifying the product's configuration, the price in Euros, and the order delivery date. When the customer accepts the terms in the contract, the sales representative keys this information into the ERP system, and the following actions are automatically executed by the system:

- The customer's credit limit is verified, and if approved, the order is recorded;
- The sales and production plan is immediately updated;
- A bill of materials is created for the order and a material requirements plan is executed;
- The shipment is scheduled, the best routing is identified, and working backward from the delivery date, the necessary materials are reserved from inventory;
- Any needed parts from suppliers are ordered, and final assembly is scheduled in the company's factory in Taiwan;
- The sales representative payroll account is credited with the corresponding commission in Euros, and his travel account is credited with the expense of the sales call; and
- The actual product cost and profitability are calculated, in U.S. dollars, and the divisional and corporate balance sheets, the accounts-payable and accounts-receivable ledgers, the cost-center accounts, and the corporate cash levels are all automatically updated.

multi-language
a property of ERP systems to simultaneously operate in multiple languages

multi-national
a property of ERP systems to handle the accounting standards of multiple countries

multi-currency
a property of ERP systems to handle multiple currencies

In short, the ERP system performs nearly every business transaction resulting from the sale, by integrating the required business processes within the computer manufacturing company, and along its supply chain.

REALITY CHECK LO-5

When you buy a ticket from a commercial airline via its website, you are interacting with its ERP system. What evidence do you have that the airline is using an ERP system?

SUMMARY

Global operations and supply-chain management has been used successfully by many firms around the world to achieve sustainable competitive advantage. Sourcing—what to make in-house and what to buy from suppliers—is a strategic decision which precedes global procurement and global production. The sourcing decision is dynamically revised as conditions around the world change, and may lead to outsourcing or to insourcing.

Once a firm has settled upon a sourcing strategy, global procurement is the business function that will manage the global suppliers, and global production is the business function that will manage the different facilities around the globe that will be producing the raw materials, components, and finished goods. The location and number of these global facilities will be determined by the location decision.

The level of business competition has increased from firm versus firm to supply chain versus supply chain. Consequently, global supply-chain management has become a key strategic component that companies use for their survival and success. World-class supply chains require coordination and collaboration, which has been made possible in part by information technologies such as the Internet and ERP systems. These two information technologies provide the day-to-day information exchanges among companies, which are members of a supply chain.

KEY TERMS

production system, *p. 314*
manufacturing system, *p. 314*
service system, *p. 314*
production facility, *p. 315*
components, *p. 315*
raw materials, *p. 315*
production stages, *p. 316*
operations management, *p. 316*
make-or-buy decision, *p. 317*
global procurement, *p. 317*
global production, *p. 317*
outsourcing, *p. 319*
domestic outsourcing, *p. 319*
global outsourcing, *p. 319*
offshoring, *p. 319*
hollow corporation, *p. 320*
insourcing, *p. 320*
dual sourcing, *p. 323*
location decision, *p. 324*
supply chain, *p. 327*
supply-chain management, *p. 327*
telecommunication networks, *p. 328*
internetworking, *p. 328*
enterprise resource planning (ERP) systems, *p. 328*
multi-language, *p. 330*
multi-national, *p. 330*
multi-currency, *p. 330*

CHAPTER QUESTIONS

1. How can global operations management be used as a source of competitive advantage?
2. List the factors that a firm should consider when making an outsourcing decision.
3. Argue why some companies should pursue global production and other companies should not.
4. How should a business organization choose a location for its production facilities?
5. Do you think that supply-chain management and ERP Systems have helped both businesses and consumers? Why or why not?

MINI CASE: WHEN IS AN AMERICAN CAR REALLY AMERICAN?

Is it possible for an American car to be more American that the Jeep Patriot? Joseph B. White writes that no other vehicle "says American more proudly than Jeep, the rugged brand that helped America win World War II." However, according to White, there could be a more American sport utility vehicle (SUV) than the Jeep Patriot: the Toyota Sequoia, which is 80 percent "domestic" according to the National Highway Traffic Safety Administration (NHTSA). In contrast, the Jeep Patriot is only 66 percent domestic. So what defines an "American" car, or, what defines an "American" car company?

The car industry transcends national boundaries. When one considers the "domestic content" as defined by NHTSA, cars or trucks sold by "Detroit" automakers such as Chrysler, Ford, or General Motors (GM), could be less American than cars or trucks sold by "Japanese" companies such as Toyota, Honda, or Nissan, despite that they all own and operate major components and assembly plants in the United States

According to Thomas H. Klier, an economist with the Federal Reserve Bank of Chicago, and James M. Rubenstein, a Miami University professor, the distinction between "American" and "foreign" vehicles is not so clear: Some models produced by the American-owned "Detroit Three" carmakers have a smaller share of domestic parts than models produced by foreign-owned carmakers. In 2006, approximately 25 percent of parts used in vehicles assembled in the United States were imported, and an equal percentage were produced by U.S.-based operations of foreign parts makers. Klier and Rubenstein add, "Against a background of global supply chains, it has become quite difficult to identify and label products such as autos by nationality."

QUESTIONS:

1) How would you decide what defines an American car and an American car company?
2) What is the impact of global operations and supply-chain management on the "nationality" of goods and services?

Sources: Joseph B. White, "What is an American Car?" The Wall Street Journal, January 26, 2009; H. Klier and James M. Rubenstein, "Whose Part is it—Measuring Domestic Content of Vehicles," Chicago Fed Letter, no. 243, October 2007.

Outsourcing Clinical Trials

India, officially called the Republic of India, is the seventh-largest country by geographical area, and the second-most populous nation with more than 1.2 billion people. For the past few years, India has increasingly attracted foreign investment, especially from Western firms, due

(continued)

to India's vast and skilled workforce, which is very competitive on productivity and labor cost. In recent decades, the gross domestic product (GDP) growth rate of India has been approximately 6 percent, which makes India one of the world's fastest-growing economies.

The economic sectors which have attracted the most foreign investment in India are services, telecommunications, construction activities, and computer software and hardware. The foreign investment in computer software and hardware, telecommunications, and some services has been the result of outsourcing from Western firms. Recently, big pharmaceutical companies have also started to outsource their clinical trials to India. As a result, while some welcome the resulting jobs and economic benefits, others question the impact on the health and safety of Indian citizens. Developing new drugs is very expensive, especially because the Research & Development (R&D) process has increased in complexity. Clinical trials in particular have become more complicated because recruiting and retaining volunteers is increasingly difficult, the diseases being studied are more challenging, and more testing is needed against comparator drugs. As the complexity of the R&D process has increased, the corresponding costs have increased as well. It is estimated that on average, pharmaceutical companies spend approximately $1.25 billion on bringing new drugs to market, which represents an increase of $500 million since 2000.

Because clinical trials take most of the time and represent most of the cost in the development of new drugs, pharmaceutical companies are trying to reduce the time and cost by outsourcing clinical trials to developing countries, India being one of them. In fact, India's Health Ministry has proposed an amendment that would permit pharmaceutical companies to test their new products on Indian patients. This development has caused controversy among different groups in India. Medical experts in India are worried about the possibility of treating patients that could get sick by the drugs being tested, especially in a country that does not have the medical resources to take care of them. Even more worrisome, India's Ministry of Health has learned of several cases where drugmakers running clinical trials had not compensated survivors of most participants who died during their studies.

If pharmaceutical companies wanted to expedite the clinical trials, they would have to recruit a large number of subjects, which is not an easy task in western countries, where most potential patients either have health insurance or government aid and thus are unwilling to participate. On the other hand, the situation in India is different; most of its citizens do not have health insurance and government health services are disastrous. Finding a large number of Indian patients to participate in clinical trials should not be a problem. Getting free and regular medical care by enrolling in a clinical trial is too attractive to be declined.

POINT The benefits of allowing the clinical trials industry to grow in India outweigh the costs. A clinical-trial outsourcing firm in India argues that the country should not be kept behind other countries and close its doors to business, especially when one considers India's supply of more than 700,000 physicians, 16,000 general hospitals, and more than 300 medical colleges. This firm adds that because clinical trials for foreign sponsors must follow international rules, the trials actually help raise Indian health-care standards. And the competition for clinical-trial dollars creates pressure for the Indian health-care standards to stay high. Other supporters note that outsourced clinical trials bring to India better and new technology, diagnostics, and treatments, consequently improving India's current medical practices. These supporters also observe that drug companies bring expensive and modern equipment and spend money on training people. Moreover, as the workload flows from big institutes in first-tier cities to smaller ones in second-tier cities, the benefits spread even more.

COUNTER-POINT The benefits of allowing the clinical trials industry to grow in India do not outweigh the costs, several of which cannot even be quantified. First, given that many Indian patients sign up for clinical trials because they do not have a better alternative to get health care access, makes the practice questionable at best and immoral at worst. Second, because a vast majority of Indian patients that enroll in clinical trials are illiterate, there is not certainty whether they truly

(continued)

Outsourcing Clinical Trials *(continued)*

understand the consent documents that they sign. To complicate matters further, clinical trials in India frequently are not advertised as such, and despite regulations to ensure otherwise, in many cases the patients are never informed by their physicians that they are participating in clinical trials. Third, of the four stakeholders in a clinical trial—sponsors or drug companies,hospitals, investigators, and patients—three of them are on the same side and have vested interests in completing the clinical trial. Even worse, participating physicians are lured by offers of foreign travel, funds, and fame. Fourth, while it is true that India does have more than 700,000 doctors, only a small percentage of them received a world-class medical education, while many of them have medical degrees of questionable quality. Finally, oversight of the clinical trials by sponsors or drug companies does not guarantee that the trials will be conducted in an ethical and safe manner.

Sources: Madhur Singh, "Should Clinical Trials be Outsourced?" Time, August 7, 2008; J. A. DiMasi, "Measuring Trends in the Development of New Drugs: Time, Costs, Risks andReturns," presentation to the SLA Pharmaceutical & Health Technology Division, Spring Meeting, 2007; Tufts Center for the Study of Drug Development, "Growing Protocol Design Complexity Stresses Investigators, Volunteers," Impact Report 10, January/February 2008; J. A. DiMasi and H. G. Grabowski, "The Cost of Biopharmaceutical R&D: Is Biotech Different?" Managerial and Decision Economics 28 (2007) pp. 469-479.

What Do *You* Think?

Which viewpoint do you support and why? How could you make this R&D outsourcing decision a win-win for all the stakeholders—drug companies, hospitals, investigators, and patients?

INTERPRETING GLOBAL BUSINESS NEWS

1) Car manufacturers GM and Chrysler are in serious need of improving their operations. Describe how these two car companies could benefit from global operations and supply-chain management.

2) Many businesses around the world have outsourced goods and services to India and China. However, some of these businesses have reversed course and are now insourcing these goods and services. Argue how this course reversal may be justified.

3) Nokia, the world's largest mobile phone manufacturer in 2008, had 17 percent of its phones made by suppliers. This will now reduce to almost zero percent as Nokia has decided to cut production owing to the contraction of the mobile handset market by 10 percent in 2009. The company hopes that this move will help it save $5 billion in revenue. The company has, however, confirmed that it has not given up on outsourcing as a permanent policy and that it would resume the process should the need arise and market conditions improve. Key manufacturers affected by this announcement include Foxconn, China's BYD, Jabil Circuit, and Elcoteq. How do you think that Nokia negotiated this reduction with its suppliers?

4) As discussed in the chapter, Boeing is considering to dual source some of the components of its 787 Dreamliner. This implies that a certain percent of Boeing's requirements, say X percent will be produced in-house, and 100-X percent will be purchased from suppliers. How would you determine the value of X percent?

PORTFOLIO PROJECTS

Exploring Your Own Case in Point: Global Operations

After reading this chapter, you should be prepared to answer some basic questions about your favorite company.

1) Is the company practicing global procurement? Is the company practicing global production?

2) If the company is procuring globally, what goods and services is it procuring and from which countries? If the company is producing globally, what goods and services are produced globally and in which countries?

3) Has the company outsourced goods and services? Has the company insourced goods and services?

4) Is the company a member of one or more supply chains? If yes, can you identify the major members of the supply chain(s)?

Developing an International Strategy for Your Own Small Business: Operations and Supply-Chain Management

From an operations and supply-chain management perspective, the first major decision that you have to make is to determine the organizational boundaries of your firm. The following questions will help you to make this decision:

1) What goods and services would you buy and what goods and services would you produce in-house?

2) What goods and services would you buy domestically and what goods and services would you buy globally?

3) Should you have one or more production facilities?

4) Should your production facility or facilities be located domestically or globally?

5) Will your company be a member of supply chain(s)? If yes, and there are alternative supply chains, how do you decide which supply chain or chains to join?

CHAPTER NOTES

[1] Jane Spencer, "Lenovo Looks to Expand Global Reach," The Wall Street Journal, July 27, 2007.
[2] For an excellent treatment of domestic operations management, the reader is referred to Julian E. Gaspar et al., Introduction to Business, Houghton Mifflin, 2006.
[3] R. H. Hayes et al., Operations, Strategy, and Technology: Pursuing the Competitive Edge, Wiley, 2005.
[4] "Outsourcing," Economist.com, September 29, 2008.
[5] K. Hall, "Can Outsourcing Save Sony," Business Week, January 30, 2009.
[6] "Outsourcing," Economist.com, September 29, 2008.
[7] J. Heizer and B. Render, Operations Management, 10th ed., Prentice Hall, 2011.
[8] Nike, Inc. 2011 Annual Report.
[9] J. Weber, "Boeing to Rein in Dreamliner Outsourcing," Business Week, January 16, 2009.
[10] S. Chopra and M. S. Sodhi, "Managing Risk to Avoid Supply-chain Breakdown," MIT Sloan Management Review, Fall 2004.
[11] J. Weber, "Boeing to Rein in Dreamliner Outsourcing," BusinessWeek, January 16, 2009.
[12] Q. Fottrell and J. Scheck, "Dell Moving Irish Operations to Poland," The Wall Street Journal, January 8, 2009.
[13] A. Tan, "Motorola Makes Big Supply Chain Investment in Singapore," BusinessWeek, June 6, 2006.
[14] L. Chao, "IBM Opens a Research Center in China," The Wall Street Journal, March 14, 2009.
[15] T. H. Davenport, "Putting the Enterprise into the Enterprise System," Harvard Business Review, July-August 1998.

CH 14

Global Financial Management

© C Miller Design/Getty Images

vario images GmbH & Co.KG/Alamy Limited

After studying this chapter, you should be able to:

LO-1 **Explain how foreign exchange risk affects firms and investors.**

LO-2 **Describe different ways to hedge exchange rate risk.**

LO-3 **Discuss sources of funds to finance international trade and investment.**

LO-4 **Apply net present value analyses to the capital budgeting decisions facing firms with international operations.**

LO-5 **Discuss how exchange rate risk affects firms' cash flows and its impact on stock returns.**

CULTURAL PERSPECTIVE

Oil Prices and the Dollar

Oil prices are denominated in terms of U.S. dollars in international commodities markets. In 2007 and 2008 the dollar price of a barrel of crude oil increased from about $60 to more than $140 at its peak (see Exhibit 14.1). The surge in oil prices more than doubled the cost of a gallon of gasoline in the United States. While oil firms and crude oil exporting countries experienced higher revenues and profits, higher gasoline prices hurt consumers and business firms around the world.

The impact of higher oil prices affected some countries more than others. During this time period, the falling value of the dollar against the euro increased dollar costs of oil for U.S. gasoline buyers. In contrast, Europeans did not see as large increases in their gasoline prices due to the rising value of the euro against the dollar. Because oil is sold in dollars, the rising euro enabled them to buy more oil per euro than a U.S. buyer could purchase per dollar.

EXHIBIT 14.1 THE PRICE IN DOLLARS OF ONE BARREL OF CRUDE OIL, MARCH 2007 TO MARCH 2009

When the dollar is falling in value, the cost of oil to the U.S. tends to rise.

High oil prices caused gasoline buyers to change their habits worldwide. People began to drive less, and they also bought fewer vehicles with low gasoline mileage. Changes in behavior were more pronounced in the United States due to the low dollar value and higher relative cost of oil compared to other countries. U.S. automakers suffered from falling car and truck sales, which tended to worsen the U.S. recession starting in December 2007. As the global economy cooled, lower demand pushed oil prices down to the $40-per-barrel range. Unfortunately, as unemployment increased in the global recession, car and truck sales declined further, endangering the survival of U.S. and some other countries' auto manufacturers.

These historic events highlight the challenges of financial managers in today's global markets. How do changing energy costs and global economic activity affect business firms? Is there a way to reduce the risk of changing currency values on business profits? Managers today must understand international finance and investment principles to help answer these questions.

Introduction

Imagine a world with only one currency. In this hypothetical world, there would be no risk associated with one currency changing in value relative to another currency, or **exchange rate risk**. However, there are more than 150 currencies that circulate today, which leads to complex exchange rate risk effects on firms. Floating exchange rates can randomly change over time as currencies are traded in world currency markets. The movement of exchange rates, such as the euro-to-dollar rate, can have short-term and long-term effects on firms, investors, and others. In turn, exchange rates can significantly affect different kinds of risks facing market participants. While some exchange rate risk can be hedged (or reduced) with derivative instruments, including futures, forward, options, and swap contracts, firms with international operations respond to movements in the values of currencies as they receive revenues and expense their costs.

Another aspect of exchange rate risk is that firms competing in the global economy need to acquire funds for their investment projects from global financial markets. International banks, bond markets, and stock markets are continuing to grow with expanding foreign trade and international business activities. Government financing sometimes provides further assistance to firms, enabling them to compete in overseas markets.

Firms incorporate the effects of exchange rate risk in capital budgeting decisions that determine their future investments. The cost of capital is used to discount cash flows and calculate net present values of potential investment projects. While the cost of debt is easy to compute, the cost of equity is subject to some controversy. Should equity be priced on a domestic or global basis? How does exchange rate risk affect the cost of equity for a firm? This chapter will address these questions. It will also discuss the operating and financing effects of exchange rate movements on firms with international business activities.

exchange rate risk the impact of random change in the value of one currency with respect to other currencies

LO-1

Explain how foreign exchange risk affects firms and investors.

Measuring Foreign Exchange Exposure

Two kinds of short-term effects of currency movements are transactions risk and translation risk. The long-term effects of currency movements are associated with economic risk.

Transactions risk arises from the import and export of goods and services. For example, consider a U.S. firm that pays for its labor and materials in dollars, but then sells its products to Europe and earns revenues in euros. If the euro decreases in value relative to the dollar (i.e., the euro-to-dollar exchange rate rises, implying a stronger dollar against the euro), the U.S. firm would experience no change in dollar-based operating costs, but its dollar revenues would decrease as euro-based revenues yield fewer dollars, thereby squeezing profits. This transactions risk affects both exporters and importers. In this example, a U.S. importer would convert its strong dollars to weak euros and buy European goods, thereby decreasing its cost of imported goods, which would boost profits. Of course, if the dollar decreased in value relative to the euro, the U.S. exporter would gain profits, and the U.S. importer would lose profits.

Translation risk is associated with the short-term effects of currency movements on the **consolidated accounting statements** of a firm. Multinational corporations (MNCs) that have subsidiaries abroad are required by home country tax authorities to report in their financial statements (income statement and balance sheet) the financial performance of all subsidiaries abroad. Converting the subsidiary's financial statements from their operating currency to the MNC's home country reporting currency satisfies this requirement. U.S. firms will naturally express accounts in dollars, European firms in euros, and so on. Some international firms provide accounting reports in two currencies due to significant trading in the firm's stock by investors in different countries' financial markets. Changes in currency values over time will affect accounting values. For example, if the total assets of a U.S. firm increase from $100 million to $120 million in one year, this 20 percent increase in total assets is affected by the change in the value of the dollar over time. If the total assets were expressed in euros, and the value of the dollar decreased from €1 per dollar to €0.80 per dollar, the euro value of total assets would have decreased 4 percent from €100 million to €96 million. It is clear that the currency denomination of accounting statements can affect their interpretation. Translation risk can affect all firms reporting accounting information with operations abroad.

In contrast, **economic risk** is associated with the ways in which long-term exchange rate movements affect firms. Protracted swings in exchange rates over a period of time can affect a firm's long-run cash flows and thereby alter the firm's value. Research has demonstrated that exchange rates have larger impacts upon the stock prices of firms in the long term than in the short term.[1] For example, currency values could potentially be advantageous or disadvantageous to firms in a country. Prolonged periods of relatively high dollar values in world currency markets would be a disadvantage to U.S. exporters and an advantage to their foreign competitors.

A convenient way to measure a currency's value in world currency markets is to use a basket of currencies. On its website, the International Monetary Fund (IMF) reports daily exchange rates between individual currencies and a basket of currencies consisting of U.S. dollars, European euros, British pounds, and Japanese yen, known as the **Special Drawing Right (SDR)**. Weights on the currencies are based on world trading patterns of goods and services. The U.S. Federal Reserve reports similar exchange rates using a basket of more than ten major currencies (i.e., the major currency index, or MCI). *The Wall Street Journal* uses the J.P. Morgan index of currencies to report daily values of the dollar. While other currency baskets exist, these examples can be used to evaluate how an individual currency is valued in world currency markets. If the SDR-to-USD exchange rate is increasing (or decreasing) over time, it means that the dollar is depreciating (or appreciating) over time in world currency markets. In this regard, large swings in SDR-to-USD values over an extended period of time would increase economic risk for firms affected by dollar movements.

transactions risk
how short-term changes in exchange rates can affect operating costs and revenues of firms engaged in international business activities

translation risk
the short-term effects of currency movements on the consolidated accounting statements of a firm

consolidated accounting statements
the income statements and balance sheets of multinational corporations and of all subsidiaries abroad due to home country tax requirements

economic risk
the ways in which long-term exchange rate movements affect firms

Special Drawing Right (SDR)
a basket of currencies consisting of dollars, euros, pounds, and yen created by the International Monetary Fund (IMF)

REALITY CHECK LO-1

Imagine buying a car to be built in Germany and then shipped to the United States. You pay an initial small amount to sign the contract and proceed with the order. The contract shows the balance due in dollars when you pick up the car from a local dealer in four months. Are you exposed to exchange rate risk? What about the car manufacturer in Germany?

LO-2

Describe different ways to hedge exchange rate risk.

Hedging Forex Risk with Derivatives

Firms and investors exposed to short- and long-term foreign exchange (forex) risks can hedge them using various derivative contracts. **Hedging** intends to reduce potential transaction, translation, and economic risks of currency movements that could lead to volatile cash flows and losses. It is important to note that speculation is the opposite of hedging. **Speculators** attempt to earn profits from trading in currencies or currency derivatives. Speculators can be instrumental in aggressively pricing currency contracts, which makes the forex market efficient when prices reflect all available information. Unlike speculators, hedgers seek to reduce forex risk and, therefore, are not engaged in efficiently pricing currency contracts. Hedges are similar to insurance contracts where a premium is paid to protect against potential losses. Forex risks can be hedged through the use of several different contracts including futures, forwards, options, and swaps.

hedging
using currency derivatives to reduce potential transaction, translation, and economic risks of currency movements that could lead to losses for a firm or investor

speculators
attempts in currencies and currency derivatives to earn profits from trading them and help to make prices efficient

Futures Contracts

Currency futures contracts are standardized agreements to buy or sell a specified amount of currency on a particular date in the future at a pre-determined price. They are similar to debt, equity, and commodity futures contracts. The buyer agrees to take delivery of a set amount of the currency on the future date at the set price and is considered to be in a **long position** due to profiting on an increase in the value of the currency. The seller agrees to make delivery of the currency according to the agreed terms, and is considered to be in a **short position** due to profiting on a decrease in the value of the currency. **Organized exchanges** such as the Chicago Mercantile Exchange (CME) trade selected futures contracts in major currencies, for example:

- EUR (quoted as the number of U.S. dollars per one euro, EUR-to-USD)
- GBP (U.S. dollars per British pound)
- CHF (U.S. dollars per Swiss franc)
- AUD (U.S. dollars per Australian dollar)
- CAD (U.S. dollars per Canadian dollar)
- RP (British pounds per euro)
- RF (Swiss francs per euro)

Other important forex derivative markets are the pan-European Euronext.liffe and Tokyo Financial Exchange.[2]

There are some common rules in trading currency futures contracts. For example, forex derivatives specify the third Wednesday in March, June, September, and December as the expiration dates for contracts. Futures contracts are **marked-to-market** daily,

currency futures contracts
standardized agreements to buy or sell a specified amount of currency at a date in the future at a pre-determined price

long position
buying a currency in a currency futures contract and profiting on an increase in the value of the currency over time

short position
selling a currency in a currency futures contract and profiting on a decrease in the value of the currency over time

organized exchanges
the trading of futures contracts in major currencies and offering price transparency and efficiency in addition to elimination of counterparty risk due to guaranteed payments on contacts

marked-to-market
futures contracts in which gains (losses) are earned (paid) in cash at the end of each trading day

AP Photo/M. Spencer Green

The Chicago Mercantile Exchange is just one of the organized exchanges trading in major currencies.

which means that gains and losses in futures positions are reconciled at the close of trading each day by the exchange organization. At that time, buyers and sellers must pay them immediately in cash. Another interesting feature of futures contracts is that buyers and sellers can close them at any time prior to the delivery date. The flexibility to unwind forex hedges when they are no longer needed is a convenient advantage. Organized exchanges offer the further advantages of price transparency and efficiency, as well as the elimination of counterparty credit risk (e.g., the possibility that a buyer will not buy a security later that you sold at a previously agreed upon price). The exchange clearinghouse manages all gains and losses and guarantees payments on contracts related to counterparty credit risk. Finally, contracts can be purchased for a small commitment fee known as the **margin**. This low cost of futures contracts makes them very affordable to use as a way to manage exchange rate and other market risks. If losses occur causing a market participant's balance to fall below the maintenance margin at the end of the trading day, a **margin call** occurs that requires the customer to replenish the margin account.

Example of a forex futures hedge. Suppose a U.S. firm exports its products to European countries and is paid in euros at a later date. If it sells 100,000 units at 1,000 euros each, the revenues it will later receive will equal €1 million. If the current spot EUR-to-USD exchange rate increases from 1.50 to 1.70 between the time of sale and time of payment (i.e., the cost of one euro increases from $1.50 to $1.70), the €1 million will increase from $1.5 million to $1.7 million for a gain of $200,000. Here the weakening dollar actually increases the revenues of the U.S. exporting firm.

What if the dollar strengthens against the euro? If the EUR-to-USD spot exchange rate falls to 1.30 over the same period, the firm could lose $200,000 in revenues. To hedge this forex transaction risk, the firm can short EUR futures contracts on the CME. As the EUR-to-USD spot exchange rate declines, the futures price will also fall, but not

margin
small commitment fee needed to purchase a futures contract

margin call
losses that are incurred and that cause the participant's balance to fall below the maintenance margin at the end of the trading day

exactly as much as the spot rate. If the firm sells short a EUR futures contract for 1.4815 and later buys the contract for 1.2850, given that each contract represents €125,000 such that 1 point = $.0001 per euro = $12.50 per contract, the gain would be as follows: ($1.4815 – $1.2850) × €125,000 = $24,562.50.[3] Futures and spot prices are typically not the same. In this example, to hedge a potential loss of $200,000 in revenues, the firm would need to sell 8 EUR futures contracts. This would result in a gain of $24,562.50 × 8 = $196,500 on the short EUR futures position, which offsets all but $3,500 in lost revenues.

Exhibit 14.2 summarizes the gains and losses on futures contracts. The price of a futures contract to buy (long position) and sell (short position) is denoted at P_0. If the difference between the sell and buy prices is positive, the payoff on the futures contract is a gain, and the converse if the difference is negative. Long positions earn gains as prices rise over time, while short positions earn gains as prices fall. Hedging involves using a *futures position* (i.e., buying or selling futures contracts) in an attempt to offset losses in the *cash position* (i.e., the sale of products to Europe by the U.S. exporter in the above example). Speculating, in contrast, implies holding unhedged futures positions with no cash position.

Forward Contracts

currency forward contracts
futures contracts available in currencies of emerging-market countries by large banks in the OTC market

over-the-counter (OTC) market
derivatives market run by large banks

Foreign currency contracts are one of the most popular forward futures. However, a problem with currency futures contracts is that they are typically available only for major currencies. For emerging-market countries' currencies there is only limited ability to obtain futures contracts. Consequently, **currency forward contracts** in other currencies can be arranged with large banks in the **over-the-counter (OTC) market**. Unlike futures contracts, forward contracts are less standardized, can be customized to meet the hedging needs of the buyer, and are not marked-to-market daily. Because they are not marked-to-market, there is no liquidity risk related to immediate cash access to pay for possible losses. Because there is no organized exchange to trade forward contracts, for every buyer there is a seller who is a counterparty. Examples include currency forward contracts in the Thai baht, Mexican peso, Czech koruna, and so forth. Most contracts are

EXHIBIT 14.2 PAYOFFS FOR FUTURES CONTRACTS

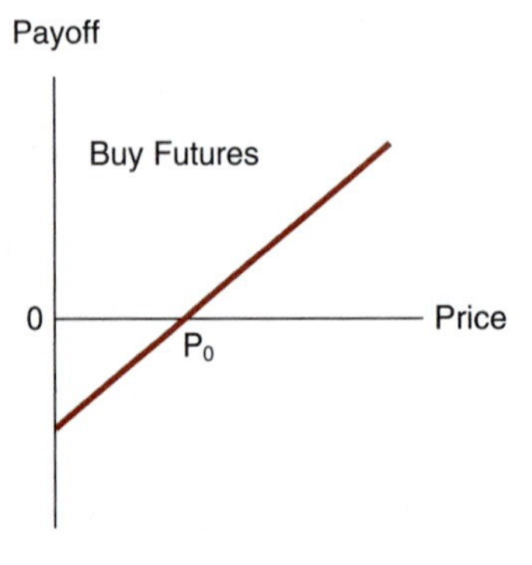

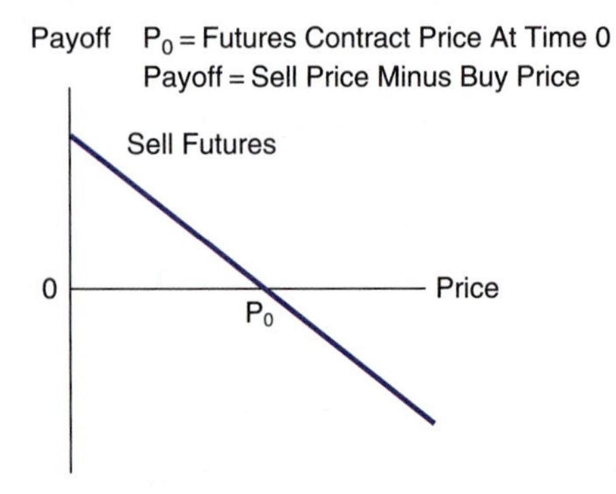

completed on the expiration date, as closing out early may require negotiation with the counterpart. Credit risk exists in forward contracts if the counterparty fails to perform their side of the agreement.

Options Contracts

Currency option contracts give an investor the right—but not the obligation—to buy (**call option**) or sell (**put option**) a specified amount of currency at a date in the future at a pre-determined price (known as the *strike price*). The buyer pays a **premium** to the seller for this right.[4] Buyers are said to be in a long position, and sellers in a short position. The buyer will not execute the option in the case of loss, such that the seller will earn the premium. If the option is executed by the buyer due to a gain, the seller will lose the amount of the buyer's gain. Most currency options are traded in the OTC market by large banks, but organized exchanges such as the CME and Philadelphia Options Exchange do handle some currency option volume. OTC options are typically European options that can only be exercised on the expiration date. American options offered by U.S. exchanges can be exercised prior to the expiration date.

In the previous example of a forex futures hedge, it was assumed that the EUR-to-USD exchange rate declined over time as the euro declined against the dollar. The U.S. exporter achieved a gain on the short EUR futures position. What if the EUR-to-USD exchange rate had increased over time? Then a loss in the futures position would cancel out the gain in the cash position (i.e., the increased revenues on export sales to Europe). To prevent this outcome, the U.S. firm could purchase a put option on the EUR-to-USD rate. If this forex rate declined over time, the U.S. firm would exercise the option for a gain by selling euros at the agreed upon exchange rate or strike price, and buying them back at the lower spot market price for a profit in dollars. This would offset the U.S. firm's cash position dollar losses. However, if the forex rate increased over time, the option would not be exercised and the cash position gain would be realized. This potential gain in the cash position causes the cost (premium) of option contracts to be considerably higher than the cost of a futures contract.

Exhibit 14.3 diagrams the payoffs on call option and put option contracts. The call option offers gains to buyers and sellers as shown relative to the agreed upon strike price. The put option offers opposite gains to buyers and to sellers. Hence, call and put options are the reverse of one another. Note that a put option in EUR-to-USD contracts is the same as a call option in USD-to-EUR contracts. Option contracts are typically favored over futures contracts when cash flows are uncertain. In the previous example, if the U.S. exporter is promised €1 million for its products upon delivery, there is no cash flow uncertainty and the futures contract is the preferred forex hedge. If the payment is uncertain due to an agreement to set the price on the delivery date according to world prices at that time, then the option contract is preferred. If a futures contract was used, it could generate gains (or losses) that are less than (or greater than) the opposite cash position losses (or gains), with the result of net losses on the hedge.

call option
an investor's right (but not obligation) to buy an asset (e.g., a currency) at a pre-determined price

put option
an investor's right (but not obligation) to sell an asset (e.g., a currency) at a pre-determined price

premium
the price paid by the buyer to the seller for an option contract

Swap Contracts

As another way to hedge exchange rate movements, firms can agree to swap currencies in the future at a previously agreed exchange rate. **Currency swaps** can be established over a period of up to ten years. Some exchanges offer currency swaps, which lower counterparty risk due to guaranteed performance by the exchange. Large banks offer swaps in the global OTC market. In the above example, the U.S. exporter and a European importer buying a considerable volume of products could arrange a currency swap of €1 million for

currency swaps
allow firms to exchange currencies at a previously agreed exchange rate as a way to hedge exchange rate movements

EXHIBIT 14.3 PAYOFFS FOR CALL AND PUT OPTIONS CONTRACTS

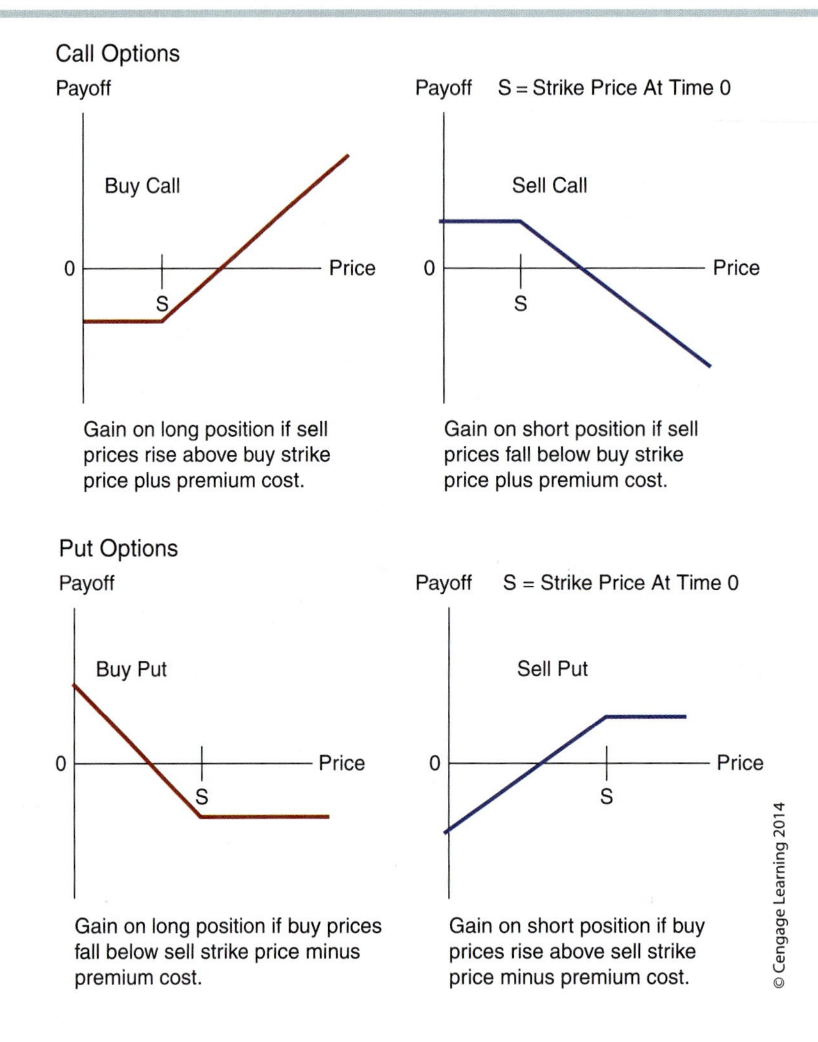

$1.5 million over a five-year period. The EUR-to-USD exchange rate will move up and down over time (i.e, the dollar cost of one euro), therein giving an advantage to the U.S. exporter when this rate decreases, and to the European importer when it increases. On average, these exchange rate fluctuations will often cancel one another out, unless there is a long-term decrease or increase in the exchange rate. In the latter instance, it may be possible to unwind or cancel a swap, but this would be costly due to penalty payments to the other party in the swap.

Currency swaps are often combined with interest rate swaps, which are commonly known as **plain vanilla currency swaps**. Consider a U.S. firm that arranges a five-year loan from a Japanese bank for ¥10,000 million at a fixed annual rate of 4 percent. A Japanese firm arranges a five-year loan from a U.S. bank for $100 million at a floating interest rate plus 1 percent. The two firms could engage in a swap at the spot rate of 100 yen for $1. Typically a bank will help find swap counterparties, negotiate the details of the swap, and take care of payments and accounting services. All cash flows, including the initial receipt of principal, all interest payments, and later return of principal would be paid in each firm's home country currency. Exhibit 14.4 summarizes this vanilla currency swap. Why would the firms seek loans from foreign banks in this example? They are able to secure credit on more favorable interest rates or other loan terms from the foreign lender. Hence, firms can use currency swaps to save on credit costs.

plain vanilla currency swap
an interest rate swap, often combined with a currency swap, if the interest being swapped is in different currencies

EXHIBIT 14.4 VANILLA CURRENCY SWAP

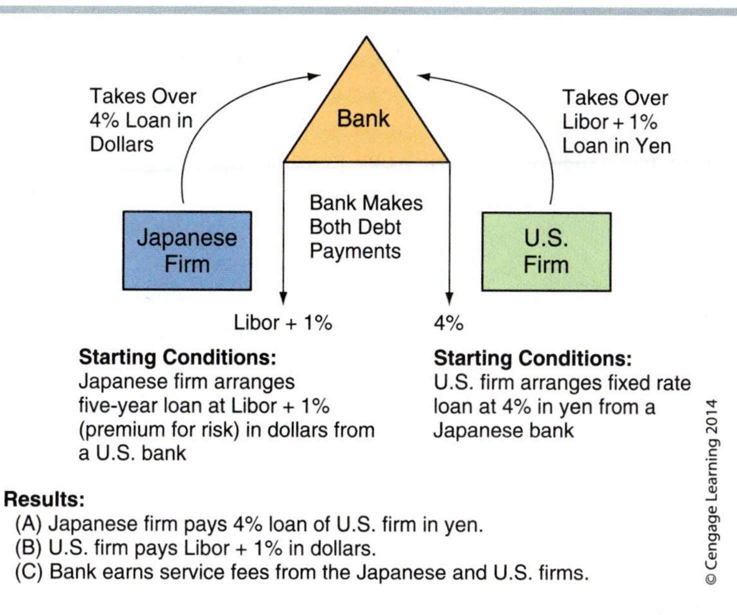

REALITY CHECK LO-2

Assume that you are a manager for a U.S. company that is selling products to a Japanese company that will pay you in yen. Do you have exchange rate risk? How could you hedge this risk to protect your company?

Financing International Trade and Investment

LO-3
Discuss sources of funds to finance international trade and investment.

Firms finance their international operations in a variety of ways. Large banks normally handle short-term financing of goods and services. Accessing international bond and stock markets provides long-term financing of capital equipment, land, and buildings. Government financing is also available to help meet international trade policy goals in a particular country.

International Banking

Large, **money center banks** in different countries dominate international banking. In the United States the top 15 banks would be included in this category, and globally there are about 200 such banks. Large, wholesale payments by businesses, banks, and governments are made via **CHIPS** (Clearing House Interbank Payments System) in New York City for dollar payments. **SWIFT** (Society of Worldwide Interbank Financial Telecommunications) provides secure communications for contracts, invoices, and other trade documents that normally accompany cash payments. A foreign importer paying for U.S. goods would order its local bank to electronically transfer the required dollar payment to a correspondent bank in the United States with whom it regularly cooperates in payments services. Funds are then transferred from the correspondent bank to the beneficiary bank of the United States exporter, which could be accomplished in the United States by means of the Fedwire operated by the Federal Reserve. Banks earn fees on these payments and documentation services.

money center banks
large global banks

CHIPS (Clearing House Interbank Payments System)
organization in New York City that provides large, wholesale dollar payments services for businesses, banks, and governments

SWIFT (Society of Worldwide Interbank Financial Telecommunications)
organization that provides secure communications for contracts, invoices, and other trade documents that normally accompany cash payments

A number of payment methods exist that differ in terms of their risk. **Payment in advance** is the safest method, but this exposes the importer to some risk concerning delivery of the goods. For this reason, the exporter and importer may split the payment with half due immediately and half due upon delivery. A **commercial letter of credit (LC)** offers payment protection to both parties, as the importer's bank writes a guarantee of payment. The importer's bank makes payment when goods are delivered and bills of lading and other shipping documents are presented. A LC is usually irrevocable, which means that the importer bank guarantees payment if the conditions of the sale are met. The exporter can take the LC to its bank and obtain the credit financing needed to pay for producing the goods for shipment. Then, the bank can sell the LC into the financial marketplace as a money market instrument known as a **banker's acceptance**. Note that the exporter has been paid for its goods, the bank has recouped its funds loaned out to the exporter, and market investors have a money market instrument that is backed by both the bank and the importer. When the importer finally pays for the goods, the funds are transferred to the banker's acceptance investors. Finally, an **open account** is a simple agreement wherein the exporter sends an invoice with the goods and the exporter pays upon their receipt. Larger firms with good relations are more likely to use this method of payment due to low risk of default on the payment.

Large international firms deal in considerable volumes of goods and often must obtain a *participation loan* from a group of banks known as a **syndicate**. A lead bank negotiates the loan terms with the firm and communicates with a group of managing banks that will underwrite the loan. Smaller participating banks may be contacted by the managing banks to accept portions of the loan. Loans are priced using floating international interest rates plus a premium for credit risk. LIBOR (London interbank offered rate) is a common international interest rate used in the United States, Europe, and other countries. SIBOR (Singapore interbank offered rate) is often used in the Pacific basin region. Additionally, the syndicate of banks each charge underwriting fees, commitment fees, and fees for other related expenses.

payment in advance
the safest method available to an exporter, but that which exposes the importer to some risk related to delivery of goods

commercial letter of credit (LC)
payment protection to both exporters and importers, as the importer's bank writes a guarantee of payment

banker's acceptance
when a bank sells a LC into the financial marketplace as a money market instrument

open account
a simple agreement wherein the exporter sends an invoice with the goods and the exporter pays upon the receipt

syndicate
a group of banks that collectively make a loan to a firm

International Bond Markets

For most of the 20th century, only large multinational corporations (MNCs) of developed industrial countries could issue long-term bonds in international markets. Their market visibility and financial soundness enabled them to attract investors around the world. Coca-Cola, General Electric, Royal Dutch Shell, and Toyota Motor Corporation are examples of MNCs. However, a number of changes have occurred in the last 20 years that have greatly expanded international bond markets. The fall of Soviet communism in the early-1990s led many emerging-market countries to open their financial markets to foreign investors. Moody's and Standard and Poor's rating services subsequently expanded their ratings of foreign bonds by opening offices outside the United States. These **bond ratings** are important in assessing the credit quality of bond issues. Another important event was the advent of the euro in the 12 European Monetary Union countries in the late-1990s. The availability of bonds denominated in the common euro currency has increased access of European companies to a larger pool of investors, and has enabled them to cross national boundaries to acquire long-term debt capital. In general, international bond markets have contributed to world economic growth by increasing capital flows to larger firms requiring substantial capital to produce goods on a global scale.

Bonds can be categorized three ways: domestic, foreign, and Eurobond. **Domestic bonds** are debt contracts sold by firms domiciled in a country in the home currency; they are not part of the international bond market. **Foreign bonds** are issued by foreign firms in

bond ratings
Moody's and Standard and Poor's rating services which are important in assuring foreign investors of the credit quality of bond issues

domestic bonds
debt contracts sold by firms domiciled in a country in the home currency

foreign bonds
bonds that are issued by foreign firms in another country in the home currency of that country

ECONOMIC PERSPECTIVES How Securitization of Home Loans Triggered a Global Financial Crisis

One of the greatest financial innovations after WWII in the 1940s was the securitization of home loans. Banks could make home loans and sell them to large government-owned or sponsored agencies (e.g., GNMA, FNMA, and FHLMC). The agencies then packaged the home loans into pools and sold bonds called *mortgage-backed securities* (MBSs) into the world financial markets backed by monthly payments on interest and principal by homeowners. Most MBSs were considered to be high quality bonds and carried the highest investment grade credit rating of AAA.

Securitization allowed individuals to tap into the global bond market to get home financing, rather than depend solely upon deposits held by banks that shrink in economic recessions, and may not be sufficient to meet demand in growing communities. Banks received benefits from securitization, too, because the home loans did not appear on their balance sheets, therefore posing no credit risk. Acting as agents to collect the mortgage payments, banks retained service fees, and then passed the home payments on to the mortgage financing agencies. Subsequently, many mortgage brokers emerged to generate loans, sell them, and then collect service fees.

In the 1990s, banks began repackaging mortgage loans and MBSs into more complex securities called *collateralized debt obligations* (CDOs). Also, many mortgage lenders started to provide loans to below median-income home-loan applicants under new government programs (e.g., the 1992 Housing and Community Development Act). This innovation, which brought the dream of home ownership to so many U.S. citizens, reduced credit risk in banks, and created new high-quality bond markets, would also be responsible for the recent global financial crisis.

What happened is that the securitization process channeled too much bond money into home loans in specific regions of the United States including the southwestern states of California, Arizona, and Nevada, as well as Florida, Michigan, Ohio and other selected areas. Many loans were issued to subprime borrowers unable to pay back their home loans, and new interest-only mortgages were invented to enable low earning households to buy homes. Unfortunately, rating agencies such as Moody's and Standard & Poor's continued to rate such risky bonds AAA, and regulators did not stop institutions from excessive home-lending and securitization practices. When the market values of MBSs and CDOs plummeted due to recognition of underlying credit risk problems, the losses immediately impacted the balance sheets of financial institutions holding these otherwise safe investments, including banks and securities firms. Home values that were heavily financed by the securitization process plummeted in some parts of the country. Insurance companies such as AIG offering credit insurance to market participants also were adversely affected. The magnitude of the crisis was truly global because bonds were sold to financial institutions, governments, and other investors around the world.

QUESTIONS:

1) Describe the securitization process for home loans. Is this financial innovation beneficial to some participants in the financial system?
2) What went wrong with securitization of home loans in the United States? Did government also play a role in the situation?

another country in the home currency of that country. Lastly, **Eurobonds** are sold in any country outside the home country, but in the home country's currency.

The Eurobond market was initially dominated by Eurodollar bonds issued by U.S. firms in Europe denominated in dollars. Currently, the market has expanded to include all major currencies and also some emerging-market countries' currencies. More generally,

eurobonds
bonds that are sold in any country outside the home country, but in the home country's currency

the Eurobond market is part of the Euromarkets, including Eurocurrency and Euroequity markets, in which buyers and sellers of money and capital market instruments borrow and lend funds internationally in multiple currencies. Large global banks play an important role in facilitating these over-the-counter (OTC) markets. In this way, a U.S. firm for example, can find dollar-based deposit rates that are the highest earning and dollar-based bonds that are the lowest cost.

Exhibit 14.5 shows that the size of the international bond market has increased from about $6 trillion in 2000 to almost $27 trillion in 2010. Fixed rate bonds are favored over

EXHIBIT 14.5 INTERNATIONAL BONDS AND NOTES BY CURRENCY AND ISSUER

Amount outstanding (in billions of U.S. dollars)	December 2000	December 2010
Total issues	5996.367	26750.79
Floating rate bonds	1470.745	7870.982
US dollar	782.963	2164.022
Euro	469.043	4300.815
Yen	84.381	195.111
Pound sterling	112.369	934.926
Swiss franc	8.663	23.352
Canadian dollar	3.305	32.166
Other currencies	10.021	220.59
Financial institutions	1315.496	7484.243
Governments	54.262	155.746
International organizations	21.278	61.547
Corporate issuers	79.709	169.446
Fixed rate bonds	4283.866	18394.38
US dollar	2119.26	8090.763
Euro	1227.557	7382.804
Yen	351.379	514.066
Pound sterling	331.466	1128.187
Swiss franc	113.29	373.323
Canadian dollar	48.13	309.635
Other currencies	92.784	595.605
Financial institutions	2565.36	12228.22
Governments	710.707	2231.991
International organizations	352.37	820.209
Corporate issuers	655.432	3113.964

Source: Bank for International Settlements, International Debt Securities by Type, Sector and Currency, Table 13b, www.bis.org/statistics/secstats.htm.

floating rate bonds. While dollar-denominated bonds had the highest volume in 2000, euro-denominated bonds were the largest in volume in 2010. It is also important to note that financial institutions issue more international bonds than governments, international organizations, and corporations combined.

International Stock Markets

Stock markets enable firms to issue new equity and raise long-term capital. However, it should be recognized that bonds are a much more important source of long-term financing for capital investments in land, buildings, equipment, and fixed assets. Unlike bonds that often are purchased by institutional investors such as insurance companies that hold the debt securities to maturity, outstanding stocks are actively traded on a daily basis. Stock markets in developed countries and emerging-market countries allow investors around the world to invest in firms on a global basis. Many individuals have retirement savings in pension plans that can be invested in a myriad of mutual funds, which are funds managed by investment companies that pool savings and invest in stocks, bonds, real estate, commodities, and so forth. A mix of bond and stock investments is normally recommended. Stock investing is popular due the fact that stocks have outpaced other types of financial instruments in terms of returns over periods of five years or more. For example, Chinese stock markets have provided about 70 percent returns on stock investments between 2003 and 2008. By comparison, U.S. long-term bond investments have earned about 4 percent per year for a total return of about 22 percent over this same time period.

Of course, there is the possibility that stock prices can fall dramatically and result in large losses to investors. For example, the Dow Jones Industrial Average of the 30 largest U.S. firms decreased from about 13,000 in May 2008 to 7,500 in February 2009 for a loss of more than 40 percent in an eight-month period. Diversifying stock investments in different sectors of the economy and different countries can help to manage this risk. When stock prices in one sector or country rise, they may fall in another sector or country.

Exhibit 14.6 shows the stock prices of two stocks (which will be called "stock 1" and "stock 2") over time. Stock 1 has more volatile price movements than stock 2. If a person invests half of his or her money in stock 1 and half in stock 2, the combined portfolio (P) would have much lower volatility than either stock. This reduction in volatility proves that **diversification** reduces risk to investors. Professor Harry Markowitz discovered this fundamental investment concept. He argued that investors need to buy securities with price patterns that were different from one another over time. If two securities had the same price pattern, they would not afford any diversification. If their price patterns were the opposite of one another, all risk could be eliminated; however, it is not typically possible to find such a situation. Markowitz received a Nobel Prize in Economics for his work on diversification.

In view of Markowitz's well-known concept of diversification, it is surprising that investors typically invest most of their retirement and other savings in their home countries. This so-called **home bias** means that investors are not reducing their risk as much as possible. A variety of reasons may explain this potentially irrational behavior. Investors may prefer domestic companies due to a belief that they have a better understanding of their products and services, or perhaps due to the desire to support businesses in their own countries. The home bias is somewhat reduced if investors buy stocks in large domestic firms with international activities, which represent international investments. Nonetheless, most experts agree that home bias likely increases investor risk.

diversification
buying securities in a portfolio with price patterns over time that are different from one another, which reduces the volatility of the portfolio

home bias
investing most of retirement and other savings in one's home country, which reduces diversification

EXHIBIT 14.6 DIVERSIFICATION CAN REDUCE RISK FOR INVESTORS

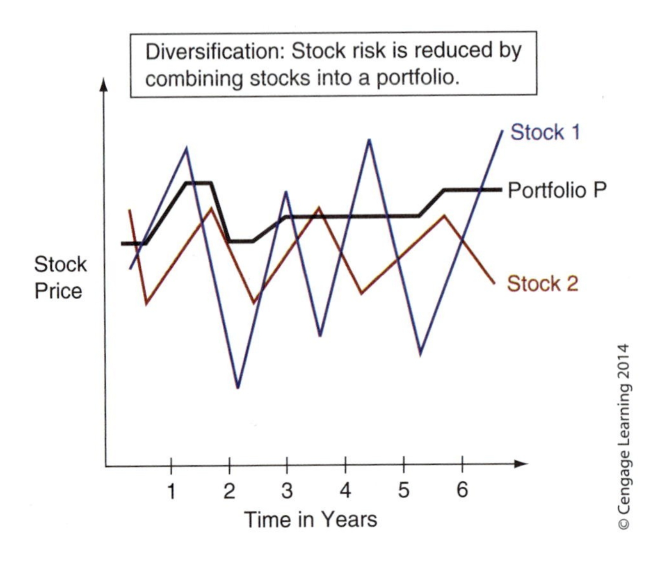

One problem in international investing is that diversification may not work when bad news affects exchanges in different countries at the same time. An example of this kind of **contagion** is the October 1987 international stock market crash, which revealed that major stock markets around the world can experience large downward price trends in tandem. On October 19, 1987 (referred to as *Black Monday*) stock prices in Hong Kong began collapsing and spread throughout the day into Europe and then North America as their stock markets opened for trading. Within one week, Hong Kong fell 46 percent, Australia 42 percent, the United Kingdom 26 percent, the United States 23 percent, and Canada 23 percent. It was the largest one-day decline in stock market history. Large stock market declines also occurred on September 17, 2001, which was the first day markets opened following the September 11, 2001 terrorist attacks. Similar concerted downward movements in global stock markets occurred from October 2008 to mid-year 2009 as the financial and economic crises at that time deepened around the world. When stock markets in many countries move down in concert with one another, international diversification benefits are reduced. Fortunately, these crisis episodes are transitory and disappear during more normal times. Hence, diversification is an effective way to reduce risk for long-term investors.

To lower the transaction costs of global investors, there has been increasing consolidation of stock exchanges over the past decade. Computer and telecommunications advances have broken barriers of distance and allowed faster and larger volume of trading in securities. Recent notable mergers include:

- New York Stock Exchange (NYSE) and Euronext, which comprises a group of European countries' exchanges
- NASDAQ (National Association of Securities Dealers Automated Quotation system) and American Stock Exchange (AMEX)
- London Stock Exchange and Borsa Italiana in Italy; and
- Chicago Mercantile Exchange (SME) and Chicago Board of Trade, which had traditionally been rivals.

contagion
when stock markets in many countries move down in concert with one another and thereby reduce international diversification benefits

PETER MORGAN/AP/Corbis

In 1987, Black Monday was the largest one-day market decline in stock market history.

It is likely that consolidation among exchanges in North America, South America, Europe, Asia, and the Middle East will continue in the future. This consolidation wave is increasing competition for securities trading with the benefits of more investment opportunities for investors and greater ability to access capital at low costs for firms. In turn, it facilitates global economic growth, thereby increasing jobs and the standards of living around the world.

Government Financing

Over the past two decades, financial crises has occurred in many different countries, including the United States, Japan, Mexico, Russia, U.K., Spain, Iceland, Italy, Ireland, Turkey, Argentina, and a number of emerging Asian and Eastern European countries. In financial crises, currency values can plummet, market volatility can cause an exodus of global investors, financial institutions can fail, and governments can lose political support. Disruption in financial markets can slow credit flows to firms, especially smaller firms that rely upon banks for financing. Without access to credit, many firms may have to curtail business activities, lay off workers, and suffer profit losses. Government financing can play an important role in providing interim credit to help business firms in a financial crisis. By providing credit, governments can reduce damage to the economy from which it would otherwise require many years to recover.

In 1944 the International Monetary Fund (IMF) and World Bank were established as agencies of the United Nations. Their purposes are to promote international monetary stability and international trade. The IMF provides short-term loans to countries in financial crisis, evaluates exchange rate policies, and gives technical assistance to countries. With more than 180 countries participating as members, the IMF can serve as a "lender of last resort" to reduce currency panics and assist troubled banks. The World Bank focuses upon long-term loans to developing countries seeking financing for economic reform purposes intended to raise the standard of living. Some examples of

World Bank mission priorities are health, education, social institutions, environmental disasters, private business formation, economic reforms, and poverty reduction. The IMF and World Bank are the major suppliers of emergency and development assistance to poorer countries.

ETHICAL PERSPECTIVES

Executive Compensation Rules in Financial Institutions

Over the past 50 years, total compensation of executives in financial institutions, including banks, securities firms, and insurance companies, has ballooned. Previously about 30 times average earnings of employees in the company, now executive compensation can reach over 400 times. Salaries and other compensation, such as stock option payments, appear to be more closely tied to the total assets than the actual performance of the firm. Also, while managers that perform well and make money earn large bonuses, often no penalties are incurred in the event of poor performance. Executives that are fired frequently receive a "golden parachute" worth millions of dollars in severance pay, cash bonuses, stock options, and other bene-fits. Some experts link high executive compensation to risk-taking by financial institutions. If a Chief Executive Officer (CEO) rapidly increased the size of an institution through mergers and acquisitions, and expanded into "hot" areas such as risky subprime mortgage lending, his or her personal wealth could be boosted. Remarkably, during the financial crisis in 2008 and 2009, a number of troubled financial institutions being rescued by the government continued to pay executives high salaries. For example, in 2008 Merrill Lynch paid out over $39 million in bonuses to a manager who had been largely responsible for over $15 billion of trading losses. On the other hand, Citibank agreed to executive compensation restrictions after receiving government support. Nonetheless, widespread unethical behavior prompted a public outcry concerning excessive executive pay in the wake of government borrowing from taxpayers to bail out failing institutions.

These problems explain why the U.S. government in early-2009 issued executive pay guidelines for large financial institutions receiving government money due to the 2008 and 2009 financial crisis. Salaries would be capped at $500,000 for executives, and stock options could not be exercised until all government support is fully repaid. In addition, there is some discussion of "clawing back" compensation paid out to executives who exhibited excessive risk taking that severely damaged their financial institutions.

Executives should be paid for creating value for shareholders, rather than taking risk. Because of this, the Federal Reserve has proposed compensation-oversight policies that seek to control salaries and excessive risk taking by all financial institutions, not only those receiving government support. These new polices would examine senior managers, traders, and other employees who take risks, loan officers, and other employees. Promoting compensation packages that are consistent with safe and sound banking and finance practices will be the primary goal.

It is now believed that excessive compensation structures at financial institutions contributed to the recent financial crisis. Some executives have sought to maximize their wealth at the expense of shareholders, workers, firms, and the greater economy. Compensation packages fostering long-term stability and growth that builds wealth more broadly across different stakeholders is needed.

QUESTIONS:

1) Are financial executive salaries and other compensation tied to performance? If not, give some examples and comment on whether they are ethical.
2) What is the U.S. government doing about ethical abuses by financial executives? Will these changes help prevent future financial crises?

Government-supported international finance is provided in developed countries by various agencies. In the United States, the **Export-Import (Ex-Im) Bank** is a government export finance agency. It seeks to level international competition by supporting U.S. firms competing against exports of other countries that are government supported. The firms receiving Ex-Im Bank financing are typically large MNCs competing globally; they are required to have at least 51 percent U.S. content to be eligible for financing. The U.S. Small Business Administration offers export financing support for smaller firms. Firms that cannot receive bank credit without a government loan guarantee can receive up to 90 percent federal guarantees for lenders on export loans. Co-guarantees from the Ex-Im Bank can be obtained in some cases.

Bank and government loans can be used by exporters to finance working capital (i.e., labor, materials, inventory, and accounts receivable)—called **trade finance**—and by importers to cover the cost of major purchases—called **term financing**. Loans can also be obtained to purchase long-term fixed assets (construction, buildings, equipment, etc.).

In Japan the **Bank of International Cooperation (JBIC)** supports exporters around the world that have at least 30 percent Japanese content. Other organizations, such as Germany's Kreditanstalt für Wiederaufbau (KfW) and Canada's Export Development Corporation (EDC) lend funds to firms based upon national interest rather than domestic content in a financed export. Large multinational firms with production facilities around the world can access government financing in many countries. However, some companies with most manufacturing operations in the United States, such as Boeing Company, are restricted to Ex-Im Bank government financing. Boeing has claimed that it lost sales in the 1990s to Airbus, which is a consortium of German, French, British, and Spanish government and private entities, with ready access to credit from KfW. International competition, as described in these examples, can be affected by government financing.

More recently, global economic and financial crises since the autumn of 2008 have moved governments around the world to implement financial assistance programs to offer government credit and investment funds to banks, insurance companies, securities firms, consumers, business firms, and others. Global credit markets froze in 2008 and 2009 and required governments to intervene through central bank and treasury actions to help get credit flowing again. In 2010 and 2011, Greece, Ireland, and Portugal suffered from credit problems that required intervention by EMU countries and the IMF. These unprecedented and historic efforts were intended to keep credit markets open and restore market confidence. Considerable government borrowing (or deficit spending) was used to finance market intervention, but the alternative of inaction was not an option in view of the dire economic consequences of a malfunctioning financial system unable to meet the credit needs of society. These government efforts to revitalize and revamp the global financial system will lay the foundation for safe and sound financial institutions in the future.

Export-Import (Ex-Im) Bank
a U.S. government export finance agency that supports U.S. firms competing against exports of other countries that are government supported

trade finance
bank and government loans used by exporters to finance working capital (i.e., labor, materials, inventory, and accounts receivables)

term financing
bank and government loans to importers to cover the cost of major purchases

Bank of International Cooperation (JBIC)
Japanese bank that supports exporters around the world that have at least 30 percent Japanese content

REALITY CHECK LO-3

Using the Internet, navigate to the Yahoo! Finance page. Look up U.S. indices and print out a chart of the past five years for the Dow Jones Composite Average. Then, look up World Indices and find a stock market index in another country. Print out the foreign country's chart for the past five years. Comparing these two charts, are there periods of time in which diversification would be obtained by investing in both stock market indices? Are there periods of time in which there would not be much diversification?

LO-4

Apply net present value analyses to the capital budgeting decisions facing firms with international operations.

Multinational Capital Budgeting

Multinational firms with operations in different countries make profits over time in different currencies. It is important to convert earnings on investments over time to their present values. Additionally, earnings in different currencies need to be converted to the home currency in order to compute their present values. In so doing, fluctuations in currency values can affect the profitability of foreign subsidiaries of multinational firms.

Parent Firm Capital Budgeting

A holding company is a conglomerate firm that is common in multinational corporations (MNCs). Suppose that the parent firm of the holding company is located in the United States, but it owns a subsidiary firm in a European country. When evaluating the profitability of capital investments (i.e., land, buildings, equipment, and other fixed assets) in its subsidiary, the parent firm needs to take the perspective of the consolidated holding company, including both the parent firm and its subsidiary. Since subsidiary profits must be repatriated to the United States to pay dividends to shareholders and be retained for future investments, it is necessary to convert all cash flows in Europe to dollars after taxes are paid overseas. Naturally, exchange rate movements will affect the dollar values of European cash flows.

The first step is to calculate the **net present value** of capital investments in the foreign subsidiary. To do this the following formula can be used:

$$NPV = \sum_{t=1}^{n} \frac{CF_t}{(1+k)^t} + \frac{Salvage_n}{(1+k)^t} - Investment,$$

where

CF_t = cash flow in period t
$Salvage_n$ = salvage value at the end of the investment's life at time n
k = the required rate of return on investment by the conglomerate firm
Investment = the initial capital investment at time 0 (now).

For example, consider a U.S. firm manufacturing computer components that outsources some of its production of new computer chips to a subsidiary in Germany. A capital investment of 20 million euros is needed to convert production lines in the German subsidiary to production of the new chips. Chips produced in Germany will be sold in Europe over the next five years. After five years, the production line will be changed to accommodate a later-generation chip, which is currently under research development. The expected net profits (cash flows in millions of euros) over the next five years, salvage value, discount factors using a 15 percent required rate of return, present value of cash flows and salvage value, and net present value in euros are as follows:

Year	Investment	CF_t	$Salvage_n$	$(1 + k)^t$	Present Values (EUR)	NPV(EUR)
0	20				20.0000	8.1584
1		5		1.1500	4.3478	
2		8		1.3225	6.0491	
3		10		1.5209	6.5751	
4		10		1.7490	5.7176	
5		6	5	2.0114	5.4688	

net present value the difference between present value of futures profits on an investment project minus the initial investment cost

In the above example, we see that the NPV is 8,158,400 euros (or €28,158,400 total present value of cash flows minus €20,000,000 initial investment). This NPV is positive and suggests good economic value added from the investment (i.e., profits well exceed those required by investors). However, we have left out an important part of the analyses. The U.S.-based MNC would not view the NPV in this way. It would convert all cash flows (including the salvage value) to dollars and then calculate their present values. Assume that the euro is falling in value relative to the dollar over this five-year period of time.

Year	Present Values (EUR)	Dollars Per Euro (EUR/USD)	Present Values (USD)	NPV (USD)
0	20.0000	1.00	20.0000	1.8000
1	4.3478	0.90	3.9130	
2	6.0491	0.80	4.8393	
3	6.5751	0.75	4.9313	
4	5.7176	0.75	4.2882	
5	5.4688	0.70	3.8282	

The NPV now is 1,800,000 dollars, which is considerably less than the NPV of 8,158,400 euros; cash flows were converted to dollars at lower exchange rates as the euro weakened against the dollar over the five-year project. However, the NPV is positive and, therefore, the capital investment should be approved.

The above example clearly demonstrates that economic risk is associated with exchange rate movements. Diversifying overseas operations in more than one foreign country with different home currencies is one way for MNCs to address the impact of exchange rates on NPVs of capital investment projects. For a U.S. MNC, if the dollar is rising against the euro, it may well be falling against the pound, yen, and other currencies. Hence, dollar exchange rates with different currencies would tend to cancel out to some degree. If diversification does not sufficiently control exchange risk, another approach is to hedge exchange rate movements using derivative contracts, including currency futures, forward, options, and swap contracts.

A variety of other risks may be involved in multinational capital budgeting decisions. For example, emerging-market countries are exposed to considerable political risk, economic risk, inflation risk, tax risk, and the like. **Country risk** means that there is uncertainty in predicting these different factors. The volatile nature of these risks in emerging-market countries makes it difficult to assess expected cash flows that extend years into the future. For this reason, MNCs must carefully evaluate long-term fixed asset commitments. Like exchange rate risk, diversifying their emerging-market activities is recommended to help reduce risk to the conglomerate firm. Gradual expansion of capital investments is also prudent, as it allows the firm to gain experience with local conditions.

Sensitivity analysis is a good way to assess risky investments abroad. Optimistic, expected, and pessimistic scenarios should be documented to better understand the range of NPVs from low to high that are possible under reasonable assumptions. If NPVs remain positive even in the pessimistic scenario, management can be more confident that the capital project will be successful.

MNCs are continuously evaluating alternative capital projects. Exhibit 14.7 gives a graphical comparison of different capital budgeting opportunities available to a MNC with a fixed amount of investment funds. Projects 1 to 4 have positive NPVs and are acceptable, while projects 5 and 6 should be rejected due to negative NPVs. Under the assumption of fixed and limited capital sources of funds, project 1 has the highest NPV and is the only project chosen. If the firm can raise additional capital by arranging bank financing, issuing bonds and stocks, or through disinvestment in less profitable operations, projects 2 to 4 may be accepted.

country risk
the uncertainty in predicting how a variety of different factors will affect an investment in a country, including political risk, economic risk, inflation risk, tax risk, etc

sensitivity analysis
an examination of optimistic, expected, and pessimistic scenarios to give a more complete picture of the risks and returns of investments abroad

EXHIBIT 14.7 SELECTING ACCEPTABLE CAPITAL BUDGETING PROJECTS

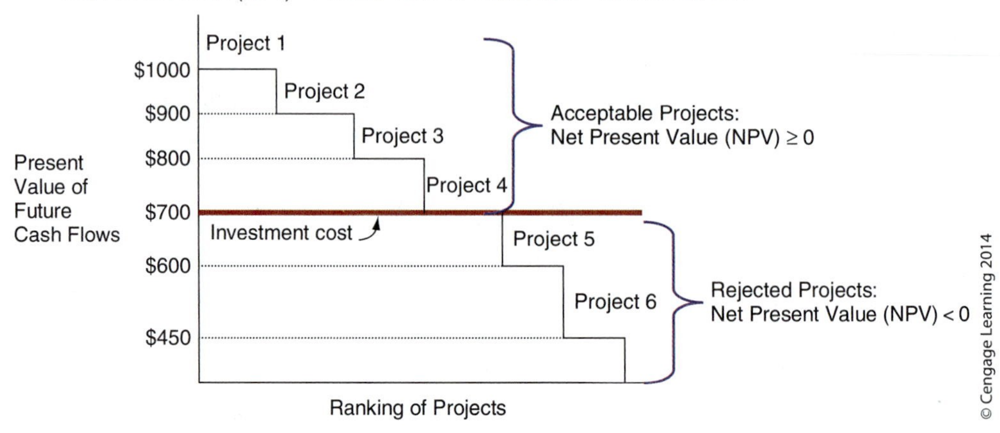

The Cost of Capital: Domestic Versus Global

The **cost of capital** is the required rate of return demanded by stock and bond investors. In the above NPV analyses, the cost of capital was the discount rate assumed to be 15 percent. The following well-known formula can be used to compute the **weighted average cost of capital** for a firm:

$$K = (\text{Equity/Total Market Value})\, R + (\text{Debt/Total Market Value})\, (1 - \text{Tax Rate})\, I$$

where

Equity = market value of common and preferred stock outstanding
Debt = market value of long-term debt outstanding
R = cost of equity or required rate of return of equity holders
I = before-tax cost of debt or interest rate
Tax Rate = marginal tax rate of the firm
Total Market Value = Equity + Debt.

The costs of equity R and cost of debt I increase as the debt, or financial leverage, of the firm increases due to increased bankruptcy risk. Notice that higher taxes can reduce the cost of capital, or K, due to higher interest deductions on debt payments. If firms can reduce their cost of capital by lowering costs of equity and debt, changes in the combination of debt and equity they use (i.e., capital structure), or tax management, they can increase the value of NPVs on investment projects. In the above example, lowering the cost of capital below 15 percent would increase the NPV on the German computer chip subsidiary.

The **cost of debt** is readily measured by calculating a weighted average of different interest rates paid by the firm on sources of long-term borrowings. MNCs are able to borrow beyond domestic borders in international capital markets and thereby minimize their cost of debt. International banks and bond markets increase access to loanable funds at competitive interest rates.

The **cost of equity** is more difficult to estimate. The Capital Asset Pricing Model[5] (CAPM) is a well-known approach to estimating the cost of domestic equity. The CAPM is written as follows:

$$R_{it} = R_{ft} + \beta_i (R_{mt} - R_{ft}),$$

cost of capital
the required rate of return demanded by stock and bond investors and is used in net present value capital budgeting analyses as the discount rate

weighted average cost of capital
the sum of the costs of equity and debt weighted by the amount of financing from these two capital sources

cost of debt
the weighted average of different interest rates paid on long-term borrowings

cost of equity
the required rate of return by stockholders in a firm and is estimated by means of the Capital Asset Pricing Model (CAPM)

where

R_{it} = the one-month return on stock i in month t

R_{mt} = the one-month return on a domestic market index (e.g., the S&P 500 index of the 500 largest U.S. firms)

R_{ft} = the one-month riskless rate of return (e.g., the U.S. Treasury bill rate)

βi = the domestic beta risk measure for the stock.

As an example, given average R_{mt} = 10 percent, average R_{ft} = 5 percent, and $\beta_i = 0.80$, the cost of equity equals 9 percent computed as 5 + 0.80(10 – 5). The **beta risk** measure is less than one, which implies that the stock has lower risk than the market index. Firms with lower betas will have lower costs of equity than higher beta firms.

One problem in estimating the cost of equity is whether the stock's equity market is domestic or global. If investors in the domestic market set the price of the stock, a segmented market for the stock exists, and the CAPM is an appropriate way to measure the cost of equity. However, if international investors set the stock price, then an integrated market exists, such that the CAPM is inappropriate. Internationally integrated equity markets require the use of the **International CAPM[6] (ICAPM)** to estimate the cost of equity. The ICAPM can be written as follows:

$$R_{it} = R_{ft} + \beta_i(R_{mt} - R_{ft}) + \beta_i^g (R_{gt} - R_{ft})$$

where

R_{gt} = the one-month return on a global market index (e.g., the Dow Jones world index of stocks)

β_i^g = the global beta risk measure for the stock other terms as before.

Now the firm's stock has both domestic and global beta risk measures. Extending the previous U.S. MNC example, given that average R_{mt} = 10 percent, R_{gt} = 11 percent, average R_{ft} = 5 percent, $\beta_i = 0.80$, and $\beta_i^g = 1.00$, the cost of equity equals 15 percent computed as 5 + 0.80(10 – 5) + 1.00(11-5). In general, MNCs should use the ICAPM to estimate their cost of equity, while domestic firms with little or no international business activity should apply the CAPM.

It should be mentioned that the CAPM and ICAPM models have been the subject of controversy for the past two decades. Extensive tests by Fama and French[7] have shown that estimates of the cost of equity can be improved by adding two other variables to these models: (1) the return on a portfolio of small firm stocks minus the return on a portfolio of large firm stocks (*SMB*), and (2) the return on a portfolio of high book-equity to market-equity ratio stocks minus the return on a portfolio of low book-equity to market-equity ratio stocks (*HML*). These **size** and **value factors**, respectively, may increase the explanatory power of the CAPM and ICAPM and, therefore, improve estimates of the cost of equity.[8] In the context of the CAPM, Fama and French propose the following cost of equity formula:

$$(R_{it} - R_{ft})_t = \alpha + \beta_i(R_{mt} - R_{ft}) + \beta_s SMB_t + \beta_v HML_t.$$

In the previous example with R_{mt} = 10 percent, average R_{ft} = 5 percent, and $\beta_i = 0.80$, if we further assume that SMB = 2 percent, HML = 1 percent, $\beta_s = 0.50$, and $\beta_v = 0.30$, then the cost of equity equals 10.3 percent computed as 5 + 0.80(10 – 5) + 0.50(2) + 0.30(1). A similar adjustment can be made to the ICAPM for MNCs facing integrated financial markets.

In sum, the cost of equity can be computed via either the CAPM for domestic firms or the ICAPM for MNCs. The Fama and French size and value factors can be added to these models to help improve their accuracy. The weighted average cost of equity and debt is the cost of capital used in discounting investment projects by the firm. The lower the cost of capital, the higher the NPVs of investment projects. In turn, the value of the firm is increased by more positive NPV projects. MNCs have an advantage over domestic firms in their ability to tap global financial markets in search of the lowest costs of equity and debt.

beta risk
a measurement of the general market risk of a stock in the Capital Asset Pricing Model (CAPM)

international CAPM (ICAPM)
an asset pricing model that includes both domestic and global market factors to estimate the cost of equity or required rate of return on stocks

size factor
whether a firm is small or large and how this size provides an estimate of the cost of equity

value factor
whether a firm has growth or value and how this firm characteristic provides an estimate of the cost of equity

REALITY CHECK LO-4

Refer again to the example in Exhibit 14.7 and re-compute the NPV in dollars for the U.S. firm. Assume that the euro increases in value over time. Insert some hypothetical EUR-to-USD exchange rates. How did the NPV in dollars change?

LO-5
Discuss how exchange rate risk affects firms' cash flows and its impact on stock returns.

Currency Risk and Stock Valuation

Foreign sales of firms will decline due to local currency appreciation. Import costs can rise when local currency depreciates. Of course, these export or import cash flow effects increase as currency movements become larger in magnitude. Suppliers and buyers that are affected by exchange rate risk can affect domestic firms with no export or import business.

Cash Flow Sensitivity to Exchange Rate Risk

Firms can experience fluctuations in cash flows due to currency movements. In the first half of 2008, the dollar rapidly declined against the euro with implications to MNCs in the United States and Europe. Coca-Cola, Caterpillar, IBM, and other companies selling products overseas gained from the falling dollar. However, many European firms, such as Finland's cell phone company Nokia, suffered losses due to the high euro value against the dollar. Reversing this trend, in autumn 2008 the dollar began to increase in value relative to the euro, which changed these cash flow effects on firms in the United States and Europe. Likewise, it is generally recognized that U.S. auto manufacturers lost market share to Japanese companies due to the strengthening dollar compared to the yen in the period 2005 to mid-year 2007. Many countries have large exports of their products to the United States, meaning that their firms are affected by dollar movements. India exports about 70 percent of its IT products to the United States and is advantaged (or disadvantaged) by a strong (or weak) dollar relative to the rupee. Also, dollar movements can affect many companies that import oil, which is normally priced in dollars. As discussed in the opening vignette of this chapter, the falling dollar in the first half of 2008 hurt U.S. firms and consumers by raising the cost of oil and related gas pump prices to a greater extent in the United States than in Europe, Japan, and other countries. High fuel costs squeezed profit margins for U.S. firms and lowered their net profits. It is clear from these recent events that exchange rate risk can dramatically affect the cash flows of firms around the world.

Stock Values and Foreign Exchange Movements

As mentioned earlier, exchange rate movements can have long-term economic effects on firms. Adler and Dumas[9] argue that stock returns are a convenient way to measure long-run exchange rate risk for a firm.

$$R_{it} = R_{ft} + \beta_i(R_{mt} - R_{ft}) + \beta_C R_{Ct},$$

where

R_{Ct} = the one-month return on local currency relative to a basket of currencies in month t

β_C = the exchange rate risk measure for the stock and other terms are the same as in equation (9.3) for the CAPM.

The rate of return R_{Ct} requires the use of a basket of currencies to measure local currency values. As discussed earlier, there are a number of well-known basket currencies, including the IMF's SDR, Federal Reserve's MCI, and others. By denominating, say, dollars in terms of

Pictorium/Alamy Limited

In 2008, Nokia was one company that suffered losses when the value of the dollar declined.

the IMF's SDR comprised of trade-weighted dollars, euros, pounds, and yen, we can more readily observe dollar value movements. If the dollars required to buy one SDR increases (i.e., SDR/USD increases), we can infer that the USD decreased in value against other major world currencies, as the value of the USD is much more volatile than the SDR over time. A currency basket represents a diversified portfolio of currencies and, consequently, has significantly lower variance than individual local currencies. In this regard, recent work by Hovanov, Kolari, and Sokolov[10] shows that major currencies can be combined into a minimum variance portfolio of currencies using Markowitz diversification that is as much as 40 times more stable than the dollar was over the period 1981-1998.

If the rate of return R_{Ct} increases, it means that the local currency depreciated in period t, and vice versa. This can be seen by defining $R_{Ct} = (SDR/USD_{t} - SDR/USD_{t-1})/SDR/USD_{t-1}$, where the rate of return R_{Ct} increases when SDR/USD_t is greater than SDR/USD_{t-1} implying a falling dollar value. The coefficient β_C measures the **exchange rate sensitivity** of the stock. Generally speaking, research evidence suggests that exchange rate risk affects only about 10-20 percent of stocks. Given that exchange rates are approximately ten times more volatile than inflation, and that most stocks are affected by changes in the level of inflation, this small percentage of stocks exposed to exchange rate risk is disappointing.

One possible solution to this puzzle is that exchange risk might be contained in the beta risk of the firm's stock. Recent work by Armstrong, Knif, Kolari, and Pynnönen (2010)[11] shows that movements in local currency affect market risk and, in turn, stock returns. They show market beta in two parts as follows:

$$R_{it} = R_{ft} + b_0 (R_{mt} - R_{ft}) + b_1 (R_{mt} - R_{ft}) R_{Ct},$$

where

b_0 = the market beta with no exchange risk

b_1 = the market beta associated with exchange risk.

Interestingly, these authors found that about 75 percent of U.S. stocks have **exchange risk betas** (or b_1) that are significant in the period 1975-2006. This evidence suggests that exchange risk affects most U.S. firms by changing their market risk.

exchange rate sensitivity
a stock value measured with the coefficient obtained by regressing the stock's return on a currency's return over time

exchange risk beta
the sensitivity of a stock to market risk affected by currency movements

To demonstrate the effect of exchange risk on the cost of equity, assume that over the past year average returns are as follows: the market return R_{mt} = 10 percent, the U.S. Treasury rate R_{ft} = 5 percent, and the SDR/USD return R_{Ct} = 2 percent. Based upon data over many years, assume that the beta coefficients are as follows: $b_0 = 0.8$, and $b_1 = 10$. Using this data, the cost of equity equals 9.00 percent computed as 5 + 0.80(10 – 5) + 10.00(10 – 5)2/100 (where the multiplication of two percentage numbers requires division by 100). Notice that exchange risk increased the cost of equity from 8 percent to 9 percent. Hence, exchange risk increases the beta without these risks from $b_0 = 0.80$ to a higher beta with exchange risk $\beta^* = b_0 + b_1 R_{Ct} + = 0.80 + 10(0.02) = 1.00$. We can infer that exchange risk changes the beta risk and, in turn, the expected return on stocks.

Finally, as mentioned earlier, emerging-market countries have country risk that may increase the costs of equity and debt. Particular countries may have political risk due to government instability and opposition, economic risk stemming from problems with rapid growth and inadequate infrastructure (roads, power, ports, etc.), and other issues. These risks require that an appropriate premium be added to the cost of capital that would decrease the NPV of emerging-market projects under consideration.

REALITY CHECK LO-5

Assume that you buy some shares of Nokia in the United States in dollars. Your friend in France buys some Nokia shares in Europe in euros. Will your rate of return over the next year be the same as your friend's? Is your market beta risk different from your friend's risk?

SUMMARY

International firms face risks and opportunities that affect their financial management. Exchange rate movements can have short-term effects on their transactions and translation risks and long-term effects on their economic risk. Transactions risk arises from changes in revenues and expenses from buying and selling goods and services in different countries. Translation risk occurs when changes in exchange rates affect the consolidated accounting statements of a firm. Economic risk comes about from currency trends over an extended period of time that adversely affect the value of a firm.

Derivatives offer a variety of ways that firms and investors can hedge (or reduce) the risks of currency movements. Futures contracts are standardized contracts that allow hedges for major currencies through an organized exchange that guarantees performance. Another important hedging instrument is the currency option contract. Lastly, swaps can be purchased that allow long-term hedges over years.

To finance international operations, firms access global banks, international bond and stock markets, and government sources. Large international banks offer wholesale payment services for businesses, banks, and governments via CHIPS and SWIFT. Some common methods of payment include payments in advance, commercial letter of credit (LC), banker's acceptances, and an open account. Groups of global banks in a syndicate provide participation loans to large firms seeking substantial funds for international business activities. International bond markets are another way to raise sizeable quantities of funds for long-term investment projects. Bonds can be categorized as domestic bonds, foreign bonds, and Eurobonds. International stock markets are another source of capital for long-term financing needs. Also, governments in countries provide import/export financing to support some sectors of their economies. The recent global economic and financial crisis prompted governments around the world to intervene in international financial markets to help maintain capital flows and restore market confidence.

Parent firms in a holding company with subsidiaries in different countries evaluate the net present value (NPV) of investment projects in terms of domestic currency values. Risks associated with currency movements can be hedged either by diversifying business operations in different countries or using derivatives contracts. Investment projects with NPVs that exceed expected investment costs are acceptable. In computing NPVs the cost of capital is needed to discount cash flows to their present values. The weighted average of the costs of debt and equity equals the cost of capital. The cost of equity can be estimated using the Capital Asset Pricing Model (CAPM). The CAPM is useful for stocks priced only in domestic markets, whereas the international CAPM (ICAPM) is recommended in the case of integrated capital markets. These asset-pricing models can be supplemented with other stock price factors to improve estimates of the cost of equity.

Firms can exhibit cash flow sensitivity in response to changes in exchange rates. Also, exchange rate movements can affect stock values of firms. Exchange risk can influence stock returns by itself or, more importantly, through its effect on market beta risk. Consequently, exchange risk affects the cost of equity of most firms.

KEY TERMS

exchange rate risk, *p. 338*
transactions risk, *p. 339*
translation risk, *p. 339*
consolidated accounting statements, *p. 339*
economic risk, *p. 339*
Special Drawing Right (SDR), *p. 339*
hedging, *p. 340*
speculators, *p. 340*
currency futures contracts, *p. 340*
long position, *p. 340*
short position, *p. 340*
organized exchanges, *p. 340*
marked-to-market, *p. 340*
margin, *p. 341*
margin call, *p. 341*
currency forward contracts, *p. 342*
over-the-counter (OTC) market, *p. 342*
call option, *p. 343*
put option, *p. 343*
premium, *p. 343*
currency swaps, *p. 343*
plain vanilla currency swap, *p. 344*
money center banks, *p. 345*
CHIPS (Clearing House Interbank Payments System), *p. 345*
SWIFT (Society of Worldwide Interbank Financial Telecommunications), *p. 345*
payment in advance, *p. 346*
commercial letter of credit (LC), *p. 346*
banker's acceptance, *p. 346*
open account, *p. 346*
syndicate, *p. 346*
bond ratings, *p. 346*
domestic bonds, *p. 346*
foreign bonds, *p. 346*
eurobonds, *p. 347*
diversification, *p. 349*
home bias, *p. 349*
contagion, *p. 350*
Export-Import (Ex-Im) Bank, *p. 353*
trade finance, *p. 353*
term financing, *p. 353*
Bank of International Cooperation (JBIC), *p. 353*
net present value, *p. 354*
country risk, *p. 355*
sensitivity analysis, *p. 355*
cost of capital, *p. 356*
weighted average cost of capital, *p. 356*
cost of debt, *p. 356*
cost of equity, *p. 356*
beta risk, *p. 357*
international CAPM (ICAPM), *p. 357*
size factor, *p. 357*
value factor, *p. 357*
exchange rate sensitivity, *p. 359*
exchange risk beta, *p. 359*

CHAPTER QUESTIONS

1. What is the difference between foreign exchange risk arising from translation, transactions, and economic risks?

2. What derivative securities can be used to hedge the effects of fluctuations in currency values on the cash flows of firms and investors?

3. Briefly describe the main sources of finance for international trade and investment. Distinguish between short-term and long-term finance sources.

4. Based on multinational capital budgeting principles, how should a parent firm evaluate investments in its international subsidiaries? How could an estimate of the cost of capital for discounting purposes be estimated?

5. Can changes in exchange rates affect the stock returns of firms? Use stock return models to explain your answer.

MINI CASE: CITIGROUP IN DISTRESS: ONE OF THE WORLD'S LARGEST BANKS STRUGGLES TO SURVIVE

With more than $2 trillion in total assets, Citigroup is one of the largest and most global banks in the world. It has more than 200 million customers in more than 100 countries. Some of its brand name components include Citibank, CitiFinancial, Primerica, Smith Barney, Banamex, and Nikko. It offers a vast array of financial services, including basic payments services, credit cards, loans and mortgages to consumers and businesses, securities services, derivatives risk management services, treasury and cash management services, and more. While Citigroup historically has been a highly profitable and successful money center bank, in 2008 its fortunes turned for the worse. Massive losses on securities related to home loans (i.e., mortgage-backed securities and collateralized debt obligations) and other asset-backed securities caused negative profits and damage to its capital that threatened the bank's solvency. The U.S. government injected more than $40 billion of new capital by buying preferred stock from the bank in an effort to prevent a catastrophic large bank failure that could damage the U.S. and global economy. The government also provided guarantees on more than $300 billion of risky loans made by Citicorp. Under the terms of the bailout, the bank cannot pay more than $0.10 per share in quarterly dividends to common shareholders for three years without government approval. In March 2008, its shares sold for as high as $55, but by March 2009 had fallen below $1 per share. One of the mightiest banks in the world had become a penny stock!

A controversy surrounds the government bailout. Some experts contend that the best strategy is to let the bank fail, have the government temporarily take it over (i.e., a bridge bank solution), remove the bad assets from its balance sheet, and put them into a separate government run entity, and divide the bank up and merge out the pieces with solvent banks. Others argue that letting the bank fail is not an option, as such an event would trigger panic in global financial markets and worsen the ongoing global recession in 2009.

QUESTIONS:

1) What are some arguments in favor of continuing government support of Citigroup? Discuss who would be hurt by the bank's failure. Is the failure of Citigroup different from that of other firms? Does the government have people to manage such a global financial enterprise?

2) What are counter arguments in favor of letting the bank fail? Discuss concepts of free markets and capitalism that create competition and allow unsuccessful firms to fail. Does bailing out large banks cause them to take excessive risks on the theory that they are "too big to fail"?

Point Counter-Point: Are Bond Rating Agencies to Blame for the Mortgage Mess?

Standard & Poor's, Moody's Investors Service, and Fitch Ratings provide bond ratings on publicly-issued debt. Since the 1980s, these companies rated mortgage-backed securities (MBSs), which are bonds backed by individuals' payments on their home mortgage loans. In the 1990s, investment banks started to repackage MBSs and other asset-backed bonds (bonds based on credit cards, auto loans, small business loans, etc.). The cash flows on MBSs and other securities were divided into interest and principal components known as tranches and marketed as collateralized debt obligations (CDOs). The top four ratings are investment grade, and lower ratings are junk bonds. Interestingly, many CDOs had higher bond ratings than the underlying MBSs. Investors around the world bought the investment-grade CDOs believing that they were safe investments. However, as increasing defaults happened by individuals on their home loans in the United States from 2007 to 2010, the CDO values plummeted. It was revealed that many CDOs were based on cash flows from MBSs that were junk bonds. Because over 25 percent of CDOs were sold into international bond markets, investors around the world are paying the price for poorly-rated bonds. Wall Street had turned a sow's ear into a silk purse! Naturally, an important question arises: Are the rating agencies to blame for the mortgage mess?

POINT The rating agencies say that they did nothing wrong. They applied long-standing procedures to establishing the probability of default on the CDOs and rated them according to rigorous rules. Analysts in the agencies were deluged with huge volumes of new CDO issues that stretched their resources. Also, CDOs became increasingly complex including CDOs contained within other CDOs. Analysts were not paid more for the number of ratings they produced or for giving high ratings on bonds.

COUNTER-POINT Critics argue that the ratings agencies were competing for rating business. If an investment bank could not get a fast response from a rating agency, or the rating was below investment grade, they would go to another rating agency. Rating agencies make their money by charging a fee for the ratings. For these reasons a possible conflict of interest existed for the rating agencies. While the Securities and Exchange Commission (SEC) was responsible for regulatory oversight of the rating process to make sure that conflicts of interest did not interfere with the accuracy of ratings, they had not investigated potential problems in rating CDOs until after defaults on CDOs began to appear in late-2008.

What Do *You* Think?

Which viewpoint do you support and why? What would you do to prevent future problems in rating CDOs?

INTERPRETING GLOBAL BUSINESS NEWS

Financial news is everywhere in the popular press and media. How do you interpret the following examples of financial news related to the concepts in this chapter?

1) Bernie Madoff's hedge fund, Ascot Partners, failed in 2008 with the shocking news that Mr. Madoff had lost $50 billion of investors' funds by using a Ponzi scheme (i.e., not investing new investment funds but merely using them to pay off other investors pulling funds out). When the economy slowed and more investors requested withdrawals, the scam was revealed. Investors around the world lost money, in more than a few cases their life savings. The largest fraud in history, Mr. Madoff faced criminal charges and was sentenced to 150 years in prison. How does this tragic incident affect financial investors and markets? What could you do to help reduce the risk of such an investment problem?

2) The Japanese yen began to fall in 2009 against both the dollar and euro due to the global economic slowdown. Will the falling yen help the Japanese economy, which exports a lot of electronics and vehicles? How will it affect the U.S. and European economies?

3) In 2008 and 2009 major stock market indices fell 50 percent or more in many countries. Also, international bond markets dried up for all but the highest quality firms. How do these market trends affect the cost of capital for international firms? What will be the effect on the NPVs of their investment projects?

4) In the midst of the 2009 global recession, the Group of 20 largest industrial countries was scheduled to consider government options to the economic and financial crises around the world. At such times, what do you think global leaders should be talking about to help the economy recover and promote prosperity in the future?

PORTFOLIO PROJECTS

Exploring Your Own Case in Point: Understanding Your Favorite Company's Exchange Rate Risk

After reading this chapter you should be prepared to answer some basic questions about your target company.

1) In what countries does your company export goods? Import goods? How would changes in the values of these countries' currencies relative to the U.S. dollar affect transactions and translation risks? Economic risk?

2) What could the firm do to hedge these exchange rate risks?

3) How would you determine whether the stock of your company is sensitive to exchange rate movements?

Develop an International Strategy for Your Own Small Business: Evaluating Foreign Exchange Risk and Weighted Average Cost of Capital

Consider how exchange rate movements might affect the profits of export sales to a target country and determine the cost of capital if you set a subsidiary abroad. Focus on one target country and its currency relative to the U.S. dollar. Here are some questions to evaluate for your small business:

1) What does a graph of the target country currency or dollar look like?

2) If the dollar rises in value against the foreign currency, how are sales revenues and profits affected? What occurs with a decrease in the value of the dollar?

3) How could your firm hedge exchange rate risk?

4) Calculate the weighted average cost of capital of your subsidiary abroad.

CHAPTER NOTES

[1] For example, see E. H. Chow, W. Y. Lee, and M. E. Solt, "The Exchange-Rate Risk Exposure of Asset Returns," Journal of Business 70, 1997, pp. 105–123.
[2] Direct quotes are in terms of dollars/foreign currency (e.g., 1.35 EUR-to-USD means that it costs 1.35 dollars to buy one euro), as opposed to indirect quotes of foreign currency/dollar (e.g., 0.74 USD-to-EUR means that costs 0.74 euros to buy one dollar).
[3] Note that each tick, or point equal to $0.0001 per euro, yields a gain of $12.50 per contract—that is, 1,965 points x $12.50 = $24,562.50 again.
[4] The Black-Scholes option pricing model and related models can be used to compute the premium price of options contracts. See Black, F. and M. Scholes, "The Pricing of Options and Corporate Liabilities," Journal of Political Economy 81, 1973, pp. 637–654.
[5] W. F. Sharpe, "Capital Asset Prices: A Theory of Market Equilibrium Under Conditions of Risk," The Journal of Finance 19, 1964, pp. 425–442; J. Lintner, "The Valuation of Risk Assets and the Selection of Risky Investments in Stock Portfolios and Capital Budgets," Review of Economics and Statistics 47, 1965, pp. 13–37; F. Black, "Capital Market Equilibrium with Restricted Borrowing," *Journal of Business* 45 (1972) pp. 444–455.
[6] B. H. Solnik, "An International Market Model of Security Price Behavior," Journal of Financial and Quantitative Analysis 9, 1974, pp. 537–554; M. Adler, and B. Dumas, "International Portfolio Choice and Corporate Finance: A Synthesis," The Journal of Finance 38, 1983, pp. 925–984.
[7] E. F. Fama and K. R. French, "The Cross-Section of Expected Stock Returns," Journal of Finance 47, 1992, pp. 427–465; E. F. Fama and K. R. French, "Common Risk Factors in the Returns on Stocks and Bonds," Journal of Financial Economics 33, 1993, pp. 3–56.
[8] J. M. Griffin, "Are the Fama and French Factors Global or Country Specific?," Review of Financial Studies 15, 2002, pp. 783–803.
[9] M. Adler, and B. Dumas, "Exposure to Currency Risk: Definition and Measurement," Financial Management 13, 1984, pp. 41–50; B. Solnik, "An Equilibrium Model of the International Capital Market," Journal of Economic Theory 8, 1974, pp. 500–524; P. Sercu, " A Generalization of the International Asset Pricing Model," Revue de l'Association Française de Finance 1, 1980, pp. 91–135.
[10] N. V. Hovanov, J. W. Kolari, and M. V. Sokolov, "Computing Currency Invariant Indexes with an Application to Minimum Variance Currency Baskets," Journal of Economic Dynamics and Control 28, 2004, pp. 1481–1504.
[11] W. J. Armstrong, J. Knif, J. W. Kolari, and S. Pynnönen, "On Stock Returns and the Exchange Risk Puzzle: Evidence from International Arbitrage Pricing Theory," Working paper, Texas A&M University, presented at the annual European meetings of the Financial Management Association, Hamburg, Germany, June 2010.

CH 15

Accounting and Taxation in Global Business

© C Miller Design/Getty Images

Nikada/iStockphoto.com

After studying this chapter, you should be able to:

LO-1 Explain briefly the function of accounting and describe the two parts of the accounting information system.

LO-2 Describe briefly the function of generally accepted accounting principles (GAAP).

LO-3 Recount the goal of the International Accounting Standards Board and describe why International Financial Reporting Standards are important to global business operations.

LO-4 Explain how auditing contributes to the usefulness of financial reporting.

LO-5 Explain how financial statement analysis can be used to evaluate a company's financial situation and compare it to other companies.

LO-6 Describe briefly tax issues that MNCs face.

New Zealand and Cybercrime

One of the world's first cases of cybercrime occurred in New Zealand, where the Michelangelo computer virus first appeared. After the virus infected one computer, it remained dormant until March 6, the birthday of Renaissance artist Michelangelo. When activated, the virus would destroy data on the hard drive of the infected computer. Some people thought that the virus was written in Taiwan, but there was never any definite proof of this. The virus spread from New Zealand to countries around the world. A computer virus is only one type of cybercrime.

Companies lose billions of dollars each year as a result of cybercrimes, also referred to as electronic crimes, or e-crimes. "Cyber" is short for cyberspace, the electronic medium of computer networks, in which online communication takes place. There are numerous news stories regarding electronic crimes and the related costs to companies. Though control techniques and other security policies and procedures are critical to the deterrence of electronic crimes, detection and resolution of successful or attempted electronic crimes are also of critical importance. Not only the cost, but also the embarrassment of such crimes is something that all companies wish to avoid.

A well-designed accounting system can enhance a company's abilities to detect and resolve electronic crimes. Is it possible to stop all criminal activity with controls and security techniques? No, even the best internal control system cannot be expected to stop every type of criminal activity. If a system was perfectly designed, fallible human beings must still operate it. For example, passwords may be set up to prevent unauthorized access to the system—but unfortunately, some employees have been known to sticky-note their passwords to their monitors. While this helps to overcome forgetfulness, it also provides an easy way for an unauthorized person to gain access to the system.

accounting
the recording, summarizing, and reporting of the economic activities and events of an organization

income statement
statement that summarizes the revenues earned and the expenses incurred by a business over a period of time

balance sheet
statement that lists the balances of the asset, liability, and owners' equity accounts of a business on a specific date

statement of retained earnings
statement that shows the beginning balance for retained earnings, additions and reductions to retained earnings, and the ending balance of retained earnings

Introduction

Accounting is the "language of business." **Accounting** is the recording, summarizing, and reporting of the economic activities and events of an organization. Accounting generates information used by people inside and outside the firm to make important decisions. For example, a financial institution like a bank may use accounting information to decide whether or not to lend money to a loan applicant. The lending institution—an external user—must predict whether the applicant can pay back the loan; this decision depends upon reliable accounting information contained in financial reports. Within the firm, business managers use accounting information to make decisions that contribute to the success of the firm. For business managers, timely and accurate accounting information is essential for managing and controlling company operations. The accounting information system contributes to developing a sound organization structure, to ensuring that employees are held responsible for their actions, and to maintaining cost effective business operations.

The most important reports produced by the accounting information system are the set of financial statements. For a corporation, these financial statements are:

- Income statement;
- Balance sheet;
- Statement of retained earnings; and
- Statement of cash flows.

Christine Webb/Alamy

An Italian friar, Luca Pacioli, authored the first book on double-entry accounting in 1494; thereby, Friar Luca earned the title of 'Father of Accounting'.

Together, these four statements represent a business in financial terms. Each statement corresponds to a specific date or a designated time period, such as a year. Together, the four financial statements reveal how much the firm has earned or lost, the change in retained earnings, the firm's ending financial position, and how much cash was generated and spent.

The **income statement** answers the question: How much income did the firm earn or lose during the period? The income statement summarizes the revenues earned and the expenses incurred by a business over a period of time. The result is a net income or net loss. Knowing whether or not the firm made a profit is of great interest to the owners and managers of a company.

A **balance sheet** lists the balances of the asset, liability, and owners' equity accounts of a business on a specific date. For a corporation, owners' equity is replaced by the term stockholders' equity, because stockholders are the owners. A balance sheet answers the question: What is the firm's financial position at a designated point in time (i.e., 12 midnight on the balance sheet date)? A firm's financial position is what the firm owns (assets), owes (liabilities), and the residual interest of the owners (stockholders' equity) on a specified day.

Retained earnings refers to the part of the stockholder equity generated from operations and kept for use in future operations. In other words, retained earnings is the stockholder's claim to assets earned from company operations and reinvested into the company. The **statement of retained earnings** is simple; it shows (1) the starting balance for retained

H.-D. Falkenstein Image Broker/Newscom

A stock certificate signifies ownership of one or more shares of stock in a corporation.

earnings, (2) additions and reductions to retained earnings, and (3) the ending balance of retained earnings. The statement of retained earnings answers the question: In what way did retained earnings change? Net income increases retained earnings. Net losses and the payment of dividends decrease retained earnings.

The **statement of cash flows** shows the company's cash receipts and cash payments, that is, the inflows and outflows of cash. The statement of cash flows answers the question: How much cash was taken in and paid out during the period?

To summarize, there are four essential questions that are answered by the four financial statements, shown in Exhibit 15.1.

statement of cash flows statement showing the company's inflows and outflows of cash

EXHIBIT 15.1 FUNDAMENTAL FINANCIAL QUESTIONS AND ANSWERS

Financial Statement	Question	Answer
Income Statement	How much did the firm earn or lose from operations during the period?	Revenues – Expenses = Net income (or Net loss)
Statement of Retained Earnings	In what way did the firm's retained earnings change during the period?	Beginning retained earnings + Net income (or – net loss) – Dividends = Ending retained earnings
Balance Sheet	What is the firm's financial position at a designated point in time?	Assets = Liabilities + Owners' Equity
Statement of Cash Flows	What amount of cash was generated and spent during the period?	Operating cash flows ± Investing cash flows ± Financing cash flows = Increase (or decrease) in cash during the period

LO-1

Explain briefly the function of accounting and describe the two parts of the accounting information system.

Accounting and Financial Reporting in Global Business

The **accounting information system (AIS)**, like all systems, has specific objectives, inputs, processes, outputs, and controls. A typical AIS has two principal objectives: (1) to provide all the financial information internally needed by management for business decision-making, known as management accounting; and (2) to provide financial information to various external users concerned with the financial activities of the organization, known as financial accounting. The following text will explore each of these in detail.

Management Accounting

The component of the accounting information system that provides information to management is referred to as **management accounting**. Management accounting is strictly concerned with the information needs of management—the only internal user of accounting information. Although internal information requirements may vary substantially between organizations, management accounting in most business firms includes similar kinds of financial analysis (e.g., cost-volume-profit analysis, capital budgeting, and inventory planning). Specific steps in performing these types of analyses are nearly standardized. Additionally, most business firms use similar types of internal documents and reports, such as sales invoices, purchase orders, receiving reports, and budgets. There are widely accepted guidelines on how these internal documents and reports should be prepared.

Like other areas of business, technological innovation has had a profound effect upon how management accounting tasks are performed. For example, specialized software is available to assist management accountants in performing many different types of financial analysis. Specialized hardware devices such as bar code readers may be used to help keep track of inventory. Telecommunication systems allow purchase orders to be placed electronically. Despite these technological advances, standard costing and variance analysis are done in much the same way today as they were in decades past, but computers have reduced the time required to complete such tasks. The competitive nature of the marketplace drives all functions within a business firm, including accounting, to become more efficient and productive. Using the latest technology is an essential ingredient for successful business operations, including accounting.

accounting information system (AIS)
a system which has two principal objectives: (1) to provide all the financial information needed internally by management for business decision making, known as management accounting, and (2) to provide financial information to various external users concerned with the financial activities of the organization, known as financial accounting

management accounting
the component of the accounting information system that provides the financial information needed internally by business managers for efficient (timely) and effective (correct) decision-making

financial accounting
the component of the accounting information system that provides financial information needed by external users such as investors and lenders

Financial Accounting

The component of the accounting information system that supplies information to external users is **financial accounting**. External users of accounting information fall into two major categories: organizations that require or expect information to be reported, and organizations that receive information on an as-needed basis.

Organizations that require accounting information to be reported to them include federal, state, and local government agencies. These agencies require business firms to regularly report specific types of information. The Social Security Administration, for example, requires regular reporting of payroll information, including the amount of social security taxes withheld from the employees and matched by the employer. The Internal Revenue Service (IRS) requires the filing of an annual tax return as well as the submission of other financial information (e.g., federal income tax withholdings from employees' pay) throughout the year. The government requires publicly traded corporations to provide annual financial statements to stockholders. This information is filed with the Securities and Exchange Commission (SEC) on Form 10-K. The same financial statements are widely used by other external users for a variety of purposes.

In addition to government units that require certain information to be reported, numerous other external users of accounting information may expect certain information to be provided

EXHIBIT 15.2 EXTERNAL USERS OF ACCOUNTING INFORMATION

	External User	Information Required or Expected
1.	Governmental Units	In the United States, the Internal Revenue Service, for example, requires an annual tax return.
2.	Lenders	Financial statement information, specifically information concerning ability to meet financial obligations.
3.	Vendors (Suppliers)	Financial statement information, specifically information regarding ability to pay back purchases made on credit. Also, the vendor will receive business documents such as purchase orders from a customer.
4.	Credit-Rating Agencies	Similar to information required by lenders and vendors. Lenders and vendors often purchase the credit-worthiness assessments made by credit-rating agencies.
5.	Stockholders (Investors)	Financial statements as well as personal information regarding stock and dividend transactions.
6.	Customers	Billing statements, sales invoices, amounts owed, account status, date due, and product information.
7.	Employees	Individuals expect payment of wages and specific payroll information, such as payroll deductions for social security withholdings, income tax withholdings, and insurance premiums. Employee groups, such as labor unions, may want aggregate information, such as profits, payroll expense, and pension funding and liability.

to them despite that it is not required. For example, a business firm may wish to borrow money from a financial institution so that the firm can expand operations. The financial institution will probably ask the firm to provide certain financial information, typically the most recent financial statements. If the firm is publicly traded, then these statements already exist, as they have been prepared for stockholder use. The financial statements will enable the lender to assess the borrowing firm's ability to meet its financial obligations, specifically the ability to pay back the loan. The lender will likely assess other factors as well, such as management's competence and general economic conditions. However, the financial statements, or information derived from them, may be the most important factor in the lender's loan decision.

Other external groups that use accounting information include credit-rating agencies, vendors (suppliers), employees, and customers. Exhibit 15.2 lists external users and the type of information with which they are typically concerned.

In many cases external accounting information is prepared in a specific format. For example, the IRS requires tax-related information to be prepared according to specific procedures and instructions, and submitted on specific IRS forms.

REALITY CHECK LO-1

Have you filed a federal tax return? The tax authorities require taxpayers to submit very specific tax-related information on the appropriate forms on a regular basis. During the year, do you keep track of the information needed to prepare your tax return?

generally accepted accounting principles (GAAP)
the principles by which financial statements are prepared

Generally Accepted Accounting Principles (GAAP)

LO-2
Describe briefly the function of generally accepted accounting principles (GAAP).

The financial statements of publicly traded companies must be prepared according to **generally accepted accounting principles** (GAAP). GAAP provides the guidelines by which financial statements are prepared. In the United States, GAAP is primarily developed by the Financial Accounting Standards Board (FASB), whereas in most other countries, there are equivalents to the FASB that develop accounting standards in those countries. In each country of the world, accounting practices have developed that relate to the culture and business environment of that country. Differences in culture and business environments have led to differences in GAAP among different countries. In the 1970s, a movement was started to create one set of GAAP that could be used in all countries. In the past decade this movement has gained great momentum.

U.S. GAAP

The FASB issues **Statements of Financial Accounting Standards** (SFAS), which provide the procedures for dealing with specific accounting matters. Additional accounting guidance is provided in a number of places. Exhibit 15.3 lists the primary sources of authoritative accounting literature.

Statements of Financial Accounting Standards (SFAS)
part of the highest level of generally accepted accounting principles (GAAP), issued by the Financial Accounting Standards Board (FASB)

Determining the appropriate accounting treatment for a particular transaction or event is sometimes a complex process requiring careful research. This research process is carried out by the accounting information system. GAAP is constantly evolving. Consequently, financial accountants in the AIS must be careful to stay abreast of current developments. For example, when a new accounting standard changed how to translate foreign currency transactions, corporate accountants had to adopt the new standard. As a result, accountants in multinational corporations had to read and apply the new methodology.

EXHIBIT 15.3 AUTHORITATIVE ACCOUNTING LITERATURE

Highest level of accounting authority:

1. Non-superseded sections of the Accounting Research Bulletins issued by Committee on Accounting Procedures
2. Non-superseded sections of the APB Opinions issued by the Accounting Principles Board
3. Statements of Financial Accounting Standards issued by the FASB
4. Interpretations issued by the FASB
5. Statements and Interpretations of the Governmental Accounting Standards Board (for governmental units)

Next level of accounting authority:

1. AICPA Industry Accounting Guides
2. AICPA Statements of Position
3. FASB and GASB Technical Bulletins
4. Industry accounting practices
5. AICPA Accounting Interpretations

Lower level of accounting authority

1. Guidelines published by SEC and other regulatory agencies
2. FASB and GASB Concept Statements
3. APB Statements
4. AICPA Issues Papers
5. Minutes of the FASB Emerging Issues Task Force
6. Other professional association statements
7. Accounting textbooks, reference books, and articles written by recognized authorities in the field

There are three primary fields of work for accountants:

- in the AIS of a business firm;
- in a public accounting firm; and
- in the AIS of a government entity or other nonprofit organization.

Accountants who work in the public accounting field need to be licensed by the state or states in which they work; the license is designated Certified Public Accountant (CPA). CPA firms provide three basic types of services: auditing, tax, and consulting. The licensing requirements for CPA include passing a rigorous exam and acquiring a certain amount of work experience. Accountants in industry, government, or public accounting may attain the CPA designation; however, public accounting is the field most closely associated with CPAs because it is a professional requirement. Other notable professional designations are the CMA (Certified Management Accountant), CIA (Certified Internal Auditor), and CFE (Certified Fraud Examiner).

Government and nonprofit accounting is not focused upon identifying the profit resulting from revenues and expenses. While the focus of for-profit businesses is to make a profit, the focus of government and nonprofit organizations is to effectively allocate services. There remain important similarities in accounting at for-profit businesses and accounting at government and nonprofit organizations. In both settings, keeping track of money flowing in and money flowing out is important. Accountability of how money is spent by government organizations is of paramount importance to citizens who pay the taxes that support government operations.

International GAAP

While the United States GAAP determines what is included in financial reports of companies based in the United States, the GAAP used by companies based in other countries is determined by the governments of those countries. Historically, every country has had its own unique GAAP: U.S. GAAP in the United States, German GAAP in Germany, Japanese GAAP in Japan, and so forth. As a result, GAAP in one country could be significantly different from GAAP in another country.

Different GAAPs made it difficult for investors and other financial statement users to meaningfully compare financial reports of companies from different countries. Due to different GAAPs, how profit is determined in one country could be quite different from how profit is determined in another country. The solution to this problem would be to develop one set of GAAP, an "international" GAAP, which could be used by all companies in all countries around the world. In the 1970s, a movement began to develop an international GAAP. Widespread acceptance of an international GAAP seemed very unlikely at the time it was first introduced. As this chapter discusses, since the 1970s, the idea has gradually gained acceptance, and international GAAP is now used in many countries around the world. International GAAP is developed by the International Accounting Standards Board. The Board's international GAAP is called International Financial Reporting Standards, or IFRS.

Differences Between U.S. and International GAAP

Generally accepted accounting principles are different among countries due to the factors that influence the development of accounting and financial reporting. These factors are unique to each country and include:

- political and legal systems;
- sources of capital;

- business complexity;
- inflation;
- taxation;
- culture; and
- accidents of history, such as one country taking over another in a war.

International Financial Reporting Standards are different from U.S. GAAP in a variety of ways. A key reason for these differences is that IFRS are regarded as being more principles-based and U.S. GAAP as being more rules-based. Principles provide broad, general guidance; while rules provide narrow, detailed guidance. The detailed rules of U.S. GAAP may be (at least partly) the result of extreme business complexity and the extremely high rate of litigation in the nation. If printed out, U.S. GAAP is estimated to be about 25,000 pages; while IFRS is estimated to be only about 2,000 pages.

There are many areas of difference between U.S. GAAP and IFRS, but there are more similarities than differences. The differences that do exist can be categorized as cosmetic or substantive. IFRS does not prescribe a particular format for presentation of financial statements; as a result, multiple formats have evolved in practice. In the United States, a common format has evolved. An IFRS-based balance sheet of a U.K. company usually lists fixed assets, such as equipment, at the top of the balance sheet and next lists the current assets, such as cash. Assets on a U.S. company's GAAP-based balance sheet would start with current assets, cash at the top, and then show fixed assets. This different arrangement of assets is an example of a cosmetic difference between U.S. GAAP and IFRS.

An example of a substantive difference between U.S. GAAP and IFRS concerns leases. Under U.S. GAAP, leases are classified as capital if one or more of the following four criteria are met:

- title transfer;
- bargain purchase option;
- lease terms are equal to or greater than 75 percent of the asset's economic life; and
- minimum lease payments are greater than or equal to 90 percent of the asset's fair market value.

Under IFRS, criteria are less rigid. For example, under IFRS, regarding the third criterion, instead of setting a number (i.e., 75 percent) as in U.S. GAAP, the IFRS criterion is that the lease term is for the "major part" of the economic life of the asset. The criterion "major part" is more a subjective principle than a rules-based specific number, 75 percent. Both approaches, rules-based and principles-based, have their respective advantages and disadvantages.

In October 2002, the FASB and the IASB issued a memorandum of understanding (referred to as the Norwalk Agreement or MoU) formally announcing their commitment to converging U.S. GAAP and IFRS. In recent years, both the FASB and IASB have issued rules that converge (or almost converge) their accounting standards with the standards of the other body.

Differences Between U.S. GAAP and Selected Countries

Due to the global movement to adopt or require IFRS, there are fewer countries that maintain their own GAAP. In 2003, less than 30 countries required or accepted IFRS for corporate financial reporting. By 2013, more than 120 countries required or accepted IFRS. Consequently, comparing U.S. GAAP to GAAP in other countries is becoming less necessary. What is more often necessary is comparing U.S. GAAP to IFRS. IFRS is described in more detail in the next section.

REALITY CHECK LO-2

Have you ever encountered a difficulty due to different measurement scales such as hand tools based on English standards (one inch, 1/2 inch, 3/8 inch, etc.) versus metric standards (10 mm, 9 mm, 8 mm, etc.) or container capacity (e.g. converting ounces to liters)? Different accounting standards create a similar problem.

International Financial Reporting Standards

LO-3

Recount the goal of the International Accounting Standards Board and describe why International Financial Reporting Standards are important to global business operations.

The **International Accounting Standards Board** (IASB) issues International Financial Reporting Standards. The IASB is an independent, privately funded accounting standard-setter based in London. As discussed earlier, **International Financial Reporting Standards** (IFRS) is a set of international accounting standards stating how particular types of transactions and other events should be reported in financial statements. IFRS is designed to provide a single set of GAAP that can be used by companies in all countries around the globe.

Board Members of the IASB come from nine countries and have a variety of functional backgrounds. The IASB is committed to developing, in the public interest, a single set of high quality, understandable, and enforceable global accounting standards that require transparent and comparable information in general purpose financial statements. In addition, the IASB cooperates with national accounting standard setters to achieve convergence in accounting standards around the world.

The IASB represents more than 100 worldwide accounting and financial organizations from more than 80 counties. Most projects require a minimum of three years from formation to standard issuance. Each IASB Member has one vote on technical and other matters. The publication of a Standard, Exposure Draft, or final SIC Interpretation requires

International Accounting Standards Board (IASB)
an independent, privately funded accounting standard-setter based in London, U.K., that issues International Financial Reporting Standards

International Financial Reporting Standards (IFRS)
a set of international accounting standards stating how particular types of transactions and other events should be reported in financial statements

L. Murphy Smith

London is home to the International Accounting Standards Board.

approval by nine of the Board's 15 Members. As previously mentioned, the IFRS is designed to provide a single set of GAAP that can be used by companies in all countries worldwide.

The objectives of the IASB include:

- increasing harmonization of accounting standards and disclosures to meet the needs of the global market;
- providing an accounting basis for underdeveloped or newly industrialized countries to follow as the accounting profession emerges in those countries; and
- increasing the compatibility of domestic and international accounting requirements.

The rapid growth in international capital markets, cross-border mergers and acquisitions, and other international developments have created pressures for harmonization of accounting standards beyond those that were contemplated when IASB was first formed. Arthur Wyatt, former chairman of the IASB, indicated that harmonization is no longer merely a philosophical notion about which to argue, but rather essential to global trade and commerce.

The goal of the IASB is to formulate and publish standards to be observed in the presentation of audited financial statements and to promote their worldwide acceptance and observance—that is, to achieve internationally recognized or harmonized standards of accounting and reporting. These standards are designed to reflect the needs of the professional and business communities throughout the world. Acceptance and implementation of international accounting standards has been impeded by cultural and ethnic differences. The IASB seeks to resolve these differences in a manner that benefits everyone.

Multinational companies will benefit if they must prepare financial reports based on only one set of GAAP, that is IFRS, in all the countries where they conduct business, rather than a different GAAP in each country. Investors and other financial statement users will benefit if all the financial reports of all companies use the same set of GAAP (i.e., IFRS). Among other advantages, this would greatly enhance the comparability of financial statements from one firm to another.

REALITY CHECK LO-3

Have you studied a foreign language? If so, you know how difficult it can be to translate a story from one language into another. The same is true for accounting information. Translating accounting information from one GAAP to another GAAP is a challenging process.

LO-4

Explain how auditing contributes to the usefulness of financial reporting.

The Role of Auditing and the Sarbanes-Oxley Act

People who rely upon financial statements are very concerned about the validity of the reports they receive. The management of a firm has the primary responsibility for designing its accounting information system (AIS). A key concern for a firm's management is the reliability and integrity of the reports produced by the AIS. Many business firms have a separate internal audit function charged with the responsibility of ensuring that the internal control structure, especially as it relates to the AIS, is operating effectively. In the case of a publicly-traded company, users of its annual financial statements (such as investors) need some form of assurance that they do not contain material misstatements, either intentional or unintentional. Assurance is provided by the independent external auditor who examines the firm's financial statements, and provides an audit opinion indicating whether those statements are fairly presented according to generally accepted accounting principles.

The two major categories of auditing are external auditing and internal auditing. In the United States, external or financial statement audits must be conducted by independent Certified Public Accountants (CPAs). Independent auditors have various designations in countries around the world. For example, in the U.K., independent auditors are designated chartered accountants. External audits are required of publicly traded companies in order for their stocks to be traded on the stock market in the United States, and on most stock exchanges around the world. The external auditor must maintain his or her independence by having no material financial interest or stake in the outcome of the audit.

Audits are characterized by the following common set of steps:

- plan the audit;
- obtain and evaluate evidence;
- arrive at an audit opinion; and
- communicate audit results.

Planning an audit involves gaining an understanding of the company being audited. Knowledge regarding the company's management and the company's goals and objectives is especially important in this process. Financial information from prior years can be analyzed to identify potential problem areas. Planning also involves identifying key personnel in the company being audited and what information that is needed to complete the audit. At this stage, the auditor will specify what audit procedures will be done and select the people who will be carrying out those procedures.

Obtaining evidence to support the audit opinion involves the application of a series of audit procedures to verify the accuracy of assertions being made by the company being audited, also called the auditee. For financial statement audits, these assertions are representations made in the financial statements relating to the auditee's income, expenses, assets, and liabilities. Audit procedures for financial statement audits include reconciling bank accounts, obtaining confirmations of accounts receivable from customers of the company, and physically counting inventory. For a financial statement audit, these procedures are applied with the objective of ensuring:

- the existence of assets and liabilities and occurrence of income and expenses;
- the completeness of the financial statements (all assets, liabilities, income, and expenses are accounted for);
- proper valuation of assets, liabilities, income, and expenses;
- that the auditee owns the assets and is obligated to the extent of liabilities shown; and
- that all financial statement items are properly presented and all disclosure regulations have been followed.

After evaluating the evidence, the auditor reaches an opinion. In a financial statement audit, the auditor's opinion states whether the financial statements were presented fairly according to GAAP. In the United States, the auditor's opinion on the financial statements is included in the annual report that the publicly traded company files with the Securities and Exchange Commission. Thereby, the auditor's opinion provides some assurance to investors, lenders, and others, who rely upon the information contained in the financial statements.

Internal audits, also called management or operational audits, are generally concerned with evaluating the economy and the efficiency with which scarce resources are used.

Internal auditors often review all aspects of operations performed in a firm to determine whether any improvements can be made in departmental operations. The efficient utilization of resources by the various departments and their accomplishment of established objectives are evaluated by internal auditors in their performance of a management audit.

Internal audits can also evaluate internal controls. Internal control structure comprises those policies and procedures established in order to provide reasonable assurance that established objectives will be achieved. In performing an audit of internal controls, internal auditors review the internal control structure (which includes the control environment, the accounting system, and control procedures) and test specific controls to determine whether they are operating as anticipated. One key objective of an internal control audit is to ensure that the internal control structure is sound and provides a reasonable degree of assurance about the integrity of information output, such as the financial statements, by the accounting system and that the firm's assets are safeguarded.

ETHICAL PERSPECTIVES

Can Government Regulations Prevent Financial Crises?

The financial crisis of 2008 led to a historical decline in stock markets throughout the world. In the United States, the market eventually bottomed out at 53.7 percent below its previous high value. Almost two years later, the U.S.'s SEC Commissioner, Luis Aguilar, observed that the SEC still was a long way from understanding the financial crisis and identifying who should be policed to avoid another similar crisis.

To improve the SEC's oversight function, Aguilar proposed that the SEC establish a capacity to carry out surveillance of market behavior in real time. He said, "Real-time market participation is necessary for effective, regulatory fact-finding, oversight, and enforcement." In addition, the SEC has proposed a new rule mandating that stock exchanges establish a "consolidated audit trail system" that would enable regulators to track information pertaining to trading orders received and executed across the securities markets.

In response to the 2008 financial crisis, a report, "Risk and Reward—Tempering the Pursuit of Profit," was issued by the U.K.'s Association of Chartered Certified Accountants (ACCA). The report encourages businesses to pay more attention to ethical responsibilities. In addition, the report urges businesses to give top priority to recruit senior executives and financial staff that have strong ethical compasses.

The ACCA report considers areas in which the financial system went awry prior to the crisis, in particular the ethical lapses of many people. Paul Moxey, ACCA's head of corporate governance and risk management, helped write the report. Moxey observes, "The financial crisis has highlighted serious ethical failings." He notes that businesses of all types, such as banks, have been increasingly regulated by burgeoning rules and regulations. Yet, at a time of crisis, despite the numerous regulatory requirements, or perhaps because of them, holes in the regulations have been exploited by unethical persons.

The report makes the case that a robust commitment to ethical business practices on the part of directors and key personnel provides a tough line of defense against reputational damage and should be a fundamental component of any risk management strategy. Recommendations of the report include setting the right tone at the top and promoting a sense of ethical responsibility, not merely complying with external rules. By doing so, a business will ensure a vibrant ethical culture that will lead to socially responsible business practices.

QUESTIONS:

1) Do you think the U.S. SEC will be able to ensure that there will not be another financial crisis like the one in 2008? Do you think that real-time surveillance of market behavior will help?
2) Do you think that with enough regulations, people's ethical failings can be prevented?
3) Why do you think the ACCA report recommended setting the right tone at the top?

Sources: Jaclyn Jaeger, "Barney Frank, SEC's Aguilar on Financial Crisis," Compliance Week, www.complianceweek.com/article/5968/barney-frank-secs-aguilar-on-financial-crisis, accessed June 2, 2010; WebCPA, "Accounting Group Calls for Better Business Ethics," WebCPA, www.webcpa.com/news/Accounting-Group-Calls-Better-Business-Ethics-54459-1.html, accessed June 3, 2010.

When the Sarbanes-Oxley Act was passed in 2002, it established the Public Company Accounting Oversight Board (PCAOB), to oversee auditors of publicly traded companies. In addition, SOX increased prison sentences for fraud. The Public Company Accounting Oversight Board sets auditing, attestation, quality control, and ethical standards for auditors. As a result of SOX, the U.S. auditing profession moved from a self-regulatory environment under the American Institute of Certified Public Accountants' peer review system to the regulatory framework under the PCAOB.

REALITY CHECK LO-4

English historian Lord Acton is famous for his quote: "Power tends to corrupt, and absolute power corrupts absolutely." In a country with no checks and balances on the power of government officials, do you think citizens are more concerned about corruption there than in a country like the United States, which has a checks and balance system? If there were no audits of financial statements of publicly traded companies, do you think stockholders would be concerned about the accuracy and reliability of those statements?

Financial Statement Analysis

LO-5
Explain how financial statement analysis can be used to evaluate a company's financial situation and compare it to other companies.

Financial statement analysis is an evaluation of the financial statements to identify significant trends or relationships among the items contained within them. For example, financial ratios are often used to identify important relationships. Financial statement analysis begins with the information directly provided on the financial statements and builds upon that information to provide a more comprehensive understanding of a company's financial situation. On the surface, financial statements can provide answers to key questions asked by management, investors, lenders, and other parties interested in a firm's performance. For example, the income statement answers the question: How much did the firm earn or lose from operations during the period? However, while it may be useful to know how much a company earned or lost, this may not be sufficient information by itself to determine whether to invest in the company or loan money to it.

Financial statement analysis goes beyond the surface details. For example, a trend analysis of net income would examine how net income has changed from year to year for the past five or ten years. Another analysis of net income would compare it to sales revenue; net income divided by sales revenue equals profit margin. Investors and other financial statement users may be interested in whether profit margin is increasing or decreasing. An investor may be interested in how one company's profit margin compares to another company's profit margin.

Financial Ratios

A **financial ratio** shows the relationship of one number on a financial statement to another number. Financial ratios are designed to assess different aspects of the firm's financial situation. Financial ratios enable meaningful comparisons among companies of different sizes, to assess which companies are performing better and which are performing worse. For example, when comparing two companies, the total dollar amount of debt is less important than the ratio of total debt to total assets. The debt ratio is calculated as follows:

$$\text{Debt Ratio} = \frac{\text{Total Liabilities}}{\text{Total Assets}}$$

financial statement analysis
an evaluation of a company's financial statements in order to identify significant trends or relationships among the items

financial ratio
the relationship of a number on the financial statements to another number

The company with the most debt may be in better financial condition because it has proportionately much more in total assets. A company with a $10 million in debt may be better than another company with only $5 million in debt. What if the company with $10 million in debt also has $50 million in total assets and the company with $5 million in debt also has $5 million in assets? The first company has a debt ratio of 0.20 ($10 million/$50 million) and the second company has a debt ratio of 1.00 ($5 million/ $5 million). Financial ratios equalize companies of different sizes for comparison of financial performance.

One of the most frequently used financial ratios is called the current ratio, which is calculated as current assets divided by current liabilities. The current ratio shows the firm's ability to pay its current liabilities using current assets. The formula is as follows:

$$\text{Current Ratio} = \frac{\text{Current Assets}}{\text{Current Liabilities}}$$

Assume that the balance sheet of ABC Company shows current assets of $200 million and current liabilities of $50 million. The balance sheet of XYZ Company shows current assets of $300 million and current liabilities of $300 million. Which company is better situated to pay its current liabilities? XYZ Company has more current assets than ABC Company, but XYZ's current ratio is only 1.00 ($300 million/$300 million). ABC Company has fewer current assets than XYZ Company, but ABC's current ratio is 4.00 ($200 million/ $50 million). ABC, therefore, has a stronger current ratio than XYZ. ABC is better situated to pay off its current liabilities.

A publicly traded company's current ratio is tracked by financial analysts, investors, lenders, and company managers. Normally a higher current ratio indicates a better financial position, for it implies that a company has adequate liquidity to carry out business operations.

What is a good current ratio? To evaluate any financial ratio, a comparison should be made using one or more past years of a company's data and benchmarking it against industry averages and similar ratios from key competitors. A rule of thumb is that companies should have a current ratio between 1 and 2.

The current ratio is often important in debt covenants. When a company borrows money, the lender will specify certain requirements to maintain the loan. These lending requirements, also called debt covenants, may indicate that the borrower must maintain a specified minimum current ratio, such as 2.5. This helps ensure that the borrower will have the money necessary to pay its interest obligations and later repay the loan.

Evaluating Trends

Financial analysts, investors, lenders, and other parties analyze the financial statements to determine how well the company is performing and how well it is likely to do in the future. Positive trends in financial performance are indicators that the company has positive future prospects. This is good news for investors and typically leads to higher stock prices. Negative trends suggest a difficult future for the firm. In the worst case, the firm might even face financial ruin and bankruptcy.

Positive trends in financial performance are equally good news for lenders, as they indicate a high likelihood that loans will be repaid. For example, suppose Disney Corporation applies for a loan from Wells Fargo Bank. In deciding whether to loan the money, Wells Fargo may look at Disney's financial statements to determine whether the company has a positive trend in net income. If net income has been steadily increasing during recent past years, this suggests that Disney will be profitable in the future and more likely to be able to pay back its loan.

REALITY CHECK LO-5

If you had a half million dollars to invest, would you prefer to invest in a company that has made steadily increasing profits year after year? Or would you prefer instead to invest in a company that has experienced dramatic ups and downs in profitability, some years with huge profits and other years with huge losses? Explain the reasons for your preference.

Global Tax Matters

LO-6
Describe briefly, tax issues that MNCs face.

Multinational corporations face many challenges conducting business in countries around the world, such as adapting to different cultures, complying with laws and regulations, hiring competent and ethical employees, and making a reasonable profit while providing a quality product or service. Another part of international operations is paying taxes in the various countries where the corporation does business. Tax rates and the types of taxes vary greatly from one country to another. Types of taxes include income tax, sales tax, property tax, payroll tax, goods and services tax (GST), and value-added tax (VAT). The tax type that receives the most attention is the corporate income tax.

Tax Rates Among Selected Countries

Almost every country imposes a corporate income tax. Countries that have little or no corporate income tax are referred to as tax havens. Conducting business in a tax haven does not mean that there are no taxes, as the company may still have to pay other taxes such as property taxes, payroll taxes, and sales taxes. The amount of the other taxes may be higher than in countries where there are income taxes. As a result, the total amount of taxes paid may be about the same in a country that is a tax haven and in a country that is not. Furthermore, taxes are just one factor to consider when locating business operations in a country. Other important considerations include factors such as economic conditions, quality of the labor force, access to transportation systems for shipping products, legal systems, political stability, and culture.

While the corporate income tax is not the only factor corporations must consider, it is nevertheless a very important factor in deciding to set up operations in another country. Tax rates and other business-related information can be obtained from various sources, including the Organization for Economic Cooperation and Development (OECD). The OECD is an international organization of 30 countries that accept the principles of representative democracy and free-market economy. Most OECD countries are high-income economies and are regarded as developed countries. The corporate income tax rates in OECD countries are provided in Exhibit 15.4.

As shown in Exhibit 15.4, corporate income tax rates vary from a high of 35 percent in the United States to a low of 12.5 percent in Ireland. When state corporate income tax rates are added to the federal rates, Japan edges out the United States for the highest combined federal and state corporate income tax rate. Japan's combined rate is 39.54 percent, while the combined rate of the United States is only slightly lower at 39.27 percent. Given the high corporate income tax rates in the United States and Japan, why would companies choose to set up business operations in these countries? The answer is that other factors make the United States and Japan excellent locations to conduct business. For example, both countries have strong economies, a quality labor force, good access to transportation systems, a well-established legal system, and political stability.

EXHIBIT 15.4 CORPORATE INCOME TAX RATES IN OECD COUNTRIES

Rank	Country	Federal Corporate Income Tax Rate Adjusted	Top State Corporate Income Tax Rate	Combined Federal and State Rate (Adjusted)
1	Japan	30	11.56	39.54
2	United States	35	6.57	39.27
3	Germany	26.38	17.0	38.9
4	Canada	22.1	14	36.1
5	France	34.43	0	34.4
6	Belgium	33.99	0	33.99
7	Italy	33	0	33
8	New Zealand	33	0	33
9	Spain	32.5	0	32.5
10	Luxembourg	22.88	7.5	30.38
11	Australia	30	0	30
12	United Kingdom	30	0	30
13	Mexico	28	0	28
14	Norway	28	0	28
15	Sweden	28	0	28
16	Korea	25	2.5	27.5
17	Portugal	25	1.5	26.5
18	Finland	26	0	26
19	Netherlands	25.5	0	25.5
20	Austria	25	0	25
21	Denmark	25	0	25
22	Greece	25	0	25
23	Czech Republic	24	0	24
24	Switzerland	8.50	14.64	21.32
25	Hungary	20	0	20
26	Turkey	20	0	20
27	Poland	19	0	19
28	Slovak Republic	19	0	19
29	Iceland	18	0	18
30	Ireland	12.5	0	12.5

Source: OECD (2008) The OECD tax database PART II. Taxation of Corporate and Capital Income HYPERLINK www.oecd.org/dataoecd/26/56/33717459.xls

ECONOMIC PERSPECTIVES Corporate Income Tax Rates and Economic Activity

The income tax is the primary source of revenues for national governments around the world. To pay for increases in the size of national governments in recent decades the amount of income tax collected has greatly increased in most countries. For example, in the United States, total government expenditures relative to gross domestic product (GDP) are now more than three times higher than before the Great Depression. Total government expenditures increased to 42.7 percent of GDP in 2009, a proportion greater than any prior year except for three years during World War II, 1943–1945.

Before the Great Depression, state and local government expenditures in the United States were much higher than federal expenditures. Since 1939, that has been the opposite. Government expenditures on defense as a percentage of GDP have declined to historic lows, such that today the percentage is similar to what it was in the 1920s. The great majority of U.S. government expenditures are on nondefense items such as health, income support, and education.

An examination was made of the relationship between corporate income tax rates in OECD countries and economic activity, including GDP growth, unemployment, and savings. OECD stands for Organization of Economic Cooperation and Development. The OECD is a Paris-based international economic organization comprising 30 countries. The OECD includes large economies such at the United States, Japan, and Germany; and small economies such as Greece, Turkey, and Poland. The OECD is one of the world's largest and most reliable sources of comparable statistics and economic and social data. The OECD monitors trends, analyzes and forecasts economic developments, and studies social changes or evolving patterns in trade, environment, agriculture, technology, and taxation. Concerning taxation, collaboration among OECD nations has contributed to a global web of bilateral tax treaties.

From 2005 to 2008, average GDP of OECD countries increased from $1,184 billion to $1,455 billion. A comparison of the higher corporate tax rate countries versus lower corporate tax rate countries shows that the average increase in GDP was higher for the lower tax rate countries. In the same time period, average unemployment decreased from 7.05 percent in 2005 to 5.76 percent in 2008. A comparison of higher tax rate countries to lower tax rate countries reveals that the average percent change in the unemployment rate was more favorable for the lower tax rate countries than the higher tax rate countries.

From 2005 to 2007, the average gross savings rate of OECD countries increased from 24.26 percent to 26.50 percent. Savings rate data was not available for 2008 at the time of the study. Comparing higher tax rate countries to lower tax rate countries indicates a significantly higher proportionate increase in the gross savings rate for the lower tax rate countries. In summary, lower tax rate countries of the OECD have experienced more favorable economic activity than higher corporate tax rate countries of the OECD.

QUESTIONS:

1) Why do you think government expenditures as a percentage of GDP have increased in the United States and other countries?

2) Why do you think a lower corporate income tax rate would be associated with more favorable economic activity such as an increase in GDP?

3) If you were a CEO making a decision upon where to locate future business operations, would you locate in a low-tax or high-tax country, all other factors being equal? As a practical matter, why is this a complicated decision?

Source: L.C. Smith, L.M. Smith, and William C. Gruben, "A Multinational Analysis of Tax Rates and Economic Activity," Journal of International Business Research, vol. 10, special issue no. 1, 2011, pp. 95–113.

Transfer Pricing

The majority of multinational corporations use transfer pricing. Transfer pricing refers to the pricing of goods and services that are transferred (bought and sold) internally between members of a corporate family, including from parent to subsidiary, from subsidiary to

Achim Baque/Shutterstock.com

The Tokyo skyline. Of all the countries in the world, Japan and the United States have the highest corporate income tax rates.

parent, and between subsidiaries. Internal transfers can involve a variety of goods and services, including any or all of the following:

- raw materials;
- semi-finished and finished goods;
- allocation of fixed costs;
- loans;
- fees; and
- royalties for use of trademarks and copyrights.

When the members of a corporate family are located in different countries, transfer pricing affects taxes owed and thereby company profits. Due to this ability to affect profits, before and after tax, top management must set appropriate transfer prices so that profitability and resources used are properly assigned to the parent corporation and its subsidiaries. This not only makes transfer pricing a very large matter of operational importance, but also creates a significant corporate tax issue.

Consider the following example of two related companies, a parent and a subsidiary, which together form a consolidated corporation. The parent and subsidiary are located in two different countries. The consolidated corporation potentially can lower taxes as a result of a transfer pricing arrangement between the parent and its subsidiary. In scenarios in which one country has a much lower tax rate than the other, the consolidated corporation's potential benefits from transfer pricing are greatly increased.

In Scenario 1, a company subsidiary is located in country "A" in which the tax rate is 20 percent. The subsidiary manufactures a product at a cost of $100, and then exports the product to the parent company, located in country "B" at a transfer-selling price of $200. The parent company sells the product for $300. Consequently, each company, the parent and subsidiary, makes a profit of $100. In country "B" the tax rate is 60 percent, which is much higher than the tax rate of 20 percent in Country "A." As shown in Exhibit 15.5, the MNE's consolidated after-tax profit is $120.

In Scenario 2, the subsidiary company sells (transfers) the product for $280, while the parent sells the product for $300, the MNE's consolidated profit increases because more of

EXHIBIT 15.5 TRANSFER PRICING SCENARIOS

Scenario 1:

	Subsidiary	Parent	Consolidated
Selling Price	200	300	300
Cost of Goods Sold	100	200	100
Profit Before Tax	100	100	200
Tax	20	60	80
Profit After Tax	80	40	120

Scenario 2:

	Subsidiary	Parent	Consolidated
Selling Price	280	300	300
Cost of Goods Sold	100	280	100
Profit Before Tax	180	20	200
Tax	36	12	48
Profit After Tax	144	8	152

Adapted from: Molly Dean, F.J. Feucht, and L.M. Smith, "International Transfer Pricing Issues and Strategies for the Global Firm," *Internal Auditing*, 23, no. 1, 2008, pp. 12–19.

the pre-tax profits are shifted to the subsidiary in country "A," in which the tax rate is lower. The subsidiary company now earns a profit of $180 and 20 percent of that is paid out in taxes. The parent now earns only $20 on the transaction, which is subject to a 60 percent tax rate; thus, the parent pays out $12 in taxes. For the two companies combined, the consolidated profit rises to $152, as shown in Exhibit 15.5.

These scenarios illustrate the potential benefit of transfer pricing, at least in situations in which a company has the ability to set the transfer price as it chooses. In this example, setting a higher transfer price shifts more of the before-tax profit to the lower tax country, which results in higher after-tax profits for the consolidated corporation. In many countries, however, a company cannot arbitrarily set the transfer price. A country may have laws and regulations that specify how transfer prices are determined.

REALITY CHECK LO-6

Are corporate taxes in the United States too high? Search the Internet for an economist's or other expert's opinion on the subject. Why would multinational corporations compare tax rates among countries before setting up business operations in a specific country?

SUMMARY

Accounting is the "language of business." Accounting is the recording, summarizing, and reporting of the economic activities and events of an organization. Accounting generates information used by people inside and outside the firm to make important decisions. For example, a financial institution like a bank may use accounting information to decide whether or not to lend money to a loan applicant. The lending institution—an external user—must predict whether the applicant can pay back the loan; this decision depends upon reliable accounting information contained in financial reports.

The accounting information system (AIS), like all systems, has specific objectives, inputs, processes, outputs, and controls. A typical AIS has two principal objectives: (1) to provide all the financial information needed internally by management for business decision making; and (2) to provide financial information to various external users concerned with the financial activities of the organization.

The financial statements of publicly traded companies must be prepared according to generally accepted accounting principles (GAAP). GAAP provides the guidelines by which financial statements are prepared. In the United States, GAAP is primarily developed by the Financial Accounting Standards Board. Historically, GAAP varies from country to country. Starting in the 1970s, a movement began to create a single set of GAAP that could be used in every country of the world. The International Accounting Standards Committee, now called the International Accounting Standards Board (IASB), was the leader of this movement.

The IASB issues International Financial Reporting Standards. The IASB is an independent, privately funded accounting standard-setter based in London, U.K. International Financial Reporting Standards (IFRS) are designed to provide a single set of GAAP that can be used by companies in all countries around the globe. IFRS are international GAAP.

In the case of a publicly traded company, investors and other users of the company's financial statements need assurance that the statements do not contain material misstatements, either intentional or unintentional. Assurance is provided by the independent external auditor who examines the firm's financial statements, and provides an audit opinion indicating whether those statements are fairly presented according to generally accepted accounting principles.

Financial statement analysis is an evaluation of the financial statements in order to identify significant trends or relationships among the items contained within them. For example, financial ratios are often used to identify important relationships. Financial statement analysis is a tool for evaluating a company's success or failure. Financial statement analysis begins with the information directly provided on the financial statements and builds on that information to provide a more comprehensive understanding of a company's financial situation.

Types of tax and tax rates vary from one country to another. As a result, when a MNC is deciding in what countries to locate its business operations, the company is wise to consider taxes in those countries. Nearly all countries impose a corporate income tax. Tax havens are countries that have little or no corporate income tax. However, doing business in a tax haven does not mean that there are no taxes, as there are other taxes such as property taxes, payroll taxes, and sales taxes. In addition, taxes are only one factor to evaluate when locating business operations in a country. Additional important factors include economic conditions, quality of the labor force, access to transportation systems for shipping products, legal system, political stability, and culture.

KEY TERMS

CHAPTER QUESTIONS

1) What is the difference between management accounting and financial accounting?

2) Describe U.S. GAAP and why it differs from GAAP in other countries.

3) What are the benefits of every country using the same GAAP, that is, International Financial Reporting Standards (IFRS)? Why haven't all countries adopted IFRS?

4) How does auditing contribute to better financial reporting?

5) How does financial ratio analysis enable an investor to compare two companies?

6) Before locating operations in a country, why should a multinational corporation evaluate that country's tax system?

MINI CASE: MCDONALD'S CORPORATION

McDonald's Corporation operates in more than 100 countries. There are approximately 31,000 McDonald's restaurants worldwide; on an average day they serve over 58 million people. Most McDonald's restaurants are franchises owned and operated by independent local men and women. Operations outside the United States generate approximately 65 percent of corporate revenues. Because more than 95 percent of the world's population lives outside the United States, substantial profits can be generated from global sales.

The success of McDonald's is a function of the corporation's consistent quality standards, good management, and effective marketing that began in 1955. McDonald's accountants face several challenges when operating in global markets, such as:

- fluctuations in currency exchange and interest rates;
- different tax rates and laws;
- cost and deployment of capital;
- differing food, labor, and operating costs; and
- diverse accounting policies and practices.

For example, financial reporting in the United States values assets according to the historical cost (the amount paid). But in Mexico, where inflation is much higher, asset values are adjusted for the impact of inflation.

As a multinational business, McDonald's Corporation must comply with the rules and regulations of the countries where it operates. The United Nations is concerned that globalization of business makes it difficult for external stakeholders, including governments, to verify a multinational firm's data. The problem is considered at least partly the result of a lack of uniform reporting requirements and standards. International Financial Reporting Standards have been developed that can be used for financial reporting by companies in countries around the world; however, not all countries have agreed to use International Financial Reporting Standards.

QUESTIONS:

1) Why is it difficult to compare the financial statements of a U.S. company with those of a company in India or Germany?

2) How would McDonald's benefit if International Financial Reporting Standards were adopted for use in all countries worldwide?

Should Minimizing Taxes be the Only Goal of Transfer Pricing?

When the members of a corporate family, such as a parent corporation and subsidiary, are located in different countries, transfer pricing affects taxes owed, and, therefore, company profits. This makes transfer pricing a very large matter of operational importance, but also creates a significant corporate tax issue. Consider the following scenario: A company subsidiary is located in Country A, where the tax rate is 30 percent. The subsidiary builds a product at a cost of $100, and then exports the product to the parent company, located in Country B at a transfer-selling price of $300. The parent company sells the product for $500. Thus, each company, the parent and subsidiary, earns a profit of $200. The tax rate in Country B is 60 percent, which is much higher than the tax rate of 30 percent in Country A. The company's consolidated, after-tax profit is $220, computed as shown:

	Subsidiary in Country A	Parent in Country B	Consolidated
Selling Price	300	500	500
Cost of Goods Sold	100	300	100
Profit Before Tax	200	200	400
Tax	60	120	180
Profit After Tax	140	80	220

POINT If the transfer price was increased from $300 to $400, then the consolidated profit would increase from $220 to $250. This is good for the corporation and its stockholders. Computations based on the higher transfer price are shown below:

	Subsidiary in Country A	Parent in Country B	Consolidated
Selling Price	400	500	500
Cost of Goods Sold	100	400	100
Profit Before Tax	300	100	400
Tax	90	60	150
Profit After Tax	210	40	250

COUNTER-POINT Changing the transfer price to $400 will allow more of the profit and related taxes to remain in Country A. Only $60 of taxes are collected in Country B. This may be regarded as unfair to the government of Country B, that needs taxes to pay for government services. The government in Country B may respond by requiring the transfer price to be set at $100, which would move all the profit and related taxes to Country B. Alternatively, the government in Country B may respond by expelling the company from the country. This would not be good for the company or its stockholders.

What Do *You* Think?

Which viewpoint do you support and why? How would you balance the needs of company stockholders with those of taxpayers who fund the national infrastructure the company uses in Country "B"?

INTERPRETING GLOBAL BUSINESS NEWS

Financial news is everywhere in the popular press and media. How do you interpret the following examples of financial news related to the concepts in this chapter?

1) In the early-2000s, many news stories reviewed the questionable accounting practices and financial collapses of major corporations such as Enron, Worldcom, and other companies. Do you think accounting rules can be developed and applied in a way that would prevent corporate failures?

2) In a news article regarding audits of major publicly traded companies, the writer said that a typical company has to pay a lot of money to hire a CPA firm to audit the company's financial statements. The writer said that audit fees were too high and that companies and their stockholders would save a lot of money if audits were not required. Do you think that's a good idea? Why or why not? Search the Internet for news articles to support your answer.

3) International Financial Reporting Standards (IFRS) are being used in over 100 countries worldwide. A news article states that generally accepted accounting principles in the United States have worked well for more than 100 years. The article says that when something is not broken, do not fix it. Is U.S. GAAP broken? How would U.S. companies benefit if the United States adopts International Financial Reporting Standards? Search the Internet for news articles to support your answer.

PORTFOLIO PROJECTS

Explore Your Own Case in Point: Company Financial Statements

Find the current stock price and price-to-earnings (P/E) ratio of your selected company. The P/E ratio is the current stock price divided by the company's net income. A number of websites, such as Yahoo! Finance (http://finance.yahoo.com/), provide stock price quotes. The Yahoo! Finance website also provides links to recent news stories about the company. In addition to finding the current stock price and P/E ratio, prepare a short summary of recent news stories about the company.

1) Find your selected company's financial statements. Now, look at the income statement, also called the statement of earnings, and find how much profit the corporation made in its most recent year. Can you imagine how difficult it would be for investors if there was no accounting information on which to base investment decisions?

2) Compare your selected company's P/E ratio to several other companies. Why do you think investors are willing to pay more or less, relative to earnings, for the selected company's stock?

3) Summarize a news story about your selected company. In the long term, do you think this news story will have positive or negative effects on the company's stock price?

Develop an International Strategy for Your Own Small Business: Accounting Standards and Taxation

Identify a country where you would like to set up business operations and produce a particular product or service. Do as much research as necessary to find out the accounting and tax matters that pertain to that country. What generally accepted accounting principles are used in that country? Is the GAAP developed by accounting standard-setters in that country, or does that country use International Financial Reporting Standards, developed by the International Accounting Standards Board? What is the country's corporate income tax rate? Is it higher or lower than the U.S. corporate income tax rate?

Subject Index

A

B

D

E

F

G

H

I

J

K

L

Q

R

S

T

U

Z

Organization Index

A

B

C

J

K

L

M

N

Z